THE
unofficial GUIDE®
ᵀᴼ Cruises

9TH EDITION

THE *unofficial* GUIDE®
TO Cruises

9TH EDITION

KAY SHOWKER *with* BOB SEHLINGER

WILEY

Please note that prices fluctuate in the course of time, and travel information changes under the impact of many factors that influence the travel industry. We therefore suggest that you write or call ahead for confirmation when making your travel plans. Every effort has been made to ensure the accuracy of information throughout this book, and the contents of this publication are believed correct at the time of printing. Nevertheless, the publishers cannot accept responsibility for errors or omissions or for changes in details given in this guide or for the consequences of any reliance on the information provided by the same. Assessments of attractions and so forth are based upon the author's own experience, and therefore, descriptions given in this guide necessarily contain an element of subjective opinion, which may not reflect the publisher's opinion or dictate a reader's own experience on another occasion. Readers are invited to write the publisher with ideas, comments, and suggestions for future editions.

Published by:
John Wiley & Sons, Inc.
111 River Street
Hoboken, NJ 07030

Produced by Menasha Ridge Press

Cover design by Michael J. Freeland

Interior design by Michele Laseau

For information on our other products and services or to obtain technical support please contact our Customer Care Department within the U.S. at (800) 762-2974, outside the U.S. at (317) 572-3993 or fax (317) 572-4002.

John Wiley & Sons, Inc. also publishes its books in a variety of electronic formats. Some content that appears in print may not be available in electronic formats.

ISBN 0-7645-7863-4

Manufactured in the United States of America

5 4 3 2 1

CONTENTS

PART THREE Cruising Alternatives 529

List of Maps and Illustrations

LAURELS
for the
LABORERS

THIS EDITION MARKS THE 10TH YEAR that the *Unofficial Guide to Cruises* has been in publication. It goes almost without saying that a book of this scope—covering more than 100 cruise lines with upwards of 400 ships sailing to destinations from the North Pole to the South Pole and around the world—is the work of many people. Over the decade it has required extensive research, interviews with passengers, seemingly endless discussions with specialized travel agents and other knowledgeable people about cruises, not to mention the incredible amount of follow-up due to the constantly changing nature of the cruise industry.

So many people have been tireless in their effort to help that it would take another book to name them all, but we would be remiss not to mention some.

Steve Gordan, publisher and managing editor of *Star Service*, which issues reports and evaluations on hotels and cruise ships worldwide for its travel agency subscribers, generously allowed us access and use of the publication's material. Mike Dricoll's online newsletter, *Cruise News;* George Devol's monthly publication *Ocean Cruise News* and its online version by Bill Miller; Anne Campbell's *Cruisemates;* and *Travel Agent* magazine's online edition have been steady sources of information helping us to keep abreast of the constantly changing cruise industry.

Lloyd Cole of Valerie Wilson Travel, Dr. Bradley Feuer of Pace Travel, and Lisa Haber of Cruise Professionals have given us plentiful insights and never seemed to tire of our endless questions.

We are grateful to all our public-relations friends at the cruise lines who helped us check the nitty-gritty details and who have been our hosts over the years without any obligation.

TEXT CONTRIBUTIONS

TIME CONSTRAINTS IN WRITING A BOOK such as this make it impossible for two people to visit and revisit every ship prior to our deadlines, as we would want to do. Throughout the years, we called on colleagues for help, particularly on writers who specialize in cruising and are as qualified as we to write this book.

Some of these folks contributed material written specifically for the book, others shared their knowledge from recent cruises or allowed us to use material from recently published research, while still others reviewed or helped with the updating of information we had already written. Specifically for Part Two, sections were written by; Dave Houser (Cruise West); Ted Scull (American Safari Cruises) and Susan Young (Oceania Cruises); for Part Three, Ted Scull (Norwegian Coastal Cruises and European Cruise Ferries); Dave Houser (Freighter Cruises); Ted Scull and P. J. Mooney (Hapag-Lloyd Cruises), and Ann Kaloosh and Susan Milne, who not only wrote parts of this book but also generously contributed their insights and information to many of the cruise lines and ships profiled in Part Two. Part Three, Shann Davies (Yangtze River Cruises in China), Susan Milne, who prepared the itineraries, and Susan Young who fact-checked and edited this last edition from cover to cover

Many other writing colleagues shared their firsthand experience with us, too. We particularly want to thank Arlene and Sam Bleecker, Anne Campbell, George Devol, Michael Driscoll, Marilyn Green, Mary Ann Hemphill, Michael Iachetta, Marcia Levin, Susan Pierres, and Molly Staub.

Many, many friends, friends of friends, travel agents, and cruise passengers along the way willingly gave us their time for interviews, helped with ship ratings, and phoned and sent us letters about their latest cruise, and to them we express our heartfelt thanks.

Last but not least, we thank the staff of Menasha Ridge Press, who worked tirelessly on the manuscript every step of the way.

Kay Showker
Bob Sehlinger

THE
unofficial GUIDE®
ᵀᴼCruises

9TH EDITION

INTRODUCTION

ABOUT THIS GUIDE

HOW COME "UNOFFICIAL"?

THE MATERIAL IN THIS GUIDE has not been edited or in any way reviewed by the cruise lines profiled. In this "unofficial" guide we represent and serve you, the consumer. If a ship serves mediocre food, has cramped cabins, or offers poor shore excursions, we will say so. Through our independence, we hope we can make selecting a cruise efficient and economical and your cruise experience on-target and fun.

MAKING IT EASY

IN THE NEARLY TWO YEARS it took to write the first edition of this book, Kay had pinned on a wall in front of her a note that read: "This book has one purpose: To help readers select the right cruise— i.e., the cruise that's right for them." She kept it there to make sure we never lost sight of that goal.

Most guides to cruising approach their subject on a ship-by-ship basis, giving only the briefest attention to the cruise line and emphasizing ships—the hardware. But people don't buy ships, they buy cruises, and those cruises—the software—have been designed according to cruise lines' business plans, which define the types of cruises they offer. The cruise lines are challenged daily by their competitors and all the other leisure products vying for your attention—from the latest car and computer to a Disney vacation—to make their cruises irresistible. Yet they freely admit that although there's a cruise for everyone, not every cruise is for everyone. What it boils down to is that you can listen to Beethoven's Ninth Symphony played by an amateur band, or you can hear it played by the New York Philharmonic. It's the same music, but it's going to come out differently.

This book is designed to help you recognize the differences. By understanding the cruise lines and the experiences they offer, you will be able to recognize the different types of cruises available and identify the ones likely to appeal to you. Each line offers cruises with features that distinguish them from the others. It is these features—or "style" as we call it—that are the essence of the cruise experience.

A Carnival cruise is a Carnival cruise, for example. Each Carnival ship offers a "Fun Ship" vacation, and, except for the cruise's length and destinations, the experience varies little among their ships. Carnival has designed it that way.

The same is true of Costa, Holland America, Seabourn, and every other line that has built ships of a class or style from the same mold. However, a Carnival cruise is as different from a Princess, Holland America, Crystal, or Seabourn cruise as night is from day.

As cruise lines continue to standardize their operations to keep costs down and distinguish themselves from their competition, it becomes more important for you (or your travel agent), as you select a cruise, to understand the line and the type of cruises it offers. With that goal in mind, this guidebook is organized in three parts:

Part One, Planning Your Cruise Vacation, covers basic information on what cruises contain, tips on finding the best values, and preparing for your cruise.

Part Two, Cruise Lines and Their Ships, profiles all major "mainstream" cruise lines that sell primarily to U.S. and Canadian travelers. At the end of Part Two are cruise lines—some small, some also in the mainstream—but not necessarily on this side of the Atlantic. Most, but not all, are based in Europe, cruise less-traveled routes, and cater mainly to Europeans.

Part Three, Cruising Alternatives, describes other options, such as river, adventure, and expedition cruises, plus freighters, coastal ships, cruise ferries, and sailing ships.

LETTERS, COMMENTS, AND QUESTIONS FROM READERS

MANY WHO USE THE *UNOFFICIAL GUIDES* write to us with questions, comments, or their own strategies for planning and enjoying travel. We appreciate all such input, both positive and critical. Readers' comments are frequently incorporated into revised editions of the *Unofficial Guides* and have contributed immeasurably to their improvement. Please write to:

Kay and Bob
The Unofficial Guide to Cruises
P..O. Box 43673
Birmingham, AL 35243

Please put your return address on both your letter and envelope; the two sometimes become separated. Also, include your phone number if you are available for a possible interview. And remember, our work often requires that we be out of the office for long periods, so forgive us if our response is slow. If you'd like a faster response, you can also try e-mailing us at unofficialguides@menasharidge.com.

A Reader Survey is included at the end of the book. We urge you to copy or clip it out, add your impressions, and send it in.

CRUISING: A LOOK BACK, A LOOK AHEAD

IN 2006, MODERN CRUISING will mark its 40th anniversary. December 19, 1966, is recognized as a landmark because on that date a series of cruises was launched that, for the first time, had been created and packaged as a mass-market product and sold on a year-round basis. The ship, the *Sunward* of the Norwegian Caribbean Line (later renamed the Norwegian Cruise Line), sailed from Miami to Nassau with 540 passengers on the first three- and four-day cruises to be offered year-round between Miami and the Bahamas. No one, including the creators, imagined where that small step would lead. Indeed, many in the steamship business dismissed the idea as crazy, declaring there was not enough of a market to support such cruises.

Cruising, of course, did not actually start in 1966; it evolved over a time span of 150 years. But it's true that until the 1960s the closest most people got to a big ship was on the big screen, either in movies about glamorous people living romantic lives, or in newsreels of the duke and duchess of Windsor arriving on the *Queen Mary*, or F. Scott and Zelda, the Astors, the Vanderbilts, and other celebrities sailing stylishly to Europe aboard an elegant oceanliner.

From the start of the first regular transatlantic steamship service by Samuel Cunard in 1840, a voyage on a great liner became the ultimate dream shared by people worldwide. In the early days, a sea voyage was more of an expedition, requiring passengers to endure hardships with few amenities on-board ship or at ports. Passenger comfort, even in first class, was not a priority, but as competition developed and steamship travel gained popularity, each generation of ships brought enhanced comfort.

Then, too, throughout the late 19th century and up to World War I, ships carrying passengers had other purposes. Among them was transporting thousands of immigrants to the New World and a new life. To meet the demand—and reap large profits—many steamship companies were born and ships built, and, except for the war years when the vessels transported troops, oceanliners paraded across the Atlantic and Pacific in an endless stream, with the world's elite in their top decks and the huddled masses below.

Then in 1921, passage of the Immigration Act, intended to slow the torrent of new arrivals, forced steamship companies to change course. To make up for lost revenue from steerage, companies created cabin or tourist class in the several decks below first class and unwittingly took the next step toward modern cruising. Although a voyage remained a means of getting from one continent to another, it was no longer a pastime only for the privileged. Cabin class did not have the elegance and panache of first class, but it wasn't bad. It found a ready market in the GIs who had fought in Europe and wanted to return with their families, immigrants who had made good and wanted to visit relatives in their homelands, and America's growing middle class, who wanted to emulate the celebrities and aristocrats in first class.

THE GOLDEN AGE

THE ROARING TWENTIES WAS A GOLDEN AGE for steamship travel. It was a time of new prosperity, blithe spirits—and Prohibition in America. With alcoholic beverages legal at sea, ship companies offered a new type of short cruise—the party, or booze cruise—that made getting there half the fun.

In the dining room, passengers sat at long tables on chairs bolted to the floor (ships did not have stabilizers). In 1910, Ritz restaurants, replicating the setting of their shore-side operations, introduced round tables and carpeted floors in first class on ships of Hapag-Lloyd of Germany. The style soon became the standard for other ships. Private bathrooms were available in first class on the grandest liners, but in cabin class, passengers shared bath facilities until the 1950s. Air-conditioning was introduced by P&O Lines in the 1930s but did not become common until the 1950s.

The first indoor swimming pool appeared in 1910 on the *Olympic* of White Star Line. (It was the first of the line's three superliners; the others were the *Titanic* and the *Gigantic,* later renamed *Britannic.*) Known as a plunge bath, it had a balcony where others could watch the bathers. The first permanent outdoor pool was introduced in 1926 on the *Roma* of Italian Lines. Until the late 1950s, the top deck was fitted with machinery and was off-limits to passengers. Today, it's usually a sports deck.

A NEW ERA

After weathering the Great Depression and another war, oceanliners resumed their traditional role, and by the 1950s were conveying hordes of students to Europe and masses of refugees to U.S. shores. The glamour returned with the comings and goings of a young Liz Taylor and the sailing of Grace Kelly to her fairyland prince. After World War II, the addition of radar and improved navigational equipment made passenger ships safer and more accurate in regard to arrival times, enabling operators to plan reliable itineraries. By the mid-1950s, most oceanliners had stabilizers. Radios were added in staterooms. The tradition to separate first class and tourist class on transatlantic service continued, but in 1958, Holland America launched the *Rotterdam,* which could be converted to one class. However, by decade's end, most elite passengers had taken flight—literally.

The final blow came in 1958, when the first commercial jets streaked across the Atlantic, cutting travel time from five days to just over five hours. Instead of dying out, however, the ships changed course and became part of the revolution that took place on the sea as well as in the sky.

THE CRUISE REVOLUTION

THE TURNAROUND OF THE 1960S brought radical changes. New cruise lines, untethered to the past, exchanged formality for fun and brought a new atmosphere to shipboard life. The barriers of separate classes were removed, and the space was used for sports, recreation, and entertainment, turning the ships into floating resorts. Getting there was no longer half the fun—it was the fun. Passengers no longer bundled under blankets in deck chairs. Instead, they bounced in aerobics classes, swung at golf and tennis balls, plunged into the sea with masks and fins, soaked in hot tubs, and luxuriated in shipboard spas. Bingo survived, but it now competed with jazzy casinos, Broadway shows and discos, wine and piano bars, comics and cabarets. New and younger passengers were attracted by the activity and informality. Families with children, too, were finding cruises to be ideal vacations.

But change came wrapped in skepticism. For example, the hot news in 1968 was the new, mod look of the *S.S. Independence.* With a red, orange, and yellow sunburst splashed across the length of its sides and a riot of interior color, it was quickly dubbed the psychedelic ship. A magazine called the shakedown cruise a "floating water pad for the turned on generation" and suggested that "dancing until the wee hours . . . the informal atmosphere of the one-class ship, and ever-changing program of *top-talent* entertainment may prove a real drawing card."

The 1970s began with Royal Caribbean Cruise Lines making its debut with a fleet of ships built specifically for Caribbean cruising. It was followed two years later by Carnival Cruise Lines, which developed the "Fun Ship" concept to scuttle the elitist traditions of oceanliners and appeal to a mass market of younger, first-time passengers from all walks of life.

As the revolution's final irony, the spectacular growth in cruise vacations really took off in the 1970s, when cruise lines joined forces with airlines, which had almost put the steamship companies out of business. The union created air/sea programs that combined air transportation and ground transfers with a cruise in one package at one price. The programs enhanced the value of cruise vacations, simplified their purchase, and eliminated hassles for travelers. With the packages, cruise lines virtually brought their ships to people's doorsteps, regardless of where they lived. The marriage enabled cruise lines to base their ships in warm-weather ports from where they could cruise year-round and to fly passengers from faraway places to begin their cruises.

A relaxed, informal holiday in the sun—and available year-round— became the essence of modern cruising. Flying passengers to their ships saved time and enabled cruise lines to offer shorter, less expensive cruises that have fitted into the national trend toward shorter vacations. People who might never have considered taking a cruise booked them. It also allowed cruise lines to open new parts of the world to cruising; itineraries multiplied. No matter how many cruises a person took, new ones remained. Or so it seemed, until the oil crisis of the early 1970s, when dark clouds again threatened the future of vacations at sea.

Then, in 1978, despite skyrocketing fuel prices and predictions that cruising was doomed, Carnival Cruise Lines ordered a large, technologically advanced passenger ship. It became the forerunner of the 1980s superliners. Two years later, Norwegian Cruise Line shocked the cruise world by buying the fabulous *France* and transforming her into the *Norway*. The floating resort set cruise trends for the decade, introducing innovations, including a variety of entertainment lounges, a theater for Broadway-scale productions, a shopping plaza, and a "sidewalk" cafe. Holland America followed with *Nieuw Amsterdam* and *Noordam,* twin ships with square sterns that allowed over 20 percent more deck space for recreation, including two swimming pools. The ships also introduced computer keys to open cabin doors and other innovations.

Princess Cruises' stylish *Royal Princess,* which debuted in 1984, set new standards of comfort with all outside cabins fitted with minibars, television, and baths with tubs in every category. About the same time, the *QE2* introduced the first Golden Door spa at sea, the first computer learning center, and the first satellite-delivered newspaper.

Among the most interesting entries in the 1980's was the *Windstar,* a cruise ship with computerized sails. *Windstar* married the romance of sailing under canvas with the comforts of a cruise ship and the electronic age. At the same time, Carnival's superliners, *Holiday, Jubilee,* and *Celebration,* were introduced. Their madcap design totally changed the look of ship interiors and the use of public space.

Yet nothing since the *Norway* caused as much excitement as the 1988 debut of Royal Caribbean Cruise Line's *Sovereign of the Seas.* The world's largest cruise ship at the time, she became the pacesetter for the 1990s. Among her features was the first shipboard atrium, rising through five decks and creating a new environment. The ship offered such numerous and varied entertainment and recreation options that passengers needed several cruises to experience them all.

As the decade closed, some old lines disappeared in mergers, and new lines popped up. Health and fitness facilities were integrated into cruising. Healthful foods were readily available. Well-equipped gyms, elaborate spas, VCRs, cable television, and worldwide direct-dial telephones were rapidly becoming standard amenities. Small boutique ships, including those of the Seabourn and Silversea lines, brought new levels of luxury to cruising. Special-interest lines were finding their niche. Increased interest in adventure and nature cruises caused some traditional cruise lines to add them.

Environmental concerns had a major impact on cruise ship technology. The late 1960s and early 1970s saw the conversion of oceanliners to cruise ships and the first ships built specifically for cruising, but the 1980s and 1990s became the decades of innovation, particularly aboard ships designed to sail in warm climates.

IN THE NEW MILLENNIUM

NOW APPROACHING ITS FIFTH DECADE, the cruise boom shows no signs of letting up. In that time, the number of passengers has swelled from under 500,000 annually to over 13 million in 2004. Ten of the nineteen members of the Cruise Lines International Association, the major cruise trade association, did not exist 20 years ago.

The 1990s were a blockbuster decade, with more than three dozen new ships costing an estimated $12 billion in the water; and followed by another $15 billion in the new century, resulting in at least five dozen more ships by 2005. Most of the ships are bigger, with more dazzle, and travel specialists are asking, "Where's the sky?"

The ships over 80,000 tons—and particularly those over 100,000 tons—represented a new generation of megaliners. Most had new design features and facilities—such as the highly publicized 18-hole miniature golf course on *Legend of the Seas,* the virtual-reality theater on Princess Cruises' *Grand Princess,* and the interactive computers on Celebrity's *Century* and *Galaxy.*

But the capper was *Voyager of the Seas,* the first of the three 142,000-ton ships built by Royal Caribbean, which debuted in November 1999 with cruising's first rock-climbing wall and ice rink. The rock-climbing wall proved to be so popular that RCL has installed them fleetwide.

Meanwhile, Cunards's *Queen Mary 2,* which debuted in December 2003, assumed the title as the biggest, widest, longest and most expensive ship ever built, and at 150,000 tons she dwarfs all predecessors. The much-anticipated *QM2* came with the first and only spa at sea operated by the world-famous Canyon Ranch health resorts; the world's first and only planetarium at sea; the largest ballroom at sea; the largest library at sea; the largest wine cellar at sea;

ten different dining venues, including the first and only shipboard restaurant by popular American chef Todd English; and a learning center with guest lecturers from Oxford University.

However, the QM2 will lose her "biggest" status next year, when RCCL launches its first ultra-megaliner, as the 162,000 ton, *Freedom of the Seas,* is being called. But that may not be the end to the contest. Carnival Cruises, Cunard's owners, is said to be planning an even larger 180,000 ton ultra-megaliner with a cost of one billion dollars.

Along with innovations, the new ships have enhanced the cruise experience. Standard cabins on most new ships are larger and there are more verandasacross the price spectrum. More dining options are becoming standard, as are more entertainment choices, more sports opportunities, greatly expanded childrens' facilities; larger, more elaborate spas, Internet cafés; in-cabin Internet access; wireless facilities and cell phones that work at sea.

Other ways the cruise experience is being enhanced are through innovative enrichment programs, such as Crystal Cruises' Creative Learning Center, offering courses in cooking, art, business, technology, and health, and on the line's new *Crystal Serenity,* even learning to play the piano in an arrangement with Yamaha that provides instructors. Passengers can also take classes in fine art, drawing, sculpture, painting, floral design, and interior design by faculty from the Parsons School of Design in New York. Another such program is Princess Cruises' Scholarship Sea (which Princess calls "edutainment"), introduced on the *Coral Princess* with topics ranging from cooking taught in a demonstration kitchen like those seen on television, to pottery classes with the first shipboard kiln; and Holland America's Culinary Arts Institute, which is part of the line's ambitious $225 million Signature of Excellence, a multi- faceted program to upgrade and expand facilities and amenities to appeal to maturing babyboomers, the growing family and multi-generation vacationer market.

There has also been a vast improvement in the variety and number of shore excursions (although not an improvement in price), particularly in the Caribbean, for active passengers to enjoy hiking, biking, kayaking, golf, swimming with dolphins, and more. Now, too, many cruise lines provide the facility to enable passengers to book shore excursions online. Cruise lines faced with intense competition—again, particularly in the Caribbean—have looked for new and more varied itineraries, but the biggest shift, particularly after 9/11, has come with a new emphasis on "homeland" cruising. That has resulted in more ships based in new U.S. ports and many more itineraries along the East and West coasts of the United States, Mexico, and Central America. In addition to attracting travelers who do not want to stray far from home, this has stimulated a market of drivers who do not want to fly out of fear or who prefer not to deal with the security hassles and delays at airports.

Although innovation and product refinement is common throughout the cruise industry, Princess Cruises and Norwegian Cruise Lines have led the way. Most of the innovations address longstanding complaints of cruise passengers (they really do read all those survey forms). For cruisers who disliked being relegated to a specific seating for dinner, or for that matter, eating in the same restaurant each night, many vessels, particularly the newest ones, now offer multiple dining venues that operate like shoreside restaurants. Make a reservation or just show up at the restaurant of your choice.

Specialties at these standalone eateries cover a wide variety of cuisines, from Japanese to Mexican and Italian to Chinese. Princess and Holland America, for example, have installed steakhouses on their fleets. The Princess Personal Choice Dining program also includes an Italian trattoria, a Southwestern restaurant, and a 24-hour buffet and bistro. Norwegian Cruise Line's Freestyle Cruising offers as many as ten different restaurants on a single ship, each with its own identity and area of specialization. On the Disney Cruise Line, passengers rotate to a different restaurant each night. The line also features a reservations- and adults-only Italian restaurant on each ship.

Carnival introduced "Total Choice" dining, enabling passengers to choose from four seating times in the main dining room instead of the usual two. The four seatings stagger the arrival of diners, preventing the galley from being inundated and allowing the waitstaff to concentrate on a smaller number of passengers at any given time. Carnival has also add a supper club with gourmet cuisine on all its new ships which has proven to be enormously popular.

Although more choice in dining sounds like a definite perk, there's a downside. A great number of singles and couples depend on meeting new friends at their assigned table in the main dining room. For many, their assigned dinner companions become their social circle for the duration of the cruise. Each night, they meet over dinner and discuss the day's activities. Some coordinate shore tours or enjoy each other's company outside the dining room, and it is a common occurrence for tablemates to become close friends and to keep in touch once they return home. Needless to say, it's much harder to get acquainted and form friendships when your assigned dinner companions are off trying the alternative dining venues each night.

Among other notable initiatives is the Princess FlightChoice program that confirms air itineraries purchased through Princess 60 days prior to the cruise date, allowing passengers ample time to make changes if desired. In a related program, Princess has also established an express check-in, where passengers can avoid the hassle of dockside check-in by completing boarding documents online or mailing them to Princess in advance.

Norwegian Cruise Line has taken a much-welcomed and long-overdue crack at easing the discomfort of disembarkation. On most large vessels, you are run off the ship by 8 a.m. to make way for passengers going on the next cruise. Norwegian's program allows passengers to occupy their stateroom until midmorning and enjoy a leisurely breakfast before disembarking. Along similar lines, the Disney Cruise Line allows passengers to disembark whenever they please as soon as the ship has been cleared by customs. If ever there were initiatives that we'd like to see emulated industry-wide, it's these.

More and more cruise lines enable passengers to "stay connected" by providing Internet access, including wireless connection. A few offer it free, but most charge a high fee per usage. Some have a plan for unlimited Internet access during a cruise for a single rate, which is a better deal for frequent users. Crystal Cruises enables passengers to have their own shipboard e-mail address. Crystal, as well as several other lines, have computer schools at sea.

For those who believe it is better to receive than send, there has been a proliferation of live, real-time television available on your stateroom. In addition to CNN, the Discovery Channel, ESPN, TNT, and CNBC are now available on many cruise liners, depending on their location.

THE BIG THREE

ALTHOUGH NOT MANY CRUISERS know it, three companies control the lion's share of the American cruise market. These companies set the pace and establish norms for the mass-market cruise industry. Then, too, when there's a depressed travel market as there was after 9/11, their discounts impact even the luxury end of the market.

First of the three is Carnival Corporation, which owns Carnival, Holland America, Cunard, Seabourn, Windstar, Costa Cruises, and its most recent acquistion, P&O/Princess Cruises (which in turn included P&O Australia, Swan Hellenic Cruise Lines, and several small lines created to serve specific markets, such as Germany).

Next is Royal Caribbean International (RCI), which operates Royal Caribbean Cruise Line and Celebrity Cruises. RCI made a bid to buy Princess Cruises, but lost out to Carnival Cruises.

Number three, Star Cruises, is Asia's largest cruise line and owns Norwegian Cruise Line and Orient Line; together, they have almost as many ships as Carnival Cruises or RCI. The deep pockets of Star Cruises have enabled NCL to grow with new ships that are among the most innovative and put NCL once again in its role as the trendsetter of the cruise industry. In 2003, to the envy of its rivals, NCL launched Project America, which gives it a near monopoly in the Hawaii market (see the NCL profile in Part Two for details).

Cruise lines big and small got off to a rough start in 2001. First, there was the soaring price of fuel, followed by a serious dip in the economy. These hit at a time when the big three, as well as several other lines, were awash with new ships with thousands of extra berths to fill. By the time the first quarter of calendar year 2001 ended, ships were sailing with empty cabins, and the fight for available passengers was running at full tilt.

Then came the events of September 11, 2001, as cruising, along with travel in general, came to a screeching halt. By the 2001 Christmas season, cruising had begun its slow comeback, and the winter season, particularly in the Caribbean, was better than anticipated. Nonetheless, three cruise lines went out of business, and a fourth declared bankruptcy.

Among the casualties were American Classic Voyages, parent company of American Hawaii and Delta Queen Steamboat Company, and Renaissance. Just the year before, two other smaller cruise lines, Premier and Commodore, went belly-up, while several others struggled and remained vulnerable. By 2003, two more— Regal Cruises and World Explorer Cruises—had departed. The loss of these lines is especially sad because they were small, moderately priced operators serving areas that the big lines had ignored or could not serve with their huge ships.

On the bright side, Delta Queen Steamboat Company was bought by a financially strong company and restarted; and two new cruise lines were launched in summer 2003: Oceania Cruise Lines, using two of Renaissance Cruises' former vessels and modeling itself, more or less, after that now-defunct line and Discovery World Cruises, sailing on less traveled routes. Despite the soft travel market, Oceania has done well and recently added a third ship. Other former Renaissance ships have found their way to exploration and cultural cruise lines, such as Swan Hellenic Cruises, and as a result, set a new deluxe standard for these types of cruises.

The big three have staying power. They don't like compromising yields, but they'll do it to fill cabins and build their customer base. As we have already seen, the cruise lines that really felt the pinch were the smaller and medium-sized ones—lines that don't have the advertising dollars or market clout to compete head-to-head with the big guys and that cannot afford to offer comparable discounts.

The loss of each small or medium cruise line is important because it diminishes competition and concentrates more power in the larger lines, especially in the American market. And while cruise passengers might enjoy bargain prices now, that will likely not be the case in the future if consolidation and diminution of competition continue.

THE FUTURE

THE TWO OVERRIDING FACTORS that will influence all travel and particularly cruises for years to come, will be the Internet and the maturing of the baby boomer generation. With someone in the United States turning 50 every seven seconds, it's easy to see who the cruise lines passengers will be and why so many trends already in place or developing are a result, directly or indirectly, of these elements.

With regard to new ships, the trend toward larger ships will continue with capacity approaching 4,500 passengers before the end of the decade. These ships will have features designed to attract and satisfy the growing market of family and multi-generation vacationers and will further develop the concept of the ship as the destination with more and more elaborate spas, rock climbing walls, demonstration kitchens, and children's facilities. Most cabins on new ships will have balconies.

Look, also, for ships more than eight years old to have major modifications and conversions that go beyond the required refurbishing, in order to cater to the changing tastes of consumers and the maturing baby boomers. Holland America's $225 million investment in its "Signature of Excellence" program; Seabourn Cruises' doubling the size of their gyms; Costa Cruises' adding balconies to one of it newest ships which did not have them, are examples.

At the same time that ships continue to get larger, we are likely to see the entry of more small ships, tailored to specific markets. It's already happened in Europe—German ships for German speakers, British ships for Brits and Anglophiles—and those designed for specific segments of the market, such as easyCruise, the new no frills cruise line, similar in concept to low cost, no frills airlines. Small and mid-ships are likely to gain in popularity as a segment of travelers, particularly among experienced cruisers, will look for greater privacy, ships with fewer people and fellow passengers with more common interests.

The average price of cruises will remain low in order for cruises lines to remain competitive and continue broadening the market. However, they will be under the constant pressure of rising operating costs for food, labor, ship building, fuel, amenities, and entertainment. Thus, they must look for ways, particularly through onboard revenue, to offset these increased costs, since there is a limit to reducing operating costs without weakening the product and little elasticity in prices.

Already labor cutbacks can be seen on the large, mass-market ships. In the past cabin attendants might have been assigned 12 cabins but now, they care for 20. In the dining rooms, headwaters and wait staff might have had a dozen tables to serve, but now they have 20 and the wine steward is gone. There have been cutbacks in food quantity (and in some cases quality) as reflected in fewer courses at breakfast and lunch and/or fewer selections for each course.

New cruisers may not be aware of these changes and experienced ones may not care if it helps keep down prices. Then, too, there has always been too much food and too many choices served on most ships. What's more, people's interests and lifestyles have changed. As a result, cruise lines are switching their emphasis to activities and amenities, rather than food, as in the past. Food is still important but changing.

Look for a wider range of amenities and dining options with more venues, more types of food and specialty restaurants onboard. We've seen the beginning of a trend—restaurants run by well-known chefs or shore side restaurants. Todd English on the QM2 is an example. The downside: passengers will be charged for their use, not only in the food outlets but perhaps for such items as movies and entertainment. Already it has been shown that passengers are willing to pay for some enhancements.

Another trend to watch: Ships staying overnight in port, giving passengers the opportunity to explore ports in more depth. This could be particularly appropriate for destination-oriented cruise lines and be a result of a maturing cruise market. It would reflect a shift from the old formula of more ports being seen as value to experienced cruisers understanding the value of overnight port stays.

Now that ResidenSea has shown the way, look for new lines to try a variety of new ideas, such as cruise ships with apartments for sale as time-share; or cabins booked for one to four months at a time or even a year.

Another trend that has picked up steam in recent years is cruise lines investing in port development in the United States—Royal Caribbean in Philadelphia and Bayonne, New Jersey; Carnival in Mobile, Alabama and Jacksonville, Florida—as well as in Mexico, the Caribbean, and Mediterranean, often giving the line exclusive rights as well as new or vastly improved ports.

The availability of Internet access on cruise ships has grown by leaps and bounds in the last two years and now, the availability of wireless connection and cell phone use is being added almost as rapidly. At the same time, the acceptance of personal computers as part of our lives and the ease of using them to book travel will have more and more people booking cruises on the Internet and the number of mom-and-pop travel agencies shrinking. Already those agencies have dropped from 33,000 in 2001 to about 17,000 in 2004, and some predict there will be less than 5,000 by the end of the decade. Meanwhile, the number of home-based travel agents has skyrocketed and now account for one-third of all cruise sales. They are expected to reach half-million agents before the decade ends. And, the Internet may even force cruise lines to simplify their pricing, including, we hope, brochure prices which today have no relation to reality.

Despite the setbacks and uncertainties, cruising as a vacation choice continues to attract new travelers by the thousands and has devotees returning year after year. That's because the fundamental attraction of cruising—value for money—has not and is not likely to change.

PART ONE

PLANNING YOUR CRUISE

UNDERSTANDING CRUISES

THE INCLUSIVE CRUISE VACATION

MOST CRUISES ARE INCLUSIVE, and when you buy a cruise, you generally are buying the basic components of a cruise vacation together rather than a la carte. Generally, a cruise—or what a travel agency or cruise line might describe as a "cruise-only" product—includes:

1. Shipboard accommodations.
2. Three full-service dining room meals daily (breakfast, lunch, and dinner), plus alternative breakfast, lunch, evening buffets, and late-night snacks. On most ships, room service meals do not cost extra. Many ships also offer options, such as early-bird breakfast, morning bouillon, and afternoon events, including tea, pizza snacks, ice cream parties, and poolside cookouts.
3. Most shipboard entertainment, including music, dancing, and shows in the lounges, discos, live bands, Las Vegas–style productions, nightclubs, karaoke, and movies.
4. Most shipboard sports and recreational facilities, including swimming pools, health club or exercise room, promenade or jogging track, whirlpool, sauna, library, game room, and child-care facilities. (Spa and beauty treatments, some specialized exercise classes such as Pilates, and sports equipment normally cost extra.)
5. Most shipboard activities, including casino entry, on-board games and contests, lectures, demonstrations, and most children's programs (where applicable, baby-sitting services are extra).
6. Stops at ports of call on the itinerary.

The features listed above are almost universally a part of any cruise vacation, and an inclusive cruise vacation is often a very good value, particularly when compared to the cost of similar pieces booked on a resort vacation. That said, other inclusions or lack of inclusion are line specific. Some cruise lines do include transfers—basically a bus or van ride from the airport to ship and ship to airport. Other lines charge for those transfers, unless you buy your air tickets through the line in what travel agents call an air/sea package.

Port charges (usually noted in the bottom fine print of any cruise advertising or brochure) are usually included in the cruise price. Still, it pays to check carefully or ask your travel agent, as port charges can range from $120 to $200 or even more on a seven-day Caribbean cruise, depending on the itinerary.

Taxes, optional shore excursions, alcoholic beverages and soft drinks, casino play, onboard shopping, some computer classes, use of Internet connection, and tips are not included in most cases. On a few very upscale lines, gratuities and wine and alcoholic beverages are included in the cruise price. On some, tips are pooled (you are asked to contribute a suggested amount per day to be divided among all staff except officers and senior staff) and now, more and more cruise lines are adding a service charge to your shipboard account in lieu of tipping. With most lines you have the option of paying it or having it removed and handling the tipping yourself. We include a section on tipping in Part Two.

CRUISING'S UNFORTUNATE STEREOTYPES

YOU HAVE PROBABLY HEARD that "cruising is not for everyone." But that's like saying travel is not for everyone. If you like to travel, you will almost certainly enjoy cruising. It's that simple. Cruising, however, has accumulated unfortunate stereotypes, which continue to recycle.

MYTH NO. 1: I'LL BE BORED Many people, particularly men and younger, active folks, believe cruising is dull and sedentary. They picture bulk loaders crowding buffets while active folks sit bored and unstimulated. Sorry, not so.

Today, most cruises offer around-the-clock activities. Ships have workout rooms with high quality equipment, jogging tracks, pools, and daily exercise classes. Some larger ships have volleyball courts, basketball courts, and even rock climbing walls, golf simulators, and ice rinks. At ports of call, a variety of sports—from golf to cycling, snorkeling to kayaking—are offered. There are far more opportunities for sports and athletics than most of us have at home. Some lines now even offer extreme adventures like off-road vehicle trips or mountain biking. If you go on a cruise and sit on your butt, that's your decision.

For the active but less athletic, most ships offer swimming, shuffleboard, table tennis, walking areas, and spa amenities, including hot tubs and saunas. Many ships offer yoga or stretching classes. At night, for the energetic, there's dancing in many forms, from ballroom to reggae to line dancing to salsa.

A range of organized activities targets gregarious and fun-loving people. Versions of television game shows are popular, as are more traditional events, such as bridge tournaments, arts and crafts classes, and dancing lessons. Most cruise ships have casinos, and almost all have bingo.

If learning is your goal, dozens of cruises specialize in providing educational experiences and exploration of a region accompanied by experts. Like floating graduate schools, these cruises may focus on political and natural history, or may even offer lectures on topics unrelated to the ship's destinations.

Finally, there is no place better than a cruise ship to relax. The favorite cruise activity for many people is curling up in a comfortable deck chaise with a good book. Even a big ship with constant activity offers quiet spots for meditation, reading, or just enjoying the beauty of the sea.

MYTH NO. 2: CRUISING IS FOR RICH PEOPLE; I CAN'T AFFORD A CRUISE
If you take a vacation of three or more days during which you stay in hotels and eat in restaurants, you can afford a cruise. In fact, a cruise may be cheaper than a deluxe resort vacation.

Let's compare cruising to a modest vacation: Vic and Edna's one-week trip to Gatlinburg, Tennessee, and the Smoky Mountains. Driving from their home near Cleveland, Ohio, Vic and Edna spent about $400 on gas for the Chevy. They averaged $75 a night plus tax for motels, or $577 for the week. For breakfast and lunch, it was Shoney's- or Denny's-type restaurants. They'd go more upscale for dinner, and they liked beer or wine with their meal. Total for seven days' food: $588. In the mountains, they mostly hiked and drove around. One day, however, they played golf; on another they visited a museum and a theme park. On the Friday before heading home, they rented horses for half a day. Golf, admissions, and horses came to approximately $260. Recapping:

Vic and Edna's Splendid Vacation	
Lodging	$577
Gas	$400
Meals	$588
Admissions	$260
Total	$1,825

During the same period, a good middle-of-the-market cruise line (not super-budget or super-luxury), offered a seven-night Caribbean cruise for $899 per person, including round-trip airfare. The cruise visited San Juan, St. Thomas, Martinique, Tortola, the British Virgin Islands, Antigua, and St. Maarten. Even better values could have been had with promotional fares, which were as low as $579.

These were promotional rates, not the "rack" rates listed in the brochures. The point is, on the seven-night cruise, Vic and Edna could have enjoyed the amenities of a full resort, dined in grand style, danced to live music, visited six beautiful tropical islands, and soaked in a whirlpool under the Caribbean moon for about the same amount they spent on their road trip. We are not suggesting Vic and Edna should swap the Smokies for the Caribbean, only that they could afford to do so if they are inclined.

MYTH NO. 3: CRUISES ARE STUFFY, ELITIST, AND FORMAL Most cruises are none of the above, though the description might fit some passengers. Cruises cover a broad range of dress and social protocols. You can choose a cruise at whatever level of formality or casualness feels right for you. Overall, cruises have become very casual and informal. Even on "formal" nights—such as the captain's welcome-aboard party and/or farewell party—only half of the men wear business suits, and women don cocktail or party dresses. Newer ships offering alternative (to the main dining room) dining options make it possible to avoid formal events entirely. Yet, on the most informal ships, like Carnival, people dress to the nines—and it's often the men more so than the women. And they love it.

MYTH NO. 4: CRUISES ARE TOO REGIMENTED FOR ME Granted, it takes organization to get everyone on board a cruise ship. It takes similar regimentation to get everyone off at the end of the cruise. At ports, you need only get back on board before the ship sails.

Some folks lump cruises into the same category as whirlwind bus tours—eight countries in five days and that sort of thing. A cruise might visit eight countries in five days, but you will have to check in and unpack only once. That's the beauty of cruising—you can hang out on the ship and just enjoy the ride, or you can get off at each port and pursue your own agenda.

Also, the trend toward more relaxed dining hours and alternative (to the main dining room) dining venues has resulted in notably less regimentation aboard ship.

MYTH NO. 5: I'M AFRAID I'LL GET SEASICK Well, you might, but the vast majority of people don't, particularly on a Caribbean cruise. Even those who get queasy in a car can usually handle a cruise. Over-the-counter antinausea medications like **Bonine** (doesn't make you drowsy) or **Dramamine** get most folks over the acclimatization period of the first few hours at sea. Bring some: You may never need it, but having it is comforting. Usually, Dramamine or Bonine is available from the purser's desk or the ship's medical unit.

Some guests swear by **Sea Bands**—a pair of elasticized wristbands (similar to tennis bands), each with a small plastic disk that applies pressure to the inside wrist, according to acupressure principles. They are particularly useful for people who have difficulty taking medication. Sea Bands are sold in drug, toiletry, and health-care stores (sometimes onboard ships as well) and can be ordered from **On the Go Travel Accessories** (5603 NW 159th Street, Miami, FL 33014; ☎ 888-303-3039; **www.onthegoaccessories.com**). If you take precautions and become seasick anyway, the ship's doctor can administer more powerful medication.

In regard to seasickness, remember: Don't dwell on your fear, and if you become queasy, take medicine immediately. When you deal with symptoms quickly, relief is quick.

Minimize the probability of getting seasick by choosing an itinerary in calmer waters: Alaska's Inside Passage, the Caribbean, the Mediterranean, and the Gulf of Mexico. Less smooth are voyages on the Atlantic, Pacific, or Indian oceans or the South China Sea. And remember the time of year may also matter. The Caribbean can be less smooth during hurricane season. You are unlikely to be in the storm's way, but water conditions can kick up far from the trouble zone.

MYTH NO. 6: I'M APPREHENSIVE ABOUT WALKING ON A MOVING SHIP If you are not agile or fit on land, you might envision tortuous trips down narrow gangways or climbing ladders through tiny hatches while the ship rolls and pitches. But those images are really in the past. Generally, if you can handle a hotel, you can handle a cruise ship. Large vessels have wide, carpeted halls with hand railings, and slip-resistant outside decks. Elevators serve all passenger decks, so using the stairs may not even be necessary. Passengers use no tricky ladders or tiny hatches.

Modern cruise ships have state-of-the-art stabilizers, and even in bad weather and heavy seas they are amazingly stable. Small ships, depending on their draft and build, may be more subject to the motion of the ocean and are a little more challenging to get around. Being smaller, however, there's less territory to cover. Most ships launched in the last ten years were built with consideration for healthy passengers as well as those with ambulatory disabilities. Most new ships offer wheelchair-accessible cabins and ramps.

A TYPICAL DAY ON A CRUISE

LET'S SAY YOU'RE CRUISING the Caribbean. You can start your morning with an early-bird breakfast or a walk or jog around deck, or you can have breakfast from the menu in the dining room. Late sleepers can order breakfast from room service or catch the breakfast buffet, which stays open later than the dining room. It may be served on the "lido" deck—a casual indoor/outdoor dining facility on the same deck as the swimming pool or sports facilities. The lido buffet has longer and more flexible hours, enabling you to come and go at will.

Days at sea are the most relaxing of the cruise itinerary. The casino, shopping arcade, spa, exercise room, and shore-excursion desk are open. Programs and activities are virtually nonstop on large ships; many folks, however, hang out by the pool or on deck to enjoy the beauty of the sea and the relaxing movement of being underway. The captain may update passengers over the public-address system on the ship's progress toward the next port. The captain or cruise director may also point out interesting sights.

Lunch works much like breakfast: You can eat in the dining room and order from the menu, or you can stay in your swimsuit and eat burgers or pizza by the pool, where there is likely to be a music combo playing upbeat rhythms. You can join the pool games—always a good way to meet people—or just watch or ignore them. You then might work out, read, nap, play bridge, learn the latest dance steps, or attend orientation lectures about the next port. Recently released movies are shown in the ship's movie theater or on cabin television in the afternoon. On some ships, afternoon tea is a big deal—white gloves and all. At cocktail hour, there is usually live music by the pool, often with special drinks or appetizers, or happy hour in one of the bars.

As dinner approaches, it's time to dress for the evening. The dress code generally is specified on the daily agenda slipped under your door every evening. It is also spelled out in the cruise line's brochure, so you can pack accordingly. (More information on dress codes is available under "Preparing for Your Cruise.")

Some passengers stroll the deck before dinner, particularly at sunset, a beautiful time at sea. Others have a drink in one of the lounges. Dinner in the dining room is a social culmination of the day's activity. Spirits are always high.

After lingering over several well-prepared courses, it's off to the showroom, where live entertainment, ranging from Las Vegas–style variety shows to Broadway musicals, is offered nightly. After the show, early risers and those who had a long day of touring retire to their cabins. The more active or party-minded guests head for the casino, disco, or a lounge with entertainment. Midnight buffets are about "gone" these days. On select nights there may be a special late-night buffet or light snack fare. Now, too, on many ships, you have another option—a 24- (or almost 24-) hour alternative restaurant, often dressed up for the evening with table service and music. Before turning in, stretch out in a chaise lounge on deck with a glass of wine. Breathe in the balmy salt-sea air and be caressed by the warm breeze. Lose yourself among the million stars of the Caribbean night.

Usually, cruise ships sail through the night and arrive at the next port early in the morning. If you have risen in time to enjoy the early morning—the most beautiful time at sea—you can watch your ship dock. It's interesting and fun. After breakfast, the captain announces that the ship has been cleared by local officials and that passengers may disembark. Those signed up for shore excursions are given last-minute instructions about when and where to meet and are normally first to go ashore.

Although port calls range from two hours to two days (with an overnight at dock), most are four to ten hours—enough time to get a taste of an island or city. As you disembark, crew members remind you of the sailing time and make sure you are carrying your cruise identification, which you must present to reboard. Once ashore, some people explore on foot on their own, take walking tours, shop, and perhaps try a shoreside restaurant. Others hire a cab for a driving tour, and most take shore excursions purchased aboard ship.

Shore excursions take many forms. Some are passive (bus tour), but others are active (snorkeling, sailing, hiking, biking, or fishing). Surprisingly, many folks, particularly repeat cruisers, stay aboard ship. It's quiet—almost empty of passengers—but it's in full operation, except for casinos and shops. Lunch is served on schedule in the dining room.

About an hour before sailing, you reboard the ship. Don't be late. The ship will not wait for you! Just before castoff, go topside to watch the crew prepare for departure. Leaving port is always interesting, and a ship's higher decks offer a great viewing platform. Once at sea, the ship settles into its normal nighttime routine, and so do you.

SO MANY CRUISES TO CHOOSE FROM

TO THE FIRST-TIME CRUISER and even many veterans, the number of cruise lines, ships, and itineraries is staggering. Travel agencies that sell only cruises ease their customers into the array of choices by comparing cruise lines with well-known hotel chains, and such comparisons are useful. They might see Carnival, for example, as the Holiday Inn of cruises. Holland America and Celebrity Cruise Line are up a notch, perhaps at the Hyatt level.

Ritz-Carlton-type cruises might appeal to the most discriminating cruisers and are at the upper end of price, service, and amenities. Large and medium ships in this class include those of Crystal Cruises and Radisson Seven Seas Cruises (which also has a small ship in Tahiti). Boutique cruises overlap the luxury category and include the smaller, all-suite ships of Silversea, Seabourn, as well as the cruise/sail ships of Windstar.

Be aware that none of the hotel chains mentioned (except Radisson and Hyatt) have anything to do with cruising, and these are only a handful of the lines available. Though the foregoing comparison may help you see where you fit into the general scheme, you must dig much deeper to find your perfect cruise.

GETTING YOUR ACT TOGETHER

CRUISES VARY WIDELY. To pinpoint your requirements and preferences in a cruise, you need to ask yourself dozens of questions. Once you settle on what you want, it's easier to match your demands and budget with the appropriate line and ship.

What Is My Vacation Budget?

Unless price is no object, one place to start planning is your general budget. How much can you afford, and what are you willing to spend for your cruise? Consider what you must or may add to the cruise price: port charges and taxes, shore excursions, shopping, drinks and dinner wine (on most ships), gambling in the casino, spa services, laundry, and tips for crew members. Once you figure a range within your uppermost limit for all costs, you can begin to explore what kind of cruise you can buy. A good travel agent may tell you about a special promotion that provides value or added perks on a cruise you may think is beyond your price range. In the end, it may cost less, and if it does cost more, you may decide it is the best choice due to "extras" you receive. In other words, use your budget as a starting point.

unofficial **TIP**
Have flexibility and an open mind.

Although we will revisit this issue in "How to Get the Best Deal on a Cruise," let's say three-day cruises start at about $295 a person, assuming two people to a cabin. Seven-day cruises begin at about $650, and ten-day cruises are about $920 and up. These prices are deeply discounted and represent the least you would expect to pay, usually for a cabin without windows.

How Many Days Do I Want to Cruise?

Your available vacation time and budget are among the factors in your ultimate cruise selection. Generally, the larger your budget, the more cruise days you can buy. That is, the longer the cruise, the more it will cost. If your budget isn't up to the number of days you have your heart set on, you still have options. First, trade luxury for cruise days; consider a cruise on a less-luxurious ship. The fee for a week on an upscale ship will easily buy two weeks on a midrange vessel. Second, cruise during the off-season, when prices are lowest. Third, consider the least expensive cabin. Once aboard, all passengers have the same privileges, eat the same meals, and enjoy the same entertainment. Unless you plan to spend an extraordinary amount of time in your cabin, you might select less-expensive accommodations. We're not talking about special suites, just the difference between the highest deck outside cabin (with a window or veranda) and the lowest deck inside cabin (no window). For example, on a seven-day Celebrity Cruise Line itinerary to Bermuda, the upper-deck outside cabin costs more than twice as much as the lower-deck inside cabin.

unofficial **TIP**
Don't veer too far from your lifestyle or expectations, or you will be disappointed with your cruise.

In the Caribbean and Mexico, a seven-day cruise is about right for your first trip, but a three- or four-night cruise will give you a good enough overview of ship life that you can determine whether cruising is something you'll enjoy again in the future.

Where Do I Want to Go?

You can cruise just about anywhere there is enough water to float a ship. This includes all of the world's oceans and seas and many rivers. Where you want to cruise depends primarily on your own "wild goose." It also hinges on your preferred style of cruising and whether you enjoy the destinations or the ship more.

Some destinations, including Alaska and Europe, are seasonal. Others, including the Caribbean and Mexico, are year-round. Almost all cruises worldwide are tailored to the market and the weather. Many to the Caribbean and Mexico, for example, are festive and high-spirited, emphasizing activity and fun. Mild temperatures allow time outdoors, and passengers tend to be younger. By contrast, Alaskan, Canadian, North Atlantic, Scandinavian, and Baltic Sea cruises are more passive, focusing on the beauty of the forests, islands, fjords, and glaciers. Still, Alaska cruises can have very active shore trips. For these northerly venues, longer cruises and colder temperatures contribute to a more sedate experience and attract families or older passengers. Mediterranean itineraries generally revolve around antiquities and port cities of southern Europe, northern Africa, and the Middle East. Most ships visit a port each day, and sightseeing is the backbone of the vacation. On ships where English is spoken and the majority aboard are Americans, the passengers are likely to be 50 years of age or older, and affluent. On cruise ships where Europeans predominate, passengers are often younger, and sun and fun are emphasized, like in the Caribbean.

Hawaiian cruises occupy the middle, emphasizing both festivity and scenery, though passengers are, at times, older on average than those in the Caribbean. For other North Pacific, South Pacific, Indian Ocean, and South China Sea settings, the distance of the cruise areas and home ports from the United States ensures an older, wealthier market. Like Mediterranean cruises, sightseeing and cultural attractions are the focus.

Though a great way to see exotic places without shuffling among hotels, cruises allow only a cursory glimpse of the countries visited. Ten hours in Venice on a cruise is no substitute for visiting Italy. Even in the Caribbean, short stopovers on small islands leave much undiscovered. Yet, many guests will enjoy seeing something new, and probably would never travel to all these destinations on their own.

If you are interested in further exploring a destination, consider the add-ons most lines offer at the beginning and end of cruises. Two- or three-night packages include a hotel and some sightseeing. They are usually well priced and can be booked at the time you buy your cruise. Also consider picking an itinerary that offers "overnights"

unofficial **TIP**
Some travelers use cruising to sample cities and countries to determine whether they might want to return later for a more prolonged visit.

in certain high-profile ports such as St. Petersburg, Russia, or Venice. These cruises offer more intense destination time ashore.

DEFINING THE CARIBBEAN On a map with the arm of the compass pointing north, the islands closest to the United States are the Greater Antilles; they include Cuba, the Caymans, Jamaica, Haiti, the Dominican Republic, and Puerto Rico. All but Cuba are visited by ships from U.S. ports and have daily, direct air service from major U.S. cities.

The Bahamas and the British colony of the Turks and Caicos lie north of the Greater Antilles and southeast of Florida. They are entirely in the Atlantic Ocean, but because their tropical environment is similar to that of the Caribbean, they are viewed as part of the region. The Bahamas, and occasionally the Turks and Caicos, are cruise stops; both have air service from the United States mainland.

In the eastern Caribbean are the Lesser Antilles, starting with the Virgin Islands in the north and curving south to Grenada. The northern of these many small islands are called the Leewards and comprise the U.S. and British Virgin Islands, Anguilla, St. Maarten, St. Barts, Saba, St. Eustatius, St. Kitts, Nevis, Antigua, Barbuda, Montserrat, and Guadeloupe. The south islands, called the Windwards, include Dominica, Martinique, St. Lucia, Barbados, St. Vincent and the Grenadines, and Grenada.

The Virgin Islands, St. Marten, Antigua, Guadeloupe, Martinique, St. Kitts, St. Lucia, and Barbados are frequent cruise stops and have direct air service from the United States mainland or via Puerto Rico. The others are reached through local airlines, and most are stops for small ships, particularly during winter cruise season. In the south are Aruba, Bonaire, Curaçao, and Trinidad and Tobago, which lie off Venezuela. Aruba and Curaçao are major ports on southern Caribbean and Panama Canal cruises. In the western Caribbean are Jamaica and the Cayman Islands, and off the Yucatán Peninsula are the Mexican islands of Cancún and Cozumel. All are major cruise destinations.

Along the 2,000-mile Caribbean chain, nature has been extravagant with its color, variety, and beauty. Verdant mountains rise from sun-bleached shores. Between towering peaks and the sea, rivers and streams cascade over rocks and hillsides and disappear into mangrove swamps and deserts. Fields of flowers, trees with brilliant blossoms, and a multitude of birds and butterflies fill the landscape. The air, refreshed by tropical showers, is scented with spices and fruit.

Yet what makes the Caribbean islands unique is their combination of exotic scenery and the kaleidoscope of diverse cultures. The cultures have evolved from traditions, music, dance, art, architecture, and religions from around the world.

To be fair, we should warn you that the exponential growth of cruising in the Caribbean has had a tremendous, and many would say negative, impact on some islands. Cruise ships disgorging thousands

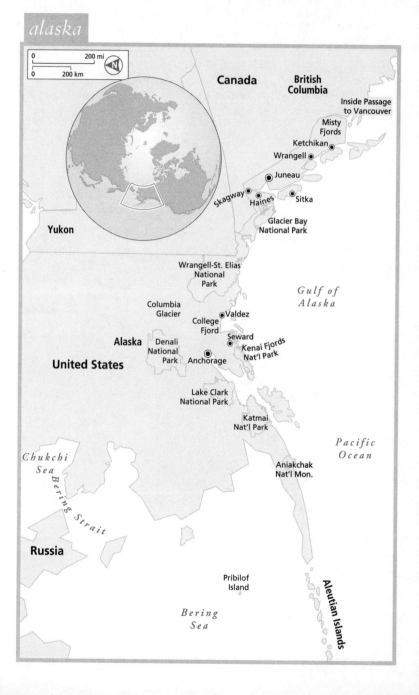

alaska

Canada

British Columbia

Inside Passage to Vancouver

Misty Fjords

Ketchikan

Wrangell

Juneau

Skagway

Haines

Sitka

Glacier Bay National Park

Yukon

Wrangell-St. Elias National Park

Gulf of Alaska

Columbia Glacier

College Fjord

Valdez

Alaska

Denali National Park

Seward

Kenai Fjords Nat'l Park

United States

Anchorage

Lake Clark National Park

Katmai Nat'l Park

Pacific Ocean

Chukchi Sea

Aniakchak Nat'l Mon.

Bering Strait

Russia

Pribilof Island

Aleutian Islands

Bering Sea

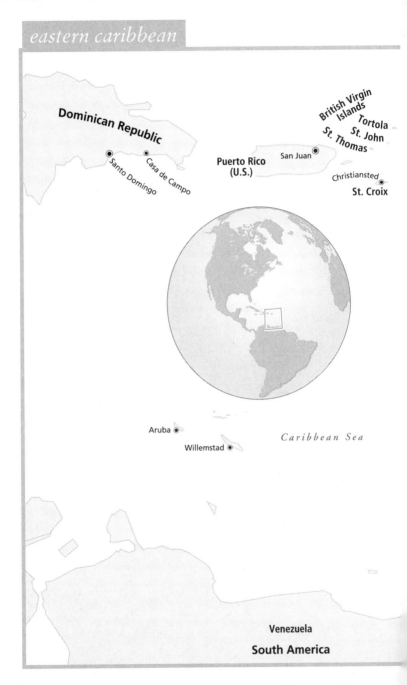

eastern caribbean

Dominican Republic

British Virgin Islands

Tortola

St. John

St. Thomas

Puerto Rico (U.S.)

San Juan

Santo Domingo

Casa de Campo

Christiansted

St. Croix

Aruba

Willemstad

Caribbean Sea

Venezuela

South America

western caribbean

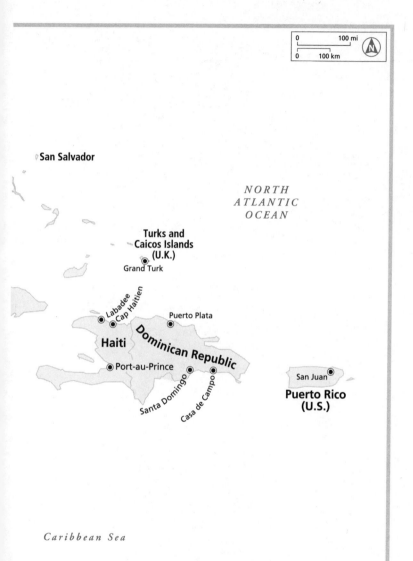

San Salvador

NORTH ATLANTIC OCEAN

Turks and Caicos Islands (U.K.)
Grand Turk

Labadee
Cap Haitien
Puerto Plata

Haiti

Dominican Republic

Port-au-Prince

Santa Domingo

Casa de Campo

San Juan

Puerto Rico (U.S.)

Caribbean Sea

Aruba
Oranjestad

Curaçao
Willemstad

Bonaire
Kralendijk

south america

Caribbean Sea

Los Roques

Margarita Island

Trinidad and Tobago

Cartagenta

La

Puerto La Cruz

Caracas

Venezuela

Angel Falls

Guyana

Suriname

Devil's

French Guiana

Cayenne

Atlantic Ocean

Columbia

Galapagos Islands

Quito

Guayaquil

San Cristobal
Santa Cruz
Ferandina

Iquitos

Manaus

Alter Do Chao

Amazon River

Santarem

Belem

Fortaleza

Peru

Lima

Brazil

Salvador

Bolivia

Chile

Paraguay

Sao Paulo

Antofagasta

Rio de Janeiro

South Pacific Ocean

Argentina

Uraguay

Santiago

Buenos Aires

Punta Del Este

Montevideo

Puerto Montt

South Atlantic Ocean

Falkland Islands (U.K.)

Tierra Del
Ushuaia
Cape Horn

0   1000 mi

0   1000km

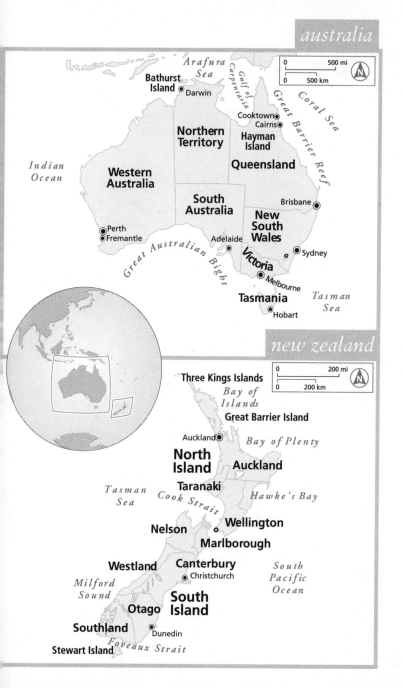

australia

Arafura Sea

Bathurst Island

Darwin

Gulf of Carpentaria

Cooktown

Cairns

Northern Territory

Hayman Island

Great Barrier Reef

Coral Sea

Indian Ocean

Western Australia

Queensland

South Australia

Brisbane

Perth
Fremantle

New South Wales

Adelaide

Great Australian Bight

Victoria

Sydney

Melbourne

Tasmania

Tasman Sea

Hobart

0   500 mi
0   500 km

new zealand

Three Kings Islands

Bay of Islands

Great Barrier Island

Auckland

Bay of Plenty

North Island

Auckland

Tasman Sea

Taranaki

Cook Strait

Hawke's Bay

Nelson

Wellington

Marlborough

Westland

Canterbury

South Pacific Ocean

Milford Sound

Christchurch

South Island

Otago

Southland

Dunedin

Stewart Island

Foveaux Strait

0   200 mi
0   200 km

the orient

indian ocean

southeast asia

eastern mediterranean

western mediterranean

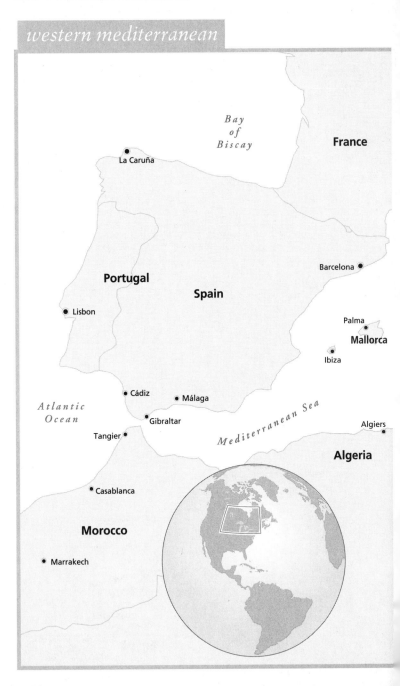

Bay
of
Biscay

France

● La Caruña

Portugal

Spain

Barcelona ●

● Lisbon

Palma
●
Mallorca

Ibiza
●

● Cádiz   ● Málaga

Atlantic
Ocean

● Gibraltar

Mediterranean Sea

Algiers
●

Tangier ●

Algeria

● Casablanca

Morocco

● Marrakech

scandanavia and northern europe

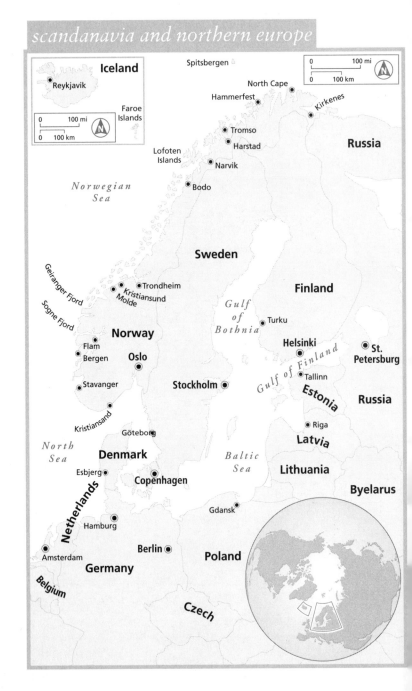

of passengers a day on a tiny island disrupt the normal rhythms, changing a quaint, sleepy, laid-back port into a frenetic, artificial tourist attraction. Sprawling malls have sprung up like ragweed around the docks, and whole local populations have abandoned their lifelong vocations to cater to tourists. Some Caribbean islands have become the equivalent of private islands owned by several cruise lines: plastic, idealized versions more familiar to fans of *Gilligan's Island* than to veteran Caribbean travelers.

When Do I Want to Go?

Cruises follow the sun, visiting destinations during their best weather. Hence, for some exotic destinations and such seasonal cruise areas as Alaska, the British Isles, Canada, and Antarctica, you have only a two- to five-month window of opportunity. For the Caribbean, Mexico, Hawaii, and Asia, among others, cruises are available all year.

Following is a sampling of popular destinations and cruising seasons.

Africa	Year-round, but mostly May–October for north Africa; November–April for eastern and southern Africa
Alaska	May–September
Asia and the Orient	Mainly October–March
Baltic	May–October
Bermuda	May–October
Black Sea	April–October
Canada	May–October
Caribbean	Year-round
Hawaii	Year-round
India and Southeast Asia	Year-round, but mostly November–April
Mediterranean	Year-round, but mostly March–November
Mexico	Year-round
New England	May–October
Panama Canal	Year-round, but mostly September–May
South America	North coast, year-round; other areas, September–April
South Pacific	Year-round, but mainly November–April

For every area, periods of peak demand are called high season; moderate demand, shoulder season; and low demand, low season or value season. Usually high season occurs when good weather in the cruise area coincides with times when people want to take vacations. In the Caribbean, that's between Christmas and the middle of April, and from June 15 to August 15. But in the Caribbean, for example, immediately after the Christmas–New Year holiday, demand drops and the first two weeks in January offer value-season rates. If you can be flexible, shifting cruise dates a week or two may offer big savings. Ask your travel agent to compare pricing on a week-to-week basis before you book. Always check the period immediately before or after your selected dates to find out your options.

unofficial **TIP**
Within high season, there are often valleys when prices are likely to be their lowest for the year, offering you an opportunity to save a bundle.

The January to April market targets seniors and Northerners seeking a respite from the winter. Although weather in summer is not generally as good as between January and April, families create high demand during midsummer. When demand tapers off, shoulder season follows, giving way to low season as cruise demand continues to decline.

During high season, ships generally are full and cruises are more expensive (because demand is high). If your plans are flexible, it is usually possible to identify several times in the year when your destination's weather is predictably good but cruise demand is moderate or low. Cruising during these periods provides lower prices, less-crowded ships, and good weather. Caribbean cruises in November and early December, before Christmas, are good examples. Hurricane season is over, prices are lower, and ships are significantly less crowded. Early May for Alaska is another excellent time.

If your travel schedule is not flexible, shoulder seasons (early June or late August) may be your best bet. Still, in 2005, one trend surfacing was that nearly all ships were sailing full, so discounting was far less than in 2004, 2003, or 2002.

What Sort of Lifestyle or Activity Level Am I Seeking?

As baby boomers enter middle age and relative affluence, and as younger couples and families discover the economy of cruise vacations, cruising's demographics are changing. On most midmarket cruises of two weeks or less, passengers are amazingly diverse. Responding to a widening range of energy and interests among these passengers, lines have developed activities that offer something for almost everyone.

Even so, lines continue to fine-tune their product for their primary markets. Thus, although Celebrity Cruises might develop programs and activities for younger clients, these cruisers continue to be a secondary market. The line's real focus is the 45 to 65 age group. That means a younger person will have a good time on Celebrity, but an over-40 person will probably have a better time because the cruise is built around the latter's preferences.

How cruise lines serve their primary, secondary, and even tertiary markets makes relevant the question, "What sort of lifestyle or activity level am I seeking?"

In each of our cruise-line and ship profiles, we pinpoint the style, tenor, and activity level of the cruises offered. Look for an activity and social mix that seems right for you, but don't get bogged down in demographics. Many older people are active, athletic, and like to party, and many young people appreciate a sedate cruise and may spend their days doing nothing more than reading in a lounge chair.

The choice to participate in activities or party all night is entirely yours. Do, however, pay attention to the ship's size. A small ship carrying 250 or fewer passengers may have only one or two lounges and limited deck space. If you don't care for a full day or evening of shipboard activity, you'll enjoy its low-key ambience. Large ships have the resources to offer considerable variety. Carnival Cruise Lines, for example, pretty much wrote the book on party cruising, but even on a Carnival ship it is possible to relax. Ships carrying 1,000 or more passengers have plenty of places to escape the festivities.

Most ships offer a variety of dance music. Many even have separate nightclubs offering different types of music, dancing, and entertainment. Some even offer teen night spots.

Cruise lines design their promotional brochures to appeal to their target markets. If you identify with the people and activities depicted in the brochure, you probably will feel at home on one of that line's ships. Lines that do not cater to families, for instance, do not feature them in their literature. Study the brochures from your travel agent. Are the passengers pictured your age or of varied ages? Is the emphasis on shipboard activities or ports and scenery? Does shipboard life look like a 24-hour party, or do photos show a more laid-back experience? On-board facilities need no interpretation. They're spelled out.

What Level of Formality Do I Prefer?

Most cruises give passengers an opportunity to play dress-up. On certain evenings in the main dining room, men may be requested to wear jackets, tuxedos, or dark suits, and women to wear cocktail dresses or gowns. Most ships have a dress protocol that passengers are expected to observe, and it varies widely by line. (See "Dress Codes" under "Preparing for Your Cruise.")

Formality (or lack thereof) is a way cruise lines set themselves apart. A luxury line targeting highly affluent passengers may be more formal than a midmarket line. Family and budget lines can be less formal, but even the "fun ships" of Carnival have some formal nights, and adventure cruises are usually the most informal.

The bottom line is how much formality you want. The great majority of cruises vary attire from night to night and won't punish someone who breaks the dress code. If, for example, a man wears a dark suit instead of a tuxedo for the captain's party, it's likely no one will turn him away. Check the ship's dress code before you book.

unofficial **TIP**
Even an informal ship might ask passengers not to wear shorts and tank tops in the dining room and be strict about it.

What Standards Do I Require for Dining and Food Quality?

Food—its quality and the overall dining experience—is cited by most passengers as a critical element of their cruise. The fare on cruise ships is generally very good—impressive considering that shipboard meals represent the ultimate extension of catered banquet dining.

Feeding 300 to 1,400 persons at a sitting is challenging under any circumstances. Doing it at sea with attention to detail, quality ingredients and preparation, multiple courses, and beautiful presentation is one of cruising's miracles. Ships have made an art of serving palatable food to crowds of diners. Hotel food and beverage managers could learn a lot from cruise ship chefs.

However, you can't expect the same excellence from a galley serving hundreds of dinners as you can from an upscale restaurant cooking to order for a small number of guests. A few small ships have cuisine rivaling better land-based restaurants, and small alternative or specialty restaurants on newer large ships can hold their own with the best of them.

The quality of meals and sophistication of the dining experience vary considerably among ships. Although luxury ships serving fewer passengers in single seatings have the greatest potential for serving memorable meals, midmarket lines like Celebrity, Holland America, and Princess have shown they can approach similar standards of excellence serving larger numbers.

If you have a refined palate and eat exclusively in the finest restaurants, you may meet your dining requirements only in the high-end group of cruise ships. If, however, you dine regularly in restaurants of varying quality, are acquainted with the world's major cuisines, and understand the limitations of cruise food service, you will find numerous ships capable of meeting or exceeding your expectations.

For those not hung up on gourmet food, there are many suitable, and even better, affordable cruises. You can use your cruise dining experience to broaden your culinary horizons, or you can save bucks aboard a ship specializing in good but less-expensive American fare.

Many people pay for food much fancier than their taste requires. Meat-and-potatoes people get a better deal putting their dollars into a cabin upgrade on a midmarket line rather than paying for fancy food on a luxury line.

Cruise lines have tended to offer good dining-room meals or good buffets, but seldom both. Almost all lines have eliminated the midnight buffet, except for one special late-night extravaganza on some ships when chefs go all out to show off their culinary skills.

Under Norwegian Cruise Line's "Freestyle Cruising" program, you can eat in one of two main dining rooms, at whatever time you choose during normal hours of operation, or you can make reservations at any of six alternative restaurants. On the *Norwegian Sun,* for example, Le Bistro serves French cuisine; East Meets West offers Pacific

Rim and Asian fusion fare; Las Ramblas offers tapas bar fare; Il Adagio offers Italian cuisine; Pacific Heights specializes in healthy, light California cuisine; and Ginza offers sushi, sashimi, and teppanyaki dining. If none of that works for you, the Garden Café operates a buffet around the clock, or alternatively there's 24-hour room service. The reservations-only alternative restaurants impose a surcharge of $10 to $25 per person, but it's worth it. The restaurants are elegant, quiet, and intimate, and the food rivals that of good onshore restaurants—or perhaps more relevant, the fare served on ships in the luxury market. Boomers love the flexibility these multiple restaurants provide. Aside from the surcharge, the main downside is that you don't have the opportunity to meet people and form friendships as you would in a conventional dining arrangement, where you eat in the same place, at the same assigned table, and with the same people, every night—a feature important to more "traditional cruisers."

Among other cruise-dining innovators, Princess's Personal Choice Dining program offers multiple restaurants and no assigned seating; or alternatively, passengers can opt for the traditional dining arrangement. The Disney Cruise Line also features several dining venues, but on the Disney ships, passengers rotate among three different themed restaurants according to a prearranged schedule. And, in a concession to those passengers who develop a fondness for their wait staff, their waiter and assistant rotate right along with them. Carnival, with yet another approach, offers "total choice" dining, where passengers can choose from four seating times in the main dining room, instead of the usual two; some other lines are also doing this. The four seatings stagger the arrival of diners, preventing the galley from being inundated, and allowing both chefs and wait staff to concentrate on a smaller number of diners at a given time.

Weather and lifestyle have clearly affected cruise dining. Because most ships spend all or part of the year in the Caribbean and Mexico, where passengers remain in their bathing suits most of the day, the lines found that it makes sense and saves money to expand the lido breakfast and lunch. Lido dining also gives passengers relief from the regimentation of dining-room hours.

A recent trend in onboard dining is the availability of stand-alone specialty restaurants in addition to the main dining room and buffet. Found mostly on ships carrying 1,000 or more passengers, and operating like a restaurant on shore, these specialized eateries offer an intimacy and ambience impossible to match in the ship's grand dining room. Like most upscale restaurants, the sea-going versions accept reservations; or alternatively, you can just show up during operating hours and hope to get a table. Cuisines and specialties available run the gamut from steak to sushi, Cantonese to California nouvelle cuisine. Almost all charge a fee ranging from $10 to $30, and most are worth every penny. Especially notable are *QM2's* Todd

English, Princess's Sabatini, and Carnival's ship-top steak and seafood restaurants.

How Gregarious Am I (Are We)?

Generally, it's easier to meet folks on a small ship if that is one of your prime goals onboard. There are fewer passengers, and you see the same people more often. Conversely, on a large ship, the only folks you see regularly may be your dinner-table companions (hope you like them!). On larger ships, if you meet somebody you would like to see again, get their name and cabin number. We once met a nice woman checking in on the 2,300-passenger *Monarch of the Seas*. In a week aboard, we never again saw her. Then again, many people who are frazzled in their everyday work life come aboard for escapism and personal pampering. Some don't need or want this socializing.

Large ships offer many social settings. It's possible to meet people in bars, lounges, and nightclubs; on shore excursions; in the health club; around the pool; and in the casino. But the easiest time to meet them is at planned activities. Whether it's aerobics and line dancing or bridge and wine tasting, such activities help people with similar interests come together.

The style of a cruise is important. If you are gregarious, you might prefer a ship that promotes a party atmosphere. If you are more solitary or are taking a romantic cruise with your significant other, you may prefer a less-frenetic social agenda.

Most cruisers solve the problem of companionship by taking significant others, friends, relatives, or all of the above with them. As on Noah's ark, the majority of passengers arrive already paired up. This is attributable in part to the double-occupancy norm for cabins. On most ships, solo passengers pay a hefty "singles supplement" for the privilege of having a cabin to themselves. Ships schedule gatherings where singles can meet, and some try to seat singles at the same dining tables, but singles generally have to scout around to find other people who are sailing solo.

The Other Passengers: What Kind of People Am I Most Comfortable With?

The less expensive the cruise, the more varied the passengers. Aboard a recent, affordable four-day cruise were retired seniors, middle-aged professionals, 20-something newlyweds, a bowling team from Pennsylvania, families with young children, a group of pipe fitters, and college students on spring break.

On upscale cruises of two weeks or longer, the cost ensures that passengers are somewhat more affluent and perhaps less diverse. On a seven-day Caribbean or Mexico cruise with midmarket lines, such as Princess, Celebrity, and Holland America, you will find more seniors, more professionals, fewer tradespeople, fewer families with children (except during summer), and fewer people younger than age 25. Passengers are even less varied on the same lines' seven-day or longer cruises to the more expensive destinations of Alaska and the Mediterranean.

On the most upscale lines, including Seabourn, Radisson Seven Seas, and Silversea, the average passenger is older than age 50 and affluent. Passengers younger than age 20 are likely traveling with parents or grandparents. Some lines don't take children or discourage their presence because they do not have the facilities or atmosphere for them. Couples account for 80% of those on board. Singles are likely to be widows, widowers, or mature singles able to afford the lifestyle. Many lines get a fair number of mother-daughter pairings.

For our profiles of cruise lines and ships, we carefully scrutinized their passengers so you'll know what to expect. We believe the inclusion of this information is one element that makes this book different from other guidebooks on cruises. If you have strong feelings about whom your fellow passengers will be, pay close attention to these descriptions.

Warning: Children Aboard

One person's darling can be another person's pain in the neck. We have received a surprising number of complaints from readers about children on their cruises. However, most referred to cruises during holidays, spring break, and summer, when there can be 400 or more children aboard a ship. On Disney Cruise Line, the number could be much greater. In such cases, even people who adore children might find their patience wearing thin if the children are rowdy and ill-behaved, or if the cruise lines fail to supervise them adequately. As cruise popularity and family travel increase, the two converge with greater frequency.

If you do not want to cruise with children, avoid holiday periods, particularly on mass-market lines that promote family travel and cruise to the most popular Caribbean, Mexican, and Alaskan destinations. If, however, these are the only times you can travel (if you are a teacher, for example), search for ships that sail off the beaten track or focus on enrichment rather than entertainment. Finally, an experienced travel agent should be able to help you find the right ship—or the ones to avoid.

unofficial **TIP**
The simple fact is that cruising can be a wonderful family vacation.

What Kind of Itinerary Do I Prefer?

Among itineraries, there's a world to choose from. You can have mostly days at sea, mostly days in port, or a balance of the two. Your cruise can be educational or just fun. There are theme cruises where entertainment or education is the focus, such as a jazz festival, and cruises where specific activities are emphasized, such as scuba diving, golf, sailing, or viewing wildlife.

Start by deciding how much time at sea versus time in port you prefer. If you are more interested in visiting ports, seek an itinerary with many of them. (Be aware that when a ship visits more than five ports on a seven-day cruise, some stops will be half-day.) Port-intensive itineraries are most plentiful on Mediterranean and eastern Caribbean cruises. Compare itineraries for different lines listing the same ports. When figuring your time in each port, remember that your ship must clear customs on arrival before passengers are allowed to disembark. A ship making port at 8 a.m. may not put passengers ashore before 9 or 9:30 a.m. Most ships require passengers to be aboard 30 minutes or more before leaving port. Thus your time in port could be trimmed by an hour or more coming and going.

Another important consideration, if you want to maximize your time in port, is whether your ship ties up at the dock or anchors offshore. Having to use a tender (a small commuting boat) to reach shore can take a big bite out of your port time. The larger the ship, the more likely the need to use a tender. The published itinerary or your travel agent will provide information on tendering.

Many passengers, particularly older, experienced cruisers who have "been there, done that" relish the serenity of being at sea. In recent years, they have been very vocal in opposing cruise lines' cramming ports into their itineraries to attract first-time cruisers who commonly perceive value in the number of ports visited. Increasingly though, as boomers and even younger travelers—both renowned as "collectors" of destinations—come onboard in greater numbers, the port or land focus has become more important to cruise lines. As a result it's more difficult to find itineraries featuring days spent at sea than to uncover itineraries with daily port calls. Some itineraries actually tout "overnights" in highly desirable ports like St. Petersburg or Venice. Most three-, four-, and seven-day cruises spend more daylight hours in port than at sea. Longer cruises typically feature more time at sea. Itineraries list days spent under way as "cruising" or "at sea."

A map highlighting ports of call in the world's cruise areas shows the hundreds of ports ships can add to their itineraries. With the possible exception of the Atlantic coast of Africa, most ports are close enough to one another to allow a port visit every day. Fortunately, most itineraries of seven or more days strike a balance. A typical seven-day itinerary includes two days at sea. Three or four days of cruising is typical of ten-day itineraries; 4 to 5 days on 12- to 14-day itineraries.

Repositioning cruises occur at the end of the season in a cruise area

unofficial **TIP**
Repositioning cruises are the best buys for those who crave more days at sea. They are also the best bargains.

when lines reposition their ship(s) by dispatching them to other areas where new seasons are beginning. Thus, Princess, Holland America, and many other lines reposition some of their Caribbean fleet in late April (the end of Caribbean high season) to the Pacific Northwest for summer cruises to Alaska. At the same time, Costa, Celebrity, Holland America, MSC Cruises, Princess, and others might dispatch ships from the Caribbean to Europe or the Mediterranean. Repositioning cruises stop at some ports, but there usually is a high ratio of sea days to days in port. Because such voyages occur only twice a year, they are difficult for lines to promote, and passage usually is discounted significantly.

Specialized Itineraries and Specialized Ships

Passengers aboard most large ships determine for themselves how they will use their time. Specialty cruises, by contrast, focus on a specific activity or pursuit. Some may specialize in whale-watching, others in exploring ancient ruins. Sometimes the vessel sets the focus. Smaller (20- to 150-passenger) ships can dock in small ports and anchor in secluded coves. This facilitates fishing, swimming, snorkeling, scuba diving, and water skiing (participants sometimes carry their own sports equipment) and makes a difference in the way passengers use their time.

Traditional ships sometimes offer theme cruises. For example, professional football players may be aboard and reruns of famous games are shown. Passengers should inquire about themes and book the cruise only if they're interested. A cruise ship can be the medium for countless activities and themes. For additional information on specialty cruises, see Part Three, Cruising Alternatives.

Big Ships versus Small Ships

Hardly a week passes that some cruise line doesn't announce plans for another ship—bigger and, of course, better than the last. But bigger isn't necessarily better for a cruise.

New words have crept into the cruise lexicon. Not everyone agrees on their definitions, but for the purpose of comparison, these are the parameters we will use:

ULTRALINER A cruise ship over 140,000 tons and with a basic capacity (i.e., 2 people per cabin) of over 2,500 passengers.

MEGALINER A cruise ship with a basic capacity of more than 2,000 passengers.

SUPERLINER A cruise ship with a basic capacity of about 1,000 to 2,000 passengers.

MIDSIZE A cruise ship with a basic capacity of 400 to 900 passengers.

SMALL SHIP A cruise ship with a basic capacity of under 400 passengers.

BOUTIQUE SHIP A luxury cruise or expedition ship with a basic capacity of under 300 passengers.

OCEANLINER Generally, any oceangoing passenger vessel, but tends to be used for ships that provided transatlantic and worldwide service and have since been converted into cruise ships. Although the new *QM2* could be called an oceanliner, she's also an ultraliner since she holds 2,800 passengers and offers transatlantic service on a regular basis.

Until you sail on small ships, you may not realize their special pleasures. Small ships are fewer but more diverse in style than larger ones. They range from traditional sailing ships, such as Star Clipper's tall ships, to computer-driven ones like Windstar Cruises' ships, and in the degree of comfort and service from the modest vessels of American Canadian Caribbean Lines to Silversea's ultraluxurious quartet. Prices likewise vary from the moderate Windjammer Barefoot Cruises to *très cher* Seabourn Cruises.

unofficial **TIP**
Small ships are people-sized. It's easy to learn the layout on the first day. Life aboard is casual, even on the most luxurious ships. Informality and friendliness go hand in hand. Passengers are fewer, and making friends is easy—an advantage for singles.

It's difficult to generalize, but all small ships are cozy, imparting warmth never felt on a superliner. The smallest ones, such as American Safari's 12- to 21-passenger ships, are like private yachts—yet surprisingly affordable. The congenial atmosphere also enhances interaction between passengers and crew, who are likely to call you by name from the first day. If you covet privacy and personal space, though, this type of cruise may not be your best bet.

Small ships with their shallow drafts, turn-on-a-dime maneuverability, and fewer passengers can gain access and acceptability in places where large ships simply cannot go. Their size makes them welcome at private islands and exclusive resorts and allows them to nudge into shallow bays and hidden coves. Their ports tend to be offbeat and uncommercialized.

Some small cruisers have bow or stern ramps, enabling them to disembark passengers directly onto beaches or into remote villages. Others carry Zodiacs and/or sea kayaks to transport passengers into wilderness. Some have retractable marinas, enabling passengers to water ski or swim from the ship.

A small ship offers exclusivity, even if it is unintended. Seating is unassigned at single seatings for meals. (On luxury ships, dining may be at the time of your choosing.) There are no crowds, no long lines, almost no regimentation. Best of all, on shore, you don't feel like part of a herd, unless you book a bus tour.

Today's superliners, megaliners, and ultraliners are self-contained floating resorts with facilities that operate almost around the clock. The bigger the vessel, the more the ship becomes the focus, although itineraries and ports are still important.

For small ships, destinations are key, and sightseeing is the main activity. These ships offer more varied and unusual itineraries than larger ships can, and often carry experts to discuss destinations and accompany passengers on shore excursions.

Small ships draw experienced, discriminating, and independent travelers who enjoy low-key ambience and often appreciate what is *not* available as much as what is. Many neither want nor need nonstop activities. Still, check with your agent, as some small ships, like *Celebrity Xpedition,* are also great for active pursuits like diving, hiking, or hefty nature activities. A few small vessels have tiny casinos and small-scale entertainment, but most substitute conversation and companionship, or lectures by various experts, for chorus lines and cabarets.

The smaller size attracts all age groups. Sailing ships, particularly schooners, draw the young and adventuresome, attracted by the lower price and the opportunity to work alongside the crew. Deluxe ships and those with longer itineraries attract older travelers, many of whom are young in spirit and intellectually curious. They appreciate an island's culture and are eager to interact with the locals.

Sound appealing? Then consider one of the three basic types of small ships: Ultraluxurious liners offer privacy and pampering, exclusivity and elegance, tastefully opulent suites, gourmet dining, and often formal evenings. In sharp contrast are adventure-oriented ships, whose destinations are chosen for their natural beauty, wildlife, or cultural interest. Activities include hiking, kayaking, and birding. Cabins usually are modest, service minimal, and cooking downhome. They appeal to many people who spurn luxurious pampering but are keenly interested in participatory travel. A third type strikes a middle ground, offering comfortable (but not lavish) accommodations, good food, and attentive service. There is some adventure, some history and wildlife, and some time for sports. Evening entertainment includes games, movies, local talent, and guest speakers.

Even with these choices, small-ship cruising is not for everyone. Some would find it boring or confining. But if you abhor lines or regimentation, can operate on your own juices, yearn for a more intimate environment, or want to try trimming the sails or floating in luxury, small ships might be right for you.

Old Ships versus New Ships

Poets praise the beauty of sailing ships. But observers of classic cruise ships like the *QE2* have been equally captivated by noble grace that is both massive and subtle. Unfortunately, *Norway* is gone—out of the U.S. fleet and possibly headed for the scrap yard. Alas, such ships will never be built again.

Are old or new vessels better? The debate rages. Classic ships still in service, as opposed to those merely old, offer ambience that no newer ship can duplicate. But the newest cruise vessels have advantages only dreamed of in 1960. Because there are well-maintained and up-to-date older ships in service, you have a choice between the old and the new afloat. Find your preference by surveying what each type of ship has to offer.

Notice first the appearance of any vessel, old or new. The newest ships are designed from the inside out to provide more and better public rooms and the most amount of usable deck space. These vessels spend most of their days in calm seas. None but *Queen Mary 2* will cut through the North Atlantic at full speed to maintain a schedule, so the fine lines and razor-sharp bow of the *QE2* aren't needed. Instead, new ships have squared sterns and chunky superstructures that provide many benefits internally but none externally.

As with some prima donnas, most new ships have one or two good angles. Publicity materials show profile shots and aerials of raked stems and funnels and broad decks for recreation.

Once inside your cabin, however, you may forget your ship's outward appearance. The space available to modern designers has generally made possible standard, usually larger, cabins for everyone. Some older ships offer comfortable space in every cabin, but they can't match the improved bathrooms and lighting of newer ships.

Luxury versus Midprice and Economy Cruises

Some of the most extraordinary spas, gyms, pools, lounges, and showrooms are found on the megaships of affordable midmarket lines such as Carnival and Princess. Likewise, dropping big bucks will not ensure that your ship is newer, nicer, or more competently and courteously staffed. (Check the ratio of passengers to crew. The lower the ratio, the more service you should get.) Booking a luxury cruise may get you a larger cabin (suites aboard Silversea or Seaborn Cruise Line) and almost certainly buys a roomier bath with tub and shower.

Regarding food, luxury lines have the edge. Usually they feed fewer passengers at a single seating spanning a couple of hours. Passengers arrive at the dining room a few at a time, like at a restaurant ashore. The staggered arrivals allow the galley the flexibility to provide more choice and cook dishes to order.

*un*official **TIP**
Spending more on a cruise does not necessarily get you more or better facilities.

Most midmarket and economy cruises have two seatings for each meal. When their seating is called, passengers stampede into the dining room like marines hitting the beach. Surprisingly, however, the quality of meals on some luxury ships is only marginally better than that of better midmarket lines. A number of mid-market cruise lines such as Princess, Norwegian, and Disney offer exclusive, stand-alone specialty restaurants in addition the to their main dining rooms. These restaurants require reservations and passengers must pay a surcharge (usually between $10 and $20), but some serve fare that rivals the cuisine served in dining rooms aboard luxury vessels.

SPECIAL PEOPLE WITH SPECIAL NEEDS

SOME PASSENGERS REQUIRE special services or accommodations. If you are a honeymooner, single, disabled, require a special diet, or plan to travel with young children or teens, read on.

Singles

Safety and security, comfort, convenience, companionship, fun, and freedom—all are reasons that cruises are among the fastest-growing options available to travelers who want to go it alone.

A cruise ship is about the safest, most secure environment you can find. A woman might hesitate to talk with someone in a hotel bar, dine alone in a fancy restaurant, or walk alone into a nightclub, but such barriers don't exist on a ship. As always, though, for female travelers, common sense remains a good attribute.

Furthermore, the fun is at your fingertips. The nightclub, disco, casino, and theater are walking distance from your cabin. Relieved of the need for an escort and with ready-made companions for dinner or activities, single people—men and women—vacation on their own terms.

Cruise prices are based on two people sharing a cabin. For one person to occupy a cabin alone, cruise lines impose an extra charge over the per-person double-occupancy rate. This "single supplement" varies from 10% to 100% (expressed as 110–200%), depending on the line, ship, itinerary, season, and cabin category. The most frequent charge is 150% except for suites, which usually go for 200%. Brochures always publish the rate. Your choices are to pay it, bring a friend, or take one of these options:

GUARANTEED SINGLE RATE You pay a set price published in the brochure, which is comparable to the low end of a per-person double-occupancy rate. The line assigns your cabin at embarkation. You don't have a choice, but you do have a guarantee of price and privacy.

You are likely to be assigned an inside cabin. If you select low season (October in the Caribbean), the start of a new season (May in Alaska), or a repositioning cruise when the ship is unlikely to be full, you might get a nice outside cabin. Currently, however, ships are sailing at full occupancy, making even these upgrades less likely than in past years. Royal Caribbean International and Norwegian Cruise Line offer a guaranteed single fare. Some lines do not show a guaranteed single rate in their brochure but will accept a reservation when bookings are light. Be sure to ask.

LOW SINGLE SUPPLEMENT Some lines have single supplements of 115% or less. Seabourn offers 110% on some cruises; Silversea has a few at 110%, though most are at 150%. In all cases, you pay slightly more than the per-person double rate, but you get privacy, and in the case of Seabourn and Silversea, all accommodations are deluxe suites.

FLAT RATE Clipper Cruise Line, Star Clipper, and some other lines charge a flat rate for single occupancy. You pay more but are ensured privacy and choice.

GUARANTEED SHARE The line plays travel matchmaker. You pay the per-person double-occupancy price, and the line matches you with a cabin mate (same gender and smoking preference). If the line does not find a suitable mate, you get the cabin to yourself at no extra charge. The savings—and drawbacks—are obvious. It's a bit of Russian roulette. You stand a better chance of having a cabin to yourself during low season or on a repositioning cruise. Some lines don't publicize a guaranteed share program but will accept a reservation. Be sure to ask.

CRUISING FOR SINGLES

S = Single cabins available
GSP = Guaranteed share program available
Single Supplement = Percentage of fare based on per-person double-occupancy rate

CRUISE LINE	S	GSP	SINGLE SUPPLEMENT
American Canadian Caribbean	Yes	Yes	175%
American West Steamboat	No	Yes	150–200%
Carnival Cruise Lines	Yes	No	150–200%
Celebrity Cruises	Yes	No	200%
Clipper Cruise Line	No	Yes	Varied
Costa Cruise Lines	Yes	No	150–200%
Cruise West	Yes	Yes	150%
Crystal Cruises	No	No	125–150%
Cunard Line	Yes	No	175–200%
Delta Queen	Yes	Yes	150–200%
Disney Cruise Line	No	No	150–200%
Glacier Bay Cruiseline	No	No	175%
Holland America Line	Yes	Yes	150–190%
Norwegian Cruise Line	No	No	150–200%
Oceania Cruises	No	No	200%
Orient Lines	No	Yes	105–200%
Princess Cruises	No	Yes	125–200%
Radisson Seven Seas Cruises	No	No	125–200%
Royal Caribbean International	No	No	200%
Seabourn Cruise Line	Yes	No	110–175%
Silversea Cruises	No	No	110–175%
Star Clippers	No	No	150%
Windstar Cruises	No	No	175%

SINGLE CABIN Some older ships have single cabins. The price is set but not necessarily comparable to a per-person double rate. More likely, a surcharge has been built into the price.

Also, some lines charge singles minimal or no surcharge for less desirable cabins, such as inside rooms, particularly when bookings are slow.

Helpful Hands

Golden Age Travellers (Pier 27, The Embarcadero, San Francisco, CA 94111; ☎ 800-258-8880 or 415-296-0151; **www.gatclub.com**), offers about 300 cruises a year and provides a cabin-mate matching service and lower supplements based on bargaining clout. Limited to those age 50 and up. Annual fee is $10 per person; $15 per couple.

Travel Companion Exchange (P.O. Box 833, Amityville, NY 11701; ☎ 800-392-1256 or 631-454-0880; **www.travelcompanions.com**), offers membership, a matching service, and bimonthly issues of a 20-page newsletter for $159 (first-time enrollment; regular annual rate is $298).

Finally, watch for specials and find a knowledgeable travel agent to help you. A smart, experienced agent knows which, when, and how cruise lines make special deals for singles, and they can often unearth ways that advance purchase and special promotional fares, even though based on double occupancy, can be applied to single travelers.

OTHER TIPS FOR SAILING SOLO The cruise industry has a long way to go in handling the singles market. The probability of finding love at sea varies according to age group. Twenty-somethings should look to the Caribbean on cruise lines that target a younger market, though the average passenger age remains above age 35.

Singles wanting to meet people should participate in activities, shore excursions, and sports. On a small ship, the chances of meeting many singles are slim. Big ships are considered better for meeting a wide range of people and also often have a get-acquainted session or other event for singles. Among small ships, adventure and educational cruises are singles' best choices; camaraderie quickly develops among passengers. Also, the number of unattached men is likely to be higher than on traditional cruises.

If you're 40-something or an older single woman who loves to dance, book a ship that employs gentlemen hosts—single males, age 50 or older, who dine and dance with all unattached women—no favoritism or hanky panky allowed. Crystal, Cunard, Delta Queen, and Holland America have them.

On singles cruises offered several times annually, Windjammer Barefoot Cruises all but guarantees a 50–50 ratio of males and females. Ages vary widely. You get no break on price—the single supplement is 150%—unless you are willing to share.

A common complaint we hear from singles concerns table assignment for dining. Some singles are unhappy because they're seated with married folks. Others are annoyed because they're seated with other singles and resent the cruise line playing matchmaker. Response varies, but your best bet is to submit a written request in advance outlining your preference in dining companionship. Aboard, if you are disenchanted with your table mates, ask the maître d'hôtel to move you; you may, in fact, even talk with the maître d' before the first night at a table, to state your preferences.

Honeymooners

If there is a better honeymoon option than a cruise, we can't think of it. There is nothing more romantic than balmy nights and sunny days under a Caribbean or Mediterranean sky. Your cabin is your honeymoon suite; room service usually is complimentary, so you never have to leave unless you want to. Forget the car, unpack only once, and still visit exotic places. Many lines (with advance notice) will provide a cozy table for two in the dining room. Regardless, tell the cruise line you are newlyweds. You will probably get preferential treatment, a bottle of champagne, flowers in the room, a souvenir photo, or even a cabin upgrade.

If you are contemplating a cruise honeymoon, consider: If you marry on Saturday, then Sunday or Monday departures are most convenient. Check on the availability of bathtubs versus showers if that is important to you. Ask whether room service is available at all three meals and whether you can choose from the regular menu (room service menus are often limited).

Nonambulatory Disabled Passengers

Many people who use a wheelchair or other mobility aids have discovered the pleasures of cruising firsthand. However, you need to be very direct and specific when exploring your options. Dining rooms, showrooms, or public rest rooms are not wheelchair-accessible on many older or smaller ships. A few small ships have no elevators; on others, particularly older ships, elevators do not serve every deck. Most ships require that you bring your own wheelchair, often one that is collapsible or narrow-gauge. Do not count on a lot of wheelchair-accessible facilities or cabins. On the most wheelchair-accessible ships, no more than two dozen cabins will have wheelchair-accessible bathrooms, and there usually is no way to get a wheelchair into a regular cabin's bathroom. If you need an accessible cabin, book well in advance. We list the number of wheelchair-accessible cabins available under each line's Standard Features and each ship's Cabin Specifications. Look for a ship with a lot of elevators relative to its complement of passengers. Divide the number of passengers by the number of elevators. Generally, the lower the calculated number, the less time you will spend waiting for elevators.

It is important that you book your cruise through an agency specializing or experienced in travel for physically challenged guests.

If you power your own wheelchair, unaided by a companion, bring something to extend your reach. A rubber-tipped teacher's pointer is good, a collapsible one is ideal. You need the pointer to reach elevator buttons, some light switches, and the closet rod and higher storage space in your cabin, even in some wheelchair-accessible rooms.

Make sure that dining rooms, restrooms, showrooms, lounges, promenade decks, and the pool areas are wheelchair accessible. Determine whether gangways are accessible at ports. If tenders are used, will you be able to board in a wheelchair? In the dining room, will your table accommodate your wheelchair, or must you shift to a regular chair? If you cannot shift yourself, will you need a companion to help or are crew members allowed to assist? Can crew members help in your cabin and elsewhere aboard ship? Must you sign a medical waiver or produce documentation from your physician to obtain a wheelchair-accessible cabin? No matter how dependable your travel agent is, call the cruise line and double-check all important arrangements yourself.

Partially Ambulatory Disabled

If you use a wheelchair sometimes but can walk a little way, you will do fine on most ships large enough to have elevators. You will be able to get around your cabin and into the bathroom on foot. A collapsible wheelchair will enable you to cover longer distances. Crutches are iffy on ships, walkers better, but the safest way for the partially ambulatory to get around is in a wheelchair.

Larger ships have wide passageways, spacious public areas, and, most likely, an adequate number of elevators. Smaller ships may have tight passageways, steep stairs, and no elevators. Older vessels may have bulkhead doors with raised thresholds, blocked passageways with steps to the next level, and no elevator access to some decks.

Choose a cabin near the elevators. Book one with a shower (with metal chair or stool); many ships' bathtubs are higher and/or deeper than yours at home. Ask whether the cabin's bath has sturdy hand grips.

Consider booking an itinerary on calmer water, such as Alaska's Inside Passage or the Mississippi River. If you cruise on the open sea, choose a cabin on a lower deck in the vessel's center; this area is least susceptible to motion.

Passengers with Sight and/or Hearing Impairments

Many people with sight or hearing impairments travel with a nondisabled companion. Regardless, be sure to inform your cabin steward of your disability. In the event of an emergency, he should know to check your cabin immediately to make sure your companion is with you and to assist you if not. If you are hearing-impaired, your steward should be given permission to enter your cabin in an emergency if there is no response to a knock.

Passengers with Diet Restrictions

Diet restrictions usually pose no problem on cruise ships. The galley will prepare meals to your specification and serve them at regular seatings in the dining room. Orthodox religious practitioners who must verify that a meal is prepared in a certain way should ask whether such verification will be possible. All lines request advance notice—either at the time of booking for some lines, or no less than 30 days prior to departure for others—for specific needs. We provide this information under cruise lines' Standard Features. Also, cruise line brochures detail procedures for diet requests.

Families with Younger Children

Although some lines are equipped to handle younger children, we do not recommend cruising for kids younger than age 5 on most lines, and age 3 and up on lines like Royal Caribbean that have a special program for toddlers and their families. Lines that really want family business advertise that fact. If you have young children and want them to enjoy the cruise, but do not necessarily want to tend to them 24 hours a day yourself, book with a line specializing in family cruises. Its ships will have play areas, supervised activities, and sometimes a separate swimming pool for children. Best of all, the chaperoned children's program provides a respite from constant parenting. If, however, your rich Aunt Hattie wants to treat you and your little nippers to a luxury cruise, don't decline because the ship's brochure doesn't picture kids. Little ones on essentially adult cruises fare reasonably well. Although planned activities may be few or none, globally astute kids who relish history, culture, new sights, and meeting new people will get along fine. Kids who need constant entertainment and attention should not be brought along.

Usually, the children's center will be a sort of seagoing day-care facility. Group baby-sitting in the children's center is available on most ships in the evening. A few ships offer in-cabin baby-sitting. If the latter and all-meal room service are available, you've got it made. Sign up for second seating in the dining room, or go late if there is only one. Let the kids enjoy room service in the cabin, or take them to the buffet or informal dining area. Then turn the fed-and-scrubbed munchkins over to the sitter and head for the dining room. Of course, you can take your children to the dining room, but if they are age 6 or younger, once may be enough. If you prefer to dine with your children in the dining room, you should sign up for the early seating.

If your ship has a supervised children's program, your kids will be on the go all the time. However, we've seen children who scarcely countenance their parents at home refuse to leave them and go to the children's center aboard ship. To avoid this issue, before you leave home, explain how things work and negotiate what time you will spend together and apart. If your children are too young to negotiate such deals, save the family cruise for another year or put the kids into the children's center and deal with any fallout.

Consider accommodations: Cabins are much more confining than children's homes or bedrooms. Your kids will size up your cabin in about ten seconds and figure there is not much to do there. From that point, they will be obsessed with running loose around the ship. Anticipate this response. Set limits in advance about bedtime, naps, meals, and parental private time, and plan for each day. Television, when available, is usually limited to a news channel, movies, and information about the ship and shore excursions. While family-focused lines may offer a cartoon channel or Nickelodeon, it's still good to bring games, books, and toys to keep the children reasonably content in the cabin.

If you can afford it, putting the children in an adjoining cabin is best, if the line's policy permits. If you buy kids their own cabin, the cruise line will sometimes include airfare in the deal. If you bunk the young ones in your cabin, you have to buy their airfare as an add-on. A few cruise lines offer a discount on a connecting cabin, where available, especially during low seasons.

Families with Teens

Teens do pretty well on cruises. They are old enough not to need constant supervision, will definitely eat their money's worth of food, and collect new experiences they can talk about back home. Teens are allowed to enjoy everything aboard except the casino and some lounges. On some ships, teens accompanied by parents are allowed in the disco and other adult areas. Family and midmarket ships often have clubs where teens can dance, and arcades with Ping-Pong, pool, or electronic games.

A cruise is a totally new environment for children—some embrace it with gusto, eager to learn, to find every nook and cranny, but others are intimidated and need help. For the right kids, it's a fabulous, fun, learning experience. With teens, as with younger kids, negotiate and set your limits before you leave home. Because teens can be messy and monopolize the bathroom, we stress our recommendation that you get them an adjoining cabin, again, if the line's policy permits. Finally, though we believe teens on their own are safe aboard ship, we suggest you keep them under tight rein ashore. If this is your first cruise and you have qualms about taking children, go without them and size up the situation. All of you might enjoy it more if you know the territory.

Additional Information

In both the cruise lines' Standard Features and the cruise ship profiles, we include a section on children's facilities. These references are a start.

Cruising for Children

This chart includes only those cruise lines with facilities for children; for details, see the line's profile in Part Two. Many lines not included on this chart accept children and offer cruises appropriate for them, but have no special facilities for children. Also, note that age limits vary from "no age restriction" to "no children younger than age 18 permitted." Always check with the cruise line before making plans.

KEY

A = All ships

S = Some ships and/or destinations

T = No 4-berth cabins available, but some triples

H = Only seasonal, usually Christmas, Easter, or summer holiday periods. Whenever children are aboard, most ships strive to accommodate them and their needs; the more children are aboard, the greater the variety of special activities."

CARNIVAL CRUISE LINES		CELEBRITY CRUISES		COSTA CRUISES	
REDUCED CRUISE RATE (with 2 full-fare adults) [1]	A	REDUCED CRUISE RATE (with 2 full-fare adults) [1]	A	REDUCED CRUISE RATE (with 2 full-fare adults) [1]	S
AIR/SEA RATE (same or less than full-fare passengers)	A	AIR/SEA RATE (same or less than full-fare passengers)	–	AIR/SEA RATE (same or less than full-fare passengers)	A
BABY-SITTING AVAILABLE [2]	A	BABY-SITTING AVAILABLE [2]	AH	BABY-SITTING AVAILABLE [2]	A
CRIBS AVAILABLE [3]	A	CRIBS AVAILABLE [3]	A	CRIBS AVAILABLE 3	A
QUAD/FAMILY CABINS AVAILABLE	A	QUAD/FAMILY CABINS AVAILABLE	A	QUAD/FAMILY CABINS AVAILABLE	A
ESCORTED SHORE TOURS	S	ESCORTED SHORE TOURS	–	ESCORTED SHORE TOURS	–
MENUS	A	MENUS	A	MENUS	A
MOVIES	A	MOVIES	A	MOVIES	A
PARTIES	A	PARTIES	A	PARTIES	A
POOL (just for kids)	A	POOL (just for kids)	S	POOL (just for kids)	S
TEEN CENTER OR DISCO	S	TEEN CENTER OR DISCO	S	TEEN CENTER OR DISCO	S
TEEN COUNSELOR	A	TEEN COUNSELOR	A	TEEN COUNSELOR	S
VIDEO GAMES	A	VIDEO GAMES	A	VIDEO GAMES	A
YOUTH CENTER/PLAYROOM	A	YOUTH CENTER/PLAYROOM	A	YOUTH CENTER/PLAYROOM	A
YOUTH COUNSELOR	A	YOUTH COUNSELOR	A	YOUTH COUNSELOR	A

CRYSTAL CRUISES		CUNARD LINES		DISNEY CRUISE LINE	
REDUCED CRUISE RATE (with 2 full-fare adults) [1]	A	REDUCED CRUISE RATE (with 2 full-fare adults) [1]	A	REDUCED CRUISE RATE (with 2 full-fare adults) [1]	A
AIR/SEA RATE (same or less than full-fare passengers)	A	AIR/SEA RATE (same or less than full-fare passengers)	A	AIR/SEA RATE (same or less than full-fare passengers)	A
BABY-SITTING AVAILABLE [2]	A	BABY-SITTING AVAILABLE [2]	A	BABY-SITTING AVAILABLE [2]	A
CRIBS AVAILABLE [3]	A	CRIBS AVAILABLE [3]	A	CRIBS AVAILABLE [3]	A
QUAD/FAMILY CABINS AVAILABLE	T	QUAD/FAMILY CABINS AVAILABLE	A	QUAD/FAMILY CABINS AVAILABLE	A
ESCORTED SHORE TOURS	–	ESCORTED SHORE TOURS	–	ESCORTED SHORE TOURS	A
MENUS	AH	MENUS	A	MENUS	A
MOVIES	A	MOVIES	A	MOVIES	A
PARTIES	AH	PARTIES	–	PARTIES	A
POOL (just for kids)	AH	POOL (just for kids)	S	POOL (just for kids)	A
TEEN CENTER OR DISCO	S	TEEN CENTER OR DISCO	S	TEEN CENTER OR DISCO	A
TEEN COUNSELOR	AH	TEEN COUNSELOR	–	TEEN COUNSELOR	A
VIDEO GAMES	AH	VIDEO GAMES	A	VIDEO GAMES	A
YOUTH CENTER/PLAYROOM	A	YOUTH CENTER/PLAYROOM	–	YOUTH CENTER/PLAYROOM	A
YOUTH COUNSELOR	AH	YOUTH COUNSELOR	–	YOUTH COUNSELOR	A

HOLLAND AMERICA LINE

REDUCED CRUISE RATE (with 2 full-fare adults) [1]	A
AIR/SEA RATE (same or less than full-fare passengers)	A
BABY-SITTING AVAILABLE [2]	A
CRIBS AVAILABLE [3]	A
QUAD/FAMILY CABINS AVAILABLE	A
ESCORTED SHORE TOURS	S
MENUS	A
MOVIES	A
PARTIES	A
POOL (just for kids)	S
TEEN CENTER OR DISCO	A
TEEN COUNSELOR	A
VIDEO GAMES	A
YOUTH CENTER/PLAYROOM	A
YOUTH COUNSELOR	A

NORWEGIAN CRUISE LINE

REDUCED CRUISE RATE (with 2 full-fare adults) [1]	A
AIR/SEA RATE (same or less than full-fare passengers)	A
BABY-SITTING AVAILABLE [2]	A
CRIBS AVAILABLE [3]	A
QUAD/FAMILY CABINS AVAILABLE	A
ESCORTED SHORE TOURS	S
MENUS	A
MOVIES	S
PARTIES	S
POOL (just for kids)	S
TEEN CENTER OR DISCO	SH
TEEN COUNSELOR	AH
VIDEO GAMES	A
YOUTH CENTER/PLAYROOM	S
YOUTH COUNSELOR	AH

ORIENT LINES

REDUCED CRUISE RATE (with 2 full-fare adults) [1]	A
AIR/SEA RATE (same or less than full-fare passengers)	A
BABY-SITTING AVAILABLE [2]	–
CRIBS AVAILABLE [3]	–
QUAD/FAMILY CABINS AVAILABLE	A
ESCORTED SHORE TOURS	–
MENUS	–
MOVIES	–
PARTIES	H
POOL (just for kids)	–
TEEN CENTER OR DISCO	H
TEEN COUNSELOR	–
VIDEO GAMES	–
YOUTH CENTER/PLAYROOM	–
YOUTH COUNSELOR	H

PRINCESS CRUISES

REDUCED CRUISE RATE (with 2 full-fare adults) [1]	–
AIR/SEA RATE (same or less than full-fare passengers)	–
BABY-SITTING AVAILABLE [2]	S
CRIBS AVAILABLE [3]	S
QUAD/FAMILY CABINS AVAILABLE	S
ESCORTED SHORE TOURS	–
MENUS	A
MOVIES	A
PARTIES	A
POOL (just for kids)	S
TEEN CENTER OR DISCO	S
TEEN COUNSELOR	S
VIDEO GAMES	S
YOUTH CENTER/PLAYROOM	S
YOUTH COUNSELOR	S

RADISSON SEVEN SEAS CRUISES[4]

REDUCED CRUISE RATE (with 2 full-fare adults) [1]	–
AIR/SEA RATE (same or less than full-fare passengers)	–
BABY-SITTING AVAILABLE [2]	–
CRIBS AVAILABLE [3]	–
QUAD/FAMILY CABINS AVAILABLE	–
ESCORTED SHORE TOURS	–
MENUS	–
MOVIES	S
PARTIES	S
POOL (just for kids)	–
TEEN CENTER OR DISCO	–
TEEN COUNSELOR	–
VIDEO GAMES	–
YOUTH CENTER/PLAYROOM	–
YOUTH COUNSELOR	S

ROYAL CARIBBEAN INTERNATIONAL

REDUCED CRUISE RATE (with 2 full-fare adults) [1]	–
AIR/SEA RATE (same or less than full-fare passengers)	–
BABY-SITTING AVAILABLE [2]	H
CRIBS AVAILABLE [3]	A
QUAD/FAMILY CABINS AVAILABLE	A
ESCORTED SHORE TOURS	–
MENUS	A
MOVIES	A
PARTIES	A
POOL (just for kids)	S
TEEN CENTER OR DISCO	S
TEEN COUNSELOR	A
VIDEO GAMES	S
YOUTH CENTER/PLAYROOM	A
YOUTH COUNSELOR	A

SEABOURN CRUISES[4]

REDUCED CRUISE RATE (with 2 full-fare adults) [1]	–
AIR/SEA RATE (same or less than full-fare passengers)	–
BABY-SITTING AVAILABLE [2]	S
CRIBS AVAILABLE [3]	–
QUAD/FAMILY CABINS AVAILABLE	–
ESCORTED SHORE TOURS	–
MENUS	–
MOVIES	–
PARTIES	–
POOL (just for kids)	–
TEEN CENTER OR DISCO	–
TEEN COUNSELOR	–
VIDEO GAMES	–
YOUTH CENTER/PLAYROOM	–
YOUTH COUNSELOR	H

SILVERSEA CRUISES

REDUCED CRUISE RATE (with 2 full-fare adults) [1]	–
AIR/SEA RATE (same or less than full-fare passengers)	A
BABY-SITTING AVAILABLE [2]	–
CRIBS AVAILABLE [3]	–
QUAD/FAMILY CABINS AVAILABLE	T
ESCORTED SHORE TOURS	–
MENUS	–
MOVIES	–
PARTIES	–
POOL (just for kids)	–
TEEN CENTER OR DISCO	–
TEEN COUNSELOR	–
VIDEO GAMES	–
YOUTH CENTER/PLAYROOM	–
YOUTH COUNSELOR	–

NOTES

1. On most cruises, infants travel free. Where applicable, maximum age is 1 to 3 years.

2. Where available, baby-sitting is arranged on board and not guaranteed.

3. Where available, cribs arranged for at time of booking.

4. Children under age of 12 not encouraged.

Source: Cruise Line International Association (CLIA)

Also consult **Family Travel Times** (40 Fifth Avenue, New York, NY 10011; ☎ 212-477-5524;**www.familytraveltimes.com**), an online publication of TWYCH (Travel With Your Children) that frequently reports on family cruises, down to the last playpen and high chair. Annual subscriptions are $39, which buys you access to six online issues.

SHOPPING FOR *and* BOOKING YOUR CRUISE

GATHERING INFORMATION

NOW THAT YOU HAVE OUTLINED your requirements and preferences, compare them against the profiles of the cruise lines and ships described in this book. After you, or you and your travel agent, identify several lines that seem to meet your needs, obtain promotional brochures either through the agent or by contacting the lines directly, using phone numbers and addresses in the profiles.

A travel agent specializing in cruises or selling them routinely can be a tremendous source of information. Many agents who have sailed repeatedly can provide firsthand information about ships and lines. Also, many will put you in touch with clients willing to share thoughts and opinions. However, always understand from a self-interest perspective that cruise lines pay the agent a commission on every cruise the agent sells.

In addition to obtaining promotional materials, buy several Sunday newspapers: (1) one in a primary geographic market for the cruise industry, including New York, Chicago, Dallas, or Los Angeles; and (2) the paper of the largest city within 200 miles of your home. The travel sections in these papers indicate where the itineraries and deals are. If you live in a medium-sized city like Charleston, South Carolina, for example, you may uncover cruise deals in the Atlanta paper that beat anything in your local paper.

Finally, here are some helpful magazines, periodicals, and Internet sites: **www.cruisecritic.com** and **www.cruisemates.com,** written and hosted by Anne Campbell, former author of *Fielding's Guide to Worldwide Cruises,* and a veteran cruise writer. Their candid ship reviews are based on firsthand experience. They also have cruise-line information, news updates, information on promotions, and best deals. Another Web site, at **www.cruiseopinion.com,** offers lots of detailed ship evaluations written by passengers who submit monthly reviews. We also recommend **www.cruisenewsdaily.com** and **www.cruisediva.com.**

A fourth Web site worth checking out is found at **www.i-cruise.com,** which has a "beat your best price" feature. The sites listed sell cruises in addition to providing comparative information. Also check **www.cruise.com.** All provide reviews, deck plans, tips for singles, and, of course, hot deals.

Cruise Reports (25 Lindsley Drive, Suite 101, Morristown, NJ 07960: ☎ 973-605-2442; fax 973-605-2722; cruises@cruise-reports.com; **www.cruise-reports.com**) offers evaluations and firsthand comments by travel agents. Annual-subscription price to be determined, as publication is being revamped.

Cruise Travel magazine (P.O. Box 342, Mt. Morris, IL 61054; ☎ 800-877-5893; **www.cruisetravelmag.com**) is unabashedly rah-rah cruising and contains no critical content, but it's a good source of information. Its six issues a year contain ads from dozens of cruise discounters, consolidators, and cruise-specialty travel agents. Subscriptions run about $20 a year in the United States, $40 in Canada.

Cruise Week (Lehman Publishing, 503 Crooked Creek Road, Wilmington, NC 28409; ☎ 800-593-8252; fax 910-790-3983; cruise-week@aol.com; **www.cruise-week.com**), a two-page weekly industry newsletter available by fax or e-mail, is produced by an editor who has reported on the industry for many years. It's directed to the travel industry, but consumers interested in tracking news about cruising will find it a timely resource. Subscriptions are $125 annually.

Ocean & Cruise News (P.O. Box 4850, Stamford, CT 06907; ☎ 203-329-2787; **www.oceancruise.com**) reports on the industry and reviews a different ship in each issue. A much-publicized annual evaluation of lines and ships in the February issue is based on subscribers' votes, which tend to reflect seasoned cruisers' preferences for established lines. Subscriptions are $30 annually for 12 issues for U.S. readers ($36 elsewhere).

Porthole (P.O. Box 469066, Escondido, CA 92046-9066; ☎ 800-776-PORT; **www.porthole.com**) is by far the most attractive and lively magazine on cruises. It offers a range of interesting articles by knowledgeable writers, although criticism is rare. Subscriptions are $20 annually.

TravLtips magazine (P.O. Box 580188, Flushing, NY 11358-0218; ☎ 800-872-8584; info@travltips.com; **www.travltips.com**) is a good bet if you are interested in freighter cruising, expedition cruising, or bargain around-the-world cruising on conventional cruise ships; it's published bimonthly. Subscriptions are $20 annually.

HOW TO READ A CRUISE LINE BROCHURE

CRUISE BROCHURES ARE VERY ELABORATE. Because they contain so much information, we offer a systematic approach to evaluating and understanding their contents.

Look at the Pictures
All photos in the brochures have been carefully chosen to excite the people for whom the cruise line tailors its product. If you identify

with the activities depicted, this may be a good cruise line for you. Pay attention to ages of the people shown. Do you see yourself in the activities?

Sizing up the Ships

Look at the ships. Are they too big, too small, about right, or you don't care as long as they float? Talk to a travel agent about your vacation style. A good agent can help you make the right fit with a line and ship. Most brochures also contain a deck-by-deck schematic of the ship. Concentrate first on the ship's layout, looking for features important to you. If you work out, look at the relative size of the exercise room and try to find a photo of it so you can check the equipment. Ask about exercise classes, the spa, and such features as a jogging track or lap pool. If you have mobility problems, look for elevators. Because upper decks offer the best views at sea, note inside and outdoor public areas, particularly on the top two and promenade decks.

Itineraries

Read the itineraries, making preliminary selections on where and how long you want to cruise. On what days and at what times does the cruise begin and end? Do these work for you? Focus on a couple of cruises. Read the itineraries, observing how much time the ship spends at sea and in port, how much cruising is during waking hours, and whether the number of ports and the time allowed to see them suits you.

For practice, let's look at a 10-day itinerary from Copenhagen to London/Tilbury.

DAY	DATE	PORT	ARRIVE	DEPART
Sunday	June 4	Copenhagen		6 p.m.
Monday	June 5	Cruising		
Tuesday	June 6	Helsinki	8 a.m.	6 p.m.
Wednesday	June 7	St. Petersburg	8 a.m.	
Thursday	June 8	St. Petersburg		6 p.m.
Friday	June 9	Stockholm	4 p.m.	
Saturday	June 10	Stockholm		3 p.m.
Sunday	June 11	Cruising		
Monday	June 12	Oslo	8 a.m.	5 p.m.
Tuesday	June 13	Cruising		
Wednesday	June 14	London/Tilbury	7 a.m.	

The cruise sails at 6 p.m. Sunday, allowing several options. Because most flights from the United States to Europe depart in the late afternoon and evening, a person living in the eastern United

States could work most or all of Friday and catch an evening flight to Copenhagen, arriving Saturday morning. They would have until about 3:30 p.m. Sunday to rest and see Copenhagen. Alternately, they could fly out Saturday evening and arrive in Copenhagen on Sunday morning with four or five hours at their disposal before boarding, although we do not recommend this. Remember flights do cancel or have serious delays at times. Come in the day before. Why take a chance of missing your ship? A third possibility, of course, would be to arrive before Saturday and enjoy a leisurely weekend. The first day (Monday) at sea is a wonderful start, providing a chance to catch up on jet lag and explore the ship.

This cruise calls on four ports, not counting ports of origination and termination. This is fewer than average for a ten-day cruise, but all are major cities. The itinerary gives lots of time in each port. In St. Petersburg and Stockholm, the ship anchors overnight. If you're interested in St. Petersburg and Stockholm and a lot of sightseeing, this works well. If not, it's a long time in port. Full days (8 a.m. to 5 or 6 p.m.) are planned in Helsinki and Oslo. In total, the cruise is 229 hours, of which 153 hours (67%) are at sea and 76 hours (33%) are in port. However, only 71 hours of the 153 hours at sea are during waking hours (7 a.m. to 10 p.m.).

Rates

Flip to the rate charts to determine whether the cruises you like fall roughly within your budget. We do mean roughly: You should antic-ipate paying 10% to 50% less depending on the line, ship, itinerary, season, and market condi-tion. We describe available discounts in "How to Get the Best Deal on a Cruise." Note however that cruise industry experts expect much less dis-counting in 2005 through 2007 than in 2001 through 2004.

unofficial **TIP**
Almost nobody pays the brochure rates. Brochure rates are helpful only in providing a base for cal-culating discounts.

Most lines present their fares in a chart like the one on the next page for Princess Cruise Line's *Grand Princess* on a seven-day western Caribbean itinerary in Novem-ber. The fares are per-person at the brochure rate, based on two persons sharing a cabin (double occupancy). If the per-person fare for a cabin on the Lido Deck, category BA, with private balcony and two lower beds is $1,569; you and your traveling companion would pay $3,138 ($1,569 x 2) for the cabin. For singles supplement, see "Singles" in this chapter for a rate explanation.

As many as four persons may share a cabin, depending on its con-figuration. Rates for the third, fourth, and fifth persons are deeply discounted, sometimes as much as 66% off the double-occupancy fare. Let's say Tom, Ed, John, and Earl are willing to share a Dolphin Deck, Category AC cabin that goes for $1,749 per person double occupancy. The line charges the double-occupancy price ($1,749) for two of the four men, and the third/fourth person rate of $399 for the remaining two. Thus, the tab for all four:

PERSON 1	$1,749	Cruise Only
PERSON 2	$1,749	Cruise Only
PERSON 3	$399	Cruise Only
PERSON 4	$399	Cruise Only
TOTAL	$4,296	

Usually, for cruise lines that bundle airfare to the port into the total price of the cruise (as part of an air/sea package), the airfare is normally included only for the two persons paying the double-occupancy rate. The cruise line will arrange airfare, often at a discounted rate, for the third and fourth persons.

If Tom, Ed, John, and Earl want to split the cost of their Princess cruise equally, here's the way the finances average out:

Cruise fare for all four guys	$4,296
Final cost per person	$1,074

Because standard cabins on almost all cruise ships are small with tiny bathrooms and little storage, we do not recommend cruising with more than two persons in a cabin unless, for budgetary reasons, there's no other choice. If you do elect to cruise with extra people in your cabin, select your roommates with care. Make sure everyone is compatible regarding smoking, snoring, and sleeping hours. Most of all, be tolerant and bring your sense of humor. Start with a cruise in a warm clime, when you can spend more time on deck than in your cabin. In the Caribbean, you might find yourself doing little more than sleeping and changing clothes there.

Most newer cruise ships are distinguished by the number of cabins with private balconies. These cabins become more affordable year by year and are highly recommended for those who want a quiet private space to relax.

Sailing Dates

Check the sailing dates of cruises that interest you, looking for those compatible with your schedule. Check dates around these to see if a slight shift puts you into a lower-priced season.

Cabin Category and Ship Deck Plans

Now look at the types of cabins available. Many brochures include floor plans for several types of cabins showing their size, configuration, and placement of furniture and fixtures. Some brochures include color photographs of cabins.

Grand Princess rate chart

Single-occupancy fares for categories GS–AD, BA–BD, and CC is 200% of the double-occupancy fare. For categories C–G and K: 150% of the double-occupancy fare.

STATEROOM CATEGORIES		LIST PRICE PER PERSON	EARLY BOOKING PRICES STARTING FROM
Balcony Staterooms/Suites			
Lido Deck	GS	$2,949	$2,949
Baja Deck	OS	$2,449	$2,449
Caribe Deck	PH	$2,149	$2,149
Baja & Caribe Decks	PS	$2,099	$2,099
Dolphin & Emerald Decks	VS	$2,049	$2,049
Dolphin Deck	XS	$1,999	$1,999
Dolphin Deck	AA	$1,949	$1.349
Dolphin Deck	AB	$1,849	$1,249
Dolphin Deck	AC	$1,749	$1,149
Emerald Deck	AD	$1,649	$1,049
Lido & Caribe Decks	BA	$3,599	$1,749
Aloha, Caribe, & Dolphin	BB	$1,569	$969
Aloha & Baja Decks	BC	$1529	$929
Baja Deck	BD	$1,449	$849
Oceanview Staterooms (no balcony)			
Lido Deck	CC	$1,429	$829
Aloha Deck	C	$1,419	$819
Emerald Deck	DD	$1,399	$799
Plaza Deck	D	$1,370	$799
Plaza Deck	EE	$1,359	$759
Oceanview Staterooms (partially obstructed view)			
Emerald Deck	E	$1,339	$739
Emerald Deck	FF	$1,319	$719
Emerald Deck	F	$1,309	$709
Emerald Deck	GG	$1,299	$699
Interior Staterooms			
Lido & Aloha Decks	II	$1,139	$639
Aloha & Baja Decks	I	$1,129	$629
Baja & Caribe Decks	JJ	$1,119	$619

Grand Princess rate chart (continued)

STATEROOM CATEGORIES		LIST PRICE PER PERSON	EARLY BOOKING PRICES STARTING FROM
Interior Staterooms *(continued)*			
Caribe, Emerald, Dolphin	J	$1,109	$609
Plaza Deck	K	$1,099	$599
3rd/4th Guests			
Suite/Minisuite		$499	$499
Balcony		$399	$399
Oceanview		$299	$299
Interior		$199	$199

Rates include port charges. Air transportation and certain taxes and fees are additional. All rates quoted in U.S. dollars, per person, double occupancy.

Although some upscale lines offer only suites, most ships provide a choice of cabins. The top of the line—usually on the top decks—are the palatial owner's suite or royal suite, comparable to the presidential suite in a good hotel. Next are a small number of one- or two-bedroom suites, followed by a larger number of minisuites. After these deluxe accommodations come standard cabins, which account for about 85% of accommodations on most ships. Now, on more of the new, large ships, many standard cabins have verandas. In fact, on some ships 60% to 80% of all accommodations feature these balconies, which are becoming a "must have" feature for many guests. Outside standard cabins with a window are generally preferred to inside standard cabins without windows, but they are more expensive. Usually, the higher the deck, the higher the cabin's price. For outside standard cabins with windows, many cruise lines offer different categories and rates for windows with an unencumbered view, versus windows that are mostly or partially blocked, by a lifeboat for example.

Standard cabins on ships built since 1988 generally are the same throughout the ship. Windows may decrease in size as you descend from deck to deck. If the window view is obstructed, this information should be indicated on the rate charts. If not, ask.

Cabins toward the middle of the ship are considered more desirable than cabins on either end, because center cabins are closer to stairs and elevators and are less affected by the ship's back-and-forward motion (pitching). The side-to-side motion (rolling) is more pronounced the higher you go and is felt least on lower decks. But the fact is, on large cruise ships, you will feel very little motion of the sea, except perhaps on the highest decks.

MINISUITE WITH
PRIVATE BALCONY

(Categories AA, AB, AC,
AD, and AE)

Large bedroom with twin beds, which make up into a queen bed. Sitting area with sofa bed and desk. 2 TVs, walk-in closet, refrigerator. Bath with tub and shower.

OUTSIDE DOUBLE WITH
PRIVATE BALCONY

(Categories BA, BB, BC,
BD, BE, and BF)

Two lower beds, which make up into a queen bed. TV, closet, refrigerator. Bath with shower.

OUTSIDE OR
INSIDE DOUBLE

(Categories C, DD, D, EE, E, FF, F,
GG, G, HH, II, I, JJ, J, K, L, and M)

Outside staterooms have a picture window. (Categories E–HH obstructed.) Two lower beds, which make up into a queen bed. Many staterooms with two upper berths. Television, closet, refrigerator. Bath with shower.

PRINCESS CRUISES

GRAND PRINCESS

Plaza Fiesta Promenade Emerald Dolphin

Caribe   Baja   Aloha   Lido   Sun

Before selecting a cabin category, study the ship's deck plan. Normally, the schematic is near scale and is color-coded for cabin category. Checking the Princess Cruise Line rate chart with the ship schematic for the *Grand Princess,* the most expensive accommodations are on the Lido, Baja, and Caribe Decks, the first, third, and fourth highest decks respectively with passenger accommodations. All three decks are removed from noise of the galley, engines, lounges, pool area, and showroom.

Check the drawing for decks where passengers walk or jog. Avoid cabins beneath jogging tracks or promenades. Similarly, avoid cabins where the window overlooks a track or walkway. Pinpoint lounges, showrooms, the casino, discos, and other potentially noisy, late-night areas. Avoid cabins directly above or below them. Engine noise may be audible in lower-deck cabins toward the stern.

Though private verandas, or balconies, have become increasingly popular and affordable, not all balconies are created equal. When shopping, always ask about balcony size and configuration. Some are barely large enough for a chair, while others can accommodate a chaise lounge, a couple of chairs, and a table. Some balconies are covered, providing both shade and privacy, but others are open to the weather, perfect for sun bathing, but also subject to the nosy gaze of passengers on higher decks. Balconies on the bow face forward and are often subject to a great deal of wind when the ship is under way. Stern balconies on the other hand offer more protection and additionally provide sweeping views to either side of the ship.

Even veteran cruisers have difficulty gleaning this information from a deck plan, but a knowledgeable travel agent knows how to check out these details when you ask. Analyze what you get for a few dollars more or less. In the chart above, for example, a balcony cabin on Baja Deck is only $20 more than an oceanview (no balcony) cabin on the higher Lido Deck.

Be aware that the newer megaships are very long indeed. The *Grand Princess* is 951 feet long, more than the length of three football fields. If you have a cabin toward the stern, it's quite a trek to the ship's main theater near the bow. One roundtrip would be roughly a half-mile. With the way that the ship's public areas are distributed throughout the ship, it's easy to log upwards of four miles of walking an average day.

A PRELIMINARY LOOK AT DISCOUNTS AND INCENTIVES

YOU SHOULD NOW KNOW whether you are interested in a cruise offered in the brochure you are reading. If you are, the next step is to check the line's price incentives and discounts.

After two decades of steady growth, with dozens of new ships coming on-line, the supply of cabins outstripped demand (the number of people to fill them). Competition put pressure on cruise lines to cut deals to keep their ships filled, and a buyer's market prevailed. But that began to change in 2004, and for 2005, it's a seller's market with high occupancy and fewer discounts. The next two to three years will see a decrease in the number of new ships being added to the inventory and a double-digit increase in the number of passengers. As a result, competitive pressures will lessen and prices will increase. There will still be bargains but they may be harder to find, available less frequently, and will tend to be seasonal, directed toward a specific sailing, or be a last minute "fire sale."

Incentives and discounts offered in the lines' brochures are varied. First, the line sets prices according to times of greatest demand. High season is most expensive, followed by shoulder season, then low season. Savings may not be spectacular, judging from the brochure prices.

Remember: Fares in the brochure are base prices to which discounts are applied. Also, ships are less crowded and cabin upgrades somewhat more available during low and shoulder seasons.

After studying seasonal discounts, check early-booking discounts. Lines offer substantial discounts to travelers willing to book six months to a year ahead. The line has use of your money in advance and gets critical information on whether a particular cruise is filling. Early-booking discounts commonly are 15% to 50% off the seasonal rate, or may be expressed as a two-for-one deal. Either way, early-booking incentives are generally the largest discounts given directly by the lines, and once they're gone, they're gone. You get other benefits, too: your choice of cabin, often the most direct air routing, and your dining-room seating preference (if the line bases seating on first-come, first-served). That's the kind of information available in fine print or from an experienced travel agent.

Cruise lines also may offer cabin upgrades, credit for shipboard purchases, receptions with the captain, or a couple of nights at a hotel at the originating or terminating port. In addition to an early-booking discount, almost all lines offer other discounts (often up to 50%) to repeat passengers. Some discounts from cruise lines, travel agents, wholesalers, and consolidators never appear in the cruise lines' basic brochures. For help in finding them, read the section "How to Get the Best Deal on a Cruise."

ROUND-TRIP AIRFARE

UNLESS YOU LIVE WITHIN DRIVING DISTANCE of your cruise's originating port, you will require transportation to it. Until a few years ago, most lines included air transportation in the cruise cost and promoted it as "free air." But times have changed.

What Happened to "Free Air"?

First, check the cruise brochure to determine whether prices include air transportation. When lines include air transportation in their packages (for a higher cruise cost, of course), they agree to fly you round-trip from specific "gateway" cities. These gateway cities vary among cruise lines, but usually include all major U.S. and Canadian cities and many smaller cities. If air transportation is part of the cruise package but your gateway city is especially far from the port, an air supplement—an extra charge—may be levied.

Until the late 1990s, air/sea packages were touted as all-inclusive, with "free" airfare. Nothing, of course, was ever free. Cruise lines built air transportation into the cruise cost and called it "free." By buying in advance and in large volume, lines could negotiate big discounts on airfares. These discounts enabled the cruise lines to offer complete vacation packages—the cruise with airfare—for a good price. Since 1997, however, cruise lines have increasingly published their rates as "cruise-only" fares and sell the air transportation as an add-on. The reason for the change is that as demand for air travel increased, airlines radically reduced the availability and size of discounts for cruise lines. Even in a post-9/11 world, airlines can fill their planes without offering reduced fares to major ports, particularly for weekend flights when cruise lines need them most. Today, cruise lines can obtain the discounts required for a good air/sea package only by buying airlines' least desirable flights, including late-night flights, circuitous routes, and multiple stops. Luxury cruise lines are the exceptions, as they continue to offer air-inclusive packages to ensure that their customers get the most direct and convenient flights.

At the same time, many passengers often are discovering they can get better airfares and routing on their own or by using their frequent-flyer points. Plus, they receive their tickets well in advance. Often with air/sea packages, airlines issue tickets only at the last minute (to distribute passengers equally among available flights). The practice panics cruise passengers near departure who wonder where their tickets are. As it happens, cruise lines accumulate reservations for several months before contacting the airlines and nailing down flight itineraries and seats. Standard practice is to advise you of your air itinerary 30 to 45 days prior to sailing (Princess has a program called Flight Choice, where flight notification is made 60 days in advance). Understand, however, that we're only talking about flight *information*. Actual ticketing does not begin until about 30 days from your sailing date, and your tickets might not arrive until a week or two before you walk out of the door. The process affords the cruise line maximum flexibility but vastly increases the probability of your receiving an inconvenient itinerary with multiple connecting flights, and with little time left to make changes. As a kicker, you may be surprised to discover that making your reservations well in advance doesn't mean that you'll get one of the better flight itineraries. A few lines give priority to early bookers, with flight itineraries based on the "seniority" of cruise reservations that are paid in full. With many other lines, it matters not whether you booked eight months or eight weeks ahead—you'll get what's available at the time the cruise line finally books the air travel.

If the air itinerary provided by the cruise line is not acceptable, you can request a change or a particular routing through your travel agent. Many cruise lines maintain "Air Deviation" desks to handle requests from passengers who want to change their assigned routing. Changes can cost $35 to $100 (as if you changed a ticket directly with an airline), and an additional air supplement may be charged if no seats are available in your designated airfare category. So, you ask, how bad can flight itineraries arranged by the cruise line be? A California couple was ushered off their ship and shuttled to the San Juan, Puerto Rico airport at 9:30 a.m. for a flight home that departed at 6 p.m. Following a cruise, a family of six were split up with four of the party scheduled for an early flight and the other two reserved for a flight that arrived eight hours later.

If you purchase an air-inclusive cruise vacation but elect to arrange (and pay for) your own air transportation, the cruise fare will be decreased because you are not using the air-travel part of the package. The amount to be lopped off your package price is shown at the bottom of the rate sheet as "Cruise-Only Travel Allowance." The allowance, for example, is about $250 on one-week Caribbean air/sea packages.

Price and itineraries, however, are not the only considerations in buying air from the cruise line. When you buy the line's air add-on or an air-inclusive cruise, transfers are almost always included. The cruise line will meet you at the airport and transfer you to the ship. Likewise, at the end of the cruise, the line will return you to the airport.

When you purchase your air transportation independently or if you use frequent-flier awards, you can usually buy airport transfers from the cruise lines. Carnival, for example, offers one-way and round-trip transfers, which must be booked 14 days in advance; price varies with location. Without such an arrangement, you must set up your own transfers. This seems complicated, but a travel agent can handle such details for you—and we advise you to let them. Be aware that at cruise's end only, some lines provide this transportation service regardless whether you bought your air through them.

When arriving at the embarkation airport, you will claim your baggage. Those on an air/sea package or with transfers will board a bus and their luggage will be transported with them to the pier.

unofficial **TIP**
Flights arranged by the cruise lines are often not eligible for frequent-flier mileage. Plan to call the airline directly after the ticket has been issued to try and get proper credit.

There, luggage will be taken by porters, and you will see it several hours later, after it is delivered directly to your cabin. If the airline booked by the cruise line loses your luggage, the cruise line will do its best to get it to you (once it's recovered), even if the ship has sailed.

During busier times, cruise lines may fly you to the port city a day in advance and provide hotel accommodations. If you live in the western United States and are sailing from an eastern port, the cruise line may fly you to the port city on a late-night flight with arrival between midnight and 9 a.m. More considerate lines arrange hotel day rooms where you can rest before boarding your ship later in the day. Similar arrangements are sometimes made for East Coast passengers embarking on the West Coast, and passengers on European or Asian cruises.

The line, when it puts you in a hotel, assumes responsibility for transporting you to the pier. If you are to be accommodated in a hotel before embarkation, pack an overnight bag; you may not have access to your luggage until you're aboard ship.

Most air transportation purchased through cruise lines is coach class. Your travel agent can arrange seat assignments, boarding passes, and upgrades (when available).

If you are cruising during autumn (excluding holiday periods) or when airfares are discounted in your city, or if you can reach the port on a discount airline (like Southwest), you may want to book your own air travel to save money. If you can book your flights at or near the cruise line's air allowance, you will be able to choose your airline, ensure a good flight itinerary, accrue frequent-flier miles, and receive your tickets well before your departure date.

If you choose the air-inclusive package or buy air transportation as an add-on, take these precautions:

1. **DO YOUR HOMEWORK.** Ask the cruise line if preferred air itineraries are allocated according to reservations seniority (i.e., those who book earliest get the best itineraries). Also ask when your booked flight itinerary will be available. If the cruise line does not give priority to those who book early or does not provide flight information far enough in advance to make changes, book your own air.

2. **CALL EARLY TO RESERVE.** Remember that cruise lines contract for a specific number of seats for every cruise—when they're filled, the line has to scramble for additional ones. That's when you're likely to get a circuitous routing. But, to put this in perspective: The airline crunch comes at holiday times—Labor Day, Thanksgiving, Christmas, spring break through Easter—and can be exacerbated by bad weather. So, if you plan a cruise during a holiday period, arrange it early and save yourself a pile of headaches. As a veteran travel agent advised, "Passengers should seriously consider taking the air/sea package from the cruise line during the winter months, especially if they are flying from a cold-weather gateway. If there are weather- or equipment-related delays, the cruise line

will help air/sea passengers get to the ship. If passengers have booked their own air, they are on their own if they miss the ship. Passengers who do their own air would also be well advised to purchase third-party travel insurance that covers trip interruption, delay, or cancellation due to weather- or equipment-related problems."

The travel agent's advice is valid, but only up to a point. The cruise line sees itself as merely an airline ticketing agent. As a matter of customer relations, many cruise lines will step in and assist a passenger who is delayed or misses the boat because of problems with flights that the cruise line booked. The salient point, however, is that the cruise line is under no obligation to help. If you read the terms and conditions of your Passage Contract, you'll almost immediately bump into language like the following: "Under no circumstances does [X Cruise Line's] responsibility extend beyond the ship. All arrangements made for the guests with independent contractors [such as airlines] are made soley for the convenience of the guest and are at the guest's risk." We'll explore the ramifications of this and related issues later under "When Things Go Wrong." For now, let us add that we recommend third-party travel insurance whether you book air through the cruise line or not.

3. ASK YOUR TRAVEL AGENT WHEN YOU CAN EXPECT YOUR TICKETS. Most cruise brochures tell this in the fine print. If not, your travel agent will know from experience or can ask the cruise line. Normally, they arrive two to three weeks before departure. Smaller cruise lines generally deliver earlier than the big lines do.

4. PLAN YOUR ROUTE. If you have a specific route you want to fly to your departure port, tell your travel agent when you book or as soon as possible, so that your plane tickets can be issued properly. If you receive tickets requiring layovers and a change of planes, have your agent contact the cruise line's Air Deviation desk.

HOW TO GET THE BEST DEAL ON A CRUISE

TO GET A GOOD DEAL on a cruise, know the players and how the game is played. In the case of cruising, game rules pivot on the unalterable reality that a cruise is a time-sensitive product. If a cabin is not sold by sailing time, it loses all of its value. This makes selling cruises like playing "Beat the Clock." From the time a cruise is announced, the line is on a countdown to sell all the cabins. The immense expense of operating a cruise ship makes the selling a high-pressure, big-stakes endeavor. Yet, for 2005 and beyond, lines are running well ahead of the norm in advance bookings, and this is tightening up the availability of discounts.

For consumers, the time sensitivity is a major plus. Any time a dealer must make a sale or write off the inventory (empty cabins, in this case), wheeling and dealing are likely, and this almost always benefits the buyer. However, we emphasize that there's more to buying a cruise than its price. If you allow yourself to be influenced only by "getting the best deal," you are likely to end up on the wrong cruise. Talk to your agent and evaluate all factors.

Note that in American ports, it is no longer possible to show up at the dock, suitcase in hand, and negotiate a last-minute fare with the purser. For security reasons, cruise ships must submit passenger manifests to the FBI about a week prior to departure.

The Players: Cruise Lines

Lines have sales offices and, more and more, Web sites that can sell cruises directly to consumers. But as many as 95% of all cruises are sold through travel agents or other players, and you usually get a better price by buying from them. To their credit, cruise lines are loyal to those who sell their product and usually won't undercut the prices available to them. Practically, the lines don't want the bother, and until the Internet came along, it wasn't cost-effective. It costs cruise lines far more to maintain sales offices to serve the general public than it does to maintain a sales network through travel agencies and Internet sellers (which are expected to increase to 25% over the next few years). Note, however, that sales directly to consumers on the Internet are not necessarily at a discount.

But now many lines have "equalized" pricing and will penalize and even ban agencies from selling their products if they advertise a lower price. Carnival Cruise Lines, saying that it "would rather have 35,000 people selling Carnival than 10," closed ranks with the little guys by offering the same prices to all of its accounts. Royal Caribbean has gone even further: Whether small agencies or giants, it announced recently that it would no longer deal with any agency that is found undercutting prices by rebating commissions. In addition, Celebrity, Oceania Cruises, and Norwegian Cruise Lines now have similar antirebating practices. Other major lines say, off the record, to be prepared for others to follow suit. For now, some lines continue to offer large operators preferential pricing, but that practice is dwindling. To gain an even greater advantage, the big sellers also use their extensive resources to gobble up blocks of cabins at group rates and then resell the cabins one at a time to individual travelers. That too may eventually become passé as major lines are beginning to forbid this practice as well. They hope to stabilize prices and avoid abuse of their policies.

The smaller agencies are also smacked by the way the cruise lines handle "distressed inventory," for example, cabins yet unsold as the sailing date for a cruise approaches. Once again, not unexpectedly, these bargain-basement goodies are sometimes handed over to the line's big-volume brick-and-mortar and Internet accounts to move. Though most of us like to root for the underdog, it's tough to walk away from the great prices offered by larger sellers. It's worth remembering, however, that the big guys usually can't compete with a good hometown travel agent when it comes to service, accessibility, and peace of mind.

With the cruise industry expanding exponentially, be alert for foreign cruise lines and new cruise lines trying to break into the American market. Sometimes these lines offer incredible deals to lure customers from the United States. In 2005, for example, the up-and-coming Italian Line, MSC Cruises, was offering seven-night Caribbean cruises for as little as $545 for an inside cabin and $945 for a balcony stateroom. Your travel agent may not be familiar with new players in the market, so you'll probably have to ask or do some research on your own, and you may want to use a cruise-only agent who knows a host of cruise products.

The Players: Wholesalers and Megasellers

Wal-Mart founder Sam Walton taught Americans that the more of something you buy, the lower the price should be. Businesspeople call it buying in quantity or volume discounting. In cruising, travel wholesalers and megasellers are volume buyers. Booking well in advance, they buy large numbers of cabins on specific cruises with the intention of reselling the cabins at a profit. Advance purchasing and volume discounts, coupled with the fact that the cruise lines do not have to pay commissions, allows them to buy at prices substantially below what an individual could obtain. Some cabins that go unsold can be returned to the cruise company by a certain date; others are bought on a nonreturnable basis. In the latter case, the wholesaler or megaseller absorbs the costs of any cabins that aren't sold. The biggest cruise discounts available to any player go to those who buy cabins in bulk on a nonreturnable basis. Wholesalers sell to travel agents and, often, like megasellers, directly to consumers. If the wholesaler sells a cruise through a travel agency, then the wholesaler pays the agent a commission.

Note that these players generally deal with lines having large ships, or they offer the best deals on a limited number of ships and lines. If they spread themselves too thinly over the spectrum of cruises, they diminish their clout with specific lines. Remember: It's in the wholesaler's or megaseller's interest to steer you to ships where they get the best deal. That may or may not be in your best interest.

The Players: Travel Agents

Travel agents act as sales representatives of the cruise lines. Unlike wholesalers and consolidators, they don't buy cabins. Instead, they sell from the line's inventory, on commission. Like cruise lines and wholesalers, however, agents earn the most when they sell in volume.

Some full-service travel agencies specialize in cruises, whereas others are cruise-only agencies, selling nothing but cruises and cruise-related travel. The latter sell so many cabins for certain lines that they earn "override commissions"—a higher percentage level of commission over the norm. There is usually a volume threshold where the override kicks in. Some general travel agencies and independent agencies cash in on override commissions by joining a consortium—a group of agencies that pool their sales to receive the overrides.

To make the most in commissions and overrides, some agents push selected cruise lines, known in the industry as preferred suppliers. If the line that interests you is among your agent's preferred suppliers, great. If not, your agent may try to interest you in a line with which the agency has such an arrangement. However, a good agent who wants to stay in business will never put a customer on an inappropriate cruise just to earn one commission check. Remember, agents rely heavily on good word-of-mouth for their business. Their goal is to satisfy you, so you will come back. Most will sell you any cruise if you specifically ask for it.

Because most cruises are sold by travel agents, it is critically important for cruise lines to develop extensive systems of loyal travel agents. Competition among cruise lines to influence agents is so heated that consumers sometimes become pawns in a marketing chess game.

Over the years, for example, Holland America has awarded its agencies bonus points redeemable for chocolate, picnic lunches, dinners in local restaurants, or any number of other choice perks. Such incentives may influence agents' recommendations and narrow consumers' choices. All cruise lines are not necessarily a good fit for all of an agent's customers. Good agents place their clients' needs and preferences first, but some agents go for the largest commissions and the most goodies.

As we noted earlier, in the past, many agents sacrificed part of their commission or override to make a cruise more affordable to a good customer and to compete with large-volume discount agencies. Some agencies selling cruises in volume still take lower commissions to underprice other agencies. But again, recent cruise-line policy changes have cut these practices but have not eliminated them. In many locations, competition among agencies for cruise business is as keen as it is among cruise lines, particularly with the proliferation of cruise-only agencies and large Internet sellers. And now, with airlines having decreased agents' commissions, the competition for cruise business has grown even hotter.

In the final analysis, buyer beware. Protect yourself best by developing a long-term relationship with a knowledgeable travel agent who works to put you on the cruise that's right for you.

HELPING YOUR TRAVEL AGENT HELP YOU When you call a travel agent, ask whether he or she has cruised, how many times, and on what lines. Firsthand experience is invaluable. If the answer is no, find another agent or be prepared to give your agent copious direction. Ask who your agent's preferred vendors are. Just asking that question will tell the agent you are a savvy buyer. Compare the agent's recommendations with information in this guide. Request permission to contact other clients who have been on the cruise line recommended, and ask your friends. Someone you know may have sailed on the line. Also check the independent cruise Web sites listed earlier under "Gathering Information." These sites feature cruise reviews from both travel writers and the general public.

To help your travel agent obtain the best possible deal, do the following things:

1. Determine from brochures, friends' recommendations, the Internet, and this book a general idea (a framework if you will) of where and when you want to cruise, which lines offer the kind of cruise that most appeals to you, and how much you can spend. Remember that your cruise tickets are only a part of your costs. Budget also for air travel and for shore excursions, alcoholic beverages, tips, and shopping. Many a cruise passenger has rung up an onboard credit account that rivals the cost of the cruise itself.

2. Check cruise ads in the Sunday travel section of your local newspaper and compare them to ads in the newspapers of a key cruising market (New York, Philadelphia, Los Angeles, Phoenix, Dallas, Chicago, Boston, Washington, or Atlanta) near you. Look for deals that fit your plans and that include a line you like. Also, read ads in specialty magazines, such as *Cruise Travel* and *Frommer's Budget Travel,* and check out Internet sites selling discounted cruises.

3. Call consolidators or retailers (including Internet sites) whose ads you have collected. Ask about their offers, but do not book your trip with them directly.

4. Tell your agent about cruises you find, and ask if he or she can match or beat the price, or provide any "added value." Some producers may offer a bottle of wine, a fluffy robe, or another perk. Be aware that promotional ads are often bait to get your attention. The "lead" price probably applies to a limited number of cabins on a specific sailing. This element is probably the trickiest part of obtaining the best deal. Every ship has 6 to 20 categories of cabins. Often, unless you can pinpoint the date, itinerary, and cabin category being advertised, it may be hard to know whether you are getting a good deal. Nobody said this was easy.

5. Choose among options uncovered by you and your travel agent. Whatever option you elect, have your agent book it. It may be commissionable (at no additional cost to you) and will provide the agent some return on the time invested on your behalf. Also, your agent should be able to help you verify the quality and integrity of the deal, and be there to assist if any glitches arise.

HOW THE GAME IS PLAYED:
THE SALES COUNTDOWN

CRUISE LINES WORK WELL in advance to schedule cruises and develop promotional brochures. It is essential to roll out marketing campaigns quickly to avoid "fire sales" as sailing dates near.

Most itineraries and dates are announced 10 to 18 months in advance. Particularly attractive dates on popular ships and itineraries sell out quickly. Likewise, cruises to seasonal destinations like Alaska fill fast. The highest- and lowest-priced cabins sell out first. Usually the last cruises to fill are low- and shoulder-season cruises to year-round areas. Many consumers used to wait for last-minute discounts available when cruise lines hit the panic button. The lines finally wised up, reasoning that early-booking discounts could generate cash flow and indicate sales prospects for each cruise. Although some distress selling continues, cruise lines are learning to control the inventory more efficiently.

Escalating Base-Rate Model

To see how this works, let's examine a pricing model adopted by several prominent cruise lines. When the cruise is announced, the line advertises a base fare, discounted from the brochure figure by, say, 40%. The line warrants that the discounted base fare may increase as the countdown progresses, but will never be lower. Therefore, a consumer who books a November cruise in the preceding April would pay less than a passenger who books in June. That passenger, in turn, would pay less than someone booking in August, and so on.

This strategy allows the line and the travel agent to tell the customer that "this cruise will not be cheaper than today." The customer knows that the rate may rise, but will never be lower. The line can maintain the discounted rate if the ship is filling slowly, or raise it incrementally as the cruise approaches being sold out. We call this the escalating base-rate model.

Identifying the pricing model is useful, because then it's easier to understand what the cruise line does to nudge the ship to capacity.

In practice, cruise lines operate two pricing systems. Primary is the escalating base-rate system. If the cruise sells to near capacity, only that system will be employed. If sales lag behind expectations, however, the line goes to its separate and collateral model: the special-situations system.

Special-Situations System

Special-situations initiatives—usually time-limited and tightly targeted efforts for boosting sales—run concurrently with, and independently of, the escalating base-rate system. Examples of such initiatives include a deeply discounted senior citizen's rate, a direct mailing to previous customers offering a big discount, a regional campaign, advertising last-minute bargains on the Internet, or a heavily discounted group-sales overture to a large company for their executives or employees.

Each special-situation initiative targets a carefully selected market segment. Initiatives may run sequentially or concurrently but usually are short-lived and end when the cruise sells out. What is really important about special-situation initiatives is that the discount offered might be much greater than the base-rate discount. If you can locate such an initiative, you may have found the lowest possible fare. If the special is advertised in Atlanta and you live in Buffalo, the package's air component will be useless to you. However, if you can buy the cruise-only part of the special and arrange affordable airfare from Atlanta, you've got a deal.

A common special-situations approach is for the cruise line to join forces with specific travel agents or Internet sellers. Like travel agents who have preferred suppliers, cruise lines have preferred retailers. When a cruise is not selling to expectations, some lines have policies permitting them to enlist favorite big-volume agencies to help move the remaining cabins; other lines' policies may prohibit this, in an effort to give all retailers equal opportunities for sales. When this tactic is used, it develops promotions with these agents featuring extra-deep discounts and special incentives, such as cabin upgrades or discounted air add-ons. Many preferred agencies and Web sites sell cruises only and field hundreds of calls daily. If they have an especially juicy deal to offer, they can sell lots of cabins fast. Big-volume, cruise-only agencies advertise in magazines, including *Cruise Travel, Travel & Leisure, Frommer's Budget Travel,* and *Condé Nast Traveler,* and in large-market newspapers.

The Dump Zone

In the cruise marketplace, anything can happen. Some lines are either unequipped to nudge sales effectively or just aren't very good at it. Sometimes, lines expert in special-situations initiatives don't fill their cruises. The upshot is that a goodly number of empty cabins may be sold at distress prices during the final eight weeks before sailing, especially in the off-season.

When time is short, agents and cruise lines know it is much easier and less complicated to sell a cruise to someone who doesn't require air transportation to the port. Florida is a huge market for late-breaking deals because of its large population of retirees and its proximity to ports. Major ports on the Pacific Coast and Northeast likewise enjoy distress sales. If you live within easy driving distance of a major cruise-ship port, you live in a dump zone. You are well situated to benefit from last-minute discounts, but you probably will have no choice in cabin selection or dining-room seatings.

Discount Alphabet Soup

Before you shop for discounts, pick the cruise type that appeals to you. Once you start looking, don't get sidetracked by price alone. Instead, stay doggedly on the trail of the cruise that meets your needs and will satisfy and exceed your vacation expectations. Never equate cheapest with best, but don't equate it with worst, either.

More than a dozen types of cruise discounts are commonly offered, other than seasonal discounts. As you encounter them, be aware that catchy marketing come-ons, like "two-for-one" or "sail three days free," aren't always what they seem. For example, a promotion advertising 50% off the second person in the cabin (a frequent gimmick) is nothing more than 25% off for both (you probably could have done better with an early-booking discount). The best method for comparing rates, with or without discounts, is to calculate the per diem (per day) cost of your cruise vacation. Add the cruise cost and the airfare cost if it isn't included, plus taxes, port charges, and other applicable fees (transfers, etc.). Divide the total by the number of nights you will stay on the ship or in hotels included in the package.

Always compare apples to apples. Some cruising areas are more expensive. For example, Caribbean cruises should be compared to Caribbean cruises, not to Alaskan or Mediterranean cruises. Remember also that cruise lines are not created equal. Comparing a seven-day Carnival (Holiday Inn–type) cruise with a seven-day Silversea (Ritz-Carlton–type) cruise is meaningless. The cruise line profiles in Part Two will describe the differences.

Early-Booking Discounts

The more common of two kinds of early-booking discounts, the escalating base-rate model, was described earlier. Each line has a different name for it. Escalating base rates are capacity-controlled and can be withdrawn or escalated without notice. Most of the major lines employ capacity control pricing. The second type of early-booking discount is the flat cut-off date. If you book before the specified date, you get the discount. This, too, is common practice on selected itineraries. Passengers who pay in full by a specified date (as much as six to nine months before the cruise) receive a 10% to 20% discount. This discount is popular with Crystal, Silversea, and others in the luxury market.

Free Days

Passengers are offered 7 days' cruising for the price of 6, or 12 for the price of 10. Variations include complimentary days (with hotel) in the port city before and/or after the cruise, or "book a seven-day cruise and receive a free two- or three-day land package." Divide the double occupancy price by the number of days in the package to get a per-diem cost for comparative purposes.

Two-for-One and Second Passenger Cruises Free

The deal is that two passengers cruise for the price of one, but some tricky math is involved. Pick your cruise and cabin category and find the double-occupancy price per person, air included, on the brochure's rate chart. The two-for-one price is this rate less the cruise line's air cost for one person from your gateway city.

Let's say the brochure's air-inclusive double-occupancy rate is $2,000. If the brochure does not give it, ask your travel agent to call the cruise line to learn the round-trip airfare cost from your gateway city. This amount is subtracted from $2,000, and the remainder is your cruise-only cost for two persons. You must then make your own air arrangements or buy airfare from the cruise line as an add-on. Celebrity, Oceania, Princess, Costa, and Holland America are among the lines frequently offering two-for-one promotional fares. These fares work well if you can travel to and from the port on frequent-flier miles or by car. If you have to pay for air, however, comparative math might demonstrate that a discounted air/sea package is a better deal.

unofficial **TIP**
Normally, two-for-one fares are offered far in advance, with a cut-off date to secure early bookings.

Two-for-one offers come and go with supply and demand. It's difficult to keep up with them. They also might pop up on short notice. Such fire-sale fares aim to boost short-term sales and can be withdrawn at any time.

Flat Rates

This is an early-booking program in which every cabin in the ship, except probably the luxury accommodations, is sold for the same flat rates (one for inside cabins and one for outside cabins) on a first-come, first-served basis. The earlier you book, the nicer your cabin. Flat rates are usually cruise only, but airfare may be purchased as an add-on. Flat rates are frequently offered by Princess, Crystal, and Norwegian Cruise Lines.

X% Off Second Passenger in a Cabin

In this very common discount offered by many cruise lines: The first passenger pays the double-occupancy brochure rate and the second passenger gets 40% to 70% off. Some simple averaging demonstrates that this works out to a discount of 20% to 35% per passenger.

Reduced Rate Air Add-ons

If you purchase airfare from the cruise line separately (as opposed to included in the cruise price), that is an air add-on. Sometimes cruise lines will couple a discounted cruise-only rate (no airfare) with a very attractive air add-on. This usually occurs when the cruise line is able to negotiate an exceptionally good bulk airfare purchase with an airline from a specific gateway city. In essence, the cruise line is passing some of their savings along to the consumer. Typically, this kind of deal applies only to specific cities and is offered only for a short time. It often results from an airline's slow sales and its need to stimulate air travel from a particular area, as opposed to being a cruise-line initiative.

Senior Citizen Discounts

Because seniors have traditionally been the backbone of the cruise market, they are often one of the first groups targeted for a discount program if a line is having difficulty filling a cruise. Usually the discount requires that one person sharing the cabin must be at least 55 years old. The size of discount varies, as does the inclusion of airfare. Also, Carnival and some other cruise lines have year-round discounts for members of AARP, the American Association of Retired Persons.

Kids or Third/Fourth Passengers Go Free or at Reduced Rate

This discount is a fairly common for lines like Carnival, Disney, and Celebrity that target families and younger cruisers. Third and fourth persons or children sharing a cabin cruise free or at a substantial discount. Airfare for the third/fourth person or children is usually not included. Third/fourth person rates are generally part of a cruise line's basic rate structure (rather than promotional fares). They normally appear in the cruise line's brochure and are applicable year-round. Their promotional use might come into play seasonally by being reduced or waived altogether, perhaps in summer to stimulate family travel or in the shoulder season to stimulate first-timers to buy a cruise when three or four friends can share the cost.

Back-to-Back or Contiguous Segments Discounts

The seven-day cruise is the most popular product offered by any cruise line, as it suits the vast majority of people in terms of time and cost. However, there are people who have both the time and means for longer cruises. To satisfy both groups, the cruise lines have several choices. They may break longer cruises into seven-day segments, enabling a passenger to board in one port and depart from another. Or, they may offer two 7-day segments with different itineraries as one 14-day cruise, offering the second week at a greatly reduced price. For example, a ship departing from Miami sails one week to the eastern Caribbean and the next week to the western Caribbean. In combining the two, the only port repeated in 14 days is Miami, the departure port. Throughout our cruise line profiles, we highlight ships whose itineraries lend themselves to this sort of coupling and which offer attractive discounts for the second segment.

Repositioning Cruises

Rather than dispatch a ship empty, lines sell their repositioning cruises; to attract as many passengers as possible, they offer them at cut-rate prices. The majority of repositioning cruises are in spring and fall when the great "migration" of ships occurs—mostly when ships that have spent the winter on Caribbean, Panama Canal, and Mexico cruises are dispatched to Alaska or to New England/Canada and/or Europe for the summer; and again in autumn, when these ships return.

Repositioning cruises with interesting and unusual itineraries, such as from the Caribbean to New England via the Eastern Seaboard, are unlikely to have as much of a discount as those with few ports of call, such as transatlantic crossings. Those with more days at sea, however, appeal to folks who really love to cruise and cherish having uninterrupted days or weeks at sea. However *Queen Mary 2*, for example, has a wealth of onboard activities designed for every type of traveler.

Group Discounts

Persons traveling together can almost always negotiate a group rate. The larger the group, the better the rate. For a big group, at least one free berth or cabin is customarily provided for the organizer. What constitutes a group varies among cruise lines, but eight or more persons traveling together and occupying at least four cabins generally can obtain a discount, extra amenities, or a cabin upgrade.

Standby Rates

Lines may offer deeply discounted standby rates for specific itineraries and sailing dates. Normally, you rank your ship, departure, and cabin preferences and submit them to the line with a deposit. If your preferred date is available, the line notifies your travel agent at least 30 days in advance. If you are offered your first choice, the deposit is nonrefundable. Airfare is additional.

Cabin Upgrades

Four basic ways to get a cabin upgrade are:

1. ADVERTISED OR UNADVERTISED SPECIALS Usually publicized primarily (some are in press releases to media) to travel agents, upgrade programs give them a powerful selling tool. Upgrades apply to specific sailings and can be guaranteed by the agent and line at time of booking. Such specials allow consumers to buy the cheapest fare and be upgraded from one to five cabin levels.

2. SOFT SAILING UPGRADES A soft sailing refers to a cruise that is likely to depart at substantially less than full capacity. Booking the least expensive cabin category on a low- or shoulder-season cruise offers the best opportunity for receiving an upgrade. Early booking an inside cabin on a ship with few inside cabins (study the ship's deck plans) might result in upgrading to an outside cabin. But, with today's high occupancy rates, you might be stuck with the inside cabin. Just be prepared to accept it if you are not upgraded.

3. GUARANTEES If a cruise is sold out of the cabin category you request when booking, the line will offer a guarantee, promising a cabin in your preferred category or better. You pay the same rate as for the cabin you requested, including early-booking or other applicable discounts. Because guarantees are offered only when a cruise is sold out or oversold in a requested category, chances of getting the upgrade are good. Cabin location is up to the cruise line.

4. PAID UPGRADES A number of lines, particularly on soft sailings, sell upgrades. Sometimes the upgrades are as little as $15 per person per cabin category.

Confusion among passengers regarding cabin-upgrade availability often leads to frustration and disappointment. A travel agent wrote us:

PLEASE, PLEASE tell your readers that cabin upgrades are a privilege and not a right. . . . With most ships sailing at [near] 100% capacity, most people have a slim-to-none chance of getting upgraded—and almost certainly not from an inside cabin to an outside cabin. Many cabin upgrades are given at the time of booking, but "guaranteed cabin categories" do not mean guaranteed upgrades—these are based solely on availability. The only thing that is guaranteed is that they will get a cabin in at least the category they are booked in! Former passengers and people who book the earliest are the most likely to get upgrades, if they become available. If a certain cabin category is that important to someone, they should book it and pay for it, and not hope to be upgraded to it. . . . Plus, any travel agent that tells [clients] to take a "guaranteed" or "run of ship" rate to increase their chances of being upgraded, is setting up their clients for disaster. The agent may say one thing, but the client hears the word "upgrade" and thinks this is a given. Then when it doesn't happen, the client gets angry with the travel agent and the cruise line.

Free Stuff
Cruise lines might offer cameras, binoculars, and other goods as booking incentives. Or, freebies may be tied to a theme cruise; for example, a photography cruise sponsored by a camera manufacturer. Big-volume producers and savvy smaller agencies may offer a bottle of wine or a photo album.

Organizational Discounts
Cruise lines commonly develop relationships with organizations like the American Automobile Association or AARP. Check for discounts available through organizations to which you belong.

Credit Card Programs
Some cruise lines have credit card programs. Whenever you use the credit card, you accrue points or "cruise dollars." These can be

applied toward a cruise or taken as a credit to spend aboard. Cardholders receive mailings promoting discounts, and charging a cruise on the card may result in cabin upgrades. Similarly, miles accrued on the American Express program offering one mile for every dollar charged are redeemable for cruises.

Travel Agents' Discounts

We have found that agents selling the same discount program for a cruise may quote different prices. Usually the difference is small, 2% to 5%. What's going on is that a few retailers are sacrificing part of their override commissions to lowball the competition. Big-volume, cruise-only agencies routinely do this, but local agents frequently will knock a few dollars off their commission to retain a good customer. Ads that claim "We will beat or match your best offer" usually mean an agent is rebating some commission to his or her clients. But beware of this practice. Commissions represent an agent's costs and profit. As any businessperson knows, if you give away your profit, you will end up with red ink. In addition, cruise lines including Carnival, Oceania, Norwegian Cruise Line, Royal Caribbean, and Celebrity have cracked down on agencies that rebate in any advertised price. So the number of agencies rebating at all is greatly reduced.

Cruise Loan Programs

Pioneered by Princess, cruise loan programs are seen by the lines and travel agents as "a tool for taking away one of the clients' biggest stumbling blocks: paying in full for a cruise before sailing." Loans may also help sellers trade the customer up. Basically, you borrow your cruise's cost on a revolving line of credit (like most credit cards) and pay off the loan in 24, 36, or 48 installments, like a mortgage or car loan. The main difference between a mortgage or car loan and a cruise loan is that the former are secured by pledging your home or car as collateral. Because there is nothing to pledge as collateral on a cruise loan, interest rates are much higher. In 2004, the lowest annual percentage rate for a cruise loan was 9%; the highest, 29%. Loans are administered by participating banks that are unaffiliated with the cruise lines. If you obtain the lowest interest rate for cruise loans on a 36-installment loan, the monthly payment for a seven-day cruise costing $5,000 per couple is $161 per month. Multiply the $161 by 36 months to see you'll actually be paying $5,796 for your cruise. Most people would do better taking out a loan on their own.

Lost in the Information Haze

Deals come and go so rapidly that a travel agency has to be knowledgeable, well staffed, and computerized to keep on top of the action. Though big cruise-only agencies are the best equipped to handle the information flood, even they occasionally lag.

The National Association of Cruise-Only Agencies (NACOA) can provide a list of member agencies in your area. Check out **www.cruising.org** for a list of member agencies of Cruise Lines International Association (CLIA). Discount agencies usually advertise widely. Always check the reliability of any agency with whom you do business.

CRUISING THE INTERNET FOR CRUISES

CRUISE INFORMATION ON THE INTERNET has increased more than 1,000% in the past five years. There are thousands of Web sites to investigate. The majority are travel agencies, large and small. Even if you're a wiz at searches, you'll still need a great deal of time and infinite patience to find the facts you need. Despite Google and Yahoo and other useful search engines, cyberspace remains chaotic. We can't organize it for you, but here are facts that can help you navigate your own way on the ocean of information.

Essentially, cruise-related information on the Internet is precisely that—information. You can ask questions and order brochures, and recently, a few cruise lines have taken the next step enabling you to buy a cruise directly from them on the Internet (the numbers are expected to increase substantially over the next decade). The best way to find out if a particular cruise line is selling online is to check out its Web site. The Web addresses for all cruise lines with Web sites are included in this book.

The Internet has become a particularly handy tool for advertising last-minute specials. There are a number of sites which, after you sign up, will automatically send you an e-mail advertising deeply discounted cruises. Many sites specialize in cruises, while others offer air, hotels, rental cars, and a range of other travel products. Many sites will provide a form for you to complete listing the kind of deals (cruises, air, hotels, etc.) that you're interested in. When they send out their weekly e-mail, they limit the message to those products. Some of the best deals we've seen are on these Web sites, but buyer beware. Some Web sites have sold cruises without advising the customer of required passport and visa requirements or other pertinent information.

One of the most useful Web sites, launched in 2003, is **Cruise Compete.com,** which calls itself "the world's exclusive competitive cruise vacation pricing Web site." Recently, it added an advanced search tool to help travelers find their ideal cruise at the best available price, enabling travelers to find multiple cruise itineraries based on a preferred port of call or country. Cruisers also can narrow their search by departure port, date range, cruise length, and cruise line at the same time. After selecting a cruise based on destination, you can then click on a sail date to request competing quotes from nearly 100 member travel agencies across the country, potentially helping consumers save substantially on their cruise vacations. If, for example, you want to take a cruise to St. Kitts in the Caribbean, you type "St.

Kitts" in the search tool, and in a few seconds, CruiseCompete.com finds all of the cruises that go there. Another click and you'll get the best prices. We are not aware of any other site on the Internet offering this type of function and ease of use. Information is also available from these sources:

- **Cruise associations** Trade organizations, including Cruise Lines International Association, that have their own Web sites (**www.cruising.org**).

- **Travel agencies** Hundreds of agencies have Web sites, and others participate through their trade organizations. Most take bookings online or via e-mail.

- **Travel publications** Major travel magazines, such as *Travel & Leisure* and *Travel Weekly*, and book publishers, including John Wiley & Sons (which publishes this book), have Web sites.

- **Individuals** Recognized travel experts and some people who consider themselves cruise experts or are interested in cruises have created their own sites.

- **Subscriber services** Many, such as AOL, have specialized programs on cruises and most feature special deals.

The typical cruise-line Web site offers about the same information available in a cruise brochure. However, fares are likely to be sample prices only. Cabin sizes or configurations aren't specific. You usually can request a brochure by e-mail or on the Web (you may be required to give a phone number or e-mail address), but such sites are most useful when you know where and when you plan to cruise. Information, of course, covers the host cruise line only.

Some sites are well done, fun, clever, and even amusing, and they are getting better. Others are basic and slow to load—you would learn more by reading the line's brochure. The best sites have special features, such as itineraries with links to maps and port information, or the facility to search by ZIP code for travel agencies near you. Often, the site is linked to other cruise-related information.

The range of information is as broad as it is voluminous—Princess Cruises' Web site is huge! But it is also one of the best. Among other things, it enables you to book shore excursions in advance—a service that is becoming available from more and more cruise lines. There is no uniformity in presentation, style, or amount of detail between cruise lines. On Windstar Cruises' Web site, you can go through a typical day on board, see a sample dinner menu, review itineraries with sailing dates, and read about special fares and onboard credits for Internet users. Carnival Cruise Lines, with one of the most extensive sites, offers pictures and descriptions of each cabin category, including drawings and pictures of cabin layouts—a rare feature. Some of the smallest cruise lines have the best Web sites; of course, with fewer or smaller ships, it easier to provide information and easier for consumers to navigate the site.

For news, guidance, and evaluations, **www.cruisecritic.com** is maintained by a team of cruise specialists and knowledgeable persons.

Included are candid, continuously updated ship reviews and evaluations on more than 100 ships, with descriptions on facilities, activities, amenities, itineraries, and fellow passengers; news on industry developments; and features ranging from seasickness to bargains. The Cruise Critic library contains trip reports and travel tips.

Similar information is available from **www.cruisemates.com,** a site by veteran cruise writer Anne Campbell and a group of established writers who specialize in cruises. When Campbell cruises, she sometimes offers daily reports with video. In addition to constantly updated information on special deals, Cruisemates promotes several specially priced cruises throughout the year. Campbell and others host message boards where people can ask questions or post their opinions on cruises, ports, and related matters.

Cruise Opinion (**www.cruiseopinion.com**) claims to have the largest database of cruise ship reviews on the Web. All are recently written and based on personal experiences. Each reviewer evaluates the ship in 42 categories using a rating of 0 to 100 and describes the cruise experience. Most reviews were provided within the last year. A recent check showed over 4,500 reviews on file, with more added daily.

CruiseReviews (**www.cruisereviews.com**) is limited but more current than Cruise Opinion. The site lists about 20 major cruise lines and all their ships. About a third had been reviewed recently. Those we checked were short, but pointed.

Other sites you might want to check out include:

- **Expedia.com, orbitz.com,** and **travelocity.com.** The three big players in Internet travel sales. Besides offering copious content, each post weekly discounts on a broad range of travel products.

- **Lastminutetravel.com** offers a full range of travel products, including cruises and air.

- **Lowestfare.com** sells all travel products but limits its e-mails to a small number or particularly hot deals.

- **Cheaptickets.com** posts a weekly newsletter advertising mostly air and hotel deals.

- **Bestfares.com** is a good all-purpose travel discount site.

Additional Web sites specializing in cruise information and discounts include **seasaver.com, cruise.com, i-cruise.com, cruiseplanners. com, cruiseholidays.com,** and **cruise411.com.**

Many of these Web sites offer deck plans; ship descriptions and reviews; tips on insurance; advice for couples, singles, seniors, and the disabled; and of course, hot deals. Last-minute specials and bargain rates can be found on all of the sites.

Buying on the Internet

If you want to purchase a cruise from an Internet company, first try to run the transaction through your travel agent. If possible, make the booking through the site's phone number as opposed to purchasing electronically. Even if you handle the entire transaction electronically, verify by calling the seller's phone number that competent help in the form of a live person is available if you need it. Because many online sites specialize in last-minute deals, you probably won't have much time to resolve a problem should one occur. Before you book, ask the seller when your reservation will be recorded as fully paid in the cruise line's system. Repeat the process with the airline if you buy air from the cruise line. On the date provided by the seller, call the cruise line and airline directly to confirm that everything is order. If time is short when you make your reservations, you should request overnight delivery; it's worth the cost for the peace of mind. Regarding air travel purchased through the cruise line, you are likely to get electronic ticketing. At least it saves you from having to worry about paper tickets being delivered on time.

unofficial **TIP**
If the deal is only available through the Internet direct to the consumer, make sure before you buy that the site provides a phone number so that you can get a real person on the line if something goes amiss.

Online Auctions

A twist in discounting is auctioning cruises online at such sites as **www.onsale.com, www.ubid.com,** and **www.allcruiseauction.com.** If ever there were a need for "buyer beware," it is here. We know that some people have scored true bargains, but we also hear of people bidding more for a cruise than they would have paid through their travel agent. The bottom line: If you want information, cruising the Internet can be useful and fun. It can also be frustrating and time-consuming. You will learn quickly which sites are worthwhile.

We believe that this book—we say in all modesty—together with cruise lines' compendiums and a knowledgeable travel agent, remains the most efficient and effective way to help you select the right cruise—that is, the cruise right for you.

unofficial **TIP**
Be cautious about comments on message boards, forums, and chat rooms from unidentified sources whose reliability you can't check.

Price Protection

The airlines and cruise lines encourage you to book early to obtain the lowest fares. But what if you plunk down $1,200 for a cruise and discover a few months later that the same class of cabin on the same cruise is selling for $800? Getting a refund for the difference or being able to cancel and rebook at the lower rate is known as price protection. The cruise lines claim to be flexible and cooperative in this regard, but when it comes to giving back money already in their pocket, things usually get sticky. Sometimes customers must "qualify" for deals offered at lower prices. These qualifications sometimes make sense, as when a deal is offered to persons over 65 years of age, or to a promotional fare offered on a strictly regional basis, for example to residents of Dade Country, Florida. Often, however, the qualifications for obtaining the lower rate are specious in the extreme. A common practice among cruise lines is to reject requests to rebook after the passenger has made his final payment. If you have been a good little passenger and paid on time, you're rewarded for your punctuality by being prohibited from taking advantage of lower fares available to most everyone else. Another way cruise lines accomplish the same thing is to limit the lower fare to "new bookings only." In other words, if the right fist doesn't get you, the left will.

Almost all cruise lines assess penalties for canceling within a certain number of days from the sailing date. If you cancel before the applicable penalty date, you're free to rebook at the lower promotional fare. Problem is, cruise lines time the announcement of cut-rate deals to fall well inside the penalty period.

The most straightforward and consumer-friendly policy we were able to uncover is offered by Royal Caribbean and Celebrity. These lines will allow a passenger to rebook at any lower rate for which they qualify until the "sailing closes" (usually one or two days prior to departure). If you're age 50 and try to take advantage of a senior deal, you won't qualify, but for deals offered to the broader market, you'll be allowed to rebook without penalty.

Finally, the best price protector you'll ever have is a good travel agent. A good agent can often use her influence and clout to beat some of the silly arbitrariness out of the cruise lines. If the agent can't arrange an actual rebate, she frequently can get you compensated through other concessions such as cabin upgrades, shipboard credit, and the like. Remember that your agent will probably have dozens, if not hundreds, of clients booked on various cruises at any one time. Thus, it's unrealistic to expect her to monitor discount deals circulated by the cruise lines. It's your job to check for lower prices periodically, and if you find something, bring it to her attention. But again, increasingly, lines are cracking down on retailers who advertise low-ball pricing, and there will be less of this battle mentality in pricing for different agencies.

PULLING IT ALL TOGETHER

YOU KNOW THE PLAYERS and how the game is played. Now it's time to put your knowledge into action.

Step 1. To Agent or Not to Agent

Your first big decision is whether to use a travel agent. This guide, cruise lines' brochures, Sunday newspaper travel sections, cruise specialty magazines, and the Internet will enable you to narrow your

choices. Even so, a reliable travel agent can contribute immeasurably in offering advice and
facilitating the process. If you have a travel agent
who has served you well, particularly if you're a
volume customer, you should use her. If you
don't have a regular agent, ask your friends for
recommendations. Make sure the agency has a good reputation and
that the agent with whom you are dealing is experienced in selling
cruises. Using a travel agent will not cost you more, since the cruise
line pays any commissions.

unofficial **TIP**
Try to select a travel
agent near your age or
one who shares your
interests and lifestyle.

Step 2. Narrow Down

Using this book and the other material, make a priority list of four
lines, ships, and cruises. Be flexible. Also be alert to the possibility of
travel agents' pushing their preferred suppliers, who may not be on
your list. If so, ask why the agent feels the supplier might meet your
needs. You might be surprised at the response. Sometimes consumers
are not the best judge of the right cruise fit for themselves.

Step 3. Scout the Discounts

Using information collected from newspaper travel sections, Internet,
and other sources, ask your agent if she can meet or top any special
deals you have found or provide extra "value" in some way. Call a few
high-volume, cruise-only agencies on your own. Ask about cruises on
your priority list, then ask what's the best deal the agency is selling.
Always ask for the bottom-line cost in dollars
rather than the percentage discount. Repeat the
quote to the agent and verify what is included
(airfare, accommodations, transfers, and so on).
Take notes.

Your top priority is to determine which cruise
is right for you. Only then is it time to scout
deals. The best way to ruin your cruise vacation
is to book the wrong ship or the wrong cabin in
an effort to save a few dollars.

unofficial **TIP**
Never fall into the trap of
buying a cruise simply
because it sounds like a
great deal—especially if
you are buying your first
cruise.

Step 4. Buy Early or Buy Late

As we said, the biggest discounts are usually given for buying early
(four to eight months before sailing) or late (during the last six
weeks). First-time cruisers have greater choice and peace of mind
taking the early-bird route. Experienced cruisers are in a better position to play the best-deal game. But any time you hold out for a deal,
you decrease your options for getting the cabin, dining room seating,
and airline routing you prefer. In the long run, these factors are much
more important to the quality of your cruise than saving $50 or $100.

Step 5. Give the Seller a Price to Beat

When you've narrowed the field to one or two cruises and you're ready to buy, call the three or so agents who quoted the best prices in your first round of inquiries. Say, "I've been quoted a price of $X for this particular cruise; can you beat it?" Give your travel agent a chance to match it. If he can't, he may be able to verify the deal's integrity or uncover hidden problems. If the deal is commissionable, have your agent book it, or if the agent has invested a lot of time on your behalf, offer a $50 or $100 consultation fee.

Step 6. Check It Out

If you decide to buy from an agency outside your city or state, try to determine whether it's bonded and a member of its local Better Business Bureau and/or Chamber of Commerce. Also check whether it's a member of the American Society of Travel Agents (ASTA), the Association of Retail Travel Agents (ARTA), the National Association of Cruise Only Agencies (NACOA), or Cruise Line International Association (CLIA). Membership isn't a guarantee of ethical business practices, but the organizations have a vested interest in maintaining the good reputation of cruising and try to attract only upstanding members.

American Society of Travel Agents	☎ 703-739-2782 **www.astanet.com**
Association of Retail Travel Agents	☎ 800-969+6069 www.artonline.com
Cruise Line International Association	☎ 212-921-0066 **www.cruising.org**
National Association of Cruise-Only Agencies	☎ 305-663-5626 **www.nacoaonline.com**

To find out how consolidators and wholesalers respond to questions about their affiliations and accreditations, we called all of the cruise discounters advertising in *Cruise Travel* and *Condé Nast Traveler* magazines. Some agencies were gracious and seemed to understand that customers have a right to check their credentials. An amazing number, however, were surly and uninformative. "Who are you?" and "What do you need to know that for?" were typical responses. Representatives from four agencies said they didn't know the answers to our questions but would call us back. Of course, we never heard from them. When you call to check an agency, accept nothing less than complete courtesy, openness, and cooperation. Life's too short, and your cruise is too important, to deal with rude salespeople. Remember to show the same respect. Good travel agents will work hard for you, but they can spot someone on a fishing expedition. Just be prepared. Some agents will not put quotes in writing if they feel you are only "shopping around" and will buy on price alone and not on price *and* service.

Step 7. Protect Yourself

When you pay for your cruise, use a credit card and insist that the charge be run through the cruise line's account, not the agency's account. This precaution is important. Financially shaky agencies sometimes use their customers' payments to settle agency debts instead of to secure the customer's booking. If these agencies fold, the customer is often left with no cruise and no refund. Paying with a credit card allows you to cancel payment if the cruise is not provided as promised. Reputable travel agents and other sellers are more than happy to run the charge through the cruise line's account and will absolutely not be offended by your request. Financially sound sellers make a practice of running credit card charges through the cruise line's account anyway. This is done so that the cruise line will have to pay the credit-card merchant fees. If you purchase your cruise from any seller other than your usual travel agent, ask the seller when the paid reservation will be posted in the cruise line's system. On the date provided, call the cruise line directly to confirm the reservation.

Protect your cruise investment with travel insurance. Most comes with lots of bells and whistles, but three things should concern you: (1) loss of your paid fare if you must cancel or if your cruise is interrupted, (2) the potentially huge costs of emergency medical evacuation, and (3) major medical expenses while traveling that your primary health insurance doesn't cover.

Though overpriced at about $5 to $8 per every $100 of coverage, travel insurance nevertheless is a prudent expenditure. You never know when you might become ill, have a death in the family, or miss your sailing because of a flight cancellation or delay.

Although travel insurance coverages can be purchased separately, they are usually "bundled." We recommend you purchase good coverage for trip cancellation/interruption and emergency medical evacuation. Trip cancellation/interruption insurance covers the insured traveler and traveling companion(s) against losses caused by illness, injury, or death. Most policies cover losses resulting from the interruption of your trip by the death, serious injury, or serious illness of a close family member back home. **Access America** (**www.accessamerica.com**) and **Travel Guard** (**www.travel-guard.com**) also offer coverage for the illness, injury, or death of a business partner.

If you must cancel your cruise before departure, most cancellation/ interruption insurance plans will reimburse you for the cruise's full cost, less any refund you receive from the cruise line. Though cancellation and refund policies vary, most lines provide a full refund if you cancel 61 or more days before your departure date. Remember that these policies generally cover only the extent of your investment. If you are buying a $1,500 cruise, you don't need $10,000 in insurance.

Ideally, insurance will allow you to cancel your trip for any reason. Most policies, however, stipulate situations that qualify for coverage.

unofficial **TIP**
If you buy a cruise at the double-occupancy rate and your companion must cancel, your policy should cover the single supplement if you want to continue alone.

At a minimum, insist on being covered for death, injury, illness, jury duty, court appearances, accidents en route to the airport or pier, and disasters at home, including fire or flood. The same coverage applies to your traveling companion(s).

Policies usually cover airline or shipworker strikes, but not earthquakes or other disasters at scheduled ports of call. Cruise lines reserve the right to alter the itinerary once under way to avoid bad weather or other problems. Also, please keep in mind that some insurance companies may only allow you to cancel *for any reason* up to 24 or 48 hours *prior* to scheduled departure.

The fine print in many policies can be tricky, and seemingly innocuous loopholes limit the carrier's obligation. One essential question regarding cancellation/interruption insurance is whether it covers preexisting conditions: any for which you were treated by a physician in the 60 days (90 days in Maryland) before the policy was purchased. In better policies, if the pre-existing condition is controlled by medication, it is covered. In insurance company language, however, "controlled" is very different from "treated." If you have high blood pressure and medication maintains it at normal, safe levels, your condition is controlled. If you have a tumor and are receiving radiation, carriers would say you are being treated, but that your condition is not controlled. If your tumor caused you to cancel your cruise, the policy would not reimburse you. The same stipulations regarding preexisting conditions apply to your family back home. If, for example, your mother dies while you're traveling, your trip interruption coverage would be void if her death was related to a preexisting condition. We recommend that you question the insurance carrier directly about any health problems, obtaining written confirmation of coverage if necessary. One reputable travel agency advised us that you stand a better chance of having preexisting conditions covered with private insurance than with many cruise-line insurance plans.

Pregnancy is covered by most policies if you cruise during your first two trimesters. If a complication arises, the policy will pay. Amazingly, if you deliver your baby normally while on a cruise, you are not covered. Many cruise lines won't accept a pregnant passenger in her third trimester.

Another potential land mine in cancellation/interruption insurance is operator failure. What if your travel agent, airline, or cruise line goes belly up? Although brochures and most policies say they will pay in the event of operator failure or default, fine print sometimes defines *failure* and *default* as bankruptcy. Because many businesses fail without declaring bankruptcy, this is an important distinction. Note that most policies exclude the failure of the company that sold the cruise (usually a travel agent) or the company that sold the insurance. If you buy insurance from a travel agency, you're covered if the cruise line or airline fails, but not if the agency fails. This is yet another reason you should pay for your cruise with a credit card and insist that the charge be run directly through the cruise line's account, not the travel agent's. It's also a good reason to buy travel insurance directly from the insurance company, something easily done on the Internet. If all of this sounds far fetched, think again. Four established cruise lines—Commodore, Premier, Renaissance, and American Hawaii—went under within the past few years.

Trip interruption coverage, sold with trip cancellation policies, supplements what you recover from the cruise line if something goes wrong during your trip. If a family member dies, for example, and you must fly home from a port mid-cruise, the interruption coverage will pay for your plane ticket home plus reimburse you for the unused portion of your cruise (less any refund you receive from the cruise line). The policy also would pay the single supplement of your cabin companion if he or she remains on the cruise. Some insurance companies also place a certain dollar limit on their trip interruption coverage and normally list the amount in their policy. Try to find a company with the highest percentage—say 150% of the trip cost rather than just 100%. Remember, when plans change you may incur additional air or hotel charges

Trip interruption insurance covers fire, flood, vandalism, burglary, and natural disaster as it affects your home, but does not cover similar catastrophic events if they occur at your place of business. In our estimation this is a huge gap in travel insurance coverage. As it turns out, it's also a gap in standard business-casualty insurance. If your office building burns down while you're cruising in Alaska, chances are about 99 to 1 that your business insurance will decline to reimburse you for the cost of returning home or for the unused portion of your cruise.

Something much less likely than a fire at your office, however, is now covered. As a consequence of the September 11, 2001 terrorist attacks, most travel insurance policies offer coverage for cancellation or interruption occasioned by an act of terrorism. Coverage varies from policy to policy.

A common but very important coverage exclusion relates to "travel arrangements canceled or changed by an airline, cruise line, or tour operator, unless the cancellation is the result of bad weather or financial default." What this means is that your trip cancellation/interruption insurance doesn't cover you if, say, your flight is cancelled for reasons other than weather, and you miss the boat. Logically, one would think, this is exactly the sort of circumstance for which you need travel insurance. When we asked the insurance companies why such events are excluded, their response, to quote one company representative, was, "Oh, we couldn't cover that. It happens too often." Isn't that reassuring?

Bundled with trip cancellation/interruption is emergency medical evacuation insurance. This pays to transport you to a place where you can obtain high-quality medical care. In some areas of the Caribbean and even more remote cruise areas in Africa, Asia, or Latin America, you might prefer not to entrust your care to local doctors. The insurer in conjunction with a qualified physician usually must verify your condition and authorize the evacuation. Once authorized, the insurer usually selects the means of transportation.

As a rule, evacuation insurance does not cover hospital stays, doctors, diagnostic procedures, treatments, or medications, though medical coverage sometimes is bundled with a comprehensive policy covering trip cancellation/interruption. Ask your primary health insurer, Medicare, or HMO whether you are covered for medical attention required when traveling abroad. If you are not covered, buy supplemental insurance.

If you book an upscale cruise and pack Rolex watches, gems, and other valuables, check your homeowners policy to determine what's covered when you travel. If you aren't covered, take out a rider. When you travel, carry your valuables on your person, not in checked luggage. Even better, leave them at home.

Cruise lines and travel agencies, as a rule, do not self-insure. In other words, the policy they sell is an off-the-shelf or customized product of an independent travel insurance company. This is true even when the policy has the cruise line's name in the title, for example, "Happy Sea Cruise Line Total Protection." As mentioned earlier, any third party selling a policy is automatically excluded from "supplier default" coverage. Thus, if you buy that Happy Sea travel insurance and Happy Sea Cruise Line goes belly up, you could get caught holding the bag. Because of many cruise lines, wholesalers, and travel agencies defaulting (going out of business) in the wake of 9/11, most travel insurance companies now maintain a list of travel suppliers, including cruise lines and cruise retailers, that they will *not* cover. Most of the failed cruise lines were on those lists prior to their ultimate collapse.

Finally, most travel insurance companies post their policies, as well as their list of excluded travel suppliers, on the Internet. Read the policies before you buy, and call the company's customer service representative if you have any questions. Here are several major insurers and their phone numbers and Internet sites:

Access America Service Corporation ☎ 866-807-3982
www.accessamerica.com

CSA Travel Protection ☎ 800-873-9855
www.travelsecure.com

Travelex	☎ 888-457-4602
	www.travelex-insurance.com
Travel Guard	☎ 800-826-4919
	www.travelguard.com
Travel Insured	☎ 800-243-3174
	www.travelinsured.com

There are also other smaller firms that may have good plans as well; ask your agent. When shopping for travel insurance, remember that language in the brochure is marketing language. The language in the policy legally defines the carrier's obligations.

If your cruise line underwrites its own policy, compare it with one or more of the policies listed above. If the cruise policy is comparable and the line's in good shape financially, consider it. The line has a greater interest in your satisfaction than an insurance company does and may be more helpful in a crisis. Be aware, however, that there is some risk involved with buying your insurance from the cruise line. If the line goes out of business, as Commodore, Renaissance, American Hawaii, and Premier did, your claim will be thrown in with claims of all of the cruise line's creditors waiting to be reimbursed, and you may get back only pennies on the dollar, if anything.

When you buy travel insurance, make sure the policy covers you *from the date of purchase until the day you arrive home from your vacation.* This is extremely important: You can't imagine the problems some folks have had with policies that did not take effect until departure time or that didn't cover the travelers' whole time away from home. In one example, a couple from Texas bought travel insurance from a cruise company. On their own, they scheduled a two-night hotel stay at their originating port and another two-night stay at their port of disembarkation. When the husband became ill on the second day after the cruise, they tried to invoke the medical coverage on their travel insurance. Much to their chagrin, they were told that their policy only covered the days of the cruise, not the extra precruise and postcruise days the couple had arranged themselves. This is yet another example of why it's usually preferable to purchase your policy directly from the travel insurance company.

Finally, be aware before you leave home that if you need to make a claim, the travel insurance companies will hold you to an exacting standard of documentation. From the time you book your cruise, hang onto every correspondence, invoice, statement, canceled check, and receipt. For trip cancellation/interruption, travel delay, and/or medical claims, you will need some or all of the following:

1. Proof of complete trip payment.
2. Proof of insurance payment.
3. Invoice from your travel agent or tour operator showing complete trip costs and cancellation penalties.

4. If your situation involves illness, accident, or death, you'll need to produce doctor's medical records, hospital records, and/or a death certificate.

5. Paid receipts for all expenses incurred.

6. Original travel documents.

A final note: If you have made the decision to forego travel insurance, consider a few important points before declining. Understand the serious financial and personal difficulties you could find yourself in should an unexpected illness or family emergency develop. First, most travelers decline because they say "Oh I have insurance with my company or Medicare." Understand that these plans generally only cover you while you are within the United States, not overseas. If a serious illness develops, you will be taken off the ship and sent to a foreign land with no resources. Travel insurance almost always comes with resources, such as a 24-hour help line to provide support while you are dealing with medical problems in a foreign land. Yes, travel insurance may not immediately pay the bills on site at a foreign hospital, but it will reimburse you later for those fees so you don't forfeit your kids college fund or your own retirement nest egg unnecessarily. Understand as well that treatment while onboard a ship is not free and not necessarily inexpensive. For example, one travel agent reports she had a 29-year-old customer who was in excellent health prior to his cruise. He took no travel insurance, then suffered a massive heart attack; his bill for one day in the ship's medical center until he could be evacuated was $6,000. That didn't count the charges from the land-based hospital. Travel insurance is not really a nicety, but a necessity.

WHEN THINGS GO WRONG

AS YOU'VE ASCERTAINED FROM the discussion of travel insurance above, there are number of things that can go wrong between the time you book your cruise and the day when you arrive back home. Long-range planning minimizes bad surprises and generally allows sufficient time to work out any snags. Last-minute deals can sometimes save a ton of money, but cramming all of your planning and arrangements into a few short weeks or days before departure increases the probability of a problem arising with little or no time to resolve it.

Eliminating problems should be an integral part of your long-term planning. Begin by analyzing your risks. Take a look at your health and the health of your family and business associates. There may be foreseeable risks which suggest that it's not really the best time to take a cruise. Before you book your cruise, get a handle on the financial stabilty of your intended cruise line. Make sure you pay with a credit card and have the charge run through the cruise line's account as opposed to the travel agent's or other third-party sellers. Buy travel insurance that takes effect on the date of purchase and provides coverage until you get home. Buy it directly from the insurance company. If you are traveling to a part of the world where you'd prefer not to be treated by the local health-care industry, make sure emergency medical-evacuation coverage is included in your policy. Go over all preexisting medical conditions with the insurance carrier before you buy. Make sure you have already acquired trip cancellation/interruption coverage. If you have special concerns, such as the possible death of an aging parent or business partner, make sure those situations are covered by the policy. Realize that there are a number of circumstances besides death that may require your unexpected return home. We have readers whose cruises were interrupted by a fire at their place of business, a tree falling on their home, a burglary, and an unexpected lawsuit, to name a few. In short, the broader and more inclusive your trip cancellation/interruption coverage, the better.

Problem 1: Missing Flight Information

If you purchased your air from the cruise line, or if air was included in the price of your cruise, you should receive your flight *itinerary* 30 to 45 days prior to departure. If less than 30 days remain prior to departure and you haven't received your information, call your travel agent and have her find out what's going on. If everything checks out, phone the seller. Work your way from reservationist to supervisor to manager to owner as required until you get a satisfactory explanation. Take the same approach with the seller if the cruise line has no record of your reservation.

unofficial **TIP**
If you bought your cruise through the Internet or from a nonlocal seller, call the cruise line first to make sure your reservation is in their system and that full payment has been received.

Problem 2: Missing Cruise Documents or Airline Tickets

Your date of departure is looming, but you haven't received your airline tickets and/or cruise documents. If you have a good travel agent, you are virtually assured that everything will get sorted out in plenty of time. If you purchased on your own through a print ad, the Internet, or from a seller with whom you do not ordinarily do business, the situation is much iffier. In that case, start by calling the cruise line directly and making sure that your reservation is in order and *that payment has been received*. If you purchased air with your cruise, and you know your flight itinerary, go through the same process with the airline. If everything is properly recorded, next call the seller. You'll probably be told that late delivery of documents, especially airline tickets, is standard practice (unfortunately true) and not to worry. Most of the time this will be valid advice, but if something is actually screwed up (documents lost in mail, misplaced, etc.), you won't have much time, once the seller acknowledges a problem, to resolve it. The one thing you can count on is that the cruise line and airline are going to refer you back to the seller for resolution.

The only exception to this is when your cruise reservation is paid in full and the cruise line knows that the seller has gone belly-up. In this case, the cruise line will usually arrange for you to pick up your cruise documents at the pier. Regarding the airline, if your reservation is in the system and fully paid, and if you have an electronic ticket, you're home free. Just go to the airport and produce your photo ID and confirmation. If paper tickets are lost, you're back to dealing with the seller. If it's a weekend or holiday and you can't contact the seller, call the airline and ask for a customer-service representative. All airlines have different policies, but the representative will usually try to help if the reservation is in the airline's system and fully paid.

If your reservations, either air or cruise, are not in the cruise line's or airline's system, you've got a big problem. It could be a simple as a transmission error between the seller and the cruise line, or it could mean that the seller lost your reservations; failed to record your payments; erroneously cancelled your reservations; or is about to, or has, gone out of business. Assuming the seller is still in business, call the seller, explain your situation, and then start working your way up the chain of command until you get someone on the phone with the knowledge and authority to address your problem.

Most of these situations can be avoided, of course, by doing business with a brick-and-mortar travel agent in your hometown, by a reputable Internet seller affiliated with a reliable travel consortium, and by arranging your air itinerary through the travel agent (or on your own) rather than through the cruise line. Buying your own air, unfortunately, puts you at some risk for a couple of other unpleasant eventualities having to do with missing the ship and losing your luggage, but we'll deal with those problems later. Finally, on the topic of arranging your own flight itinerary, we don't want to overstate the case. While working on this section of the guide, we received a direct-mail promo from an excellent European cruise line offering outside cabins at half price with air to Europe included. Would we hesitate to buy because the cruise line is providing air? Not for a second.

Problem 3: Bad Weather or Air-Traffic Delays on Departure Day

When you book your air, either on your own or through the cruise line, give some thought to what weather and air-traffic conditions are likely to be on your day of departure. If you're traveling the same day as your cruise departure, over a holiday period, or at a time of year when bad weather is likely, you might want to take some precautions. Begin analyzing your airport choices. In the New York area, for example, be aware that Newark and Kennedy have longer runways, more de-icing equipment, and electronic traffic-control systems that often allow them to function when La Guardia is shut down. New Yorkers can also take a Washington-bound train directly to the Baltimore–Washington Airport (BWI) from Penn Station in under three hours. (Washingtonians can do the same on a northbound train.) BWI has a better track record than any of the three New York airports for on-time departures.

During holiday periods or bad weather, the chance of a serious snafu increases exponentially with every flight connection you have to make. If, with a little inconvenience, you can eliminate a connection, it's usually worthwhile to do so. Let's say you live in Louisville, Kentucky; Columbus, Ohio; or Charleston, West Virginia, and you're flying to Fort Lauderdale for a cruise out of Port Everglades. If there's no direct flight, you might be better off driving to the Cincinnati Airport (located in northern Kentucky) and taking a direct flight from there to Fort Lauderdale, thereby eliminating the connecting flight.

> *unofficial* **TIP**
> Always book the earliest flight of the day on an airline that offers a number of flights throughout the day to your destination.

Early morning flights have a much better on-time record than do flights later in the day. Plus, if there's an equipment problem or a cancellation, the airline can put you on a later flight. *For maximum peace of mind, travel to the port of departure one or two days prior to your sailing date. If things go awry on your travel day, you've still got sufficient time to make alternative arrangements.* Why risk jeopardizing a cherished vacation? Arrive a day early at minimum.

You've probably heard the ongoing debate regarding electronic versus paper airline tickets. Generally speaking, we prefer electronic tickets with the proviso that you double-check with the airline to insure that your correct itinerary is in their system and that your reservations are shown as fully paid. The one situation where paper tickets are preferable is when your flight is cancelled and your airline cannot book you on another flight. In this case, you'll want to make arrangements with an alternative carrier. Most carriers will honor the tickets of another airline in the event of cancellations or labor actions, but they will require paper tickets or some form of documentation as proof of purchase.

Problem 4: Missing the Boat

This is the nightmare scenario that haunts all cruisers. If you're savvy in your travel planning, and especially if you plan to arrive at your departure port a day or so ahead of time, you'll almost eliminate the likelihood of missing the boat. We all know, however, that travel, like life, can get mixed up in ways that we never anticipate.

If you purchase your air from the cruise line, the cruise line will do its utmost to get you on the ship. There are many, many documented cases of ship departures being delayed while awaiting the arrival of a delinquent flight full of cruise passengers. Likewise, cruise lines have flown passengers who actually missed the boat to rendezvous with the ship at the first port of call. The more passengers that are affected by late flights, the more likely the cruise line is to hold the ship. The most important thing to understand, however, is that the cruise is absolutely not under any legal obligation to hold the ship or to assist in any other manner. If you read the terms and conditions of your Passage Contract, you'll almost immediately encounter language like the following: "Under no circumstances does [X Cruise Line's] responsibility extend beyond the ship. All arrangements made for the guests with independent contractors [such as airlines] are made solely for the convenience of the guest and are at the guest's risk." What you *can* count on, exclusively as a matter of customer relations, is for the cruise line to do what is practicable. Do 30 late-arriving guests on a weather-delayed flight from Cleveland justify delaying the departure of a 3,000 passenger cruise ship? Perhaps, but don't count on it. We know of at least one situation when the ship sailed while two busloads of flight-delayed passengers waited at the airport to be driven to the port, 20 minutes away.

Sometimes, when air is arranged through the cruise line, and passengers miss the boat owing to flight delays, the airline will help out. Assistance usually comes in the form of a meal and perhaps a hotel room. If the airline flies to your first port of call, it will try to book you on a flight so that you can meet the ship. Because the airline is not responsible for weather or air-traffic delays, it has no legal obligation to help. Like the cruise line, any assistance rendered is primarily a matter of customer relations.

If you book your own travel arrangements to the departure port, you're on your own. As far as the cruise line is concerned, you're totally responsible for getting to the ship. If you miss the ship through no fault of your own, however, as in the case of a delayed flight, you will have that travel insurance we recommended to fall back on. Travel insurance is also your safety net if you miss the boat because of sickness, or because of bankruptcy of the cruise line. Missing the boat because of an airline strike is also usually covered by travel insurance, though the conditions for coverage vary from policy to policy. If you or your cruise line book you on an airline involved in a labor dispute, discuss the situation with your insurance carrier to determine under what circumstances you're covered. When it comes to travel insurance, don't, as the saying goes, leave home without it. Also, ask a ton of questions and compare plans carefully.

Problem 5: Lost Luggage

If you book air through the cruise line, the cruise line will make every effort to get your luggage to you (once it's recovered), including flying it to meet you at a port of call. Once again, this assistance is purely voluntary as opposed to obligatory. If you handle your own air, you must depend on the airline (generally without any assistance from the cruise line) to get your recovered luggage to you. In such situations, the probability of your luggage catching up with you while on your cruise is slim. Minimize the chances of your luggage being lost by arriving in port a day early and/or eliminating connecting flights where possible. Buy travel insurance, and make sure it pays if your bags are delayed more than 24 hours. The possibility of lost luggage is a good reason to pack essentials for an overnight in your carry-on luggage.

Problem 6: You Get Sick during Your Cruise

Although most cruise ships carry a physician and usually one registered nurse, only the new large ships are equipped to handle serious problems; and some, such as Princess' ships, maintain satellite contact with state-side hospitals when serious diagnosis is needed. Nonetheless, the majority of cruise ships fly under foreign flags, and hence their physicians are not required to be licensed to practice in the United States. From the cruise physician's perspective, shore-based facilities are better equipped to handle serious illness and emergencies. In practical terms, this means that the cruise physician will want to transfer you to a hospital on shore at the first opportunity if he anticipates your illness taxing the limitations of his clinic. Also, you should know that according to the fine print in your passage contract, the cruise line is not responsible for medical care you receive while on board. As with the problems discussed earlier, travel insurance is a must. When you purchase your policy, make sure any preexisting condition is covered and understand the policy's medical evacuation coverage.

In the last several years there has been a media circus swirling around the periodic occurrence of gastrointestinal viruses aboard cruise ships. Referred to in the media as "outbreaks" and "epidemics," the press has so sensationalized cases of the viruses that they have become known as the "cruise ship disease." The facts, however, tell a different story. The viruses, known as Norwalk virus, Norwalk-like virus, and norovirus (collectively known as NLV) occur everywhere (on land as well as at sea), ranking second only to the common cold in the number of cases reported. Because of the extraordinary sanitation practices aboard cruise ships (operated and monitored in partnership with the Centers for Disease Control [CDC]), these NLV occur far less frequently on cruise ships than among the general population. Expressed differently, NLV is a very common ailment and incidents occur far more often in the home, office, and at school than on cruise ships. Most cruise ship outbreaks are not caused by a "sick ship" but by sick people who bring it onboard.

Symptoms can include vomiting, diarrhea, abdominal cramps, and a low-grade fever. NLV is not an upper respiratory virus such as the flu, and is usually not life-threatening, unless someone has other, more serious, medical problems.

NLV is transmitted from person-to-person through direct contact, and indirectly from surfaces that are then touched by another person. NLV can also be transmitted through a food or water source; the CDC has concluded that person-to-person transmission has been the means of transmission on almost all cases reported on cruise ships.

"We continue to work very closely with the cruise lines," said David Forney, chief of Vessel Sanitation Program of the U.S. Centers for Disease Control and Prevention (CDC). "These ships are maintaining the highest standard of sanitation in the world."

If cases of a gastrointestinal virus are reported, cruise lines take extensive precautions to contain the spread through aggressive sanitation measures and open communication with their guests prior to boarding and while onboard the ship. Some of the measures employed when responding to reported cases may include:

- Passengers with obvious symptoms may not be allowed to board.

- To avoid the risk of spreading the virus, passengers who experience typical gastrointestinal symptoms are usually told to remain in their cabins until they are noncontagious but could be asked to disembark at the next available port. The CDC endorses this procedure.

- Crew with symptoms may be similarly quarantined until they are noncontagious but may also disembark the ship at the next available port.

- An aggressive on-board communications effort to encourage guests to frequently wash their hands. Washing one's hands regularly (each hour or two) is a very good way to reduce the spread of contact viruses.

- Aboard ship, staterooms and public areas are cleaned and disinfected daily, including, but not limited to, counters, bathroom surfaces, door handles, railings and grab bars, exercise equipment, and TV remote controls. Some lines also offer hand sanitizers at the entrance to the gangway or at a buffet line.

- On turn-around days, extra crew are brought on board to disinfect the ship with the CDC recommended chlorine-based solution from top to bottom before additional passengers board.

- Onboard medical facilities and staff are always available to prescribe medication for symptomatic treatment of gastrointestinal symptoms.

Be aware that the cruise lines are so sensitive to bad press surrounding NLV and the need to assure that as many guests as possible remain well that some have enacted rather draconian policies, endorsed by the CDC. A man from Maryland on a Caribbean cruise sought care for gastrointestinal symptoms and was notified that he would be involuntarily disembarked at the next port of call. Though there were any number of alternative explanations for the symptoms, and no diagnostic testing was done, the man and his wife were ordered ashore the next day. Quarantined until time of disembarkation, his symptoms completely resolved after about ten hours. Onboard medical staff, realizing then that the symptoms could not be attributed to NLV, apologized but informed the couple that the decision was made by the line's home office and could not be reversed. After the man's return home, laboratory tests ordered by his doctor showed no evidence of a viral infection. The cruise line was so intent in getting the man off the ship that they evidently failed to clear the couple's entry into the port. Later, when they went to the airport for their flight home, they were detained by immigration for supposedly entering the country illegally. In case you're wondering, the cruise line did pay the couple's travel expenses home. Granted, this is a worse-case scenario, but it always helps to know what could happen.

Problem 7: Onboard Complaints

If your stateroom toilet backs up, the air conditioner conks out, or the showroom performers quit, don't expect a refund. If it's not resolved onboard when it happens, the best you are likely to get is a discount on a subsequent cruise. Once again, it's that pesky passage contract that purports to absolve the cruise line from all responsibility, anytime, anywhere. In point of law, however (as any attorney who specializes in travel will tell you), some of the language is nothing but smoke, totally unenforceable and made part of the contract as a bluff to inhibit you from taking legal action. Understand, however, if you decide to sue, that cruise lines operate under maritime law, and you might have to file the lawsuit in the country where the ship is registered. It's not an accident that so many cruise ships fly under the so-called flags of convenience, particularly those of Liberia and Panama.

Legalities aside, it's always preferable to settle problems on the spot. Usually, you will direct your complaint to the chief purser or to the hotel manager, and usually they will be quite responsive. Be polite and friendly, and keep your anger under control. As a last resort, if your complaint is not addressed, fax the president of the cruise line. Resend each day until your problem is resolved. Keep copies of your faxes in case the complaint goes unremedied for the entire cruise. As of this writing, Carnival is the only cruise line that will allow you to cancel your cruise and disembark at the first port of call once underway if things are not satisfactory. You can get a refund for the *unused* portion of your cruise fare.

If you are really unlucky, like when your cabin is for some reason uninhabitable and the ship is completely full, your only option is to negotiate the best deal you can or leave the ship on your own initiative at a port of call. If you jump ship, regardless of the reason, you're on your own. Consequently, we recommending contacting your travel-insurance carrier for advice about how to best proceed before taking action.

Problem 8: Credit Hold

It has become common practice for cruise lines to ask passengers to complete a form prior to leaving home authorizing the cruise line to hold X dollars in credit per day for each day of the cruise. On a Holland American cruise, for example, the line held $60 per day. The same credit card covered both husband and wife, so the credit hold amounted to a not insignificant $2,160. In practicality, if the card had a $3,000 credit limit, the credit hold would only leave only $840 of available credit on that card for the couple to use for onshore shopping, restaurants, etc.

Cruise lines use credit holds to make sure a passenger's onboard charges are covered. On land, each transaction on your card is approved and processed individually. On a cruise it doesn't make sense for the line to pay $10 or so in satellite telecommunications to process that $4 beer you enjoyed on the Lido Deck. Consequently, charges are recorded but not processed until the end of the cruise. At that time they are totaled and the ship runs through a single transaction. To make sure you have the credit available to pay your onboard charges, the line puts a credit hold on what it estimates you'll charge. Among other things, the practice largely eliminates messy credit problems at the time of disembarkation.

Though using credit holds addresses a legitimate problem (passengers without sufficient funds or credit to pay their onboard tab), there are a couple of problems. First, the cruise lines do not communicate what they are doing very well, and some of the credit-hold preauthorization forms are confusing. Because many passengers don't realize what's going on, they are surprised and embarrassed when their credit card is subsequently rejected while they attempt to purchase something ashore.

The second problem is that the cruise line may hold much more per day that you'll actually charge onboard. The solution to these problems is to carefully review any form the cruise line sends, particularly one that requires your signature. If the credit amount the cruise line holds is out of line with your normal onboard spending habits, negotiate with the purser a lower per-day amount when you board the ship. Remember, however, those spa treatments and shore excursions are expensive. Your onboard spending may very likely exceed your bar bill and a couple of T-shirts for the grandchildren.

Be aware that cruise lines that do not send preauthorization forms for credit holds will probably put a similarly calculated credit hold on your card when you present it during embarkation. The salient point in the latter case is to ask the amount of the credit hold. Finally, remember that a credit hold is not a charge on your credit card. The credit hold is an amount reserved, and nothing is actually charged to your card until your total onboard bill is processed at the end of the cruise.

Problem 9: Itinerary Changes/Cancelled Ports of Call

You will discover that the cruise line has complete discretion in regard to changing the itinerary or canceling a scheduled port stop. This discretion is necessary in order to insure the safety of the passengers, ship, and crew. It is this flexibility that permits a ship to circumvent storms or offload a passenger at a nonscheduled port for medical reasons or other emergencies.

Problem 10 : Shore Excursion Problems

Because shore excursions are conducted off the ship and produced by local tour companies, the cruise line will decline responsibility for any problem you have, however serious. Sometimes, however, as a matter of customer relations, a cruise ship might offer you a refund or assist you in obtaining satisfaction from the tour operator. Nevertheless, you should always register your complaint with the cruise line immediately after the tour. Though of little comfort to you, so doing may result in the cruise line forcing an errant tour operator to clean up its act.

WHAT'S THE REAL COST OF A CRUISE?

SOME READERS REPORT being surprised by all the extras that are not covered by their cruise fare: items like beverages on board, spa services, photos taken by the ship's photographer, shore excursions, wine tastings, specialized cooking, exercise or computer classes, and even designer ice cream treats. Although all these things add up to a hefty sum, we don't consider them to be "hidden" charges. Except for port charges (if the cruise line doesn't include them in the fare), such purchases are optional. Any travel provider will try to sell you stuff; it's like the popcorn or beer vendors at the ballpark. You know they'll be there and that what they sell will be expensive. Buy or not as you see fit, but don't be surprised by their presence. The cruise lines find these services to be very lucrative profit centers, which help them keep basic cruise prices down. Also, these multiple options increase guest choices onboard, which attracts different types of customers to cruise ships. Because most folks don't like to scrimp on their vacation, however, it's wise to anticipate these expenditures. Even the little stuff like beverages and photos can tack on $200 to $400 to a week-long cruise. So be forewarned.

Concerning port charges, after some lawsuits in Florida seeking to redress the less-than-forthright ways that certain cruise lines represented port charges, almost all cruises from Florida to the Caribbean now include port charges in the cost of the cruise rather than tack them on as a separate charge. Still, watch out for port charges, particularly for Europe and Asia.

PREPARING *for* YOUR CRUISE

A CRUISE MAY BE ABOUT the easiest vacation you can take when it comes to making preparations, because so much is done for you, particularly when you buy an air/sea package. During the cruise, entry formalities are handled by the ship for its passengers in most cases, sparing you the need to fill out immigration forms or clear customs in each port of call.

In most ports you can simply walk off your ship after it has been cleared by local authorities; spend the day sightseeing, shopping, enjoying a sport or other pleasant pursuits; and return to your ship without having to do anything more than pass through metal detectors and put your purchases through an x-ray machine for security reasons, and show your boarding pass.

The destination of your cruise will make some difference—the more exotic the location, the more you may have need for planning ahead, perhaps for inoculations, visas, and the like. And of course, the weather during your cruise will determine the wardrobe you select.

Such advice may seem obvious to those who have traveled, and if it does, let this information serve simply as a reminder or checklist. Even the most seasoned travelers have been known to pack their cruise tickets and passports in their checked luggage or leave their traveler's checks at home.

CRUISE LINE BROCHURES

THE EASIEST PLACE TO START your preparation is by reading the brochures from the cruise line you selected for your cruise. These have a wealth of useful information. To be sure, much of it is glossy pictures and promotional puff to entice you to take a cruise, but almost all materials contain several pages, usually toward the back, aimed at answering the questions people ask most often.

These include the specifics about dining hours, smoking/non-smoking provisions, paying for incidentals on board ships, embarkation and sailing times, and similar tips. In this book, too, each of the major cruise line profiles in Part Two includes a chart entitled Standard Features, which will answer similar questions pertaining to a specific cruise line and its ships.

CRUISE LINE VIDEOS/DVDS

MOST CRUISE LINES HAVE VIDEOTAPES or DVDs of the cruise you are taking that they would be happy to send you—for a fee. Most cost about $15 to $20. Essentially, it is a promotional video, but it will give you an idea of what to expect, particularly if your cruise is to an area of the world in which you have not traveled previously. You will probably receive a flyer from the cruise line to order the tape directly from a distributor. Some cruise line Web sites allow for purchasing the video online; some sites feature virtual ship tours and shore excursions.

TRAVEL DOCUMENTS

IN 2005, THE U.S. STATE DEPARTMENT BEGAN phasing in a new border-control program that will ultimately require a valid passport to both enter and leave the country. The Western Hemisphere Travel Initiative brings an end to decades of travel to Mexico, Canada, and the majority of Caribbean nations with only a birth certificate as proof of citizenship. The implementation dates are as follows:

- **December 31, 2005** Passport required for all air and sea travel to or from the Caribbean, Bermuda, and Central and South America.

- December 31, 2006 Passport required for all air and sea travel to or from Mexico and Canada.

- December 31, 2007 Passport required for all air, sea, and land border crossings.

Aliens residing in the United States need to have valid alien registration cards and passports. All non-U.S. citizens must have valid passports and necessary visas when boarding any cruise ship departing from and returning to U.S. ports.

Passengers on some cruises visiting Europe, former Soviet bloc countries, Asia, Africa, and South America may also be required to have a visa. *A valid passport usually means one that will not expire for at least six months.* If yours has less than six months left, it may be rejected by either the cruise line or ports of call.

Often, on cruises to these destinations, ship authorities will ask you to surrender your passport when you check in and will keep it until the end of your cruise. This enables them to clear the ship more quickly in foreign ports. In such cases, you do not need to worry about giving over your passport to the ship. The passports are locked away securely and are taken out only if local authorities ask to see them. Finally, never pack your passport in your suitcase; carry it with you at all times.

TRAVEL REQUIREMENTS

SPECIFIC REQUIREMENTS for passports, visas, and vaccinations will be provided by your cruise line or travel agent. However, obtaining the necessary visas and any other documentation required for embarkation, debarkation, and reentry into the United States is your responsibility; if you do not have the proper documents, you will be denied boarding. If you buy your cruise on the Internet or from a seller not located in your city, the seller may neglect to inform you of required travel documents and other pertinent information. Even when you purchase from your local travel agent, however, it's a good idea to independently confirm document, visa, and vaccination requirements for the countries you'll be visiting. Nobody likes a last-minute surprise.

Documents that will be accepted as proof of identification vary with each cruise line. You will need to inquire in advance if the information is not provided in the cruise line's brochure, which it usually is—in the fine print.

Children traveling with anyone other than their parents or legal guardian must have permission in writing for the child to travel. Failure to comply with this requirement can also result in denial of boarding.

*un*official **TIP**
U.S. passengers under 18 years of age are usually not allowed to board a cruise ship at initial embarkation without a passport. No refund of the cruise fare will be given to families without such identification.

DRESS CODES AND PACKING

WHAT TO PACK will be determined by your ship, its destinations, and, to some extent, the itinerary. An adventure cruise might be three weeks long, but not a single night will be formal or even very dressy. The dress code is usually explained in the cruise line's brochure; we also note it in the Standard Features in each cruise line's profile in Part Two.

There are no limits on the amount of luggage you can bring on board, but most cabins do not have much closet and storage space. More importantly, because you are likely to be flying to your departure port, you need to be guided by airline regulations regarding excess baggage. All airlines have weight restrictions. Buy too many souvenirs and you will pay. So pack light on the outbound journey with that in mind.

As a consequence of the September 11th, 2001 terrorist attacks, all checked and carry-on luggage is carefully screened before being allowed on board. Even if you pack something in your checked baggage as seemingly innocuous as a corkscrew, knitting needles, or a pair of small scissors, these items might possibly be confiscated and not returned until you disembark. Moreover, none of your checked luggage will be delivered in the normal fashion to your cabin. After an hour or two of panic, thinking your baggage is lost, you'll be summoned to ship security. There you will be asked to identify the offending luggage and objects and to sign forms acknowledging that you brought such items aboard, and that they have been impounded for the duration of the cruise. While on your cruise, be aware also that purses, bags, and packs that you carried ashore will be searched before you're allowed back on board. Ditto for anything you purchased while ashore.

Despite the image you may have about fancy parties and clothes, the reality is that shipboard life is very casual. You will spend your days in slacks, shorts, T-shirts, and bathing suits. Lightweight mix-and-match ensembles with skirts, shirts, blouses, shorts, and slacks are practical. For women, colorful scarves are another way to change the look of an outfit. Cocktail dresses or dressy pants suits are appropriate for evening wear.

Men usually are asked to wear a jacket at dinner in the dining room. A dark suit and white shirt work fine in place of a tuxedo if the evening is black tie. Add a selection of slacks and sport shirts, and one or two sports jackets. If you are heading for a warm-weather cruise (Caribbean, Mexico, Hawaii, Tahiti), pack as you would for any resort destination. Lightweight, loose-fitting clothing is ideal, and cotton or cotton blends are more comfortable than synthetic fabrics for the tropics. Include two bathing suits if you are likely to be spending much time in the sun and at the beach. Don't forget a cover-up and flip flops for the short jaunt between your cabin and the pool or other outside decks, as cruise ships ask passengers not to wear bathing suits or go barefoot in the public rooms.

Take along cosmetics and suntan lotion, but don't worry if you forget something. It will most likely be available on board or in portside duty-free shops. Sunglasses and a hat or sun visor for protection against the sun are essential. A tote bag comes in handy for carrying odds and ends, as do plastic bags for wet towels and bathing suits on returning from a visit to an island beach. You might also want to keep camera equipment in plastic bags as protection against the salt air, water, and sand.

The first and last nights of your cruise are usually casual, and the nights your ship is in port almost always call for informal dress. At least one night will be the captain's gala party, where tuxedos for men and long dresses for women are the norm, but a jacket and tie for men and a cocktail dress for women are also just fine.

Bring your most comfortable walking shoes for shore excursions. Tennis, deck, or other low-heeled rubber or nonskid shoes are recommended for walking about the ship, up and down gangways, getting in and out of the ship's tenders, and for sightseeing. And you will need a sweater for breezy nights at sea or for the air-conditioning in the dining room or shore-excursion bus. A small flashlight, a fold-up umbrella, and a light jacket are often handy.

unofficial **TIP**
For a one-week or shorter cruise, you should be able to fit everything you need into one suitcase.

Pack lightly. But most of all, be comfortable. You do not need to rush out and buy an expensive wardrobe. Obviously, if your cruise is in a cool or cold climate, you will need to plan accordingly. A Baltic or Scandinavian cruise in summer is likely to encounter colder temperatures than you might think—similar to a New England fall—but then can quickly turn to a hot summer day. Plan for layers when the weather is uncertain.

As we mention elsewhere, it's a sound practice to have a small carry-on bag for your medications and cosmetics and to include a change of clothing for your first afternoon aboard your ship, in the event of a delay in the delivery of your luggage. Also, bring a fold-away bag to carry all those souvenirs, gifts, and duty-free bargains that probably won't fit in your suitcase.

Every evening, an agenda for the following day is delivered to your room; it states the dress code for the following evening. It may be:

CASUAL Comfortable daywear, such as slacks, shorts, or jeans, but some cruise lines will state specifically that T-shirts, tank tops, or shorts are not allowed in the dining room for dinner.

INFORMAL Dresses and pantsuits are suggested for the ladies; jackets for the men, but ties are optional.

FORMAL Cocktail dresses or gowns for the ladies, and tuxedo, dinner jacket, or dark business suit for men; jacket and tie are required.

It varies greatly by line, but as a general rule, the lineup might be like this:

3- TO 4-NIGHT CRUISES One formal, one informal, and one or two casual.

7- TO 8-NIGHT CRUISES Two formal, two informal, two or three casual.

10- TO 14-NIGHT CRUISES Three or four formal; four or six informal; four or five casual.

You are asked to comply with the ship's stated dress code, if for no other reason than out of respect for your fellow passengers. Generally, the suggested attire is respected throughout the evening or at least until after the shows in the main showroom and the late-night buffet, when it is a gala event. Often, those who want to stay up late for the disco or casino change to more comfortable dress, if they prefer.

COSTUMES

A FEW SHIPS still have one night as a masquerade party, and others have theme nights for which some people bring an outfit—a 1950s and 1960s night or a country-and-western night, for example. It's entirely up to you whether or not to participate. The cruise line's brochure usually tells you about theme nights, or you can ask your travel agent for theme nights featured on your cruise, if you want to join in. If you don't have space for a costume, the cruise staff can help you make one.

SPORTS EQUIPMENT

IF YOU PLAN to play golf or tennis frequently, you might want to bring your own equipment, and of course, you'll need the appropriate clothes and shoes. Ships that have golf practice facilities and shoreside golf programs sometimes supply the equipment for a nominal fee. Inquire.

Fins and a snorkeling mask (particularly if you have one fitted with your eyeglass prescription) are bulky, but might save you a $10 to $20 fee each time you go snorkeling on your own. If you buy the ship's shore excursions, the snorkeling equipment is included. Scuba gear is usually included in dive packages, too, and except for your regulator, is impractical to bring on a cruise.

Hiking boots, jogging shoes, riding attire, and other sporting gear will depend entirely on you and the nature of your cruise. For adventure or expedition cruises, such as to Antarctica, your cruise line will give you ample information about dress and the equipment you need; some supply guests with winter parkas and boots.

MONEY MATTERS

DOLLARS ARE READILY ACCEPTED throughout the Caribbean and in some other regions, as are traveler's checks and major credit cards. In Europe or Asia, the ship's purser or front office usually offers foreign currency exchange facilities, or the ship brings someone aboard to provide the facility in each port of call.

If you do exchange money (it's a great opportunity to teach kids about other currencies—euros in Martinique, Dutch guilders in Curaçao, pesos in Mexico), exchange only small amounts for your immediate use. Seldom will you have time to exchange the money back before returning to your ship, and you lose money every time you make the exchange. An exception is a European cruise. If you are visiting multiple European countries, say France, Italy, Spain and Greece, simply exchange a lot of dollars in advance for euros, which can be used in many countries.

Even with U.S. dollars, always carry small denominations—ones, fives, tens. Chances are, if you are owed change, it will be returned in the local currency. Incidentally, U.S. coins are seldom accepted in foreign countries and are impossible to exchange except in quantity at foreign-exchange banks. Likewise with foreign coins when you want to exchange them back into U.S. currency. Most become souvenirs.

Some travelers report problems cashing traveler's checks in foreign cruise ports, especially on the weekend. Major credit cards have become the currency of travelers worldwide and are accepted in most places. On a cruise, you will often find them the most convenient method of payment for settling your account aboard ship, for shopping at duty-free shops, and for payment of local restaurant or hotel bills. However, do not expect to use them in select off-the-beaten-track locations. The Cuna Indians of the San Blas Islands—an exotic stop on Panama Canal cruises—want your greenbacks. After you return home and receive your credit card bills, review them carefully. The theft of credit card numbers is a worldwide problem and cruise passengers, who are normally in for only a day, are easy prey.

PRESCRIPTION MEDICINE AND OTHER MEDICAL REQUIREMENTS

AS WITH ANY TRIP, whether on land or sea, you should have all your required medicine with you and carry it in original bottles and in your hand luggage, not packed in your suitcase. As a further precaution, bring copies of your medicine prescriptions—and for your eyeglasses, too.

If you have dietary requirements, you or your travel agent should communicate them to your cruise line at the time you book your cruise. Most ships can accommodate normal requirements of low salt and low fat, but more complex ones that require special stores be carried aboard require planning. Do not take anything for granted. Inquire. For example, many ships do not normally stock skim milk. In each of the cruise line profiles in Part Two under Standard Features, the amount of advance notice a cruise line requires to handle special diets is indicated.

Cruise ships that travel beyond coastal waters are required to have a doctor on board; most large ships have nurses and adequate medical facilities for normal circumstances. The doctor and nursing staff have limited daily office hours, which are printed in the ship's daily agenda, and they are always on call for emergencies. There are charges for most medical services.

SUNBURNS

YOU WILL NEED TO TAKE PRECAUTIONS against the sun when you are on a Caribbean, Mexican, Antarctic, southern European, or southeast Asian cruise. The sun in these regions is much, much stronger than the sun to which most people are accustomed. Always use a sunscreen with an SPF of 15 or higher, preferably 30 and above, and do not stay in the direct sun for long stretches at a time. Nothing can spoil a vacation faster than a sunburn.

LEARNING THE LINGO

CRUISE SHIPS HAVE A LANGUAGE all their own. Though it is not necessary to enroll in a Berlitz course to learn it, becoming familiar with a few terms will be worthwhile so you won't feel lost at sea, if you will forgive the pun.

Passengers don't reserve rooms on a ship, they book **cabins,** which cruise lines sometimes call by a fancier name, **staterooms.** The price level of a cabin is known as its **category.**

When you reach your ship, you will **board** or **embark;** when it's time to leave the ship, passengers **disembark.** If the ship arrives at a port where it cannot pull into the dock, the ship will **anchor** and passengers are taken ashore in a **tender,** one of the small ancillary vessels or lifeboats that travel onboard the ship.

Several terms will assist you in finding your way around the ship. The **bow** is the front of the ship, the **aft** is the rear, and the center portion is **midship.**

Heading forward, toward the **bow,** the right side of the ship is known as the **starboard side;** the left side of the ship is called the **port side.** Ships have **decks,** never floors. Decks are named after such things as precious stones (Emerald Deck), activities (Sports Deck), places (Monte Carlo Deck), and planets (Venus Deck).

If you've built up an appetite from all this exploring, you can go to the **main seating** (or sitting) and eat early, or the **second seating** and dine late. Both times are assigned by the line. Some lines also offer two early and two late seatings. Some ships have **single seating,** which means that all passengers eat at the same time for all three meals. Some ships also have **open seating,** in which case you may sit anywhere—at any unoccupied table or join others. By invitation, you may even find yourself at the **captain's table.**

Onboard, there are people to help you decode ship lingo. The **purser's office** is the information center, similar to a check-in desk at a hotel. The **hotel manager** is in charge of all passenger-related shipboard services, such as dining, housekeeping, and so on. The **chief steward** is responsible for cabin services, and **cabin stewards** or **stew-**

ardesses take care of cabins; the **dining steward** is your waiter. The **cruise director** functions as the emcee, and the **cruise staff,** who are his assistants, run all activities and entertainment and make sure that you are having a good time. Finally, there's the **captain,** who is in charge of everything.

Cruise lingo is part of the fun, so don't take it too seriously. Here are the most common terms you are likely to encounter.

Add-on A supplementary charge added to the cruise fare, usually applied to correlated airfare and/or post-cruise land tours.

Aft Near, toward, or in the rear (stern) of the ship.

Air/sea A package consisting of the two forms of travel, that is, air to and from the port of embarkation, transfers to and from the port, as well as the cruise itself.

Astern Beyond the ship's stern.

Batten down To secure all open hatches or equipment for sea worthiness while the ship is under way.

Beam Width of the ship (amidships) between its two sides at its widest point.

Berth Dock, pier, or quay (key); also, the bed in the passenger cabins.

Bow Front or forward portion of the ship.

Bridge Navigational and command control center of the ship.

Bulkhead Upright partition (wall) dividing the ship into cabins or compartments.

Category The price level of a cabin, based on location on the ship, dimensions, and amenities.

Colors A national flag or ensign flown from the mast or stern post.

Course Direction in which the ship is headed, usually expressed in compass degrees.

Crow's nest Partially enclosed platform at the top of the mast, used as a lookout.

Deck plan An overhead deck-by-deck diagram illustrating cabin and public room locations in relation to each other.

Disembark Depart from the ship.

Dock Berth, pier, or quay (key).

Draft Measurement in feet from water line to lowest point of ship's keel.

Even keel The ship in a true vertical position with respect to its vertical axis.

Fathom Measurement of distance equal to six feet.

First seating The earlier of several meal times in the ship's main dining rooms.

Fore The forward mast or the front (bow) of the ship.

Forward Toward the fore or bow of the ship.

Funnel The smokestack or "chimney" of the ship.

Galley The ship's kitchen.

who's who on the cruise ship

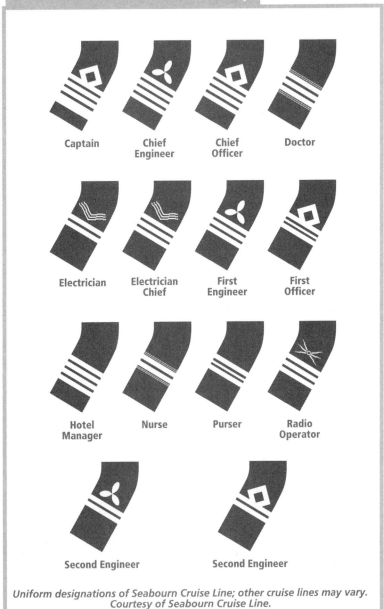

Captain   Chief Engineer   Chief Officer   Doctor

Electrician   Electrician Chief   First Engineer   First Officer

Hotel Manager   Nurse   Purser   Radio Operator

Second Engineer   Second Engineer

Uniform designations of Seabourn Cruise Line; other cruise lines may vary.
Courtesy of Seabourn Cruise Line.

Gangway The opening through the ship's bulwarks (or through the ship's side) and the ramp by which passengers embark and disembark.

Gross registered ton A measurement of 100 cubic feet of enclosed revenue-earning space within a ship (see Space ratio).

Hatch The covering over an opening in a ship's deck, leading to a hold.

Helm Commonly the ship's steering wheel, but more correctly the entire steering apparatus consisting of the wheel, the rudder, and their connecting cables or hydraulic systems.

Hold Interior space(s) below the main deck for storage of cargo.

House flag The flag denoting the company to which the ship belongs.

Hull The frame and body (shell) of the ship exclusive of masts, superstructure, or rigging.

Knot A unit of speed equal to 1 nautical mile per hour (6,080.2 feet), as compared to a land mile of 5,280 feet.

League A measure of distance approximating 3.45 nautical miles.

Leeward In the direction of that side of the ship opposite from which the wind blows.

Manifest A list or invoice of a ship's passengers, crew, and cargo.

Midship In or toward the middle of the ship; the longitudinal center portion of the ship.

Nautical mile 6,080.2 feet, as compared to a land mile of 5,280 feet.

Open seating Seating in the main dining room(s) is not assigned. You eat where and with whom you wish.

Paddlewheel A wheel with boards around its circumference, and, commonly, the source of propulsion for traditional American riverboats.

Pitch The rocking back and forth (bow to stern) motion of a ship that may be felt in heavy seas when the ship is under way.

Port The left side of the ship when facing toward the bow.

Port charge Port taxes, collected by the line and paid to a local government authority; it may include other miscellaneous charges, such as gasoline surcharge and fees, as well as fees to dock in a particular port.

Port tax A charge levied by the local government authority to be paid by the passenger.

Prow The bow or the stem (the front) of the ship.

Purser A senior management position on board ship. In most cases, the purser is like the general manager of a hotel, but in some cases, he or she is more of the financial or administration officer.

Quay (pronounced "key") A dock, berth, or pier.

Registry The country under whose flag the ship is registered and with whose laws the ship and its owners must comply; in addition to compliance with the laws of the countries at which the ship calls and/or embarks/disembarks passengers/cargo.

Rigging The ropes, chains, and cables that support a sailing ship's masts, spars, kingposts, cranes, and the like.

Roll The alternate sway of a ship from side to side.

Running lights   Three lights (green on the starboard side, red on the port side, and white at the top of the mast) required by international law to be lighted when the ship is in motion between the times of sunset and sunrise.

Second, third, or fourth seating   The later meal times in the ship's dining room(s).

Space ratio   A measurement of cubic space per passenger. Gross registered ton divided by the number of passengers (basis two) equals space ratio.

Stabilizer   A gyroscopically operated finlike device extending from both sides of the ship below the water line to provide stability for the ship and reduce its roll.

Stack   The funnel or chimney from which the ship's gases of combustion are released into the atmosphere.

Starboard   The right side of the ship when facing toward the bow.

Stateroom   Cabin or suite.

Steward   Personnel onboard ship.

Stem   The extreme bow or prow of the ship.

Stern   The extreme rear of the ship.

Suite   Upscale accommodations with more space, more in-room amenities, a bigger balcony and, at times, more rooms than standard or balcony cabins.

Superstructure   The structure of the ship above the main deck or water line.

Tender   A small vessel, sometimes the ship's lifeboat, used to move passengers to and from the shore when the ship is at anchor.

Transfers   A bus or van ride between the ship and other locations, such as airports, hotels, or departure points for shore excursions.

Upper berth   A single-size bed higher from the floor than usual (similar to a bunk bed), usually folded or recessed into the wall or ceiling by day.

Wake   The track of agitated water behind a ship in motion.

Water line   The line at the side of the ship's hull that corresponds to the surface of the water.

Weigh   To raise; for example, to weigh the anchor.

Windward   Toward the wind, to the direction from which the wind blows.

TIME *to* GO

IF YOU PURCHASE an air/sea package, your cruise begins from the moment you arrive at the airport. Here's how.

CRUISE DOCUMENTS

NORMALLY, YOU RECEIVE your travel documents—including tickets, transfer vouchers, boarding forms, and luggage tags—about two weeks before departure. Some cruise lines, particularly deluxe and smaller ones going to offbeat destinations, begin sending material a month or more in advance, and often include information on ports of call and on shore excursions sold on board ship. A "Welcome Aboard" brochure is intended to familiarize you with your ship. Read it.

The final documents will include your airline and cruise tickets. Your agent should have checked them before sending them to you. Check them yourself. If you buy your cruise late, documents may come directly to you from the cruise line. Check them, too. Remember that you must show your cruise ticket when you check in at the dock.

Luggage tags show the cruise line's name and logo. They have spaces for your name and address and the name of your ship, cruise and cabin numbers, and departure date and port. Complete the luggage tags using information contained in your cruise ticket. Attach at least one tag to every piece of your luggage, including your handbags. (An amazing number of people, in their excitement, leave hand luggage behind on an airplane, in the airport, or on a motorcoach. If it's tagged, airline or port personnel will know immediately what to do with it.)

When you arrive at the airport, you will claim luggage and it will ride on the transfer bus with you for the drive to the pier. There it will be taken by baggage handlers and will show up in your cabin in a few hours. If not, do not panic. Cruise ships, especially large ones, have thousands of bags to load and sort as passengers arrive. In our experience, luggage is moved from the airport to your cabin with amazing speed.

AIRPORT ARRIVAL AND TRANSFERS

AS YOU LEAVE YOUR AIRPLANE in Miami, Ft. Lauderdale, San Juan, Vancouver, or any major departure city, you will be met by uniformed cruise line representatives, usually holding a placard showing your ship's name. The representatives gather their charges and escort or direct them to a waiting motorcoach. Keep your transfer voucher handy; you must show it to board the bus.

If you do not spot your cruise line representative, ask airline personnel or other cruise lines' reps for help. Or go to an airport "red" phone and ask that your line's representative be paged. Or proceed to where motorcoaches pick up passengers for transfer to the pier.

ADVANCE ARRIVALS OR DELAYED RETURNS

ALMOST ALL LINES have hotel and sightseeing packages for people who choose to arrive at their port of departure in advance of their cruise or linger there afterward. Packages are described in your cruise brochure. If your cruise begins after a long flight, lines normally schedule the first day for cruising to give passengers time to overcome jet lag. If the itinerary calls for immediate ports of call, you might consider arriving a day before departure.

Give the most serious consideration to a day-in-advance arrival when you buy the cruise by itself, are arranging your own transportation to the departure port, or your travel falls during busy travel periods when weather in the northern United States often turns bad and flights are delayed (such as Thanksgiving, Christmas, New Year's, and President's Day weekend).

If you're on an air/sea program, your line has a greater incentive—although not necessarily a legal one—to get you to the ship when you've been delayed, either by postponing the sailing or by arranging a hotel room and transporting you to the first port of call. In such instances, you're likely to be one of many stranded passengers.

Your name is on a passenger list, and the cruise line representative at the airport expects you. They are in touch with the airline and your ship and probably are setting strategy before you arrive. If you're traveling on your own and are delayed, your cruise ship has no record of your flight and no obligation to help, although most will try. If you arrive at least a day early, you can avoid this hassle.

This is highly recommended whenever possible. Why risk missing the ship due to a flight snafu? Some people advise arriving early to avoid standing in line for check-in. We view this as the least valid reason unless you want to be on as early as physically possible to enjoy onboard amenities. Queues at the airport and dockside departure gates are a fact of life in mass-market travel. If you're so impatient that you cannot stand in a check-in line—even if it takes an hour—without having your blood pressure skyrocket, then you're probably on the wrong cruise. Megaships have megapassengers, and they must be individually processed. (It would speed the process if everyone arrived with all their documents completed properly.)

AT THE PIER

IF YOU'RE LUCKY, you will be among the first to arrive from the airport and the first in line for check-in. More likely, you'll be among several hundred others, and, depending on the cruise line, day of the week, size of the ship, and other contingencies, you will stand in line ten minutes to two hours. Pull out a magazine or travel book and start reading.

Large ships have a check-in system, asking you to line up behind your letter in the alphabet. Despite occasional glitches, this works well. You often have until 60 minutes before departure to board the ship. Some lines let you board until 15 to 30 minutes before departure, but we don't suggest cutting it that close.

Normally, lines begin processing passengers at noon or 1 p.m. for a 4 or 5 p.m. departure. But they seldom allow passengers to embark sooner than two or three hours before departure, because time is needed for previous passengers to disembark and the crew to clean the ship and prepare your cabin. Some luxury or premium lines will let you come aboard sooner sometimes for a fee, but you must remain in public areas.

VISITORS

FOR SECURITY REASONS, lines do not allow visitors. If your friends or family want to send you off in style, they can contact your travel agent to arrange a party for you in your cabin, complete with flowers, wine, and champagne, or a birthday cake or anniversary surprise in the dining room when the ship is at sea.

SETTLING IN

BOARDING YOUR SHIP

SOME SHIPS, PARTICULARLY the most luxurious ones, have uniformed cabin stewards and stewardesses at the gangway to take you to your cabin and carry your hand luggage. Your escort may offer a quick orientation or ask you to wait for your regular steward, whose name is probably on a small tent card on your dresser. Also in your cabin is ship's literature, including an agenda for the day's events, a deck plan, and possibly stationery.

CHECKING OUT YOUR CABIN

TAKE A QUICK LOOK AROUND the cabin to be sure everything is working—it usually is on new ships, not necessarily on old ones. Check how to operate air conditioning, lights, and the hot water faucets—some fancy new ones are tricky, and the water can scald you. Check the location of life preservers, blankets, and pillows—do you have enough? If anything is missing or not as you requested—twin beds instead of a double—report it now. If you cannot locate your steward, go to the purser or front desk. If you do not get satisfaction, work your way up to the hotel manager.

HAIR DRYERS/ELECTRIC SHAVERS

ALMOST ALL CABINS on modern ships have standard 110-volt AC electrical outlets: Your small hair dryer and electric razor won't need an adapter. A few older ships need them. Most new ships have hair dryers. We list this information in the ships' profiles in Part Two, in Standard Features, under Cabin Amenities.

LAUNDRY AND DRY CLEANING

ALMOST ALL SHIPS have laundry service. Far fewer have dry cleaning facilities. Generally, laundry service is good and reasonable but ship laundries tend to use lots of bleach. Price lists and laundry bags are in your cabin. Give your articles to be cleaned or pressed to your steward. They usually are returned in a day, and same-day service is available for an extra fee. For safety reasons, ships ask that passengers not use irons in their cabin, but many have public launderettes with an iron and ironing board, as well as coin-operated washers and dryers. The Standard Features section in our cruise line's profile details the availability of launderettes.

TELEPHONES AND OTHER COMMUNICATIONS

ALL BUT A FEW SHIPS have telephones in cabins with instructions for using them. Most phones have direct-dial to the United States 24 hours a day, but be aware of the price. Usually, you are charged $8 to $15 per minute for a ship-to-shore call. Receiving a call or a fax may cost $5 to $7 or more per minute. Policies vary. Some allow you to call collect or charge your call to your shipboard account. Shore to Ship has technology enabling passengers to dial toll-free numbers in the United States directly from their cabins. The price is $6.95 per minute, maximum 10 minutes per call. Crystal Cruises was among the first to enable passengers to send and receive e-mail with relative ease. Now, many cruise ships have added e-mail facilities.

If someone wants to reach you at sea, they can telephone the ship by calling ☎ 800-SEA-CALL, asking for the ship by name, and giving its approximate location. The specific phone number for your ship is often included in the documents you receive from the cruise line in advance of your cruise. Charges for this call will appear on the caller's long-distance telephone bill. Ship-to-shore telephone and fax services are normally available only at sea. When the ship is in port, onshore communications must be used.

Cell phones work locally in ports and up to about two miles at sea, depending on the phone and the location. But beyond two miles, they seldom are effective, except perhaps for some very expensive models. With e-mail becoming so readily available on cruise ships, it is the best, least costly means to stay in touch with family and friends, or to tend to business during a cruise. Also, "Internet stores" in ports of call have become available around the world and are usually very inexpensive to use to send and retrieve e-mail.

Almost all new ships also have an Internet cafe with a dozen or more computer terminals, and older ships and many small ones have installed at least one or two terminals for passengers use. Many older ships have also been retrofitted with these cafes. Charges range from 25 cents to 75 cents per minute, including dial-up time, which can often take five minutes or more at sea. On week or longer cruises, many ships also offer weekly rates. Wi-Fi access was recently added to the newest ships of Norwegian Cruise Line as well as to Seabourn Cruise Line's entire fleet. The new Carnival *Valor* also has bow-to-stern Wi-Fi access. More lines are following suit.

CHECKING OUT YOUR SHIP

AFTER YOU CHECK OUT YOUR CABIN, you might want to tour the ship or, alternatively, relax in a lounge or visit the spa. The ship will be your home for a while, and it's nice to feel at home as quickly as possible.

CHECKING ON YOUR DINING RESERVATIONS

WHEN YOU BOOK YOUR CRUISE, your travel agent should state your dining preference and request reservations. On ships with assigned seating times, you may request first or second seating, or on ships with four seating times, any of those. Tables for two, four, six, or eight are available; and guests can ask for smoking or nonsmoking areas, although most ships departing from U.S. ports now have smokeless dining rooms. Most lines say they honor requests on a first-come, first-served basis, yet few confirm them in advance. Generally, dining reservations are confirmed only by the maître d'hôtel on board.

Royal Caribbean International is among the few lines that print passengers' dining reservations on their cruise tickets. Why, in this computer age, all can't do the same is a mystery—unless it's to allow the maître d'hôtel to control last-minute shuffling and to ensure he gets his tips.

You may receive confirmation of your dining arrangements on check-in, or it may be in your cabin. If not, check on it. Even lines that give you a dining reservation in advance may ask you to confirm it with the maître d'hôtel. If you have a problem with your dining arrangements, know that most cruise lines will accommodate your change request, though not necessarily on the first night. Rest assured, you won't be the only one. No other item causes more consternation than dining-room reservations.

unofficial **TIP**
If assigned arrangements are not what you requested, make a bee-line for the maître d'hôtel.

If you let the cruise line or maître d'hôtel place you randomly at a table and you are unhappy with your companions, do not hesitate to ask the maître d'hôtel to move you. Nothing is worse than spending a week dining with people with whom you have nothing in common and no basis for conversation. And you don't need to.

DINING HOURS

CONSUMERS OFTEN ASK about dining hours before they cruise. They vary so much that it is difficult, if not impossible, to give an accurate generic overview. Keep in mind that each line, each itinerary, and sometimes each ship may have varied hours. You will get a complete list of hours on board, and some general information before boarding about dining times and seatings. Ask your travel agent or cruise line.

But before booking, it is more important to assess how you will dine and to pick a line that meets your needs. Do your homework up front. What type of dining do you prefer? Are you more structured or flexible in dining times? Do you like to socialize with other passengers every night or do your own thing? Check brochures, Web sites, consumer cruise bulletin boards, and ask questions of your agent or friends. Find out exactly what the dining policies and dining style are on every ship you are thinking of sailing on (see our descriptions in Part II).

For those seeking the most flexibility, some luxury lines offer open seating and anytime dining programs. On the mass-market side, Norwegian Cruise Line offers the highly flexible Freestyle Dining—guests eat where, when, and with whom they want; and guests can also access a host of onboard alternative restaurant choices in addition to the main dining room. Some are free, some come with a charge. Expedition and small ship lines may have open seating but set very specific times for their dining service.

Princess, in another twist, offers both a flexible dining experience and a more traditional fixed one; guests choose which so they can have the best of both worlds. Some lines also have open seating for breakfast and lunch, yet more structured, assigned seating times and tables for dinner. That means you are assigned a table with other guests and you dine at that same table, at that same time, every evening; of course you don't have to dine there every night. Guests often take a break and have room service one night, or visit an alternative restaurant or the buffet restaurant on another. But if you do dine in the dining room on any evening you will eat at that table and with those people each night.

Generally, there are two fixed dinner seatings between 5:30 and 7:30 p.m. and between 8 and 10 p.m. But even those times can vary. Carnival and Holland America have both adopted four seatings within the same period to offer more flexibility for guests. So if you have strong preferences, tell your travel agent, who can explain what the dining hours and choices are on individual lines.

Whichever line you pick, you won't go hungry. In addition to the regular meals, most lines offer a host of other options. These might include room service, ice cream on deck, pizza parlors (some 24 hours), a late-night snack or buffet, afternoon tea, barbecues on deck, early-bird coffee and continental breakfast in a lounge, cocktail canapés, and a host of alternative dining options.

ESTABLISHING SHIPBOARD CREDIT

MOST LINES USE A CASHLESS SYSTEM aboard ship. At check-in, you receive a card—like a credit card—which will be your identification card and probably your cabin door key. If you want to establish credit for purchases on board, drinks at the bar, wine in the dining room, and so forth, you must present a major credit card at check-in or the purser's office (you will be told at check-in) to have an imprint made and signed.

On the last night of the cruise, you receive a printout of your charges for review. You can pay the amount with cash or traveler's checks or have it billed to your credit card. In profiles in Standard Features in Part Two, we list credit cards each cruise line accepts. Also see our discussion of credit holds on page 113.

PREPARING *for* TIME ASHORE

PORT TALKS AND SHOPPING GUIDELINES

ALL SHIPS OFFER "PORT TALKS"—briefings on the country or island and port where the ship will dock. The quality of these talks varies enormously among lines and ships, depending largely on the cruise director's knowledge and the importance the line puts on such programs.

Most mainstream lines with large ships do a lousy job with port talks. On the other hand, adventure and expedition cruises offer superb talks. Small ships generally have a better track record than large ones.

Avoid being misled. If, during a port talk, the cruise director or anyone else recommends one store over another, shop around before buying. The store recommended may be the best place to buy—or it may not.

Also, be cautious of advice that fabulous buys are available in duty-free shops on board and in ports. Most often, you can do as well or better at discount stores and factory outlets at home. If you are considering sizable purchases of jewelry, cameras, china, or crystal, bring a list of prices from home and comparison shop. Be sure you are comparing similar products. Prices in shipboard shops are a good gauge; they usually are competitive with those in ports.

In the Caribbean, expect to save up to 20% on such well-known brands as Gucci, Fendi, and Vuitton, and on French perfumes, which must be sold at prices set by the makers. Any store caught undercutting the price will be dropped from distribution. The biggest savings are on cigarettes and liquor, not because the price is so much less, but because you save the hefty U.S. taxes imposed on them.

When preparing for your day ashore, be aware also that purses, bags, and packs that you carry along will be searched before you're allowed back on board. Purchases you make while shopping will likewise be inspected.

SHORE EXCURSIONS: SOME PITFALLS AND COSTS

ALTHOUGH THERE HAS BEEN much improvement recently, "Shore excursions"—the tours passengers buy from the cruise line to take at ports—are often the weakest element of the cruise vacation. Cruise lines are finally recognizing the needs of younger, more active passengers by providing more adventurous excursions featuring horseback riding, hiking, mountain biking, scuba diving, snorkeling, sailing, and even a MIG flight over Moscow. But the core product—large to medium group sightseeing tours—needs more work, given the shore excursion's importance to the cruise experience.

All the latest cruise lines' research indicates that what attracts customers to buy a particular cruise are the specific ports of call on the itinerary. Travelers often view their shore trips as one of the more important aspects of the cruise. In response, major cruise lines have beefed up their shore excursion departments to offer more compelling tours, which often includes exploring a destination on foot as well as by bus, van, or boat.

Shore excursions are available at every stop on a ship's itinerary, almost always at additional cost. The exceptions are adventure and expedition cruises, where shore visits are an integral part of the experience (and one reason these cruises appear to be more costly than mainstream ones). Also, cruises in China usually include the cost of shore excursions, not because cruise lines are altruistic, but because the Chinese want it that way.

Shore excursions have traditionally been sold aboard ship either by a shore excursion office or, rarely, from the purser or cruise director. It has been assumed that people prefer to buy excursions on board because their interests and plans change once the cruise begins. However, that assumption may have no foundation in fact. After you have been subjected to the way shore excursions are sold aboard many ships, you might say as we do: There must be a better way.

Often you must choose your excursions on the first night of the cruise, especially for the first port of call. Unless you have done your homework in advance of your cruise, you will be buying blind. The shore excursion office usually has limited hours. For the first few days of a cruise, particularly on large ships, ticket lines are long. Therefore, it really pays to read your cruise literature plus books and magazine articles about your destinations in advance.

If possible, take advantage of the opportunity to book shore excursions in advance. In addition to significantly increasing your chances of getting the excursion you want, you also avoid the hassle of booking on board. Usually, a pamphlet on shore excursions is included in the literature sent prior to your cruise. Not all brochures list prices, but they are listed on those cruise lines' Web sites that provide a booking facility. Absent that convenience, you can request prices through your travel agent, if you need them for budgeting purposes. We are happy to report that more lines are including prices in their literature. Also, more often pamphlets are specific to cruise itineraries, making it easier to select tours of interest.

unofficial **TIP**
More and more, cruise lines are enabling passengers to purchase shore excursions in advance on the line's Web site, and some, even by phone or mail.

Shore excursions normally are operated by local tour companies. Motorcoaches seating 30 to 50 passengers are the most common form of transportation, particularly on general sightseeing tours offered by large ships. Minibuses and vans are common for smaller groups; location and terrain are also factors in the choice of conveyance. Most tours assume that passengers are on their first visit to the locale—one reason shore excursions are a weak link.

Standard shore excursions vary little among cruise lines and are, for the most part, passive and unimaginative city and/or countryside tours to the best-known sights. There are exceptions, like the excursions on Greek Isles cruises, where escorts are university graduates who must pass stiff examinations to qualify as guides, and customized tours offered by smaller ships and luxury liners. Happily, many cruise lines have added a variety of sports activities and tours that emphasis nature and culture in an effort to appeal to younger travelers and in response to passengers' requests.

After years of being bad to awful, shore excursions available on Caribbean cruises have recently shown a great improvement, as cruise lines have worked with local operators to be more creative, provide greater variety of tour offerings, and enhance the tour experience with more substance and better-trained guides.

As a rule of thumb, most standard half-day tours cost $25 to $35 in the Caribbean, but they can cost twice that amount in Alaska and Europe. Adventure excursions run $50 and up, mainly because the groups are small and hence, cost more per person to operate. Full-day tours can run as much as $70 to $150, and some, like helicopter tours, might cost $200 or more. Often the most expensive are the first to sell out. That's usually because the number of participants is limited, or they are perceived as great value or a once-in-a-lifetime experience, or it's an excursion that would be difficult to arrange on one's own. Variables that affect price include the locale, the number of participants, local costs, and mode of transport.

As you study excursions offered by your line, look for options that keep things simple. Excursions that involve multiple activities, sights, and stops could drive some people nuts. It's on the bus, off the bus, back on the bus, head counts. "Wait, Thelma's in the restroom!" "Where are Harry and Louise?" "I left my credit card in the stuffed parrot shop! I'll be right back." With few exceptions, you'll spend more time driving among sites and loading and unloading the bus than you will touring or doing something interesting.

When you read descriptions of available excursions, check how long the primary activity or event is. If the written material doesn't say, ask the cruise director. You'll sometimes discover that the half-day "riverboat excursion" spends only an hour on the water. The remainder of the time is spent commuting and waiting for fellow passengers to shop.

In ports where most attractions you want to see are clustered in a small area, you may save time by taking a cab or walking. Rental cars are another option. By forgoing a $48-per-person half-day shore excursion, two people can apply the $96 toward cab fares, rental cars, and admissions to attractions. In most ports, you can see and do a lot for $96.

Ask probing questions about each port. Is it a good and safe place to explore on foot? What are the local people like? At some ports, tourists are subjected to swarms of in-your-face hucksters and peddlers. In such places, escorted tours, though regimented and inefficient, can be a less stressful way to visit.

When the ship arrives in port, people who have purchased shore excursions are allowed to disembark first and are usually asked to follow a departure schedule to avert a traffic jam at the gangway. This is seldom a problem when the ship docks and passengers can disembark quickly. It can be a problem when the ship must tender, because it cuts an hour or more (depending on ship size) from the time you have in port if you plan to tour on your own.

AT *the* END *of* YOUR CRUISE

TIPPING

THERE ARE NO DEFINITIVE RULES about tipping, but because it causes so much consternation for passengers, cruise lines offer guidelines, distributing them aboard ship. Some even publish them in their cruise brochures, which is helpful if you want to budget for tipping in advance. In Part Two, the cruise ship profiles' Standard Features includes Suggested Tipping. The guidelines are similar: Tip slightly less on budget cruises, slightly more on luxury cruises. Lines will also tell you if gratuities are included or if they are automatically added to your bill. Follow guidelines or your inclinations. Ship officers and senior management are never tipped. For all service personnel, tips are their main source of compensation. Only a few deluxe ships include tipping in the cruise cost (noted in the cruise line profiles).

In a session at voyage's end, the cruise director will discuss disembarkation procedures and outline tipping guidelines. There no longer is anything subtle about tipping. Either the line will auotomatically add the tips; if not, on the final cruise day, your cabin steward will leave a supply of envelopes for distributing your tips, possibly with guidelines. Lately, the envelopes are crassly stamped with titles—Cabin Steward, Dining Steward, Waiter—in case you did not know whom to tip!

On ships without "automatic" tipping, tips are usually given to individuals—your cabin stewards and dining room waiters. On ships with Greek crews and on many small vessels, tips are pooled for distribution to include those behind the scenes, such as kitchen staff.

The advent of alternative dining venues has confused tipping customs in recent years. Passengers sometimes were deducting from the amount given to their dining room wait staff in order to compensate for gratuities rendered at the alternative restaurants. To create a more uniform approach, a number of cruise lines add gratuities directly to your shipboard bill. Most of these offer the option of decreasing or increasing the amount on your bill depending on how you felt about the service. Whatever the tipping protocol on your cruise, you can be sure it will be explained to you in detail, probably several times.

If tips are not added to your shipboard bill, custom dictates that you distribute tips the last night of the cruise. Some lines, particularly deluxe ones, will arrange prepayment of tips. Check the Standard Features section in our cruise line profiles for each line's "Suggested Tipping" information.

DEPARTING

TO SMOOTH DISEMBARKATION, your captain and cruise director will ask you to follow procedures outlined in the cruise director's final talk and repeated on closed-circuit television in your cabin and in the daily agenda. On the last day, your cabin steward will give you luggage tags to be completed and attached to your bags. You are asked to place your bags (except hand luggage) outside your cabin door before you retire. Times vary; some lines want them out by 8 or 10 p.m.—an unreasonable hour for passengers dining at the late seating. Such requests are for the ship's convenience, because no luggage can be unloaded until the ship docks. Do what's convenient for you and tell your cabin steward what to expect.

The last night of a cruise is almost always casual; plan your packing accordingly. And don't pack everything. Remember you still need to dress the next day. It's not unheard of for people to pack shoes, underwear, and even needed travel documents in their exuberance to put their bags out.

Luggage tags use a color-coded, alphabetic system that enables the ship to disembark passengers by cabin locations and airline departure times for those on air/sea packages. (Passengers on the earliest flights disembark first.) Tags also identify your airline so that your bags will go to the correct place at the airport.

Ships normally dock about 7 or 8 a.m. the last day and require about an hour to unload luggage, meaning no passengers will disembark before 9 a.m. The ship is very eager to unload passengers as quickly as possible. Some people find disembarkation so abrupt that it's unpleasant. Try to remember that the next group of passengers will arrive soon, and staff and crew have only about four hours to prepare the ship and be all smiles for them.

Breakfast is served either at normal hours with the full menu or at abbreviated hours with a short menu. Room service usually isn't available. You will be called to depart by the color of your luggage tags. After leaving the ship, you encounter chaos that varies depending on the port. Usually, you proceed first to immigration and then to the baggage holding area, where your luggage has been placed according to the color of your tags. You are responsible for finding it and taking it to Customs. In Miami, for example, baggage handlers help you, and the Customs official stands by the exit to take the declaration form you completed aboard ship. They may check your passport, so have it handy.

After clearing Customs, your luggage will go with you to the airport on the transfer bus. Find the motorcoach going to your airline's departure area, show your transfer voucher, give the driver your luggage, and climb aboard. If you aren't on an air/sea package, you may be allowed aboard the motorcoach unless you have lots of luggage. Otherwise, taxis are nearby.

CRUISE LINES *and* THEIR SHIPS

THE HEART OF THE MATTER

PART TWO CONSISTS OF IN-DEPTH CRUISE LINE and ship profiles—the heart of this guide—serving the U.S. and Canadian markets. Listed alphabetically by cruise line, each line has three parts: a company profile, its ships' standard features, and ship descriptions. Cruise lines profiled in this section are listed in the Table of Contents. For listings of specific ships, itineraries, destinations, or for a general subject index, refer to the respective indexes at the end of this book.

CRUISE LINE PROFILES

The first three to four pages focus on the cruise line and the type of cruises it offers. At-a-glance summaries—**Type of Ships, Type of Cruises, Cruise Line's Strengths, Cruise Line's Shortcomings, Fellow Passengers, Recommended for, Not Recommended for**—help you select cruise lines of potential interest.

Summaries are followed by background on the line, its fleet, and cruise areas to reveal the company behind the cruise. The **Style** section defines the experience you can expect on any ship of that cruise line. **Distinctive Features** highlights amenities or facilities that are innovative or unusual.

Rates

The **Rates** section explains discounts, special fares, and packages and provides a range of per-person daily (per diem) costs. These figures were derived by averaging cruise-only (no airfare) brochure rates for each cabin class on every ship in the line. Calculations exclude owner's suites, presidential suites, and other extraordinary accommodations. The rate table aims to indicate the most and the least you would pay per day for a cruise if you paid brochure rates. Savvy shoppers almost certainly will be able to chip away 10% to 50% or more of the listed per diem by taking advantage of common discounts. (Our average rate is not calculated by adding the highest and lowest rates in the brochure table and dividing by two. Rather, the average per diem takes into account the number of each type of accommodation available in the line's cabin inventory. The per diem box averages rates for all ships of the line.)

Past Passengers tells what repeat customers can expect, and **The Last Word** is our summary of the line—the big picture.

Standard Features

Information on elements common to all ships of a line—including officers, staff, dining facilities, dress code, cabin amenities, and electricity—is listed in one chart for handy reference.

Cruise Ship Profiles

The cruise line's fleet, starting with its flagship (or the most representative) vessel, is covered in depth. Sister ships with identical design are clustered. Other ships that vary only in degree receive shorter treatment. We recommend that readers review the entire section for a given cruise line to have a complete picture of the cruise experience offered.

QUALITY RATINGS To differentiate ships by overall quality of the cruise experience and to allow comparison of ships from different lines, we give ships a rating of 1 to 10, with 10 being the best. The numerical rating is based on the quality and diversity of the ship's features and service, taking into consideration its state of repair, maintenance, and cleanliness; the design, comfort, decor, and furnishing of public areas; recreational and fitness facilities; meal quality and dining room service; entertainment, activities, and shore excursions; cabin comfort, decor, furnishings, and spaciousness; and hospitality, courtesy, and responsiveness of officers and crew.

We have opted for numerical ratings because some of our colleagues in the travel press have hopelessly muddled the more familiar star ratings. Traditionally, ships have been rated one to five stars. This system was easily understood by the cruising public and provided a quick way to compare critics' opinions. Several years ago, however, some writers changed the scale to one to six stars, precluding meaningful comparison. Although those guidebooks are no longer published and the writers are deceased, the practice continues, mainly because the cruise lines perpetuate it. We believe a standardized rating system helps consumers. But so long as the star system remains corrupted, we elect to abandon the star business.

VALUE RATINGS There is no consideration of cost in the quality ratings. If you want the finest cruise available and cost is no issue, look no further than the quality ratings. If, however, you seek both quality and value, consult the value rating, expressed in letters. All value ratings are based on brochure rates. Any discount you obtain will improve the value rating for a ship. Value ratings are defined as follows:

value ratings

A	Exceptional value, a real bargain.
B	Good value.
C	Absolutely fair. You get exactly what you pay for.
D	Somewhat overpriced.
F	Significantly overpriced.

A WORD ABOUT NEW SHIPS

We do not evaluate or rate new ships until they have been in service for at least one year. This allows the new ship to work out any kinks and settle into normal operation. If you are considering a cruise on a new ship, check our ratings and descriptions of other ships in the same line for a good idea of what to expect. If a ship has not completed a year of service at press time, it will be marked as a "preview" in the ship's ratings box.

American Canadian Caribbean Line

461 Water Street, Warren, RI 02885
☎ 401-247-0955 or 800-556-7450
fax 401-247-2350
www.accl-smallships.com

TYPE OF SHIPS Small, no frills, budget.

TYPE OF CRUISES Light adventure, destination-oriented, unhurried pace.

CRUISE LINE'S STRENGTHS
- innovative, small ships
- imaginative itineraries
- homey ambience
- friendly, diligent staff
- moderate prices

CRUISE LINE'S SHORTCOMINGS
- minimal service
- spartan cabins with small bathrooms
- limited shipboard facilities
- sparse pre-cruise information

FELLOW PASSENGERS Mature, experienced travelers ages 55–85; retired couples, seniors; water sports enthusiasts. Not all are sporty, but all are good sports; friendly and unpretentious, most with modest means, college-educated, well-traveled. Even affluent passengers who care little for luxury and ostentation are keenly interested in history, wildlife, and ecology. They are avid readers and play bridge and Scrabble. Most come from the northeast United States, Florida, and California.

Recommended for Travelers seeking friendship, companionship, light adventure in unusual destinations; budget-conscious travelers favoring a small ship with family atmosphere. Those who abhor large ships.

Not recommended for Swingers, hyper super-achievers, snobs, or night owls.

CRUISE AREAS AND SEASONS Spring–fall, U.S. coastal waterways between Rhode Island and Florida; Hudson River/Erie Canal, Maine, New England/Canada; small mid-America rivers and Mississippi byways to New Orleans; Great Lakes from Chicago, Hudson River and Lake Champlain. Winter, Bahamas; Virgin Islands; Eastern/Southern Caribbean, Panama; Belize, Barrier Reef, Honduras, and Guatemala.

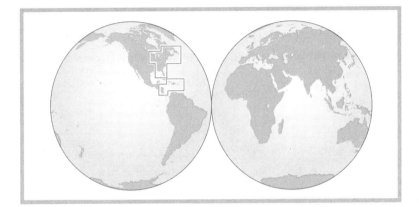

THE LINE Shipbuilder and adventurer Luther Blount designed and built his first small ship in 1964 for cruising the Hudson River, Erie Canal, and Canada's inland waterways with his friends. A loyal following developed, and his hobby became a business that pioneered innovative itineraries and ship design.

With slightly larger ships, he expanded to the Bahamas, Virgin Islands, and small islands of the Eastern Caribbean, added "Caribbean" to the line's name, and again pioneered unusual itineraries in Central America, the Southern Caribbean, and other U.S. waterways.

Each vessel, built at Blount's shipyard in Warren, Rhode Island, has had design improvements, larger cabins, and better public space. Blount was a hands-on president, designing every aspect of the ships (with design concepts adopted by many small cruise ships), supervising the building, and scouting new itineraries. ACCL remains a family enterprise. Daughter Nancy Blount, who had been vice president and director of operations, took over as company president when Luther Blount retired in 2001 at the age of 84.

THE FLEET	BUILT/RENOVATED	TONNAGE	PASSENGERS
Grande Caribe	1997	99	100
Grande Mariner	1998	99	100
Niagara Prince	1994/1999	95	84

STYLE Adventure at budget prices. Leave your Guccis at home—no one here would be impressed. Since its inception, ACCL has maintained an informal, unpretentious atmosphere with limited service and planned entertainment. Passengers receive an intimate look at places they visit. The ships' shallow drafts enable them to cruise small tributaries. Bow ramps, a Blount innovation, allow access to inaccessible places like secluded beaches for swimming and snorkeling. The ships carry a glass-bottom boat, small sailboats, and snorkeling equipment.

ACCL cruises, staffed by American officers and crew, are run like a family outing. Surprisingly good food is served family-style in a folksy atmosphere conducive to friendships. Limited table service is provided by cheerful, hard-working staff who are always ready to bring beverages or second helpings and deal with special requests.

New itineraries are offered every year, tapping pristine areas strong in natural beauty and history and providing frequent opportunities for exploring, swimming, and snorkeling. For example, a new seven-night coast of Maine includes ports where large ships cannot go.

DISTINCTIVE FEATURES Bow ramps; retractable pilothouse allowing vessels to sail under low bridges and the length of Erie Canal.

	HIGHEST	**LOWEST**	**AVERAGE**
PER DIEM	$327	$151	$246

Per diems are calculated from cruise line's nondiscounted *cruise-only* published fares on standard accommodations and vary by season, cabins, and cruise areas.

RATES Port charges are additional. Some shore excursions included.

Special fares and discounts 10% discount on certain cruises when two cruises are booked back to back; up to 20% discounts or more periodically on special promotions.

- **THIRD PASSENGER:** 15% discount for each occupant of cabin.
- **SINGLE SUPPLEMENT:** 175% for certain cabins, depending on season and time of booking. On select cruises, a single's willing-to-share program offers double occupancy rates.

Packages

- **PRE/POST:** Panama, Belize, Bahamas, New Orleans, Maine.

PAST PASSENGERS Loyalty is rewarded; after ten cruises, a passenger gets one free. Advanced mailings on new itineraries and special discounts.

THE LAST WORD Up to 68% of passengers are repeat, suggesting that ACCL has found the right formula for a certain type of passenger: one who doesn't want or need pampering and appreciates small-ship cruising, preferring conversation and friendship to chorus lines and casinos. New itineraries usually sell out quickly. ACCL reflects the owners' hands-on philosophy and personal touch with customers. Passengers who understand the limitations of a small ship and the nature of these cruises enjoy themselves immensely; those who do not may discover they're on the wrong ship.

In the past, we complained about the dearth of information on itineraries and ports of call, but we are pleased to report that ACCL's new cruise brochure includes quite a lot of information on itineraries and ports. The only thing missing now is information on shore excursions sent to passengers before their cruise. Tours are not published in advance because, ACCL says, they are so often decided by the interests of the passengers and are subject to demand and weather conditions; however, experience shows they do not change that much. It is difficult to understand why ACCL handles such information haphazardly, particularly when its cruises and passengers are destination-focused. It's even more puzzling when you know that ACCL is one of the few cruise lines that does not profit on shore excursions. They're either included in the cruise price or sold at cost—one of many reasons ACCL cruises are a truly good value.

ACCL Standard Features

Officers American.

Staff Dining, Cabin, Cruise/American.

Dining facilities One dining room with open seating; meals served at specific hours: breakfast, 8 a.m.; lunch, noon; dinner, 6 p.m.

Special diets Cruise line needs notice at booking, but chefs can accommodate basic requests.

Room service None.

Dress code Casual at all times; men never need a tie. Gentlemen might bring a jacket and women a dress in case they want to try a fancy place in a port of call.

Cabin amenities Air-conditioning/heat; upper-deck cabins have windows that can be opened. Very small bathroom with hand-held shower. Reading light; plug for hair dryers. Limited drawer and closet space.

Electrical outlets 110 AC.

Wheelchair access No designated cabins; motorized chair between main and sun decks.

Recreation and entertainment Lounge with bar setup, books, and videos; informal entertainment, occasional lectures; bridge and parlor games. No casino, swimming pool, gym, or theater.

Sports and other activities Glass-bottom boat, Sunfish, kayaks, and snorkeling equipment on board for warm-weather cruises.

Beauty and fitness No facilities. On request, cruise director will provide information about beauty/barber salons in ports.

Other facilities Ships have no doctors; "BYOB" policy.

Children's facilities None. Children under age 14 not accepted.

Theme cruises Fall foliage.

Smoking No smoking inside ships; allowed only in outside open areas.

ACCL suggested tipping $10–$15 per person per day. All tips are pooled and shared.

Credit cards None onboard. Passengers may use travelers checks or personal checks. Visa or MasterCard to book a cruise.

Niagara Prince	QUALITY 2	VALUE A
REGISTRY United States	LENGTH 175 feet	BEAM 40 feet
CABINS 30	DRAFT 6.3 feet	SPEED 12 knots
MAXIMUM PASSENGERS 60	PASSENGER DECKS 3	ELEVATORS Chairlift
	CREW 15	SPACE RATIO NA

THE SHIP The U.S.-flagged *Niagara Prince,* an innovative small ship with shallow draft, made her debut in 1994. She was designed to navigate the length of the Erie Canal and sail on coastal waters. The comfortable but basic ship has two passenger decks with homey decor and low ceilings.

The lounge and dining room are located forward on the top or sun deck and have windows at the bow and along the sides, providing enhanced views. The lounge, shaped by the bow, has the ship's only television set for videos, books, and newspapers (updated as available in ports). The dining room is an all-purpose room between meals. The sun deck has cabins and a wraparound promenade with small sitting areas at each end.

A flight of steps at the bow accesses the patented bow ramp, used when a site of interest has no dock. Extensions lengthen the ramp and allow for dry shore landings. Stairs from the promenade deck lead to a partially covered rooftop deck with chairs.

Also atop is the retractable pilothouse, lowered to pass under bridges by lifting off its roof, folding back its three sides, and disconnecting all the equipment. The captain's chair, console, steering mechanism, and equipment then are lowered to the promenade deck and reconnected so the ship can resume operation. It's quite a scene to watch, leaving you with an I-had-to-see-it-to-believe-it feeling.

Niagara Prince's profile can be made even lower with a hull feature Blount likens to letting the air out of a tire. It enables the ship to pass under the Erie Canal's lowest bridges and traverse the waterway from Troy to Buffalo, the first boat to do so in over 120 years. (Previous ACCL ships traveled about three-quarters of the way.) The feature also is used to navigate Lake Champlain and the Chicago River through the heart of the Windy City, passing under its bridges.

Niagara Prince offers a motorized chairlift for passengers who have difficulty negotiating stairs, and during recent renovations, new hallway railings were added to improve capabilities for handicapped passengers. Other changes included opening the bow area to make it more accessible for passengers, relocating the bar to increase space in the dining/lounge area, and refurbishing with new furniture and rugs.

ITINERARIES *See* Itinerary Index.

CABINS Small, spartan, but functional cabins have twin beds on metal frames. Storage space is limited to four drawers, about one square foot of counter space, and a four-foot-tall cabinet for hanging clothes; luggage goes under the beds. Accordion doors close tightly but do not lock.

Bathrooms, ingeniously designed by Blount, are tiny but utilitarian; they were improved somewhat during the ship's most recent refurbishing. They're a deluxe version of a "head" on a sailboat or RV. A very small sink with spring taps lets water run for only a few seconds at a time. The hand-held shower is very efficient and can be left in its wall mount when showering; the shower curtain is the "door" to the head. A trap in the floor lets water out. The toilet has a fill-and-flush system that works very well. However, if you do note operate it properly— refilling the water in the bowl after each use or closing the trap in the floor—an unpleasant odor develops.

All but two main-deck cabins are outside. The largest and most desirable cabins are on the sun deck. Six cabins open onto the promenade; others have large sliding windows—a pleasant feature on U.S. waterways when fresh, cool air fills the room.

Cabins are cleaned daily; linens are changed weekly. Bath towels are replaced every second day or as needed. (The ship does not have laundry facilities.) There is no room service.

Specifications 40 outside cabins (14 opening onto the promenade); 2 inside; all have private facilities and twin lower beds; some can be converted to doubles. 4 cabins have upper and lower berths. Standard dimensions, 72–96 square feet.

DINING A big advantage on a small ship is its fresh food and homemade bread and pastries. Aboard *Niagara Prince,* well-prepared American fare is much better than expected for the ship's category and better than on more expensive lines.

Menus are posted daily. One of two entrees available is lighter, healthful fare. This reflects past passengers' criticism of the ship's tendency to serve high-cholesterol foods. New menus are an improvement, but we would prefer more salads and green vegetables, and less gravy and sauces.

The main course of the hearty breakfast—eggs, pancakes, and so on—varies daily. Lunch usually includes a freshly made soup (the best we've had on any ship), salad, and dessert. Dinner features fish, chicken, or other meat; vegetables; and dessert. Meals are family-style; staff serves dessert, beverages, and second helpings. Coffee, tea, and cookies are always available in the dining room.

The dining room, which has an open kitchen, has tables for four, six, eight, and ten. The square tables for four are also used for card games.

Passengers bring their own liquor and wine, and ACCL provides storage, setups, and ice. For the captain's dinners, ACCL supplies wine and an open bar. Likewise, for Celebration Night, when passengers collectively celebrate birthdays, anniversaries, and so on, the line supplies wine. Make-Your-Own-Sundae, with many varieties of ice cream and toppings, is another popular event.

SERVICE Most crew members—young, energetic, and terrific—are from Rhode Island or neighboring states. The teams that clean the cabins also attend the dining room. They are cheerful, hardworking, unfailingly polite, and particularly accommodating to their mostly older passengers.

FACILITIES AND ACTIVITIES Except for television monitors for videotapes, local talent at some ports, and visiting lecturers, there is no evening entertainment. Most passengers are in bed by 10 p.m. Although the ship has some paperbacks, avid readers should bring their own books.

Passengers gather in the lounge for pre-dinner cocktails. A crew member helps prepare drinks. After dinner, some may linger for a film or bridge and other card and parlor games. ACCL's captains are very knowledgeable about places the ships visit and often provide running commentary.

The ship has no shop, but the cruise director does open his "boutique" to sell signature shirts, caps, and jackets at least once during each cruise.

SPORTS AND FITNESS Onboard, a mile walk on the promenade deck usually starts the morning fitness activity for most passengers. Ashore, sports activities can include swimming, snorkeling, hiking, and birding, depending on the itinerary.

SHORE EXCURSIONS On the cruise's first day, the cruise director distributes descriptions of tours. Excursions vary with itineraries, cost $4–$45 each, and often are subject to demand and weather conditions. ACCL uses local operators specializing in small special-interest groups. The line says it continuously checks tours and books the most appealing choices.

POSTSCRIPT The *Niagara Prince* is a one-of-a-kind ship, sailing unique itineraries through America's most historic waterways. It's both a great value and a great cruise experience.

Grande Caribe	**QUALITY 2**	**VALUE A**
Grande Mariner	**QUALITY 2**	**VALUE A**
REGISTRY United States	**LENGTH** 183/182 feet	**BEAM** 40 feet
CABINS 50	**DRAFT** 6.6 feet	**SPEED** 12 knots
MAXIMUM PASSENGERS	**PASSENGER DECKS** 3	**ELEVATORS** Chairlift
100/96	**CREW** 15/17	**SPACE RATIO** NA

THE SHIPS Built at Blount Marine in Warren, Rhode Island, the *Grande Caribe* and her near twin, *Grande Mariner,* are designed for coastal cruises from Labrador to the Amazon. Like other ACCL ships, they have shallow drafts and bow ramps to guarantee access to areas large cruise ships simply cannot reach. They also have a retractable pilothouse for passage under low bridges and a chairlift for passengers who have trouble negotiating stairs. On Caribbean and Central American cruises, the ships carry a Blount-designed glass-bottom boat, kayaks, snorkel equipment, and Sunfish.

Although the *Grande Caribe* is only slightly larger than earlier ACCL ships, her layout varies in several ways. The dining room is on the main deck; the lounge, with wraparound windows, is on the top deck. A new feature is a stern swimming platform.

The *Grande Mariner,* which made her debut in 1998, has more comfortable cabins than *Grande Caribe,* as well as unique features including an acoustical "floating deck" between the engine room and main-deck cabins. This special deck is meant to reduce engine noise, along with sound-deadening enclosures for the ship's main generators. (We did not find the ship quieter than her earlier sisters. In fact, our cabin, 44A, was actually noisier from the sound of the generators.)

In another first for ACCL, the hull of the *Grande Mariner* is ice-strengthened for cruising in the Canadian subarctic waters of Labrador, Newfoundland, and parts of the St. Lawrence River. Incidentally, the ship's 24-passenger glass-bottom boat and shore launch are built with the same foam-based materials found in a life raft.

The *Grande Mariner's* "vista view" lounge, a multifunctional room located forward on the upper deck, has wraparound windows to showcase passing scenery. The room has a bar, piano, and large projection screen; it can be used for lectures by visiting experts, historians, and naturalists, or for business seminars. A self-service bar has storage shelves for passengers' liquor and a fridge for chilling wine and beer. Nightly, the chef prepares hors d'oeuvres for the cocktail hour.

ITINERARIES *See* Itinerary Index.

CABINS The *Grande Caribe* has a third, lower deck (the *Niagara Prince* lacks this) with six cabins fitted with upper and lower berths and no windows. There are three similar, inside cabins on the main deck. These nine are the least expensive of the *Grande Caribe's* 50 cabins.

All other cabins are on the main and sun decks and have two beds, either side by side or in an L shape. Two cabins have double beds. Six cabins on the sun deck have doors that open to the outside promenade.

On the *Grande Mariner,* each cabin has its own air conditioner with air circulated outside through ducts. Unlike many other ships where air is recirculated, the Blount-designed system supplies fresh air continuously to the cabins, and stale air is removed.

Also, *Grande Mariner's* cabins are ACCL's most comfortable. Bathrooms, particularly, show marked improvement. Gone is the hole in the floor from which odors escaped. Toilets operate on the standard principle, but the design is more streamlined. Also new: Cabin doors can be locked from the inside. However, passengers are not issued keys, and they don't need them.

Specifications 50 cabins (*Caribe* 9, *Mariner* 7 inside/no window; *Caribe* 8, *Mariner* 9 open onto promenade); all have private facilities and twin lower beds (except *Mariner* has 2 cabins with double bed); some convert to doubles. *Caribe* 8, *Mariner* 10 have upper and lower berths; 1 cabin has 1 double and 1 single. Standard dimensions, 80–110 square feet.

SERVICE The young and energetic crew members are outstanding. They are hardworking, smiling, and unfailingly polite. The same teams that clean the cabins also attend the dining room. They seem eager to please and are particularly accommodating to their mostly older passengers.

FACILITIES AND ACTIVITIES There is no evening entertainment of the usual cruise variety. Passengers gather in the lounge for informal, pre-dinner cocktails. After dinner, some may linger for card or parlor games or to watch a film. The lounge has a television monitor for videotapes, and visiting lecturers or local talent may appear at ports of call. Most passengers are in bed by 10 p.m.

POSTSCRIPT ACCL's ships' best features are their staff, itineraries, and the camaraderie among passengers—the latter not found on a large ship. The ships are basic (at times, you feel you're camping), but passengers appear to be happy and having a good time. Clearly they are the type more interested in destinations than in creature comforts.

Note that no liquor is sold on board any ACCL vessels; BYOB basics with setups are offered.

Anyone planning a cruise on the *Grande Caribe* or *Grande Mariner* should read the entire section on ACCL to have a more complete picture of the cruise experience the line offers.

Carnival Cruise Lines

3655 NW 87th Avenue, Miami, FL 33178-2428
☎ **305-599-2600, 800-438-6744, or**
800-327-9501; fax 305-406-8666
www.carnival.com

TYPE OF SHIPS New, mod superliners and megaliners.

TYPE OF CRUISES Casual, contemporary mass market. "Fun Ships" hallmark makes the ship the destination—just as central to the cruise as the ports of call.

CRUISE LINE'S STRENGTHS
- lavish recreational and entertainment facilities
- new fleet with unusual, innovative interiors
- value
- clear, easy-to-use literature
- variety of dining outlets
- quality of cuisine for price category

CRUISE LINE'S SHORTCOMINGS
- megaliner size
- little relief from crowds and glitz
- lack of outdoor promenade deck on some ships
- long lines for facilities and services

FELLOW PASSENGERS From all walks of life, ages 3 to 93. Although Carnival's image has been that of a shipload of young swingers partying day and night (an image Carnival once cultivated to attract young people to cruising), the mix now is more likely to range from Joe Sixpack and his Nike-shod kids to Lester and Alice celebrating their 50th wedding anniversary. The cruises lend themselves to families with or without kids, honeymooners, married couples, singles, and seniors. Average age: 43. On a typical cruise, 40% are ages 35–55; 30% younger than 35 (including 500,000 kids annually); 30% older than 55. Fifty percent are first-time cruisers. Most have medium income.

Recommended for First-time cruisers who want an active, high-energy, party atmosphere; families, young singles, and couples; young-at-heart of any age; those who enjoy Las Vegas glitz or similar ambience.

Not recommended for Small-ship devotees; sophisticated travelers who prefer luxury and individual travel; anyone seeking a quiet or cerebral travel experience; those who consider Martha's Vineyard their ideal vacation spot.

CRUISE AREAS AND SEASONS Bahamas, Caribbean, West Coast and Mexican Riviera year-round. Alaska, Hawaii, New England/Canada, Europe seasonally.

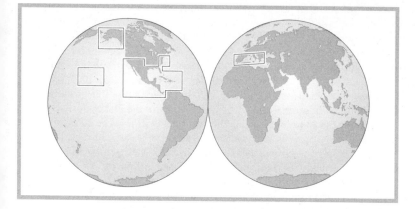

THE LINE In 30 short years, Carnival Cruise Lines went from one ship that ran aground on its maiden voyage to becoming the largest, most influential company in the cruise business, having revolutionized the nature of cruises along the way. Its story is the stuff of legends.

The late Ted Arison, a cruise executive in Florida, and a maverick travel company in Boston bought the *Mardi Gras* (formerly the *Empress of Canada*) in 1972. After three years of losses and near bankruptcy, Arison took over the company, assumed its $5 million debt, bought the assets—the *Mardi Gras*—for $1, and created the "Fun Ship" concept, turning a profit in his first year and adding two more ships.

Arison's aim was to take the stuffiness out of cruising, abandon the elitist image on which classic ocean liners had thrived, and make cruises fun and available to everyone, particularly to middle America, who never dreamed of a holiday at sea. He hit the right button. Through the 1970s, Carnival ships broke occupancy records while traditional companies were sinking all around.

Carnival continued to defy conventional wisdom. In the late 1970s, with spiraling shipbuilding costs and the oil crisis putting the future of cruising in doubt, Carnival ordered a new ship, *Tropicale,* whose technology set new industry standards, changed ship profiles, and enhanced Carnival's "Fun Ship" concept. Then, a decade after its inauspicious beginning, Carnival added three radically new ships—*Holiday, Jubilee,* and *Celebration*—which became trendsetters of the 1980s and beyond. These 1,800-passenger superliners were not the largest passenger ships ever built, but their design and madcap decor were profoundly different from ocean liners of the past.

To prepare for the 21st century, Carnival added eight megaliners, each for over 2,600 passengers, and lifted eyebrows with such names as *Fantasy* and *Ecstasy.* They were followed in 1996 with the 101,000-ton, 3,400-passenger *Carnival Destiny,* the world's largest ship at the time.

Carnival was so pleased with her performance and passenger response that it ordered four more like her, each costing $450 million or more.

Along with the Destiny class, Carnival started a new class of ships with the 86,000-ton *Carnival Spirit* in 2001, followed by three more of the group. Another new class of 110,000 ton ships started with the *Carnival Conquest* in 2002, with another three of them added by 2005, and a fourth, *Carnival Freedom,* arriving in 2007. Carnival's new ship investment in the 1990s exceeded $5 billion; those so far for the 21st century added more than $3 billion, bringing the fleet total to 21 ships by 2005. When the new ships for its sister companies—a total of 14—are added in, the expenditure reaches more than $7 billion by 2009. Meanwhile, rumor has it that Carnival has plans, dubbed the "Pinnacle Project," to build the world's largest liners at 180,000 tons for as many as 4,500 passengers.

Under Arison's son Micky—Carnival Corp's chairman since 1990—Carnival Cruise Lines' young, aggressive team has marketed cruises as the universal dream vacation for everyone. The line carries about 3.3 million passengers a year.

A publicly held company since 1987, Carnival Corp broadened its base (and buffed its image) by acquiring the classic Holland America Line and the upscale Windstar Cruises in 1989. Later, it acquired ownership of ultraluxurious Seabourn Cruise Line. In 1996, Carnival Corp bought Costa Cruises (Europe's largest line), and the following year, it stunned the cruise world by buying Cunard as well. More recently, it outmaneuvered Royal Caribbean for the purchase of Princess Cruises/P&O Cruises, adding another 18 ships to its inventory. These acquisitions give Carnival a total of 78 ships and a huge share of the world cruise market. All 12 lines operate as separate companies, each with a sharp focus; together, they give Carnival Corp tremendous clout.

In 1999, Carnival became the first major cruise line to launch direct booking on its Web site. In recent years, the line has introduced departures from new gateways, particularly new U.S. ports such as Jacksonville, Florida, advancing the "close-to-home" trend following the September 11 attacks. For 2005, the line is using 18 different North America home ports. It also launched its first Mediterranean cruise in summer/fall of 2005.

At the same time, Carnival has expanded its focus on families, adding a second children's playroom to all Fantasy-class ships and extensive children's facilities on all its newest ships. The line carries 500,000 children a year, and its children's program, Camp Carnival, employs one of cruising's largest staffs of trained personnel—over 100 child counselors spread over 20 ships on a full-time basis, with additional personnel hired during peak periods. More recently, Camp Carnival has added a family reading club, youth fitness and spa programs, hands-on science, education and art programs, and a kids dining program."Vacation Guarantee," a Carnival innovation, allows a dissatis-fied passenger, after notifying the purser's office, to leave a cruise at the first non-U.S. port of call and get a prorated refund. Another Carnival "first" is a 24-hour, toll-free hotline—☎ 877-TVL-HTLN (885-4856)—for passengers who encounter a travel emergency (such as severe weather or an airline strike) en route to or returning from their cruise. Passengers outside the United States can call collect ☎ 305-406-4779. In 2001, Carnival launched new, more flexible dining programs along with lighter cuisine, including low-carb options. It also introduced fleetwide Internet access for passengers. Recently, it began booking shore excursions on its Web site.

THE FLEET	BUILT/RENOVATED	TONNAGE	PASSENGERS
Carnival Conquest	2002	110,000	2,974
Carnival Destiny	1996	101,353	2,642
Carnival Freedom	2007	110,000	2,974
Carnival Glory	2003	110,000	2,974
Carnival Legend	2002	88,500	2,124
Carnival Liberty	2005	110,000	2,974
Carnival Miracle	2004	88,500	2,124
Carnival Pride	2002	88,500	2,124
Carnival Spirit	2001	88,500	2,124
Carnival Triumph	1999	102,000	2,758
Carnival Valor	2004	110,000	2,974
Carnival Victory	2000	102,000	2,758
Celebration	1987/2000/03	47,262	1,486
Ecstasy	1991/2000	70,367	2,052
Elation	1998	70,367	2,052
Fantasy	1990/2000/2003	70,367	2,056
Fascination	1994	70,367	2,052
Holiday	1985/94/98/2000	46,052	1,452
Imagination	1995	70,367	2,052
Inspiration	1996	70,367	2,052
Paradise	1998	70,367	2,052
Sensation	1993	70,367	2,052

STYLE Youthful and casual, "Fun Ships" have so much action and diversions that the ship itself is the cruise experience. The emphasis on fun aims to get people out of their cabins and into public spaces to become part of the action. The variety of activity and entertainment attracts a range of passengers, but the basic appeal is to the young and young at heart—at reasonable prices.

An important part of creating Carnival has been Joe Farcus, an interior architect and decorator, unique in his role among the cruise lines. He believes people go on vacation to have fun, and his job is to create the surroundings and atmosphere for it. If you accept his flamboyant decor as entertaining, you will find it ingenious. But sometimes, so much bombards the senses that the impact is more exhausting than exhilarating.

Another characteristic: Perhaps more than any line, Carnival has standardized features on its ships. If you see a water slide on one ship, you can count on its being on the others. A menu with four desserts on one ship will be on others. Even deck names are the same. The uniformity helps keep down costs, and consistency is reassuring to passengers—and to their travel agents.

DISTINCTIVE FEATURES Ships' design and decor, children's programs, 24-hour pizzerias, free ice cream and yogurt stations, sushi bars fleetwide, steakhouse supper clubs; fitness centers, areas for topless sunbathing, tuxedo rentals, vacation guarantee, golf program, travelers' hotline; self-service digital photo printing kiosks; Internet cafes fleetwide; and stem-to-stern wireless Internet access on the newest ships.

	HIGHEST	LOWEST	AVERAGE
PER DIEM	$467	$125	$286

Per diems are calculated from cruise line's nondiscounted *cruise-only* published fares on standard accommodations and vary by season, cabins, and cruise areas.

RATES All include port fees.

Special fares and discounts Super Savers early-bird program provides discounts ranging from up to $860 per cabin on three-day cruises to $2,200 on seven-day cruises.

- **CHILDREN'S FARE:** Same as deeply discounted third/fourth person rates. Passengers younger than age 21 must be accompanied by a parent, grandparent, or legal guardian 25 years old or older in the cabin. Exceptions apply to married couples and to children traveling with parents in a separate cabin.
- **SINGLE SUPPLEMENT:** 150% or 200%, depending on category. Singles matching program.

Packages
- **CRUISE/AIR ADD-ON WITH TRANSFERS:** Yes.

- **PRE/POST:** Yes. Wedding and vow renewal packages in U.S. home ports and eight Caribbean ports year-round, plus Vancouver.
- **OTHERS:** Yes.

PAST PASSENGERS No club. After their first cruise, passengers receive a two-year free subscription to *Carnival Currents,* the line's onboard magazine, which includes discounts. A repeater's party is offered on five-day or longer cruises.

THE LAST WORD Carnival has had an enormous impact on cruises, particularly those aimed at the mass market. The line wrote the book on marketing. Yet despite its success, a Carnival cruise isn't for everybody. The ships have more glitter than glamour. Some people love them; others think they redefine tacky. For the generation that grew up with shopping malls and Las Vegas–style glitz, Carnival's gargantuan, flashy ships may feel like home. But if big and boisterous is not your style, Carnival is probably not for you. Yet everyone should take at least one Carnival cruise to see for themselves. The ships are eye-popping and the atmosphere infectious. Even the most staid, buttoned-down party poopers are often turned on by the Carnival neon and end up having the time of their lives.

Carnival Standard Features

Officers Italian.

Staff Dining/International; Cabin/Central American, Asian, others; Cruise/American and others.

Dining facilities Two main dining rooms/four seatings (except Spirit class, one dining room). Breakfast and lunch cafeteria-style and Seaview Bistro dinner service in lido restaurant; midnight buffet. Lido restaurant is four-in-one: pizzeria, Asian, trattoria, American grill; New York–style deli, sushi bars; steakhouse restaurants ($25 surcharge) on newest ships.

Special diets Low-salt, diabetic, vegetarian, low-carb.

Room service 24 hours, upgraded menu.

Dress code Casual; no shorts in evening; two formal nights on 7-day; tuxedos not required, semiformal dress is acceptable.

Cabin amenities Closed-circuit television; safe. Bath with shower; international direct-dial phones. Hair dryers on Destiny and Spirit class; other ships on request. Terry robes in all outside cabins.

Electrical outlets 110 AC.

Wheelchair access 14–27 cabins, depending on ship.

Recreation and entertainment Casino, bingo, disco, library; 10 bar/lounges (16 on Spirit class; 18 Destiny class; 22 Conquest class); two-deck show lounges (three-deck on Destiny, Conquest, and Spirit classes).

Carnival Standard Features (continued)

Sports and other activities Three or four outside swimming pools, shuffle-board, jogging tracks (Fantasy, Destiny, Spirit classes), table tennis.

Beauty and fitness Barber/beauty salon, sauna. Spas on all ships; full gym, exercise classes, body treatments. Spa fare on menus.

Other facilities Boutiques, tuxedo rentals, infirmary, video of cruise souvenir ($39), and coin-operated laundry facilities; Internet cafes fleetwide.

Children's facilities Camp Carnival, year-round, with supervised activities for toddlers to teens. Video arcades, water slides, playroom, teen club/disco, children's menus, high chairs. Baby-sitting, 10 p.m.–3 a.m., $6 per hour for first child, $4 for each additional child in same family; children under age 2 also welcome. Passengers under age 21 must be accompanied by adult older than age 25 in same cabin.

Theme cruises Some.

Smoking Smoke-free dining room, main show lounge, and selected lounges.

Carnival suggested tipping $10 per person, per day added automatically to passenger's on-board account, which can also be prepaid when booking the cruise. Otherwise, $3.50 for waiter, $2 busboy; $3.60 cabin steward, per person, per day; 15% added to wine and bar bill.

Credit cards Cruise and shipboard charges: American Express, MasterCard, Visa, Discover, Optima.

Ecstasy/Fantasy	**QUALITY 4**	**VALUE B**
Elation	**QUALITY 5**	**VALUE B**
Fascination/Imagination	**QUALITY 6**	**VALUE A**
Inspiration	**QUALITY 6**	**VALUE A**
Paradise	**QUALITY 7**	**VALUE A**
Sensation	**QUALITY 4**	**VALUE B**
REGISTRY *Ecstasy/Elation/ Fantasy/Paradise* **Panama;** *Fascination/Imagination/ Inspiration/Sensation* **Bahamas**	**LENGTH** 855 feet	**BEAM** 118 feet
CABINS 1,026/1,028	**DRAFT** 26 feet	**SPEED** 21 knots
MAXIMUM PASSENGERS 2,610/2,606	**PASSENGER DECKS** 10	**ELEVATORS** 14
	CREW 920	**SPACE RATIO** 34

THE SHIPS Billed as ships for the 21st century, Carnival's eight megaliners were already dazzling passengers of the 1990s. Their flashy decor and high-energy ambience are Las Vegas, Disneyland, and Starlight Express all in one. Atrium lobbies ascend seven decks at the heart of the ship and contain huge, specially commissioned art. Throughout the vessels, there are so many imaginatively decorated bars, lounges, and entertainment and recreation outlets that they can't be absorbed in one cruise. On these ships, the senses work overtime.

Except for decor—each ship is themed—the vessels are identical, and as with all Carnival ships, even the deck names are the same. The *Fantasy*, first of the group, is dazzling with its towering atrium awash in lights. Here and in the entertainment areas, 15 miles of computerized lights are programmed to change color—constantly but subtly—from white to cool blue to hot red, altering the ambience with each change. *Fantasy* was given a multimillion-dollar refurbishing in 2000, and meeting facilities and a brand-new promenade were added. All the ships in the group are being refurbished during their annual drydock stay.

The second megaliner, *Ecstasy,* is designed as a city at sea. Carnival-watchers declared her the fleet's most elegant and sophisticated vessel, reflecting an effort to upgrade the style. But there's no mistaking this for anything but a Carnival ship. *Ecstasy's* decor takes inspiration from Manhattan's cafe society, showcasing exotic woods, Italian marbles, rich carpets, sumptuous fabrics, and a vintage Rolls Royce on the lounge-lined City Lights Boulevard. The promenade's highlights are the **Neon Bar,** a piano bar with vintage neon signs, and **Chinatown Lounge**, guarded by huge lion-headed Foo dogs.

Sensation, third in the series, resembles *Ecstasy* with decor slightly more sophisticated than her mates'. Light, sound, and color create a "sensual" environment. Public rooms range from elegant to kitschy. Among them, the **Touch of Class Lounge** is a "hands-on" experience, with gigantic hands cupping the entrance, hands supporting tables, and chairs and bar stools shaped like hands.

Fascination takes Hollywood of the 1930s, 1940s, and 1950s as its theme, mixing homage and spoofs—and kitsch galore. On the entertainment promenade, Hollywood Boulevard, are **Puttin' on the Ritz Lounge**, **Bogey's Café,** and the **Passage to India Lounge.** But the show-stoppers are 20 life-sized mannequins of movie legends posed as they might be in real life. At the **Stars Bar,** you find Gary Cooper and Rita Hayworth, and in the **Tara Library,** Vivien Leigh and Clark Gable. Purple neon dramatically edges each of the seven decks rising from the Grand Atrium's lobby, which is centered by an enormous sculpture, *Nucleus,* by British artist Susanna Holt.

Architect Joe Farcus's fertile imagination worked overtime creating the decor of the bars and lounges for *Imagination*. Images of space ships, space stations, and other futuristic technologies are incorporated into four rotating towers of stainless steel and clear plastic that are the centerpiece of *Imagination's* atrium. The 24-foot sculpture by Len Janklow is among commissioned works from five artists whose imaginations carried them from seascapes to mythical tales of ancient lands.

The ship's 24-hour pizzeria is now a feature on all Carnival ships. Favorite nightspots include **Shangri-La,** for music and dancing, and **Mirage,** a sing-along piano bar.

Farcus's concept for the *Inspiration* was drawn from the arts. Decor incorporates musical icons, themes, and motifs—from a larger-than-life replica of Elvis's guitar in the disco to the elegant **Chopin Lounge** and its piano. The ship offers the Fantasy group's multideck, glass-domed atrium and dramatic centerpiece, a promenade of lounges and bars, and sports and recreation features.

Elation boasts significant improvements over her Fantasy sisters and incorporates some of the best design elements, including the atrium lobby bar copied from *Carnival Destiny* and now a feature of many Fantasy-class ships. *Elation* was the first cruise ship with the Azipod propulsion system, which dramatically reduces engine noise and vibration. The system pulls rather than pushes the ship, eliminating the need for rudders or stern thrusters and increasing maneuverability and fuel efficiency.

Elation, the most sophisticated of the Fantasy-class ships, has a broader appeal than her older, glitzier sisters, although there is still plenty of glitter. *Elation's* theme is the mythological Muses. The ship's noticeably more elegant decor uses copper tones and inlaid woods. Prisms and fiber-optic lights create subtle lighting and mood changes. Among new features were a sushi bar, Carnival's largest children's center, a patisserie and coffee bar, a redesigned lido cafe area, a casino bar, and a conference center.

The eighth member of the group, *Paradise* was the world's first and only smoke-free cruise ship with a bright red no-smoking emblem painted on the hull. But when the ship was home ported on the West Coast, this distinction was dropped. Your first view on boarding *Paradise* is likely to be the atrium, centered by a large circular bar—a feature copied from *Carnival Destiny,* where it has been very popular. Immediately, you notice foot-tall Fabergé-like eggs. Used in decor throughout the ship, they have tiny lights to suggest the diamonds and rubies on Fabergé originals. From the bar, a stairway decorated with three kinds of wood winds upward to the Atlantic Deck, where every lounge recalls maritime history. *Paradise* immortalizes famous steamships in maritime history and evokes the era when travelers boarded famous vessels en route to foreign lands.

ITINERARIES *See* Itinerary Index.

CABINS As with all Carnival ships, the 12 cabin categories include some of the largest standard cabins and junior suites of any ship in their price category. They are finished in light oak, and although color schemes vary among ships, the furniture and decor are essentially the same—basic and comfortable.

Almost all cabins have twin beds that convert to king-size—a Carnival innovation quickly copied by other cruise lines.

Cabins have international direct-dial phones; a desk/dressing table; television with channels for movies, cartoons, and satellite programs (depending on ship's location); stereo music; and wall safes. Outside cabins have picture windows. Bathrooms are well-designed and have roomy shower stalls. They have soap and some toiletries; hair dryers are available on request. Closet space is adequate for short, warm-weather cruises. All ships have self-service laundry rooms with washers, dryers, irons, and ironing boards—a big plus for families traveling with children.

Specifications 389 inside cabins, 564 outside; 54 suites with verandas (28 suites with bathtub Jacuzzi). Standard dimensions, 183–190 square feet; 953 with twins convertible to doubles; 19 inside with upper and lower berths; no singles. All ships have wheelchair-accessible cabins.

DINING Each ship has two dining rooms with two seatings for breakfast and lunch, and four seatings for dinner at 5:45 p.m., 6:15 p.m., 8 p.m., and 8:30 p.m. The rooms are on an upper deck and have large windows with good views.

Restaurants have round tables for eight people in the center of the room; the sides are lined with rectangular tables, which are sometimes difficult to get in and out of. The *Ecstasy's* **Wind Star** and **Wind Song** and *Elation's* **Imagination** and **Inspiration** dining rooms get more kudos for stylish decor than their older sisters. All earn criticism for high noise levels. The ships no longer have wine stewards; wine is served by waiters often unfamiliar with the selections.

Breakfast, lunch and midnight buffet are served cafeteria-style on the Lido Deck. *Fantasy's* **Windows on the Sea** is one of the group's most attractive restaurants, with pastel parasols, brass highlights, and etched glass. On the *Ecstasy*, the **Panorama Bar and Grill** has floor-to-ceiling windows and a playful ambience with signal flags and blue neon lighting. *Fascination's* **Coconut Grove Bar and Grille** has imitation palm trees as columns and a bamboo bar and tables.

Seaview Bistros, an alternative casual dinner service available fleetwide, offers specialty salads, pastas, steaks, and desserts in a cafe setting. They operate each evening from 6–9:30 p.m. in the lido restaurant. Tablecloths, preset silverware, and flowers on tables set the tone. Service is buffet-style, but waiters refill drink orders and food requests. Another winner is the around-the-clock pizzeria, offering delicious pizzas with varied toppings, fresh Caesar salads, and warm garlic rolls. *Paradise, Elation, Imagination, Inspiration,* and *Jubilee* have sushi bars.

Carnival initially was not known for its cuisine, but recent efforts to upgrade the quality, selection, and variety have yielded outstanding results. The line now offers menus fleetwide with lighter, more contemporary cuisine and an expanded wine list. A typical dinner menu offers three juices; four appetizers; three soups; two salads; two fish choices; three entrees of beef, chicken, or turkey; five desserts; and a variety of ice cream and sherbet, cheese, and beverages. At least one item per course is marked as spa fare, which has lower calories, sodium, fat, and cholesterol.

SERVICE Dining staff generally earn good marks, but cabin attendants get mixed reviews. Cruise directors and their staff are very professional, but the cruise director on ships of this size is in little evidence except when he or she is on stage. Recent passengers on *Fantasy* reported that contacting their room steward or the purser's desk by phone was nearly impossible. They also complained that they encountered orientation problems on boarding. Rather than being escorted to their cabins, they were handed ship diagrams and directed to find their cabins on their own. The bottom line: Megaliners offer many wonderful facilities and options, but personal service is not among them.

FACILITIES AND ACTIVITIES The ships' array of activities include bingo, a singles party, a newlywed game, a passenger talent show, horse racing, bridge, ballroom and country line-dance classes, masquerades, wine and cheese parties, and sing-alongs. There are tours of the galleys and bridge, first-run movies daily, and abundant boutiques. The library/lounge—especially the mahogany-paneled **Explorer's Club** on *Ecstasy*—is one of the loveliest rooms in the Carnival fleet.

The Fantasy group's most distinctive feature is an indoor promenade that serves as an "entertainment boulevard" of bars, lounges, disco, casino, and nightclubs. Called the Century Boulevard on the *Fantasy,* the promenade has the **Cats Lounge,** with decor inspired by the long-running Broadway show, and **Cleopatra's,** a piano bar with every conceivable cliche in ancient Egyptian art.

At one end of the boulevard, the spectacular, two-deck **Universal** show lounge stages nightly entertainment on the scale of a Las Vegas extravaganza. It's outstanding. At the stern is the opulent **Majestic Bar**, with a king's ransom in marble and onyx. Through the bar is the flamboyant **Crystal Lounge,** where red and white lights nearly blind you. Here you can catch the naughty comedy acts. The casinos, each with over 200 slot machines, blackjack tables, roulette, and other games, are among the largest afloat.

The most amusing place on the *Fascination's* nighttime array is **Club 88,** a piano bar named for the 88 keys on a piano and decorated with huge, neon-lit keys at the door and on the columns between piano-shaped tables. At the **Passage to India Lounge,** two life-size elephant figures are a prelude to the interior draped with elaborate Indian ceremonial cloth. Furnishings include British colonial-style mahogany chairs, a statue of a multi-armed Hindu deity, a domed shrine holding a Buddha, mosaic ceiling tiles, and floral carpets. The **Puttin' on the Ritz**

Lounge, with decor inspired by Fred Astaire's top hat, offers late-night comedy acts and a vocalist.

Fascination's **Palace Lounge,** in shimmering golden beige and silvery pink with painted clouds decorating the walls, had the most technologically advanced stage at sea when she was introduced.

On the *Sensation,* the popular **Michelangelo Lounge** combines soft gray, yellow, and black in its furnishings and uses classic features, such as Ionic columns, Greek designs, and ceiling frescoes. The bar and dance floor are marble. The **Polo Lounge** was designed for those seeking a quiet spot—all the ships have at least one such lounge.

The *Elation's* **Mikado** showroom (named after the Gilbert and Sullivan operetta) strikes a Japanese theme with large fans, rice paper shoji screen walls, Japanese-motif upholstery, and gold-leaf bamboo and chrysanthemum designs sandblasted onto black fossil stone walls and tables. **Duke's** piano bar evokes Manhattan in the Jazz Age, paying tribute to Duke Ellington. Decor includes replicas of famous New York sights. A bar encircles a white baby grand piano on a turntable. The **Jekyll and Hyde Dance Club** has eight-foot-tall sculptures of Robert Louis Stevenson's fictional character with split faces, meant to convey benevolence and malice. The heads swivel to the music's tempo, and monitors set into the sculptures show live pictures of dancing guests and music videos.

On the *Paradise,* all public rooms are named for ocean liners. The **Blue Riband Library,** namesake of the international prize awarded for the fastest transatlantic crossing, pays tribute to the ships of yore in miniature models and old photographs. It contains a full-scale reproduction of the gold and onyx Hales Trophy, models of ships that won the prize, and memorabilia, including a signed photo of the duke and duchess of Windsor on Cunard's *Queen Elizabeth*.

In eye-popping contrast, the **America Bar** across from the library is named for the *SS America* and all but screams U.S.A. with its red, white, and blue color scheme, starred carpet, and stars and stripes on the walls. At the stern, the 1,300-seat, two-story **Normandie** show lounge carries an Art Deco theme and celebrates the French liner considered by some to be the best ship ever built. Another showroom, the **Queen Mary Lounge,** uses funnels from the great ship as the motif to line the bar and walls, frame the seats, and serve as table bases. From the Italian liner *Rex,* Farcus took the Latin meaning of rex (king) and conjured up the king of the jungle, giving the **Rex Dance Club** a jungle theme.

SPORTS AND FITNESS Three swimming pools (one with a slide), Ping-Pong, shuffleboard, and volleyball are available, and pool games are staged almost daily. On Caribbean and Mexican cruises, depending on ports, you can play golf, sail, ride horseback, bike, hike, snorkel, scuba dive, and windsurf.

The sports deck has a fully equipped gym with trained instructors, separate locker rooms, dressing rooms, showers for men and women, six whirlpools, saunas, and steam rooms. Or one can choose from an array of exercise and aerobics classes, and a 500-foot outside jogging track—all included in the cruise price. Instructors will also create a fitness regimen for you to follow at home. All Carnival ships have a secluded deck area for topless sunbathing.

Carnival's golf program provides play at 50 courses in the Bahamas, Caribbean, Hawaii, Europe, and Mexico. It offers one-on-one, 30- or 60-minute instruction from PGA teaching pros aboard ship and on golf excursions. Shipboard lessons are in a netted driving range where golfers' swings are videotaped and computer-analyzed. A take-home video with voice-over instruction and stop-action/slow-motion analysis is provided with each lesson. Golf packages include greens fees, instruction, cart rental or caddie, and transportation to and from courses. Prices range from $50 for on-board lessons to $225 for golf excursions. Equipment rentals include Callaway clubs and Adidas "soft spike" golf shoes.

SPA AND BEAUTY The beauty salon and spa, operated by the Steiner Group, a British-based company, has nine private rooms for body and facial treatments—including facials, pedicures, massage, and herbal packs. Any of them can become an expensive indulgence. The spas on all ships in the group are being expanded.

CHILDREN'S FACILITIES Camp Carnival, which handles 400,000 kids fleetwide annually, is a year-round program with a wide array of activities supervised by trained counselors for children in four age groups: Toddlers (ages 2–5), Juniors (ages 6–8), Intermediate (ages 9–12), and Teens (ages 13–16). Young children enjoy puppet making, finger painting, and learning the alphabet and numbers; older kids have pizza parties, scavenger hunts, and lip-synch contests and play bingo, charades, and Twister. Teens have activities ranging from disco parties and star search contests to evening deck parties. All ships have video arcades, wading pools, water slides, playrooms (two on Fantasy class), teens' club/discos, children's menus, and high chairs.

One playroom is designed for kids ages 6–11 and is stocked with age-appropriate toys, games, and puzzles, including such popular pastimes as air hockey, foosball, and "pop-a-shot" basketball, along with the latest video games. The other playroom is geared toward toddlers.

Elation and *Paradise* have among Carnival's largest children's facilities. The 2,500-square-foot **Children's World** is divided into three sections. One features an educational computer lab and computer games. The arts and crafts section has spin art, sand art, jewelry-making machines, easels for painting and drawing, and a gallery for displaying participants' creations. The third is an indoor play area with a climbing maze, toys, games, and a video wall where kids can watch movies, music videos, and cartoons. The outdoor play area has a schooner-shaped playhouse and a wading pool for toddlers. Teens get special attention, too, with **Virtual World,** photography workshops, late-night movies, and disco parties.

The latest additions include a youth fitness and spa program, introduced on *Carnival Miracle* and now featured fleetwide, allowing kids ages 12–14 and their parents to have body and beauty treatments together on port days at discounted rates. Also new is "ExerSeas," a recreational fitness program designed to encourage kids to enjoy a diversity of fun physical activity from obstacle courses and basketball to popular games. "A-B-Seas" is a new reading program in which the youth counselors read popular children's books to parents and kids in the ships' libraries, followed by parents and kids presenting their own creative interpretations of the stories through puppet shows, skits, and other group activities. A new science program, H2Ocean, offers a variety of fun, hands-on science projects, allowing kids to make their own ice cream or miniature hovercrafts. The EduCruise program has been expanded to include more interactive projects focusing on the cultures, landmarks, history, and geography of the ships' destinations. Kid-friendly dining options include special children's menus in the main dining rooms and a program that enables kids to dine with the youth counselors on Lido Deck. Recently, the line added new teen shore excursions and "Action Alley" teen clubs on Conquest-class ships.

Camp Carnival operates 9 a.m.–10 p.m. At 10 p.m., baby-sitting in the form of slumber parties in the children's playrooms becomes available through the purser's office for $6 per hour for the first child, $4 for each additional child. Carnival has a "Fountain Fun-Card" for those younger than age 21, good for unlimited sodas from the bars (the card is $9 on a 3-day cruise, $30 on an 11-day cruise).

SHORE EXCURSIONS   Recently, Carnival has tried to provide greater variety. Nonetheless, dockside in almost all Caribbean ports are plenty of vans with driver/guides eager for your business and ready to design a tour to your liking. Prices depend on your ability to bargain and the driver's eagerness, but always agree on a fee before the tour begins.

An air/sea package is recommended for cruises departing from Port Canaveral combined with Orlando attractions because the Orlando International Airport, where most passengers arrive, is about an hour's drive from Port Canaveral, where the ships depart. There is no public transportation between the two; those traveling on their own must hire a taxi or rent a car. Or, those booking "cruise-only" can buy Carnival's transfer package. Also, if you buy the Orlando package, plan to take the Spaceport USA bus tour on the day you sail. That way, the full morning can be spent at Spaceport USA, about 20 minutes from Port Canaveral. A late lunch is available aboard ship until 3:30 p.m. In Alaska, the line offers excursions for teens, along with nearly 100 tours for all ages.

Carnival Destiny	**QUALITY 8**	**VALUE A**
Carnival Triumph	**QUALITY 8**	**VALUE A**
Carnival Victory	**QUALITY 8**	**VALUE A**
REGISTRY *Destiny*/*Triumph* Bahamas; *Victory* Panama	**LENGTH** 893 feet	**BEAM** 125 feet
CABINS 1,321/1,379	**DRAFT** 27 feet	**SPEED** 22.5 knots
MAXIMUM PASSENGERS 3,400/3,470	**PASSENGER DECKS** 12	**ELEVATORS** 18
	CREW 1,050/1,100	**SPACE RATIO** 37/38

THE SHIPS The *Carnival Destiny* was the largest cruise ship ever built when she made her debut in 1996 and was the first one too wide to transit the Panama Canal. When the ship was being planned six years earlier, Carnival employees were asked to submit their wish lists for enhancing the new vessel. Apparently, they got most of their wishes.

The *Destiny* had Carnival's first double-deck dining room; a show lounge spanning three decks; a double-width promenade lined with lounges and bars; a mall-style shopping area; a 9,000-square-foot casino; 18 bars and lounges; four swimming pools and an expansive spa; a retractable glass dome over the pool area; and sports and recreation facilities similar to the Fantasy-class ships. The pool area has a stage for entertainment and teak decks cantilevered in an amphitheater. **Virtual World** is a high-tech virtual reality game center.

Destiny's configuration was a departure for Carnival at the time. Entertainment and recreation decks are between accommodations decks. The two lowest passenger decks have only cabins, followed by three decks of public rooms, then five decks of cabins and suites with balconies. To avoid big rooms and long corridors that would make the ship's huge size obvious, public rooms span two or three levels. The layout is often confusing, however.

Despite her size—nearly three football fields in length—*Destiny* does not seem as large from the inside as some of her Fantasy-class cousins. This is primarily because of the layout and the decor, which is softer and toned down—sometimes even tony—a change from Farcus's flamboyant creations on other Carnival ships.

The Rotunda (Capital Lobby on *Triumph*; Seven Seas Atrium on *Victory*), a nine-deck atrium with four glass elevators and a glass dome, is the ship's focal point. An enormous marble and onyx mural of geometric forms suggesting skyscrapers decorates the walls. The atrium has an attractive lobby bar at its base, creating a meeting place that helps humanize the huge space.

The *Carnival Triumph*, which debuted in 1999, builds on *Destiny's* success but incorporates new features. Sixty percent of cabins have ocean views with a sitting area, and more than 60% of those have verandas. The ship celebrates the world's great cities, with such venues as **Underground Tokyo** video arcade, the **Rome Theater, Vienna Café** coffee bar, and **Oxford Bar**. A huge golden globe dominates the atrium; it's inlaid with glittering fiber optics that mark the world's metropolises. Smaller globes are part of the decor shipwide. The new Panorama Deck, one level above the Lido Deck, has 42 ocean-view cabins, most with verandas, and 24 inside ones, adding capacity for 132 guests. *Carnival Victory,* whose theme is the seven seas, arrived in August 2000.

ITINERARIES *See* Itinerary Index.

CABINS The group's standard cabins are the largest and the most attractively furnished in the Carnival fleet. All have hair dryers and safes; some have interactive television. Cabin numbers pinpoint your deck and location (forward, aft, or midship). Each section has its own elevators. Sixty percent of standard outside cabins have small balconies, all with clear panels for unobstructed ocean views. Unfortunately, they do nothing to absorb sound. This and insufficient soundproofing make the cabins noisy. Particularly to be avoided are cabins on Deck 6 forward, which are directly above lounges that operate most of the night. Ocean-view cabins have a sitting area with sofa and coffee table. Veranda cabins create a new category of standard cabins for Carnival that, although larger, are comparable in price to standard outside accommodations on Fantasy-class ships. Family cabins are near the children's play facilities.

Specifications 515 inside cabins, 432 outside with verandas; 48 suites with verandas, some with bathtub whirlpools. Standard dimensions, 220–260 square feet; all cabins with twins convertible to kings; 4 inside with upper and lower berths; no singles; 25 *Destiny,* 27 *Triumph, Victory* wheelchair-accessible cabins.

DINING Carnival's first bilevel dining rooms feel roomy, and the additional space allows wider separation between tables. But the restaurants are noisy. Both dining rooms enjoy ocean views.

The two-deck **Sun & Sea** (**South Beach Club** on *Triumph*; **Mediterranean** on *Victory*), the casual lido restaurant, is dressed in shades of green with yellow, hand-blown Murano glass and hand-painted ceramic tile decorating walls and countertops. Different settings create dining options: Trattoria for pasta and made-to-order Italian dishes; Happy Valley for Chinese cuisine, stir-fried to order; and The Grille for hamburgers and hot dogs. Service has also been upgraded; waiters carry dishes and beverages to tables. The **Seaview Bistro** alternative dinner service in the lido restaurant offers specialty salads, pastas, steaks, and desserts—plus a daily special—in a cafe setting. The bistro operates 6–9:30 p.m. each evening. Also open are a 24-hour pizzeria and, on the promenade deck, a patisserie appointed with cherry wood counters and windowed banquettes. *Carnival Victory* has a New York–style deli. In 2004, Carnival introduced low-carb menu items, with each dish's carb grams designated on menus.

FACILITIES AND ACTIVITIES   In the evening, you are likely to run out of energy before you run out of choices. The flashy **Millionaire's Club** (**Club Monaco** on *Triumph*; **South China Sea Club** on *Victory*), said to be the largest casino afloat, has 321 slot machines and 23 table games. In the lavishly decorated **Apollo Bar,** the piano revolves, enabling the pianist to shine a spotlight on anyone eager to test the microphone on each table.

At the whimsically decorated **Downbeat,** where a 20-foot trumpet and French horn are suspended above the bandstand, patrons sit on clarinet-shaped barstools or at glass tables supported by oversized sections of horns.

In the **Point After Dance Club,** tricolor neon lights snake across the ceiling above a bilevel floor, and over 500 video monitors flash pictures and computer-generated graphics around the room. A staircase by the dance floor leads to the elegant **Onyx Room,** a more sedate club where backlit alabaster panels glow softly beside a neon and glass dance floor.

The three-deck **Palladium** show lounge is one of the most technologically sophisticated afloat. The additional deck below seating levels allows the orchestra pit to be retracted, and the space above enables backdrops, lighting equipment, and performers to be "flown" offstage via cables. A Venetian glass chandelier hangs from the dome; at show time, it goes high-tech with fiber optics.

To achieve three decks of seats for 1,500 people, some sacrifices were made. The main floor is almost level, making viewing more difficult the farther back one sits. Also, balcony rails partially block some views. The big production shows are top-notch.

Yet more entertainment is offered in **Virtual World,** a game center with virtual reality and electronic games, and **All Star Bar,** decorated with celebrity memorabilia, including tables bearing autographs of sports stars, and featuring seven big-screen televisions broadcasting sporting events.

SPORTS, FITNESS, AND BEAUTY   The *Destiny* has four pools, including a children's pool, and seven whirlpools. One has Carnival's trademark water slide—but here, it is three decks tall and 214 feet long. A retractable dome covers the aft pool.

The 14,500-square-foot spa and health club is on two levels, one with a beauty salon, massage rooms, whirlpools, and sauna and steam rooms, the other with an aerobics room. The spa offers hydrotherapy baths, aromatherapy, and other body treatments. There is also a "Nouveau Yu Health Environment Capsule," an egglike temperature-controlled capsule designed to induce relaxation. The gym has an array of equipment, including bikes, treadmills, step and rowing equipment, and 16 Keiser or Life-Fitnessmachines. Instructors lead exercise classes and can be hired as personal trainers. An eighth-mile jogging track is on the sun deck. On the *Triumph,* more open space was provided on the Lido Deck for deck chairs, and the forward and aft pools were enlarged and bordered by "wading" areas.

CHILDREN'S FACILITIES The two-deck-tall, 1,300-square-foot indoor and outdoor play center includes a jungle gym and pool. See the *Fantasy* profile for information on Carnival's children's program.

Carnival Legend	QUALITY 8	VALUE A
Carnival Miracle	QUALITY 8	VALUE A
Carnival Pride	QUALITY 8	VALUE A
Carnival Spirit	QUALITY 8	VALUE A
REGISTRY Panama	LENGTH 963 feet	BEAM 105.7 feet
CABINS 1,062	DRAFT 25.7 feet	SPEED 22 knots
MAXIMUM PASSENGERS 2,667	PASSENGER DECKS 12	ELEVATORS 15
	CREW 930	SPACE RATIO 40

THE SHIPS *Carnival Spirit,* the first of a new class of ships for Carnival, entered service in 2001, followed by triplets: *Carnival Pride* and *Carnival Legend* in 2002, and *Carnival Miracle* in 2004. They are among the longest ships in the Carnival fleet, but they still can pass through the Panama Canal. The ships have a number of environmentally friendly technical enhancements, and their technologically advanced Azipod propulsion system enables them to reach a maximum speed of 24 knots, and thus sail on innovative itineraries. The ships boast an exceptional space ratio of 40 (the Fantasy class is 34, Destiny class 37) with the usual array of Carnival amenities and facilities, and some new ones, such as the first Carnival ships with a wedding chapel, and more recently, self-service digital photo printing kiosks, now available fleetwide.

The theme of *Carnival Spirit* is design, particularly architectural design (which makes for an eclectic mix of decor), while that of *Carnival Pride* is icons of beauty which gave Farcus's active mind neverending inspiration—from architecture and artistic masterpieces to athletic achievement and the human body. The beauty icons start with Renaissance inspiration in the atrium lobby, elevator, and stairwell areas, where huge reproductions of murals by Botticelli, Raphäel, and other Italian painters adorn the walls. Here, too, the craftsmanship of the Italian Renaissance is reflected in rich details of wood and bronze moldings, and it's dominated by gold, sienna, and burnt-red tones.

The ships' interior promenade meanders through public rooms on two consecutive decks, linking the ship's two atriums with its dining rooms, more than a dozen bars, lounges and entertainment venues, and a shopping arcade that includes a tuxedo rental and flower shop. The ships also have a wraparound outdoor promenade on Atlantic Deck—the first for a Carnival ship in two decades. All the Spirit- and Conquest-class ships have an upscale supper club located atop a towering 11-deck-high atrium, and a large percentage of balconied cabins. They have a two-level dining room; large poolside food courts offering casual breakfast, lunch, and dinner; a 24-hour pizzeria; and a sushi bar. There are 16 lounges, ranging from an elaborate, multilevel showroom for Vegas-style revues, to an intimate piano bar, a casino, shopping mall, wedding chapel, video game room, and Internet cafe. There are several swimming pools—including one with a spiral water slide, a spa and gym, a "Camp Carnival" program for kids ages 2–15, and a comprehensive golf program.

Carnival Legend's motif is inspired by great legends of history, from the ancient Greeks in the atrium, to modern jazz in the New Orleans design of **Satchmo's Club,** and the Art Deco of **Billie's Piano Bar,** named for blues legend Billie Holiday. *Carnival Miracle* has fictional characters as its theme—but Harry Potter is not among them. *Carnival Miracle* has Tampa as her home port year-round.

CABINS The ships have several levels of suites with private balconies and have set a new standard for outside cabins, 80% of which have private balconies. Many cabins can accommodate up to four guests; other are interconnecting and are ideal for large families.

Specifications 213 inside cabins, 99 outside, 624 outside with balconies, 68 with French doors; 52 suites, 6 penthouse. 16 wheelchair-accessible.

DINING Each ship has three restaurants. *Pride's* **Normandie Restaurant** (**Empire** on *Spirit;* **Golden Fleece** on *Legend*), spanning two decks with wraparound windows, has elegant decor based on the famous ocean-liner *Normandie,* one of the most beautiful passenger vessel ever built.

Spirit's unusual **Nouveau Supper Club,** Carnival's first alternative restaurant (reservations only; $25 charge), is situated topside with one end bordering the ship's huge red-glass smokestack and the other extending out over the top of the ship's multideck atrium. Menu specialties are prime aged beef, seafood, and other gourmet selections. The restaurant's counterpart on the *Pride* is **David's Supper Club,** with a full-size replica of the famous Michelangelo sculpture, *David,* celebrating the beauty of the human body.

The **Mermaids' Grille,** the ship's lido restaurant, has a variety of food stations, each offering a different type of cuisine and including a pizzeria. It is open almost around the clock.

FACILITIES AND ACTIVITIES The ships seem to have a dance floor at every turn. From the **Beauties Dance Club** to the **Starry Night** jazz club and the grand **Taj Mahal** show lounge. On the *Pride,* a famous Van Gogh painting was the inspiration for the Starry Night jazz club (**Club Cool** on

Spirit). The beauty of ideas and intellectual achievement is enshrined in the **Nobel Library,** with a portrait of Alfred Nobel who created the famous prize. The room also houses the Internet cafe. The beauty of experience is represented in the **Perfect Game** sports bar and the **Winner's Club** casino. **Butterflies Lounge** draws on natural beauty with faux windows decorated with colorful transparent fabrics that resemble butterfly wings which disappear under special lights to illuminate the flocks of butterflies behind. Four different butterfly patterns are seen in the upholstery. Architectural beauty is celebrated in the Taj Mahal show lounge (**Pharaoh's Palace** on *Spirit*) filled with intricate Indian designs and stonework sparkling with small jewels pressed into decorative designs. Infrared listening devices for hearing-impaired passengers are available in the main lounge on most Spirit-class ships.

Other highlights include a chapel suitable for weddings or religious services, ice cream/frozen yogurt bar, and a large conference center.

SPORTS, FITNESS, AND BEAUTY The ships' **Spa Carnival** is a two-level health and fitness facility, along with huge open decks and three swimming pools, one with a two-deck-high water slide plus a children's wading pool. One of the pools is heated and has a sliding glass roof, known as a magrodome—ideal for Alaska, where *Carnival Spirit* spends her summers. A golf program, managed by Elite Golf Cruises of Florida, includes private lessons, digital teaching technology, and packages for shoreside play with priority tee times starts; it's $49 for excursions and $80 for a one-hour lesson and video. Equipment rental is available for an additional fee. Advance reservations can be made at ☎ 800-324-1106 or **www.carnivalgolf.com.**

CHILDREN'S FACILITIES A variety of new and expanded family-friendly amenities have been added to the fleetwide Camp Carnival and include choices from fun, educational geography classes and candy-making machines to special family activities on a private island, teens-only shore excursions, and "just-for-kids" port lectures. **Fun Club,** located forward on Upper Deck 5 and decorated with a colorful undersea motif, is divided into three areas, connected by a series of tunnels. The first area houses an arts and crafts center, the second has a computer lab, and the third has a play room stocked with toys and games, a video wall displaying movies and cartoons, and kid-sized tables and chairs. An outdoor play area has a mini-basketball hoop and other playground equipment. **Real Virtuality,** a high-tech game room housing video and arcade games, is one deck below the Fun Club.

A turndown service offering freshly baked chocolate chip cookies on formal nights is available. So too is the fleetwide Fountain Fun Card, a soft drink program for unlimited sodas, costing from $9 for three-day cruises to $20 for seven-day cruises for those under age 21 (21 and over, $15 and $30 respectively); and there are kids' menus. Baby-sitting is available 10 p.m.–3 a.m. in the children's play room for $6 per hour for the first child and $4 for each additional child in the same family. Strollers are available for rent at $6 per day and $25 for the week.

Carnival Conquest	QUALITY 8	VALUE A
Carnival Freedom	2007	
Carnival Glory	QUALITY 8	VALUE A
Carnival Liberty	(PREVIEW)	
Carnival Valor	(PREVIEW)	
REGISTRY Panama	LENGTH 952 feet	BEAM 116 feet
CABINS 1,486	DRAFT 27 feet	SPEED 22.5 knots
MAXIMUM PASSENGERS 3,700	PASSENGER DECKS 13	ELEVATORS 15
	CREW 1,160	SPACE RATIO 37

THE SHIPS *Carnival Conquest,* which made her debut in New Orleans in 2002, kicked off delivery of the largest class of vessels in the fleet. She also was the first to have her interior decor tied directly to her home port. Using the ship's interiors as a huge canvas, designer Joe Farcus created something of an ode to Impressionist and post-Impressionist art and the Big Easy's French legacy.

The main atrium, called the **Atelier,** has Impressionist paintings on the central ceiling dome and wall; the **Artists' Lobby** is dominated by a large hand-painted mural collage of famous paintings. The collage effect is picked up in the promenade and in other public areas throughout the ship.

Her sister ship, *Carnival Glory,* which arrived in July 2003, takes colors as a theme, with each public room done in different shades of the rainbow and reflected in their name and decor. The kaleidoscope of colors begins in the Colors lobby, **Color Bar,** and the main atrium, named **Old Glory** after the United States flag. Each deck was given a different color; looking up through the atrium, it's easy to see the color definition of each deck. The **Kaleidoscope Boulevard** has one-square-meter light fixtures subdivided into geometric modules that are backlit with strips of color. The result is thousands of different tones in a slow-moving kaleidoscope.

Carnival Valor, inspired by its name, has heroes and heroism—real and imagined—as its theme. *Carnival Liberty* was launched in July 2005, debuting the line's first Mediterranean summer with 12-day cruises round-trip from Rome (Civitavecchia). In November 2005, she will introduce Carnival's first six- and eight-day cruises from Fort Lauderdale.

Like her sister ships, both *Valor* and *Liberty* have 22 lounges and bars, four swimming pools, a 214-foot-long water slide, an Internet cafe, a

13,300-square-foot health club, a comprehensive golf program, and four restaurants, including an upscale reservations-only supper club, two bilevel main dining rooms, a sushi bar, a patisserie, and a 1,200-seat casual poolside restaurant.

Carnival Valor also scored a first—the first cruise ship to offer 100% stem-to-stern wireless Internet access, enabling passengers to surf the net from every public room, the pool decks, and any cabin.

ITINERARIES *See* Itinerary Index

CABINS By Carnival standards, the cabins are exceptionally low-key and understated, dressed in soft pastels and lovely rich wood that blends with the soft colors. A wall unit has a dresser/desk with drawers and cabinets; safe; minifridge; television with CNN, BBC, Discovery Channel, and other channels such as ABC, CBS, and NBC when available; and three closets that should be ample for most people on a week's cruise. All outside cabins have a sofa; most are sofabeds. The bathroom with a rather tight shower stall has a dispenser for shampoo and shower gel. All outside cabins get terry robes. There are a larger number of cabins with a small balcony with space for two chairs—and that's about all.

Specifications 10 penthouse suites, 42 suites, 504 outside with balcony, 343 outside without balcony, 18 outside with glass wall, 570 inside cabins.

DINING Each ship has two bilevel dining rooms. On *Conquest,* the **Monet** and **Renoir** dining rooms (**Platinum** and **Golden** on *Glory*) are identical architecturally and have panels of wood-veneered images of the Eiffel Tower in the walls and ceiling. The fabrics and colors are based on works by the two painters. *Glory's* dining rooms take their decor from their colors and are elegant in their simplicity—resembling, somewhat, the uncluttered lines of Japanese decor, with only a touch of color from a few handpainted bonsai and cherry-blossom trees on the walls and ceiling. The rooms are the most crowded of any dining rooms we've experienced on any Carnival ship. Off to each side of *Glory's* Golden dining room is a private dinning room, **Copper** (for 28 people) and **Silver** (for 36 people), which are among the most handsome rooms on the ship. *Conquest's* **Renoir Restaurant** was inspired by *Lunch at the Restaurant Fournaise*, a tranquil scene of boaters relaxing at a cafe overlooking the Seine, featured in the wall-covering fabric. In the **Monet Restaurant,** one of the artist's famous "Water Lilies" series sets the motif.

The bi-level **Restaurant Cezanne** (**Red Sail** on *Glory*, **Rosie's** on *Valor*) on the Lido Deck has the atmosphere of a 19th-century French cafe. In addition to Carnival's standard variety of Italian, Chinese, Mexican, and other food stations, you can enjoy hamburgers and hot dogs, a 24-hour pizzeria, and a self-service ice cream/frozen yogurt station. The restaurant is also the venue for an upscale seafood station on the second level of the Lido restaurant. **Café Fans** (**Creams** on *Glory*) on

Promenade Deck is a patisserie serving a variety of coffees and rather pricey desserts; next door is a sushi bar. And there's 24-hour room service with new, expanded menus.

The Point, high on Panorama Deck, is *Conquest's* reservations-only supper club, named for the style of Georges-Pierre Seurat, known as pointillism, which renders images through thousands of individual dots, or points, of color. *Glory's* **Emerald Room** has light fixtures resembling giant emeralds and a huge medallion on the wall made up of hundreds of these light fixtures. For structural reasons, the Club is divided into two separate rooms (rather than the large open space by the funnel as on the line's Spirit class). The cost is $25 per person. In our experience, Carnival's alternative restaurants are excellent, with food and service top-notch and well worth the extra charge. Reserve early in your cruise, as they are very popular and fill up fast.

FACILITIES AND ACTIVITIES The **Toulouse-Lautrec Lounge,** the main show lounge, takes its inspiration from the painter's sketches, which were drawn from the subjects he saw in the cabarets, circuses, and brothels of Paris's Montmartre. To the sides of the stage are the famous windmill signs of the Moulin Rouge cabaret; the windmill motif is repeated in the carpet. *Glory's* **Amber Palace,** the most extravagant room on the ship, is named after Russia's famous Amber Room (recently reconstructed and open to the public) in the palace of Peter the Great. The wall covering, for example, replicates the mosaics of amber as they are on the palace walls; hanging from the ceiling is an enormous crystal chandelier, with smaller ones at the sides of the room. The Russian eagle is designed into the room's carpet, and the cut velvet covering on the seats would suit any czar's palace. For those who take a backstage tour, the state-of-the-art stage and equipment is on par with the latest of Broadway.

Two new shows debuted on *Glory*: *Livin' in America* and *Rock Down Broadway*, both in keeping with the Carnival tradition of fast-paced Vegas-style revues that blend choreography with elaborate sets and costumes. *Rock Down Broadway* is one of the best shows we have ever seen on any cruise ship—or on Broadway for that matter.

Conquest's **Tahiti Casino** and **Gauguin's Bar,** a sports bar, recall post-Impressionist Paul Gauguin's paintings of Polynesia. **Henri's Dance Club** takes its theme from the exotic jungle paintings of Henri Rousseau. Painted metal cut-outs, meant to look like the coarse grass of Rousseau's paintings, are mounted on the wall, with occasional three-dimensional animal heads, similar to those lurking in the artist's works. *Glory's* **Camel Club Casino** is a bit incongruous. The camel color inspired Farcus to install statues of reclining camels (which kids love to climb, despite a sign reading "No one under 18 years of age is allowed in the Casino"), but from the camels it's a stretch to the main decor, meant to reflect the age of European rediscovery of Ancient Egypt and the Orient.

On *Glory,* the **White Heat Dance Club** has gigantic white candles, 12 to 18 inches in diameter, in silver candelabra bases from two to five feet tall and giving off imaginary white heat. One deck below, the multipurpose **Ivory Club** has an Indian theme set off with elephant tusk replicas, and the barstools and table bases replicate elephant feet. Across the way, the **Burgundy Bar** is a wine bar; **Cinn-a-Bar,** a piano bar; and the **Bar Blue,** taking its "blue" from giant peacock feathers in the motif, is the ship's jazz bar. The **Ebony Cabaret,** a multifunction show room with African decor, is one of *Glory's* most successful rooms, using ebony wood, African textiles, and handsome authentic wooden masks in the decor. **On the Green,** the sports bar, celebrates the game of golf with memorabilia from its legends. In all, the ships each have 22 bars and lounges. Daytime activity range from a Jazz & Bloody Mary Party to a Sing-Along or a Men's Hairy Chest Contest; art auctions, trivia quizzes, game shows, and adult comedy shows in the evening round out the offerings. They also have, libraries, multipurpose conference centers, boutiques, infirmaries and Internet cafes—$0.75 per minute, or packages of 30 and 60 minutes for slight savings. Cruise e-mail available for a one-time activation fee of $3.95. Local calls are $6.90 per minute within the U.S.; additional charges may be applied to your credit card.

Two high-energy Las Vegas–style revues, *Far From Over–The 80s*, a tribute to the music and the movies of the 1980s, and *Nightclub Express*, a rollicking tour—hosted by a talking, singing sofa!—of ten famous cabarets and night spots (with different sets, costumes, and music appropriate to each), are highlights on *Carnival Valor*. Both were produced by Carnival Productions, the line's in-house entertainment group. They are staged in the 1,400-seat medieval-themed **Ivanhoe Show Lounge,** which boasts the latest in shipboard technology, such as "fly-in" scenery capabilities; a turntable stage with built-in lifts allowing for multiple sets; a multimillion-dollar sound and lighting system, including laser pods; and a rising orchestra pit.

SPORTS, FITNESS, AND BEAUTY Each ship has a spa with a large variety of treatments, sauna and steam rooms, a very small indoor pool with a most unusual half-moon-shaped Jacuzzi, a gym with state-of-the-art equipment, and a beauty salon. There are four swimming pools, including one with Carnival's signature slide; seven whirlpools (although often so many kids who should not be in them reduces the number by half); and a jogging track. You can start your day in the gym as early as 6 a.m. and be treated to classes in aerobics or abs or for $10 extra per session of yoga, Pilates, or seminars on body care, diet, or cellulite. Sports include basketball, volleyball, and golf.

CHILDREN'S FACILITIES The newest feature on the Conquest-class ships is the expanded teen recreation center housing a large, high-tech video game room and teen dance club with a DJ spinning the latest hits, a bar serving nonalcoholic specialty drinks, and a video wall along, with new activities and shore excursions for teen groups.

For younger children, the *Conquest* group has the largest play areas in the Carnival fleet. The Camp Carnival program set in **Children's World** is divided into four distinct areas: an arts and crafts center with spin and sand art and candy-making machines; an all-ages playroom with toys, games, and puzzles; a video room showing kids' movies and cartoons; and children's library, along with the latest PlayStation games. Children's World is also the venue for the ship's baby-sitting service, available nightly 10 p.m.–3 a.m. for $6 per hour for the first child and $4 per hour for the second child in the same family.

Adjacent to Children's World is an outdoor play area and a wading pool, and access to Carnival's trademark water slide. Stroller rentals are available for $6 per day and $25 per week.

Kids can also make their own culinary creations through new cake-decorating and pizza-making sessions, part of a full schedule of morning-to-night activities for children ages 2–15. Children receive their own printed activities program daily. Sample activities include storytelling, sing-alongs, and "Play-Doh Fun" for younger cruisers, and disco parties, scavenger hunts, and pool parties for older kids. The ships offer a variety of kid-friendly dining choices and a "daily junior special" in the main dining rooms. Kids are also provided with freshly baked chocolate chip cookies on formal nights; youth counselors host "children's only" meals poolside with a different cuisine featured each night. Also debuting on *Carnival Valor* was "WaterColors," a new art program which is to be expanded fleetwide, teaching kids the techniques employed by professional artists in papier-mâché, oil paintings, and watercolors; and "SeaNotes," a new music program that introduces kids to different musical instruments and genres.

Like her sister ships, the new *Carnival Liberty* has enhanced family facilities with a 4,200-square-foot children's play area with an arts and crafts center and computer lab; special dining amenities for children, including a turn-down service offering chocolate chip cookies at bedtime and a program where kids can dine with the youth counselors on Lido Deck. The ship will also house "Action Alley," the teens' area with a dance club, coffee and soda bar, and a high-tech game room and video arcade.

Celebration	**QUALITY 4**	**VALUE B**
Holiday	**QUALITY 4**	**VALUE B**
REGISTRY *Holiday* Bahamas;	**LENGTH** 727/733 feet	**BEAM** 92 feet
Celebration Panama		
CABINS 726/743	**DRAFT** 25 feet	**SPEED** 21 knots

MAXIMUM PASSENGERS	PASSENGER DECKS 9/10	ELEVATORS 8
1,800/1,896	CREW 660/670	SPACE RATIO 32

THE SHIPS When the *Holiday* was unveiled in 1985, her decor was called zany. Micky Arison, Carnival's chairman, called it a "Disney World for adults." For those accustomed to the sleek lines of traditional ships, the boxy look of *Holiday* took some getting used to, but it was the innovations inside that revolutionized cruising, making the ship with its four decks for recreation and entertainment as much the destination as its ports of call. The most startling change was the main promenade deck. Instead of circling the ship, as had been typical, the deck runs double-width down only one side—a feature that became standard on all Carnival megaliners. Called Broadway on the *Holiday,* with as much glitter as its namesake, it serves as a meeting place and thoroughfare, with bars, nightclubs, casinos, a disco, and reminders of Broadway: a traffic light, street lamps, an authentic 1934 bus, and Times Square.

A decade later, after larger and more flamboyant ships had been added to Carnival's fleet, the *Holiday* is regarded as traditional. That may be pushing credibility, but it's amazing how quickly passengers became comfortable with the new ideas the *Holiday* introduced. What's more, the innovations continue. The promenade was redesigned, and **Doc Holiday's** (a country-and-western lounge) was added. A separate section contains **Cyber City,** a virtual reality and game center. The fitness center was expanded, the casino renovated, and the lido restaurant remodeled, adding another dinner option, a 24-hour pizzeria, and a deli counter.

The *Holiday* was quickly followed by the *Jubilee* (since transferred to P&O Australia, a Carnival Corp acquisition resulting from the purchase of Princess Cruises) and the *Celebration*. The trio were identical in almost all aspects except decor. Each was themed and had a generous use of wood. The trio set the course for Carnival for the decade and had an incalculable impact on cruising. Zany, yes. Successful? You bet.

The *Celebration* pays tribute to New Orleans and Mardi Gras, complete with Bourbon Street, an outdoor cafe, bistro, and a New Orleans streetcar named, yes, Desire. Sculpture by Israeli artist Yaacov Agam greets passengers in the lobby, and his wall pieces decorate public areas. But the most dramatic art is by San Franciscan Helen Webber, whose sculptured aluminum kites hang on wires the full six decks of the stairwells. The *Celebration,* like the other ships, has its own quiet corner—**Admiral's,** a library and writing room dedicated to great ocean-liners of the past. The *Celebration* recently completed a major refurbishment of all cabins, public areas, dining rooms, purser's lobby, stairs, and elevators.

Holiday set another course in 2004, being the first ship to depart from Mobile year-round.

ITINERARIES *See* Itinerary Index.

CABINS For all the unconventional elements on the ships' activity decks, cabins on the *Holiday* duo are downright sane and larger than most on other ships in the same price category. Outside cabins have picture windows; inside have backlit windows of the same size, making the cabin seem larger and less closed in.

Cabins are furnished with twin beds that can be converted to kings and have ample closet and drawer space in cabinets of genuine wood. Artwork decorates the walls and adds a touch of class.

Specifications 279 *Holiday/Celebration* inside cabins, 437/443 outside; 10 suites with whirlpool bathtubs. Standard dimensions, 180/185 square feet. 683/709 with twin beds convertible to kings; 27/16 inside, 10/8 outside with upper/lower berths. No singles. 15/14 wheelchair-accessible.

DINING The ships offer the same menus as other Carnival ships, with two dining rooms serving three meals. Carnival has upgraded and expanded lido-area food service on all its ships to meet passengers' preference for casual breakfast and lunch choices. Specialties are offered in addition to standard favorites, such as scrambled eggs, hot dogs, and hamburgers. Particularly popular are the made-to-order pasta stations and expanded salad bars. Ice cream and frozen yogurt are available all day, (cookies in the afternoon) in the lido. Wine bars have been added on the promenade decks.

FACILITIES AND ACTIVITIES The Lido Deck has acres of open space and a swimming pool with a 14-foot-tall spiral water slide, a signature on Carnival ships. A more secluded pool is at the stern; a kids' pool is a deck below. The ships have spas with separate facilities for men and women. Decks are covered with Burmese teak.

Activities are numerous, ranging from wine tastings to surviving a "Survivors" game. In the evening, there's bar-hopping and people-watching on Broadway or Bourbon Street, and action in the casino or electronic game room. A favorite spot is the piano bar, but *Celebration's* **Red Hot Piano Bar** wins the award for novelty. Red walls glow under red lights, and the bar is shaped like a red piano with the ivories as the bar counter. And the music is . . . red hot. A spiral staircase leads directly to the casino a deck above.

The ships have huge theaters spanning two decks, where Broadway-style musicals and Las Vegas–type shows are staged twice nightly. Seats are terraced on six levels, giving all 1,000 patrons unobstructed views.

The year-round children's program, Camp Carnival, offers supervised activities for four age groups. **Cyber City** incorporates cutting-edge electronic game technology.

SHORE EXCURSIONS All Carnival ships offer similar shore excursions at common rates. They can be booked on Carnival's Web site. Many are off-the-shelf tours you often could take on your own. The main reason to book excursions through the cruise line is convenience. Recently, Carnival added a group of sports-oriented shore excursions for teenagers, such as horseback riding in Cozumel, biking in Key West, and cave tubing in Belize; these are discounted 20% off the regular price.

Celebrity Cruises

1050 Caribbean Way, Miami, FL 33132-2096
☎ **305-539-6000 or 800-646-1456**
fax 800-437-511; www.celebritycruises.com

TYPE OF SHIPS Stylish superliners and megaliners.

TYPE OF CRUISES Moderately priced deluxe; ample activity at comfortable pace; emphasis on quality.

CRUISE LINE'S STRENGTHS
- cuisine
- well-designed, stylish, spacious ships
- dining room service
- children's program
- value for money

CRUISE LINE'S SHORTCOMINGS
- lack of outside, wraparound promenade deck
- excessive promotion of onboard shopping
- boarding procedures
- loud deck music on some ships

FELLOW PASSENGERS Moderately affluent, ages range from late 30s to 60s in high season; ages lower in off-season. Typical passenger is age 48, married, with a household income of $50,000+. He/she tends to be an educated, experienced traveler who understands quality, owns a house in relatively affluent suburb, and has college-age children. Fifty percent have cruised before, and of this group, 20–30% are repeaters with Celebrity. Due to the line's regular departures from northeast United States in summer, a majority of passengers live on the East Coast; the balance come from the Midwest and West Coast.

Recommended for Middle- to upper-middle-income travelers in their 40s and older, whether first-timers or experienced cruisers, who appreciate good service and cuisine and want recreation and entertainment of a large ship at an easy pace. Those with children during the holidays.

Not recommended for Small-ship devotees (except *Celebrity Xpedition*); those seeking a party atmosphere

CRUISE AREAS AND SEASONS Bahamas and Caribbean in fall-winter; Alaska, Canada/New England, Bermuda, Baltic, Mediterranean in summer; Panama Canal, Hawaii, Mexico, South America, Europe, spring, winter, and fall; Galapagos, Antarctica, winter.

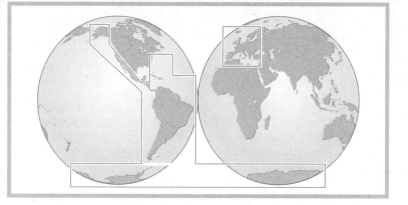

THE LINE From its inception in 1989, Celebrity Cruises' objective has been to offer deluxe cruises for experienced travelers at affordable prices. The plan was greeted with skepticism because the new line was being created by the owners of Chandris Cruises, an established company long associated with budget-priced cruises. But in less than three years, Celebrity achieved its goal and did better than anyone imagined.

Quickly it became apparent that Celebrity Cruises was more than just a new cruise line. It was a completely new product with a new generation of ships designed for 1990s travelers and new standards of service and cuisine in its price category. To their admirers, Celebrity's first vessels define the ideal size of a cruise ship and balance contemporary design and decor with traditional cruising.

Starting in 1992, Celebrity began building a new class of cruise ships for the 21st century. Once again, Celebrity's ships were winners. The Century series of ships—*Century, Galaxy,* and *Mercury*—accommodated 26% more passengers in 48% more space than Celebrity's first generation of ships and had the latest in entertainment and interactive communications systems. The addition of these ships enabled Celebrity to expand beyond the Caribbean to Alaska and Europe.

No sooner were these ships in service than Celebrity began building yet another new class of ships, the 91,000-ton Millennium group. The first of the French-built ships, *Millennium,* made her debut in 2000, followed by three more in 2001 and 2002. Celebrity was purchased by Royal Caribbean Cruises in June 1997 but operates as a separate brand.

In 2004, Celebrity took a big leap into adventure cruises with a series in the Galapagos onboard the 296-foot megayacht, *Celebrity Xpedition*. More recently, it has created a dozen or more special "Xpedition" programs in conjunction with its other cruise ships. These are as different as a "fire and ice" experience in Vancouver on an Alaska cruise, with helicopter and Zodiac tours of the Mt. Garibaldi volcano site and Howe Sound; and treks through the Alaskan wilderness in search of black bears; to an aquatic archaeology course from the platform of a 43-foot catamaran in Bermuda; to Marlin fishing in Cabo San Lucas on a Mexico Riviera cruise.

Celebrity is the first cruise line to offer "Acupuncture at Sea," now available on five of its ships. But Celebrity's most unusual innovation has been the introduction of the famous Cirque du Soleil experience in its "Bar at the Edge of the Earth" on the *Constellation* and *Summit* (see ships' profile later in this chapter for details).

In 2005, Celebrity launched its first three-, four-, and five-night cruises of the Pacific Northwest round-trip from Seattle on *Mercury;* heretofore the line's cruises were seven nights or longer. With *Bon Appétit* magazine, the line repeated its "Savor the Caribbean" series on *Millennium* featuring some of the nation's hottest chefs. Celebrity Discoveries, the line's enrichment program, has been expanded with up to four lecturers on every cruise, as varied as caricature artists on Caribbean and Bermuda sailings to naturalists on Alaska, Hawaii, and South America voyages. Also expanded is the number of Concierge Class cabins from 100 to 228 on all Millennium-class ships.

THE FLEET	BUILT/RENOVATED	TONNAGE	PASSENGERS
Celebrity Xpedition	2001	2,842	94
Century	1995	70,606	1,750
Constellation	2002	91,000	1,950
Galaxy	1996	77,713	1,870
Infinity	2001	91,000	1,950
Mercury	1997	77,713	1,870
Millennium	2000	91,000	1,950
Summit	2001	91,000	1,950
Zenith	1992/1999	47,255	1,374

STYLE From the handsome, deep-blue-and-white exteriors with their signature stacks to the elegant interiors, Celebrity ships have style, combining the glamour of traditional cruising with a contemporary look. An example: Famous contemporary artists, such as David Hockney and Roy Lichtenstein, are displayed alongside ancient Greek artifacts. On its first ships, introduced when atriums were becoming standard on cruise ships, Celebrity chose instead to make more space for public rooms, giving passengers entertainment and recreation options similar to those on megaliners, but without the glitz. Small lounges, each with its own ambience and entertainment, appeal to a broad range of tastes.

The ships were also designed for passenger comfort and flow. For example, the **Rendezvous Lounge** amidships provides a place where passengers can mingle before and after dinner, reducing crowds waiting for the restaurant or show lounge to open.

Celebrity distinguished itself from competitors by giving top priority to superior cuisine, hiring as food consultant Michel Roux, an award-winning master French chef who operates a Michelin three-star restaurant and other food enterprises in England. Roux helped design the ships' kitchens, trained its chefs, and guided food suppliers to ensure year-round quality. He's created a sophisticated but unpretentious cuisine for refined palates, emphasized quality over quantity (although quantity is there, too), and he established a new standard for competitors.

DISTINCTIVE FEATURES Computer room on *Galaxy*; shipboard passenger-service manager. Children's program and specially priced shore excursions. Martini bars. Advance bookings for **AquaSpa.** Robes in all cabins. Butler service in suites. Alternative restaurant for casual dining; sushi cafes, made-to-order pasta/pizza bars; 24-hour room service. Internet cafes. Unique restaurants, music libraries, conservatories, and concierge service.

	HIGHEST	LOWEST	AVERAGE
PER DIEM	$686	$62	$195

Per diems are calculated from cruise line's nondiscounted *cruise-only* published fares on standard accommodations and vary by season, cabins, and cruise areas.

RATES All published rates include port fees.

Special fares and discounts Early-bird discounts, called Five Star rates, represent some of cruising's best values. Advance-purchase fares offer up to 50% discounts on cruise-only rates (deluxe cabins and suites excluded). Base rates for seven-day cruises offer upgrades for a low fee. Two itineraries—such as Eastern and Western Caribbean—can be combined at a special rate.

- **THIRD/FOURTH PASSENGER:** Yes.
- **CHILDREN'S FARE:** Yes.
- **SINGLE SUPPLEMENT:** 150–200%, depending on category. Guaranteed single rate.

Packages
- **CRUISE/AIR ADD-ON WITH TRANSFERS:** Yes.

- **PRE/POST:** Yes.
- **OTHERS:** Anniversary, honeymoon, family.

PAST PASSENGERS The Captain's Club is open to all passengers after their first Celebrity cruise. The club's benefits are determined by the number of times you cruise. For Classic level (one to five cruises): one-category upgrade, custom air arrangements, presailing specialty restaurant reservations, priority embarkation/debarkation (where available) for founder classic members, exclusive party, welcome amenity gift with purchase at AquaSpa, certificates for Celebrity casino, golf clinic and special rate for simulator, wine tasting, reunion cruises, quarterly newsletter with exclusive offers. Select level (six to ten cruises): private event for members, behind-the-scenes tours, priority status for shore excursion waitlist, preferential debarkation (where available), plus all Classic benefits. Elite level (11 or more cruises): private shipboard departure lounge with Continental breakfast, plus all Classic and Select benefits.

THE LAST WORD Celebrity Cruises has been one of the industry's true success stories. It created the right formula at the right time: classic cruising updated for contemporary lifestyles and available at reasonable prices. Its immediate success resulted from exceeding everyone's expectations and reflected the extensive planning and testing that went into the ships. The line has maintained high standards for its price range and continues to enhance the product by adding new deluxe amenities as well as value items like reduced rates for children. Almost anyone would enjoy a Celebrity cruise, but first-timers with cultivated tastes and experienced cruisers who seek greater comfort and service than is common in this price range will be most appreciative of the value.

Celebrity Cruises Standard Features

Officers Greek.

Staff Dining, European; Cabin/International; Cruise/European, American.

Dining facilities One main dining room with two seatings for breakfast and lunch; midnight buffet; indoor/outdoor lido buffet breakfast and lunch. Century and Millennium class, two-level dining room. Alternative restaurants. AquaSpa cafe in Millennium class.

Special diets Request at time of booking.

Room service 24-hour menu; butler service in suites.

Dress code Casual but not sloppy during the day; informal in evening, with two nights formal or semiformal.

Cabin amenities Direct-dial phone; bath with shower; suites with marble bathrooms. Robes in all cabins. Television with CNN and music channels. Hair dryers, safes, minibars, on Century and Millennium classes.

Electrical outlets 110/220 AC; 110 AC only on *Horizon* and *Zenith*.

Wheelchair access See Cabin section for each ship.

Recreation and entertainment Card room/library, casino, three–five-deck show lounge, bars/lounges, disco, video game room. Bingo, lotto, horse racing, culinary demonstrations, wine tasting, fashion show, dance lessons, art auctions, floral demonstrations on *Millennium*. High-tech entertainment center on Century class.

Sports and other activities Two outside swimming pools; exercise classes, walks, golf putting, table tennis, deck and pool games. Golf simulators on Century and Millennium class; volleyball, basketball on Millennium class.

Beauty and fitness Barber/beauty salon; health club, gym, and sauna; jogging track on sun deck; elaborate spa with beauty treatments.

Other facilities Boutiques, hospital, laundry and dry cleaning services, meeting facilities on Century, Millennium class; Internet on all ships. No passenger-operated washers or dryers.

Children's facilities Play room; teen disco; baby-sitters; age-specific programs with counselors, year-round.

Theme cruises Occasionally.

Smoking Not permitted in dining room or theater. Other public rooms have designated areas.

Celebrity suggested tipping Per person per day: waiter, butlers (suites only), $3.50; assistant waiter, $2; restaurant, 15% service charge added to all beverage checks.

Credit cards Cruise/onboard charges: American Express, MasterCard, Visa, Discover.

Zenith	QUALITY 7	VALUE C
REGISTRY Bahamas	LENGTH 682 feet	BEAM 95 feet
CABINS 677/687	DRAFT 24 feet	SPEED 21.4 knots
MAXIMUM PASSENGERS	PASSENGER DECKS 9	ELEVATORS 7
1,374	CREW 642/670	SPACE RATIO 34.5

THE SHIPS Celebrity Cruises was launched in 1990, with the *Horizon* (which left the fleet in October 2005 for Royal Caribbean's European sister company, Island Cruises) followed the next year by the *Zenith,* her near twin. The spacious, German-built ships incorporate safety features that exceed national and international requirements. These safeguards added about $1 million to the cost of each ship.

Celebrity made a few enhancements on *Zenith,* which was completed in record time using computer-aided design. Michael and Agni Katzourakis, who created interiors for many luxury ships, designed the cabins. London-based John McNeece, another veteran of ship interiors, designed the public rooms. *Zenith* has a warm, inviting ambience supported by lavish use of fine wood and rich fabrics in soothing colors. Public rooms are on four spacious decks. Those on the entertainment deck are connected by a promenade that, in one section, has floor-to-ceiling windows looking out to sea and flooding the area with light. Original art on walls and displays of ancient artifacts add to the feeling of quality—a characteristic reflected fleetwide.

In 1999, nine public areas of *Zenith* received a multimillion-dollar makeover to add the signature elements of Celebrity's newer Century-class vessels: a martini bar, chocolates and coffee cafe, and fancy spa. On Deck 8, the disco was replaced by a new rotunda with alabaster, bronze chandelier, and wood flooring inlaid with a marble compass; it also gained **Michael's Club,** a piano bar echoing a private English club. Adjoining the club and with similar decor is a library and card room, available for parties or meetings of up to 70 people. The library offers books, iPod rentals, and electronic equipment for audiovisual presentations. Beside high-back chairs are wall units with headsets for listening to audio books and music. The **Business Center,** also in the library, has two computers and two printers for passenger use.

Under an exclusive agreement with the historic Milan coffeehouse, Pasticceria Confetteria COVA, the Plaza Bar on Deck 5 was transformed to the **COVA Café,** a coffee and chocolate bar. On Deck 7, the **Rendezvous Lounge,** the ship's most popular before-dinner area, was enlarged and given an expanded dance floor and redesigned window wall. The lounge has a small bar where a combo plays nightly for dancing and easy listening. Also on Deck 7 are a boutique, art gallery, and the Art Deco **Martini Bar.**

ITINERARIES *See* Itinerary Index.

CABINS Handsomely fitted in light wood, the spacious, well-designed cabins reflect the attention to detail that went into them. For example, all built-in furniture has been finished with rounded corners and edges for safety and durability. Decor is colorful and cheerful; space is generous, with two full-length closets and plenty of drawers. Bathrooms, large for ships in this price range, have ample counter space. Almost 75% are outside cabins. Passengers can dial toll-free numbers in the United States directly from their cabins.

All cabins are equipped with the Celebrity Network, enabling you to order meals or wine for dinner, review your account, and request other services directly from your cabin television. Stewards can be summoned by phone.

Cabins are cleaned and bathroom linens changed twice daily. In-cabin dining—full breakfast and dinner off the restaurant menu—and massage are also available. Both are amenities normally found only on luxury ships. Missing from this ship are passenger-operated washers and dryers.

Lengthening the 9th, 10th, and 11th decks created space for suites and for larger royal suites. The roomy suites have marbled bathrooms with Jacuzzi tubs and excellent showers. Most have a king-size bed and sleeper loveseat. Suites have butler service, but unless you can easily afford the higher cost, the true value is in the standard cabins.

In summer and holidays when many children are apt to be aboard *Zenith*, avoid cabins on Europe Deck aft near the playroom—unless some are your own kids.

Specifications 146 inside cabins, 541 outside; 22 suites. Standard dimensions are 172 square feet; 462 with twin (260 convert to doubles); 74 double/king; third/fourth persons available; no singles.

DINING Chef Michel Roux's highly praised cuisine was a major factor in the line's immediate success. Roux's credo was to use the best-quality products and keep menus seasonal. To maintain his high standards, Roux or one of his sous-chefs sails on every ship during the year. Food presentation receives as many accolades as preparation. A typical lunch menu offers a choice of four appetizers, two soups, two salads, two cold and three hot entrees, a selection of vegetables, and four desserts, plus ice creams, sherbet, and cheeses.

Dinners have even more choices. Every menu includes at least one lean-and-light dish. There is a separate, full-week's vegetarian menu. Wines are suggested on menus; prices are moderate to very expensive.

Celebrity eschews themed nights for dinner—common on other lines and often more show than authenticity. Rather, themes are given to the lunchtime buffets, when chefs are better able to do justice to ethnic cuisine. A popular nightly feature is the presentation of "Gourmet Bites," a chef's sampling provided in public rooms and available fleetwide.

Dining-room service is exemplary, and the gracious ambience is enhanced by piano music at lunch and dinner. Although the dining room seats 840, its H layout with raised center lessens the feeling of being in a huge room. Nonetheless, when the ships are full, which they usually are, tables are set close together, and the room is crowded. A few tables seat two; most accommodate four, six, or eight passengers.

Alternative casual dinner service is available in the **Windsurf Café.** The limited menu includes an appetizer, soup, salad, pasta, choice of meat, and dessert. Freshly made pizza is also available. The open rotisseries and large grills enable diners to see food being cooked to order.

Breakfast and lunch in the Windsurf Café offer hot and cold selections. When the ships are full, long lines develop, particularly on days at sea when passengers don't need to be up for early excursions. To relieve the problem, waiters at the buffet lines carry your tray to your table. The most informal setting, the outside **Grill,** serves hamburgers and hot dogs cooked to order.

SERVICE Particularly in the dining room, service distinguishes Celebrity from other midprice cruise lines. Among the line's innovations is a passenger service representative, who is usually found in the main lobby, ready to help with problems that crop up.

FACILITIES AND ACTIVITIES Scheduled activities are so numerous that it would be virtually impossible for one person to do them all. But the variety ensures there is enough to suit almost every passenger. Choices range from exercise and dance classes to contests and karaoke. The week's activities might include a singles' party, poolside Island Night, honeymooners' champagne party, a jazz concert, and seminars on cuisine, the stock market, stress management, and estate planning. Art auctions draw mild interest. First-run movies are shown daily in the show lounge, and older films play on cabin television; a week's schedule is provided in your cabin. The ship has lounges for peace or pleasure, with entertainment ranging from a sing-along piano bar and dance music to Broadway-style productions in the two-deck showroom. The popular **Rendezvous Lounge,** convenient to the dining room and crowded for cocktails, is great for people-watching anytime.

The *Zenith's* **Fleet Bar** is among the most attractive rooms afloat. The top-deck, club-like piano bar has a small dance floor and an expanse of windows. It's a favorite spot for drinks and dancing—light and cheerful by day, softly aglow at sunset, and sophisticated at night. The ship also features champagne and caviar service in the observation lounge and martini bars.

Evening entertainment is balanced between specialty acts (acrobats, comedians, magicians) and big production shows, all of which are appropriate for families. In the bilevel show lounge, which doubles as a meeting room, most seats have good sight lines. During a week's cruise, two big stage productions are presented. From the upper level, passengers can walk aft to the casino, offering blackjack, roulette, and slot machines, or to the shops.

SPORTS AND FITNESS Wide, open decks have plenty of space for deck chairs, even when the ship is full, and quiet corners for reading, sunning, or snoozing, but shady areas are limited. At sea, there are swimming pool games, Ping-Pong, trapshooting, darts, shuffleboard, and golf putting. In port, golf, snorkeling, and other sports are offered, depending on location. The ship has a large, well-equipped fitness center and a one-fifth-mile jogging track on its top decks, but no outside, wraparound promenade deck. A full fitness program encompasses four or five activities daily. The cruise price includes use of the facilities, saunas, and exercise classes.

SPA AND BEAUTY A major addition to the ship in its makeover was an **AquaSpa** on the Sun Deck. Although smaller than those on Century- and Millennium-class ships and lacking their thalassotherapy pool, the spa offers many of the same treatments. It houses a beauty salon; six treatment rooms; sauna, fitness, and aerobics area; and separate changing rooms for men and women. All Celebrity ships offer the AquaSpa program by Elemis, a spa operator owned by Steiner of London. Services are expensive. Spas on all Celebrity ships have a barber shop and beauty salon and offer massage, facials, and body treatments for additional fees. Spa programs may be booked in advance. Beware: Steiner's staff pushes their products aggressively; you should not feel any obligation to buy.

CHILDREN'S FACILITIES During summer and major holidays, Celebrity ships offers supervised, daily programs for five age groups: Ship Mates (ages 3–6), Celebrity Cadets (ages 7–9), Ensigns (ages 10–12), and Admiral T's (ages 13–17). Younger children enjoy painting, drawing, songs, dances, movies, and other age-appropriate activities. Celebrity Summer Stock lets young actors participate in theatrical shows with dances and costumes. The Young Mariners' program showcases the operations of the ship and provides the opportunity to meet the captain and learn navigation by the stars.

Junior Olympics offer water volleyball and basketball, golf putting, Ping-Pong, and other games. At meals, kids can join their peers at the Celebrity Breakfast Club and at dinner, order from their own or the regular menu. The program also has family activities and a masquerade parade.

Century	QUALITY 7	VALUE C
Galaxy	QUALITY 8	VALUE B
Mercury	QUALITY 8	VALUE B
REGISTRY Liberia	LENGTH 815/866 feet	BEAM 105/105.6 feet
CABINS 875/935	DRAFT 25/25.5 feet	SPEED 21.5 knots
MAXIMUM PASSENGERS	PASSENGER DECKS 10	ELEVATORS 9/10
1,750/1,870	CREW 858/909	SPACE RATIO 40

THE SHIPS Celebrity got a jump on the millennium with the 1995 debut of the *Century,* first of a new fleet designed for 21st-century cruising. *Galaxy* followed in 1996 and *Mercury* in 1997. More than ten teams worked with *Century's* builders to achieve a comfortable, inviting, integrated design. With 48% more space than their cousin ships but only 26% more passengers, this spacious trio has one of cruising's highest passenger-to-space ratios in their category. Public rooms range in style from an elegant wood-paneled bar to a futuristic disco. Sony Corporation of America designed a sophisticated, interactive communications and entertainment system, and the company's music, pictures, and electronic publishing divisions provide products and expertise.

Century's focal point is a three-deck **Grand Foyer** encircled by a staircase and topped with a painted glass dome lit as if by sunlight during the day and as a starlit sky at night. The piazza has marble floors, burled woods, brass trim, suede furniture, and a waterfall with changing fiber-optic images. Nearby are boutiques and the **COVA Café,** a floating version of Pasticceria Confetteria COVA, the Milan-based pastry shop famous for its exquisitely packaged chocolates, pastries, and signature coffees.

The *Galaxy* is essentially *Century's* twin in layout, but she is slightly larger with improvements over her sister ship, including the atrium, with a 40-foot-tall video panel projecting changing images, and a high-tech center offering free computer classes. The atrium has been improved further on *Mercury* with a spiral staircase leading to the promenade deck, where the port side has the COVA Café (now found on all Celebrity ships).

The *Galaxy's* best new feature was a retractable glass dome covering a swimming pool and the surrounding deck. The **Oasis,** one of the ship's most popular areas, has an indoor/outdoor grill and bar that in the evening offers alternative casual dining, now available fleetwide.

The ships have multilevel, multipurpose observation lounges that become discos in the evening. One of the ships' two atriums, positioned aft and spanning three decks, opens onto the casino, **Rendezvous Lounge,** the dining room's foyer, and a champagne bar.

Century-class vessels, like their predecessors, have multimillion-dollar art collections that are virtually contemporary art museums at sea. The focus for *Century* is contemporary masters; for *Galaxy,* the avant garde; and for *Mercury,* works by artists who emerged after pop art in the 1960s and 1970s. The collections were assembled by Christina Chandris, the ships' curator and former fine art advisor, in collaboration with the Marlborough Gallery of New York. The line provides information for a self-guided art tour.

At press time, Celebrity announced a $55 million remake of the *Century* in April 2006, transforming the decade-old ship into one closer to the line's Millennium class. The most important change will be the addition of 325 large, new balconies to cabins throughout the ship and 24 new cabins and suites (2 handicapped-accessible) on the stern of Deck 12 . Deck 12 will also get a Sushi cafe and an alfresco dining area. Another big addition will be a specialty restaurant with tableside cooking. The Spa will be expanded and a cafe added. A new sports deck will be added on Deck 14—complete with basketball court and table tennis. Cabins will get new decor and flat-screen television.

On Deck 7, the sports bar will become a martini bar. The computer station will become a "High Seas Computing" learning center with newly dedicated space for courses ranging from basic computer use to Web site creation to digital photography. On Deck 4, six cabins will be removed to enlarge the children's area and add a new teen area and video arcade. The new *Century* will sail on short cruises from Miami, the first time Celebrity will have a ship departing regularly from Miami

ITINERARIES *See* Itinerary Index.

CABINS Each deck has its own color scheme, with cabins on each using complementary colors for carpeting and bedspreads. Windows in the spacious cabins are framed in rosewood, conveying luxury and comfort. All *Century* cabins have built-in vanities; generous closet and drawer space; large bathrooms with showers, hair dryers, and terry robes; telephones, safes, and minibars; and radios and televisions. Interactive cabin television enables passengers to order breakfast or room service, book spa appointments, buy shore excursions, gamble (charged to the room), order merchandise from shops, and watch pay-per-view movies (including adult selections). Interactive televisions located throughout the ship provide information and entertainment.

Although cabins on *Century* are similar to those on *Zenith,* they were modified on *Galaxy* to accommodate more features. Some storage space was lost; drawer space, particularly, is inadequate. All have minibars, and upper-category cabins have VCRs. The ships have penthouse and royal suites, and all suites have marble bathrooms, whirlpool tubs, verandas, and butler service.

Specifications Century, 304 inside cabins, 571 outside; 52 suites, 61 suites and deluxe cabins with verandas. Standard dimensions, 172 square feet; 806 with twin beds, all convertible to doubles; third/fourth persons available; no singles. 8 wheelchair-accessible. *Galaxy/Mercury,* 296 inside cabins, 639 outside; 50 suites and 170 minisuites with verandas. Standard dimensions, 172 square feet; 877 with twin beds, all convertible to doubles; third/fourth persons available; no singles. 8 wheelchair-accessible.

DINING *Century's* stylish **Grand Restaurant,** the main dining room, was Celebrity's first two-tiered dining room; a majestic staircase leads to a colonnaded center aisle reminiscent of the Karnak Temple in Egypt. Each of two galleys prepares food for half of the dining room, thus providing speedier service, consistent temperatures, and freshness. The **Orion Restaurant** aboard *Galaxy* has a larger second tier to accommodate the ship's greater capacity, and decor is lighter, more contemporary, and less pretentious than on *Century*. The room's focal point is an enormous, backlit ceiling panel of a hemisphere with continents superimposed. The *Mercury's* **Manhattan Restaurant,** with a backdrop depicting the Big Apple skyline, is completely different from those of its sisters. Food, however, is the same on all three ships and meets the line's high standards.

Other dining areas are the casual **Veranda Grill,** adjacent to the pool, and **Islands Café,** with four buffet stations and two bars. The cafe serves an afternoon tea buffet that's in addition to Celebrity's traditional Elegant Tea. *Galaxy's* **Oasis** (**Palm Springs Grill** on *Mercury* and the **Sky Bar** on *Century*) is a casual-dining alternative restaurant. As something of an afterthought, the restaurant is a disappointment compared to the ships' other venues and to Celebrity's dining reputation. The outdoor section has a small swimming pool in a garden setting and is covered by a dome (particularly appealing on Alaska itineraries). Celebrity was the first line to offer complimentary pizza delivered to cabins—a service now available on many cruise ships.

SERVICE European-style service distinguishes Celebrity from other mid-price cruise lines. It's one of the ships' best and most rewarding features.

FACILITIES AND ACTIVITIES The two-deck **Celebrity Theater** used for Broadway-style revues and cabaret shows has a sloping orchestra section and cantilevered balconies providing unobstructed sight lines. The venue has a revolving stage, the ability to handle multiple backdrops, an orchestra pit with adjustable height, sophisticated lighting, and other special effects.

The Art Deco **Crystal Room** (**The Savoy Nightclub** on *Galaxy;* **Pavilion** on *Mercury*), a low-key night club for evening dancing, has etched-glass panels, luminous alabaster dome ceiling, rotating bronze globe, and chic color scheme of red, black, and gold that recalls 1930s New York. The Savoy employs a jungle motif in its late-night cabaret, and **Fortune's Casino** has the full roster of games. Rendezvous Square, next to the dining room, is a lively place for cocktails or socializing before and after dinner.

High atop *Century*, **Hemisphere** (**Stratosphere Lounge** on the *Galaxy* and **Navigator Club** on *Mercury*) is an airy, sunlit observation lounge by day transformed into a futuristic "disco under the dome" at night, when window blinds lower automatically, etched-glass room dividers illuminate one by one, and a special table "glows." The hemisphere then rises—casting light from within—and the dance floor appears. Telescopes are placed around the room's edge for stargazing. On *Galaxy*, the Stratosphere has three sections. The outer one next to the floor-to-ceiling windows is a quiet zone for reading and daytime viewing of scenery. The middle level is ideal for cocktails at sunset, and the innermost can accommodate meetings during the day as pull-down screens separate it from other areas of the lounge. In the evening, the inner room becomes the disco, as sophisticated equipment transforms it and provides a terrific laser light show.

Michael's Club aboard *Century* is an intimate lounge fashioned after a private gentlemen's club, paneled in rich woods and furnished with leather chairs and couches. On *Galaxy,* the room is contemporary in decor and lacks the cachet of the club on *Century.* The three ships also have martini bars. Flexible walls fold into pillars in a conference center, allowing it also to serve as cinema, meeting room, library, or card room. Keypads in the armchairs can be used for responses to questions or for interactive movies.

Activities are numerous and varied to appeal to a range of passengers and include exercise and dance classes, contests, singles parties, honeymooners' champagne party, and karaoke. Informational seminars also may be scheduled. First-run and adult pay-per-view movies are shown daily on cabin television; a schedule is provided in your cabin.

SPORTS, FITNESS, AND BEAUTY   The spacious ships have 62,000 square feet of open decks and sports, including simulated golf, Ping-Pong, volleyball, basketball, darts, and jogging. The *Century's* two swimming pools have cylindrical waterfalls and are rimmed with teak benches.

AquaSpa, the ships' health and fitness center, is among the most popular feature on all three ships. It's one of the best-equipped gyms at sea, with a hydropool, saunas, steam rooms, cardiovascular machines, and weight stations. Personal trainers are available to create individualized training programs. Aerobics classes are ongoing. The spa offers a variety of beauty and health treatments. The most unusual is rasul, based on an Oriental ceremony with a seaweed soap shower, medicinal mud pack, herbal steam bath, and massage. Not to be missed is the tranquilizing thalassotherapy treatment taken in a 115,000-gallon pool with waterjet massage stations. Spa treatments are expensive; they may be booked in advance of your cruise.

CHILDREN'S FACILITIES   With every new ship, Celebrity's children's facilities improve. The **Fun Factory** on *Galaxy* and *Mercury* is a 1,600-square-foot playroom, and there's also a kids' splash pool. As on other Celebrity ships, supervised daily programs are geared to five age groups. See previous section for details. Teens have a private lounge with a dance floor, plus a video game room. The program also offers family activities.

SHORE EXCURSIONS   Passengers can review and make reservations on line at **www.celebritycruises.com.**

Constellation	QUALITY 8	VALUE B
Infinity	QUALITY 8	VALUE B
Millennium	QUALITY 7	VALUE B
Summit	QUALITY 8	VALUE B
REGISTRY Bahamas	LENGTH 965 feet	BEAM 105.6 feet
CABINS 975	DRAFT 26.3 feet	SPEED 24 knots
MAXIMUM PASSENGERS 2,038	PASSENGER DECKS 11	ELEVATORS 10
	CREW 999	SPACE RATIO 46.6

THE SHIPS When the *Millennium* debuted in 2000, she launched a new class of ships for Celebrity—somewhat larger than her sister ships and with many of the same facilities, but even more spacious and with contemporary refinements sure to please maturing baby boomers. These include the line's largest spa, a unique specialty restaurant with a dine-in wine cellar, a large boutique of designer fashions, a music library, floral conservatories with full-service florists, and huge suites.

The *Millennium*, the first of four sister ships, also enabled Celebrity to expand its cruise horizons. *Infinity*, which debuted in 2001, offered the line's first cruises to Hawaii. *Summit*, launched in October 2001, will sail on the lines first cruises to Australia and Asia in 2005; while *Constellation* entered service in Europe in 2002.

These ships are powered by environmentally friendly gas-turbine engines, which reduce exhaust emissions by up to 90% and lower noise and vibration levels considerably. The way these ships glide out of port is reminiscent of the smooth sailing aboard steam-driven, classic liners from the past. The only vibration noticed was in the aft section when the Azipod propulsion system was altering the ship's course. That same propulsion system also allows the ships to cruise at 24 knots, enabling them to sail to more destinations in shorter time. They are also able to transit the Panama Canal. Changes in the exterior design—a lean, chiseled profile with a new stack design and hull striping—make the group look like the faster ships that they are.

The interiors, created by some of the same design teams that worked on other Celebrity ships, are the line's most sophisticated and elegant to date. They have something of a back-to-the-future decor, blending the glamour and grandeur of turn-of-the-19th-century luxury liners with the amenities and state-of-the-art technology that passengers in the new millennium expect. The ships also boast Celebrity's signature features: museum-quality contemporary art collections, an enormous **AquaSpa, COVA Café di Milano, Michael's Club** piano bar, martini and champagne bars, and cuisine by Michel Roux.

Passengers are introduced to the *Millennium* via the **Grand Foyer** with a translucent, backlit onyx staircase. Opposite the shore excursion desk is a bank of four glass elevators—the first external-facing ones ever built on a cruise ship—that capture panoramic views as they rise. One passenger, enjoying her elevator ride with Amsterdam views, said, "It was almost as good as a shore excursion." Next to the elevators, a paneled wall of wood and metallic vinyl rises from the entry to the top of the ship through a series of atria.

In 2003, the line introduced "Celebrity ConciergeClass," an enhanced level of accommodations with new amenities and priority services with the notion that little extras make a big difference. The amenities include a bottle of chilled champagne on arrival, fresh flowers and fruit, afternoon canapés, a leather key holder, personalized stationery, an oversized tote bag, and an umbrella to use during the cruise. In 2005, the number of cabins in ConciergeClass was more than doubled from 100 to 228.

Sleeping comfort is enhanced with pillow-top mattresses; lush duvets; pillow selections, such as goose down, Isotonic, and others; and a new room-service breakfast menu. In the bathroom, ConciergeClass passengers find oversized Egyptian cotton towels, Frette bathrobes, two hair dryers, a Hansgrohe shower head, and a selection of fine toiletries. On the veranda, they have a table for alfresco dining, cushioned chairs, and high-powered binoculars.

Priority service gives them priority luggage delivery, dining time and seating preferences, shoe-shine service, VIP invitations to exclusive shipboard events, priority shore excursion bookings, early embarkation and debarkation privileges, and a one-touch phone button direct to a ConciergeClass desk representative.

Unique to the ships are their floral conservatories and the silk floral displays by Emilio Robba of Paris, renowned for his silk floral artistry. Both the conservatories and the floral displays add to the serene character of these beautiful vessels. The floral conservatories—the first at sea—provide an attractive botanical environment, ideal for romantic occasions and reflective moments. Designed by Robba, they combine natural flora with his silk creations. The floral boutiques are operated by full-time florists who produce flower arrangements and corsages for passengers and hold classes in flower-arranging several times a week. Following the facility's success on *Infinity*, a small conservatory and boutique were added to *Millennium*, replacing the little-used teen center. On the three newer ships, the larger conservatories replaced *Millennium's* sports bar. The Millennium-class ships also have **Online@Celebrity Cruises** Internet cafe, a computer training and education program, acupuncture-at-sea, and meetings space with a business center.

ITINERARIES *See* Itinerary Index.

CABINS Of the 975 cabins, 80% are outside, and of those, 74% (or 56% of the total) have verandas. All cabins have air-conditioning, minibar, safe, telephone with voicemail, shower, hair dryer, and multifunction interactive television. The standard cabins are furnished with twin beds that are convertible to queen size. *Infinity, Summit,* and *Constellation* have Connect@ Sea and in-cabin Internet access. The spacious cabins are well-appointed and beautifully finished. Added touches, such as a silver carafe of fresh water replenished regularly, heighten the level of service. There are no self-service launderettes—particularly missed on long sailings.

The Penthouse suites, measuring 1,432 square feet plus 1,098 square feet of veranda, have marble-floor foyers, separate living and dining rooms; baby grand piano; butler's pantry; master bedroom with generous closets; exercise equipment; dressing room with vanity; marble master bath with twin sinks; whirlpool tub, separate shower, toilet and bidet area; powder room; motorized draperies, lights and security system, two interactive audio/visual entertainment systems with flat-screen television, and a fax machine; veranda with whirlpool, wet bar, and lounges.

The Royal suites have floor-to-ceiling glass doors; separate living room with dining and sitting area; two entertainment centers with flat-screen TVs and VCRs; walk-in closet; bath with whirlpool tub and stall shower; and a veranda with whirlpool tub. There are also Celebrity suites, each with themed decor and floor-to-ceiling windows; and Sky suites (including six wheelchair-accessible) also with floor-to-ceiling glass doors, sitting area with sofabed and lounge chair, similar entertainment center, minibar, walk-in closet, and bathroom with whirlpool tub. All but a few suites have verandas, and all have butler service.

Specifications 639 outside; 296 inside. 2 penthouse suites; 8 Celebrity suites; 8 Royal suites; 26 Sky suites, plus 6 wheelchair-accessible—all with verandas. 5 inside and 4 outside cabins are wheelchair-accessible and have flat floor entrances and 35-inch-wide cabin bathroom doorways. Public elevator doorways are 39 inches wide.

DINING The **Metropolitan Restaurant,** the main dining room spanning two levels, features bold, geometric motifs in reds, blues, and golds based on French designs from the late 1940s/early 1950s, which the designers describe as "restrained exuberance." At night, panels with dramatic architectural scenes are lowered onto the room's expansive windows, with a quintet providing a quiet, elegant accompaniment. It's called **The Trellis** on *Infinity* and has an 18th-century-garden theme.

The **Olympic,** Celebrity's first specialty restaurant, is the *Millennium's* show-stopper. It takes its name from a rare maritime treasure—a section of the original Edwardian wood-carved paneling from the *Olympic,* the sister ship of the *Titanic*. First discovered in a private English residence, the exquisite French walnut paneling ornamented with gold leaf in Louis XVI style was bought at auction at Sotheby's. Seating only 134 people, the intimate dining room uses an Edwardian theme for its decor, to convey a nostalgic ambience of the elegant golden days of steamship travel. The Olympic restaurant also was the cruise industry's first demonstration galley (an open kitchen where guests can see their meals being prepared). The reservations-only restaurant (surcharge, $30 per person) has its own menu of gourmet cuisine, and to make the dining experience even more memorable, some dishes are presented and finished table side. One treat is Waldorf pudding—a re-creation of an original dessert from the *Olympic*. There is a piano/violin entertainment. Memorabilia from the *Olympic* includes White Star Line china and the ship's bell, which is on exhibit in the foyer. Adjoining the room is a separate wine cellar, which can be used as private dining room for small groups of eight persons or so. The wine list has almost 200 international selections, some of them quite prestigious. Passengers may also order recommended wines by the glass with each of the four courses. Wine and after-dinner espressos can increase the tab to $100 or more for a couple.

The same theme of honoring a different liner from the past, with superb design and decor and recreating the first-class dining experience of a past era, is found on *Millennium's* sister ships. *Infinity's* **S.S. United States** restaurant has etched glass panels from the famous American liner's first-class ballroom. The French liner *Normandie* is featured in *Summit's* alternative restaurant; **Ocean Liners** on *Constellation* salutes the classic ships of the past with memorabilia and paintings of famed liners and original lacquered panels from the *Ile de France*.

At the entrance to each restaurant, glass cases containing memorabilia from the famous ships are found. The ambience of the great liner era is enhanced by cutlery and china reproduced from classic ship designs and the style of music performed throughout the evening. The three-hour dining experience is a unique opportunity to enjoy fine dining in the style of a bygone age. It is certainly worth the $30 per-person service charge added to your shipboard account when booking these restaurants.

The **Ocean Café** (**Seaside Café** on *Constellation*), an indoor/outdoor restaurant designed to resemble a Portuguese outdoor cafe, is the casual dining venue for breakfast and lunch buffet, while the **Ocean Grill,** with a separate entrance, is an alternative dining venue featuring steak, fish, rotisserie chicken, pizza, and pasta. There is no fee for this by-reservation, partial-waiter-service restaurant. Recently, Celebrity added fleetwide what it calls the "Casual Dining Boulevard" on the Lido Deck, a nightly alternative to the more formal atmosphere in the main dining rooms. There, you will find a sushi cafe and a pizza and pasta bar.

Savvy travelers discover the **AquaSpa Café,** where they can select light, healthy food and fruit plates, whole-grain cereals and breads and yogurt at breakfast, and cold poached salmon and chicken and crudités at lunch. Smoothies and fresh vegetable and fruit juices are available for an extra charge.

SERVICE Service in the main dining rooms is very attentive and up to Celebrity's high standards. In the buffet-style cafe, you never have to carry your tray; waiters are ready to assist you. The alternative dining rooms have the highest level of service of any ship of this category and price range.

FACILITIES AND ACTIVITIES The Celebrity Theater is the line's first three-tiered show lounge, seating 900 passengers in a classically inspired but contemporary setting with a full circular balcony. Designed by premier theater designers, the stage, orchestra pits, and lighting can accommodate most any Broadway-style show at sea. Sight lines are excellent and seats extremely comfortable with room between rows. The use of dazzling laser and lighting effects, movable stage levels, and the big-screen video is stunning, but they are frequently more remarkable than the quality of entertainers.

The ever-popular **Rendezvous Lounge,** an elegant cocktail lounge that leads to the dining room, has music for dancing, and the **Platinum Club,** on a balcony overlooking the lounge, is a martini bar and a champagne bar. **Michael's Club,** another Celebrity tradition, is a richly appointed piano bar with traditional English Georgian decor and natural cherry paneling. **Extremes,** at the top of the ship overlooking the pool deck, was Celebrity's first sports bar.

High above the ship on Sunrise Deck is a glass-sheathed observation lounge for panoramic viewing by day. It is transformed into an early evening cabaret and piano bar with a dance floor and a late night disco. The richly decorated **Fortune's Casino** has 228 slot machines, 23 game tables, and a huge selection of video casino games. Overlooking the Grand Foyer is a card and games area; the **COVA Café de Milano,** with a separate tea room and well-attended classical music performances each evening; The cafe quickly becomes a favorite hangout for many, especially non-American travelers who enjoy the European flair of this onboard version of the classic Milan coffeehouse. Passengers are served a variety of coffee drinks, champagne cocktails, and morning and afternoon pastries, often accompanied by music from a harpist or pianist.

In 2005, Celebrity Cruises in conjunction with the famous Cirque du Soleil debuted *The Bar at the Edge of the Earth* onboard *Constellation,* followed by *Summit,* transforming the observation lounge into the new bar. The unusual attraction features surreal characters—Wave Correspondent, The Abyss Gardener, Lantern Tuner, and Pez Erizo—who emerge in the evenings to greet passengers as friends and wander joyfully throughout the bar where exotic food and beverages are served. The room has been redecorated and furnished with small beds (curtains on two sides) replacing what had been observation seating. There are white slip-covered easy chairs on either side for daytime viewing of the passing scene; they remain in place during evening. Abstract designs are projected on veil-like screens that are hung in varying locations throughout the room as backdrop for a single figure dancing. The veils change constantly, with veils drawn, then removed, all in an otherworldly ambience. In addition to the nightly activity, a Cirque du Soleil Masquerade Ball is held once on every cruise. Innovative as the concept is, it has met with mixed reviews and perhaps some disappointment from passengers, since Cirque du Soleil does not stage its unique acrobatic performances on the ship.

Words is a two-level library where passengers can check out books and rent iPods. **Online@CelebrityCruises,** the line's Internet cafe, has 18 individual stations enabling passengers to check their e-mail and other services. The charge is a flat $2 per message, incoming or outgoing, or 75 cents per minute. There are reduced rate packages of $70 for 100 minutes; $120 for 200 minutes; and $250 for 500 minutes. If you want to use your laptop, there is a $10 daily charge for rental of the Connect@Sea kit plus the above charges for minutes. Computer classes are available for $20 an hour. Similar facilities have been added fleetwide.

Another innovation on the Millennium-class ships is the Acupuncture-at-Sea program, in which two to four doctors offer treatment for pain management, smoking cessation, weight loss, and stress management; present lectures about acupuncture, feng shui, nutrition, and healing with herbs; and diagnose and treat specific syndromes with medicinal herbal formulas. The acupuncture program is being added to the other ships this year.

The ship's conference room is designed to hold more than 300 people in auditorium-style seating and offers the latest audiovisual technology, including seat voting/interactive systems and full control booth. The center also can double as the ship's cinema. Five flexible rooms, each offering television, monitors, computers, teleconferencing, Internet connections, fax machines, and private satellite telephones, are available for meetings and other functions.

The **Emporium,** the *Millennium's* European-styled shopping arcade, has designer boutiques, an art gallery, a signature Celebrity shop, and COVA Café store.

SPORTS, FITNESS, AND BEAUTY The Resort Deck has the Riviera pool with four freshwater whirlpools and plenty of areas for sunbathing as well as shaded spots. The deck also houses an entertainment area with a canopied stage and bandstand, a teakwood dance floor, two outdoor bars and the **Grill.** Forward is the **AquaSpa, Aqua Dome,** and the fitness area. The Sunrise Deck overlooking the pool area has a running track and golf simulator (reserve at the Purser's Deck), and the Sports Deck holds a full-size basketball court, paddle tennis, volleyball, and quoits, a game similar to horseshoes.

The 25,000-square-foot AquaSpa, which Celebrity says is the largest and most extensive spa of any cruise ship, is an impressive facility that includes a large fitness area; a gym with an enormous array of equipment (rowers, exercise bikes, recumbent bikes, treadmills, steppers), and an aerobics area, indoor hydropool with air beds, whirlpools, sauna, steam, and tropical showers. The Persian Garden is a tranquil, aromatherapy oasis which can be booked by the hour. The AquaSpa has a beauty parlor and 16 treatment rooms, including a dry float room with shower, Alpha Massage Capsule, a disabled-accessible, full-body treatment room, and other specialty rooms.

The spa offers Celebrity's water-oriented treatments of Middle Eastern, Asian, and European origin, as well as such specialties as thalassotherapy, hydrotherapy, a new aromatic bath, and first-at-sea treatments such as hot stone therapy. Spa charges range from $33 for a 30-minute body composition test, $109 for a 50-minute well-being massage and fitness consultation, to $305 for a two-and-a-half-hour haiku ritual facial and aroma stone massage. Fitness consultants are on hand to assist with programs and assessments. In addition to the equipment in the fitness area, there are four daily classes, two of which, such as yoga and spinning, carry a $10 fee. Four decks down, the promenade does not completely circle the ship, as the lower level of the main dining room takes up the aft portion of Promenade Deck. Still, the long and wide promenade is a fine place for walkers and passengers for whom being on deck, close to the sea, is one of the great joys of cruising.

CHILDREN'S FACILITIES The **Fun Factory** for children ages 3–12 offers a variety of activities with an ocean-travel and exploration theme. Children enjoy a puzzle wall, movie room, and colorful play area under the supervision of experienced counselors. A separate arts and crafts room is available for younger children, whereas the older children have their own broadcast room (though sometimes used by the younger children), video game arcade, dance floor, and CD jukebox.

SHORE EXCURSIONS A variety of tours from adventure activities to cultural experiences is available. In Alaska, they include the Mendenhall Glacier helicopter tour in Juneau, $216–$242; kayaking tours, $66–$89; or panning for gold, $30–$42. In Hawaii, there's a Hilo and Kilauea seven-and-a-half-hour volcano tour, $69–$79; or, two hours whale-watching in Maui, $19–$35. In France, tours are often full-day trips to cities away from the port of call. From the Seine Valley, a ten-hour visit to Paris costs $68–$111; from Le Havre, an 11-hour excursion to Paris with a lunch cruise is $110–$185. On the Russia and the Baltic voyage, a 13-hour excursion by train to Berlin from Rostock is $295 and includes highlights of East and West Berlin, a breakfast snack on the train, buffet lunch at a Berlin hotel restaurant, and dinner snack on the return trip.

POSTSCRIPT Each Celebrity ship has been an improvement on its predecessor. Gracious service combines with inviting decor, high-tech wizardry, and just enough glitz to keep the vessels competitive. The fleet will please travelers who prefer large ships for their high-energy entertainment, extensive facilities, state-of-the-art equipment, and elegant restaurants. The vessels' spaciousness is particularly appealing and unusual in their price group and provides a great deal of value for money.

Celebrity Xpedition	(PREVIEW)	
REGISTRY Ecuador	LENGTH 292 feet	BEAM 48 feet
CABINS 50	DRAFT NA	SPEED 15 knots
MAXIMUM PASSENGERS 94	PASSENGER DECKS 10	ELEVATORS NA
	CREW 64	SPACE RATIO NA

THE SHIP Celebrity's newest ship, added in 2004, is completely different from the rest of the fleet. Small and deluxe, it is used for year-round sailing in the Galapagos Islands. But even eco-focused travelers appreciate fine cuisine, wine, and modern amenities, and indeed, Celebrity Cruises uses as a tag line for *Celebrity Xpedition's* Galapagos cruises: "Where the untamed meets the indulged."

Celebrity is able to offer these cruises by having purchased an Ecuadorian tour operator that held the necessary government permits for Galapagos sailings and ensuring that the 100-passenger *Xpedition* (formerly the *Sun Bay*) was Ecuadorian-flagged and crewed. The German-built vessel is headed by an experienced Royal Caribbean or Celebrity captain, assisted by Ecuadorian and international officers. Most of the staff are experienced in cruise service but have been retrained by Celebrity.

The cruise includes all meals, naturalist guides, folkloric entertainment, enrichment program, shore excursions, gratuities, and Zodiac rides, as well as bottled water, soft drinks, and alcoholic beverages (except premium brands) onboard. On cruise-tour packages, passengers fly to Quito for a two-night stay at the luxurious J.W. Marriott hotel and a city tour by bus and on foot. In addition, the package includes airport transfers; round-trip flights between Quito and Baltra via Guayaquil; Galapagos entry fee; one or two night's hotel stay in Quito on return; and some meals in Quito.

Despite its small size, *Xpedition* has a spacious feel. The **Discovery Lounge** includes a large bar, comfortable seating, and a library with books and games. Here, passengers attend folkloric presentations, lectures, and naturalist discussions about each day's program. The ship also has a small exercise room with sauna, several bars, outdoor deck lounging space, and a small boutique.

The open-seating **Darwin Dining Room** is elegant but not stuffy. It serves breakfast and luncheon buffets with cooked-to-order dishes including omelets and pastas, and full-service dinner. Waiters eagerly bring drinks and special sandwiches or entrees beyond the regular menu choices. Guests can also dine alfresco on many occasions at the outdoor **Beagle Grill.**

Cabins and suites have television, telephone, fluffy cotton bathrobes, Egyptian cotton towels, safe, and hair dryer. Standard cabins (145 square feet) have a large rectangular window and are furnished with two twin beds or one queen bed, a small sofa, desk area with minifridge, and mirror. There is ample closet space and a well-appointed bathroom. The one penthouse suite (460 square feet) has two single beds and one double bed as well as two verandas. Other suites measure 230 square feet.

Xpedition does not have a passenger elevator and is not equipped to accommodate wheelchair passengers or those who can't climb two or three flights of stairs. The ship has a doctor onboard for every voyage, but it does not have Internet access. The ship has a modern waste management system that is being upgraded further this year.

Passengers enter and leave the ship via a platform incorporated into the vessel's structure. To explore ashore, they are tendered via Zodiac craft and proceed on foot. The ship stops at several islands for wildlife viewing. Snorkeling and swimming are included on several excursions; a dive trip can be booked for an additional charge. As on all Galapagos cruises, naturalist guides or the ship's staff accompany all excursions, providing commentary and discussions.

Clipper Cruise Line

11969 Westline Industrial Drive, St. Louis, MO 63146-3220
☎ 314-655-6700 or 800-325-0010;
fax 314-655-6670
www.clippercruise.com

TYPE OF SHIPS First-class small ships.

TYPE OF CRUISES Destination-oriented, light adventure, low-key, intellectually stimulating cruises for nature- and culture-oriented travelers on the byways of the Americas and exotic, offbeat destinations.

CRUISE LINE'S STRENGTHS
- itineraries
- small-ship experience
- cuisine
- accompanying naturalists and experts
- maneuverability of small ships

CRUISE LINE'S SHORTCOMINGS
- lack of cabin amenities and service on oldest ships
- limited shipboard activities
- shallow-draft older vessels in turbulent waters

FELLOW PASSENGERS Relatively affluent, educated, usually professionals, often retired or semiretired and part of a university alumni group. They come from throughout the United States and prefer small ships—often after trying a larger vessel—for the camaraderie, ambience, and small number of passengers. They are not looking for last-minute specials. They are mature, well-traveled, low-key, and, often, seasoned cruisers and Clipper repeaters. Most are environmentally minded and intellectually curious. Some prefer remote, relatively unknown areas; others seek destinations closer to home with strong cultural and natural history appeal, particularly places where small ships have access but large ships must pass by.

Recommended for Experienced travelers who like the coziness of a country inn where people are called by name; big-ship refugees turned off by mainstream cruises and seeking quieter, more substantial travel experience; inquisitive minds who travel to learn.

Not recommended for Night owls, swingers, party seekers, unsophisticated travelers, people who want to be entertained, those with marginal interest in history and nature; and people who like to wear finery.

CRUISE AREAS AND SEASONS Caribbean, South and Central America, Panama Canal, New Zealand, Antarctica in winter; Pacific from Australia, Southeast Asia to Japan to Alaska; Europe, Mediterranean, and North

Africa; eastern seaboard from Florida to Maine, New England/Canada, St. Lawrence River, Great Lakes, West Coast from California to Alaska, Mexico/Sea of Cortés, Alaska, Russia/Alaska, Arctic/Greenland in spring, summer, and fall.

THE LINE Clipper Cruise Line was created in 1982 to provide cultural- and nature-oriented cruises on small coastal ships along historic byways of the United States and the Caribbean. Central and South America. Antarctica, Australia, New Zealand, and Asia were added as oceangoing ships joined the fleet.

The *Nantucket Clipper* and *Yorktown Clipper* are United States–built and registered and have American crews. Their shallow drafts and turn-on-a-dime maneuverability enable them to sail into places where larger ships cannot go. Destinations are as diverse as the Alaskan fjords and tours of the Antebellum South.

In 1997, Clipper Cruise Line was acquired by INTRAV, an established St. Louis group-tour operator, and acquired another vessel, the 122-passenger *Clipper Adventurer*. The ship's ice-hardened hull enables her to sail from the Arctic to Antarctica. The following year, the more deluxe, 128-passenger *Clipper Odyssey* joined the fleet. The ship added a completely new dimension to the cruise line, both in her style, amenities, and in her destinations. In 1999, Kuoni, a prominent Swiss tour company, acquired INTRAV and Clipper Cruise Line.

THE FLEET	BUILT/RENOVATED	TONNAGE	PASSENGERS
Clipper Adventurer	1975/1998	4,364	122
Clipper Odyssey	1989	5,218	128
Nantucket Clipper	1984/95	1,471	100
Yorktown Clipper	1988/97	2,354	138

STYLE Clipper cruises emphasize destinations rather than shipboard fun and games. The ships' size provide intimacy and a sense of place often missing on large ships, plus cordiality resembling that in a country inn. There are passengers enough to ensure an interesting mix. It's easy to meet everyone in the course of a week and for camaraderie to develop effortlessly. The convivial crew members bolster the friendly atmosphere. Absent but not missed are casinos, discos, staged entertainment, and organized diversions of large ships.

The ships cruise mostly at night, stopping during the day for passengers to tour an island, hike in a rain forest, enjoy a secluded beach, or snorkel in reef-filled waters. Life aboard is casual, unregimented, and leisurely. The experience is enhanced by naturalists and experts who, in addition to presenting seminars, talk informally with passengers during shore excursions and cocktail hour.

Clipper is proud of its role in providing environmentally responsible travel, saying that ship size and the nature of the cruises have a minimal impact on destinations.

DISTINCTIVE FEATURES Historians, naturalists, and other experts travel as guides on ships; Zodiac landing craft aboard. Excellent precruise literature. Consumer protection plan.

	HIGHEST	LOWEST	AVERAGE
PER DIEM	$712	$251	$452

Per diems are calculated from cruise line's nondiscounted *cruise-only* published fares on standard accommodations and vary by season, cabins, and cruise areas.

RATES Published rates include port fees; some include shore excursions and gratuities, and frequently may include special events.

Special fares and discounts Some advance booking discounts available and detailed in cruise line's brochure.

- **THIRD PASSENGER:** Specific to each cruise, quoted in brochure.
- **SINGLE SUPPLEMENT:** Specific for each category, quoted in brochure; otherwise, 150% of brochure rate on other cabins, when available.

Packages
- **AIR/SEA:** Yes.
- **PRE/POST:** Alaska; train tours combined with Sea of Cortés, northern California, and Pacific Northwest; Asia, among others.
- **OTHERS:** No.

PAST PASSENGERS In 2003, Clipper launched its Pinnacle program to reward past passengers for multiple cruises with special benefits, like travel certificates to be used for future cruises, in-room gifts, as well as acknowledgment by the captain and crew during the cruise. The program has three levels, with varying benefits: Explorers (2 to 5 trips), Grand Explorers (6 to 15 trips), and Elite Explorers (16 or more).

THE LAST WORD Clipper has been transformed from a coastal cruise line to a worldwide operation since obtaining its new ships. Nonetheless, it continues to attract people who recoil at the notion of today's mega-ships. Yet anyone who does not fit into Clipper's country-club, somewhat academic atmosphere could quickly feel out of place. To compare Clipper's small-ship cruise experience with that of large ships is comparing apples to oranges. In terms of the published prices, however, they are comparable. The difference is that Clipper does not usually discount its prices, even for early-bird bookings—a practice almost standard elsewhere. Prices, particularly for cruises on the two older ships, seem high given their lack of some shipboard services and facilities—no swimming pool, elevator, beauty shop, laundry room or laundry service, or cabin telephone and television. Clipper's last two acquisitions with their amenities come closer to the mark. Precruise information sent by Clipper is thorough; some papers are the length of a book. These excellent reference materials reflect the line's commitment to making its cruises stimulating, enriching, and memorable.

Clipper Cruise line Standard Features

Officers American; *Clipper Adventurer*, European; *Clipper Odyssey*, Australian and European.

Staff *Nantucket*, *Yorktown*, Dining, Cabin/American; *Adventurer*, *Odyssey*, Dining, Cabin/Filipino; Cruise/American, all ships.

Dining facilities Single-seating dining room for three meals with open seating, buffet breakfast and lunch in lounge, and occasional lunch buffet on sun deck or picnic on shore. Self-service juice, coffee, and tea in lounge.

Special diets Accommodated with advance notice.

Room service None.

Dress code Casual but smart; coat and tie recommended for special occasions or going to fashionable restaurants in ports of call.

Cabin amenities Radio, but no television or phones; bathrooms with showers; hair dryers. *Odyssey*, television for movies, safe, bathroom with small tub and shower.

Electrical outlets 110 AC, except *Adventurer,* 220 AC.

Wheelchair access One cabin and elevator, on *Odyssey* only.

Recreation and entertainment Seminars by naturalists, historians and other experts; movies; occasional local entertainers. *Adventurer*, *Odyssey*, two lounges, bars, library.

Sports and other activities Gym on *Adventurer* only. Swimming, snorkeling, beach walks, wilderness and rain-forest hiking. Swimming pool on *Odyssey* only.

Beauty and fitness *Nantucket, Yorktown*, no beauty/barber shop; services generally available in port; *Adventurer* and *Odyssey* have both.

Other facilities *Adventurer, Odyssey*, infirmary with doctor, gift shop, laundry service; e-mail service. *Nantucket, Yorktown*, no laundry service; no doctor aboard except Costa Rica, Sea of Cortés, and western Caribbean cruises.

Children's facilities None.

Theme cruises None.

Smoking No smoking allowed in any interior areas, including cabins, at any time. Smoking permitted only on outside decks.

Clipper suggested tipping Tips pooled. $10 per passenger per day, deposited in a box at cruise's end. No service charge added to wine or bar bill. Tips are included in cruise fares for *Adventurer* and *Odyssey*.

Credit cards For cruise payment: American Express, Diner's Club, Discover, MasterCard, Visa. On-board *Nantucket Clipper* and *Yorktown Clipper*: American Express, MasterCard, Visa; *Clipper Adventurer* and *Clipper Odyssey*: MasterCard and Visa.

Nantucket Clipper	**QUALITY 5**	**VALUE C**
Yorktown Clipper	**QUALITY 5**	**VALUE C**
REGISTRY United States	**LENGTH** 207/257 feet	**BEAM** 37/43 feet
CABINS 51/69	**DRAFT** 8 feet	**SPEED** 7/10 knots
MAXIMUM PASSENGERS	**PASSENGER DECKS** 4	**ELEVATORS** None
100/138	**CREW** 32–36/38–42	**SPACE RATIO** NA

THE SHIPS United States–built and flying the American flag, the *Nantucket Clipper* and the slightly larger *Yorktown Clipper* are almost identical. With their shallow drafts, the ships glide into small places as easily as they tie up in small ports, sailboat-filled harbors, and coves.

The *Nantucket Clipper* has three passenger decks and the *Yorktown Clipper* four, including a spacious top sun deck aft of the bridge—a comfortable place for watching the passing scene.

Cabins and lounges are decorated with quality furnishings. No glitter, no glitz.

Both ships have a single forward observation lounge and bar on the center deck that serves as a social center. Three sides of the cheerful room have large windows trimmed with light wood. Textured fabric and neutral colors give the lounge a warm, contemporary look. During cruises, the room has the air of a club, with passengers conversing, reading, writing postcards, or simply watching scenery. It is also the scene for lectures, early breakfast buffet, afternoon cookies, and hors d'oeuvres at cocktail time.

ITINERARIES *See* Itinerary Index.

CABINS All six categories of cabins are outside, and all but the lowest category have picture windows.

Cabins on the promenade deck open onto an outdoor, wraparound deck (as on river steamboats). Although these have an airy feel, some passengers might prefer cabins that open onto a central corridor. On the *Yorktown*, four cabins on the sun deck are the largest and most private.

The cabins are small but adequate, well-lighted, offer ample storage, and appear more spacious because of a large wall mirror. Beds are parallel or at right angles; the latter provides more floor space. The furnishings have a clean, modern look, with pastel curtains and bedcovers, closets and dressers in light wood, and landscape paintings on the wall. The bathrooms have showers only and are small, with limited shelf space. In an effort to let passengers get away from it all, cabins have neither telephones nor televisions. Radios, however, provide wake-up calls, ship information, and music. Some cabins get noise from the hydraulic lift that raises and lowers the gangplank in port.

There is no room service. Laundry, beauty shop, and barber shop are usually available in port. The ships carry no nurses or doctors except on specific cruises. However, the vessels are almost always near shore in case of medical emergency. Lack of medical staff and the difficulty of walking on steep gangways make the ships unsuitable for many physically disabled persons.

Specifications All outside cabins; no suites. Standard dimensions range from 122–139 square feet on *Yorktown Clipper;* 106–123 square feet on *Nantucket Clipper*. All have 2 lower beds, some with pull-down third bunk; no singles. None are wheelchair-accessible.

DINING The dining room, on the lower deck, has large windows and pleasant decor reflecting quality. Passengers dine at a single, open seating at round or square marble-topped tables, which are covered with cloths for dinner. The food is American cuisine overseen by a chef trained at either the prestigious Culinary Institute of America or at Johnson and Wales. Meals feature excellent soups, good-quality beef, fresh seafood, vegetables, and fruit. They're presented in a straightforward manner by the young, cheerful staff. Selections are not as extensive as on larger ships—dinner menus offer four entrees—but all menus include a regional specialty. A small but moderately priced selection of wines is available.

An early light breakfast is served in the lounge; lunch buffets are offered on the sun deck, weather permitting. Snacks, including fresh fruit, are available throughout the day. In the afternoon, freshly baked chocolate chip cookies are set out in the lounge, welcomed by passengers who have gathered in anticipation. The bar is open from 11 a.m. to midnight.

SERVICE The clean-cut staff of young American men and women are cheerful, attentive, friendly, and unfailingly polite. Most are college students from the U.S. heartland, where Clipper is based, who sign on for a year of employment. They take care of the restaurant, bar, and cabins, working 12 hours a day, 6 days a week, and smile through it all.

FACILITIES AND ACTIVITIES Daily seminars by naturalists, historians, or other experts on places visited on the cruise precede follow-up discussions after the visits. The naturalist also acts as guide for nature walks, bird-watching, and study of the local environment. Afternoons at sea, a movie plays in the dining room. A local folklorist or other interesting characters may come on board for a lecture, discussion, or entertainment. The cruise director briefs passengers daily about upcoming adventures. Activity centers around the destination, whether it's a tour of a historic town, a golf game, or a forest hike. There are no organized fun and games. Deck space is adequate for a destination-oriented ship, and most people use it to sunbathe, read, or watch the scenery—often through binoculars. Evenings in port enable passengers to explore local nightlife. Otherwise, passengers gather in the lounge after dinner to visit, or they retire to the dining room to watch videos. Most are in their cabins by 10 p.m.

SPORTS AND FITNESS Walkers can circumnavigate the promenade deck, and when the ships tie up at night, as they often do, passengers walk into town. Depending on itinerary and weather, snorkeling directly from the ship is available, and scuba diving, windsurfing, deep-sea fishing, golf, or tennis can be arranged. The ships have no pools, whirlpools, exercise equipment, or fitness centers.

SHORE EXCURSIONS Cruises usually call at ports seldom visited by other ships and often tie up at small, out-of-the-way marinas and yacht harbors, enabling passengers to explore remote islands and coastlines on foot. Where *Nantucket Clipper* cannot dock, passengers go ashore by Zodiac boat; *Yorktown Clipper* has dib launches. In urban areas, ships often tie up within walking distance of cultural attractions and offer above-average tours at reasonable costs.

POSTSCRIPT Although the adventures are light and seldom far from civilization, many itineraries entail walking, wet landings, and climbing in and out of Zodiac boats in remote areas. Some involve traversing open sea, and with the ships' shallow drafts, passengers may have a bumpy ride for several hours. Because the ships do not carry doctors and do not have elevators, they are not able to handle passengers with serious health or physical limitations.

Clipper Adventurer	QUALITY 8	VALUE C
REGISTRY Bahamas	LENGTH 330 feet	BEAM 53.5 feet
CABINS 61	DRAFT 16 feet	SPEED 14 knots

MAXIMUM PASSENGERS 122	PASSENGER DECKS 4	ELEVATORS None
	CREW 72	SPACE RATIO NA

THE SHIP The *Clipper Adventurer* is the former *Alla Tarasova,* a Russian expedition vessel with an A-1 Super Ice-class rating. Her itinerary is designed by Hasse Nilsson, the widely known former master of the *Lindblad Explorer* and the first captain to take passengers through the Northwest Passage.

Built in 1975 in Yugoslavia, the ship received a $15-million renovation before joining Clipper's fleet in 1998. As a result, she is one of the most comfortable and stylish expedition ships afloat, designed to be more elegant than Clipper's older craft while retaining the feeling of an adventure ship. The renovations added a window-lined observation lounge, library/card room and bar, small gym, beauty salon, covered promenade, and observation platform directly below the bridge. To ensure comfort even further, stabilizers were added in 1998. the ship's public rooms are mahogany-paneled and the furnishings upholstered in handsome colors of deep blue, red, and aquamarine.

The refined decor and upgraded amenities helps the line merge INTRAV's more upscale passengers with Clipper's eclectic mix. the ship is well suited for exploration with her ice-class hull, great maneuverability, and shallow draft that enable her to sail near shorelines, in polar waters, or along scenic riverbanks.

ITINERARIES *See* Itinerary Index.

CABINS *Adventurer* has 61 all-outside cabins averaging 130 square feet, including three suites. All have large windows or portholes. There are eight categories.

Cabins are designed to be comfortable rather than posh. Twin lower beds are in an L shape or parallel (no queens). Bathrooms are tiled, with showers. Closet and storage space is ample. The suites on Boat Deck have separate seating areas with desks and chairs.

DINING A window-lined dining room accommodates all passengers at one leisurely seating at tables for two to seven. American and regional dishes are prepared by trained chefs. Service is provided by a Filipino staff who are cheerful, pleasant, attentive, and accommodating.

FACILITIES AND ACTIVITIES The main lounge and bar of the cozy, club-like ship is the center for informal talks by staff naturalists, historians, and other specialists. Also in the lounge are breakfast and lunch buffets, before-dinner hors d'oeuvres, and musical performances. The **Clipper Club** lounge near the dining room is the favorite spot for cocktails. One level up, the small library offers books on wildlife and literature. The quiet retreat, furnished with silk-covered armchairs, doubles as a card room, with board games and puzzles.

One of the ship's best features is a large observation platform directly below the bridge. It's ideal for viewing wildlife or scenery. (Also, the captain usually maintains a 24-hour open bridge.) Promenades on two decks provide additional viewing venues. The wide Boat Deck promenade has a partially covered area aft and provides teak benches perfect for scene-watching or conversation. The Promenade Deck has a wide, enclosed deck, allowing exercise out of the elements. Other facilities and amenities include a small gym, beauty shop, a full-time physician, gift shop, and laundry service—the first time such amenities have been available on a Clipper ship. *Adventurer* is equipped with ten Zodiac landing craft for exploring hard-to-reach places.

Clipper Odyssey	QUALITY 9	VALUE B
REGISTRY Bahamas	LENGTH 340 feet	BEAM 51 feet
CABINS 64	DRAFT 14 feet	SPEED 14 knots
MAXIMUM PASSENGERS 128	PASSENGER DECKS 5	ELEVATORS 1
	CREW 72	SPACE RATIO 83

THE SHIP In September 1998, less than seven months after launching the *Clipper Adventurer*, the cruise line acquired a fourth ship, the deluxe *Oceanic Odyssey*, from Spice Islands Cruises. When Clipper took over operations in November 1999, the ship was renamed the *Clipper Odyssey*.

Designed in Holland and constructed in 1989 by Japanese craftsmen, the ship is beautifully built with quality furnishings and the detail of a deluxe yacht with an intimate and casual ambience. The decor is warm and comfortable, with traces of its Japanese origins in the pictures and other art.

The center of activity is the main lounge and bar on the main deck, which is used for most activities—lectures, socializing, or waiting for the warm chocolate chip cookies served in the afternoon. At cocktail time, when most passengers gather in the lounge, the dining staff lays out generous hot and cold hors d'oeuvres. Usually, the expedition staff gives a briefing on the day's activity ashore and preparations for the following day. After dinner, passengers usually return to the lounge for a lecture by one of the expert guides accompanying the cruise. Adjacent to the lounge is a library with good collections of reference books for each of the areas the ship visits.

One deck up, the **Day Lounge,** when not in use for light meals, becomes the card and reading room. Here, a self-service counter has coffee, tea, and juices around the clock. Directly outside is an outdoor deck and swimming pool. In good weather, this deck is used for informal parties. All five passenger decks are served by a central elevator.

The ship spends the year in the Pacific region roaming as far south as New Zealand and Australia, west to Vietnam, and north to the Russian Far East.

ITINERARIES *See* Itinerary Index.

CABINS Accommodations are spacious, all-outside cabins with sitting areas, spread over four decks. All standard cabins are the same size—approximately 186 square feet—and have large windows, except for a few on the lower deck, which have portholes. Each cabin provides a high degree of comfort, with television for videos and movies, a safe, minifridge, music system, and hair dryer—amenities lacking from Clipper's older ships. Bathrooms have a small, Japanese-style tub and shower. The rooms are furnished with a blonde wood, built-in dresser/desk with shallow drawers, and two small hanging closets, plus bedside night tables with drawers. Beds can be configured as twin or queen size. One cabin is designed for disabled travelers. The one suite and eight deluxe cabins on the uppermost accommodations deck have verandas. Instant News from London (faxed news) is available daily.

Specifications 60 outside cabins; 1 suite and 8 deluxe cabins with verandas. Standard dimensions, 180 square feet. All have 2 lower twin or queen beds; no singles. 1 wheelchair-accessible.

DINING The attractive **Main Dining Room** offers open, single seating at set hours for three meals. It serves high-quality, well-prepared cuisine with regional accents using fresh ingredients, often bought from local markets on the ship 's route. As with other Clipper ships, the chef is a graduate of the Culinary Institute of America or another reputable culinary school.

Breakfast in the dining room is a buffet feast of fruits, cereals, breads, eggs cooked to order, and a specialty of the day. Lunch and dinner menus are varied and creative and offer a choice of two soups, fish, chicken, meat, or vegetarian entree, and dessert. Dinner has similar selections with even more choices. In addition, there is a daily healthy menu. Passengers may order half-portions of any course. A wine is suggested for each course of dinner; wine is available by the glass for an additional charge. Continental breakfast and light lunch are also served indoors in the sunny **Day Lounge** or poolside. Dress is casual throughout the day and only slightly more fashionable in the evening.

SERVICE The service rendered by the Filipino staff in the dining room, bar, decks, and cabins is among the ship's best features. It is the equal of some of the most luxurious ships afloat. They are smiling, pleasant, thoughtful, hardworking, and gracious at every hour of the day. Dining room waiters make a point of learning passengers' names from the first day, and even though passengers sit where they choose, the waiters seem to remember their individual likes and needs.

FACILITIES AND ACTIVITIES The ship has a swimming pool and Jacuzzi; a small, well-stocked reading room; and a boutique. The ship's band plays dance music in the main lounge. The INMARSAT telecommunications system permits worldwide, 24-hour telephone and fax communication, and there is a computer station for passengers to send e-mail. All activity is focused on and determined daily by the port or location and weather, docking and tender or Zodiac landing condition, whether it is sight-seeing, hiking, water sports, or other sports.

SPORTS, FITNESS, AND BEAUTY The small gym on the Bridge Deck has a treadmill, step machine, bicycle, and free weights. There is a jogging track on the top deck. *Odyssey* has ample teak-covered deck space and the broad upper deck for sunbathing.

At the beginning of the cruise, passengers are issued snorkeling gear to keep for their entire trip. Depending on the area of the cruise, the expedition staff takes passengers in Zodiac landing craft on shore excursions in remote areas and for swimming and snorkeling. The staff will arrange scuba diving where it is available for an additional charge.

The tiny hair salon on deck three has two chairs; the attendant, who also manages the ship's tiny boutique, can do a simple wash and set or blow dry. Next door is the small clinic staffed by a registered physician.

Costa Cruise Lines

Venture Corporate Center II
200 South Park Road, Suite 200, Hollywood, FL 33021-8541
☎ **954-266-5600 or 800-462-6782; fax 954-266-2100**
www.costacruises.com

TYPE OF SHIPS New, modern superliners.

TYPE OF CRUISES Mass market, designed for Europeans as much as North Americans—hence, more European in service and ambience.

CRUISE LINE'S STRENGTHS
* Italian style and service
* friendly, attentive crew
* itineraries

CRUISE LINE'S SHORTCOMINGS
* noise level in dining rooms
* excessive announcements on European-based ships
* language problems

FELLOW PASSENGERS Costa has two seasons: Caribbean from late fall to early spring, and Europe, mainly from spring through fall, although some European cruises are now year-round. This results in two sets of passengers. In the Caribbean, up to 70% of passengers are North Americans, depending on the cruise; average age is 54 years, with annual household income of $50,000+. A bevy of Italian-American fans and newlyweds are attracted by the line's Italian style. Most have cruised before.

In Europe, 80% or more are Europeans likely to have traveled abroad, probably even cruised before. Among the North Americans, average age is about the same as Caribbean cruisers, but they would be inclined to rent a car and drive through Europe on their own instead of taking an escorted tour. They enjoy traveling with and meeting people from other countries.

Recommended for Italophiles; first-time cruisers and less experienced travelers who want to sample European ambience, but with facilities typical of a large ship; and repeat cruisers who want to try something different.

Not recommended for Those who like small ships as well as an all-American atmosphere or those who prefer to travel with Americans.

CRUISE AREAS AND SEASONS Caribbean, Mediterranean, Greek islands, the Holy Land, Black Sea, Northern Europe, Norwegian fjords, the Baltic, Russia, South America, and transatlantic cruises.

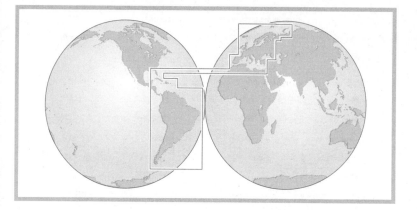

THE LINE Genoa-based Costa Crociere, parent company of Costa Cruise Lines, had been in the shipping business for over 100 years and in the passenger business for almost 50 years when it was bought jointly by Carnival Corp and Airtours, a European tour company, in 1997. (Three years later, Carnival acquired Airtours' shares as well.)

Costa, Europe's largest cruise line, was among the earliest lines to offer one-week Caribbean cruises from Miami (1959) and the first to introduce an air/sea program (late 1960s). Despite its long Florida-Caribbean association, Costa changed course in the 1990s to become more Europe-focused. Of its nine ships, only two sail from U.S. ports, and they sail only in winter. The others, including Holland America's former *Westerdam*, which joined the Costa fleet in April 2002 as *Costa Europa,* are positioned in Europe and elsewhere.

Costa launched the 1990s with four new ships costing more than $1 billion and intended to serve a broad spectrum of passengers. The ships combine modern and classic qualities with new design features. The line added the larger *Costa Victoria* in 1996, followed by the even larger *Costa Atlantica* in 2000; the latter's sister ship, *Costa Mediterranea,* followed in 2003. With the arrival of two 105,000-ton ships, *Costa Fortuna* and *Costa Magica* in 2003 and 2004, another billion-dollar expansion continued—the last three ships alone doubled the line's passenger capacity. Costa's largest ship to date, the 112,000-ton *Costa Concordia,* is under construction and expected to debut in 2006, while her yet-to-be-named twin will follow in 2007.

THE FLEET	BUILT/RENOVATED	TONNAGE	PASSENGERS
Costa Allegra	1990/2001	28,430	820
Costa Atlantica	2000	85,619	2,114

THE FLEET	BUILT/RENOVATED	TONNAGE	PASSENGERS
Costa Classica	1991/2001	52,926	1,308
Costa Concordia	2006	112,000	3,300
Costa Europa	1986/90/2002/03	53,872	1,494
Costa Fortuna	2003	105,000	2,720
Costa Magica	2004	105,000	2,720
Costa Mediterranea	2003	86,000	2,114
Costa Romantica	1993/2003	53,049	1,356
Costa Victoria	1996/2004	75,166	1,928
Unnamed	2007	112,000	3,300

STYLE In the early 1980s, Costa coined the phrase "cruising Italian style" to celebrate its Italian basis in everything from design to cuisine. Its fleet is designed and built in Italy by Italians, with floors and walls of Italian marble, splendid wood cabinetry, designer fabrics and linens, and Italian art throughout. They reflect the sophisticated architecture and decor of modern Italian designers rather than the classic Italian look. The Finnish-built *Costa Atlantica* was the first to depart somewhat from the Italian style.

Life on board is made to seem *molto Italiano,* from the pasta and espresso to Italian language lessons, Italian cooking classes, Italian ice cream, pizzas in the pizzerias, and toga parties. Theme nights such as the "Festa Italiana" feature an Italian street festival with bocce ball games, tarantella dance lessons, pizza dough–tossing contests, Venetian mask-making, and more. Yet for all the trimmings, the Italian ambience has been diluted, mainly because Costa ships no longer have all-Italian crews.

The ships are very much "today" with gyms, spas, and fitness programs, and Costa's Caribbean shore excursions emphasize outdoor activities. One of Costa's most popular innovations is its "private" beach on Isla Catalina off the Dominican Republic. The island is near the sprawling resort of Casa de Campo, which, among its many facilities, has a tennis village, four of the Caribbean's best golf courses, and a marina village with restaurants and shops, enabling Costa's ships on Eastern Caribbean cruises to spend the day at the island and the evenings at the marina.

All dining and public rooms on Costa ships are nonsmoking, but that doesn't mean passengers, especially European ones, don't light up. The ships do not have self-service launderettes, a much-appreciated amenity available on most new large ships. Laundry and pressing services are available from the ships' facilities, but these are costly.

DISTINCTIVE FEATURES Free hot pizza throughout day. On Caribbean cruises, couples can renew their wedding vows in a shipboard ceremony. Alternative dining on the new ships; unusual private island; Fiesta nights; toga party.

	HIGHEST	LOWEST	AVERAGE
PER DIEM	$538	$86	$161

Per diems are calculated from cruise line's nondiscounted *cruise-only* published fares on standard accommodations and vary by season, cabins, and cruise areas.

RATES Port charges are included.

Special fares and discounts Andiamo Fares provide 12–25% discounts, depending on category, for bookings 120 days in advance in the Caribbean and 90 days in Europe. Additional discounts on Andiamo Fares are available in some categories for seniors and for friends and families traveling together. Combining Eastern and Western Caribbean or two Mediterranean cruises into 14-nighters offers savings, too.

- **CHILDREN'S FARE:** Same as third/fourth passenger fares (works for single parents, too); also $199 for children ages 17 and younger on some cruises.
- **SINGLE SUPPLEMENT:** 180–200%.

Packages
- **AIR/SEA:** Yes, for Europe; mostly as add-ons for Caribbean.
- **PRE/POST:** Yes, in Amsterdam, Copenhagen, Genoa, London, Nice/ Monte Carlo, Paris, Rome, Venice, Ft. Lauderdale, or Orlando, depending on cruise.
- **OTHERS:** Spa, seniors, honeymoon, family.

PAST PASSENGERS Costa Club is the line's new passenger club which passengers can join after their first cruise. With each subsequent Costa cruise, you receive points based on the number of days of the cruise and expenditures charged to your cruise card. The Costa Club card is valid for three years. Depending on your category, members receive discounts in the beauty salon, fruit basket, free dinner in an alternative restaurant that has a charge; and discounts on cruise fares, ranging from 5–18%, among others. Past passengers also receive mailings announcing new itineraries and a Costa magazine.

THE LAST WORD Costa has dared to be different in style and in the markets it pursues, preferring to be number one in Europe, where it has a strong base and years of experience, rather than struggling in the fierce competition of the Caribbean. The strategy virtually guarantees that when you take a Costa cruise in Europe, the experience will be European rather than catering to American tastes.

Some Americans welcome the opportunity to take a European vacation with Europeans. Others are turned off by cliques in lounges and bars and the steady stream of announcements—for bingo, shopping talks, and shore excursions—in five languages, even though English-speaking hostesses are aboard to cater to North Americans. The multilingual announcements on Caribbean cruises are kept to a minimum and normally are used when matters of safety are being broadcast.

Areas are designated as smoking or nonsmoking on Costa ships, but some European smokers flout the restrictions—defiantly.

Costa Cruise Lines Standard Features

Officers Italian.

Staff Dining/Italian, other European, Asian, Central American; Cabin/International; Cruise/International.

Dining facilities One main dining room (two on *Costa Victoria*), two seatings for breakfast and dinner, one for lunch, midnight buffet featuring Italian cuisine; indoor/outdoor buffet breakfast and lunch. Alternative dining; *Victoria, Atlantica, Mediterranea, Magica, Fortuna* (extra charge). Pizzerias and pastry cafes on most ships.

Special diets Should be requested four weeks in advance.

Room service 24 hours, limited menu; butler service in suites with full service for meals from dining room menus.

Dress code Casual; informal evenings; two nights formal/semiformal.

Cabin amenities Phone, radio, private shower, hair dryer, safe, television; suites have whirlpool bath, minibar, and veranda.

Electrical outlets 110/220 AC; adapters available onboard.

Wheelchair access 6 cabins on *Classica, Romantica, Victoria;* 8 on *Allegra, Atlantica, Mediterranea;* 24 on *Magica, Fortuna.*

Recreation and entertainment Casino, bars and lounges with nightly entertainment, showrooms, disco, dance and Italian language lessons, bingo, bridge, horse racing, library, card room.

Sports and other activities Three swimming pools, *Atlantica, Mediterranea, Magica, Fortuna* (one for children); two, *Classica, Romantica, Victoria* (plus one inside); one, *Allegra, Marina, Riviera.* Exercise classes, snorkeling lessons, paddle tennis, Ping-Pong, deck and pool games. *Victoria, Atlantica, Mediterranea, Magica, Fortuna* tennis/basketball. Golf Academy on *Atlantica, Mediterranea, Magica.*

Beauty and fitness Barber shop and beauty salon, spa, sauna, European beauty treatments, fitness centers, jogging track, whirlpools.

Other facilities Boutiques, medical facility, laundry and dry cleaning services, meeting room, chapel. Internet access on all ships.

Children's facilities Costa Kids year-round; babysitters. (No baby-sitting service in cabins.)

Theme cruises Golf, food and wine, others.

Smoking Smoking in designated public areas; all dining and public rooms are nonsmoking.

Costa suggested tipping (*Caribbean*) Per person per day: cabin steward, $3; waiter, $3; busboy, $1.50, head waiter, $1; (*Europe*) Costa will add €7.50 per person per day to your shipboard account. 15% gratuity added to all beverage bills (including mineral water in the dining room).

Credit cards For cruise payment and onboard charges: American Express, Carte Blanche, Diners Club, Discover, MasterCard, Visa.

Costa Atlantica	QUALITY 7	VALUE C
Costa Mediterranea	QUALITY 7	VALUE C
REGISTRY Italy	LENGTH 960 feet	BEAM 106 feet
CABINS 1,057	DRAFT 19.5 feet	SPEED 24 knots
MAXIMUM PASSENGERS 2,114	PASSENGER DECKS 12	ELEVATORS 12
	CREW 920	SPACE RATIO NA

THE SHIPS *Costa Atlantica,* debuted in 2000, and her twin, *Costa Mediterranea,* launched in 2003, were the largest, fastest ships in the fleet at the time they entered service and have drawn positive reviews from passengers. After Costa came under the Carnival umbrella, and with interior design in the hands of architect Joe Farcus, who is known for creating the flamboyant decor of Carnival ships, there was considerable concern that he would "Carnivalize" these Costa ships. Farcus's imprint is unmistakable, but he has combined touches of his trademark fantasy and glitter with European elegance that seem to work and delight most—but not all—of the North Americans and Europeans who have sailed on them. It's safe to say that Farcus's decor is the antithesis of the modern, spare interiors created by Italian designers for some of Costa's other ships.

Atlantica, because of her balconies and large windows, has a more open, lighter appearance than *Costa Victoria,* which recently had balconies added to 246 of her cabins. Most of the public rooms are on decks two and three, anchored by a spectacular glass-ceiling atrium. The decor of *Atlantica,* including the use of Murano glass and inlaid mosaic, is flamboyant. For example, passengers take turns enjoying the Alice in Wonderland–style red-leather chairs with extremely high backs in the atrium bar.

The Farcus touches are everywhere—the red-leather benches near the theatrical multilevel fitness room have little boots on them; whimsical or fantastic motifs are worked into the carpets, the banquettes, and the tables, with subtlety and taste.

Atlantica is dedicated to Federico Fellini, the great Italian filmmaker, with her 12 passenger decks named for movies directed by him and huge blow-ups from his work placed in public rooms. (Although, as one passengers pointed out to us on a recent cruise, none of Fellini's movies are to be found among the ship's movie selections.) Besides the impressive large public spaces, there are intimate quiet areas, like the small Italian garden by the chapel. The ship also pays homage to Venice with **Caffe Florian,** a replica of the 18th-century landmark in St. Mark's Square, with a menu and music taken from the original. Traditionalists will probably find these rooms to be the ship's most attractive area. *Costa Mediterranea* is dedicated to the history, art, and architecture of Italy and the Mediterranean. The decks, for example, are named for historic figures—Medea, Pandora, Cleopatra, etc.

Atlantica was the first Costa ship to offer Internet access, available in a center that doubles as the library and in some cabins and suites, where guests can bring their own laptop computer or rent one. The cost is a steep $0.50 per minute. The ships are equipped with a dual Azipod propulsion system, technology that was introduced on the *Carnival Destiny* and contributes to smooth sailing. They have received the Green Star from the Italian Register of Shipping for innovative environmental protection design.

ITINERARIES *See* Itinerary Index.

CABINS The ships have 13 categories of cabins, most on decks 1 and 4–8. Of the total 1,057 cabins, 78% are outside. The 678 cabins or almost 65% of cabins and suites have verandas with clear acrylic barriers in front, enabling passengers to lie in bed and look out at the port of call or the sea. Another 68 cabins have French balconies, but these have views obstructed by the lifeboats as noted in the deck plan.

Cabins are stylish in decor and very well designed, with an unusual amount of polished hardwood floors as well as carpets and fine leather. All cabins have direct-dial telephone, television, minibar, safe, hair dryer, amenities, and ample storage. In the suites, the bedside lamps have exceptionally attractive Murano glass shades with smaller, concentrated lights attached for nighttime reading. The suites also have plush robes, marble baths, double sinks, and Jacuzzi tubs. In standard cabins, showers are much larger than on the line's previous vessels.

Specifications 824 outside; 233 inside; 678 cabins (including 58 suites) with verandas. Cabins with verandas measure 210 square feet; inside cabins, 162 square feet; suites with verandas, 360 square feet. 8 are wheelchair-accessible.

DINING The ships have several dining venues. The two-level **Tiziano Restaurant** (**Degli Argentieri** on *Costa Mediterranea*) is the main dining room serving undistinguished Continental cuisine with some Italian specialties; the Botticelli Buffet offers breakfast and lunch in an informal setting with a rather limited, repetitive selection; and the **Napoli Pizzeria** serves a variety of fresh hot pizzas throughout the day. Surprisingly, there are no pasta stations in either the dining room or the lido buffet, as on Costa's other ships.

The dining rooms are comfortable, but the noise level is high, depending on where you sit. Healthful menus with low-fat, low-carb, low-calorie, and low-cholesterol courses are available in the dining rooms for lunch, dinner, and at the informal breakfast. A generous number of vegetarian dishes is offered, and there is a separate children's menu.

Club Atlantica by Marchesi (**Club Medusa** on *Costa Mediterranea*), the alternative, by-reservation restaurant, is located at the top of the ship, above the Lido restaurant. It is modeled after its namesake in Venice and has an extra charge of $23 a person—and worth every penny. It offers two appetizing single-choice menus and wines served amid candles, flowers, and live musical entertainment. If you come only once, you might want to mix and match selections from both menus. The cuisine here is so outstanding that it shows up the dining room's mediocre results and makes one wonder why there is such a marked difference.

SERVICE Not everyone agrees about the service. Some say it's excellent, warm, and efficient; others say it's often haphazard. But for sure, long-time Costa fans will miss the verve of an Italian crew as the only Italians in the restaurants are the maître d'hôtel and his assistant. On a recent cruise, we found service throughout the *Costa Atlantica* to be excellent and its top attraction. There are no wine stewards in the dining room.

FACILITIES AND ACTIVITIES Daytime diversions include dance, gaming and golf lessons, port and shopping talks, the ubiquitous art auctions, health and beauty workshops, bridge, handwriting analysis, tennis singles, arts and crafts, and quizzes. The cruise staff is one of the most active this writer has every encountered, keeping passengers busy with games, dancing, and other activities, and creating an atmosphere that reminded me of traditional cruises of the past. The library and card room are handsome and well-used, but the multinational nature of the passengers means a somewhat limited number of books in English. The Internet center, which is part of the library, has five terminals. **Via della Spiga** is the ship's shopping promenade, and there's a full-service conference center.

Evening entertainment is designed for the multinational nature of the passengers, with more dance, music, and magic than comic routines. The **Caruso Theater** (**Osiris** on *Costa Mediterranea*), the impressive three-level main show lounge at the front of the ship, has very few columns to interrupt sight lines. En route to the theater, passengers pass the **Paparazzi Lounge** with bigger-than-life, black-and-white photographs of celebrities, such as Joe DiMaggio.

Caffe Florian, replicating the famous St. Mark's Square landmark, serves afternoon tea, coffees, liqueurs, and aperitifs with background music evoking the romance of the Venetian legend that captivated such luminaries as Vivaldi, Dickens, Stravinsky, and others. The **Madame Butterfly Grand Lounge** is a large multifunction room and bar used for activities throughout the day and evening. The **Coral Lounge,** used for seminars and special entertainment, has an underwater quality with blue walls and huge white coral trees behind etched glass.

The glittering **Fortuna Casino** (**Grand Canal Casino** on *Costa Mediterranea*) is well laid-out, with comfortable access to slots, roulette, and blackjack tables. It has its own bar—one of 12 on the ship—and is adjacent to the **Madame Butterfly Grand Lounge.**

Dancing in the evenings ranges from disco to swing, and bands playing for guests waiting to enter the dining room inspire impromptu dance sessions along the lounges. The two-level **Dante's Disco** with an outstanding sound system is positioned on the bottom two passenger decks—a good choice because the action tends to go to the wee hours of the night.

Theme nights are offered in the Costa tradition and include "Fiesta Italiana" and "Notte Mediterranea," street-festivals-at-sea with bocce ball and tarantella dance lessons, costumes, music, and finger food from Spain, France, Greece, and Turkey. Then, too, the last night is the always popular "Toga Party-at-Sea," when passengers show their ingenuity—or lack thereof—creating a toga out of a bed sheet that the ship supplies.

SPORTS, FITNESS, AND BEAUTY Each ship has three outdoor pools plus Jacuzzis. One pool has a retractable roof that converts the central pool deck into an 11,000-square-foot solarium, thus providing all-weather swimming. At the top of the ship is a stand-alone water slide which does not empty into a pool. The Aurora Pool, the third pool located in the rear of the ship, is a quiet hideaway. It adjoins the dramatic two-level **Ischia Spa and Gym,** which has thalassic therapy and a broad range of other treatments, as well as sauna, steam, and whirlpools—and all well used. Costa has full- and half-day spa packages as well as à la carte, all of them pricey. Above the spa is a tennis court, where undersized racquets are used; it converts to a basketball or volleyball court.

The workout area is theater-style with a main floor and balcony; it has an array of Technogym equipment like that found in a major health club, plus sophisticated electronic aerobic monitoring equipment. Exercise classes are offered for all fitness levels, including children's jogging and aerobics.

Costa's **Golf Academy-at-Sea** on Caribbean cruises offers onboard golf clinics, private lessons with a PGA pro, and play in port. Video swing analysis and lessons range from a 15-minute swing-check for $25 to a 60-minute golf lesson for $80. Other activities include golf seminars, putting competitions, tournaments, and range practice. Golfers can rent top-of-the-line clubs and shoes. Courses available include Mahogany Run (St. Thomas) and Teeth of the Dog (Casa de Campo, Dominican Republic), among others. Fees vary. The PGA instructor accompanies participants when they play in port.

CHILDREN'S FACILITIES The large and well-fitted **Pinocchio's Children's Room** is the center of children's activities. Costa Kids, a year-round program available on Caribbean and European cruises, offers daily activities geared to two age groups: Costa Kids Club, 3–12 years; and Costa Teens Club, 13–17 years. Two youth counselors are aboard each ship year-round; counselors are added when there are more than 12 children on a cruise. Youth Center activities include video-game competitions, bridge and galley tours, arts and crafts, a treasure hunt, Italian lessons, bingo, board games, karaoke contests, pizza parties, ice-cream socials, face painting, cartoons, and movies.

At sea, Kids Club hours generally are 9–11:30 a.m., 2–5:30 p.m., and 8–11 p.m. On Caribbean cruises, group baby-sitting for ages 3 and up (children must be out of diapers) is available on request from 6:30–11 p.m. In port, hours are 8:30 a.m.–12:30 p.m. and 2:30–6:30 p.m. There is a charge. Costa also offers "Parents Night Out." On two different nights, parents can enjoy evenings alone while their children have the evening with their peers at a supervised buffet or pizza party with activities designed especially for them.

European cruises have three clubs: Baby Club, 3–6 years; Junior Club, 7–12 years; and Teens Club, 13–17 years. Baby Club offers a story hour, crafts, games, and ice-cream parties. Junior Club has aerobics, puppet theater, mini-Olympics, and team treasure hunts. Teens Club offers sports and fitness programs, guitar lessons, video productions, and a rock-and-roll hour. In Europe, free group baby-sitting for ages 3–6 is available, subject to staff availability. A disco and teen club offer a dance floor, video games, four computer stations, and a large television monitor.

SHORE EXCURSIONS On Eastern Caribbean cruises, the ship stops at Isla Catalina, where Costa developed facilities for a fun day at the beach with games and water sports. The ship also offers tours to **Casa de Campo,** one of the Caribbean's largest resorts, for tennis, horseback riding, and golf on world-famous Pete Dye courses. You must buy the ship's shore excursion to go to Casa de Campo; cruise passengers are not allowed to venture there on their own during the day. The ship docks at Isla Catalina for the day and the Casa de Campo marina for the evening, enabling passengers to enjoy the resort's elegant dining and nightlife. The ship offers diving and snorkeling at selected ports.

In Europe, shore excursions generally are as varied as the cruises and range from a glacier walk in Norway to a visit to Egyptian pyramids. Itineraries are port-intensive, rarely including more than one or two days at sea during a week.

COSTA CRUISE LINES EUROPEAN FLEET

Costa Fortuna	(PREVIEW)	
Costa Magica	(PREVIEW)	
REGISTRY Italy	**LENGTH** 890 feet	**BEAM** 124 feet
CABINS 1,358	**DRAFT** NA	**SPEED** 20 knots
MAXIMUM PASSENGERS 3,470	**PASSENGER DECKS** 13	**ELEVATORS** 18
	CREW 1,068	**SPACE RATIO** NA

THE SHIPS If the name is any indication, then good fortune will shower Costa with the *Costa Fortuna,* launched in late 2003, followed by her twin, *Costa Magica,* in 2004, as part of line's enormous expansion program, that added four superliners and megaliners in four years. And there's more to come with the 112,000-ton *Costa Concordia* in summer 2006, followed by her twin in 2007.

Not only are *Costa Fortuna* and *Costa Magica* the largest ships in Costa's history, they are also the largest ships in Italian maritime history and the first post-Panamax ship (a ship too wide to transit the Panama Canal) for a European cruise line. They are also the first post-Panamax ships to sail in Europe year-round.

Although the ships are not quite as large, their "footprint" is similar to *Carnival Destiny* with a three-story show lounge, two main dining rooms, a casual lido restaurant, large spa and fitness facilities, three swimming pools, shops, a chapel, Internet cafe, and children's and teen's areas. But there are differences, too. For example, the casino was made smaller to accommodate the Grand Bar with a large dance floor because Costa's Italian and European passengers like to dance more than gamble. Also, in place of the sports bar on the Carnival ships, the ships have cigar bars.

Costa Fortuna's interiors pay tribute to the great Italian liners of yesteryear; public rooms are named for these classic ships and the year they entered service. The Michelangelo 1965 Restaurant has a 20-foot-long model of the liner *Michelangelo* in its foyer. Exhibited for years in Milan's central railway station, it is believed to be the second-largest ship model in the world.

Inverted scale models of Costa vessels, past and present, glide across a blue ceiling over the bar of the *Costa Fortuna*'s nine-deck atrium. The models are among the 38 found on the vessel, which is awash in art and memorabilia, including a collection of antique nautical objects and antique globes. *Costa Magica*'s theme is the magic of Italy's enchanting small villages.

ITINERARIES *See* Itinerary Index.

CABINS More than half (853) of the 1,358 cabins are outside. Of those, 522 cabins and 64 minisuites and suites have balconies. All come with hair dryer, safe, and stocked minibar. Standard cabins have showers only, but minisuites have bathtubs, and suites are equipped with whirlpool tubs. Minisuites and suites also have butler service.

Specifications 474 inside (160 square feet); 335 outside standard (174–190 square feet.); 458 outside with balcony (210 square feet); 64 suites (360–650 square feet); 27 wheelchair-accessible (220 square feet).

DINING Italian specialties like homemade pastas are highlights in the bilevel main restaurant, **Michelangelo 1965** (with big windows in the stern), and **Raffaello 1965** at mid-ship (**Costa Emerald** and **Portofino** on *Costa Magica*). Casual meals and pizza are served in the spacious **Cristoforo Columbo 1954** buffet restaurant; and perched high on Deck 11 is the **Conte Grande 1927** supper club (**Vicenza Club** on *Magica*), a reservation-only venue where you dine on dinnerware by Versace and Italian cuisine by Zeffirino, the famous Genoa restaurant with a branch in Las Vegas. The cover charge is $23.

FACILITIES AND ACTIVITIES The ships' main gathering spot, morning and night, is the centrally located **Conte di Savoia 1932 Grand Bar** named for Italy's most elegant ocean liner (**Grand Bar Salento** on *Magica*). People gather here from early morning for cappuccinos until late into the night when a live band plays for dancing. The room has a huge parquet dance floor, sweeping black granite bar, and gilded fabrics in yellow, blue, and green. At 11,000 square feet, it may be the largest bar afloat.

In the **Vulcania 1927 Disco,** a glass wall surrounds the upper level, enabling gamblers in the casino one deck up to look down on the dancers. Named after the liner *Vulcania*, the disco has a large mechanized figure of Vulcan, the mythical god of fire, who pounds out fiber-optic sparks on an anvil in time to the music.

Other appealing rooms are the **Leonardo Da Vinci 1960 Lounge,** displaying reproductions of masterpieces like the "Mona Lisa" etched onto large glass canvases. The room has a combo for dance music and becomes the venue for late-night cabaret. A more intimate bar/dance venue is the **Conte Verde 1923 Lounge.** Inspired by the grand ballroom of the *Conte Verde* liner, the room sports an emerald-green ceiling and large malachite vases of Murano glass that sprout topiary trees ("verde" means green in Italian). The **Conte Rosso 1921 Piano Bar** pays tribute to *Conte Verde*'s sister ship and is colored red ("rosso" means red in Italian).

The **Rex Theater 1932,** where big production shows are staged, is an enormous room stretching over three decks and seating 1,100 passengers. The stage is flanked by towering funnels to recall the powerful *Rex*, which held the transatlantic speed record from 1933–1935. The *Rex* was Italy's fastest and most famous ocean liner. Along the corridor to one theater entrance is a display case containing a historic model of the *Rex*, which was built at the same yard as the liner. Outside another entrance is a case of bejeweled theatrical costumes and masks from famous plays like *Macbeth*.

POSTSCRIPT Although these ships are designed for European cruisers, Americans who want to cruise the Mediterranean on a very large, new ship with all the latest amenities will find the facilities, activities, and entertainment to be similar to those on mainstream U.S. lines like Carnival. There's plenty of action for children, teens and adults, from games and sports contests to classes, shopping, shows and dancing from ballroom to hip hop—plus, an international flair and very active nightlife centered around dancing and dining on Italian cuisine.

Costa Victoria	QUALITY 5	VALUE C
REGISTRY Italy	LENGTH 828 feet	BEAM 105 feet
CABINS 964	DRAFT 24 feet	SPEED 23 knots
MAXIMUM PASSENGERS 1,928	PASSENGER DECKS 10	ELEVATORS 12
	CREW 800	SPACE RATIO 38.9

THE SHIP Costa's first megaship made her debut in 1996. Designed by well-known naval architect Robert Tillberg, she was the largest passenger liner built in Germany when she was launched. Despite her large size, her shallow draft provides exceptional maneuverability and gives the ship access to smaller ports and the Suez Canal. Her size also makes possible more choices in dining and entertainment.

Ultra-modern and sophisticated, the circular Planetarium Atrium spans seven decks and has four glass elevators connecting the lobby with the pool deck above. It's capped by a large glass dome admitting sunlight that reflects off a colored glass sculpture by Milanese artist Gianfranco Pardi on the Boheme Deck (Deck 5). Deck 5 also has the purser's office, shore excursion desk, and a piano bar. All but one of the ten passenger decks are named after Italian operas.

The most dramatic room is the Concorde Plaza, an observation lounge at the bow. It spans four decks; a floor-to-ceiling glass wall provides spectacular ocean views. Opposite the windows is a marble dance floor adjoining a center stage; its backdrop is a waterfall inspired by Leonardo Da Vinci's drawings of the moon eclipsing the sun. Decorated in blues, silver, and gold, the lounge serves as an elegant area for socializing, special events, and evening entertainment, including cabaret shows, games, bingo, and port lectures.

ITINERARIES *See* Itinerary Index.

CABINS The majority of cabins are on the upper decks. Sixty percent are outside cabins with a porthole or large, square window.

Cabins are small compared to those on *Costa Romantica*. Originally, the ship had no cabins with balconies, which was definitely a drawback for the ship, but in 2004, full balconies were fitted to 246 cabins. *Victoria* was the line's first ship to have a minibar, safe, hair dryer, and interactive television in every cabin. All cabins have direct-dial telephones and sliding doors that separate the living area and bathroom. Circular bathrooms have rounded showers and vanity areas.

The six top suites and 14 minisuites, forward on the pool and sports decks, are decorated with Laura Ashley fabrics and trimmed with pearwood. They have sitting areas, whirlpool baths, walk-in closets, and queen beds, plus one upper berth and a Murphy bed, thus accommodating up to four people. Butler service is provided.

The *Victoria*'s unique "fan coil" system allows each cabin to be refreshed with its own recycled air or outside air. Thus, nonsmokers' air isn't mixed with smokers'. The ship does not have self-service laundromats for passenger use.

Specifications 391 inside, 553 outside; 20 suites; 250 cabins with balcony; 6 wheelchair-accessible. Standard cabins range from 120–150 square feet.

DINING *Costa Victoria* was the first Costa vessel to have two dining rooms: **Sinfonia Restaurant** aft and **Fantasia Restaurant** amidships. Both are decorated with marble and pine walls and glass chandeliers from Murano. Their picture windows are transformed from ocean views by day to Italian scenes by night by murals that drop in place like window shades.

Dinner menus have fewer selections than offered on some ships in Costa's price group, but choices are ample and of good quality, balancing Italian and European dishes with American favorites. A different pasta is featured at lunch and dinner; American audiences rave over them. A typical dinner menu offers three appetizers, two soups, two salads, three pastas, four entrees (one vegetarian), three or more desserts, ice cream, sherbet, cheese, and fresh fruit. The presentation is always attractive.

Ristorante Magnifico by Zefferino is modeled after the famous Zefferino's in Genoa. Passengers must make reservations and pay an extra charge of $23 per person, but given the uneven quality of the dining rooms' fare, it's worth it and has proven to be a popular alternative. Walls are hung with ten paintings of earlier Costa passenger ships by artist Stephen Card and contribute to the cozy atmosphere created by the addition of candlelight, flowers, soft music, and excellent service.

Passengers dine informally at an indoor/outdoor buffet serving breakfast and lunch. **Bolero,** the indoor buffet, is surrounded by glass windows and furnished with rattan chairs and marble tables. The outdoor **Terraza Café,** similar to one on *Romantica* but much larger, is protected by a large white canopy made by Canobbio, an Italian firm specializing in circus tents and sports arena coverings. Other dining options include two buffets, a pizzeria, ice cream bar, and grill.

FACILITIES AND ACTIVITIES Daytime diversions include lessons in dance, Italian language, and gaming; bingo; bridge; backgammon; culinary demonstrations; port and shopping talks; horse racing; and the Not-So-Newlywed Game. The teen center has a video game room, and there's a library, card room, and Internet center. Movies are shown on the in-cabin televisions.

The two-deck **Festival Show Lounge** is decorated in rich reds with Tivoli lights twinkling in the ceiling. The stage can be raised for variety and production shows or lowered for dancing.

The **Grand Bar Orpheus,** with a bar trimmed in rare, blue Brazilian marble, is popular for cocktails and after-dinner espresso. It's connected by a curved glass stairway to the big, bright **Monte Carlo Casino.** Just outside the casino is **Capriccio Lounge,** an intimate piano bar decorated with floor-to-ceiling mosaics by Italian painter Emilio Tadini.

Theme nights may include Notte Tropical, the lively Festa Italiana, and the rollicking Roman Bacchanal. The full-service conference center offers meeting space, audiovisual equipment, movable leather chairs equipped with flip-top desks, and a board room for 20. The center has its own front desk, which meeting planners applaud.

SPORTS, FITNESS, AND BEAUTY The **Solarium,** a top-deck viewing and sunning area, has pipes that continuously emit mists of cool water. The two outdoor pools are surrounded by six whirlpools and two shuffleboard courts. Nearby is the **Wimbledon Tennis Court,** a miniature court using smaller racquets and balls. It can be converted to a basketball or volleyball court.

In addition to the beauty salon, the **Pompei Spa** has an indoor swimming pool centered with a large mosaic and surrounded by Roman columns and teakwood lounge chairs. The spa offers a Turkish bath, saunas, massage, thalassotherapy, hydrotherapy, and other beauty treatments. A 1,312-foot jogging track connects the spa to the gymnasium, which is equipped with weight-training equipment and an aerobics room. This is the first ship to carry products from Tuscany's chic Terme di Saturnia.

CHILDREN'S FACILITIES Costa Kids Club for children ages 3–12 is further divided by age group depending on the number of children on a particular sailing. Activities include ship tours, video game competitions, arts and crafts, Italian language lessons, games, Coke-tail and pizza parties, ice cream socials, and kids' karaoke. The programs are not usually active when the ship is in port. Two nights of Parents Night Out (with free entertainment for children from 5 to 11 p.m.) are offered, and group baby-sitting for ages 3 and up is available for a fee.

Costa Classica	QUALITY 7	VALUE C
Costa Romantica	QUALITY 7	VALUE B
REGISTRY Italy	LENGTH 722/610 feet	BEAM 102 feet
CABINS 654/678	DRAFT 24 feet	SPEED 18 knots
MAXIMUM PASSENGERS	PASSENGER DECKS 11	ELEVATORS 10/8
1,998/1,356	CREW 650/722	SPACE RATIO 41.5/40

THE SHIPS *Costa Romantica* and *Costa Classica* are almost identical. These spacious ships with public rooms on the upper four decks have ultra-modern Italian interiors using a king's ransom in marble, dramatic window walls, futuristic sculptures, clean lines, angular shapes, and fine art. The result is a look that reflects modern Italian design and is a radical departure from traditional Italian ocean liners of the past.

Passengers are introduced to the ship in its dramatic **Grand Lobby,** set low on the Copenhagen Deck, which is dedicated entirely to cabins, as are the deck below and the two decks above. White-gloved room stewards escort passengers to their cabins. The background music of Vivaldi and other Italian composers is meant to underscore the start of a week of "Cruising Italian Style." The ships' layouts are easy to follow, with one lounge or public space flowing to the next, creating openness and harmony. Decks are named after European cities.

The dramatic centerpiece of *Romantica*'s lobby is a moving sculpture by Japanese artist Susumu Shingu. Installed in 1992 to commemorate the Columbus quincentennial, it's a mobile with panels that move continuously and change color against the area's Cararra marble walls and floors.

Romantica's heart and social center is the **Piazza Italia** on the Verona Deck—an atrium furnished as a lounge, with a small bandstand and dance floor on one side and a bar on the other. The lounge is the favorite gathering spot for pre-lunch and pre-dinner drinks, as it's a short walk from the dining room. Forward are meeting rooms, the library, chapel, card room, and the ground floor of **L'Opera,** the bilevel show lounge. From the Piazza, a double stairway leads up to the Vienna Deck and the popular **Romeo's Pizzeria** and **Juliet's Patisserie.** Forward are shops on the Via Condotti, named for Rome's fashionable shopping street.

ITINERARIES *See* Itinerary Index.

CABINS Spacious and well-designed, cabins are these ships' best feature. Standard cabins are fitted in cherry wood furnishings, including a dresser/desk unit with large mirror, bedside tables, a control panel for lights by the bed, ample closet space, and two chairs, one of which opens into a bed suitable for a child.

Elegant touches are the white curtain spanning the room, which can be raised and lowered to cover the oversized porthole; designer amenities; and high-quality bed and bath linens. All cabins have television, radio, safe, direct-dial satellite phone, and hair dryer. The 24-hour room service offers sandwiches and beverages.

Specifications *Costa Romantica*, 216 inside cabins, 428 outside, no singles. 16 suites, 18 minisuites. Standard dimensions, 175 square feet inside, 200 square feet outside. 242 take third and fourth persons. *Costa Classica*, 216 inside cabins, 688 outside; 4 grand suites, 16 with verandas. Standard dimensions, 175–200 square feet. 359 cabins take third and fourth persons. 6 singles. 6 wheelchair-accessible.

DINING *Romantica*'s **Botticelli Restaurant,** similar to *Classica*'s counterpart, **Tivoli,** is beautifully laid out almost entirely in off-white and brown Carrara marble with coffered ceilings. Elegantly designed wicker-backed chairs encircle round tables, most seating eight, dressed in starched white cloths, fine china, glassware, and flowers. Movable side panels faced with a variety of scenes—a European city, landscapes, or Italian gardens—are changed each evening. They were designed by Giorgio Cristini, set designer for Milan's famous La Scala opera house.

The lovely room lacks carpeting or wall coverings, causing an extraordinarily high noise level that hinders conversation. Acoustical material was added, particularly in the ceiling, which helped—but not enough. Side tables toward the back of the room get less noise.

Il Giardino, the lido cafe for indoor breakfast and lunch buffets, is among the ship's prettiest informal settings; its rattan chairs are dressed in English country fabrics against aquamarine glass walls and wood floors. At least two evenings per cruise, a dinner buffet is offered. The midnight buffet's setting changes depending on weather and the theme.

Adjacent to the lido cafe, the **Terrazza Café** reproduces the *Classica*'s popular **Al Fresco Café,** the ship's most pleasant location from dawn to dusk. Set with wicker chairs and tables under a high-peaked canvas canopy, it provides a cool, inviting outdoor setting for breakfast and lunch.

The other big hit is **Romeo's Pizzeria,** where pizza is served throughout the day. It's free, but you might want to buy a glass of wine or beer to wash it down. Romeo's neighbor, **Juliet's Patisserie,** open from 9 a.m. to midnight, serves pastries (without charge) and espresso. It's also the **Martini Bar.**

Afternoon tea, with fabulous desserts, is served daily; a cart dispenses Italian ice cream from 10 p.m. to midnight, and **Notte Tropical** is an outdoor tropical buffet.

SERVICE In recent years, Costa has changed its crews' makeup, with major impact. No longer are the ships all-Italian but rather multinational, as most other cruise lines. As a result, Costa lost an edge that distinguished it. Italian officers still command the ships, and Italians supervise the restaurants, but the flair and fun that Italian waiters create is often missing. Service is attentive, friendly, and good—often, very good—but for those who knew Costa before, the ambience isn't the same. The cruise staff cheerfully runs daily activities, but you're unlikely to see the cruise director except to open the nightly show.

FACILITIES AND ACTIVITIES Lessons in dance, Italian language, and gaming; bingo; bridge; backgammon; and culinary demonstrations are some of the daytime diversions. Evening entertainment is designed to appeal to the multinational passenger mix. *Romantica*'s main show lounge, the **L'Opera Theater** (**Colosseo** on *Classica*), is a modern interpretation of a classic, horseshoe-shaped concert hall. Creating a glamorous setting are red and royal blue carpets, blue velvet seats against a wall of blue mosaics, and brass accents. Most seats have good sight lines, and back-pain sufferers will like the hard, stiff balcony seats. L'Opera has shows nightly.

Romantica's casino is spectacular, with stucco walls inlaid with gold accents and a large crystal chandelier. The **Tango Ballroom,** a multipurpose lounge with large dance floor, becomes a high-energy nightclub with live music. The room has window walls and is a lovely daytime retreat. The **Diva Disco** atop the ship, a daytime observation and cocktail lounge with floor-to-ceiling windows, is the late-night hot spot. Everyone's favorite is the toga party, when passengers create Roman garb from sheets provided by the ship. It's remarkable how many ways passengers find to make togas, and almost all passengers join in and have a great time.

SPORTS, FITNESS, AND BEAUTY Two outdoor pools are separated by Costa's distinctive yellow stacks. One has four Jacuzzis and is surrounded by three terraces of teak decks with lounge chairs. The second is inlaid with ceramic tiles; suspended above it is a Susumu sculpture in red metal, which changes shape in the wind.

The **Caracalla Spa** on the *Classica* has floor-to-ceiling windows. *Romantica*'s smaller spa is beside the stack. In addition to weights, life cycles, and treadmills, the spa has sauna, steam, and massage rooms, plus a beauty salon offering personalized hair and body treatments. A partial deck above the swimming pools has a jogging track and sunbathing space.

CHILDREN'S FACILITIES *See Costa Victoria section.*

POSTSCRIPT After heavy criticism for seemingly endless shipboard announcements in five languages beginning at 8 a.m., Costa says it has trimmed the intrusion; however, we still hear complaints. Because most of this information is in the daily agenda, the broadcasts seem quite unnecessary.

Costa Europa	QUALITY 7	VALUE B
REGISTRY Italy	LENGTH 798 feet	BEAM 101 feet
CABINS 747	DRAFT 75.5 feet	SPEED 24 knots
MAXIMUM PASSENGERS 1,773	PASSENGER DECKS 9	ELEVATORS 7
	CREW 650	SPACE RATIO 36.4

THE SHIP The *Costa Europa,* the former *Westerdam* of Holland America Line, joined the Costa fleet in spring 2002. She is not a new superliner, but she fits well with the fleet. She is longer, more narrow, and has fewer decks than the newer ships, and a lower space-to-passenger ratio, but she's a spacious ship nonetheless. (Moviegoers saw her in *Out to Sea,* the 1997 comedy starring Jack Lemmon and Walter Matthau.)

When she debuted in 1989, she was hailed as one of the decade's most magnificent ships. She combines the style and refinement of great liners with state-of-the-art facilities. To increase her capacity from 1,000 to 1,494 passengers and update her facilities, the ship was stretched. A 130-foot section was added, providing space for a two-tiered show lounge, more bars, a sports deck, fitness facilities, library, larger restaurant, and second buffet. Before entering service for Costa, the ship got a $6 million facelift.

Comfortable, classy, and contemporary, the *Costa Europa* is dressed in pastels with lovely woods and interesting art and antiques. Most public rooms are on the Promenade Deck, anchored by the casino and several lounges forward and a bilevel lounge aft.

The dining room is on the lowest passenger deck. The main section has an interesting wood and Plexiglas dome. Dining is elegant and menu choices extensive; linen-covered tables are set with fine china, silver tableware, and fresh flowers.

The *Costa Europa* has two lido restaurants, where buffets are available. You can have breakfast and lunch—as well as alternative dining several nights—in the pleasant settings of the veranda by the Sun Deck pool or the **Lido Restaurant** by the Upper Promenade pool.

ITINERARIES *See* Itinerary Index.

CABINS The ship has 13 cabin categories and boasts standard cabins with comfortable sitting areas. Minimum cabins are only slightly smaller, and suites are more than double average size. Most are fitted with twin beds; more than a third can be converted to queens. All have ample drawer and closet space. The comfortable decor employs the same soothing colors of public rooms. All cabins have telephone, closed-circuit television, multichannel music system, and fine toiletries; all outside cabins (except a few lower-priced ones) have bathrooms with a tub and shower.

Specifications 326 inside cabins, 421 outside. Standard dimensions, 200 square feet for outside cabins. Some upper/lower berths; no singles; 4 wheelchair-accessible.

FACILITIES AND ACTIVITIES The theater on Sun Deck is particularly pretty, with gray velour seats and deep blue carpets and walls. Current films are shown daily. The space is also used for religious services, meetings, and lectures. Other daytime activities include bridge tournaments, dance lessons, karaoke, and bingo.

Entertainment and activities are similar to those on her sister ships. Promenade Deck has a cluster of lounges and bars. In one, an orchestra plays for predinner cocktails. Later, the space becomes a disco. Next door is a sports bar, and across the way, another bar with a small dance floor.

The **Book Chest** is a delightful spot for those reading in quiet comfort. The nearby **Ocean Bar,** where every table has a sea view, is the best for people-watching because everyone passes en route to the main lounge, a multipurpose room with evening entertainment. The ship has a children's facility.

SPORTS, FITNESS, AND BEAUTY The Sports Deck has an unobstructed 40-by-40-foot jogging track, glass windbreaker walls, and two tennis practice courts. A retractable roof protects the Sun Deck swimming pool, two Jacuzzis, and bar. The fitness center on Navigation Deck offers exercise equipment, saunas, and massage rooms. The beauty salon and barber shop are on Promenade Deck.

THE LAST WORD Another Costa ship, *Costa Allegra,* has seasonal sailing from Florida to the Caribbean, primarily for European passengers. More typically, she sails to South America from Europe, and thus is not covered as these markets are outside the focus of this book. Recently added to Costa's European portfolio is Aida Cruises, which specializes in cruises for the German market.

Cruise West

2301 Fifth Avenue, Suite 401, Seattle, WA 98121-1856
☎ 888-851-8133; fax 206-441-4757
www.cruisewest.com

TYPE OF SHIPS Six small, informal, minicoastal cruising vessels, one luxury oceangoing ship, and one day-touring boat.

TYPE OF CRUISES Casual, close-up, light adventure, with emphasis on scenery and wildlife in coastal areas.

CRUISE LINE'S STRENGTHS
- innovative itineraries
- enthusiastic crew
- itinerary flexibility allows extra time for wildlife viewing
- small ships

CRUISE LINE'S SHORTCOMINGS
- small cabins; noisy lower-deck cabins on older ships
- small bathrooms with handheld showers on older ships
- limited shipboard facilities and evening activities

FELLOW PASSENGERS Mature, physically active; mid-40s to mid-80s. Retired couples and seniors. Passengers somewhat older on Columbia River cruises; younger on Alaskan cruises. Up to 70% have college degrees or some college education; passengers are well-traveled and more curious about nature, history, and ecology than typical passengers on mainstream cruise ships.

Passengers are outgoing; most would rather rise early to catch the sunrise than party late. Most are from California, Florida, New York, the Great Lakes region, Pacific Northwest, and Texas; some from Canada. About 40% are repeaters. Regardless of age, they like the intimacy of a casual cruise to places larger liners cannot reach.

Recommended for Small-ship devotees; people looking for light adventure, to experience a region up-close; those preferring wildlife to nightlife.

Not recommended for Travelers who need to be entertained; seek a lavish, resort-like experience with emphasis on nightlife; prefer facilities and activities of large ships; gamblers.

CRUISE AREAS AND SEASONS April–October, Alaska and western Canada; June–August, Aleutian Islands and Bering Sea; spring and fall, Columbia and Snake Rivers, Pacific Northwest; fall, California; winter, Sea of Cortés and South Pacific; December–April, Costa Rica and Panama; March–October, Japan.

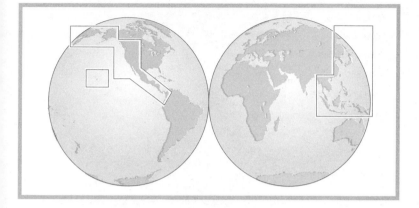

THE LINE After flying "The Hump" in the China-Burma-India theater in World War II, Charles B. "Chuck" West moved to Alaska to become a bush pilot. Flying over the northern wilderness, he recognized Alaska's great tourism potential. In 1946, he organized, sold, and piloted the first all-tourist air excursion north of the Arctic Circle. From that, he built the largest tour company in Alaska—Westours—which he sold to Holland America Line in 1971.

Starting over again at age 60, West built the tour company that became Cruise West, beginning in 1986 with a luxury cruiser for day tours on Prince William Sound. In 1990, adding its first overnight coastal cruising vessel sailing from Juneau to Glacier Bay, and six vessels in seven years, the line became America's largest small-ship cruise company. Other ships followed as the company expanded its operations. In 1997, *Spirit of Endeavour,* the line's most luxurious ship to date, began offering a more upscale level of cruises. In 1998, the line took another major step, sending two ships to cruise Mexico's Sea of Cortés for the winter, thus becoming a year-round operator. The line's American-built and -flagged vessels are subject to Federal Maritime Commission bonding and strict U.S. Coast Guard inspections.

In 2001, Cruise West added *Spirit of Oceanus* and launched a new era for the line, enabling it to develop new worldwide itineraries and attract new audiences. The all-suite ship, formerly *Renaissance V,* was the line's first oceangoing vessel and the most luxurious ship in the fleet by far. And in the autumn of the same year, it added the *Pacific Explorer* (formerly *Temptress Explorer*), offering cruises in Costa Rica and Panama.

THE FLEET	BUILT/RENOVATED	TONNAGE	PASSENGERS
Pacific Explorer	1995/1998	575	100
Spirit of Alaska	1980/1995	97	78
Spirit of Columbia	1979/1995	98	78
Spirit of Discovery	1976/1992	94	84
Spirit of Endeavour	1983/1999	95	102
Spirit of '98	1984/1995	96	96
Spirit of Oceanus	2001	1,263	114
Sheltered Seas (DAY-CRUISER)	1986/1999	95	70

STYLE Cruise West believes that responsible travel means having enriching experiences that cause minimal impact on the environment. The company encourages environmental education and understanding through unusual, up-close experiences, while respecting wildlife and natural habitats.

The small, shallow-draft vessels can nose into shore for close views of scenery and wildlife and navigate intricate waterways, narrow locks, and small marinas inaccessible to larger ships. Their size and casual atmosphere inspire instant friendships not always possible on larger ships.

Two of the vessels have bow-landing capabilities, enabling them to pull up to wilderness beaches or shoreside parks. En route, narration and occasional talks by park rangers, historians, and other specialists inform passengers of the history, geology, and wildlife of areas they're visiting. Otherwise, onboard style is unstructured.

Passengers entertain themselves by immersing in the scenery and wildlife, reading, playing cards and games, or socializing with other passengers and the crew.

Cruise West's young, mostly college-age crew is recruited primarily from the Pacific Northwest and Alaska. Their caring attitude and enthusiasm are some of the line's strengths. Also notable is the cuisine, which is more sophisticated than is normally associated with small-ship, light-adventure cruising.

DISTINCTIVE FEATURES Bow ramp on *Spirit of Columbia;* bow stairs on *Spirit of Alaska.* Open bridge. Dib launches (inflatable, Zodiac-like motorized launches with covers, seats, and railings) on *Spirit of '98* and *Spirit of Endeavour* provide shore access in Alaska and the Sea of Cortés. Both have Zodiacs to use.

	HIGHEST	LOWEST	AVERAGE
PER DIEM	$850	$207	$491

Per diems are calculated from cruise line's nondiscounted *cruise-only* published fares on standard accommodations and vary by season, cabins, and cruise areas.

RATES Port charges included.

Special fares and discounts Look for early-bird discounts and refundable/changeable air on seven-day or longer cruises when booked by specific deadlines.

- **SINGLE SUPPLEMENT:** Varies from 125% to 200%; single cabins on *Spirit of '98* and *Spirit of Discovery*. A twin rate is available for singles on select cruises and all inside "B" and "C" cabins.

Packages

- **AIR/SEA:** Air add-ons available from up to 75 gateways.
- **PRE/POST:** Variety of cruise-tour Alaska packages with up to nine days of land touring.

PAST PASSENGERS The Quyana Club (the name means "thank you" in Yu'pik Eskimo) offers passengers newsletters, shipboard credits, and 5% savings on all cruises and pre/post packages.

THE LAST WORD The company remains faithful to its founder's vision that small groups maximize travelers' enjoyment without overwhelming villages, small ports, and wilderness areas they visit, and that the focus should be outward, on nature and culture, rather than inward, on nightclubs and gambling. By focusing on wildlife—passengers are likely to see whales, bears, seals, and eagles—and the wilderness, Cruise West says it is increasing awareness and support for protection of natural treasures. And now, Cruise West has a whale of a guarantee: On any of its Inside Passage Daylight Yacht Tours or Wilderness Inside Passage Cruises, you are given a guarantee that whales will be sighted—if not, Cruise West will refund $250 of your cruise price after your return home.

Most passengers try an Alaskan cruise first. If they like it, they graduate to cruises elsewhere. Baja California, Costa Rica, or Panama give Cruise West alumni a complete contrast to Alaska or the Northwest. Yet the Sea of Cortés offers similar attractions—wildlife, beautiful scenery, and interesting culture—and much the same appeal. Cruise West's Web site is particularly useful regarding cabins. There are diagrams with precise measurements of each of the six cabin categories along with a readable deck plan.

Cruise West Standard Features

Officers American.

Staff Dining, Cabin, Cruise/American.

Dining facilities One dining room with open seating; meals served at specific hours. Early continental breakfast and 6 p.m. appetizers in forward lounge. Coffee, tea, fresh fruit available throughout day.

Special diets Vegetarian, low-fat, low-salt, and other heart-healthy requests accommodated; notice required at time of booking.

Room service None, except for owner's suite on the *Spirit of '98*.

Dress code Casual at all times. Most passengers wear jeans, chinos, and layer with shirts, sweaters, and windbreakers in cooler climates.

Cabin amenities Air-conditioning/thermostat; upper-deck cabins have windows that open. Most bathrooms on older ships are small, some with handheld showers; some have sink and vanity in room, separate from bathroom. Reading lights over bed; limited closets, storage on older ships. *Spirit of Endeavour, Spirit of '98, Spirit of Oceanus,* television monitor and VCR, satellite phone, Internet access.

Electrical outlets 110 AC.

Wheelchair access *Spirit of '98* and *Spirit of Oceanus* have elevators.

Recreation and entertainment Forward lounge with bar setup, television, small library with reference books of area, informational videos, movies; informal entertainment by crew; occasional talks by historians, park rangers, and other experts. Bridge, other card and board games. Ships stock binoculars, but it's wise to bring your own. Musical entertainment on Sea of Cortés cruises.

Beauty and fitness Some fitness equipment, such as stair steppers and exercise bicycles. No beauty/barber shop.

Other facilities Doctor on Sea of Cortés cruises and on *Oceanus*; at least one crew member on each vessel is trained in "First Response."

Children's facilities None.

Theme cruises Some on American history.

Smoking Not allowed in public rooms or cabins; smoking allowed only on designated outside area.

Cruise West suggested tipping No tipping is expected or required for either cruise or land-based service. Any tips offered are pooled and shared by nonofficer staff.

Credit cards For cruise payment and on-board charges: American Express, Visa, MasterCard.

Spirit of Oceanus	QUALITY 6	VALUE C
REGISTRY Bahamas	LENGTH 295 feet	BEAM 50 feet
CABINS 57	DRAFT 13.25 feet	SPEED 14.5 knots
MAXIMUM PASSENGERS 114	PASSENGER DECKS 5	ELEVATORS 1
	CREW 65	SPACE RATIO NA

THE SHIP Cruise West took possession of its new ship, *Spirit of Oceanus,* in spring 2001 in Singapore. Built in 1991 as the *Renaissance V,* the ship was renamed *Sun Viva* when she was purchased by Sun Cruises, and later became *MegaStar Sagittarius* under Star Cruises, from whom Cruise West purchased her. After some cosmetic refurbishing, the ship sailed on a 32-day voyage from Singapore to Whittier, Alaska, entering Alaska service in June—at which time she became the line's flagship, taking over that honor from *Spirit of Endeavour.*

The luxurious *Spirit of Oceanus* was Cruise West's first oceangoing vessel and, as such, opened up new horizons for the line, from new destinations worldwide to newer, more upscale cruises that would appeal to a completely new market. In addition to Alaska in summer, she sails on 13- to 24-night voyages to the Bering Sea from Anchorage or Nome. She is adding cruises of the South Pacific from December 2005 to February 2006, and to Japan from March through October. In 2005, the ship was refurbished with two additional suites, new carpeting, mattresses, upholstery, window treatments, and passenger phone and Internet access.

Registered in the Bahamas—another first for Cruise West—the ship has American officers, an onboard naturalist guide, and an English-speaking crew whose numbers constitute the highest crew-to-guests ratio in the line's fleet.

ITINERARIES *See* Itinerary Index.

CABINS *Spirit of Oceanus* has spacious, all-outside suites, each with a large picture window or porthole, ranging in size from 215 to 353 square feet. The 12 suites on the Sun and Bridge Decks have private teak balconies—another first for Cruise West ships. Other cabin amenities include a walk-in closet, marble-topped vanity, and a lounge area separated from the bedroom by a curtain. All suites can be configured with two twin beds or a full queen-size bed and have a television/VCR, safe, minibar, satellite telephone, and private bathroom with a marble sink and shower. In the renovation, Cruise West added minifridges, safes, and hair dryers.

Specifications 57 cabins, from 215–353 square feet; 12 suites with teak balconies.

FACILITIES AND ACTIVITIES The handsomely appointed *Spirit of Oceanus* has marble and polished hardwood interiors, sumptuous fabrics, and fine art. There are two large lounges (one with a grand piano) and several elegant bars, providing havens for conversation, reading, or playing board games. Among other new features passengers enjoy on a Cruise West ship for the first time are a hot tub on the aft Sports Deck, a health facility, a patio bar, and a pool in warm climates.

The ship has a library, an elevator providing access to all five passenger decks, and spacious outside viewing areas and walkways on four of the five guest decks. The elegant dining room accommodates all guests at a single seating. Among the changes in the latest renovations, the casino was removed to make room for more public space, and a small room with exercise equipment was added. The ship has a small clinic staffed by a doctor.

Spirit of Endeavour	QUALITY 3	VALUE C
REGISTRY United States	LENGTH 217 feet	BEAM 37 feet
CABINS 51	DRAFT 8.5 feet	SPEED 12 knots
MAXIMUM PASSENGERS 102	PASSENGER DECKS 4	ELEVATORS None
	CREW 28	SPACE RATIO NA

THE SHIP Built in 1983 in Jeffersonville, Indiana, *Spirit of Endeavour* (formerly *Newport Clipper* of Clipper Cruise Lines) was launched for Cruise West in 1996 after a $5 million refurbishing. She was Cruise West's most luxurious ship at the time and added a new level of comfort to the line's fleet until the *Spirit of Oceanus* was acquired. One of the more deluxe small vessels sailing in Alaska and the Sea of Cortés, *Endeavour* has teak decks, a wide companionway, and comfortable lounges.

In the renovations, all cabins and public areas were refurbished, passenger phone and Internet access were added, and cabin furnishings renewed. Safety features were updated, and new engines and bridge electronics were installed. New bow and stern designs increase the ship's fuel efficiency by more than 22%. A "bulbous" underwater bow extension splits the water, reducing the bow wake and water resistance. A stern ferring forces water to flow closer to the surface, reducing drag.

The *Spirit of Endeavour*'s clean lines and raked bow make it look most like a small cruise ship. Viewing breathtaking scenery in Alaska is a major activity on this ship, which appeals to those looking for quiet social life and a relaxed itinerary; in the Sea of Cortés, there are daily excursions that appeal to those eager for light adventure.

Passengers give high marks to the ship's educational programs, and they appreciate finding two pairs of high-powered binoculars and umbrellas in their cabins. The ship does not have an elevator. The decor throughout is understated and pleasing. The ship does not have a promenade deck completely surrounding the ship.

ITINERARIES *See* Itinerary Index.

CABINS Cabins are large compared to her older sister ships and have wide picture windows. They're equipped with phone, television monitor/ VCR, and tiled baths with showers. Refurbishing in 1999 added new closets, lighting and window treatments, wall coverings, artwork, and furniture, as well as the upgrading of all the bathrooms.

Cabins are on three decks and of four types: The 100 series on the Main Deck includes eight of the AAA category measuring 109 square feet, and four A cabins of about the same size. The Lounge Deck has 4 A's that open onto the outside deck, 12 AAA's, and 2 deluxe cabins measuring 155 square feet. Upper Deck has 20 AA's and one deluxe cabin, all opening to an outside veranda. The A and AA have twin or double beds, and some cabins accommodate three passengers; most have large picture windows.

Specifications 51 cabins. The cruise line's brochures show precise lay- outs of each category.

DINING The **Resolution Dining Room** accommodates all passengers at a single open seating; most tables seat six or eight persons, none are for two. Mealtimes may vary depending on the itinerary, but generally, breakfast served at 7:30 a.m., lunch at 1 p.m., and dinner at 7:30 p.m. The food gets high praise from passengers, and there's a good selection of wines. An unusual custom onboard: The chef personally introduces the evening menu and invites passengers to dinner. As with most small ships, there is a great deal of camaraderie among passengers and friendly interaction with the ship's staff.

FACILITIES AND ACTIVITIES The spacious **Explorer Lounge** is a multipur- pose room and the heart of the ship's activity, beginning with continental breakfast in the morning and coffee, tea, and cocoa avail- able throughout the day. It is also used for most of the lectures. A wide selection of videos and magazines, are available in the library, along with a good selection of books and reference works pertaining to the area of the cruise.

The main activity on an Alaska cruise is sightseeing, which Alaska offers like no other place in the country. A Baja California and Sea of Cortés cruise during the winter months offers more sports activities, such as hiking, swimming, snorkeling, and kayaking, as well as sightsee- ing and spotting wildlife. Among the highlights are an opportunity to swim with sea lions, watching dolphins play, and photographing a colony of blue-footed boobies, but the most anticipated activity of all is whale-watching. From about mid-January to mid-March, large numbers of California gray whales assemble in the lagoons of Bahia Magdalena, which passengers visit.

Spirit of '98	QUALITY 3	VALUE C
REGISTRY United States	LENGTH 192 feet	BEAM 40 feet
CABINS 49	DRAFT 9.3 feet	SPEED 13 knots
MAXIMUM PASSENGERS 96	PASSENGER DECKS 4	ELEVATORS 1
	CREW 26	SPACE RATIO NA

THE SHIP Added to Cruise West's fleet in 1993, *Spirit of '98* previously sailed as the *Pilgrim Belle, Colonial Explorer,* and *Victorian Empress.* The handsome vessel has the profile and interior of a turn-of-the-19th-century riverboat (she had a role in the 1994 movie *Wyatt Earp*).

Built in 1984, the decor recalls a Victorian country hotel. Accenting a handsome mahogany and mirrored bar in the forward observation lounge are fanciful wall lamps and wood columns trimmed with strip mirrors. Continuing the theme on her four decks are extensive use of wood, wingback chairs, leaded glass, and old-fashioned brass lamps. The ship has one elevator operating between Main and Upper decks.

ITINERARIES *See* Itinerary Index.

CABINS All cabins are outside and have varied arrangements. They're roomy, with closet and storage space adequate for a casual cruise. All are decorated in rich Victorian-style colors and fabrics. All have TV/ VCR combinations, are air-conditioned, and have windows that open— a welcome feature.

Cabins on lounge and upper decks open onto promenades. Main-deck, lower-priced cabins have windows on the outside hull, a benefit for those who like privacy but want to keep their curtains open.

The ship has an amazingly large, two-room owner's suite on the top deck with picture windows on both sides. The only cabin on the deck, just behind the bridge, it has a sitting area, a game and meeting area, complimentary bar, television, VCR, king-size bed, and bathroom with full-size tub. Occupants may have their meals served en suite.

Specifications 48 outside cabins; 1 suite. Standard dimensions, 100–120 square feet. 40 with twins; 2 with upper/lower bunks; 4 with queen, 6 with doubles. 2 singles.

DINING The **Klondike Dining Room** provides seating at a variety of table configurations, including booths next to the picture windows. One open seating is offered at each of three meals. The cuisine is better than expected for this type of cruise. It's mostly Pacific Northwest fare encompassing fresh seafood, local produce, and Northwest wines and local specialty beers. In Mexico, meals have Mexican choices. Bread and pastries are baked onboard. Coffee, tea, cocoa, and fruit are available all day.

An early continental breakfast is available in the forward lounge; full breakfast is at 7:30 a.m. in the dining room. Lunch features soups, salads, and sandwiches. Appetizers served between 6 and 7 p.m. may include Alaskan Dungeness crab and artichoke dip or baked Brie.

Entrees at dinner are attractively presented and surprisingly sophisticated. They may include fresh halibut in Dijon sauce, veal piccata with white wine and capers, or Oregon razor clams grilled with garlic aïoli.

SERVICE The young, enthusiastic crew are friendly, caring, and especially considerate of older passengers. These "customer service representatives" perform a variety of duties, including cleaning cabins and serving in the dining room.

FACILITIES AND ACTIVITIES Unusual in coastal cruise ships, **Soapy's Parlor** is a second, quiet lounge with wraparound windows at the stern, a good spot for watching the vessel's wake. Tea is served in the afternoon. The bridge deck has ample space for sunning, viewing scenery, or lounging. A barbecue lunch is offered in good weather. A small area serves as a gift shop, where caps, mugs, and similar items are sold. A shuffleboard and huge checkerboard are on the bridge deck, along with two exercise machines.

The forward lounge is the ship's social center at night. Most entertainment is provided by the passengers interacting with each other in conversation, cards, or board games in the lounge or dining room. Absent are a pool, casino, aerobics class, bingo, midnight buffet, or napkin-folding classes. The crew provides informal talent and lively entertainment on Crew and Casino nights. Vegetable races are amusing, and can be lucrative for those who wager correctly on such entries as Percy Potato or the Lemon Sisters. A television shows evening movies. Guest lectures, talks by the cruise coordinator/naturalist, and entertainment from the old-style player piano are offered.

Spirit of Discovery	QUALITY 2	VALUE D
REGISTRY United States	LENGTH 166 feet	BEAM 37 feet
CABINS 43	DRAFT 7.5 feet	SPEED 13 knots
MAXIMUM PASSENGERS 84	PASSENGER DECKS 3	ELEVATORS None
	CREW 21	SPACE RATIO NA

THE SHIP Built in 1976 as the *Independence* and renamed *Columbia*, the vessel cruised the East Coast and Puget Sound before being acquired by Cruise West in 1992 and renamed *Spirit of Discovery*. The forward lounge of this three-deck vessel is the ship's social center and cool-weather retreat. Nicely decorated in blue, soft grays, teals, and mauves, it has a bar with standard spirits plus Pacific Northwest wines and specialty brews. Furniture is arranged in conversational groupings. These, along with mirrored ceiling and chrome accents, give it the look of a private yacht or small, European-style hotel.

The lounge offers good views to both sides and over the bow through vertical windows at the front. Passengers at the bow can almost touch the vegetation when the ship noses up to shore. The bridge has a wraparound viewing area and is open to passengers at most times. A stair stepper, exercise bicycle, and rowing machine are available.

ITINERARIES *See* Itinerary Index.

CABINS Cabins on all three decks are outside with large windows. Most are small but adequate and furnished with a vanity, desk, and chair. Bathrooms have showers. Closets could use more hangers. Two sought-after smaller cabins, sold as singles, are amidships on the bridge deck.

Four spacious, deluxe cabins on the top level have a queen-size bed, desk and chair, television/VCR unit, and fridge/minibar. All bridge-deck cabins and most lounge-deck cabins open onto a promenade. The two lowest-priced cabins are on the lower main deck forward, reduced in size to fit the hull's curvature.

Specifications 43 outside cabins; no suites. Standard dimensions, 64 square feet (single cabin) to 127 square feet. 34 with twins, 1 with double, 4 queens, 2 with upper/lower berths, 2 singles.

DINING The **Grand Pacific Dining Room,** aft on the main deck, is pleasant and airy, but a bit noisy because it's over the engine room. The food is imaginative and quite good, encompassing Pacific Northwest versions of classic American fare with fresh local produce and seafood. All passengers dine in one open seating; table configurations vary.

A continental breakfast is available for early risers. Sit-down breakfast, lunch, and 6 p.m. appetizers are served. Two entrees are offered at dinner; they may include lingcod baked in parchment or a superb rack of Ellensburg lamb roasted with Dijon rosemary crust.

SERVICE Customer service, galley and engine crew, and deck hands are young Americans, most from the Pacific Northwest. They're attentive, enthusiastic, and outgoing. Friendships form between crew and passengers, and many crew members receive holiday greetings from passengers for years after they meet.

Spirit of Alaska	QUALITY 2	VALUE D
Spirit of Columbia	QUALITY 2	VALUE D
REGISTRY United States	**LENGTH** 143 feet	**BEAM** 28 feet

CABINS 39	DRAFT 7.5/6.5 feet	SPEED 12/10 knots
MAXIMUM PASSENGERS 78	PASSENGER DECKS 4	ELEVATORS None
	CREW 21	SPACE RATIO NA

THE SHIPS *Spirit of Alaska* and *Spirit of Columbia* are identical in size, similar in layout, and are smaller versions of their sister ships. *Spirit of Alaska,* built in 1980 as the *Pacific Northwest Explorer,* was extensively renovated when acquired by Cruise West in 1991, and she was renovated again in 1995. *Spirit of Columbia* (formerly *New Shoreham II* of American Canadian Caribbean Line) joined in 1994 after being refitted in a "Western National Park Lodge" theme.

Both ships have four decks, with most cabins on the lower and upper decks and a forward lounge and dining room amidships on the main deck. The lounge is the center of social life and site of briefings. It has a small bar, gift shop, reference library focused on the cruise area, television, and movie videos. The upper deck has an unobstructed walking and jogging circuit and several exercise machines.

On *Spirit of Alaska,* the bridge deck provides open and covered seating and a good-weather venue for buffet lunches. Bow ramp stairs enable passengers to walk directly onto shore; some complain the stairs are steep and difficult to negotiate.

Besides decor, *Spirit of Columbia* differs in having a large owner's suite with windows overlooking the bow, three additional suites, a raised wheelhouse with 360-degree viewing, and a unique bow ramp. A hinged, V-shaped segment of the bow can be lowered to form a ramp, giving direct access to shore from the forward lounge.

ITINERARIES *See* Itinerary Index.

CABINS Cabins on both ships range from roomy—for ships of this size—to very small. *Spirit of Alaska*'s suites and deluxe cabins have small sitting areas and open to promenades. Three bridge-deck suites have oversized double beds, windows on two sides, and accommodate a third person.

Spirit of Columbia's 11 suites and deluxe cabins have a television monitor/VCR, refrigerator, side tables, and a chair. Suites have a double bed; deluxe rooms, twins. The owner's suite has a queen-size bed, tub/shower, and complimentary bar. Upper- and bridge-deck cabins open directly onto promenades.

On both ships, main-deck cabins are on the short passage between the dining room and forward lounge, a high-traffic area, but convenient for those who want easy access to activities and facilities. Windows in these cabins are on the outside hull, ensuring privacy. Lower-deck cabins have portlights high on the bulkhead and not for viewing. Baths are small units with handheld showers and curtains on tracks. Most cabins have twin beds; all have reading lights, closets, and under-bed storage.

They're just above the engine room and can be noisy when the ship is underway, but they are a good buy for budget-watchers.

Specifications *Alaska,* 12 inside; 24 outside; 3 suites. Dimensions range from 81–130.5 square feet. 26 with twins; 13 with doubles; 7 cabins accommodate third persons; no singles. *Columbia,* 12 inside; 20 outside; 7 suites. Dimensions range from 73.5–176 square feet.

DINING Meals are served at a single, open seating. Cuisine is good American fare, emphasizing fresh Pacific Northwest and Alaskan seafood and local produce. The *Spirit of Alaska*'s **Grand Pacific Dining Room** has small round and square tables with upholstered banquettes running bow to stern underneath side windows.

SERVICE The young American staff helps set the friendly ambience and, despite the considerable workload, remains courteous, enthusiastic, and helpful, especially to seniors. Most retain a sense of awe about the magnificent region the vessel sails, often sharing passengers' excitement for wildlife sightings or glacier calvings, when enormous pieces of a glacier break off and crash into the sea.

Pacific Explorer	QUALITY 3	VALUE C
REGISTRY Honduras	LENGTH 185	BEAM NA
CABINS 50	DRAFT 7 feet	SPEED 12 knots
MAXIMUM PASSENGERS 100	PASSENGER DECKS 4	SPACE RATIO NA
	CREW 25	

THE SHIP Built in 1995 and remodeled in 1998, the *Pacific Explorer* specializes in cruises of Costa Rica and Panama. The historic Panamanian port of Portobello, dating from 1502, was added to its itinerary in 2003. The ship is staffed with English-speaking Costa Ricans and guides. A lounge and dining room are on the lower of four decks, cabins and a forward lounge are on Main and Upper decks, and the Bridge, Sun area, and outdoor bar are on the Sun Deck.

All cabins have picture windows and are air-conditioned. They have television monitor/VCR and private baths with showers. There are three types of cabins—deluxe (152 square feet), AAA/AA (122 square feet), and A (107 square feet)—and they are furnished with either twin or double beds. International cuisine and Central American specialties are served, along with breads and desserts made onboard by the pastry chef.

DAY CRUISES *Sheltered Seas,* a day-cruiser, is not covered here because her type of cruises are outside the scope of this book. For more information, contact the cruise line.

POSTSCRIPT Readers considering a cruise on any Cruise West ship should read the entire section for a more complete picture of the cruise experience the line offers.

Crystal Cruises

2049 Century Park East, Suite 1400, Los Angeles, CA 90067
☎ **310-785-9300 or 888-799-4625; fax 310-785-3891**
www.crystalcruises.com

TYPE OF SHIPS Modern, luxury superliners.

TYPE OF CRUISES Modern version of glamorous, traditional cruising with a touch of California glitz, for upscale, sophisticated travelers.

CRUISE LINE'S STRENGTHS

- service
- beautifully designed ships
- alternative restaurants
- globe-roaming itineraries
- interesting, unusual, and varied shore excursions
- enrichment program

CRUISE LINE'S SHORTCOMINGS

- two seatings in main dining room
- some cabins with restricted views, except on *Serenity*

FELLOW PASSENGERS Professional, retired or semiretired, experienced travelers; likely to be business owners, entrepreneurs, and executives rather than staff; ages 45–70. Typical passenger is affluent, active, friendly, fashion-conscious, and often a 55–60-year-old couple or mature single.

Recommended for Quality-conscious travelers who appreciate style with flash and want large-ship facilities; urbane first-time cruisers who can afford it.

Not recommended for Anyone uncomfortable with or uninterested in sophisticated ambience.

CRUISE AREAS AND SEASONS Caribbean, Mexico, Central America, Panama Canal in fall and winter; South America and Amazon, and world cruise, January–March; Europe, Baltic, North Cape, Arctic Circle, and Mediterranean, April–September. Fall, New York–New England–Montreal.

THE LINE Two years before her first ship debuted in 1990, Crystal Cruises promised it would return grand ocean liner elegance and personalized service to modern cruises for the "upscale mass" market—an apparently inconsistent term. The line not only delivered on its promise, but *Crystal Harmony*, its first ship, was even better than its advanced billing. It quickly became the ship by which others in her class—or aspiring to be in her class—were measured.

And therein lies the tale. There were no other ships in her class. Crystal Cruises created a niche all its own: a ship the size of most superliners but carrying a third fewer passengers (some comparably sized ships carry twice as many passengers) and offering the best of all worlds—the facilities of a large, spacious ship with the personalized service of a small vessel.

Crystal Cruises' first ship was built in Japan by its owners, Mitsubishi Heavy Industries, a subsidiary of Nippon Yusen Kaisha, the Japanese shipbuilding giant known for its technologically advanced ships. The ship incorporated state-of-the-art engines, radar, and navigational equipment. Comfort and amenities went far beyond the norm. Ironically, its second ship, *Crystal Symphony,* was built in Finland, for cost-saving reasons. *Crystal Serenity*, a third ship which debuted in summer 2003, was built in France. Somewhat larger than her sister ships, *Crystal Serenity* has set a new direction for Crystal Cruises with facilities for greater focus on enrichment programs and enhanced onboard amenities.

The much-loved *Crystal Harmony* is slated to leave Crystal Cruises in December 2005 to join a new cruise line created by its owners for the Japanese market.

THE FLEET	BUILT/RENOVATED	TONNAGE	PASSENGERS
Crystal Harmony (to 12/2005)	1990/2003	49,400	940
Crystal Symphony	1995	51,044	940
Crystal Serenity	2003	68,000	1,080

STYLE Exceptionally spacious ships with superliner facilities and Rodeo Drive style are designed for affluent travelers willing to pay for luxury and personal attention and who appreciate quality in details. The cruises provide fine food and service in a gracious atmosphere; stimulating enrichment programs, a year-round roster of celebrity and expert speakers, and varied itineraries with more structure than ultraluxurious lines but less formality than luxury ships of old. Itineraries generally include more days at sea than is the norm, so passengers have time to fully enjoy the luxury and pampering that Crystal offers.

Not one to rest on its laurels—Crystal consistently sweeps the awards ratings—the line continues to add enhancements and interesting options and, thus, value to its cruise experience. There are more and more adventure-type shore excursions, additional programs in the onboard Creative Learning Institute, an expanded roster of theme cruises including fashion, gardens, and comedy, among others; and a new series of extended land programs.

DISTINCTIVE FEATURES Computer University@Sea. Personal Web sites. Creative Learning Institute. Two specialty restaurants at no extra cost; gentlemen hosts; close-captioned television for hearing-impaired passengers; free self-service laundromat on each deck; business center with audiovisual equipment, fax machines, and office equipment; secretarial, translation, and e-mail services; take-out laptops; air-conditioned tenders with toilets.

	HIGHEST	LOWEST	AVERAGE
PER DIEM	$1,594	$271	$840

Per diems are calculated from cruise line's nondiscounted *cruise-only* published fares on standard accommodations and vary by season, cabins, and cruise areas.

RATES Port charges additional.

Special fares and discounts Crystal has advance-purchase discounts ranging from 10% to 30% and more, depending on the cruise; they may be used with other promotional rates and Crystal Society savings. Another group marked with a V in Crystal's brochure offers two-for-one savings.

- **THIRD PASSENGER:** Age 12 and older: minimum fare for cruise.

- **CHILDREN'S FARE:** Younger than age 12, half-fare with two full-paying adults and free on certain cruises.
- **SINGLE SUPPLEMENT:** Crystal's single's fare begins at 125% of the double-occupancy rate for the lowest categories and is applicable to advance-purchase discount rates (130% for World Cruises).

  Packages
- **AIR/SEA:** Yes.
- **PRE/POST:** Yes.
- **OTHERS:** Honeymoon; extended land programs.

PAST PASSENGERS Crystal Society past-passenger club offers amenities that increase with the number of cruises. These include business- and first-class air upgrades, confirmed stateroom and penthouse upgrades, shipboard credits, free cruises in staterooms and penthouses, limousine transfers, prepaid gratuities, and private luncheon and dinner parties.

Passengers are automatically enrolled after their first Crystal cruise and receive financial bonuses with every subsequent cruise. The higher reward levels are 5–30 cruises, 50, 70, and 100 cruises, but all members receive a 5% cruise discount, an additional 5% savings for reservations made while on a cruise, priority check-in, a Crystal Society travel bag, membership card, recognition pin, quarterly newsletter, and, beginning with the tenth cruise, a complimentary bottle of wine and fresh flowers on every cruise. Several cruises, including the annual president's cruise, are Crystal Society Sailings (marked with a C in the compendium) and feature a personal escort, exclusive events, and special gifts.

THE LAST WORD Crystal Cruises identified a market of experienced travelers (but not necessarily experienced cruise passengers) who weren't being served by other cruise lines and created a product that set new standards of luxury for large ships. Those who can afford the cruises get quality all the way. Compare Crystal's quality and extra amenities with those of other lines in the same price bracket, and you find Crystal's cruises are among cruising's best values.

Crystal Cruises Standard Features

Officers Norwegian and Japanese.

Staff Dining/European; Cabin/International; Cruise/American.

Dining facilities One main dining room, two seatings for dinner with open seating for breakfast and lunch; buffet breakfast and lunch on Lido Deck; alternative dinner restaurants; cocktail hour; midnight buffet; tea.

Special diets Requests should be made when reservations are confirmed (or at least one month in advance). Kosher, 90 days advance notice.

Crystal Cruises Standard Features (cont'd)

Room service 24-hour menu; butler service on penthouse deck.

Dress code Casual by day; casually elegant in the evening, with two formal evenings per week of cruising.

Cabin amenities Direct-dial phone with voicemail; television with CNN and ESPN, VCR or DVD; stocked minibar; safe; bathroom with tub, two hair dryers, robes; suites with marble bathrooms and whirlpool tubs.

Electrical outlets 110/220 AC.

Wheelchair access 4 cabins on *Symphony*; 8 *Serenity*.

Recreation and entertainment Casino, disco, nightclub, show lounge, piano bar, coffee/wine bar, cinema/theater, six lounges, observation lounge, card/meeting room, video game room, smoking room. Guest lecturers, area specialists, celebrities. Bingo, bridge, dancing, and crafts classes. Computer classes.

Sports and other activities Two outdoor swimming pools, one with retractable roof; two Jacuzzis; teak deck for walking/jogging; paddle tennis; table tennis, golf clinics and practice corner; deck and pool games.

Beauty and fitness See text.

Other facilities Boutiques, concierge, hospital, laundry/dry cleaning, valet service, launderettes, photo processing center, video camera rentals, meeting facilities, business service center, e-mail facilities.

Children's facilities Playroom, baby-sitters, youth programs.

Theme cruises Food and wine; Asian art and literature, jazz and blues, fashion and style, garden design, Crystal Comedy Club at Sea, Sotheby's and Smithsonian, and others.

Smoking Dining rooms nonsmoking; public rooms smoking in designated areas.

Crystal suggested tipping Per person per day, cabin stewardess, $4; butler $4; waiter, $4, $5 for single travelers; assistant waiter, $2.50; $6 per person per dinner in specialty restaurants; 15% added to bar bills.

Credit cards For cruise payment and on-board charges: all major credit cards, cash, and traveler's checks. Ship uses a charge system, with the bill settled at the end of the cruise.

Crystal Harmony (to 12/2005)	**QUALITY 9**	**VALUE B**
Crystal Symphony	**QUALITY 9**	**VALUE B**
REGISTRY Bahamas	**LENGTH** 790/781 feet	**BEAM** 105/99 feet

CABINS 408	DRAFT 25 feet	SPEED 20 knots
MAXIMUM PASSENGERS 940	PASSENGER DECKS 8	ELEVATORS 9
	CREW 545	SPACE RATIO 52.6/54.3

THE SHIPS Gleaming white inside and out, Crystal Cruises' ships are a symphony of Japanese technology and artistry, European service and tradition, and American flair for fun and entertainment. The elegance is in their simplicity, clean lines, and extraordinary attention to details. The line's quality, luxury, and spaciousness—one of the highest ratios of passenger-to-space of any ships—are immediately evident. The decor— a bit glitzy but always in good taste—was created by Swedish, Italian, and British designers influenced by Japanese artistic understatement. Quiet colors and quality furnishings harmonize. Fine fabrics and tex- tures set off marble and woods accented with brass and stainless steel. The generous use of glass gives interiors an airy ambience.

Passengers' introduction to the ship is the **Crystal Plaza,** an atrium lobby with cascades of Lucite lights, stairways, and railings that appear to float in space. They're outlined with brass fixtures against white mar- ble walls. Fresh greenery, hand-cut glass sculpture, and a waterfall provide accents. Summing up the feeling of opulence is—what else?—a crystal piano. The beautiful vessel has lounges for many purposes and moods. The **Palm Court,**one of the most handsome lounges afloat, is an airy space in white and mint green with graceful palms under sky- lights. It wears the atmosphere of a traditional palm court in the afternoon when tables are set for tea with crisp linens and gleaming sil- ver, and a harpist strums. Forward of the Palm Court is the fabulous **Vista Lounge,** a trilevel observation room with white leather chairs on sky-blue carpets and floor-to-ceiling windows that frame a 270-degree view. All designed in accordance with the principles of Feng Shui, the ancient practice of balance and harmony.

Crystal Symphony, introduced in 1995, was essentially a duplicate of the first ship with some enhancements. The **Crystal Cove Lounge,** Crys- tal Plaza, and **Lido Cafe** were doubled in size; the casino and shopping arcade expanded; the two alternative restaurants were enlarged, and a video room added. A spiral waterfall highlights *Symphony*'s atrium. Other important changes were in the cabins—all outside, about a third more with verandas, and all with larger, better-designed bathrooms.

In 2004, Crystal invested $12 million to renovate the *Crystal Symphony* with a completely new Feng Shui–designed spa and fitness center, an expanded Computer University@Sea, and a new **Vintage Room,** as well as a refurbished dining room, library, and penthouse suites and cabins.

ITINERARIES *See* Itinerary Index.

CABINS Large, comfortable, and handsomely appointed with fine fabrics and quality furnishings, the well-equipped cabins have sitting areas. Quality European fabrics provide a warm combination of textured wheat colors. Standard cabins have adequate closet and storage space, although some complain that hanging space is limited for long voyages. Large down pillows and comforters on beds, plush robes, fluffy towels, fine toiletries, and voicemail on the direct-dial telephone reflect attention to detail. All cabins have fresh flowers, two hair dryers, television with CNN and ESPN (when available), and Internet access.

More than half of all cabins have private verandas. Lifeboats obstruct views from some cabins, but *Crystal*'s literature notes them as "limited" or "extremely limited" views and prices the cabins accordingly.

The ship's ultimate luxury is on the all-suite, concierge-attended Penthouse Deck. Suites have large bedrooms, large sitting areas, and luxurious marble bathrooms with Jacuzzi bathtubs. The four most extravagant suites encompass 982 square feet, including verandas. In the recent renovations on *Symphony*, all penthouses and cabins were updated with new decor of Italian-made fabrics in blues, peaches and lavenders. CD players and DVD televisions were added.

The suites are attended by European-trained, white-gloved butlers and Scandinavian stewardesses. The young men, dressed in formal attire (some find this pretentious) are as competent as they are eager to serve. They will unpack your bags (and repack them at cruise's end), arrange a party or a dinner in your suite, and attend to other special requests. Nightly at cocktail time, they serve hors d'oeuvres and pour drinks from your fully stocked bar.

During a day at sea, passengers are given a ship tour on which they visit other cabin categories—a useful sales gimmick! Should the impulse seize you to book your next Crystal voyage right there, a "cruise consultant" is aboard to make the arrangements—at a discount.

Symphony's standard cabins are roomy. All are outside, and 278 have verandas and overall dimensions of 246 square feet. Other standard cabins cover 202 square feet and have large windows. All have a sitting area with love seat. Some Penthouse Deck suites are arranged to allow for larger closets. Standard-cabins have large bathrooms and all have two sinks in a six-foot counter, bathtubs plus showers, and large closets with more hanging space than in the line's first ship. All Penthouse Deck suites have verandas.

Specifications *Symphony*, 480 outside cabins, including 19 penthouse suites with verandas and 214 deluxe cabins (246 square feet) with verandas; 202 deluxe cabins (202 square feet) without verandas; 7 wheelchair-accessible. No singles. All twins convert to queens or kings.

DINING Super in quality and stunning in presentation, cuisine is one of Crystal ships' best features, on par with top restaurants in New York

and Los Angeles. Food is served on fine china by waiters who are as polished as the silver. The spacious dining rooms with floor-to-ceiling
windows and modern chandeliers are elegant and well-designed. More
space than usual is allowed between tables, helping keep noise down.
Tables for two are more numerous than usual.

In the latest renovations, *Symphony*'s **Crystal Dining Room** was
redesigned with rich, dark paneling offsetting a bronze and peach color
palette. Along with the new decor came new lighting, window treatments, and an acoustically-designed, elegant ceiling. Also added is **The
Vintage Room,** a classic boardroom with access to the ship's extensive
wine cellar—a copy of the one on *Crystal Serenity*. It is located in a newly
constructed space at the heart of the ship's entertainment area on Deck
6. Designed for the line's exclusive wine-and-champagne–maker's dinners, The Vintage Room accommodates 12 in a luxurious setting of
deep green colors and rich polished woods.

Dinner menus, placed in cabins in advance, are greatly varied during
a cruise. Typically, they include a choice of four appetizers; three soups;
two salads; pasta; five entrees of fish, poultry, and meat; vegetables; and
an array of desserts. Low-salt, low-fat, low-carb, and low-sugar choices
are available. The maître d'hôtel often asks passengers for their favorite
dishes, which the kitchen will prepare with advance notice. The wine list
has over 170 varieties. The ships' most innovative features—the first for
cruising and starting the trend—were the intimate, alternative dinner
restaurants, available at no extra cost to all passengers. The alternative
restaurants have a hidden charm: Dining in the same surroundings on a
long cruise can sometimes become boring. The two additional restaurants offer a change of ambience and cuisine—a great bonus. One of the
alternative restaurants, **Jade Garden,** serves Japanese specialties and
other Asian cuisine, while **Prego** features Italian dishes. Each restaurant
has its own kitchen; dishes are cooked to order. Reservations are
required. Make yours early because both are enormously popular.

Symphony's Prego has a waiting list almost every night and probably
ranks as the ship's main attraction. Decorated to suggest Venice, the
room has banquettes and high-backed chairs around tables seating four
or six. Dishes are outstanding. The Jade Garden stresses Asian simplicity of design. Light-hued screens with bamboo patterns cover the
windows and multi-colored carpeting and upholstery provide an
upbeat and modern look to this popular restaurant. Food is excellent,
prepared to order by an Asian chef and relies heavily on seafood, but
beef and chicken entrees are also available.

The level of service and cuisine in the dining room and alternative
restaurants is meant to compensate for the lack of the single-sitting dining room traditional on luxury ships. (Die-hards consider this Crystal's un-
forgivable sin. However, two seatings accommodate the many passengers
who like to eat early. What's more, it has not had an adverse effect on

Crystal's success.) The indoor/outdoor **Lido Cafe** serves breakfast, mid-morning bouillon, and lunch. Luncheon and themed buffets set up around the pool are very popular. The **Trident Bar,** an extension of the Neptune Pool swim-up bar, offers hot dogs, hamburgers, and other snacks, and there's a bar for ice cream and frozen yogurt. Moving the *Symphony*'s alternative restaurants to Deck 6 enabled its designers to double the size of the Lido Café, add a second buffet counter, and connect the cafe to indoor/outdoor seating for breakfast and lunch.

Crystal ships now serves a late-risers breakfast from 10 a.m. to noon, as well as a Sunday brunch in the **Crystal Cove** on Sundays at sea. The line also offers casual dining with an informal menu on deck on select evenings, usually after a day in port; passengers dress as they like in slacks, jeans, or shorts, and eat when they wish.

A sumptuous tea is served daily in the **Palm Court,** and the Crystal Plaza is the setting for a weekly dessert extravaganza set to the music of Mozart. Should you still suffer hunger pangs, the fruit basket in your cabin will have been replenished, or your cabin attendant will bring any item on the extensive 24-hour room service menu. You also may dine in your cabin, with courses served one by one.

The attractive **Bistro Café** serves coffee and pastries for late risers and wine and cheese, coffees, teas, and desserts during the day. Charming French prints that decorate the wall are reproduced on the cafe's pottery. On several sailings, a wine and food festival features guest chefs and wine experts.

SERVICE The ships have among the highest crew-to-passenger ratios in cruising. The well-trained staff is young, cheerful, and eager to please; service is thoroughly professional and consistently excellent. Dining room staff primarily are European; cabin attendants, European and Filipino; and the cruise and entertainment staff, American. A European-style concierge and purser service are available around-the-clock.

FACILITIES AND ACTIVITIES Cultural and destination-oriented lectures by experts, political figures, and diplomats are a regular afternoon or after-dinner feature. Daytime pursuits include card and other games, dancing classes, golf clinics, and arts and crafts. The well-stocked library has added videos, DVDs, books, and periodicals.

Crystal has expanded its **Computer University@Sea** and upgraded the room's computers. Depending on cruise length, classes range from "PC Basics" to "How to Create Your Own Home Page." The classroom aboard *Symphony* has 25 computer work stations and hands-on lab sessions. In the recent renovations, the facility was nearly doubled in size. Passengers may also schedule private instruction in their cabins. Rental laptop computers are available. Crystal was among the first to introduce e-mail service on its ships. Passengers have their own e-mail address, which they receive with their cruise ticket. There is an initial $5 set-up fee and a range of charges thereafter, depending on use. The line also offers a selection on packages based on the number of days used. Internet access has also been added to all cabins.

The **Library,** with more than 1,400 titles, was relocated to a new facility in the ship's atrium amidship. A door with brushed bronze finish opens to an inviting room of warm woods and Andrew Martin leather chairs. The VHS tapes collection were replenished with DVDs.

The **Hollywood Theatre,** with high-definition video projection and hearing-aid headsets, runs films each afternoon and evening. Films and other programs also are available on cabin televisions. For further diversion, pricey temptations with designer names are sold in the pretty shops on **Avenue of the Stars.**

Pre-dinner options include cocktails in the **Vista Lounge** or wood-paneled **Avenue Saloon** (enlarged on the *Symphony*), or a classical concert by a harpist or trio. The **Connoisseur Club,** adjacent to the Avenue Saloon, is a cigar and cognac lounge with private club atmosphere.

A cabaret show in **Club 2100** and two Broadway-style, full-scale, high-quality productions in the **Galaxy** show lounge are offered at night. Local entertainers may perform at ports of call. One evening is a masquerade party.

"Repertory Theatre at Sea," is a delightful innovation for the ships' entertainment and enrichment program. It includes well-known comedy and light drama performed by professional actors on every cruise. The diverse roster offers up to 91 scenes, excerpts, or reading from larger works as varied as Shakespeare, Edgar Allen Poe, and Henry James.

Symphony's Art Deco **Starlite Club** is one of the ship's most attractive lounges. It is used for the captain's cocktail and past-passenger parties, pre- and post-dinner cocktails, and dancing. In late evening, it becomes the disco, depending on passenger preference during each sailing.

Galaxy Lounge, the main show lounge, offers an array of first-rate productions that might range from classical ballet to a Broadway revue. Crystal has its own production team, Gretchen Goertz and Kathy Orme, who create all the production shows and are very original and very good. The talented show troupe includes former dancers from the Bolshoi Ballet and London's West End. The shows usually have spectacular costumes—some valued at $10,000 apiece—and sets by award-winning designers.

The ships boast the only casinos at sea operated by Caesars Palace of Las Vegas. They have Roman columns at the entrance and offer blackjack, slots, and roulette. Before sailing, passengers receive an application for credit at the casino, if they care to have it.

SPORTS, FITNESS, AND BEAUTY A lap pool has adjacent whirlpools, and an indoor/outdoor swimming pool has a swim-up bar and a retractable roof. There's generous sunning space on deck, plus Ping-Pong, shuffleboard, pool games, golf, and the only full-scale paddle tennis court at sea. Deck 7 offers a wraparound, unobstructed route for walking or jogging.

On *Symphony,* the spa was completely reconstructed and enlarged following the design principles of Feng Shui. The new facility with sweeping ocean views has eight treatment rooms, a new relaxation area, a private canopied teak sundeck, a state-of-the-art steam shower and sauna area, and custom-designed manicure/pedicure areas with sunken foot bowls. A new dry float bed suite, appropriate for singles or couples, has a sensory bed to create a feeling of weightlessness, ideal for "Aroma Spa" and other treatments. The enlarged **Fitness Center** now has a separate room for yoga, Pilates, aerobic and personal training instruction, and an expanded gym with state-of-the-art fitness equipment, all with heart-rate sensors.

Crystal's new alliance with TaylorMade showcases its prestigious r7 quad driver and other TaylorMade equipment. Crystal's golf program includes right and left-handed clubs for men and women, golf clinics, instruction by PGA golf pros, a putting green, practice cage, and golf driving ranges aboard the ships. A golf pro is generally onboard offering lessons and tips and the line schedules several golf cruises during the year.

CHILDREN'S FACILITIES Supervised youth programs are provided only when the line knows in advance that a sizable number of children will be aboard. **Fantasia,** a children's playroom, is more of an entertainment center, with video games for children ages 3–16. In-room baby-sitting can be arranged with crew members for $7.50 per hour for one child, $10 per hour for two children, and $12.50 per hour for three children.

SHORE EXCURSIONS Shore excursions are sold onboard, but they can also be booked in advance. Details are in the shore excursion brochure passengers receive before their cruise. Crystal's efficient tenders have air-conditioning—a much-appreciated amenity. Crystal provides good maps and information about each port. The concierge and excursion desk helpfully suggest and arrange independent port programs.

Crystal continues to add interesting and ambitious excursions, particularly on Alaska cruises. They range from hiking and kayaking to rafting, horseback riding, and wildlife viewing. One exotic option is a 70-mile float-plane ride from Ketchikan to Anan Creek, where only 48 people each day are permitted to watch black and brown bears feeding from the creek. Another is a wildlife tour in dugout canoes on a Botswana safari offered on the occasional Africa cruises.

Crystal Serenity	**QUALITY 10**	**VALUE C**
REGISTRY Bahamas	LENGTH 820 feet	BEAM 105.6 feet
CABINS 550	DRAFT 25 feet	SPEED 22 knots
MAXIMUM PASSENGERS 1,080	PASSENGER DECKS 9	ELEVATORS 8
	CREW 655	SPACE RATIO 63

THE SHIP Crystal's third ship, built at Chantiers de l'Atlantique in France, made her debut in July 2003. The ship combines the best features of her sister ships with new ones added, including more dining venues, more penthouse suites, more cabins with verandas and butler service, more entertainment lounges, and more fitness options, among others. The new ship is also almost 20% roomier and is richly decorated in very good taste, incorporating soft, muted colors which complement the beautiful crystal-glass signature touches throughout the vessel.

Some of the new features are a new-style, alternative Asian restaurant and sushi bar, which is the third evening alternative; a boardroom with a wine cellar for special dinners and wine tastings at an extra charge; a second paddle tennis court; a new learning center for creative and educational hands-on classes; and a club lounge off the atrium for Crystal Society members, one of the first ships to have a room dedicated specifically to its past passengers.

The familiar favorites from other Crystal ships include a contemporary rendition of the **Palm Court**, a spacious observation lounge with potted palms set into hexagonal skylights, the clubby **Avenue Saloon,** and the **Connoisseurs Club.** The **Computer University@Sea** classroom is more than 50% larger than the facility on the other ships and has a 24-hour Internet center, plus a private area for one-on-one computer instruction. The *Serenity*'s spa and fitness center, approximately 40% larger than on her sister ships, are quite lavish. Located high up and aft, the two sections have separate entrances and good soundproofing—hence the thumping of exercise machines does not intrude upon the serenity of the treatment room or the **Lido Café** below. *Crystal Serenity* has an even greater space ratio (63) than her sister ships, with 34% more public space and one deck more than *Crystal Symphony*. The ship was designed by an international team headed by well-known Swedish naval architect Robert Tillberg, who worked on Crystal's other two ships. Tillberg says *Serenity* is a sister, not a twin, to the other Crystal ships. His team was responsible for most of the public rooms and all passenger and staff accommodations. Other firms designed the specialty lounges and restaurants, spa, and retail shops.

ITINERARIES *See* Itinerary Index

CABINS Like *Crystal Symphony,* the ship has no inside cabins, and approximately 85% of the outside cabins and suites have private verandas. None have obstructed views, as the lifeboats are stowed below the cabin decks. One and a half decks of *Serenity* are devoted to 100 Penthouse accommodations with verandas (56% greater than on *Crystal Symphony*). Of those, the most lavish are four Crystal Penthouses, each measuring 1,345 square feet—or 37% larger than those on sister vessels.

In addition to the suites, there are 368 outside cabins with verandas and 82 outside staterooms with large picture windows. The eight wheelchair-accessible cabins are found in various categories: two penthouses, two veranda cabins, and four cabins with picture windows.

The deluxe cabins with veranda (Categories A and B) are virtually identical to the penthouse cabins with veranda (Category P), all being 269 square feet, but the former do not have butler service. The cabins are furnished with a comfortable sofa with a pop-up coffee table for in-cabin dining; queen or twins beds with two night tables and lamps rather than reading lights. The entertainment center has a remote-control television and DVD player. The minibar and refrigerator are stocked with complimentary soft drinks and bottled water. All cabins have a dataport for laptop computer hook-up. The veranda is furnished with two white plastic chairs and a table; chaise lounges can be requested. The bathrooms have full-size tubs and showers and twin sinks.

DINING Passengers on *Crystal Serenity* have the choice of five evening dining venues: the main **Crystal Dining Room** (two seatings); **Tastes,** an indoor/outdoor poolside area for casual evening dining; and three specialty restaurants: **Prego** for Italian fare; a sushi bar, a first for Crystal; and **Silk Road** for pan-Asian cuisine. The latter features eclectic creations by famous master chef and Crystal consultant Nobuyuki "Nobu" Matsuhisa, known for his innovative blend of classic Japanese dishes with Peruvian and European influences. Two of the alternative restaurants operate on a reservations-only basis for no extra charge. No reservations are needed for the sushi bar. In general, service seems better and a bit less harried in Silk Road, perhaps because the menu is less extensive.

Serenity's Prego, the Italian specialty restaurant, is entirely different in style than on her sister ships. It is a long two-level room located aft on the starboard side, decorated in white and gold with bas-relief urns filled with fruit on the bulkhead pilasters. The decorative panels show Tuscan city scenes using two-dimensional depictions: the front panel low in height and the rear one in full height, with indirect lighting between to brighten the settings and create depth. Two Italian favorites on the menu are pumpkin ravioli flavored with apricot, and filet of Angus beef topped with gorgonzola. The restaurant also offers mouthwatering blends of seafood and pasta.

Among the "Nobu" selections on Silk Road's pan-Asian menu are lobster with truffle yuzu sauce, black cod with miso, and chicken with teriyaki balsamic. The airy portside setting is executed in lime green and soft blue lighting, with the sushi bar at the entrance.

During the day, passengers have choices similar to her sister ship, plus some new ones. Permanent hot-food stations aft of the ship's second pool serve luncheon buffets with a theme. The ship also offers stylish versions of its popular **Bistro,** a coffee and wine bar for morning and afternoon snacks such as cold meats, salads, cheeses, and desserts; the **Lido Café** for breakfast and lunch; the **Trident Grill** for casual, poolside lunches throughout the afternoon; an ice cream/frozen yogurt bar; and 24-hour room service. Recently, Crystal expanded its healthy breakfast options at **Tastes** with gluten-free, lactose-free, sugar-free, fat-free, and whole grain selections.

FACILITIES AND ACTIVITIES The **Galaxy Show Lounge** is the main entertainment venue for production shows and has improved sight lines and state-of-the-art sound and lighting systems. It's truly a showroom for the 21st century. Several new shows are being offered. A second cabaret lounge, the **Stardust Club,** provides a venue for daytime activities, such as dance classes and wine tasting, as well as for evening dancing and cabaret entertainment.

The **Palm Court,** with floor-to-ceiling 270-degree panoramic windows, is a splendid, roomy top deck lounge in blue-gray with rattan seating, used for afternoon tea with a menu of about a dozen regular and herbal teas. It's also a good spot for evening dancing and entertainment, special events, and for simply enjoying the changing scenery. New room extensions offer unusual views of the glass-enclosed bridge wings one deck below. Other public facilities include the **Crystal Plaza** and **Crystal Cove,** the lobby area with a two-story atrium and **Crystal Piano Bar;** the **Avenue Saloon,** Crystal's clubby signature piano bar; the **Connoisseurs Club**, a cigar lounge for after-dinner drinks; **Caesars Palace at Sea** casino; **Pulse**, a disco/nightclub for late-night dancing and karaoke; **Hollywood Theater,** a cinema-conference center with theater-style seating for day and evening movies, lectures, and religious services; a staffed library with books and DVDs—and even a great selection for kids—and comfy reading bays; a card room for Crystal's avid bridge players; and a gallery of high-end retail shops.

Passport to Music, Crystal's latest innovation which debuted on *Crystal Serenity,* is a partnership with Yamaha to offer a program of music instruction as part of the line's new **Creative Learning Institute** (CLI), perhaps the most original experiential and interactive "edutainment," as Crystal calls it, offered at sea. Music instruction is offered in **The Studio,** *Crystal Serenity's* handsome, high-tech facility created expressly for CLI programs.

The Studio is outfitted with 15 portable grand-piano keyboards—Yamaha's newest state-of-the-art model—and supported with the Clavinova digital piano. Certified Yamaha music teachers are aboard to teach groups of 12 to 15 guests. Depending on the length of the cruise, the average curriculum offers six 60-minute sessions; guests receive a certificate at the program's completion. A selection of software created by Yamaha enables guests to continue their musical journey at home.

Other Crystal partnerships for the Creative Learning Institute allow well-known organizations and schools, such as Berlitz, the Cleveland Clinic, Society of Wine Educators, Pepperdine University, Tai Chi Cultural Center, and Barnes & Noble, among others, to bring experts aboard to share their knowledge in a classroom setting. The CLI curriculum offers progressive levels of instruction on a single subject or several one-class sessions of related topics. The main categories are Arts and Entertainment, ranging from Asian woodblock printing to acting workshops; Business and Technology, estate planning to fundraising to patent applications; Lifestyle, dealing with topics such as book clubs, candlemaking, or menu planning; Wellness, with health and fitness topics and serious medical subjects, such as prostate cancer, led by an expert from the Cleveland Clinic; and Wine and Food. The CLI is very popular—a kind of Elderhostel at sea. Thus, when the ship is full, it's wise to sign up early. There is no charge for any of the courses.

"Repertory Theatre at Sea," similar to that on *Crystal Symphony*, features well-known comedy and light drama performed by professional actors. The diverse roster offers scenes, excerpts, or reading from larger works as varied as Shakespeare, Edgar Allen Poe, and Henry James.

SPORTS, FITNESS, AND BEAUTY *Serenity*'s 8,500-square-foot spa and fitness centers are approximately 40% larger, with more treatment rooms and a larger gym and aerobics studio than her sister ships with state-of-the-art equipment. In response to passenger feedback, the ship has a second paddle-tennis court, an outdoor lap pool flanked by two whirlpools, a second indoor/outdoor pool covered by a sliding roof, a full promenade around the exterior of the ship for walking, jogging and shuffleboard, and a sports deck with two golf driving ranges, putting green, and table tennis.

CHILDREN'S FACILITIES *Crystal Serenity* has a **Fantasia** children and teen center with video games, both small and located high up and aft of the Palm Court foyer. Programs apply when there are children aboard, which is not often on long cruises. Holiday cruises bring out families. Then, too, Crystal, like most cruise lines, is seeing a steady increase in multigenerational as well as family cruising.

POSTSCRIPT The *Crystal Serenity* is an evolutionary ship for the line. The recent refurbishment of the *Crystal Symphony* reflects the newer ship's lead. Roominess is probably the most obvious improvement, enabling Crystal to expand where the line excels, such as in the expansive and spectacular Palm Court, the Creative Learning Institute, Computer Learning Center, standard cabin size, more accommodations with butler service, and additional seats in the alternative restaurants. All in all, *Crystal Serenity* has gone a long way to keep Crystal Cruises ahead of any competition.

Cunard Line, Ltd.

24303 Town Center Drive, Suite 200, Valencia, CA 91355-0908
☎ 661-753-1035 or 800-7-CUNARD; fax 661-259-3103
www.cunard.com

TYPE OF SHIPS Large, traditional ship; deluxe megaship.

TYPE OF CRUISES Wide range of destinations and durations, from warm-weather vacations to transatlantic summer service for affluent, demanding travelers; distinctively British pedigree.

CRUISE LINE'S STRENGTHS
- name recognition
- distinctive ships
- itineraries
- accommodations and service
- single cabins on older ship

CRUISE LINE'S SHORTCOMINGS
- mixed products on ships

FELLOW PASSENGERS Cunard attracts a broad spectrum of passengers—from first-timers eager to visit many ports to veterans who seldom leave the ship—but most are upscale, mature, experienced travelers. Depending on time of year, the makeup is about 50-50 American and British, with large contingents of Europeans and repeaters. QE2's world cruises attract a crowd—affluent and older, taking long winter vacations—very different from that on other itineraries. QM2 passengers may be all ages, incomes, and professions, as well as families with children, and people eager to take an ocean voyage on the famous ship.

Recommended for Those who enjoy a certain amount of formality and tradition, and are accustomed to luxury and willing to pay for it.

Not recommended for Those uncomfortable in elegance who prefer a casual or nonstop party atmosphere.

CRUISE AREAS AND SEASONS Around the world in winter; transatlantic, April–November; Europe, spring–fall; Caribbean, South America, Baltic, Mediterranean, New England/Canada, and Panama Canal, seasonally.

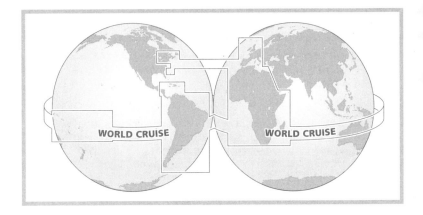

THE LINE Cunard Line, with a history stretching back to 1840, sailed into the new millennium with new owners, new management, and a new direction. But reinventing itself is nothing new for Cunard. With the postwar birth of the jet age and the demise of transatlantic passenger service, traditional steamship companies like Cunard had to adapt to the new realities to survive. Some converted their ships for modern cruising, some built new ships, and some bought or merged with other cruise lines. Cunard took all these steps and more.

During the era of the grand ocean liners, Cunard Line was best known for its queens—the *Queen Mary* and *Queen Elizabeth*—which set the standard of elegance at sea for decades. *Queen Elizabeth 2* made her debut in 1969, when the future of transatlantic service was uncertain.

In 1971, Cunard was acquired by Trafalgar House, a multinational conglomerate headquartered in London, but doubts persisted throughout the decade on whether the line would survive. Having the only ocean liner on regular transatlantic service helped keep her going. In 1982, the *QE2* was pressed into Her Majesty's service during the Falkland Islands War. For Cunard and the *QE2*, it was a blessing in disguise, giving the ship a new lease on life with the publicity and a much-needed refurbishment by the British government before her return to passenger service.

In 1998, Cunard was sold to Carnival Corporation, and the following year, Cunard's other ships were moved to other lines, leaving only the *QE2* and *Vistafjord*, renamed *Caronia* under the Cunard brand. The new owners spent millions renovating the *QE2* and rebuilding Cunard with new ships.

The first, *Queen Mary 2*, christened by Her Majesty Queen Elizabeth II on January 8, 2004, was billed as the "grandest and largest passenger liner ever built" according to Cunard. She is intended to evoke a bygone era of seagoing luxury while representing the next era of ocean liner evolution, to create "a new golden age of sea travel for those who missed the first." After the *Queen Mary 2* entered service, the *QE2* was transferred to England to serve primarily the British market. Later in the year, Cunard's offices were integrated with Princess Cruises and moved to the West Coast for back-office economies.

Cunard also plans to build the *Queen Victoria,* for delivery in December 2007. The *Caronia* was sold.

THE FLEET	BUILT/RENOVATED	TONNAGE	PASSENGERS
Queen Elizabeth 2	1969/1987/1994/1996/1999	70,327	1,778
Queen Mary 2	2004	150,000	2,620
Queen Victoria	2007	NA	NA

STYLE The legendary *Queen Elizabeth 2* has a style all her own, and the *QM2* is developing a similar yet different style, too. Today, the *QM2* is the only passenger ship sailing the Atlantic on a regular schedule, from April to November, with three levels of service. Now based in Southhampton, the *QE2* sails on an annual world cruise from January to April. Both ships offer shorter cruises, usually in the Caribbean and Europe, that fill the weeks between.

To many, the Queens are the ultimate cruise experience—both cities at sea that dwarf all but the newest mega liners. The Queens are proud, elegant, formal, and as British as—well, yes—the queen. Throughout its history, Cunard has been an innovator in response to changing lifestyles. *QE2* was the first ship to have a full-fledged spa, and now the *QM2* has Canyon Ranch's first spa at sea. Recognizing the impact of the electronic revolution, Cunard installed the first computer learning center, satellite editions of world news delivered daily to passengers, and an electronic library on the *QE2*.

DISTINCTIVE FEATURES Year-round gentlemen hosts, computer learning centers, British nannies, driving range and putting green, florist, tuxedo rental, electronic library, bookshop. *QM2*: Canyon Ranch Spa, Royal Academy of Dramatic Art performance, and Illumination, the only planetarium at sea.

	HIGHEST	LOWEST	AVERAGE
PER DIEM	$596	$266	$431

Per diems are calculated from cruise line's nondiscounted *cruise-only* published fares on standard accommodations and vary by season, cabins, and cruise areas.

RATES Most port charges are included.

Special fares and discounts

- **EARLY-BOOKING DISCOUNTS:** Time-sensitive discounts called BEST fares range from 20% for booking and deposit a year in advance, to 30% for payment in full a year in advance; 10% for Cunard World Club members; 15% for World Cruise Society members; and others when two or more cruises are combined.

- **THIRD/FOURTH PASSENGER:** Specific fares listed in chart in brochure.

- **CHILDREN'S FARE:** Children age 1 and 2 years travel free (plus port and custom charges). If the child is the second person, they are charged full published fare. If the child is the third or fourth person, third/fourth person fare applies.

- **SINGLE FARES:** Single-occupancy cabins listed in brochure. Supplement for single occupancy of double cabin is 140–200%, depending on cabin.

Packages

- **AIR/SEA:** Yes.
- **PRE/POST:** Yes.
- **OTHERS:** Yes.

PAST PASSENGERS Cunard World Club, the past passenger program, has three levels: Silver (after the second cruise); Gold, third to seventh voyage; and Platinum, eight or more cruises or completion of 48 consecutive days. Benefits include savings on sailings, onboard Club representative, special mailings with savings offers; access to members-only Web site, and more. Platinum members get priority check-in and embarkation in New York and Southampton.

THE LAST WORD Cunard has long been known for luxury, but if you don't understand the differences in the levels of luxury, it can be somewhat misleading. For example, the popular image of the *QE2*, and now for *QM2*, is glamour, grand luxury, and haute cuisine. For those who buy the highest-priced suites and deluxe cabins and dine in the grills, this picture is accurate—but that's less than 30% of passengers. On her transatlantic run, *QM2* has three levels of service determined by cabin category, which is a polite way of saying three classes based on price. Each of three categories is assigned specific restaurants, and entry by the others is restricted accordingly. The redeeming factor is that all entertainment, sports, recreational facilities, and shops are available to everyone, regardless of their cabin location.

In March 2005, Cunard launched "White Star Service," a training program for officers and staff focusing on three pillars: the legendary, the elegant, and the memorable. Each member of the ship's crew wears a black enamel pin on which the three words are inscribed. Named for the White Star Line with which Cunard merged back in 1934, the new service is intended to acquaint the ship's crew with Cunard's long history, and through it, instill in them the pride and high level of service that is the Cunard tradition.

Although Cunard has been carrying passengers for 165 years, just now it has to be called a work-in-progress as it reinvents itself once again. The years prior to the launch of the *QM2* were ones of change and setting the line's new direction. That mission is still in development and probably will be for several years as new ships are added to its fleet. Stay tuned.

Cunard Line Standard Features

Officers British and International.

Staff British and International.

Dining facilities *QE2*, single seating in five dining rooms for three meals, except Brittania, two seatings; informal lido cafe for three meals and midnight buffet; snack bar. Casual indoor/outdoor cafe for breakfast and lunch buffets. Alternative Italian restaurant. *QM2*, Todd English restaurant, 3 dining rooms, pub and a lido-style King's Court with an Asian section, one featuring Italian specialties plus the carvery, salads and such.

Special diets Diabetic, low-calorie, low-cholesterol, low-salt, and vegetarian.

Room service 24-hour room service.

Dress code Formal/informal, for dining, depending on evening.

Cabin amenities Radio, direct-dial telephone, 20-channel television with CNN. Bathroom with tub and shower in mid and top categories. Refrigerator, walk-in closet, TV/VCR, bathrobes, hair dryer, safe, fruit baskets, nightly turn-down service and verandas.

Electrical outlets 220/110 AC.

Wheelchair access *QM2*, 30 cabins; *QE2*, ramps; four cabins; bathtubs with grab bars, wide doors, low sills, two elevators designed for the handicapped.

Recreation and entertainment Casino, cabaret, revues. Life-enrichment seminars, guest lectures. Lounges, bars, disco, bingo, dance lessons, gentlemen hosts, computer learning center, planetarium.

Sports and other activities Indoor/outdoor pools, deck sports, golf putting and driving net, jogging track, paddle tennis, Ping-Pong.

Beauty and fitness Spa, fitness center, gym, barber/beauty salon, exercise class. See text for more details.

Other facilities Cinema/theater, launderette, laundry/dry cleaning service, library, bookshop, shops, hospital. *QE2*, tuxedo rental shop, foreign exchange, Harrods, Hermes, Chopard, florist, board room, synagogue.

Children's facilities Teen center, video, supervised children's playrooms, nursery, nannies, baby-sitting; special children's evening meal served daily in the Lido at 5:30 p.m.

Cunard Line Standard Features(continued)

Theme cruises Year-round selection.

Smoking Designated areas in public rooms.

Cunard suggested tipping $11–$13 per day added to bill, depending on cabin category. Both ships include 15% gratuity for bar and salon services. Gratuities included in fare for cruises of 90 days or more.

Credit cards For cruise payment and on-board charges: American Express, Diners Club, Discover, MasterCard, Visa.

Queen Mary 2	QUALITY 8	VALUE B
REGISTRY Great Britain	LENGTH 1,132 feet	BEAM 135 feet
CABINS 1,310	DRAFT 32 feet	SPEED 30 knots
MAXIMUM PASSENGERS 3,090	PASSENGER DECKS 17	ELEVATORS 22
	CREW 1,253	SPACE RATIO 57.25

THE SHIP The *Queen Mary 2*, Cunard's new flagship, is not only the biggest, widest, longest, and most expensive ship ever built—her debut has given birth to a new Cunard cruise line.

The ocean liner is meant to be reminiscent of great transatlantic steamships and, in Cunard's words, "re-launch the golden age of travel for those who missed the first one"—but with refined interiors that have a contemporary rather than a classic liner look. Designed as an ocean liner for the 21st century and intended to appeal to baby boomers who Cunard sees as the ship's main market, the overall impression is one of quiet grace, conservative and a bit formal in a British manner without being stuffy.

The spacious *QM2*, costing upward of $800 million and constructed at Alstom Chantiers de l'Atlantique in Saint-Nazaire, France, was christened by Her Majesty Queen Elizabeth II on January 8, 2004. The 150,000-ton vessel's slick hull, with a height of 237 feet from keel to funnel top, travels at speeds of up to 30 knots, making her one of the fastest cruise ships and able to undertake unusual itineraries. She can carry up to 3,090 passengers in a "quasi-class system" similar to that on *QE2*, with the cabin category determining restaurant assignments.

QM2 has the first and only spa at sea operated by the world-famous Canyon Ranch health resorts; the world's first and only planetarium at sea; the largest ballroom at sea; the largest library at sea; the largest wine cellar at sea; and ten different dining venues, including the first and only shipboard restaurant by popular American chef Todd English.

There are 14 lounges and bars, a two-story theater, a casino, five indoor and outdoor swimming pools including a children's pool, an adults-only pool, another pool with a magrodome, hot tubs, boutiques, and a children's facility, complete with British nannies. The learning center has guests lecturers from Oxford University. The ship's $5 million art collection includes over 300 original works of art.

On departing the ship at ports of call, passengers use four lounges— **Kensington, Chelsea, Knightsbridge,** and **Belgravia**—named for London's best-known upscale neighborhoods and tube stops; those in wheelchairs are transferred to tenders or docks by a hydraulic platform.

QM2 is following a similar pattern as the QE2 had for many years, sailing on regularly scheduled transatlantic crossings between New York and Southampton from spring to November and longer world-wide cruises at other times. As a result of her unprecedented publicity and instant popularity, the number of her transatlantic cruises were doubled for 2005.

CABINS The three main cabin categories correspond to the ship's dining rooms—Britannia, Princess, and Queen. Britannia offers 17 cabin levels ranging from standard (about 194 square feet) to deluxe (248 square feet). Princess accommodations are 381-square-foot junior suites, while Queen encompass five levels of suites, ranging from 506 square feet to two-story Grand Duplex apartments at 2,249 square feet each.

Seventy-five percent of the 1,310 cabins have eight-foot-deep balconies. Thirty cabins for disabled passengers are available in various categories. The cabins are well laid out and very comfortable. The decor throughout is a quiet, tony quality, using light apricot, beige and other soft pastels. All have interactive television with multi-language film and music channels, direct-dial phone, hair dryer, 110/220-volt outlets, and bathroom with tub and/or shower.

The five duplex apartments (Balmoral, Windsor, Holyrood, Buckingham, and Sandringham suites) are two stories high and cover more than 1,650 square feet. They have two-story glass walls at the ship's stern, providing great sea views. The lavish suites have their own exercise area, veranda, two full bathrooms with tub and shower, a walk-in closet, a separate sitting area, and refrigerator. Occupants in duplex apartments will be pampered by butler service and room-service dining prepared by chefs from the Queen's Grill. Apartments can be connected to a penthouse to create a 2,220-square-foot suite.

Four deluxe penthouses (Queen Mary, Queen Anne, Queen Elizabeth, and Queen Victoria suites) overlooking the ship's bow measure between 861 and 1,076 square feet. Each features a marble bathroom with tub and shower, walk-in closet, refrigerator, separate dining area, and sitting area with large picture windows.

Suite amenities include two plasma, flat-screen televisions, an entertainment system, a bon voyage bottle of champagne, personalized stationery, a bar with selected spirits or wine and soft drinks, plush terry cloth bathrobes, slippers, and daily fresh fruit and predinner canapés. Penthouses can also be connected with two of the suites to create more than 5,000 square feet of living space. In addition to dining at the Queen's Grill restaurant, suite passengers have an exclusive lounge for afternoon tea, cocktails, and an after-dinner aperitif. Several suites have a private elevator entrance.

Specifications Duplex apartments, 5; deluxe penthouses, 4; penthouses, 6; suites, 82; outside standards with veranda, 782; outside standards, 138; inside standards with atrium view, 12; inside standards, 281. 30 wheelchair-accessible.

DINING Seating in the three main restaurants corresponds to the category of the passenger's accommodation. The elegant **Queen's Grill** is reserved exclusively for luxury penthouses, duplexes, and suites, and the **Princess Grill** for passengers in junior suites. Both have single-seating dining and operate much like an upscale à la carte restaurant. If there has been any disappointment voiced with the ship, it's with the Queen's Grill. Given the exclusivity of the venue, the quality of the service is not convincing for the price. Aware of the criticism, however, Cunard has worked to improve it and recent reports are much more favorable than in the beginning.

The **Britannia Restaurant** accommodates all other cabin categories with 1,347 seats and offers open seating for breakfast and lunch and two seatings for dinner. The three-deck-high room spans the width of the ship, with a dramatic central staircase meant to recall the grand dining rooms of past Cunard liners. Despite the large number of passengers being served at one time, many give the food and service high marks.

Another vast space is the **King's Court,** the lido restaurant serving buffet breakfast and lunch and four casual dining alternatives for dinner. At lunch, there are regional specialties and carved meats. In the evening, King's Court is transformed into sit-down restaurants: **La Piazza** for Italian specialties, **Lotus** offering Chinese and Asian cuisine, the **Carvery** serving carved meats, and the **Chef's Galley** for chef's selections. Here, passengers can watch and learn the preparation of their meal from Cunard or guest chefs sponsored by *Gourmet* magazine.

Other dining options include **Todd English,** featuring the innovative Mediterranean cuisine of its renowned namesake, open for lunch (surcharge, $20) and dinner (surcharge $30) with indoor/outdoor seating overlooking the aft pool terrace. Reservations are required. The cuisine is outstanding, and indeed the restaurant was so popular that Cunard added the surcharge in order to handle the demand. The **Golden Lion** and **Boardwalk Grill** are casual venues for fast food or pub grub, offering hot dogs, hamburgers, and other grills, a daily specialty, soups, and salads. Afternoon tea is served in the colonial-style **Winter Garden**.

FACILITIES AND ACTIVITIES In a six-day transatlantic crossing, the *QM2* offers a roster of over 200 activities. Some are traditional cruise-ship fun and games, but many are designed especially for this ship. The **Royal Court Theatre,** the main showroom with tiered seating for 1,100 passengers, boasts concert-hall acoustics, a hydraulic proscenium stage, and sophisticated lighting and sound equipment. The theater is the venue for full-scale, West End– or Broadway-type productions and other entertainers. The **Empire Casino** offers blackjack, roulette, and slot machines. The **Queen's Room** is the elegant ballroom.

Illuminations, the first-of-its-kind planetarium-at-sea, has stadium-type seating where passengers are entertained with celestial shows, movies, lectures, and other programs. Movies are also shown alfresco near the funnel high atop the ship.

ConneXions, the ship's enrichment program, has seven function rooms to use as classrooms or meeting rooms; they can be separated or joined to adjust for class sizes. The programs, ranging from wine appreciation and cooking to seamanship and navigation, are taught by expert guest instructors, some from Oxford University. Computer classes and business services are also available. The facility has the latest electronic equipment and Internet access.

Also falling under ConneXions are the plays and workshops being conducted by England's famous Royal Academy of Dramatic Art, which supplies the actors and conducts the workshops.

The *QM2*'s 8,000-volume library and the **Bookshop,** similar to those on the *QE2,* are furnished with comfortable leather sofas and armchairs and directed by a full-time librarian. The library also has books on CD. Mayfair Shops, a shopping gallery, offers a myriad of items from sundries to fine leather goods and formalwear for sale and rental. Also in this area is the elegant **Champagne Bar,** created by the famous champagne house Veuve Clicquot Ponsardin, its first and only venture on a cruise line. In addition to a variety of champagne, the bar has a menu including caviar and foie gras.

SPORTS, FITNESS, AND BEAUTY The *QM2* boasts the largest spa afloat designed by the famous Canyon Ranch, which also operates it. The **Canyon Ranch Spa Club,** covering 20,000 square feet on two decks, has a staff of 50 to provide treatments and lead classes in yoga and tai chi as well as health-related workshops. The spa has 24 treatment rooms, a thalassotherapy pool, whirlpool, saunas, reflexology, an aromatic steam room, a gym with state-of-the-art equipment, a juice bar, and men's and women's locker rooms. The spa is very popular. You should plan to book your treatments early as it fills up fast.

You should know that the *QM2* proves that passengers are willing to pay extra for many shipboard amenities—in this case, *QM2*'s fitness facilities and Canyon Ranch Spa. The spa issues a Canyon Ranch Spa-Club Passport, covering the locker rooms and aquatic center for these charges: One-day Passport, $29; three consecutive days, $49; five consecutive days, $79. The fee is the same for at-sea or in-port days. The Passport is issued free with the booking of a spa treatment.

CHILDREN'S FACILITIES   The **Play Zone** for small children and **The Zone** are located all by themselves on Deck 6 aft. The area has a small splash pool and toddlers are supervised by nannies. The older children have a separate facility with computer terminals and activities.

Queen Elizabeth 2	QUALITY 7	VALUE C
REGISTRY Great Britain	LENGTH 963 feet	BEAM 105 feet
CABINS 950	DRAFT 32 feet	SPEED 28.5 knots
MAXIMUM PASSENGERS 1,791	PASSENGER DECKS 12	ELEVATORS 13
	CREW 921	SPACE RATIO 36

THE SHIP   Until the arrival of *QM2*, *Queen Elizabeth 2* had been the lone survivor of Cunard's long, rich history of ocean travel. Extensive facelifts between 1995 and 1999 helped her retain her uniqueness: a grand ocean liner with the flexibility to provide a modern cruise experience.

Major remodeling of most public areas were directed by John McNeece, Britain's leading cruise-ship interior designer, and MET Studio, an architectural and design firm that worked with James Gardner, the *QE2*'s original designer. They improved passenger flow and added new decor, facilities, and ambience that address today's lifestyle while retaining the ship's distinctive character. By integrating *QE2* and Cunard history into the decor, the designers created a floating museum, named Heritage Trail, as well as a ship as modern as the 21st century. Escorted tours of the 24 exhibits underscore her traditions.

Public rooms are on three decks—Quarter, Upper, and Boat—with new links and stairways to let traffic flow naturally and to reflect passengers' activities at different times of day. Promenades echo the earlier Queens. Passengers enter the *QE2* through the Midships Lobby, a two-story atrium on Deck 2 elegantly decorated in mulberry and green against honey-colored cherry wood trimmed in bronze, where a harpist is usually in residence during embarkation. A four-part mural by Peter Sutton depicting the history of Cunard and the *QE2* covers the atrium's circular walls. The bell from the first *Queen Elizabeth* and the *Spirit of Atlantic* statuette are displayed.

ITINERARIES *See* Itinerary Index.

CABINS Comfortable and convenient, all cabins were refurbished, and their bathrooms retiled and given new fixtures in recent renovations. Two new Grand suites (QS category), including one that is wheelchair-accessible, and two Princess Grill cabins were added.

The *QE2*'s complex arrangement of cabin categories is different for the world cruise and the transatlantic service. Because dining assignments are determined by cabin category, it's important to understand precisely what you're buying. In principle, when you pay more, you get more.

The top 6 among 23 categories—plus the 4 named suites—dine in the Queen's Grill. The next group, ultradeluxe, is split between the Princess and Britannia Grills. Assignments continue on down the line.

Categories don't completely reflect the variety of configurations. The top two decks, Signal and Sun Boat, have the largest, most luxurious suites with verandas and penthouse service, which includes butlers whose duties range from planning parties to arranging priority disembarkation and customs preclearance. Ultradeluxe cabins are amidships on Sun Deck, Deck 1, and Deck 2; other categories are fore and aft on Decks 2 and 3 as well as the two lower decks.

All cabins have television with 24-hour CNN, information, and movies. Cabins in grill and deluxe class have refrigerators, VCRs, and bathrooms with tub and shower; premium class has bathrooms with shower only. Bathrooms of 55 penthouse suites are in marble. *QE2* has a total of 136 single cabins covering five categories.

Specifications 97 single and 222 double inside cabins; 39 singles and 592 doubles outside; 700 with 2 lower beds; 7 ultra-luxury suites. Some wheelchair-accessible cabins. Standard dimensions not available.

DINING Four of the dining rooms have single seating for each meal. The **Mauretania Restaurant** has an early and a late seating. Named for an early Cunard ship, this restaurant has as the centerpiece *White Horses,* a sculpture by Althea Wynne that depicts four horses riding waves, emblematic of the British sailors' term for whitecaps. On transatlantic service, this restaurant has two seatings.

The **Caronia Restaurant,** named for another Cunard ship of legendary opulence, is now one of the ship's most attractive rooms. At the entrance is a 15-foot model of the *Mauretania* (one of the Heritage Trail's largest items) on display. In the style of an English country house, it has rich mahogany-paneled walls and columns and a white-painted ceiling with Murano glass chandeliers in a spreading leaf design. On the back wall behind the captain's table is a lovely Italian hill-country scene.

The **Princess** and **Britannia Grills** have their own separate entrances from the **Crystal Bar.** The latter's name honors Cunard's first ship, *Britannia,* a model of which is displayed in the Heritage Trail group entitled

"Samuel Cunard and the Paddle Steamers." The **Queen's Grill** is reserved for passengers booked in Queen's Grill class only. Among its latest additions were etched glass doors and a completely new galley.

Menus are identical in all restaurants, except the Queen's Grill, where cuisine is meant to be of the highest gourmet standard and patrons enjoy tableside preparations. The rooms' sizes and ambience differ more than the food. Fare includes hors d'oeuvres, three soups, sorbet, five entrees, two salads, four or five desserts, cheese, ice cream, sherbet, and fruit. A spa menu is available.

The **Lido** is the ship's most obvious bow to current lifestyles. It was transformed into a buffet-style restaurant, providing an informal setting for breakfast, lunch, dinner, and the midnight buffet. Coffee and drinks are served all day. From our experience, with the exception of the Queen's Grill, the food—and certainly the service—are the best aboard, surpassing even the Princess Grill. Floor-to-ceiling windows open to the outside deck, making the room light and airy. White, beige, and mint decor is set off by two murals by Italian artist Giancarlo Impiglia depicting the QE2 cruise experience. Stairs lead from the cafe to the Deck 1 lido area and the **Pavilion** bar and grill.

SERVICE Officers are British, but most hotel and cabin staff are European, many of them women. The level of dining room service rises with the dining room and price. In grill class, service is meant to be luxurious. For other passengers, it's, well, British. Most passengers say it's friendly and attentive. Unless you're in a top suite, do not expect cabin and dining service to be any different or better than most mainstream ships.

FACILITIES AND ACTIVITIES Varied lounges and public rooms provide an array of activities. A day could begin with exercise in the fitness center or jogging, progress to a lesson in the computer center, and move to a seminar or workshop in the theater. The latter also functions as a lecture hall, conference room, and cinema. There is also a business center. Passengers can send and receive e-mail and faxes at more than a dozen computer stations. The Life Enrichment Program offers seminars, workshops, and lectures by experts. Bingo, horse racing, arts and crafts, and beauty demonstrations are available. Theme cruises add such attractions as jazz or classical concerts.

The QE2 and her sister ship have the only libraries at sea with full-time professional librarians. Doubled in size with a book shop, the QE2 library has more than 6,000 books, hundreds of videos, and a multimedia reference library. Red leather seats and desks are provided, but the library is so popular there's often no place to sit.

Lifestyle updates were central to the ship's renovations as evidenced in the **Golden Lion,** a large, classic English pub decorated in mahogany and plaid. It's the ship's informal social center with an upright piano, television, karaoke, and darts. Many lagers, stouts, and draught beers are served. The classy **Grand Lounge** showroom has a fully equipped curtained stage, dance floor, a new audio system, and improved sight lines. The latest addition brings fledgling Broadway and West End shows for development aboard ship. Passengers may attend rehearsals, workshops, and improvisation sessions performed by the cast that may appear on opening night.

The popular **Yacht Club,** aft, with handsome nautical decor and America's Cup memorabilia, is a lounge and bar by day and a sophisticated nightclub in the evening. The **Chart Room** on Quarter Deck showcases Cunard's nautical antiques. A piano from the *Queen Mary* plays for cocktails and after dinner. A bust of Queen Elizabeth II decorates the blue and gold **Queen's Room,** which has retained its dignified best with royal blue carpeting interwoven with gold Tudor roses. The royal connection is showcased in exhibits of the Queen's Standards, presented to the ship by Queen Elizabeth.

The room is the setting for afternoon tea with live music and evening ballroom dancing. (Gentlemen who forget their formal attire may visit the *QE2* tuxedo rental shop.) Gentlemen hosts are there to dance with the unescorted ladies. Lounges offer varied dance music and celebrity performers, who in the past have included Bill Cosby and Dick Clark, among others.

SPORTS, FITNESS, AND BEAUTY The ship has indoor and outdoor pools. Deck sports include golf (putting and driving area), shuffleboard, Ping-Pong, and jogging on a track. Exercise classes are available daily in the fitness center and gym on Deck 7. The European-style spa on Deck 6 offering sauna, massage, and beauty and body treatments, is operated by Steiner of London; the barber shop and beauty salon are located on Deck 1.

Among her extensive facilities, the *QE2* has one of the largest, best-equipped hospitals afloat.

CHILDREN'S FACILITIES **Club 2000** teen center is on Quarter Deck, and a supervised children's playroom and nursery are available high up on Sun Deck.

Delta Queen Steamboat Company

Robin Street Wharf, 1380 Port of New Orleans Place
New Orleans, LA 70130-1890
☎ 504-586-0631 or 800-543-1949; fax 504-585-0630
www.deltaqueen.com

TYPE OF SHIPS Classic steamboats.

TYPE OF CRUISES River cruises through America's heartland.

CRUISE LINE'S STRENGTHS
- the steamboats
- the setting
- turn-of-the-19th-century atmosphere

CRUISE LINE'S SHORTCOMINGS
- limited shipboard activities
- small cabins on the *Delta Queen*

FELLOW PASSENGERS Mix of ages, nationalities, families, couples, singles, and grandparents traveling with grandchildren. Group is likely to be cosmopolitan: Norwegians, Dutch, British, Germans, Canadians, and Americans. Average age is 62 years; it drops on shorter trips, which usually include more families. Most passengers are retired, with annual incomes over $35,000. There are young and middle-aged honeymooners and repeaters who have sailed on the steamboats many times. A surprising number of passengers live near the river and cruise to enjoy it in a different way. Fifty-five percent have been to Alaska; about 70% have cruised on an upscale, traditional line.

Recommended for Anyone interested in American history, culture, and literature or just good, old-fashioned values regardless of age. Those who enjoy the relaxed pace and shoreline visibility that river cruises offer. Dixieland jazz fans. Anyone uneasy about ocean voyages or straying far from home.

Not recommended for Travelers expecting European-style elegance, elaborate cuisine, and polished service. Those who don't enjoy a certain amount of hokum. Families with young children (for lack of children's facilities). Those requiring large-ship amenities, such as cabin television.

CRUISE AREAS AND SEASONS Mississippi, Atchafalaya and Red (Louisiana), Cumberland, Tennessee, Ohio, Kanawha (West Virginia) rivers; intracoastal waterways of Louisiana, Texas, and Mississippi year-round.

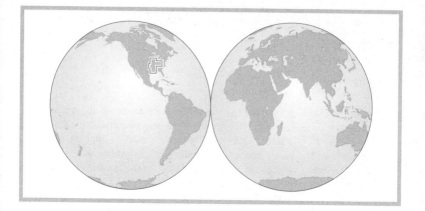

THE LINE The Delta Queen Steamboat Company is the oldest line of American-flagged cruise vessels. Of the few authentic, steam-powered paddle wheelers in the United States, Delta Queen's are the only ones offering overnight accommodations and traveling the length of mid-America's inland rivers.

The forerunner of the present cruise line was founded in 1890 by Capt. Gordon C. Greene, who pioneered riverboat vacations, and his wife, Mary, also an accomplished river pilot and steamboat captain. The couple and their sons owned and operated 28 steamers over the years. After World War II, Tom Greene purchased the *Delta Queen* in California, remodeled her, and inaugurated her with Mississippi River cruises in 1948. In 1973, new owners renamed the line Delta Queen Steamboat Company and added the *Mississippi Queen*, which is twice as large as her sister steamer; in 1995, they added the *American Queen*, which was the largest steamboat ever built.

Within a short time after the tragedy of September 11, American Classic Voyages, the owner of Delta Queen Steamboat Company, as well as American Hawaii Cruises, United States Lines, and Delta Queen Coastal Voyages, declared bankruptcy. Then in May 2002, the Delaware North Company of Buffalo, New York, a privately-held hospitality and food service group of companies with annual revenues of $1.6 billion, bought three steamboats—*Delta Queen, Mississippi Queen,* and *American Queen*—from the Delta Queen Steamboat Company at auction for $80 million. All three boats were back in service before the year's end, along with 98% of the boats' staff and many members of the former management.

THE FLEET	BUILT/RENOVATED	TONNAGE	PASSENGERS
American Queen	1995	3,707	436
Delta Queen	1927/1984/1998	3,360	174
Mississippi Queen	1976/1996	3,364	416

STYLE A cruise on one of the Queens differs from an ocean voyage. *Delta Queen* calls the experience "Steamboatin'," a unique visit with the American soul and character. While floating down the Mississippi on one of these "wedding cakes" at a lazy nine miles per hour, visions of Huck Finn and Tom Sawyer are sure to arise—as they have for thousands of folks who have come before you. Nostalgia is thick when a morning mist hangs over the shoreline, and the only sounds are the low hum of engines and the red paddle wheel churning the river's muddy water. Mark Twain wrote that the Mississippi at morning has a "haunting sense of loneliness, isolation, remoteness from the worry and bustle of the world. The dawn creeps in stealthily, the tranquillity is profound and infinitely satisfying."

After breakfast, the cruise "Riverlorian" relates colorful bits of river history. Later, your boat, festooned in red, white, and blue flags, arrives in a port with its calliope (an organlike instrument with whistles sounded by steam or compressed air) in full song. Most likely, you'll be met by townfolk, who personally offer passengers directions. It's an experience not likely found on standard cruises.

DISTINCTIVE FEATURES Paddle wheel, calliope, *Delta Queen*'s authentic interiors, Dixieland jazz, Southern specialties, immersion in 19th-century life on the Mississippi.

	HIGHEST	LOWEST	AVERAGE
PER DIEM	$993	$265	$550

Per diems are calculated from cruise line's nondiscounted *cruise-only* published fares on standard accommodations and vary by season, cabins, and cruise areas.

RATES Port charges included.

Special fares and discounts Early-booking bonus available on most cruises.

- **CHILDREN'S FARES:** One child age 18 or younger cruises free in some cabins on the *Mississippi Queen* and *American Queen* when sharing a cabin with two full-fare adults.
- **SINGLE SUPPLEMENT:** 175–200%, depending on vessel and cabin category.
- **THIRD/FOURTH PASSENGER:** An adult sharing accommodations with two full-fare adults on the *Mississippi Queen* and *American Queen* will only be charged $100 per night.

Packages
- **AIR/SEA:** Yes.
- **PRE/POST:** Packages in New Orleans, Memphis, St. Louis, Minneapolis/St. Paul, and other main ports.
- **OTHERS:** Theme cruises, such as Kentucky Derby and Fall Foliage.

PAST PASSENGERS Members of the Paddlewheel Steamboat Society of America receive a newsletter welcome aboard reception, advance notice of schedules, and discounts on future cruises and in the ships' gift shops.

THE LAST WORD For most passengers, the real destination of these cruises is the steamboats. Most people love this homespun, star-spangled slice of Americana, from the Huck Finn picnic to the foot-stomping Dixieland jazz. The riverboats have universal appeal and transcend age barriers. Aboard a recent cruise was an under-40 couple with sons 8 and 12 years old. The boys got a daily lesson in American history on the boat and in ports, but they also enjoyed romping on the Mississippi shoreline, à la Huck Finn. Then, one night in the lounge, the older boy was seen playing chess with a 96-year-old passenger.

Delta Queen Standard Features

Officers American.

Staff Dining, Cabin, Cruise/American.

Dining facilities One dining room with two seatings for dinner; three meals daily, plus tea and moonlight buffet; open seating breakfast and lunch.

Special diets Diabetic, kosher, low-calorie/cholesterol, and low-salt. Request with cruise reservations. Vegetarian and heart-healthy selections on menus.

Room service Continental breakfast served in cabins on request.

Dress code Casual but neat during the day; fashionable dress for evening—jacket and tie for men, dress or stylish suit for women.

Cabin amenities Some cabins with brass beds, Tiffany-style windows, veranda, sitting area, baths with shower, writing area.

Electrical outlets 110 AC.

Wheelchair access Companion recommended. See text. Some cabins on *Mississippi Queen* and *American Queen*.

Recreation and entertainment Jazz, big bands, cabaret, and Broadway stage revues in lounges; riverboat shows; bridge; bingo; calliope concerts; crafts and cooking demonstrations; sing-alongs. Riverlorian talks.

Sports and other activities Jogging on decks, kite flying, Ping-Pong; bathing pool on *Mississippi Queen, American Queen*.

Delta Queen Standard Features (continued)

Beauty and fitness Small exercise room, aerobics, beauty salon on *Mississippi Queen* and *American Queen*.

Other facilities Gift shop; *Mississippi Queen, American Queen,* conference centers, fax service, library, theater.

Children's facilities No special facilities but family programs with counselors during summer and holidays on *Mississippi Queen* and *American Queen*.

Theme cruises Newly expanded offering; see specific steamboats.

Smoking *Delta Queen,* smoking on outside decks only; *Mississippi Queen, American Queen,* smoking section in lounges.

Delta Queen suggested tipping Per person per night, $15, detailed information found in cabin; $2.50 per bag for on and $2.50 per bag off for the porter. Porter's tips are left at purser's office; cash only. Gratuities may be prepaid by credit card.

Credit cards For cruise payment and on-board charges: American Express, Discover, MasterCard and Visa. Only gift shops and gratuities are accepted in cash. Traveler's and personal checks can be cashed at purser's office.

Delta Queen	QUALITY 3	VALUE C
REGISTRY United States	LENGTH 285 feet	BEAM 60 feet
CABINS 87	DRAFT 9 feet	SPEED 6 knots
MAXIMUM PASSENGERS 174	PASSENGER DECKS 4	ELEVATORS None
	CREW 80	SPACE RATIO 19

THE SHIP The *Delta Queen* is the only remaining authentic example of the thousands of overnight paddle-wheel steamers that once plied the nation's rivers. She has the warmth of a bed-and-breakfast inn, and her small-town friendliness mirrors the heartland ports she visits.

From the outside, this waterborne piece of history looks rather ordinary, except for her paddle wheel. Inside, however, she enchants with Tiffany-style stained glass, brass fittings, and rich, polished woods from another era. Simply knowing the *Delta Queen* is the real thing makes you appreciate every ceiling molding and creak in the floor. There's no other cruise vessel like her, and there never will be, because passenger vessels can no longer be built of wood. Indeed, *Delta Queen*'s elaborate superstructure, which adds so much to her character, was almost her undoing.

In the 1920s, the boat was one of two steamers commissioned by the California Transportation Company for luxury overnight travel on the Sacramento River between Sacramento and San Francisco. Their steel hulls were fabricated in Scotland, then dismantled and shipped to California for reassembly. The wheel shafts and cranks were forged in Germany. Her American-built superstructure was crafted from pine, oak, teak, mahogany, and Oregon cedar.

The *Delta Queen* and her twin, *Delta King*, were launched in 1927 at the astounding cost of $875,000 each and became famous for their deluxe appointments. The *Delta Queen* might have died as other steamboats did, but at the outbreak of World War II, the U.S. Navy commandeered her, painted her battleship gray, and used her to ferry troops across San Francisco Bay.

At war's end, the U.S. Maritime Commission auctioned the boat. Tom Greene, president of Cincinnati-based Greene Line Steamers, forerunner of the Delta Queen Company, bought her for just $46,250. Greene had the vessel towed 5,378 miles in a 37-day trip to New Orleans via the Panama Canal. From Louisiana, she steamed on her own up the Mississippi and Ohio rivers to Pittsburgh, where she was refitted to her original state. She made her Mississippi River debut in June 1948.

By 1962, the ship's demise seemed imminent, but publicist Betty Blake revived the tradition of steamboat races to draw attention to the venerable steamer. It worked. In 1969, the *Delta Queen* returned to death's door when federal safety standards banned wooden vessels as fire hazards. Blake organized a letter and petition campaign that won a congressional exemption the boat still enjoys. The riverboat was made fire-resistant, but in November 1970 she again faced demise. Another act of Congress, however, saved the *Delta Queen*, placing her on the National Register of Historic Places. More than a million dollars was spent to enhance fire resistance. In 1989, she was designated a National Historic Landmark.

To ocean veterans, a cruise on the *Delta Queen* requires reorientation. Large cruise ships take at least a day to figure out; *Delta Queen* requires under an hour. The small, intimate boat is like an inn. Arriving passengers are greeted by riverboat dandies and Southern belles in hoop gowns, the reception setting the cruise's tone.

At the speed of six to eight miles per hour, the ship averages 100 miles a day (an automobile covers that distance in 90 minutes), but after a day, distance and speed become irrelevant. Life aboard is a tonic for stress. Seasickness is no issue. The steamboat's hush—scarcely a murmur—is immediately apparent.

Passengers settle in to watch the passing scenery—forested banks, marshy coves, and high bluffs—and a lively parade of barges and towboats heaped with grain, coal, scrap iron, and fuel. (Binoculars are helpful.)

Approaching ports becomes a major event. The *Delta Queen*'s throaty whistle and cheerful tunes from her century-old calliope announce her arrival and draw people to the river. During docking, people ashore and passengers at the rails chat.

The engine room, open to passengers at all hours, is a marvel—immense pistons pushing huge beams that cause the giant red paddlewheel to turn. Engineers keep fresh coffee ready to welcome visitors.

ITINERARIES *See* Itinerary Index.

CABINS Cabins fall into eight categories, all outside with private showers. Hair dryers are allowed. Four of six suites have picture windows framed by stained glass, a conversation area, queen-size bed, bathtub, and shower; the other two have smaller sitting areas and shower only. Suites are furnished with antiques, while the homey furnishings in standard cabins range from good reproductions to collectibles and include patchwork quilts and wooden shutters. A few standard cabins have double beds; the remainder have twins.

The lowest-priced cabins have upper and lower berths. All are small but comfortable and clean. They range from 44 square feet for the smallest quarters, to 68 square feet for mid-priced cabins, to 135 and 156 square feet for top accommodations.

Cabins on two of the three decks face wide promenades dubbed the "front porch of America." Rooms on cabin deck open inside onto the quiet **Betty Blake Lounge,** but they have outside-facing windows. Bathrooms are small but functional; many have sinks outside the bathroom door. There's a dresser, and instead of a closet, an open rack with brass rods.

Specifications 87 outside cabins; 6 suites. Standard dimensions, 100 square feet. 56 with twin beds; 4 with double; 8 queens; 19 with upper and lower berths.

DINING The **Orleans Dining Room** offers two seatings. Most tables accommodate four, although some seat two or six. Wide windows on two sides frame a river panorama. A pianist entertains throughout dinner.

A continental breakfast is served in the **Forward Cabin Lounge.** All other meals are in the dining room, with choices from the menu or buffet at breakfast and lunch. The breakfast buffet offers oatmeal, grits, fruit, ham, eggs Benedict Cajun (with crawfish sauce), and flavored pancakes. Southern specialties like biscuits and gravy can be ordered.

Menus feature American favorites—steak, stew, ribs, catfish, fried chicken, roast duck, and roast lamb—and Southern recipes. Portions are relatively small, yet sensible for those who sample all five courses. Preparation ranges from good to excellent. One of the four entrees at each meal is labeled Traditional River Fare. Possibilities include creamy red beans, rice with Cajun sausage and ham chunks, and crawfish pie. The **Forward Cabin Lounge** has coffee and iced tea available all day, afternoon tea, and a moonlight buffet at 10:30 p.m.—not as elaborate as aboard seagoing cruise ships, but offering desserts, fruits, and several hot items.

SERVICE Fresh-faced young Midwesterners provide cheerful service. The staff seems to be a well-integrated, clean-cut, happy family. Their attitude is infectious and genuinely appreciated by passengers. Cabin attendants keep everything neat as a pin.

FACILITIES AND ACTIVITIES The laid-back *Delta Queen* offers simple pleasures. Televisions are absent, and the only telephone is for ship-to-shore communication. Despite images of riverboat gamblers, there's no casino; passengers must settle for bingo or horse racing. They can also head for a casino ashore in some destinations.

Days aren't packed with activities, but there's enough to do, including some things you'd never encounter on an oceanliner: flying kites from the deck, for example. The musically inclined—or curious—can try their hand at the calliope. Everyone who tries the keyboard gets a commemorative certificate.

Other daytime activities include card tournaments, lessons on *Delta Queen* history, radio trivia games, pilothouse tours, wine and cheese parties, sing-alongs, a Mardi Gras costume party, champagne receptions, and walking and jogging to calliope music. Riverlorian talks are well-attended. The softly lighted **Betty Blake Lounge,** furnished with armchairs, sofas, desks, and bookcases, is fine for reading, board games, or writing postcards (a *Delta Queen* postmark is available in the adjacent purser's office).

The **Forward Cabin Lounge,** distinguished by mirrors and wooden pillars, is a popular place to prop your feet and watch the passing scenery through the windows. The lounge also has tables for card games and dining. Loaner binoculars are available free from the shore excursion desk.

The *Delta Queen*'s centerpiece is the **Grand Staircase,** which links the Forward Cabin Lounge to the **Texas Lounge** upstairs. An ornate bronze filigree railing, scrolled latticework, and hardwood paneling accent this impressive stairway, which is crowned by a Tiffany chandelier. The ship is casual, but a lady in flowing skirts could make a grand entrance on the staircase.

At the Texas Lounge entrance is plaque recognizing the *Delta Queen*'s landmark status. The wood-paneled lounge's piano bar is a magnet for the sing-along crowd. Passengers come here for popcorn, hot dogs, or hors d'oeuvres at cocktail hour. Wide windows provide the ideal setting for watching the river and sunsets.

The **Orleans Dining Room,** the boat's largest room, doubles as the entertainment lounge after the second-seating dinner. Tables are rearranged to accommodate a stage. Entertainers dazzle audiences with ragtime piano, Dixieland jazz, or banjo artistry with a different show each night. After the show, many passengers retire to the Texas Lounge for dancing and music. The wholesome entertainment is in keeping with the boat's character, and passengers get involved in festivities and hokey contests. By 11 p.m., most of the crowd has turned in.

SHORE EXCURSIONS Rural and urban ports offer visits to an array of heartland attractions, including Antebellum Southern plantations, Mark Twain's boyhood home, the Gateway Arch in St. Louis, Civil War sites, and many museums.

THEME CRUISES Perennial themes are the Kentucky Derby in May, Great Steamboat Race in June, Fall Foliage in October and November, and Old-Fashion Holidays in December. Cruises with educational themes have been enhanced to appeal to travelers seeking a learning vacation. The new "Gardens of the South" cruises, for example, have a roster of writers, landscape designers, and gardening experts who accompany different sailings. Among other new ones are Golfing, Springtime in Texas, and Legend of the 50's cruises.

POSTSCRIPT The *Delta Queen* has been called a romantic anachronism; there is nothing like her. To cruise on her is to experience another time. Her small size and leisurely pace are conducive to meeting and chatting with fellow passengers. It's a small-town atmosphere that might not suit everyone.

Mississippi Queen	QUALITY 6	VALUE C
REGISTRY United States	LENGTH 382 feet	BEAM 68 feet
CABINS 208	DRAFT 9 feet	SPEED 7 mph
MAXIMUM PASSENGERS 416	PASSENGER DECKS 7	ELEVATORS 2
	CREW 157	SPACE RATIO 8

THE SHIP If the *Delta Queen* is a floating country inn, her larger sister, *Mississippi Queen,* is a stately Victorian showboat. Proud and pretty, she rolls down the river like the grandest float in a parade. On board, it's the Fourth of July—a red, white, and blue celebration of Americana amid Victoriana. And for good measure, one day's lunch is always an old-fashioned barbecue picnic with all the trimmings.

Polished brass railings, beveled mirrors, crystal chandeliers, and Victorian-style chairs—all of which were recently refurbished—evoke the turn of the century, yet the *Mississippi Queen* offers seven decks of comfort and many modern cruise ship amenities, including bathing pool, six lounges and bars, a small gym, library, gift shop, elevators, cabin telephones, some private verandas, and a beauty salon.

Modern comforts aside, this ship is a true steamboat, powered by an authentic steam engine. Her huge paddle wheel is not just for show. Visit the **Paddle Wheel Lounge** on Texas Deck and watch through floor-to-ceiling windows as the bucket planks churn to drive the vessel. The boat has a full roster of theme cruises, including a new one. All are listed in the line's literature.

ITINERARIES *See* Itinerary Index.

CABINS The *Mississippi Queen*'s modern side is best appreciated in her cabins. All accommodations have air-conditioning, wall-to-wall carpeting, telephones, and private bathrooms. Standard cabins are compact and have tiny bathrooms with showers. Suites and outside deluxe cabins have private verandas, but only suites have bathrooms with tubs and showers. Each cabin displays historical art pertaining to its name. Cabin staff attend rooms twice daily to replenish towels and ice.

Specifications 73 inside cabins, 135 outside; 26 suites (114 with verandas). Standard dimensions are 123 square feet. 151 with twins; 36 with double; 21 with upper and lower berths; 1 wheelchair-accessible cabin.

DINING Two seatings are offered at dinner; open seating for breakfast and lunch. Menu choices are similar to the *Delta Queen*'s and change daily. Five-course dinners include appetizers, soup, salad, entree, and dessert. Grazers find a light lunch buffet in the **Grand Saloon,** a late-night snack in the **Upper Paddlewheel Lounge,** and hot dogs and ice cream all day at the open-air **Calliope Bar.** A room-service continental breakfast may be ordered the previous night, although delivery may not be prompt.

FACILITIES AND ACTIVITIES Entertainment is G-rated and genuine, emphasizing big-band hits of the 1940s and 1950s, Broadway favorites, ragtime, and Dixieland jazz. The band plays nightly for dancing in the **Grand Saloon.** The *Mississippi Queen,* like her sister boats, features a Riverlorian who regales passengers with tales from the past, historic tidbits about the river, and explanations of river activity.

SHORE EXCURSIONS Land tours cost extra and are purchased onboard unless arranged beforehand by a tour group. Tours in port last about three hours and cost from $12 to $70 per person per excursion and may be reserved in advance.

American Queen	QUALITY 7	VALUE C
REGISTRY United States	**LENGTH** 418 feet	BEAM 89.4 feet
CABINS 222	**DRAFT** 8.6 feet	SPEED 10 mph
MAXIMUM PASSENGERS 436	**PASSENGER DECKS** 6	ELEVATORS 2
	CREW 160	SPACE RATIO NA

THE SHIP The *American Queen* returned to service in January 2003. Constructed in Amelia, Louisiana, *American Queen* was the largest passenger vessel built in a U.S. shipyard in more than four decades when she made her debut in 1995. No expense was spared in re-creating the luxurious setting of yesteryear. The vessel merges the best features of the *Delta Queen* and the Victoriana of the *Mississippi Queen,* both of which are smaller, and the grand style of 19th-century steamboats with modern shipbuilding technology and selected cruise-ship amenities. Her white exteriors are laden with gingerbread filigree, and a 45-ton red paddle wheel turns at the stern. Inside are a bathing pool, gym, conference center, movie theater, and elevators.

The vessel is powered by two 1930s Nordberg steam engines salvaged from the *Kennedy,* a dredge belonging to the U.S. Army Corps of Engineers. Each of the rebuilt engines generates 750 horsepower.

The *American Queen* rises 97 feet from the waterline to the top of its fluted stacks, making quite a show. The stacks and pilothouse can be lowered to enable the vessel to pass under low bridges.

The boat's special program combines a three- or four-night cruise with a three- or four-night stay in New Orleans, during which you have a choice of top-rated restaurants, hotels, and tours.

ITINERARIES *See* Itinerary Index

CABINS A Victorian theme employs period wallpaper, floral carpets and fabrics, brass fixtures, etched glass, and antiques or good reproductions. Even modern plumbing and electrical fixtures are disguised as antiques. Each cabin is named after a river town or historic steamboat.

Seven categories are distributed on all but the lowest passenger deck. Some cabins have bay windows; 27 have verandas. Three-fourths are outside; some have windows or private verandas, but most have French doors. Mid-range standard cabins are considerably larger than on her sister boats.

Cabins are more "senior friendly," with larger bathrooms, emergency call buttons by each bed, and levers (rather than handles) on doors. As on *Delta Queen,* many cabins open onto promenade decks. Although *American Queen* is much larger, such touches provide a sense of community and make it easy for passengers to meet.

Specifications 54 inside cabins, 168 outside; 27 suites and cabins with veranda. Standard dimensions are 141 and 190 square feet. 208 with twin beds; 2 with doubles; 4 queens; 8 singles; 9 wheelchair-accessible.

DINING Interior designers borrowed liberally from historic steamboats, particularly the 1878 *J. M. White,* called the most graceful and spacious steamboat of her time. Her dining saloon—which Mark Twain described as "dainty as a drawing room; when I looked down her long, gilded saloon, it was like gazing through a splendid tunnel"—has been copied and named the **J. M. White Dining Room.**

Located on main deck, the lowest passenger deck, the dining room spans two decks. Tall windows have ornate fretwork arches. A dropped ceiling divides the room and gives each half a soaring appearance. Each side has a vaulted space with huge mirrors in spectacular gilt frames dating from the 1880s. Providing music is a custom-built mahogany Victorian piano bar accenting the vessel's Victorian decor.

FACILITIES AND ACTIVITIES   The **Mark Twain Gallery** around the upper level of the dining room honors the author whose *Life on the Mississippi* captured the essence of steamboating. Books and curio cases contain exhibits on regional wildlife and steamboat history and river memorabilia. Furnishings include Tiffany-style lamps and writing tables. Window areas provide cozy nooks for reading, writing, or watching the scenery.

Forward from the gallery to starboard is the **Gentlemen's Card Room,** a masculine room meant to resemble Teddy Roosevelt's library. Cases are filled with books typical of late-19th-century homes, with many first-person accounts of exploration and vintage how-to books. One of the ship's two television sets is tucked behind cabinet doors.

To port is the **Ladies Parlor,** a Victorian drawing room where afternoon tea is served. From the gallery to amidships is the purser's lobby and grand, gilded staircase under a spectacular filigreed ceiling, also harking to the *J. M. White*. Beyond are the **Grand Saloon's** upper level and the lively **Engine Room Bar** overlooking the paddle wheel. The engine room viewing area is open to passengers around the clock.

Forward on Texas Deck is the cruise line's signature "Front Porch of America," complete with swings and rockers. Above, the Promenade Deck has a full-circuit walkway and the **Calliope Bar.** Stairs behind the bar lead to the topmost sun deck, small exercise room, and bathing pool (essentially a large hot tub). The Observation Deck also has a full-circuit promenade (seven laps equal a mile).

A lounge and bar at the dining room entrance links the lobby and Grand Saloon below, used for nightly entertainment and dancing. Designed as an idealized 1880 opera house, the theater has a proscenium stage and is ringed with private boxes on the second-story balcony.

The **Chart Room** on Observation Deck has authentic old piloting instruments and navigational charts as well as the boat's 1,500-pound bronze bell. At the end of the ship's first season, names of all inaugural passengers were engraved on the bell.

Disney Cruise Line

P.O. Box 10210, Lake Buena Vista, FL 32830
☎ 407-566-3500 or 800-DCL-2500; fax 407-566-7417
www.disneycruise.com

TYPE OF SHIPS Modern ocean liners with classic steamship lines.

TYPE OF CRUISES Family-oriented mainstream cruises combined with a Walt Disney World vacation, designed for all ages.

CRUISE LINE'S STRENGTHS
- Disney name recognition
- innovative ships
- dining venue variety and presentation
- friendly, conscientious staff
- outstanding private island
- children's facilities
- family cabins

CRUISE LINE'S SHORTCOMINGS
- intrusive, loud public announcements
- Disney overdose
- over-regimentation of children's programs
- uneven cuisine
- unnecessary pressure to vacate ship on disembarkation

FELLOW PASSENGERS A cross-section of the nation—similar to patrons at Disney theme parks.

Recommended for Families with children or grandchildren. But, like the Disney parks, a Disney product for kids of all ages.

Not recommended for Anyone who isn't enraptured by Disney.

CRUISE AREAS AND SEASONS Bahamas, Caribbean year-round.

THE LINE When Disney does something, it does it big, in a spare-no-expenses way. So, we were ready for the Disney Cruise Line to make a huge splash when its first ship, *Disney Magic,* was launched in 1998. What you see here and on her twin, *Disney Wonder,* is the result of three years of intensive planning by cruise industry veterans, Disney creative talent, and dozens of the world's best-known ship designers. Their task was to design a product that makes every adult feel the vacation is intended for them, while at the same time giving every child the same impression. The results may surprise people, including adults without children.

The ships are both classic and innovative. Exteriors have traditional lines, reminiscent of great ocean liners. Inside, they're up-to-the-minute technologically and full of novel ideas in dining, entertainment, cabin design, and entertainment facilities. Even Disney's exclusive cruise ter-

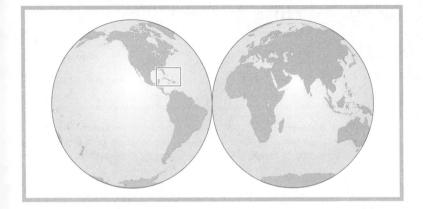

minal at Port Canaveral is part of the overall strategy, aiming to make enjoyable even embarkation and disembarkation.

Disney offers a "seamless vacation package," combining a three- or four-day stay at Walt Disney World with a three- or four-day cruise, as well as some seven- and ten-cruises. Disney Cruise Line passengers are met at the airport by Disney staff and transported to the terminal in easily identifiable buses. During the hour's ride, they watch a cruise video. When your cruise is packaged with a stay at a Disney hotel, you check in once. The key that unlocks your hotel room door also opens the door to your cruise cabin.

The major innovation is in dining. Each evening on board, you dine in a different restaurant with a different motif, but your waiters and dining companions move with you.

To cater to varied constituencies, some facilities, services, activities, and programs were designed specifically for adults without children, seniors, and honeymooning couples. For example, in addition to the themed restaurants, each ship has an alternative restaurant, swimming pool, and nightclub for use by adults only, as well as entertainment for all the family. Disney continues trying to enhance the adult experience with such new facilities as an adults-only cafe, an adults-oriented sports bar, and a new area for teens.

Overcoming the hassle of tendering passengers was an important consideration when Disney selected its private Bahamian island visited on all cruises; deep water enables ships to pull dockside. In 2000, the line inaugurated a seven-day Eastern Caribbean itinerary, and two years later, it added an alternating Western Caribbean one. In 2005, *Disney Magic* ventured to the West Coast, in conjunction with Disneyland's 50th anniversary celebrations, sailing from Los Angeles to Mexico. While there appears to be no plans to repeat the West Coast series in the near future,

Disney has added Costa Maya and some new ports to its Western Caribbean itineraries as well as offering two nights at Castaway.

THE FLEET	BUILT/RENOVATED	TONNAGE	PASSENGERS
Disney Magic	1998	83,000	1,754
Disney Wonder	1999	83,000	1,754

DISTINCTIVE FEATURES Three themed restaurants with "rotation" dining, sports bar in a funnel, children's facilities, cabin design, port terminal. Pagers for adults to locate their kids participating in programs.

	HIGHEST	LOWEST	AVERAGE
PER DIEM	$650	$123	$348

Per diems are calculated from cruise line's nondiscounted *cruise-only* published fares on standard accommodations and vary by season, cabins, and cruise areas.

RATES Price includes port charges.

Special fares and discounts Early booking can save on three-, four-, and seven-night cruises and packages; consult Disney's brochure for details.

- **CHILDREN'S FARES:** Prices range from a start of $229–$1,199 on three- or four-night cruises; $399–$2,199 on seven-night cruise; children age 3 and under are $99 for three or four nights and $139 for seven nights.
- **SINGLE SUPPLEMENT: 175–200%.**

Packages Weeklong packages pair a visit to Walt Disney World in Orlando with unlimited admission to the theme parks and a three- or four-night cruise. A seven-day, cruise-only package is available. Most people buy the week-long cruise/park package. Consult the Disney brochure for these prices.

- **AIR/SEA:** Yes.
- **PRE/POST:** Yes.
- **OTHERS:** Honeymoon.

THE LAST WORD Cruise experts questioned whether Disney could fill its ships when kids are in school, but Disney estimated that if 1–2% of the estimated 40 million annual visitors to Disney's resorts and parks bought a Disney cruise vacation, the ships would sell out. The vessels are complex and innovative, breaking the mold of traditional cruise ships.

Disney Cruise Line Standard Features

Officers European, American, and International.

Staff Cabin, Dining/International, Cruise/American and International.

Dining facilities Three themed family restaurants with "rotation" dining; alternative adults-only restaurant; indoor/outdoor cafe for breakfast, lunch, snacks, and buffet dinner for children; pool bar/grill for burgers, pizza, and sandwiches; ice cream bar.

Special diets Request at the time of booking for low-sodium, kosher, and other dietary requirements.

Room service 24 hours.

Dress code Casual by day; resort casual and informal in the evenings. Jacket requested for men in Palo, Lumiere's, Triton's in evening; one formal night on *Magic* seven-night cruises.

Cabin amenities Direct-dial telephone with voicemail; tub and shower, two-in-one bathrooms; television, safe, hair dryer. Beachside massages on private island for a fee.

Electrical outlets 110 AC.

Wheelchair access Yes.

Recreation and entertainment Showroom, theater, family nightclub, adult nightclub, pub, lounges.

Sports and other activities Sports deck, basketball, paddle tennis, family sports, adult, family and kids' pools, Ping-Pong, shuffleboard, biking and water sports on Castaway Cay (extra charge).

Beauty and fitness Spa with sauna, steam rooms; beauty salon.

Other facilities Self-service launderettes; digital photographic services and camera and video recorder rentals; dry cleaning; satellite phone services; medical facilities; guest services desk; 24-hour front desk service; fax and secretarial services; conference facilities.

Children's facilities Age-specific supervised children's program, year-round youth counselors; group baby-sitting; teen club; nursery for ages 12 weeks to 3 years.

Smoking Smoking not allowed except in designated areas.

Disney suggested tipping Per guest per cruise for a three-night, four-night, and seven-night cruise: dining room server, $11, $14.75, $25.75; assistant server, $8, $10.75, $18.75; head server, $2.75, $3.75, $6.50; cabin host/hostess, $10.75, $14.50, $25.25. 15% service charge added automatically to bar, beverages, wine, and deck service bills.

Credit cards For cruise payment and on-board charges: all major credit cards.

Disney Magic	QUALITY 8	VALUE C
Disney Wonder	QUALITY 8	VALUE C
REGISTRY Bahamas	LENGTH 964 feet	BEAM 106 feet
CABINS 875	DRAFT 25 feet	SPEED 21.5 knots
MAXIMUM PASSENGERS 2,700	PASSENGER DECKS 11	ELEVATORS 12
	CREW 950	SPACE RATIO 35.4

THE SHIPS *Disney Magic* and *Disney Wonder* are modern cruise ships with long, sleek lines, twin smokestacks, and styling that recalls classic liners but with instantly recognizable Disney signatures. Colors—black, white, red, and yellow—and the face-and-ears silhouette on the stacks are clearly those of Mickey Mouse. Look closely and you'll see that *Magic*'s figurehead is a 15-foot Goofy (Donald Duck on *Wonder*) swinging upside down from a boatswain's chair, "painting" the stern.

Interiors combine nautical themes and Art Deco inspiration, but Disney images are everywhere, from Mickey's profile in the wrought-iron balustrades to the bronze statue of Helmsman Mickey at the center of the three-deck Grand Atrium. Disney art is on every wall, stairwell, and corridor. Some works are valuable old prints of Disney cartoon characters. A grand staircase sweeps from the atrium lobby to shops selling Disney Cruise–themed clothing, collectibles, jewelry, and sundries; classic Disney toys; and souvenirs. (The shops are always full of buyers; some people speculate that the cruise line derives as much revenue here as other lines do from their casinos, which the Disney ships do not have.)

The ships have two lower decks with cabins, three decks with dining rooms and showrooms, then three decks of cabins, and two sports and sun decks with separate pools and facilities for families and for adults without kids. Signs with arrows point the way to lounges and facilities, and all elevators are clearly marked forward, aft, or amidships. (More deck plans mounted on walls would help newcomers get their bearings.) Passengers receive a Disney Passport, a purse-size booklet covering just about everything you need to know for your cruise. Daily in your cabin, you receive "Your Personal Navigator," listing onboard entertainment and activities separated into options for teens, children, adults, and families, plus shore excursions.

Following the renovation of *Disney Magic* in 2003, *Disney Wonder* got a similar treatment in 2004 along with the addition of three new age-specific venues to appeal to adults and older teenagers—Aloft, Cove Café, and Diversions. **Aloft,** with decor that's a cross between a college dormitory and a trendy coffee shop, is a teen haven for socializing with new-found friends. **Cove Café** and **Diversions** are new areas just for adults. In the Cove Café, located next to the Quiet Cove pool, passengers can enjoy gourmet coffees, specialty drinks, and lighter fare, along with a supply of popular magazines. Diversions, a sports pub in the ship's nighttime entertainment area, is filled with flat-screen plasma televisions where passengers can watch sports or their favorite television shows.

ITINERARIES *See* Itinerary Index.

CABINS Cabins and suites are spacious with generous wood paneling throughout. About three-fourths are outside, almost half with verandas. The 12 cabin categories range from standard to deluxe, deluxe with veranda, family suite, one- and two-bedroom suite, and royal suite. Categories are similar to those at Walt Disney World hotels. Passengers who spend three or four days at a Disney hotel are matched with a cruise cabin in a comparable category.

Note: If you're staying at a Disney resort before your cruise, be sure to complete and return your cruise forms at the hotel. By showing your shoreside room key card at the cruise terminal, you can bypass lines and board directly. Cruise-only passengers may encounter a wait at check-in.

Cabin design reveals Disney's finely tuned understanding of the needs of families and children and offers a cruise-industry first: a split bathroom with bathtub/shower and sink in one room and toilet, sink, and vanity in another. This configuration, found in all but standard inside cabins, allows any member of the family to use the bathroom without monopolizing it entirely. All bathrooms have both tub and shower. *Note:* For added convenience, couples or families should pack two of essentials like toothpaste, providing one for each sink.

All cabins sleep at least three; many accommodate four or five and some up to seven. In some, pull-down Murphy beds provide additional daytime floor space. Storage space is generous. Bureaus are designed to look like steamer trunks.

Cabins have direct-dial telephone with voicemail; television; hair dryer; and cooler. The room key also opens the minibar and safe.

Specifications 256 inside, 621 outside. Two Walt/Roy Disney suites (sleeps up to 7); 2 two-bedroom suites, 18 one-bedroom suites, 80 family cabins—all sleep up to 5); 282 deluxe cabins with verandas (up to 3 or 4); 237 deluxe outside cabins (up to 4), 96 deluxe inside cabins (up to 4) and 160 standard inside cabins (up to 4). 16 wheelchair-accessible, including 4 one-bedroom suites, 6 deluxe cabins with verandas, 2 deluxe outside cabins, and 4 standard inside cabins.

DINING Disney's most innovative area is dining. Ships have three different family restaurants, plus an alternative restaurant for adults only. Each night, passengers move to a different family restaurant, each with a different theme and menu, taking along their table companions and wait staff. In each restaurant, tableware, linens, menu covers, and waiters' uniforms fit the theme.

On *Magic,* **Lumiere's**—named for the candlestick character in *Beauty and the Beast*—is a handsome, Art Deco venue serving continental cuisine. A mural depicts Beauty and the Beast (the equivalent restaurant on *Wonder* is called **Triton,** themed after *The Little Mermaid*). **Parrot Cay** dishes up Caribbean-accented food in a fun, tropical setting and seems to be the most popular for breakfast. But it's **Animator's Palate** that reflects the creative genius of Disney animation. Diners are given the impression they have entered a black-and-white sketchbook. Over the course of the meal, the sketches on the walls are transformed through fiber optics into a full-color extravaganza. Waiters change their costumes from black and white to color. The first course is a montage of appetizers served on a palette-shaped plate, and dessert—a tasteless mousse in the shape of Mickey—comes with a parade by waiters bearing trays of colorful syrups—mango, chocolate, and strawberry—used to decorate it. It's entertaining, but the food is, at times, less than inspired, and hot dishes are likely to arrive cold, but no ones seems to care—they are too absorbed in watching Disney perform its magic.

Palo, the Italian restaurant named for the pole gondoliers use to navigate Venetian canals, is the intimate, adults-only restaurant. It's the best aboard. The lovely, semicircular room has a sophisticated ambience with soft lighting, Venetian glass, inlaid wood, and a backlit bar. Northern Italian cuisine is featured. Food and presentation are excellent. More than two dozen kinds of wines are available by the glass ($4.75–$25). There's a $10 per-person cover charge. Reservations are required; make them as soon as you board or risk being shut out. (Disney underestimated demand for this venue.) Other dining options include **Topsiders** (**Beach Blanket Buffet** on *Wonder*), an indoor/outdoor cafe serving breakfast, lunch, snacks, and a buffet dinner for children; a pool bar and grill for hamburgers, hot dogs, and sandwiches; **Pinocchio's Pizzeria;** and an ice cream and frozen yogurt bar. The newest addition is a free soda fountain outside of the buffet, which is proving to be very popular. The ships also have 24-hour room service.

On seven-night cruises, the dining options are expanded. They include a "Captain's Gala" dinner with wine and French continental cuisine, and "It's a Small World dinner" as a final-night farewell, featuring dishes from throughout the world On four- and seven-night cruises, there's also a champagne brunch on sea days, high tea, and character breakfasts hosted by Chip and Dale, the latter offering kids a chance to meet and pose for pictures with popular Disney characters in Caribbean attire.

SERVICE Passengers lavishly praise Disney cast members, as cruise and park staff are called. Staff are among the most accommodating you will encounter in travel, and they try hard to smooth your way. More than once when I stopped to get my bearings, a staff member was beside me in seconds to help.

FACILITIES AND ACTIVITIES Disney diversions are geared to children, families, and adults. A day at **Castaway Cay,** Disney's 1,000-acre private island, is meant to be the ultimate escape. The natural environment has been preserved. Miles of white-sand beaches are surrounded by beautiful water. A pier allows access without tendering. A four-car, open tram (like those at Disney World) conveys passengers from the ship to **Scuttle's Cove** family beach. The shuttle runs every five minutes. You could walk the quarter-mile to the beach, but it's inadvisable in the blistering heat. (Bring sunblock and wear a hat.) Strollers are available, as are rental bikes, floats, and kayaks. Lounge chairs under pastel umbrellas are plentiful, and some hammocks swing under the palms, but otherwise there's very little shade.

Disney Imagineers have created shops, rest rooms, and pavilions that give the impression they have been there for years. A supervised children's area includes a "dig" at a half-buried whale skeleton. Water sports are offered in a protected lagoon. One snorkeling course is near shore; the other, farther out, requires more endurance. On the distant course, snorkelers see a variety of fish they identify from a waterproof card provided with rental equipment. Lifeguards watch snorkelers all around the courses. The cruise line has also planted several "shipwrecks." On one in about ten feet of water, snorkelers can see Mickey Mouse riding the bow of the ship. There's also a treasure chest, its contents guarded by large fish. Snorkel equipment to rent costs a pricey $25 for adults and $10 for children (ages 5–9). The Gateway Package, a combination of snorkel equipment and float for the day plus a one-hour bicycle rental is also available for $6 more for children; $7 more for adults. Nature trails and bike paths are provided. The main beach offers kids' activities, live Bahamian music, and shops. **Cookie's Bar-B-Cue** serves a buffet lunch of burgers, pork ribs, hot dogs, baked beans, slaw, corn on the cob, fruit, and potato chips.

A second tram connects to **Serenity Bay,** the adult beach on the island's opposite side. The adult beach is a long sweep of sugary sand. A bar serves drinks, and passengers can enjoy a massage in one of the private cabanas with shuttered doors opening on the sea. Passengers must be back on the ship by 3:15 p.m. Most say they would have liked more time on the island.

Nightly entertainment is unlike any other cruise line's and features quality, Disney-produced shows. The 1,022-seat **Walt Disney Theater** stages a different musical production each night, with talented actors, singers, and dancers. These family musicals are on the level of Disney theme parks' live entertainment rather than Broadway and may appeal more to children than to adults.

Disney Dreams has about every Disney character and song ever heard and offers a light plot wherein Peter Pan visits a girl who dreams of Disney's famous characters. It's pure schmaltz, but audiences give it a standing ovation. Another night offers *Hercules, The MUSE-ical*, a comedy that's the least saccharine of the lot. In the smaller **Buena Vista Theater** with full-screen cinema, passengers watch first-run movies and classic Disney films.

Disney added some new entertainment in 2005. The "Pirates IN the Caribbean" party on the *Disney Magic* transforms passengers into pirates for the evening and treats them to a special dinner with selections presented on a parchment menu. This is followed by a deck party with meant to appeal to every member of the family, plus classic Disney characters in pirate garb. Passengers join a conga line with the cruise staff, Goofy, and his seafaring friends to learn special dance steps. Then suddenly, the mood of the party changes as Captain Hook, Mr. Smee, and a gang of "bad" pirates take over the party with special effects including black lighting, skull-and-cross-bone projections, and an invasion of pirates rappelling from the funnel. The music changes from light pop to lightly sinister hard rock classics and heavy metal—reminiscent of earlier days for the adults. Just in time, and before Captain Hook can enlist audience dads to join his gang of pirates, Captain Mickey appears and saves the day, ridding the ship of the evil buccaneers with a swash-buckling finish. "Pirates IN the Caribbean" has been added to *Disney Wonder*, too.

Disney Magic also has a new show that includes variety acts, musical performances, and a cavalcade of Disney characters. The show tells the story of a young cruise passenger trying to achieve his dream of becoming a seafaring captain. Mickey, Minnie, and the rest of the Disney characters help the boy realize that if he believes in his dream, it can come true. Woven into the show is an overview of the events, activities, venues aboard the ship and an introduction to the officers, along with tips to make the cruise more enjoyable, such as the best time to meet the Disney characters.

There are two other new entertainment additions. *The Golden Mickeys* is a character-filled musical review using all the glitz and glamour of an awards show to honor the great animated films and characters that Disney has produced for over 75 years. The passengers, too, are treated as celebrities, given red-carpet treatment, and taken on a journey to celebrate comedy, romance, heroes, and the characters we love to hate—the villains of Disney films.

Second is a Disney-themed trivia game show (much like *Who Wants to be a Millionaire*) with state-of-the-art lighting and a stylized set. A shipboard host challenges passengers to compete in front of an audience. Contestants are selected randomly, by seat number. The lifelines are "Ask the Audience," "50:50," and "Ask the Panel." For "Ask the Panel," six contestants are onstage; they have 60 seconds to discuss their recommendation for the final answer. Prizes of logo items and such are awarded.

Studio Sea, modeled after a television- or film-production set, is a family-oriented nightclub offering dance music, cabaret acts, passenger game shows, and multimedia entertainment. The Art Deco **Promenade Lounge** is a daytime haven for reading and relaxation and a nightspot for cocktails and piano music. A pub, formally in the sports bar in the ship's forward, decorative funnel, was moved to Deck 3 to make way for **Aloft,** the new teen center. The pub has plenty of big screens for viewing sporting events and a "no children after 7 p.m. rule"—another small feature to enhance the adults' experience.

Beat Street on *Magic* (**Route 66** on *Wonder*) is an adult-oriented evening entertainment district with shops and two themed nightclubs: **Rockin' Bar D,** with live bands playing rock and roll, top 40, and country music; **Diversions,** a comfortable and casual hang-out for karaoke or sports talks; and **Sessions,** a casual yet sophisticated place to enjoy easy music. Disney ships have no casinos. (Research showed its target markets weren't interested in gambling at sea, Disney says.) They don't have libraries, either.

SPORTS, FITNESS, AND BEAUTY Of three top-deck pools, one has a Mickey Mouse motif and water slide and is intended for kids. Another is set aside for families; the third is for adults. At night, the pool area can be transformed for deck parties and dancing.

The 8,500-square-foot, ocean-view **Vista Spa and Salon** above the bridge offers Cybex exercise equipment, an aerobics room, exercise instruction, thermal-bath area, saunas, and steam rooms. It's supervised by a qualified fitness director. The spa, run by the British-based Steiner group, offers pricey beauty treatments along with a sales pitch for Steiner products. Despite high prices, the spa has proved to be very popular; it's generally booked for the entire cruise within hours of embarkation. Passengers in Deck 8 concierge-level suites can have a private massage in their suite or veranda. The Sports Deck has a paddle tennis court, Ping-Pong, basketball court, and shuffleboard. A full promenade deck lures walkers and joggers; both ships now have deck chairs.

CHILDREN'S FACILITIES Playrooms and other kids' facilities occupy more than 15,000 square feet. Programs of age-specific activities are among the most extensive in cruising. They include challenging interactive activities and play areas supervised by trained counselors. Also offered is a children's drop-off service in the evening at the **Oceaneer's Club** or **Lab.** This service is available from 9 a.m. until midnight or 1 a.m. and is included in the cost of the cruise. Children in the drop-off program are taken to dinner at Topsiders.

The ships' **Flounder's Reef Nursery** has been expanded and improved with a new reception area and enhanced lighting that creates the look of being under the sea. There are new toys from Hasbro, Disney's partner. The toddler area, doubled in size, has a special porthole for parents to check on their kids without the little ones seeing them. The ships provide parents with pagers.

The nursery holds up to 30 children (10 infants and 20 toddlers). The child/counselor ratio is one babysitter to four children (ages 12 weeks to 1 year); one babysitter to six children (ages 1–2 years); and one babysitter to 11 children (2–3 years). On embarkation day, the nursery is open 1:30–3:30 p.m. to take reservations for the cruise. Space is limited and available on a first come, first served basis, based on sitter availability.

Group baby-sitting in Flounder's Reef Nursery is available for select hours every day. (Guests should check with programming once onboard for the exact times as the hours change daily in accordance with daily activities, ports of call, etc.) Flounder's Reef is open 5:45 p.m. to midnight, nightly. Cost is $6 per child, per hour; $5 per hour for each additional child. A two-hour minimum is required.

The Oceaneer's Adventure program encompasses **Oceaneer's Club** (ages 3–7), themed to resemble Captain Hook's pirate ship, with plenty of places for activity; and **Oceaneer's Lab** (ages 8–12), with high-tech play, including video games, computers, lab equipment, and a small room for listening to CDs. Kids wear ID bracelets, and parents receive pagers for staying in touch with their playing children. Both parents and children give the youth programs high marks.

Aloft (**The Stack** on *Wonder*) sits high on Deck 11 in the ornamental smokestack with lots of space and nooks and crannies. The program also has organized activities, including volleyball at Castaway Cay. The teen program seems to be a hit, as teens enjoy having an area to themselves in the evenings as well as having their own area apart from the kids. Aloft has high-tech diversions such as a big-screen television, MP3 players, computers, a mixing studio, and video-game systems, some of which have wireless controllers. The decor is meant to resemble a college dorm room, with bean bags, a soda bar, and eclectic decor. While the room succeeds in its hardware, the activities—apparently too juvenile for teens—appear to need some work; on a recent cruise, one passenger reported that only a handful of teens hang out at any one time there, often munching on snacks, sometimes watching movies.

SHORE EXCURSIONS On some itineraries, the ships dock in Nassau for 15 hours—ample time to explore the island, enjoy a sport, visit Atlantis Resort on Paradise Island, shop, and take in a show and casino. The ship offers at least 14 excursions for Nassau, most of them fairly standard tours. Among choices are the Historical Harbor Cruise ($20 for adults; $14.50 for children), the Blue Lagoon Beach Day ($38/$23), Blue Lagoon Dolphin Encounter ($114/$89), and a Historic Nassau city tour ($22/$16). Some new ones added recently are a Powerboat ride for teens, a ride on a custom-built speedboat, and touring the island ($35).

A similar ride for families and children costs $39/$29. Children's prices apply to ages 3 through 9. Booklets on excursions for the Eastern and Western Caribbean itineraries are also available. Shore excursion descriptions are available on the line's Web site, and the excursions can be booked in advance of your cruise.

POSTSCRIPT   The Disney Cruise Line attracts a high percentage of first-time cruisers, thanks to Disney's reputation for quality, service, and entertainment, which helps dispel doubts about cruise vacations. At the same time, great effort is made to ensure that the ships appeal to adults—with or without children—as much as to families. Adults without children are catered to in myriad ways and presented with an extensive menu of adult activities. The presence of hundreds of children onboard does not diminish the adult experience.

More difficult to escape than children, however, is Disney's sugary, cute entertainment, which permeates every cruise. Expressed differently, you don't need to adore children to enjoy a Disney cruise, but you'd better love Disney. Instead of the usual ship's horn, you hear the first seven notes of "When You Wish Upon a Star."

Our main criticism of the ships' design is that all outdoor public areas focus inward—toward the pools rather than seaward, as if Disney wants you to forget you're on a ship. There's no public place on any deck where you can relax in the shade and watch the ocean (at least not without a Plexiglas wall separating you). If this quintessential cruise pleasure ranks high with you, book a cabin with private veranda.

A second characteristic, expected but nonetheless irritating, is the extent to which the ship is childproofed. There's enough Plexiglas on these ships to build a subdivision of transparent houses.

Some bothersome areas could quickly be improved. Examples: Public announcements are loud and intrusive. Bar bills include a 15% gratuity, then have an empty space marked "gratuity" below the total. This amounts to a second tip. Guest Services says the space enables passengers to reward "extraordinary" service with something "extra." But most passengers, especially first-timers, won't know that or may be too shy to ask and will add a second tip. Food and service is uneven. At Palo, food is excellent, but service is very slow. At Topsiders, food is mediocre, selections limited, and tables very crowded, but service is outstanding.

On the plus side, passengers booked on airline flights can check in for them shoreside. (Too bad all cruise lines can't provide this service.)

Glacier Bay Cruiseline

2101 Fourth Avenue, Suite 2200, Seattle, WA 98121
☎ **206-623-7110 or 800-451-5952; fax 206-623-7809**
www.glacierbaycruiseline.com

TYPE OF SHIPS Four small, no-frills coastal ships.

TYPE OF CRUISES Casual; active and light adventure, loosely structured itineraries; emphasis on nature, wildlife, and local culture.

CRUISE LINE'S STRENGTHS
- small, highly maneuverable ships
- Alaska Native culture and off-vessel activities
- all excursions included in cruise price
- friendly shipboard atmosphere
- enthusiastic staff and crew
- naturalists on every cruise

CRUISE LINE'S SHORTCOMINGS
- small, spartan cabins with minimal soundproofing
- tiny, head-style bathrooms
- lack of shipboard diversions
- ships not very stable in rough waters

FELLOW PASSENGERS On active-adventure *Wilderness Explorer* and light-adventure *Wilderness Adventurer,* age ranges from 40s to 70s, with 80-year-olds and 30-somethings in the mix. Passengers are active and interested in nature and wildlife and are attracted to the ships' itineraries, which favor wilderness areas. Many are veteran hikers and kayakers—two activities central to these cruises. All seek a trip heavy on experience and information and light on formality and glitz, and they are happy with flexible itineraries that free the captain to sail wherever passengers will get the best Alaska experience. Spartan cabins and lack of diversions suit them fine—in fact, the homey atmosphere draws many passengers.

Recommended for Outdoors enthusiasts; people interested in Alaska Native culture; escape from television, traffic, and the daily grind; people eager to reach less accessible waterways; those seeking an informal experience with camaraderie between passengers and crew.

Not recommended for People who need entertainment or casinos or would be bored without television or shopping; people wanting to remain anonymous aboard ship; those requiring large cabins and normal bathroom facilities; people taller than 6'3" (ships' ceilings are low).

CRUISE AREAS AND SEASONS Alaska, May–September.

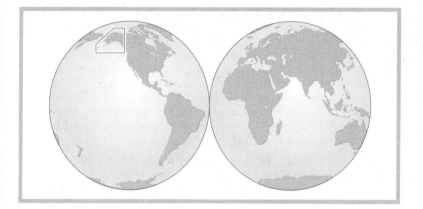

THE LINE Formerly owned by the late Seattle entrepreneur Robert Giers-
dorf (founder of the America West Steamship Company), Glacier Bay
Cruiseline and two of its ships were purchased in 1996 by Juneau-based
Goldbelt, Inc., an Alaska Native corporation set up under the Alaska
Native Claims Settlement Act and representing over 3,000 Tlingit and
Haida shareholders. Two additional ships were purchased in 1996 and
1997 from American Canadian Caribbean Line. In 2003, the cruise line
was purchased by a group of Seattle investors with extensive experience
in the travel and cruise business, particularly in Alaska. The line's focus
now is on small-ship adventure cruises, particularly in Glacier Bay,
Prince William Sound, and the Columbia River.

THE FLEET	BUILT/RENOVATED	TONNAGE	PASSENGERS
Executive Explorer	1986/1999/2005	98	49
Wilderness Adventurer	1984/97/99	89	69
Wilderness Discoverer	1992/99	99	87
Wilderness Explorer	1969/97	98	31

STYLE Glacier Bay emphasizes experiences made possible by the small
ships' ability to navigate in shallow waters and narrow passages, nose
up to shore for wildlife watching, and get closer to whales. On their
U.S.-registered adventure ships, Glacier Bay places heavier emphasis
than other lines on putting passengers in contact with nature. Through
kayaking, hikes (often directly from ship), and naturalist lectures, passengers spend much more time enjoying Alaska's natural wonders than
shopping in ports or being distracted by shipboard activities. The
adventures are offered on three levels—low, medium, and high—which
are noted in the line's brochure and on its Web site.

One naturalist sails with every cruise and may lead a group no larger than a dozen on an excursion into the rain forest, explaining flora and fauna and natural features, while another heads a kayaking trip. All the ships are casual. The informality of the passenger-crew relationship results in off-duty crew members watching nature videos with passengers and naturalists sitting topside at night with passengers, watching the stars. Most crew members are from Alaska and the western United States. The casual atmosphere and small number of passengers allow easy camaraderie. Passengers often know one another by name within days and maintain friendships long after the cruise.

DISTINCTIVE FEATURES Kayak and Zodiac adventures and some shore excursions, included in cruise price; Native culture-oriented excursions. Dry-launch platforms on *Adventurer* and *Explorer* enable passengers to step directly into their kayaks from ship. Shallow drafts and bow ramps allow ships to nose up to dockless places, enabling passengers to walk out of ship's nose onto dry land.

	HIGHEST	LOWEST	AVERAGE
PER DIEM	$695	$356	$457

Per diems are calculated from cruise line's nondiscounted *cruise-only* published fares on standard accommodations and vary by season, cabins, and cruise areas.

RATES Alaska airport transfers on disembarkation, day port charges, and tips are not included.

Special fares and discounts
- **SINGLE SUPPLEMENT:** 175% of twin rate, except for certain positioning cruises for which the supplement is waived.
- **CHILDREN:** Ages 5–18 pay 50% when sailing with an adult on designated family cruises.

Packages
- **AIR/SEA:** Air add-ons available.
- **PRE/POST:** Optional three- to eight-day Alaska packages.
- **OTHERS:** One-, two-, and six-day independent tour.

THE LAST WORD Two words—adventure and informality—sum up this line's cruise experience. The cruises are for people who want to do something really different. When your ship enters wilderness areas, you can imagine you are on an expedition into the unknown. Kayaking on a quiet lagoon or hiking through rain forest will do that to you. There is no better holiday than Alaska for children interested in wildlife and the environment. The *Wilderness Adventurer* and *Wilderness Discoverer*—which accept children—are ideal for families, particularly those who hike and camp together.

Glacier Bay Cruiseline Standard Features

Officers American.

Staff Dining, Cabin, Cruise/American.

Dining facilities One dining room with open seating, set meal times. Early continental breakfast and cocktail hour with snacks in lounge or on top deck, weather permitting. Coffee, tea, cocoa, fruit, dry snacks throughout day.

Special diets Notice required at booking. Accommodates vegetarian, low-fat, low-salt.

Room service None.

Dress code Casual at all times. Jeans, polos, and flannels the norm in Alaska. Many bring dress shirts, chinos, or dresses for the captain's dinner.

Cabin amenities Windows that open in upper-deck cabins. Reading lights over beds; small closets, limited drawer space.

Electrical outlets 110 AC.

Wheelchair access None.

Recreation and entertainment Lounge with bar, television/VCR with nature, Native-culture videos, films; small library with nature books and field guides; board games. Binoculars available, but better to bring your own. Nature and culture talks by naturalists and occasionally other experts.

Beauty and fitness None.

Other facilities No doctor. Crew trained in first aid and CPR.

Children's facilities None.

Theme cruises None.

Smoking Prohibited in cabins or public rooms; allowed outside on open decks.

Glacier Bay suggested tipping $12–$15 per person per day. Tips pooled and shared by nonofficer staff and crew.

Credit cards For cruise payment and onboard charges: American Express, Visa, MasterCard, Diners Club, Discover.

Wilderness Adventurer	**QUALITY 3**	**VALUE B**
Wilderness Discoverer	**QUALITY 2**	**VALUE B**
REGISTRY United States	**LENGTH 157/169 feet**	**BEAM 38 feet**
CABINS 32/41	**DRAFT 6.5 feet**	**SPEED 10 knots**
MAXIMUM PASSENGERS	**PASSENGER DECKS 3**	**ELEVATORS None**
69/87	**CREW 22**	**SPACE RATIO NA**

THE SHIPS Wide and low-slung, the ships reflect a function-over-form sensibility. The quiet, maneuverable vessels (formerly *Caribbean Prince* and *Mayan Prince* of American Canadian Caribbean Line) are equipped with innovative features for which ACCL founder Luther Blount is known, including his patented bow ramp, which allows a ship to crawl right up to shores where there is no dock and off-load passengers for hiking and exploration.

Furthermore, the *Wilderness Adventurer,* which was renovated in 2000, is outfitted with 23 stable, two-person sea kayaks and a dry-launch platform that allows passengers to take their kayaks directly from the ship. Several outside areas—an open bow space, a half-covered top deck, and a small stern area—are ideal for wildlife watching.

Caution: Due to their shallow drafts, these vessels tend to pitch and roll uncomfortably in rough water, but because they ply the mostly protected waters of Alaska's Inside Passage, the going is usually smooth. Also, ceilings are low—only about 6'3".

In 1999, after *Wilderness Adventurer* ran aground near Juneau, it underwent a quarter-million-dollar repair and renovation, upgrading the comfort level at the same time. All cabins were refitted with new doors and refurbished, and the soundproofing was improved. Public rooms, including the dining room, were also refurbished.

In 2001, *Wilderness Discoverer* was given a multimillion-dollar renovation that included painting and refurbishing public areas and all cabins with new furniture and new doors; remodeling the dining room and lounge; and the addition of four suites on the Observation Deck, the only cabins located on this deck. They have large picture windows and are furnished with a queen bed, television/VCR, table, and chairs.

The ship also has a new hot water system, new sprinkler system, and new sound system enabling passengers to hear the naturalist, captain, and cruise director from any location on the ship. The vessel also has wireless Internet access. More rail space on decks for wildlife and glacier observation has been provided. Also new are a flotilla of 25 two-person sea kayaks; a launching platform which allows passengers to embark easily on wilderness excursions directly from the ship; and a new custom-designed inflatable excursion craft.

In 2005, *Wilderness Discoverer* returned to the Columbia River for a series of cruises in spring and fall.

ITINERARIES *See* Itinerary Index.

CABINS Very basic cabins come in three categories (five on *Discoverer*) determined by size and location. All have private bathrooms, and all but those on the lowest deck have picture windows that open-almost as good as having a balcony. Deluxe cabins (*Discoverer* only) and AA cabins on the Sun Deck have twin beds; some accommodate a third person. Deluxe cabins have more floor space. A-level cabins on the main deck, aft of the dining room, offer twin beds (double bed in three). B-level cabins, on the lowest deck, have no windows. They are furnished with two twins or one twin and one double bed. Storage in all cabins except deluxe is minimal.

Wilderness Discoverer's bathrooms are "marine heads"—toilet, shower, and sink are in one small space separated from the main cabin area. A solid door has replaced the curtain that separated them before the renovations. Deluxe cabins on Discoverer and cabins 303–306 on Adventurer open onto the outside deck, rather than inside corridors.

Specifications Adventurer, 30 outside, 4 inside cabins. 11 cabins with double beds, 23 with twins. Discoverer, 37 outside, 5 inside cabins. 6 cabins with queen-size beds, 8 with doubles, 28 with twins. No suites. Dimensions, 99 square feet. Some accommodate third passenger. No singles.

DINING All meals are served in single, open seatings. Cuisine is basically American, with regional specialties and international touches, all freshly prepared. Snacks are served during pre-dinner cocktails; cookies are baked fresh daily.

SERVICE Friendly, cheerful, and capable service is one of the ship's best features. Most staff members are young and come from Alaska and the Pacific Northwest. They do it all: cleaning cabins, serving meals, as well as toting luggage.

FACILITIES AND ACTIVITIES Each ship has a single lounge with a full-time bartender. Entertainment is do-it-yourself, with naturalist lectures and occasional parlor games. Occasionally, a nature video or feature film plays on the lounge VCR, or the crew may challenge passengers to a board game. Passengers spend most shipboard hours reading, conversing, or watching for wildlife. Binoculars are available; most passengers bring their own. The open-bridge policy attracts passengers to the wheelhouse. Activities are typically hiking and kayaking.

Wilderness Explorer	QUALITY 3	VALUE C
REGISTRY United States	LENGTH 112 feet	BEAM 22 feet
CABINS 16	DRAFT 7.6 feet	SPEED 9 knots
MAXIMUM PASSENGERS 31	PASSENGER DECKS 3	ELEVATORS None
	CREW 13	SPACE RATIO NA

THE SHIP The line's oldest ship (another former American Canadian Caribbean Line vessel, built in 1969), Wilderness Explorer offers perhaps the most active, high-level cruise experience in Alaska.

The ship is tiny, accommodating only 31 passengers in miniscule cabins, but it's the adventure—exploration and the line's respect for the natural environment—that's the big drawing card. Underscoring this concept, the line refers to the ship as its "floating base camp." It's a means to take passengers into the Alaskan landscape rather than be a floating hotel. Nevertheless, interiors are surprisingly bright and cheerful, and the lounge has a piano.

All meals are served family style in single, open seatings in the dining room on the main deck. Snacks are served during the cocktail hour. Service is consistently friendly and professional.

ITINERARIES *See* Itinerary Index.

CABINS Except for one deluxe cabin behind the wheelhouse on the top deck, all cabins are tiny, offering upper and lower bunks, head-style bathrooms, and minimal storage. Tiny "portlights" in A- and B-class cabins admit light but can't be called real windows. AA-class cabins, next to the dining room on the main deck, have slightly more space and real windows. The deluxe cabin is considerably larger than others and has windows on both port and starboard sides.

Specifications 17 outside cabins, all with upper and lower berths. No inside cabins, suites, or singles, and none accommodate a third passenger.

FACILITIES AND ACTIVITIES There is no shipboard entertainment or exercise facility. Passengers amuse themselves with board games, a small library, a television/VCR, and a piano in the lounge. A bar operates on the honor system except during cocktail hour, when it is staffed by a crew member.

Activities center on off-vessel exploration. Passengers who take this cruise through Glacier Bay and Icy Strait focus on nature exploration and wildlife observation. They need to be in good physical condition to handle the three- to four-hour kayaking and hiking excursions. The only planned activities aboard are informal nature, culture, and history lectures by the ship's naturalists and the Glacier Bay park naturalist who accompanies the ship within park boundaries.

POSTSCRIPT A *Wilderness Explorer* cruise is a good choice for those seeking active, ship-based outdoor adventure. The port-free itinerary and small number of passengers mean your Alaska experience will be very personal and completely different from that of a large ship and most small ships. This ship requires the highest level of physical exertion by passengers of all the four ships. People requiring a lot of personal space should look elsewhere.

Executive Explorer	**QUALITY 3**	**VALUE B**
REGISTRY United States	**LENGTH 104 feet**	**BEAM 37 feet**
CABINS 24	**DRAFT 8 feet**	**SPEED 16 knots**
MAXIMUM PASSENGERS 49	**PASSENGER DECKS 6**	**ELEVATORS None**
	CREW 18	**SPACE RATIO NA**

THE SHIP Though odd-looking with its catamaran hulls and three-deck-tall, wedge-shaped superstructure, the *Executive Explorer* is Glacier Bay's most luxurious ship, sailing less adventurous port-to-port itineraries and featuring larger, better-appointed, more inviting cabins and public areas than the line's other ships. Streamlined and powerful, she's able to zip between ports faster than most other small passenger ship on the Alaska scene.

Public areas are pleasantly furnished, and like the line's other vessels, are decorated with Native Alaskan art. The **Vista View Lounge** and Vista cabins above it have a wall of windows overlooking the bow. An open top deck and covered area on the middle deck are best for wildlife viewing. An open area at the stern is another option.

The ship was out of service for the last two years, but she was relaunched in April 2005 after a complete renovation.

ITINERARIES *See* Itinerary Index.

CABINS The ship has the largest, best-appointed cabins in the line's fleet. All have large windows, refrigerator, TV/VCR, considerable closet space, and solid cabin doors rather than the accordion-style doors of the other ships.

The bathrooms are small, arranged in the line's space-saving "head style" (toilet is in the shower stall); sinks and vanities are in the main cabin area.

All but Vista Deluxe and B cabins have twin beds that convert to queen size. One B cabin, smaller than the others, has upper and lower berths and accommodates two people but is suggested as a single. The two Vista Deluxe cabins (aft middle deck, below the bridge) face the bow and have a sitting area, queen-size beds, larger closets, and a wall of windows providing a wraparound view.

Specifications 25 outside, including 2 deluxe cabins. Two Vista Deluxe with queens; 22 standard with twins (convertible to queens), measure approximately 135 square feet; 1 with upper/lower bunks.

DINING Meals are served in single, open seatings in one dining room. Cuisine, all freshly prepared, tends to be standard American fare with regional specialties, but galley staff often come up with surprising gourmet touches. There are usually two or three entrees for dinner; Alaska salmon is a staple.

The galley staff bakes fresh cookies in midafternoon and serves a snack at the predinner cocktail hour. One dinner per cruise is designated as the captain's dinner, with lobster and free champagne. With advance notice, the galley staff can accommodate special diets.

SERVICE Service is one of the line's best features—cordial and warm, capable and professional. Members of the hotel staff, most of them young and mostly from Alaska and the Pacific Northwest, do double and triple duty, cleaning cabins, serving meals, and helping carry luggage on and off the ship. All in all, the service is more like that found at a friendly bed-and-breakfast than at a resort.

FACILITIES AND ACTIVITIES The ship has only two public rooms—one lounge with the vessel's only bar (and full-time bartender), small library, board games, and videotapes; and one dining room. There are no exercise or entertainment facilities.

Shipboard activities are focused mainly on observing nature and wildlife. In the evenings, the naturalists and the ship's cruise director give talks on wildlife, Native culture, and history, and occasionally host participatory games. Other than this, entertainment is provided by Alaska itself and by passenger interaction.

Executive Explorer has low-activity positioning cruises April–May and August–September between Seattle and Juneau when the single supplement, normally 175%, is waived. The line is planning some theme cruises, including a Culinary Cruise introduced in summer 2005 that is likely to be repeated.

Holland America Line

300 Elliott Avenue West, Seattle, WA 98119
☎ **206-281-3535 or 877-SAIL HAL (724-5425); fax 206-281-7110**
www.hollandamerica.com

TYPE OF SHIPS Modern superliners.

TYPE OF CRUISES Traditional yet modern, high-quality mainstream cruises.

CRUISE LINE'S STRENGTHS
- tradition and experience
- easy-to-like ships
- consistent quality and style
- worldwide itineraries
- impeccable condition of ships

CRUISE LINE'S SHORTCOMINGS
- show lounge entertainment
- shore excursion cancellation policy
- communication problems with dining staff due to language

FELLOW PASSENGERS Experienced travelers and families who seek comfort and consistency, quality, a refined environment, and a high level of service and who choose cruises by their destinations. Many are retired business owners with some college education, executives, and professionals, but the range includes young nurses and secretaries on their first cruise, affluent seniors who cruise often, honeymooners, young families, multigenerational families, and some disabled travelers. They're social-minded, well mannered, and outgoing, but not loud. They enjoy traveling with old friends and making new ones. They're conservative, careful with money, and seek good value. They often cruise to celebrate a special occasion, such as an anniversary or a family reunion.

The average age is mid-50s in winter and can be as low as 44 on Caribbean cruises, younger in summer, particularly on Alaska cruises but varies by cruise length and itinerary. A seven-day Alaska and seven-day Caribbean cruise on the same ship attract different ages and incomes. More than 55% are couples; 50% are groups—as different as business or tour groups, or square dancing and stamp-collecting clubs.

Recommended for Those who enjoy cruise traditions and want a quality experience in a refined environment, but like the facilities and choices available on superliners. Small-ship devotees open to trying a larger ship. Budget cruisers able to move up to higher quality, families, and multigenerational vacationers.

Not recommended for Swingers, party seekers, late-night revelers, trend seekers, or pacesetters.

CRUISE AREAS AND SEASONS Caribbean, year-round; Panama Canal, fall to spring; Asia, South Pacific, Africa, fall/winter/spring; Alaska, Europe, Canada, New England, transatlantic, summer/fall; Mexico, Hawaii, Pacific coast, fall to spring ; South America, world cruise, winter.

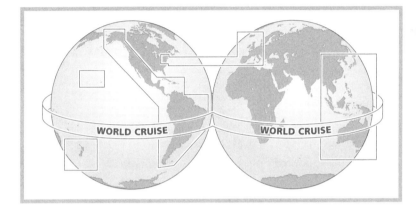

THE LINE Holland America has carried passengers since 1871. It's among the few lines to make a successful transition from a classic steamship company to a modern cruise line, and it did so better than most, managing to keep its identity and traditions intact while developing a fine mainstream product.

The turning point came in the early 1980s when the line introduced the *Nieuw Amsterdam* (sold in 2000), a forerunner of today's superliners. She was revolutionary because of such features as a square stern that provided 20% more open deck; two outdoor heated pools; a fully equipped gym, spa, and whirlpool; coded cards rather than keys for cabins; and cabin television—all features that quickly became standard on new ships.

In 1988, HAL acquired the unusual Windstar Cruises, and the following year, Holland America, Windstar, and Seattle-based Westours, which pioneered Alaska tours and cruises, were acquired by Carnival Corp. The marriage proved to be brilliant, enabling Holland America to continue its expansion (four stunning new ships in the 1990s, and another four early in the new millennium) and allowing the line to expand in Alaska, return to Europe after nearly two decades, and increase its number of longer cruises. All were factors critical to HAL's retaining its many loyal fans.

The Statendam-class ships, the first HAL ships to have private verandas, combine classic elegance with state-of-the-art technology, offering such features as multideck atriums, fountains, whirlpools, jogging tracks, and theaters even Broadway would envy. The faster *Rotterdam* and her sister ship, *Amsterdam,* with top cruising speeds of 25 knots, gave the line new flexibility in creating itineraries. They were followed by slightly larger twins, *Volendam* and *Zaandam,* and a brand-new class of 82,000-ton cruise ships, dubbed the Vista series, began arriving in 2002. Altogether, the line introduced ten new ships in ten years—a challenge for any cruise line.

In 1998, to widen its audience and meet the market's demand for short vacations, HAL offered cruises of five days or less for the first time. In 2001, the line introduced wheelchair-accessible tenders and Internet access for passengers fleetwide. More recently, the line has added shore-excursion booking to its Web site.

But these enhancements pale compared to the extensive, $225 million *Signature of Excellence* program now underway to update the line for the modern traveler while continuing to uphold the traditions that are Holland America's signature.

THE FLEET	BUILT/RENOVATED	TONNAGE	PASSENGERS
Amsterdam	2000	61,000	1,380
Maasdam	1994	55,451	1,258
Noordam	2006-	85,000	1,848
Oosterdam	2003	81,769	1,848
Prinsendam	1988/93/96/99/2002	38,000	794
Rotterdam	1997	59,652	1,316
Ryndam	1994	55,451	1,258
Statendam	1993	55,451	1,258
Veendam	1996	55,451	1,258
Volendam	1999	60,906	1,432
Westerdam	2004	81,769	1,848
Zaandam	2000	60,906	1,432
Zuiderdam	2002	81,769	1,848

STYLE HAL cruises are classic but contemporary, blending Old World traditions with modern lifestyles. They offer the full range of activities
expected on large, mass-market ships. The pace is leisurely, designed for
experienced, mature travelers and families.

To attract younger passengers, the line has progressively expanded
onboard sports and fitness facilities; added sports bars with ESPN programming, alternative dining, Internet access, sports and adventure
shore excursions for active passengers on Alaska and Caribbean cruises;
and beefed up its children's program and "Just for Kids" adventure and
learning excursions in Alaska. Now, with the introduction of *Signature of
Excellence,* some ships have special teens-only areas.

In 1997, Holland America bought the uninhabited 2,400-acre Bahamian island of Little San Salvador, renamed it Half Moon Cay, and developed it as HAL's private island destination on Caribbean itineraries. Located between Eleuthera and Cat Island, less than 100 miles southeast of Nassau, the 45-acre facility fronts a gorgeous white-sand beach. Three areas, connected by walkways and a tram, are an arrival marina and plaza built to resemble ruins of a Spanish fort, a shopping area styled as a West Indian village, and a food pavilion. In 2005, the Aqua Park was expanded to include slides and other new features.

The market has shops, an ice cream parlor, coffee shop, bar, and art gallery. There is a children's playground, wedding chapel, and post office selling Bahamian stamps—including one issued to commemorate the island. Passengers get a barbecue lunch of West Indian selections. The sports center offers snorkeling and diving on nearby reefs, Sunfish sailing, other water sports, volleyball, and basketball. Nature trails feature a bird sanctuary designated by the Bahaman National Trust. The newest additions are horseback riding and swimming with dolphins. Passengers can debit the cost of all services and sports to their cabins; cash is required for island stamps.

Holland America's vessels feel like ships, not floating hotels. The fleet shares characteristics that reinforce the line's traditions: art and antiques reflecting Holland's association with trade and exploration in the Americas; Dutch officers and Indonesian crews, linking Holland's historical ties to Asia; and the Crow's Nest, an observation bar inspired by the lookout on the main mast of the company's old sailing ships.

Now, with the new *Signature of Excellence* program, the line aims for an even more youthful look and ambience with enhancements to cabins, dining, and children's facilities, and the introduction of new features throughout the fleet, such as early boarding from 11:30 a.m. on the day of departure, four evening dining times, and the addition of the Pinnacle Grill, a steak and seafood specialty restaurant. The *Ryndam, Prinsendam,* and *Zaandam* were the first of the fleet to get the extensive makeover, followed by the *Rotterdam, Westerdam,* and *Statendam* in 2005, and the remainder by 2006 year's end. Meanwhile, expect to find differences in the ships until the refits are completed. Ever-mindful of their longtime loyal fans, Holland America is working to strike a balance between the pace and nature of the changes needed to attract a broader, younger audience, and keeping the traditions that older passengers cherish.

DISTINCTIVE FEATURES Escalators on the newest ships, self-service laundries, good libraries, fresh flowers shipwide; fruit basket, robes in cabins, hot hors d'oeuvres at cocktails, chimes played by a uniformed steward to announce dinner, private Bahamian island, alternative dining, Internet centers; Culinary Arts program, Explorations Café.

	HIGHEST	LOWEST	AVERAGE
PER DIEM	$911	$88	$371

Per diems are calculated from cruise line's nondiscounted *cruise-only* published fares on standard accommodations and vary by season, cabins, and cruise areas.

RATES Port charges are included.

Special fares and discounts Save up to 45% for early booking under the Caribbean Savings program. A similar Alaska program offers 25% off. Membership Miles, a program with American Express, offers mileage redeemable for upgrades and discount dollars.

- **THIRD/FOURTH PASSENGER:** Low rates.
- **CHILDREN'S FARE:** Reduced rates for ages 2–18; specific rates for younger than age 2. Ages 19 and older are billed as third/fourth persons sharing parents' room.
- **SINGLE SUPPLEMENT:** 150–190% of double rate or specific rate on certain cruises; guaranteed share program.

Packages
- **AIR/SEA:** Yes.
- **PRE/POST:** Yes.
- **OTHERS:** Renewal of vows and other pricey packages for special occasions. "Just for Us" includes couple massage and chilled Cordon Rouge champagne at embarkation, a guarantee of table for two in the dining room, framed photo, and more. "Romantic Voyage" offers bon voyage flower bouquet upon arrival, champagne, private card lesson with $25 in chips, chocolate truffle dessert after farewell dinner, and spa day for one.

PAST PASSENGERS Mariner Club members receive discount and upgrade offers about five times a year, amenities, recognition, theme cruises, and occasional cruises with HAL's president. New enhancements include baggage tags, separate check-in, party hosted by the captain, and certificates for third to tenth cruise, based on the number of cruises.

THE LAST WORD Holland America puts itself in the premium category, between luxury and economy, but it's at the high end of premium, a hair's breadth from luxury, and deluxe by any standard. The refinements and thoughtful touches it offers are unavailable on many comparably priced ships. HAL's consistency—even the names of most public rooms are the same fleetwide—has built a large, loyal following that doesn't find the predictability boring—rather, reassuring.

We are happy to report that Holland America has dropped its ambiguous "no tipping required" policy. Now, $10 per person per day is added to your shipboard bill. You can add to, reduce, or delete it.

Holland America Line Standard Features

Officers Dutch; *Veendam*, British.

Staff Dining/Dutch supervisors, Indonesian and Filipino staff; Cabin/Indonesian and Filipino; Cruise/American and others. Bar, deck/Filipino.

Dining facilities One dining room, four seatings. Indoor/outdoor lido restaurants for casual buffet breakfast, lunch, and alternative dining; taco, pasta, and ice cream bars.

Special diets Kosher; low-sodium, low-cholesterol, low-fat; vegetarian; sugar-free desserts; baby foods. Request 30 days in advance.

Room service 24 hours; dining room menu during dining hours.

Dress code Casual or informal with two formal/semiformal nights per week of cruise. Tuxedo rental service available.

Cabin amenities Television with CNN, TNT, ESPN, TCM, CNBC, Discovery, and children's channel; multichannel music system; hair dryers, direct-dial telephone. Suites and deluxe cabins have VCR, whirlpool bath, and minibar.

Electrical outlets 110 AC.

Wheelchair access 21 cabins on *Amsterdam*, *Rotterdam*; 22 on *Volendam*, *Zaandam*; 28 on Vista class; 4–6 on others.

Recreation and entertainment Theater for movies and lectures; show lounge; nightclub; casino, bars, and lounges; karaoke; masquerades; crew show; culinary demonstrations; kitchen tours; bingo, card games, bridge; pool games; dance classes; library. Sports bars with ESPN.

Sports and other activities Two outdoor pools, tennis, golf putting, volleyball, Ping-Pong, shuffleboard.

Beauty and fitness Beauty/barber shop, saunas, massage, fitness program, gym with professional instructors, jogging track, practice tennis. Spa treatments and fitness programs.

Other facilities Religious services, medical facilities, laundry/dry cleaning service, laundry rooms, meeting room. Credit-card phones. Wedding ceremony and amenity packages for vows renewal, honeymoons, and anniversaries at additional charge. Internet centers or Exploration Cafés.

Children's facilities Club HAL year-round youth program with counselors and age-specific activities for three age groups; "Just for Kids" adventure and learning shore excursions. Teens ages 13–18 have their own areas with sun deck, waterfall, lounge, and other features.

Theme cruises See specific ships.

Smoking Designated smoking areas in public rooms; some, such as dining rooms, card room, library, and theater, are designated nonsmoking.

Holland America suggested tipping A $10 per person per day gratuity added to passenger's shipboard account; 15% added to bar bills.

Credit cards Cruise and onboard charges: American Express, Discover, Master-Card, Visa; no cash.

Maasdam	**QUALITY 8**	**VALUE B**
Ryndam	**QUALITY 8**	**VALUE B**
Statendam	**QUALITY 8**	**VALUE B**
Veendam	**QUALITY 8**	**VALUE B**
REGISTRY *Maasdam/Ryndam/*	**LENGTH** 720 feet	**BEAM** 101 feet
Statendam Netherlands;		
Veendam Bahamas		
CABINS 633	**DRAFT** 24.6 feet	**SPEED** 22 knots
MAXIMUM PASSENGERS 1,258	**PASSENGER DECKS** 10	**ELEVATORS** 8
	CREW 557	**SPACE RATIO** 44

THE SHIPS The *Statendam* and her sisters introduced a new class of ships in the 1990s that set the style and standard for Holland America into the next century. They combine Old World tradition with state-of-the-art technology and provide an imposing yet inviting ambience. The spacious ships differ in decor but are identical in layout and offer almost identical facilities and activities.

Interiors of the Italian-built ships were designed by De Vlaming, Fenns, and Dingemans (VFD), the Dutch firm responsible for earlier HAL ships, and who helped establish the line's signature look. In the group's public areas, designers drew from Holland America's history to capture the golden age of Dutch shipping, but in a contemporary context. Multimillion-dollar collections of art and artifacts from the 17th to 19th centuries are integrated into the decor. These combine with contemporary art to enhance the ships' modern image. Together, they make the ships floating art galleries. In materials, the world was VFD's emporium. Designers used woolen fabrics from Holland; leathers from Germany, France, and England; glass from Italy. Cabins were made in Finland, a Danish company supplied teak, and furniture was built in Slovenia. Galley equipment came from the United States.

Public rooms span two decks on the Promenade and Upper Promenade in an asymmetrical pattern, allowing for bars and lounges of different sizes.

The *Maasdam,* fifth ship in the company's history with that name, is a far cry from the first *Maasdam*—a double-masted iron steamship that carried eight first-class and 288 steerage passengers. It sailed the Atlantic monthly from 1872 to 1884 at a speed of ten knots. Today's computer-piloted *Maasdam* has only one class and moves at more than twice that speed.

Passengers are introduced to the *Maasdam* by a three-deck atrium on the Lower Promenade Deck. Under a ceiling of mirrors and fiber-optic lights, the atrium sparkles with a 30-foot glass sculpture, *Totem,* by Italian artist Luciano Vistosi. The sculpture contains thousands of pieces of glass that catch the light and cast specks of color on nearby surfaces. The best place to see it is from the stairs that rim the atrium.

Atrium sculptures on *Statendam* and *Ryndam* are classic in style but out of scale with their setting. On *Statendam,* it's a huge fountain with a bronze statue of three enormous mermaids rising from the sea. On *Ryndam,* it's a tribute in marble (five tons!) to sea legends. An oversized sea dragon twines around the sculpture's top and an undersized boat at the bottom, an improbable mermaid on its bow. The decor of the *Statendam,* also the fifth HAL ship to bear the name, is more baroque than the other ships and often eclectic. Interiors range from conservative to bizarre, blending textures and earth tones with classic European and exotic Indonesian motifs. The *Veendam* is the most stylish of the group, with different color schemes, furnishings, and art. The atrium features a glass sculpture, as on *Maasdam.* Adjacent is the Crystal Terrace.

Ryndam was the first to receive the *Signature of Excellence* makeover and now sports new public rooms with brighter decor, cabin improvements, dining enhancements, and children's facilities, among others.

ITINERARIES *See* Itinerary Index.

CABINS Comfortable, contemporary furnishings in light wood are combined with continental touches. Standard cabins are almost 30% larger than comparable ones on ships of similar category. Large mirrors lighten the rooms, and in many, curtains separate the sleeping and sitting areas. Seventy-seven percent are outside cabins.

All cabins in all categories fleetwide already have comfortable euro-top mattresses. Now, the cabins on the *Ryndam* (and soon her sister ships) have a modern, very different look for HAL, with a light bed-cover and a display of pillows. The cabins also have upgraded bed linens, towels, and terry robes, flat-screen television with DVD players, massage showerheads, and lighted magnifying mirrors.

All cabins have hair dryers, direct-dial telephone with automated wake-up service, multichannel music system, and closed-circuit television. Full-length double closets and deep chests of drawers—nice features for long cruises—provide ample storage.

Standard cabins have sofas; 70% have sofa beds. All outside cabins have a bathtub and shower. Suites and deluxe cabins have a veranda, minibar, VCR, and whirlpool bath. Each suite also has a small private dining area; laundry and dry cleaning is free.

Passengers in suites have a concierge to assist with appointments and other needs, plus the new and very comfortable Neptune Lounge for the private use of Penthouse and Deluxe suite passengers only. Located on Deck 10 of the *Ryndam,* it has its own library, television, and bar.

Specifications 144 inside cabins, 485 outside (including 120 deluxe cabins and 29 suites with verandas). All with twin beds convertible to queen. Standard dimensions are 186 square feet, inside cabin; 196 square feet, outside cabin. 16 deluxe/36 standard outside have connecting doors for family suites. Some upper/lower berths and single cabins; 6 wheelchair-accessible cabins.

DINING The ships' crowning glories are their dazzling **Rotterdam Dining Rooms**. Surrounded on three sides by floor-to-ceiling windows that embrace the scenery and span the Promenade and Upper Promenade Decks, the rooms are a harmony of elegant tradition and modern technology. An impressive curved staircase connects the two levels.

On the *Maasdam,* a fountain of antique Argentine marble is the lower level's centerpiece. A ceiling canopy of a thousand morning glories is made of blown glass from Murano, Italy. Between the decks is a border of fiber-optic "florets" programmed to change color, altering the room's mood. Four large, colorful linen screens depicting day and night cover the walls on both decks.

One passenger's verdict: "The room is so beautiful it takes your breath away." The room is large but remarkably quiet; diners can converse in normal voices and hear chamber music playing on the balcony. The secret: Glass ceilings look spectacular—and absorb sound.

Dining here and on all Holland America ships is more elegant, and menu choices more extensive, than on most mainstream cruise ships. A typical dinner menu offers a choice of seven appetizers (six cold, one hot); three soups (two hot, one cold), and three salads (five dressings); six entrees, including a vegetarian selection and a light and healthy one, plus selections of cheese and fruit; six desserts; pastries; ice cream; and light and sugar-free desserts. Tables are set with white Rosenthal china bearing a gold HAL logo, silver tableware, wine coolers, and fresh flowers on starched tablecloths. Many tables have either window or balcony seats. A microphone at the captain's table on the main floor allows him or other speakers to address the room; upper-level guests view the speaker on television monitors.

An important element of the *Signature of Excellence* program has been the fleetwide addition of the **Pinnacle Grill.** The venue replaces the former private King's Room off the main dining room. Sterling beef is the grill's major draw; you can choose your cut from the display tray, including a 20-ounce Porterhouse steak. The food is superbly prepared, presented, and served. Reservations are required, and there is a charge: $10 for lunch (served on sea days only), and $20 for dinner. The true bargain is the $10 dinner on the first night of a cruise.

Responding to passengers' preference for casual, flexibly timed breakfast and lunch—and alternative dining in the evening—Holland America has worked to perfect the lido buffet, outdoing competitors in quality, choice, and presentation. More lunch choices—hot dogs, hamburgers, pasta, satay, and tacos—are available by the lido pool. A free ice cream bar is open daily. Sandwiches, desserts, coffee, and tea are available here around the clock. Hot hors d'oeuvres with Indonesian tidbits are served in public rooms before dinner, and a weekly Indonesian lido buffet is popular. And should you still be hungry, the 24-hour room service menu has been expanded, and your cabin's fruit basket is freshened daily.

On the *Ryndam*, the **Lido Restaurant** has been reconfigured into food stations, replacing the cafeteria design. Entrees from the dining room are served as part of the casual dinner option—a handy alternative after a busy day ashore.

One of the main ingredients of that *Signature of Excellence* added to the *Ryndam* and other ships is the new Culinary Arts program and **Culinary Arts Center.** It has a state-of-the-art show kitchen where cooking demonstrations, tasting events, and cooking classes take place. Some cruises offer presentations by guest chefs. In the Center, housed in the **Wajang Theater,** passengers in the audience get a up-close view of the cooking action on large, plasma screens, while broadcast capabilities provide all guests the opportunity to watch from their cabins. In addition to the onstage kitchen, the centers have portable cooking stations where up to 16 guests can participate in hands-on classes that often feature regional cuisine reflecting the ship's itinerary.

The one-hour demonstrations by the executive or guest chefs are free. The daily classes, limited to a dozen or so participants sharing six cooking stations, run one-and-a-half hours, during which an appetizer, entree, and dessert are prepared. There is a charge, which includes a set of recipes plus a 10% discount at the Pinnacle Grill or complimentary admission to a wine-tasting event. The theater is still used for movies, lectures, and religious services.

Integral to the program is Holland America's new culinary advisor, master chef Rudi Sodamin, who has been instrumental in developing the centers and instructional programs. Sodamin, who emphasizes quality ingredients and creative presentation, has added a number of his signature dishes to the menus—and there's more to come.

Across from the theater, replacing the Java Café, is the **Gourmet Shop** and wine-tasting area. In the future, the Gourmet Shop will be selling culinary items, as well as china and silverware from the Pinnacle Grill and Rudi Sodamin's cookbooks.

SERVICE HAL's efficient Dutch officers and the friendly Indonesian and Filipino crew are a good combination. Unobtrusive service by a gracious and attentive staff is a hallmark—and a reason the line has so many loyal fans. Dining room supervisory personnel are officers; many crew members have been with Holland America for many years.

Unlike most cruise ships, HAL has retained a tradition its fans love: a uniformed steward passes through the ship playing chimes to summon passengers to dine. (Older passengers are reminded of the pageboy in old Philip Morris cigarette ads.)

FACILITIES AND ACTIVITIES The *Maasdam* and her sisters each have five lounges, often with the same names and similar entertainment. The Promenade Deck is anchored by the two-deck main show lounge designed by Joe Farcus, who is known for his innovative, flamboyant ship interiors for Carnival Cruise Lines. Daytime activities include lectures, bridge tournaments, dance lessons, bingo, golf putting contests, kite flying, movies (with popcorn), religious services, and—the most unusual—guided tours of the ship's art and antiquities.

The ships have large, comfortable card and puzzle rooms, a shopping arcade, and libraries with floor-to-ceiling windows. The ships hold auctions of contemporary art. Be wary of the sales pitch. If the bargain sounds too good to be true, it probably is.

In the *Maasdam*'s **Rembrandt Show Lounge,** Delft ceramic tiles are set against brocade, gold-tinted mirrors and mahogany paneling that recall the 17th-century Dutch master whose portrait is etched into glass doors at the entrance. The **Vermeer Lounge** on the *Ryndam* honors the 17th-century Dutch master Jan Vermeer. It's Art Nouveau in style, reminiscent of great movie palaces of the 1930s, with lacy mahogany woodwork and silver columns amid dozens of luminescent tulips.

For the **Van Gogh Lounge** on the *Statendam,* the artist's *Starry Night* is the inspiration for computerized special effects, fiber-optic lighting, and curtain drawing. Staircases frame the stage, whose revolving platform facilitates set changes. The *Veendam*'s **Rubens Lounge** is named after the celebrated 16th-century Flemish painter Peter Paul Rubens and features glass sculptures in his style. The lounges offer Broadway-style shows similar to entertainment on many mainstream cruise ships.The **Ocean Bar** on the Upper Promenade showcases music by a combo. Here Matthys Roling, one of Holland's best-known artists, created her signature "drapery" art, decorating ceilings and walls in beige and red fabric. The oddly shaped **Piano Bar,** adjacent to the casino and popular for sing-alongs, is designed around a piano, with two semicircles of tables and curving sofas. Lights are programmed to change, altering the cozy room's ambience. The **Explorer's Lounge** has traditionally been passenger's favorite spot for after-dinner drinks.

The casino offers blackjack, Caribbean poker, roulette, dice, and slot machines. Outside, kinetic artist Yaacov Agam created a computer display wall that shows thousands of constantly changing images.

Another *Signature of Excellence* initiative is "**Explorations Café powered by *The New York Times*,**" a new concept, not only for Holland America, but for the cruise world. The new venue is a combination 2,000-book library, puzzle corner, Internet center, music-listening area, DVD library, and Torrefazione coffee bar. Located on Upper Promenade Deck 8, it replaced the card room, which was moved down the hall to the former Queen's Room section of the dining room.

Designed with the comfort of a living room, it is operated in cooperation with *The New York Times* and has *Times* crossword-puzzle tables with write-on, wipe-off tops, plus cases of memorabilia from the *Times* archives. The electronic edition of the *New York Times* is downloaded to the room's computers. The daily quiz and crossword puzzle can be picked up at the desk. The area also includes a huge globe, educational programs on interactive flat screens, and Discovery Channel programming on a larger screen. There's a DVD library in the **Explorations Café** where passengers can choose from 1,000 titles for $10 per week (no charge for those in suites). Internet access ranges from $0.40 to $0.70 per minute; wireless hotspots are located in various lounges around the ship for use with your own laptop.

The best java onboard is found at the coffee bar that serves Torrefazione, Starbucks' premium brand. A free snack is included with the purchase of a drink, which cost $1.50 for an espresso, cappuccino, caffe latte, or hot chocolate, or $2.25 for specialty sodas.

The **Crow's Nest,** traditionally a sedate observation lounge by day and disco by night, has gotten a big *Signature of Excellence* makeover, if the *Ryndam* is the model. Its Crow's Nest has the liveliest nightlife of any Holland America ship, thanks largely to the venue's design changes. The lounge is now outfitted in shocking pink and other bold colors, and private seating areas are cordoned off by soft curtains. There's a striking new bar of backlit onyx, disco lights, dance floor, and a high-tech video wall.

SPORTS, FITNESS, AND BEAUTY The ships' upper decks cater to active passengers. At the center of a teak expanse on Navigation Deck is one of two outdoor swimming pools. On the lido, a second swimming pool, with whirlpools and wading pool, has a retractable glass roof for use in cool weather-a great asset on Alaskan cruises. A tiled wall with a bronze sculpture of dolphins frames the area.

The topside Sports Deck has two practice tennis courts (on *Statendam*, the space is a jogging track). A teak deck encircling the Lower Promenade Deck has space for deck chairs, walkers, and joggers (four laps equal one mile). The fleetwide Passport to Fitness program awards points for daily exercises and activities that can be redeemed for prizes, such as a belt pack or T-shirt.

The *Ryndam* now has a **Greenhouse Spa and Salon,** a brand exclusive to Holland America with features developed in the Texas-based Greenhouse Spa chain, such as a Strawberry Herbal Back Cleanse, a hydrotherapy pool (day use $15, and a thermal suite, $15 for the day). Inaugurated on the Vista-class ships, the Greenhouse Spa will be added to all the fleet as part of the *Signature of Excellence* program. Operated by Steiner, the larger, more sophisticated facility has new treatment rooms, steam and aromatic room, and a new relaxation room with heated ceramic lounges and a wide range of skin, body, and hair treatments, and manicure/pedicure and massage chairs. The hair salon was actually made smaller to add spa treatment rooms, including couples' massage rooms, reflecting a change in the demands of today's passengers. The ocean-view gym is equipped with treadmills, step machines, rowing machines, life cycles, and a Hydra fitness circuit with ten resistance machines. In front of the spa is an outside deck for exercise classes.

At **Half Moon Cay**, HAL's private island, which is a stop on most Caribbean itineraries and Panama Canal cruises, passengers have new activities to enjoy as a result of the *Signature of Excellence* program. These include a horseback riding and swimming excursion, a stingray adventure, a guided personal watercraft tour, and an aqua park with large water "toys" in the shapes of whales, octopi, sharks, and dolphins. The new activities augment the island's array of excursions—scuba diving, catch-and-release deep-sea fishing, eco-tours by glass-bottom boat, kayaking, and parasailing. The island has a water-sports center, a children's playground, volleyball, basketball, nature trails, and a bird reserve. Passengers can have a beachside massage or rent a private, air-conditioned beach-front cabana for the day ($200).

CHILDREN'S FACILITIES All ships have year-round, full-time youth coordinators (one for every 30 children, more during holidays and summer). They organize and supervise programs for three age groups: generally, 5–8 years, 9–12 years, and teens. On some ships, Club HAL now accepts children as young as three years old.

Daily activities for children ages 5–8 may include storytelling, candy-bar bingo, games, arts and crafts, charades, and ice cream parties. Those age 9–12 might learn golf putting, have dance lessons or theme parties, or participate in deck sports or scavenger hunts, Ping-Pong, or karaoke. Older children have a teen disco, dance lessons, arcade games, sports, card games, trivia contests, bingo, and movies. All have pizza and Coke-tail parties and ship tours. The ships have wading pools, activity rooms with video games, and children's menus listing such favorites as hamburgers, hot dogs, fish and chips, chicken fingers, and pizza.

The "Just for Kids" shore excursion on **Half Moon Cay** offers a variety of activities, including beach parties, treasure hunts, water sports, scuba diving, and more; prices are $9–$119, and rental equipment costs $9–$19.

On the first night of each cruise, kids and their parents meet the youth coordinator, who outlines the program. At sea, there is at least one activity in the morning, afternoon, and evening; none are scheduled on port days. Baby-sitting by staff volunteers (availability isn't guaranteed) costs $8 per hour for the first child and $5 more per hour for additional children from the same family.

One of the main objectives of the *Signature of Excellence* program—to appeal to the growing market of multigenerational vacationers—can be seen in the new and expanded **Club HAL** facilities on the *Ryndam*, located on Deck 12. Teens now have their own area, which is supervised but no adults are allowed. The **Loft** lounge has a dance floor, lights, music videos, and DVDs. Upstairs is the **Oasis,** the teens' new private sun deck, complete with its own waterfall, covered snack areas, and hammocks. Two rooms loaded with games and toys for ages 3 to 7 accommodate 20 children each, with additional areas available as needed. For the 8- to 12-year-olds, entertainment includes PlayStations, Internet access, arcade games, and karaoke. Among other enhancements is a Port Day program, allowing parents to place kids in Club HAL from 8 a.m. to 5 p.m., including a boxed lunch. Mom and Dad are then free to go off the ship and enjoy the destination. From 10 p.m. to midnight, parents can take advantage of Club HAL's After Hours program, which runs $5 per child per hour.

SHORE EXCURSIONS Holland America has been a leader in Alaska travel and offers programs ranging from cruising near glaciers on dayboats to rail travel on the domed McKinley Explorer. In Ketchikan, you can have a half-day sight-seeing/flight-seeing combination, or you can kayak, fish, or pan for gold. Alaskan cruises are highlighted by a visit to Glacier Bay National Park. Every Glacier Route cruise offers visits to Sitka's Alaska Raptor Rehabilitation Center, dedicated to returning injured bald eagles to the wild.

In the Caribbean, the line offers 175 shore excursions at 30 Caribbean ports. Most are standard offerings with moderate to moderately expensive rates. Flight-seeing is available frequently, and certified divers are offered scuba excursions. Twenty "environmentally sensitive" eco-tours focusing on the islands' nature, history, and culture are designed to help passengers better understand the islands. They range from guided rain forest hikes to air tours to view the archaeological sites. European shore excursions can be expensive on any line, but HAL's seem to cost more than its closest competitor. Save money by taking standard city tours on your own and buying only those excursions that are unique or that visit attractions difficult to reach.

Note: Shore excursions can now be booked online. Be very sure of your tour choices before you buy. In addition to the industry's standard policy of no refunds for cancellations 24 hours before a tour, Holland America charges a 10% fee for any cancellation.

Amsterdam	QUALITY 8	VALUE C
Rotterdam	QUALITY 9	VALUE C
Volendam/Zaandam	QUALITY 8	VALUE C
REGISTRY Netherlands	LENGTH 780/781 feet	BEAM 105.8 feet
CABINS 690/658/720	DRAFT 29.8/24 feet	SPEED 25/23 knots
MAXIMUM PASSENGERS	PASSENGER DECKS 10	ELEVATORS 12
1,380/1,316/1,440	CREW 647	SPACE RATIO 44/47/ 42

THE SHIPS The *Rotterdam,* the line's sixth ship bearing that name, upholds Holland America's tradition in contemporary style but little resembles *Rotterdam V*. She's more like the Statendam quartet, with almost the same layout and with many of their most popular features. Passengers recognize immediately that they are on a Holland America ship. Her slightly larger sister, *Amsterdam,* followed in 2000. Both were designated as the line's flagships and introduced new features. Their speed gives HAL more flexibility in designing itineraries. Each have more deluxe cabins with verandas, an alternative restaurant, extensive facilities for the handicapped, and a private lounge and concierge desk for suite passengers.

At about the same time, Holland America introduced the *Volendam* and *Zaandam,* built at the Fincantieri in Italy, creating a new generation of luxury cruise ships that combined features from the Statendam group and the *Rotterdam*. The twins are about as long and wide as *Rotterdam,* but their tonnage is greater because they have more passenger cabins—1,432 compared to *Rotterdam's* 1,316 passengers.

The principal architect for all eight ships, Frans Dingemans, created interiors in keeping with HAL's tradition and passenger preferences. He describes the *Rotterdam's* interiors as an evolution from the Statendam group. The enhancements are a three-story atrium (oval instead of octagonal), a larger lido restaurant, and a dome over the lido pool. But *Rotterdam* differs from Statendam-class ships in other ways too: She's longer, wider, and more spacious, as well as faster. Because she's designed to be speedier, the hull is longer and more tapered. Like *Rotterdam V*, she has two funnels aft. Passenger capacity is higher—1,316 versus 1,266 passengers. Three staircases instead of two put passengers never farther than about 125 feet from access to the public rooms. The layout of the public rooms on the *Volendam* and *Zaandam* is the same as that of *Rotterdam,* including three staircases, an alternative restaurant, a lounge with additional dance floor, and a children's room on Sports Deck. The *Zaandam* was the first of these four ships to receive the new facilities and amenities of Holland America's *Signature of Excellence* program. (See the *Ryndam,* the first ship to be refitted, for details.) *Rotterdam's* interior was inspired by (not a replica of) her predecessor, though some of her namesake's rich interiors and 1930s Art Deco style have been incorporated. More woods and darker colors were used to achieve a classy as well as classic ambience.

A huge sculpture fills the *Rotterdam*'s three-deck atrium. More a curiosity than a work of art, it represents a Flemish clock tower with 14 timepieces and is embellished with mermaids, dolphins, and snakes. All HAL ships have valuable art collections, but *Rotterdam*'s is the most varied, with museum-quality antiques that evoke the Dutch maritime tradition. Works include glass wall sculptures, an 18th-century French oil painting, 17th-century Japanese armor, 18th-century Chinese silk scrolls, and antique furniture. The most memorable are life-sized replicas of the terra-cotta warriors found at Xi'an, China.

In the *Volendam*'s three-deck-tall atrium is a monumental crystal sculpture by Luciano Vistosi, one of Italy's leading contemporary glass artists. He also created the towering atrium sculptures of the *Maasdam* and *Veendam*. The centerpiece of the *Zaandam*'s atrium is an impressive pipe organ with mechanical figures of dancing musicians. The organ may be played by hand or operated automatically. Both ships showcase multimillion-dollar art collections, including works created specifically for the vessels by world-class artists.

The theme of *Volendam*'s decor is flowers—from the 17th to 21st centuries—which are featured in public rooms' fabrics, art, doors, and other design elements throughout the ship. Music is the *Zaandam*'s theme, with music-related decor throughout.

HAL invested $1 million to add a closed-loop system for the hearing impaired, Braille directories and directional buttons in the elevators, and large-print menus for the visually impaired. In cabins, light-flashing telephones and bed-shaker alarm systems are available. The *Rotterdam* has 21 wheelchair-accessible cabins (*Amsterdam*, 23); four have connecting doors for accompanying companions. The *Rotterdam* was the second ship of the fleet to install an Internet center.

The *Amsterdam* has distinctive features of her own. The atrium centerpiece is an ornate "Astrolabe" clock tower with a carillon in its base and four different faces: an astrolabe, world clock, planetary clock, and astrological clock. On display near the **Crow's Nest Lounge** is *Four Seasons,* a gold-plated sculpture of four pieces, originally created for the *Nieuw Amsterdam* of 1938 and bought from a private collector. At the lido pool, passengers will see a trio by British sculptor Susanna Holt— two brown bears fishing, their cub nearby.

ITINERARIES *See* Itinerary Index.

CABINS Standard cabins, a roomy 185–195 square feet, are similar to those in the Statendam group. On the *Rotterdam,* another 120 deluxe cabins at 245 square feet have whirlpool bathtubs, VCRs, minibars, refrigerators, and verandas with chaise longues.

Navigation Deck 7 has 40 suites, all with verandas, a private lounge, and concierge where passengers may settle accounts, book shore excursions, and make special requests. The area's glass walls overlook the corridor, but when privacy is wanted, an electric current makes the high-tech glass opaque. Each of four penthouse suites offers living room, dining area and kitchen, bedroom, and dressing areas, and steward's entrance. Two suites are wheelchair-accessible. The *Amsterdam* has 15 more suites than her sibling.

The *Volendam* and *Zaandam* have more deluxe veranda cabins than their sister ships. The penthouse, 28 deluxe suites, and 168 minisuites and deluxe cabins have large verandas, VCR, whirlpool bath, and minibar. All cabins have a sofa, hair dryer, telephone with voicemail and automated wake-up service, music system, and television. They are furnished with twin beds, convertible to a queen size.

Specifications *Rotterdam/Amsterdam,* 133/117 inside cabins, 385/381 outside; 50/36 suites; 160 cabins with verandas; some adjoining cabins. 498 standard cabins with twin beds; 618 with convertible twins or queen beds; 284 with third and fourth berths. No singles. 21 wheelchair-accessible. *Volendam/Zaandam,* 1 penthouse and 28 suites with verandas; 168 deluxe cabins (120 deluxe minisuites) with verandas, 383 standard outside; 136 standard inside; 21 wheelchair-accessible cabins.

DINING *Rotterdam*'s elegant, two-level **La Fontaine Dining Room** spans the Promenade and Upper Promenade Decks. Decor mingles Venetian, contemporary, and baroque designs. Panoramic windows overlook the stern. The ceiling represents a star-filled night sky broken by circles of colored glass. Around the balcony are hundreds of individually lighted Venetian-glass morning glories. On the back wall are two giant murals of waterbirds, recalling *Rotterdam V*'s famous Ritz-Carlton room.

At **Odyssey,** a specialty Italian restaurant, passengers dine by reservation at no extra charge. The opulent room is reminiscent of a Venetian villa, dressed in black with gold-framed mirrors in the ceiling, black and gold columns along the walls, and glass candelabras in alcoves. About 90 people can be seated in three intimate areas. Tables have a movable top that slides forward to ease access to banquettes. The restaurant also serves lunch on days at sea.

In the large, informal **Lido Restaurant,** passengers can enjoy a full breakfast and lunch, including hot dogs and hamburgers grilled to order or make-it-yourself tacos. An ice cream sundae bar, tea, and coffee are available all day. Alternative evening dining is offered several days of every cruise.

The *Volendam*'s impressive, bilevel **Rotterdam Dining Room** at the stern has huge windows and an elegant staircase connecting the two levels. Overhead, six large wrought-iron chandeliers designed by Italian artist Gilbert Lebigre hang from the ceiling; they are lighted by fiber optics. The **Marco Polo,** the *Volendam*'s alternative restaurant, evokes a California-style "artists' bistro." Italian fare, including pasta and pizza, is served in a relaxed setting. Its beechwood walls hold the drawings and etchings—reproductions and originals—of artists ranging from old masters to new talent. The restaurant has its own kitchen and staff and serves lunch and dinner daily; there is no extra charge.

FACILITIES AND ACTIVITIES The *Rotterdam*'s **Ambassador Lounge and Tropic Bar** (Upper Promenade Deck) has a movable wall allowing different configurations. After dinner, the lounge is a large room for dancing; in late evening, it's an intimate piano bar with the piano on a turntable.

Repeat passengers will recognize the ships' traditional collection of small public rooms. The adjoining **Half Moon and Hudson Rooms** accommodate up to 115 people for meetings or parties. **Ocean Bar** has replicas of items from the old Holland America building in Rotterdam; a copy of the sculpture of Henry Hudson's ship, *Halve Maen* ("half moon"), crowns the roof. The larger **Explorers' Lounge** focuses on maritime heritage of Italy and Holland in a large mural of Renaissance Venice. The dance floor is made of Italian marble in a floral pattern.

The **Crow's Nest Lounge** has floor-to-ceiling windows around three quarters of this delightful daytime observation lounge. The room has three sections. To one side is a **Tea Area** decorated with porcelain and silver. To the other is a **Captain's Area,** with leather chairs and old ship models. At center is a circular bar and dance floor that become the nighttime disco.

Queen's Lounge, the two-level main show lounge, has state-of-the-art sound and lighting equipment, a rotating stage, hydraulic lifts, and a dance floor. Deep red, burgundy, and orange decor reflects the opulent age of sea travel. Huge, gold-etched Murano glass chandeliers resemble upside-down umbrellas. Along the room's sides, statues of Moorish guards hold large candelabra. The theater curtain is hand-painted satin in maroon, gold, and black.

Volendam's main show lounge, the two-level **Frans Hals Lounge** in Art Deco design, was inspired by the city of Amsterdam's famous Tuschinski Theater. The multicolored ceiling and colonnades contrast with dark wood walls and huge, colorful ceramic vases. The **Casino Bar,** the ship's sports bar, showcases cinematic memorabilia. On *Zaandam,* the **Casino Bar** spotlights music. The ship also has the cruise line's traditional **Explorer's Lounge, Ocean Bar, Piano Bar, Library, Half Moon Room,** and **Hudson Room**, the last of which serves as a card or meeting room; **Crow's Nest,** which doubles as an observation lounge and nightclub. The **Wajang Theater,** equipped with writing tables and headphones for meetings, has become the venue for the **Culinary Arts Institute** on *Zaandam* and other ships in the fleet that have been refitted for the *Signature of Excellence* program.

On the *Volendam*, the Navigation Deck was extended aft to accommodate additional cabins, and the outdoor swimming pool moved to the Lido Deck. The arrangement provides direct access between indoor and outdoor swimming pools and the **Lido Restaurant.** For *Volendam*'s lido pool area, British artist Susanna Holt created a bronze sculpture of arcing dolphins, similar to those found on other HAL ships.

Another change on these ships that frequent HAL passengers will notice is the funnel design that more closely resembles those of the old *Noordam* rather than the *Rotterdam* or the Statendam group.

The *Volendam* was the first of the fleet to have an Internet center with eight computer terminals and a printer. Open 24 hours, it is staffed from 9 a.m. to noon, 2 to 6 p.m., and 9 p.m. to midnight. The basic charge is $0.75 per minute with a five-minute minimum; other pricing packages are available. Instructions for use are posted on each computer terminal.

SPORTS, FITNESS, AND BEAUTY The ships have a large Steiner-operated spa and fitness center with beauty salon/barber shop, dual saunas and steam rooms, six treatment rooms, juice bar, and a glass-walled exercise room with the latest equipment. The Lower Promenade Deck is a wraparound teak deck, ideal for walking or cooling off in the line's traditional wooden deck chairs. *Zaandam* has received the new **Greenhouse Spa,** similar to those on the Vista class.

All Holland America ships that call at the line's private island, **Half Moon Cay,** already benefit from some *Signature of Excellence* enhancements, such as the new horseback riding and swimming excursion, the stingray adventure, and aqua park with large water "toys" in the shapes of whales, octopi, sharks, and dolphins. The new activities augment the cay's array of excursions—scuba diving, fishing, eco-tours, kayaking, and its water-sports center, children's playground, volleyball, basketball, nature trails, and bird reserve.

CHILDREN'S FACILITIES The Sports Deck has a children's playroom with craft-making areas, video games, and a teen disco. As part of the *Signature of Excellence* program, *Zaandam* has gotten the new facilities of Club HAL (see "Children's Facilities" under the Statendam group for details).

Prinsendam	QUALITY 7	VALUE C
REGISTRY Netherlands	LENGTH 673 feet	BEAM 95 feet
CABINS 398	DRAFT 23.5 feet	SPEED 21.8 knots
MAXIMUM PASSENGERS 793	PASSENGER DECKS 9	ELEVATORS 4
	CREW 443	SPACE RATIO 48

THE SHIP The *Prinsendam* comes to the line with an illustrious history as the *Seabourn Sun* and *Royal Viking Sun,* having been the prize of Cunard's purchase of Royal Viking Line in 1994. After Carnival bought Cunard in 1998, the *Sun* was given a $15 million renovation, renamed, and moved to Seabourn, which turned out to be a mismatch.

When the ship was transferred to Holland America Line in April 2002, Swedish architect Tomas Tillberg, the vessel's original interior designer, and Holland's F. C. J. Dingemans, the architect who has created handsome interiors for all HAL ships in the last two decades, were engaged to oversee major renovations that transformed her into a HAL ship. The *Prinsendam* was named for a sentimental favorite of HAL's loyal passengers that was lost after an accident in Alaskan waters several years ago. The ship emerged with a redesigned interior, new decor, and renamed decks and public rooms to correspond with the other ships in the HAL fleet. Artwork was added, including a frosted and sculptured glass cylinder and wall murals by Bolae for the circular atrium.

The sleek vessel has a sharply raked bow and a beautiful profile, which distinguishes her from the rectangular shape of newer ships. The Finnish-built *Prinsendam* is a spacious ship. Penthouse and deluxe veranda suites are palatial; standard cabins are as large as other ships' suites. Treats include walk-in closets, comfortable lounges, a swim-up bar in the main pool, a lap pool, a spa, and a golf simulator of famous courses; and some unusual features like a same-level gangway for easy access to docks or tenders; air-conditioned tenders with lavatories and catamaran hulls for stability; and two high-speed man-overboard boats. Fine wood and high-quality fabrics are used throughout. Public rooms and facilities are on three center and two top decks.

In early 2005, the *Prinsendam* received some *Signature of Excellence* enhancements, including a Culinary Arts Center and flat-screen televisions in all cabins and suites. The ship already operates a Greenhouse Spa, a Pinnacle Grill, the line's Northwest-themed steak and seafood specialty restaurant, as well as a Neptune Lounge for suite passengers. Since the *Prinsendam* sails longer voyages around the globe and attracts a mature audience, it did not receive expanded youth facilities. Due to space limitations (she is half the size of the Vista-class ships), the *Prinsendam* also does not have the Explorations Café.

ITINERARIES *See* Itinerary Index.

CABINS Cabins are spread over eight decks. Seventeen categories offer four accommodation types: suites, deluxe veranda outside, outside with a large window, and standard inside cabins. All suites and deluxe cabins (more than a third of accommodations) have verandas. HAL spent millions of dollars upgrading cabins. The decor was recently replaced with a new, more modern look in the *Signature of Excellence* style. Dark wood cabinets have a mirrored dresser/desk. When HAL acquired the ship, bathrooms received new sinks, tile, and plumbing repairs, while verandas got new doors, teak decks, and rattan furniture.

All cabins have new flat-screen televisions with CNN, TNT, ESPN, TCM, Discovery, Boomerang, and ship's programming; phone; mini-fridge; locking drawers; safe; hair dryer; refrigerator; and walk-in closets (cruising's first, but not found in wheelchair-accessible cabins). Most bathrooms have tub and shower. All but a few have twin beds convertible to kings, and most have a small sitting area with love seat, table, and chair. Two decks have launderettes. Room service is available 24 hours a day.

The largest, most luxurious suites are on the top two decks. Dividers separate the bedroom and sitting areas. Additional amenities for deluxe cabins and suites include bathrobes, extra-luxurious towels, DVD and video library access, personalized stationery, veranda, and floor-to-ceiling windows. In addition, penthouse and deluxe veranda suites have the private Neptune Lounge, staffed by a concierge, for their exclusive use. They receive afternoon tea and hors d'oeuvres before dinner upon request; a private cocktail party with the captain; an exclusive Indonesian rijstaffel luncheon hosted by the captain and hotel manager; and complimentary corsages and boutonnieres on the first formal night, among other amenities The sole Penthouse Veranda suite was one of the first on a cruise ship to have a whirlpool bath surrounded by picture windows facing the sea. In the 2002 refit, the aft lounge on Promenade Deck was replaced with new lanai cabins complete with private deck area and whirlpool—a new concept for HAL.

Specifications 25 inside cabins, 373 outside including suites; 68 suites; 1 penthouse suite; 151 with verandas; 82 deluxe. Standard dimensions, 191 square feet. 344 outside cabins and suites with 2 lower beds, convertible to kings; 19 suites with 2 lower beds convertible to kings and a sofa bed; 3 single cabins (2 outside, 1 inside); 8 wheelchair-accessible.

DINING *Prinsendam*'s dining room on Lower Promenade Deck has large windows on three sides, providing a panorama of sea and scenery. Passengers are served in two seatings with assigned tables for dinner, and in open seatings for breakfast and lunch. Tables seating two, four, six, or eight are set with fresh flowers, fine china, crystal, and silverware. Menus are similar to those on other HAL ships, with specialties added from the region of the cruise.

A major change that HAL made with her acquisition was the switch from one- to two-seating dining, which means the main dining room no longer needs to seat all passengers at once. However, the Lido Restaurant required expansion. As a result, the forward dining room was reconfigured to include the **Ocean Bar;** an art gallery; an Internet center, and the **Pinnacle Grill at the Odyssey,** the handsome alternative restaurant, featuring steaks, seafood and Pacific Northwest wines. Entrees are prepared on a hot grill to guarantee tenderness and taste. Reservations are required, and a charge of $20 for dinner (only $10 on the first night of a cruise) and $10 for lunch (sea days only).

The **Lido Restaurant** is the venue for casual buffet breakfast, lunch, dinner, and late-night snacks. The variety of food here is impressive and includes a salad bar, soups, hot entrees, carvery, pizzeria, cafe, taco bar, ice cream bar, and dessert area; 24-hour coffee and tea are available. The restaurant, located aft on Lido Deck, has been expanded to both sides of ship with two service lines. A wall of windows overlooks the deck and sea. There's outdoor seating on the terrace, which resembles a sidewalk cafe with a teak floor. The **Terrace Grill** serves hot dogs and hamburgers poolside.

FACILITIES AND ACTIVITIES Promenade Deck holds most of the public rooms, including a casino, the **Explorer's Lounge,** a movie theater showing first-run films, a card room, the library, boutiques, shore excursions office, the 24-hour front desk, and the show lounge. *Prinsendam* offers a program of port and theme lectures similar to those on other HAL ships and has *Signature of Excellence*'s new **Culinary Arts Center** (see *Ryndam* for details).

The redesigned **Queen's Lounge** showroom was given a new stage and state-of-the-art sound and light to bring the facility up to par with newer HAL ships. Production shows feature a cast of seven top-notch entertainers. In front of the stage is a sizable dance floor. Typical of ships built in the 1980s, the lounge has a low ceiling and poor sight-lines from seats in the rear. The **Ocean Bar** with bandstand and dance floor is action central in the evening. Forward of the Ocean Bar is the new **Internet Center,** with 11 flat-screen computer stations; and opposite the center, there's a new art gallery.

The casino offers slot machines and roulette, craps, and blackjack tables. Just outside the casino is the **Java Bar and Café,** one of the ship's most popular spots. It leads to the handsome **Oak Room,** reminiscent of a men's club, with leather chairs in a wood-paneled setting. It's a cozy daytime retreat and popular for after-dinner drinks.

The popular Explorer's Lounge is situated opposite the casino and beside the Java Bar and Café. One of the *Prinsendam*'s loveliest rooms, it has a wall of windows with sea views and is decorated with Dutch etchings. In keeping with the Holland America fleet, there is a massive painting of 17th-century Dutch ships—in this case, being given a royal send-off on a voyage of exploration. Classical music is piped in during the day, and a trio plays classical favorites every evening. The lounge's comfortable leather chairs are popular with passengers who want to read, since the nearby **Erasmus Library** only seats four. Stairs lead to the dining room below. Above the bridge is an observation lounge with 180-degrees of wraparound windows facing the bow. It's a popular perch for watching the world go by wherever the ship may roam. A pianist plays here in the evenings.

SPORTS, FITNESS, AND BEAUTY A wind-sheltered swimming pool on Lido Deck has a whirlpool and swim-up bar and is ringed by a sunning area.

Outdoors are shuffleboard, Ping-Pong, and quoits. A teak deck for walking wraps the Lower Promenade Deck, and an Astroturf jogging track encircles the Sports Deck. The wood-paneled **Golf Club and Pro Shop** on Deck 5 is a cozy hangout for golfers, with comfortable seating and magazines. It has a new, sophisticated golf simulator of 22 courses, including many on the PGA tour (similar to the high-tech simulator on the *Zuiderdam*). A large golf cage is found on Sports Deck (12), but the putting area on that deck has been replaced by a versatile sports court for volleyball, basketball, and tennis.

The **Greenhouse Spa** has a lap pool with two whirlpools and a glass-enclosed fitness facility with toning and cardiovascular equipment. The spa boasts nine treatment rooms and an array of treatment choices. Also available are sauna and beauty salon.

Noordam	**2006**	
Oosterdam	**QUALITY 8**	**VALUE C**
Westerdam	**QUALITY 8**	**VALUE C**
Zuiderdam	**QUALITY 8**	**VALUE C**
REGISTRY Netherlands	**LENGTH** 935 feet	**BEAM** 105.8 feet
CABINS 924	**DRAFT** 24 feet	**SPEED** 22 knots
MAXIMUM PASSENGERS 1,848	**PASSENGER DECKS** 13	**ELEVATORS** 14
	CREW 800	**SPACE RATIO** 46

THE SHIPS Holland America has completed three of the four Vista-class 85,000-ton cruise ships that it is building. The ships take their names from the "vista" points of the compass: *Zuiderdam*, east; *Oosterdam*, south; *Westerdam*, west; and the fourth, *Noordam*, north, is scheduled to debut in January 2006. The "-dam" suffix follows the line's century-old tradition for its passenger ships.

The Vista-class name, selected from an employee contest, is meant to represent the ships' forward-looking design and HAL's future direction with ships that are the most advanced and most luxurious Holland America has ever built. Constructed at the Italian shipyard Fincantieri Cantieri Navali, three ships were delivered between 2002 and 2004, and when the fourth launches, these ships will have more than doubled Holland America's passenger capacity in less than four years.

A more contemporary image—with the use of bright colors (orange, purple, and magenta), suede walls, and jazzy patterns in Holland America's first disco—and such 21st-century amenities as dataports in cabins and a high-tech golf simulator were signals that the *Zuiderdam* was the line's determined effort to attract younger passengers, broaden its base, and lower the average age of its customers—the forerunner of the

$225 million *Signature of Excellence* program which Holland America is now installing fleetwide.

Zuiderdam definitely is a departure from past Holland America ships. Reactions have been mixed. Some people see in it the influence of Carnival Cruises and say it was time for updating the HAL look; others prefer the line's traditional style. Yet, on balance, there's no mistaking that the ship is a Holland America product.

The traditional fresh flowers are still everywhere, and so is the multimillion-dollar art collection and signature HAL rooms like the **Explorers Lounge, Half Moon, Hudson Room,** and **Ocean Bar.** There's also a three-deck-high atrium with Art Deco styling and a fascinating Waterford crystal seahorse suspended from the ceiling.

This trio are HAL's largest ships but carry only 25% more passengers. Passengers benefit by having bigger cabins and more (but not necessarily larger) lounges and other public areas in an asymmetrical layout that reduces the impression of an immense ship.

The vessels' propulsion system includes a full-scale diesel-electric power plant, backed up by a gas turbine as an additional power source, enabling the vessels to operate on diesel or gas turbine power. The ships use the Azipod propulsion system, allowing for greater maneuverability, operating efficiencies, and environmental benefits. Installed on both sides of the vessels are innovative exterior elevators serving ten decks and providing passengers with panoramic sea views.

Other new features include a cabaret-style show lounge as well as a new three-deck main show lounge; a casual "around-the-clock" cafe, an Internet cafe and dataports in all cabins, the largest spa facilities in the fleet, an extensive **Club HAL** children's facility with inside and outside play areas, two interior promenade decks, an exterior covered promenade deck encircling the entire ship, a large lido pool with a retractable dome, and the signature **Crow's Nest** observation lounge.

In 2006, the Vista-class ships will get more *Signature of Excellence* enhancement, although they already have some of them, such as the Pinnacle Grill, the Greenhouse Spa, and the euro-top mattresses.

CABINS One of the most significant differences in the Vista ships is their large number of veranda cabins. Eighty-five percent of the accommodations are outside, and two-thirds have balconies. (By comparison, on the Statendam-class ships, only suites have verandas.) The deluxe veranda outside cabins, the largest category, have 200 square feet, plus a roomy, 54-square-foot veranda. All cabins are furnished with sofas, minibars, hair dryer, safe, and telephone with voicemail and dataport. Most cabins have tubs, an amenity normally found in more costly suites on other lines. There is a Neptune Lounge with a concierge for the exclusive use of penthouse and deluxe veranda suite passengers. In addition to 28 wheelchair-accessible cabins, there is a dedicated elevator for wheelchair users, assistance with tender embarkation, and two tenders equipped with wheelchair-accessible platforms.

Specifications 924 cabins, 623 with verandas. 2 penthouse suites (1,318 square feet), 60 deluxe suites (510–700 square feet), 100 superior suites (398 square feet), 461 deluxe outside (254 square feet). Standard 165 outside (185 square feet), 136 inside (170–200 square feet). 28 wheelchair-accessible cabins.

DINING   The two-story **Vista Dining Room,** the main restaurant, has floor-to-ceiling windows on three sides and two grand staircases. Each level has its own galley, which makes for faster service. On the *Westerdam,* the dining room ceiling is made up of colorful Chihuly-designed glass around the light fixtures.

The large, bright **Lido Restaurant** has been expanded and designed in food-court style, with specialty areas offering made-to-order omelets, deli sandwiches, Italian and Asian specialties, salads, etc. Outside, the large lido pool area is covered by a retractable dome; a sculpture of polar bears is a reminder of Holland America's role in Alaska cruising.

The **Pinnacle Grill** is the ships' specialty, reservations-only restaurant and is twice the size of those on her sister ships, but the decor with elaborate silver chairs and overhead lights is in keeping with their Rococo style. The tables are set with Bulgari china for dining on the featured Pacific Northwest cuisine. There is a $20 per-person charge for dinner (only $10 on the first night of the cruise) and $10 for lunch (sea days only).

FACILITIES AND ACTIVITIES   The ships' new additions are the **Queen's Lounge,** a versatile venue where cabaret-style shows are staged and movies shown; the new **Windstar Café,** which is open 20 hours a day, offering specialty coffees, smoothies, pastries, and snacks; HAL's first disco; and the three-tier, bright red **Vista Lounge,** with a bar near the entrance, an orchestra pit, and $10 million of the latest sound and light equipment, where big production shows are staged. Currently playing are *Stage & Screen* (based on movie musicals) and *Under the Boardwalk.*

Passengers on the *Oosterdam* see *Tommy Tune's Paparazzi,* a multi-million-dollar musical extravaganza created by the nine-time Tony award–winning director, choreographer, dancer, and singer, Tommy Tune; it was the first show he created specifically for a cruise ship. The show, which pays homage to our fascination with celebrities and the photographers who chase them, was added to the *Westerdam* in 2004. As popular as ever is the **Crow's Nest,** the topside observation lounge where passengers escape for quiet by day and dancing by night.

SPORTS, FITNESS, AND BEAUTY   The **Greenhouse Spa,** operated by the Steiner Group, is more than twice the size of the spas on the original Statendam-class ships. It has 11 treatment rooms (including one for couples), a large hydrotherapy pool, and offers features such as a unisex thermal suite with aromatic steam and sauna chambers.

Zuiderdam has a golf simulator (as does *Prinsendam*) that displays 22 renowned golf courses, such as Pebble Beach and Pinehurst No. 2, on a giant projection screen, while a sophisticated computer system tracks players' shots; aspiring linksters actually play the course virtually hole-by-hole and shot-by-shot. Fees start from $30 per person for an hour of golf in a group of three or four. Private lessons are available from the onboard golf pro, with packages starting at $45 for a 30-minute session. Clubs and balls are included. Golf packages for play on the best courses are also available on all Caribbean itineraries.

As noted earlier, all Holland America ships that call at **Half Moon Cay** already benefit from some *Signature of Excellence* initiatives, such as the new horseback riding and swimming excursion and the stingray adventure. The new activities augment the island's array of excursions—scuba diving, fishing, eco-tours, kayaking, and its water sports center, children's playground, volleyball, basketball, nature trails, and bird reserve.

CHILDREN'S FACILITIES The ships already have **Club HAL** facilities, and with the *Signature of Excellence* enhancements to be completed in 2006, they will have new and expanded facilities like those on the *Ryndam*. Teens will have their own area with a lounge for dancing and hanging out, and the **Oasis** will be their own private sun deck, complete with its own waterfall, covered snack areas, and hammocks. Already there are programs for those age 3–7 and 8–12. Among other enhancements is a Port Day program, allowing parents to place kids in Club HAL from 8 a.m. to 5 p.m., including a boxed lunch while their parents go off the ship. Club HAL's After Hours program, from 10 p.m. to midnight, provides baby-sitting for $5 per child per hour.

Norwegian Cruise Line/ NCL America

7665 Corporate Center Drive, Miami, FL 33126
☎ 305-436-4000 or 800-327-7030; fax 305-436-4120
www.ncl.com

TYPE OF SHIPS Modern superliners and new megaliners.

TYPE OF CRUISES Contemporary, mainstream, emphasizing "Freestyle Cruising."

CRUISE LINE'S STRENGTHS
- sports activities
- Freestyle Cruising offering options and flexibility
- variety of dining venues
- nonsmoking cabins
- innovative ships

CRUISE LINE'S SHORTCOMINGS
- loud deck music
- small bathrooms on some ships
- disparate fleet

FELLOW PASSENGERS Norwegian Cruise Line is everyman's cruise line, with attractive ships where anyone can feel comfortable. Passengers, mostly from the United States and Canada, represent all walks of life, including young professionals, families, and seniors. Average household income ranges from $50,000 to $70,000.

Recommended for First-time cruisers, active travelers of all ages who want a fun vacation and like the facilities of a large ship. Repeaters and middle-income travelers. Those who seek an unstructured atmosphere.

Not recommended for Snobs or seasoned travelers with five-star expectations. Sedentary travelers.

CRUISE AREAS AND SEASONS Bahamas, Caribbean, Hawaii, New York–Caribbean year-round; South America, Mexico, winter; Bermuda, Alaska, Europe, spring and summer; New England/Canada, Mediterranean, fall; Panama Canal, May–March and September–October.

THE LINE On December 19, 1966, the *Sunward* sailed from Miami with 540 passengers on the first of three- and four-day cruises to be offered year-round by Norwegian Caribbean Line between Miami and the Bahamas. With this trip, NCL was born. Those cruises—the first packaged for the mass market—are credited with launching modern cruising. Since then, NCL, renamed Norwegian Cruise Line, has played a major role in shaping today's cruises. Within five years of startup, NCL had acquired three

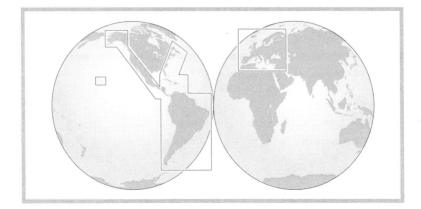

brand-new ships, pioneered weekly cruises to many Caribbean destinations, and introduced a day on a private island in its itineraries—a feature quickly copied by its competitors.

Yet for all these innovations, nothing equaled in excitement and impact NCL's purchase of the *Norway* in 1980. After buying her as the *France* for $18 million, NCL spent $100 million to transform her from a great oceanliner to a Caribbean cruise ship, setting in motion trends that transformed cruising completely.

Later in the decade, a series of costly expansion decisions, including the acquisition of Royal Viking Line and Royal Cruise Line, weakened NCL's debt-encumbered parent company, opening the way for more aggressive lines to take over its pace-setting role. However, by the 1990s, NCL had reinvented itself with a fleet of new ships, introducing superliners with innovations that made NCL a trendsetter once again. Among the most notable were alternative dining; sports bars with broadcasts of ESPN and major sporting events; and separate sitting areas in standard cabins—which is an amenity usually reserved for deluxe accommodations. These innovations soon became standard on new large ships.

In 1997, NCL became the first line to base a ship in Houston for year-round cruises to the western Caribbean. The following year, it became the first mainstream cruise line to base a ship in southern South America (which NCL dubbed Alaska South) for the winter season, sailing on 14-day cruises between Chile and Argentina. NCL also took over two ships of the defunct Majesty Cruise Line; then ordered a 2,000-passenger ship; bought an unfinished hull intended for Costa Cruises (since completed as the *Norwegian Sky*, and now, is NCL America's *Pride of Aloha*); stretched three ships; streamlined the fleet with new names; and bought Orient Lines.

At the dawn of the new millennium, a bidding war between Carnival Cruises and Star Cruises, Asia's major cruise line, ended with Star

Cruises as the sole owner of NCL and Orient Lines. By 2001, NCL's new owners had launched "Freestyle Cruising," an innovative concept challenging many cruise traditions; added a series of megaships, starting with the *Norwegian Sun* and followed by the *Norwegian Star* and *Norwegian Dawn;* and new, year-round cruises of Hawaii.

Now Number Three in the lineup of big cruise companies, NCL once again astonished the cruise world by acquiring Project America's unfinished ships (left abandoned after American Classic Voyages Co. declared bankruptcy in 2001), agreeing to finish their construction. With the help of Hawaii's powerful Senator Daniel Inouye, NCL gained Congressional exemption to reflag NCL's foreign-flagged *Norwegian Sky* to the U.S. ship registry and sail it year-round in Hawaii under the American flag—all in exchange for completing the two Project America vessels, also destined for U.S. flag operations in Hawaii. In turn, NCL created NCL America as its new brand to operate the new U.S.-flagged ships and itineraries within Hawaii.

As a next step, NCL locked up the deal even more completely by buying the two remaining U.S.-registered cruise ships—the *Independence* and the *United States*—saving the latter from the scrap yard for potential U.S. flag operations and undertaking a total reconstruction of the vessel that had sat idle for almost two decades. Now, NCL is undertaking a comprehensive evaluation to decide if it is feasible to rebuild the *United States*, a major job that would likely cost as much as building a new ship. NCL says a decision is not likely before the end of 2005.

Meanwhile, NCL has expanded its Homeland Cruising program with more new U.S. departure ports, such as seasonal cruises from Philadelphia, Baltimore, and Charleston and year-round cruises from New York and Houston. Even with all these development, NCL is not finished. The 77,000-ton *Norwegian Spirit* (formerly Star Cruises' *SuperStar Leo*) was added to the NCL fleet in 2004, while its smaller *Norwegian Sea* departed for Star Cruises. The next 2,400-passenger, 93,000-ton ship, *Norwegian Jewel*, is scheduled to arrive in August 2005, with her twin to follow in 2006.

Then in early 2005, NCL ordered two more new 2,400-passenger Freestyle Cruising ships costing approximately $1 billion. One ship will be built at Meyer Werft in Papenburg, Germany, and delivered in February 2007. The other ship will be built at the Aker Finnyards in Helsinki and delivered in May 2007 with an option for another ship for a 2008 delivery. The Meyer ship will be a copy of the *Norwegian Jewel*, which was built at that yard, and will have 2,384 lower berths, 10 restaurants, an expansive top-of-ship complex of Garden Villas and Courtyard Villas, multiple lounges and bars, and 540 cabins and suites with balconies. The Aker Finnyards' ship is a new design, incorporating the features of the purpose-built Freestyle Cruising ships, but slightly larger in capacity with 2,430 berths. More significant, every outside cabin will have a balcony.

The two new ships will bring to nine the total of new ships introduced by NCL since Star Cruises took control of the company in 2000—an investment of over $3.75 billion. NCL's plan is to transfer all her ships under 70,000 tons to Star Cruises by 2009, while adding a megaliner a year.

THE FLEET	BUILT/RENOVATED	TONNAGE	PASSENGERS
Norwegian Crown	1988/2000/03	34,242	1,078
Norwegian Dawn	2002	91,000	2,224
Norwegian Dream	1992/1998	50,760	1,748
Norwegian Jewel	2005	92,000	2,376
Norwegian Majesty	1992/1999	40,876	1,462
Norwegian Spirit	1999/2004	75,338	1,966
Norwegian Star	2001	91,000	2,240
Norwegian Sun	2001	77,104	2,002
Norwegian Wind	1993/98/2001	50,764	1,748
Unnamed	MAY 2007	92,000	2,384
Unnamed	2008	92,000	2,430
NCL AMERICA FLEET			
Pride of Aloha	1999/2004	77,104	2,002
Pride of America	2005	81,000	2,144
Pride of Hawaii	2006	92,100	2,376

STYLE NCL has always been at the heart of mainstream cruising with attractive ships reflecting contemporary lifestyles and offering a variety of activities for all ages almost around the clock. NCL ships have thoughtful amenities and "signature" items, including a full luncheon buffet served on embarkation, expanded room-service menus, and ice cream parlors and alternative restaurants; the Chocoholic Buffet, a weekly dessert extravaganza; and pool and beach attendants to provide chilled towels on warm-weather cruises. All dining rooms are nonsmoking. In some casinos, some blackjack tables are reserved for nonsmokers. On the newest ships, cabins are equipped for the hearing-impaired. An extensive, year-round children's program includes supervised activities.

Fitness centers—open 24 hours/7 days a week fleetwide—offer fully equipped exercise facilities, aerobics classes, basketball/volleyball courts, and golf practice facilities. Water-sports instruction is combined with experience in ports. All ships have a "Dive-In" snorkeling program and can arrange scuba excursions for certified divers—even in Alaska. Great Stirrup Cay, NCL's private Bahamian island, offers varied activities.

Under its new owners, NCL introduced "Freestyle Cruising" to replace some of cruising's time-honored traditions with flexibility and options. The goal has been to broaden cruising's appeal. Gone are rigid dining hours, assigned seating, and dress codes. Instead, NCL's ships' dining venues (its newest ships offer ten restaurants) have open seating and open dining with continuous service like in a restaurant. Passengers can dine when, where, and with whom they want. The dress code is also optional, from casual to formal, depending on the venue. Other elements of Freestyle Cruising include increased service, with a ratio of almost one crew member per cabin; upgraded cabins; more relaxed disembarkation at the end of a cruise; enhanced enrichment from computer classes to yoga and mountain biking; and a simplified gratuity system.

The *Norwegian Sun* and the *Norwegian Star* were the first to incorporate specific facilities for the new program during their building. The program has been phased in throughout the fleet. Also available fleetwide is wireless access, introduced in 2004.

NCL's latest innovation, rolled out on the *Pride of America* in June 2005, makes selecting a dining venue easier and more convenient. Flat-panel televisions situated around the ship tell passengers how long the wait for dinner will be. The restaurant names are color-coded according to the number of diners and, if the eatery is full, how long the wait will be. if a passenger prefers not to wait, the staff at each of the restaurants can make reservations in another restaurant. The system was tested first on *Norwegian Spirit* and is being added to the new *Norwegian Jewel* and then, to the rest of the fleet.

DISTINCTIVE FEATURES Freestyle cruising, chocoholic buffets, dive program and offbeat excursions in Alaska, single/open seating for many meals; alternative dining; full-scale Broadway shows; and sports bars. Nonsmoking cabins, cabins for hearing-impaired. 24/7 fitness centers, Internet centers, including wireless access. Children/teen programs.

	HIGHEST	LOWEST	AVERAGE
PER DIEM	$297	$76	$167

Per diems are calculated from cruise line's nondiscounted *cruise-only* published fares on standard accommodations and vary by season, cabins, and cruise areas.

RATES Port charges are included.

Special fares and discounts NCL's LeaderShip fares, available through travel agents, are capacity-controlled with discounts up to 50%. Other early-booking fares are also available. NCL's Premium Air Service handles requests for upgrades, stopovers, and flights on specific airlines and air/sea bookings. Requests for deviations must be written or faxed 60 days in advance and they carry a nonrefundable service fee, plus fare differential, if applicable.

- **CHILDREN'S FARE:** Third/fourth person's fares. Children under age 2 free with two accompanying, paying guests.
- **SINGLE SUPPLEMENT:** Guaranteed singles rate, subject to availability.

Packages
- **AIR/SEA:** Yes.
- **PRE/POST:** Yes.
- **OTHERS:** Yes.

PAST PASSENGERS Latitudes, NCL's past passenger club, provides expedited check-in and embarkation at selected ports, a captain's reception, *New York Times* news by fax, special cruises with $200 onboard credit, members' events, gifts, upgrades, discounts on selected cruises, newsletter, and customer service phone line. Members-only promotions are listed on NCL's Web site.

THE LAST WORD In the 1990s, NCL had a litany of problems and financial woes that caused its competitors to outpace it in expansion and innovations. With the deep pockets of its new owners, NCL's future has brightened, and once again, it is a trendsetter with its new direction and new ships with many new features.

   However, one of its new policies does not have our approval. That is NCL's application of a fixed "service charge" to the passenger's shipboard account that cannot be removed or adjusted, as is the case with most other cruise lines. And, it seems inconsistent and confusing to added 15% to bar tabs and spa services and call it a "suggested" gratuity which can be removed or adjusted. The policy is stated in the NCL's brochures under "What you need to know." We can't help but wonder how many passengers actually "read the fine print" and instead, are surprised to find these charges on their bills at the end of their cruise.

Norwegian Cruise Line Standard Features

Officers Norwegian.

Staff Dining and Cabin/International; Cruise/American.

Dining facilities *Majesty and Dream,* three; *Wind,* two; *Spirit,* eight; *Star* and *Sun,* seven; *Dawn,* nine; *Jewel,* ten; *Pride of America, Pride of Aloha,* six—all with open seating, some with charge, $10–$15. Embarkation lunch; Chocoholic, midnight buffets; Le Bistro ($15), Sport Bar & Grill; ice cream parlors; pizzerias; array of specialty restaurants on newest ships.

Special diets Vegetarian, low-salt/calorie, kosher; must be requested 30 days in advance.

Room service 24 hours.

NCL Standard Features (continued)

Dress code Casual for day, informal in evening. One formal night on short cruises, two on seven-day with formal/semiformal attire but with casual dress options as well.

Cabin amenities Phone, refrigerator; some bathrooms with tub, sitting areas in standard cabins on newest ships, television with CNN and ESPN; safe, hair dryers. *Majesty*, ironing board.

Electrical outlets 110 AC. *Majesty,* 110/220 AC.

Wheelchair access All have cabins with bathtubs with grab bars. *Dream, Wind,* 11; *Majesty,* 4; *Sun, Star, Dawn, Jewel,* 20; *Spirit,* 27. Newer ships: Braille indicators for elevator buttons and cabin numbers, electrical hoists for pools and Jacuzzis, tender boats accessible via wheelchair. Older ships: barriers to wheelchairs removed, ramps built. For details on each ship's facilities, contact NCL.

Recreation and entertainment Six or seven lounges, sports bars; Broadway shows, Las Vegas–style revues, comedy; nightclub; disco; casino; library. Wine tastings; singles, honeymooner parties; video arcade.

Sports and other activities Sports Afloat program with golf practice, basketball, volleyball, table tennis. Snorkeling; scuba for certified divers. Private island with rental equipment. Two swimming pools; jogging track.

Beauty and fitness Aerobics, fitness center, sauna, jogging track, barber/beauty salon. Spa on *Dream, Wind, Spirit, Jewel, Sun, Star, Dawn.*

Other facilities Medical, dry cleaning/laundry. Conference. All ships have 24-hour Internet cafe and wireless access; cost is $0.75 per minute, packages available; $3.95 per e-mail. Video e-mail, $4.95 per transmission; computer games, $3.95 per computer game application. Laptop rental, $20 per day.

Children's facilities New and enhanced year-round program for ages 2–17 in four age-specific levels with youth counselors. Children's menus, fares, baby-sitting. *Majesty, Sky, Jewel, Dawn, Star,* kids' splash pool, play room; *Dream, Majesty, Wind, Spirit, Star, Dawn, Jewel,* unlimited soda packages $16, backpack with unlimited soda program $39.50; teen passport, $34.50.

Theme cruises See text.

Smoking Nonsmoking dining room. Nonsmoking sections in public rooms.

NCL suggested tipping NCL automatically applies a service charge to passenger's shipboard account: $10 per passenger per day for those ages 13 and older, $5 per day for children ages 3–12; no charge for children under age 3. These charges, while in line with other cruise lines, are not discretionary and are not removable or adjustable, as is the case with most other cruise lines; additional tipping is not expected or required. However, the 15% added to bar tabs and spa services is a "suggested" gratuity and can be removed or adjusted.

Credit cards For cruise payment and onboard charges: American Express, Visa, MasterCard, Discover.

Norwegian Dawn	QUALITY 9	VALUE B
Norwegian Jewel	(PREVIEW)	
Norwegian Star	QUALITY 8	VALUE B
REGISTRY Panama	LENGTH 965/971 feet	BEAM 106/105/107 feet
CABINS 1,112–1,192	DRAFT 27/28 feet	SPEED 22.5/25/24 knots
MAXIMUM PASSENGERS	PASSENGER DECKS 15	ELEVATORS 12
2,224/2,376/2,240	CREW 1,100–1,154	SPACE RATIO NA

THE SHIPS The $400 million, 91,000-ton megaliner, *Norwegian Star* (formerly slated for Star Cruises as *SuperStar Libra*), was something of a prototype for future NCL ships. In 2001, she joined the *Norwegian Sun* for the first-ever dual cruise-ship christening in Miami. Her name, *Norwegian Star*, was meant to signify the link between NCL and its owners, Star Cruises. Her sister ship, *Norwegian Dawn*, was delivered in December 2002. The third ship, *Norwegian Jewel*, is scheduled to make her debut in Europe in August before arriving in the United States in September 2005.

The trendsetting *Star*, built in Germany, was outfitted to NCL specifications, and as the line's first ship to be based in Hawaii year-round, was tailored to the requirements of the Hawaii market—i.e., no casino. However, a casino (along with other enhancements) was added when the *Star* moved to Alaska in spring 2004. The most noticeable change is the new decorative artwork splashed along her hull—a burst of colorful stars and streamers in green, red, yellow, purple, and aqua running from the bow of the ship to midship. The design is meant to evoke the long-time cruise tradition of passengers throwing streamers from the bow of the ship as the vessel pulls away from the dock to embark on its voyage. Based in Seattle, *Star* became NCL's largest ship sailing in Alaskan waters in summer; in winter, she cruises from Los Angeles to Mexico. Built at the maximum size to pass through the Panama Canal, she and her near-twin, *Norwegian Dawn*, are NCL's largest and fastest ships, with a maximum cruising speed of 25 knots. They have been fitted with pod drives, which greatly improve maneuverability.

ITINERARIES *See* Itinerary Index.

CABINS The ships have set new cruise industry standards in their cabins, with rich cherry wood finishing, tea- and coffeemakers in every cabin, and larger bathrooms than the line's other ships, with toilets, shower, and washstand compartments separated by sliding doors. Seventy percent of cabins are outside, and over 70% of these have balconies.

A steel-and-glass structure on top of the ships, aft from the main sun deck, is a fantasy world, unlike anything on any other vessel today. The *Star* and *Dawn* have two six-room "garden villas," each covering

5,750 square feet and each with a roof terrace and private garden and offering open-air dining, Jacuzzis, and totally private sunning and relaxing areas—all yours for a mere $26,000 per week.

In addition, these ships have two owner's suites, two honeymoon suites, and 30 penthouse suites, and an entire deck of spacious mini-suites with balconies. There are 20 cabins of various categories for disabled passengers. The *Jewel* will have a new configuration.

Most cabins have a sofabed or pop-up trundle bed for a third lower bed and many have a fourth pull-down berth. A large number of cabins (including suites and minisuites) interconnect to create a two-, three-, four-, or five-bedroom area suitable for families.

Specifications 372 standard cabins with balconies, 250 outside; 361 inside; 107 minisuites with balconies; 2 owner's, 2 honeymoon, 30 penthouse suites; 6 multiroom villas; 20 wheelchair-accessible.

DINING In keeping with the line's trendsetting Freestyle Cruising, enabling passengers to dine where, when, and with whom they wish, the ships have up to ten different restaurants offering 11 different menus every night—more dining options than any other ships in the North American market. **Versailles** (**Venetian** on *Dawn*) is an ornate main dining room with floor-to-ceiling windows, offering the traditional six-course cruise dining experience. **Agua** (**Aqua** on *Dawn*) is a contemporary-styled second dining room, with a lighter menu. Both rooms are open 5:30 p.m.–midnight. On *Star*, **Endless Summer** (**Salsa** on *Dawn*), set around the second level of the central atrium, is a Tex-Mex and tapas-style restaurant, offering sangria, tamales, black bean soup with chorizo, enchiladas, quesadillas, and Mexican chocolate mascarpone cheesecake. On *Dawn*, it's **Impressions,** with a 1900s French bistro style. Dining in these three restaurants do not have additional charges.

The *Star's* **Soho,** a high-end Pacific Rim restaurant, features California and Asian fusion cuisine ($15 per person); **Ginza** is a Japanese restaurant ($12.50) with an à la carte section, a sushi bar (all-you-can-eat for $10), and a teppanyaki room (prices on menu). On *Dawn*, the Japanese/Chinese/Thai complex is called **Bamboo** ($12.50) with similar outlets. **Le Bistro** is a French restaurant with nouvelle cuisine and French classics on the menu. The charge is $15 per person. The restaurants with charges require reservations and its wise to reserve early.

The Market (**Blue Lagoon** on *Dawn*) is a food court for hamburgers, fish and chips, pot pies, and wok dishes; and an indoor/outdoor buffet restaurant extending over a third of a deck with "action stations" preparing made-to-order omelets, waffles, fruit soups, ethnic specialties, and pasta as well as an extensive buffet. **La Trattoria,** which takes over a corner of the Market in the evening, offers popular Italian fare and table service. In the *Star's* 2004 conversion, **Las Rambles,** a Spanish tapas restaurant was replaced by **Cagney's Steak House**—NCL's first steakhouse when it appeared on the *Dawn*—with a 1930s theme and a $20 per-person cover charge.

Garden Café, a buffet with food stations offering prepared-to-order omelets, pasta, soups, and ethnic specialties, doubles as a kids' cafe with an area that has small seats and tables. The *Star* also has an outdoor grill, an ice cream bar, and a coffee shop, plus 24-hour room service.

FACILITIES AND ACTIVITIES One of the ships' most distinctive attractions is the show lounge, spanning three decks without obstruction and seating 1,150 people. Among the offerings, passengers might get to watch *It's Fame* and *Cirque Asia,* with the incredible feats of Chinese acrobats showcasing the cultures and tradition of the Pacific. The *Star*'s biggest change was the addition of the **Star Club Casino,** which was installed where Dazzles Nightclub had been. It offers blackjack, baby baccarat, roulette, three-card poker, Caribbean stud poker, and craps as well as some games other lines don't have, such as pai-gow poker, pai-gow tiles, and even a big baccarat table (available only by special request prior to sailing). Also available is a new electronic player tracking system that logs each passenger's play and rewards them for it. The card records players earnings and offers various rewards, including onboard amenities, credit applied to their onboard account, reduced rates for future cruises and even a complimentary cruise if the level of play is high enough.

On *Dawn*, passengers are treated to two shows. *South Beach Rave!*, meant to reflect the energy and excitement of Miami's hot South Beach, has DJs from the popular Miami television show Deco Drive manning the controls, plus red-hot radio personality Nikki Night from Miami's Y-100-FM. *Rave!* rocks as musicians appear from every corner of the theater, together with horn players, guitarists, and drummers, combining for a pastiche of Latin sounds. *Bollywood* is a celebration of India's traditional film culture, founded on spontaneous song and dance. Bombay nights come alive when the audience enters the theater as the scents of spices, incense, and perfumes fill the air. Bright sarongs and turbans combine to create a tapestry of color as stilt-walkers, magicians, and jugglers assemble to present the story. Aerialists wrapped in silks, belly dancers, and snake charmers perform against the Taj Mahal in the background.

Under an exclusive partnership with the famed Second City improv troupe, six performers stage a comedy revue aboard *Norwegian Dawn* on each of her round-trip sailings from New York City. In addition to performing one night each sailing, the inventive and hilarious Second City ensemble hosts onboard workshops introducing the art of improvisation to *Dawn* passengers, exploring their artistic voices and providing the techniques needed to express those voices. The troupe also gives workshops designed especially for children. In fall 2005, Second City will begin appearing on *Norwegian Jewel* when the ship is in the Caribbean.

The *Star* has a cabaret lounge, karaoke bar with a large screen, a cigar lounge, wine cellar, champagne bar, a beer garden, an atrium cafe for coffee and pastries, an English pub, an attractive card room and library, and an Internet cafe with 16 stations. There is also a cinema/auditorium, four adjoining meeting rooms, gift shop and department store, and a wedding chapel.

The *Norwegian Dawn* has these attractions too, but its most distinctive feature is the high-quality art on loan from Star Cruises Chairman Tan Sri Lim Kok Thay's personal collection. These include paintings by Vincent van Gogh, Henri Matisse, Claude Monet, and Pierre-Auguste Renoir—all of which have been exhibited in such famous museums as the National Gallery of Art in Washington, D.C., and the National Museum in Stockholm.

Another distinction for the *Norwegian Dawn:* She is the only ship offering seven-day cruises from New York to the Bahamas and the Caribbean on a year-round basis. Highlighting this itinerary, the ship stages "Ifuacata!" parties with hot Latin rhythms and special food and drinks. "Ifuacata!" has been called the hottest party trend in Miami and is named after the Spanish word meaning "to be hit by the unexpected."

Another distinction: NCL was the first cruise line to offer wireless Internet access (WiFi) fleetwide. Passengers who bring their laptops can rent a wireless network card for $10 a day; laptops can be rented for $20 a day. Wireless Internet access costs $0.75 per minute, though buying minutes in bulk—33-, 100-, or 250-minute packages—can bring the cost down to $0.40 per minute. The wireless service functions best in certain areas of each ship, but it normally enables poolside surfing as well as access in meeting rooms and some other public areas. Now, too, NCL offers the use of cell phones at sea.

SPORTS, FITNESS, AND BEAUTY   The main pool is located amidship on Deck 12. Aft is the bilevel spa and fitness center, with a waterfall in the atrium of its reception area and an indoor pool that is said to be the longest on any cruise ship. The fitness center has state-of-the-art, cardiovascular workout equipment, aerobic and boxercise area with a sprung wooden floor, steam and sauna rooms, a jet-current exercise pool, whirlpool, and hydrotherapy facilities. The spa is operated by Mandara, one of the world's leading operators of resort spas and featured on all of NCL's ships, is in charge of pampering with an exotic menu of treatments combining Asian and Eastern techniques. On the *Dawn*, the 11,302-square-foot **El Dorado Spa** has 21 treatment rooms, with one designed exclusively for couples. There are private hydrotherapy baths, a lap pool, a Jacuzzi, two Japanese pools, sauna, and a steam room in both the men's and women's areas. Passengers may also have spa treatments in their cabins, poolside and on-deck massages on port days, and massage and de-stress treatments on secluded beaches during private island visits.

The Sports Deck has an outside jogging track, golf driving range, volleyball, and basketball court. To complement the ships' facilities, an array of active shore excursions are available, including mountain biking, sailing, and scuba diving.

CHILDREN'S FACILITIES   The ships have huge children's centers, complete with a playroom, outdoor pool, movie theater, computer rooms, teen center, video arcade, a nursery, and toddlers' nap room. There is even a special children's area in the buffet restaurant, where kids have their own low-level serving counter and kid-sized tables and chairs. *Norwegian Dawn,* constructed with families in mind, also has the **T-Rex Childcare Center,** a supervised facility with a jungle gym; a children's playroom; **Flicks Movie Theater, Clicks,** a computer learning center equipped with five terminals; **Doodles** arts and crafts area; and **Snoozes** sleeping area. A highlight is the **T-Rex Pool,** a Jurassic-themed children's pool with dino-riffic water slides, a kids-only hot tub, and a paddling and wading pool for the little ones. The **Teen Club** is a disco strictly for teens, with a video wall showing the latest music video hits, a cinema, and **Video Zone,** a huge arcade with 25 of the latest video games. NCL has eight special menus for the most finicky young eaters, including kid-size hamburgers, hot dogs, spaghetti, chicken fingers, and ice cream sundaes.

In NCL's year-round "Kid's Crew" program-coordinators plan and supervise daily activities. An NCL brochure lists activities for four age groups: Junior Sailors (ages 2–5), First Mates (6–9), Navigators (10–12), and Teens (13–17). At sea, the hours are 9 a.m.–noon; 2–5 p.m., and 7–10 p.m. First evening of cruise, 8–10 p.m. Port days, 7–10 p.m. Group-sitting in port is available from 9 a.m.–5 p.m. for a nominal charge. Children under age 2 sail free. For baby-sitting, inquire from cruise line prior to departure.

Kids meet the captain at a Coke-tail party; for the masquerade ball, they receive help in making costumes. Activities include dances and arts and crafts. There are races, treasure hunts, and games planned for the day at the beach. The ship publishes *Kids' Cruise News* and *Teen Cruise News* daily. Also available are ice cream bar and children's menus. The Kids Soda package gives unlimited soda-fountain access for $8 on a three-day cruise or $16 for seven days. A Kids' Backpack provides baseball cap, luggage tags, T-shirt, and more for $28–$39.50, depending on cruise length. "Teen Passport" for teens ages 13–17 enables them to purchase a coupon book for $34.50 to be used for up to 20 nonalcoholic specialty drinks, as well as enjoying exclusive dance and pizza parties and a farewell "Frat Party."

Norwegian Spirit	(PREVIEW)	
Norwegian Sun	QUALITY 8	VALUE B
REGISTRY Bahamas	LENGTH 881/848 feet	BEAM 106/108 feet

CABINS 985/1,000	DRAFT na/26 feet	SPEED 24/23 knots
MAXIMUM PASSENGERS	PASSENGER DECKS 12/11	ELEVATORS 13/12
1,966/2,400	CREW 965/768	SPACE RATIO NA/38

THE SHIPS *Norwegian Sun* arrived in 2001, following her sister ship, *Norwegian Sky*, which is now NCL America's *Pride of Aloha*. The handsome interior, created by Swedish marine architects Tillberg Design, is one of cool elegance. In the glass-domed, eight-deck atrium and throughout the ship, there is no glitz or bright lights, but rather an airy, refined setting with a multimillion-dollar art collection integrated into the decor.

The reception and purser's desks, concierge, and shore excursion offices are on Atlantic Deck. Neptune's Court, a second atrium, has a grand staircase just outside the **Seven Seas Dining Room,** connecting Atlantic Deck to Promenade and International Decks with the main show lounge. The *Norwegian Sun* was the first of the fleet to have NCL's Freestyle Cruising elements included during the building. Among them are more dining options—nine restaurants (some with surcharge or pay-as-you-go). They include three dining rooms, an outdoor buffet, an indoor garden buffet, pizzeria, and wine bar, the NCL signature **Sports Bar & Grill, Le Bistro,** an ice cream bar, and champagne and cigar bars.

Among other new features, *Norwegian Sun* has a "lifestyle area" for classes in computers, financial planning, yoga, and so on; a wedding chapel; a larger gym and spa than NCL's earlier ships; larger cabins, and a new cabin category—minisuites with balconies.

At the **Internet Café,** now available on all NCL ships, passengers can go online 24 hours a day. Ship's photographers have digital cameras, enabling passengers to e-mail photos home (for an additional fee). A "Skycam" on the bridge is downloaded onto a Web site so family members ashore can track the voyage. Other facilities include the Atrium Room, available for small private functions, and a medical center.

In a joint venture, dutyfree.com and Colombian Emeralds International manage *Norwegian Sun*'s gift shops. Passengers view patterns and designs at a kiosk, with home delivery available. Liquor selections, displayed in the shopping arcade, can be ordered through room service.

Norwegian Spirit (formerly Star Cruises' *SuperStar Leo*), added to the fleet in 2004, is not a twin of the *Sun*, but a close relative in her features and facilities. She has the same Freestyle Cruising elements, such as ten restaurants, a large spa and fitness center, and a 24/7 Internet cafe, among others.

ITINERARIES *See* Itinerary Index.

CABINS Cabins are similar to those on other NCL ships and are furnished with two lower beds that convert to a queen, a sitting area, dressing table, refrigerator, safe, television, radio, and telephone. Those on the

Sun have bathrooms with duvet. Other than the penthouses and owner suites, all cabins are uniform in size and efficiently laid out. Closet space is adequate. All cabins have Internet hookups. Sixteen penthouses with teakwood furnished balconies have butler service and an exclusive room service menu for breakfast, lunch, and dinner.

The *Sun*, with more than 100 additional outside cabins (67% in total) than her former twin, has larger cabins and 30 minisuites with balconies, measuring 267 square feet. Four owner's suites, located forward above the ship's bridge, have 828 square feet each.

Specifications Norwegian Spirit, 983 cabins. 591 outside cabins with 374 balconies; 374 inside; 16 penthouse suites; 4 wheelchair-accessible. *Norwegian Sun,* 675 outside (145–221 square feet), 325 inside (167–176 square feet), 52 suites with balconies (436 square feet); 16 doubles, 185 triples, 779 quads; 20 wheelchair-accessible.

DINING Both the *Spirit* and *Sun* reflect the Freestyle Cruising's concept with their dining options. On a seven-day cruise, passengers never need to eat dinner in the same restaurant more than once, if they care to pay extra in some of the eateries. Among their choices, they can enjoy either of two main dining rooms, **Four Seasons** and **Seven Seas** on the *Sun*, with open seating from 5:30 p.m. to midnight every evening; a more formal Italian restaurant, **Il Adagio** ($12.50), by reservation; French fare at **Le Bistro** ($15); a Pacific Rim restaurant complex with a sushi bar and teppanyaki room; a California/Asian fusion restaurant ($10–$15); a 24-hour indoor/outdoor cafe with food stations serving hamburgers, hot dogs, soups and salads; and a "healthy living" restaurant with a lighter, more contemporary menu, including selections from *Cooking Light* and spa menus. Note, however, that some of these restaurants have a surcharge, and some are pay-as-you-go.

Shogun, *Spirit*'s Asia complex ($12.50), has a show kitchen at the entrance where passengers are visually introduced to traditional styles of preparation. At **Maxim's,** a traditional steakhouse ($20), they can enjoy certified Angus beef, veal, pork, lamb, seafood and grilled chicken.

The casual **Great Outdoor Restaurant** and **Garden Café** (**Raffles Buffet Terrace** on *Spirit*) have "food action stations" serving up paella, sushi, Norwegian waffles, pasta, and more, intended to eliminate long buffet lines. Both cafes offer breakfast, lunch, and snack specialties that vary daily. There is a pizzeria and **Sprinkles Ice Cream Bar.** The 24-hour room-service menu offers pizza, too. **Blue Lagoon** on *Spirit* is a 24-hour food court serving hamburgers, fish and chips, pot pies and wok fast dishes and includes a buffet for kids with small seats and tables.

Passengers give the ship's cuisine, especially the alternative dining options, good reviews. The only dining disappointment is breakfast and lunch in the pool deck cafe for the lack of variety.

FACILITIES AND ACTIVITIES   The ships have similar bars, including a **Champagne Bar,** by the atrium with large glass windows and a view of the lobby area, serving champagne and premium vodkas along with caviar and pâté de foie gras. A modest but respectable half-bottle of Veuve Clicquot with pâté de foie gras accompaniment is a mere $40–$50; if you go for the works, a bottle of Dom Perignon with sevruga caviar and pâté will run you about $150.

Nonsmoking guests can select from the martini menu in the **Windjammer Bar,** and cigar connoisseurs enjoy freshly hand-rolled stogies and premium brandy behind the glass walls of the adjoining but segregated **Cigar Club** with humidor. The **Coffee Bar** has a great selection of coffees, tea, and liqueurs at fair prices, and serves pastries and cookies. *Spirit* also has the Bier Garten offering beer and cocktails and Bavarian food, such as Weisswurst and pretzels.

Sun Club Casino offers blackjack, roulette, Caribbean poker, and slot machines. Now playing in the golden, two-deck **Stardust Lounge** (**Moulin Rouge** on *Spirit*) with a proscenium stage is *Hey Mr. Producer: The Musical World of Cameron Mackintosh,* which highlights the legendary musicals Mackintosh produced, including *Cats, Miss Saigon, Les Miserables,* and *The Phantom of the Opera*. With the venue's sound, lighting, and audiovisual facilities, can be easily transformed into a disco.

Dazzles Lounge has what NCL claims is the longest bar at sea. Passengers may choose cabaret acts, illusionists, comedians, and on some cruises, the wildly popular jazz and pop show of *Jane L. Powell & Company*. The entertainment is uniformly of high standard in keeping with the NCL tradition.

The *Sun* also has a wedding chapel for ceremonies in port, a library, and the **East Indies Conference Center,** which seats 100 and can be divided into three smaller rooms.

On the Pool Deck, the **Topsider's Bar** is a long poolside bar with stools and outdoor tables; on the Sports Deck, the **Sports Bar** offers televisions with videotaped and live broadcasts of sporting events. The **Observatory Lounge** has floor-to-ceiling windows overlooking the bow. Roaming the decks is a "Skymobile" beverage cart making drink deliveries to passengers. When the ships sail in the Caribbean, pool attendants provide Evian water, suntan lotion, cold face towels, and fresh fruit.

NCL racked up another first in 2004 when it began offering onboard cell-phone service on the *Norwegian Sun*. The new technology is expected to be available fleetwide within the year. The service is available to most passengers with GSM phones that operate at 900 MHz and 1900 MHz. Consumers are charged by their cellular wireless providers at the roaming rates set by their carriers.

SPORTS, FITNESS, AND BEAUTY The two swimming pools are connected by steps and a central wading platform to four hot tubs and set off by dark wood decks and dark green lounge chairs. Also on the enormous Sun Deck is a **Spa** with therapists trained in a wide range of treatments. It has a unisex beauty salon and a gym/aerobics area with exercise equipment; exercisers can enjoy ocean views through floor-to-ceiling glass walls.

On *Sun*'s Sports Deck, passengers will find two golf driving nets, a full-size basketball/volleyball court, a batting cage, and shuffleboard. A walking and jogging track circles the Promenade Deck. *Spirit*'s Sports Deck is similar with four golf driving nets.

CHILDREN'S FACILITIES **Kids Korner** playroom on International Deck offers "Kid's Crew," a year-round, supervised program divided into four age groups; see "Children's Facilities" in the *Norwegian Star* section for details. A kids' splash pool is on Sports Deck. "Teen Passport" for teens ages 13–17, enabling them to purchase a coupon book for $34.50, to be used for up to 20 nonalcoholic specialty drinks, as well as enjoying exclusive dance and pizza parties and a farewell "Frat Party." *Spirit*'s **Teen Club** includes a disco for teenagers; the video arcade has 70 of the latest video machines. Its children's **Pirate** theme pool area has a wading pool and two small slides. See *Norwegian Star* for details of children's program.

SHORE EXCURSIONS In Alaska, NCL offers some of mainstream cruising's best offbeat excursions, such as glacier hiking, mountain biking, forest trekking, a six-hour hike outside Skagway, and three hours of sea kayaking from Juneau (you're likely to see a whale close enough to feel its spray). Flight-seeing from Juneau to a remote lodge showcases vast ice fields. The more exotic tours have few slots; book early. Among the most popular is "Dive Into Adventure," for snorkeling and scuba diving. It's active and attracts a variety of passengers. Plus, few people can say they have been diving in Alaska. At excursion's end, participants shiver out of wet suits and jump into the heated pool on Sun Deck.

Note: Alaska shore excursions are expensive on every cruise line because of the very short season in which operators have to make money and the very high costs of operating tours in Alaska.

Norwegian Dream	**QUALITY 5**	**VALUE C**
Norwegian Wind	**QUALITY 5**	**VALUE C**
REGISTRY Bahamas	**LENGTH** 754 feet	**BEAM** 94 feet
CABINS 874	**DRAFT** 22 feet	**SPEED** 21 knots
MAXIMUM PASSENGERS 1,748	**PASSENGER DECKS** 10	**ELEVATORS** 11/10
	CREW 700	**SPACE RATIO** 29

THE SHIPS The twin ships, *Norwegian Dream* and *Norwegian Wind,* were designed for people who want to know they're on a ship at sea. At almost every turn, glass walls frame the ocean and connect with the outdoors—a link that many modern cruise ships have lost. But these ships, breaking the mold on design, have unusual features inside and out. All five upper decks are open and slant downward to create a profile more sleek than those of most large new ships.

The ships have identical interiors; even names of decks, public rooms, and suites are the same. The comfortable, contemporary settings are the work of well-known Norwegian designers Petter Yran and Bjorn Storbraaten. Quality fabrics, fine woods, marble, and brass trim translate to casual elegance. Windows and use of glass bring the outdoors into the indoor decor. Light floods the interiors, giving them a lively atmosphere.

In early 1998, both ships were stretched 130 feet, and all cabins and most public rooms were refurbished. Lengthening resulted in a sleeker, more hydrodynamic profile, one captain says. The new sections increased the ships' lengths to 754 feet, their passenger capacity from 1,246 to 1,748, and added 251 cabins, but the space ratio decreased, surrendering some of the ships spaciousness.

Lengthening also resulted in a new entrance and lobby and 12 new owner's suites; expansion of the **Four Seasons Dining Room;** a larger casino and nightclub; an enlarged fitness center and spa; new children's playroom; new coffee bar and lounge; splash pool, wet bar, and two whirlpools; outdoor cafe and pizzeria; and three new passenger elevators. Show lounges and bars received additional seating, and the shopping arcade nearly doubled.

The striking new entrance on the Promenade Deck has a Nordic motif in blue and gray with wood blinds, marble accents, and Art Deco lighting. Here are a 24-hour reception desk, information and concierge desks, the purser's office, and shore excursion and "Dive In" desks. Most innovative are the dining rooms—four instead of the traditional one or two. The rooms have multiple tiers, creating more intimate settings and enabling all diners to enjoy panoramas through acres of windows.

Topside, the tiered Sun Deck becomes an amphitheater for evening entertainment. The former Sports Bar on the *Norwegian Dream* has been replaced with a buffet restaurant.

ITINERARIES *See* Itinerary Index.

CABINS The ships offer 15 categories; almost all are on the lower five of the vessels' ten decks. All portside cabins are nonsmoking; 16 cabins are equipped for the hearing-impaired, and 11 are wheelchair-accessible.

Unusual in the midprice ships, 85% of cabins are outside with large windows; standard cabins are larger than average; all have a sitting area with table and sofa chair or love seat that converts to a third bed; and a curtain separates sleeping and living areas.

There are some trade-offs. Bathrooms are small, particularly the shower stall, and storage space is insufficient. Space around beds is tight, but separate sitting and sleeping areas compensate. Almost all cabins have twin beds that convert into a queen; television with CNN and ESPN; radio; telephone; and hair dryer.

Passengers in International Deck cabins, added when the ships were lengthened, must access them through the **Four Seasons Dining Room,** which was expanded across the ship's girth. Otherwise, these passengers must detour up or down a deck.

Owner's suites measure 336 square feet and accommodate up to five people. Located on the Sun Deck, each has a separate bedroom and living room with convertible double sofa, television, stereo system, refrigerator, and balcony. Bathrooms have a tub and shower and entrances from both hall and bedroom. Other top-category suites also have balconies; most have refrigerators and floor-to-ceiling windows. They're served by an attentive concierge who provides complimentary amenities, including wine and hors d'oeuvres.

Specifications 179 inside cabins, 695 outside; 18 owner's suites; 52 penthouse suites with balcony; 62 suites. Standard outside dimensions, 152 square feet. Most cabins have 2 lower beds convertible to queen; some have third and fourth berths. 1 single; 13 wheelchair-accessible; 16 hearing-impaired.

DINING Each of the three main dining rooms has its own personality and setting; the fourth is an informal dinner cafe. All have the same menus, and food comes from a central kitchen. The diverse, distinctive settings make dining more fun and interesting, and open seating enables passengers to meet.

The three levels of **Terraces** are separated by greenery and connected by twin stairways. Some passengers say the arrangement suggests a supper club in vintage Hollywood movies. A mural covers the back wall, and a wall of glass allows splendid views.

The **Four Seasons Dining Room,** extending side-to-side in the ship, is the largest dining room. Floor-to-ceiling bay windows extend over the water and offer spectacular views. Four terraced areas provide excellent sight lines. Sun Terraces, the smallest dining room, is casually appointed in light wood and wicker. It's set on three narrow terraces with walls of glass on three sides that extend overhead. Shades protect diners when the sun is above. The view is across the aft swimming pool to the sea.

Le Bistro, the alternative restaurant, is open to all passengers on a first-come, first-served basis. The cozy, informal cafe offers a daily pasta dish prepared tableside and other light fare. Wine by the glass is available. The **Coffee Bar and Lounge** is designed as a coffee house, with such memorabilia as antique coffee machines on display. Coffee and coffee-flavored drinks are served. The area, with curved walls and quiet niches, incorporates the ship's library and card room.

The former Sports Bar has been replaced with a buffet restaurant as part of the ships' transformation to incorporate "Freestyle" dining.

Free ice cream and frozen yogurt are available poolside each afternoon. The Sun Deck splash pool has a semicircular "wet bar." Nearby, the casual **Outdoor Café and Pizzeria** serves breakfast and lunch buffets and snacks. If you aren't watching calories and are willing to stand in long lines, you can pig out at the one-night Chocoholic Buffet.

SERVICE The ships are praised for good cabin service, but complaints about service in dining areas are not uncommon.

FACILITIES AND ACTIVITIES Daytime activities include art auctions, bingo, dance classes, bridge tours, culinary demonstrations, and pool and parlor games. We repeat our warning: At art auctions, know what you're buying. Bargains are rare, despite the sales pitch. A conference center on Sun Deck accommodates 60 people and can be divided into two spaces. An Internet cafe with computer terminals is available on the International Deck; fees apply.

Fabulous entertainment is the cruise highlight. Passengers often give the shows standing ovations. *Dreamgirls* was the opener for the *Norwegian Dream,* and the ship has featured *42nd Street* in the **Stardust Lounge,** the main showroom. On alternate nights there are Las Vegas–style variety shows. The room is well laid-out in four tiers, providing comfortable seats and clear sight lines. The lounge has a dance floor, and dance music may be provided.

The Art Deco casino, dressed in hot magenta and black, offers blackjack, Caribbean stud poker, craps, roulette, "Let It Ride," and 158 slot machines. Adjacent to the casino is **Dazzles** nightclub, which has a circular granite bar, a circular dance floor, and curved sofas in velvet Harlequin patterns. **Lucky's** piano bar has a dance floor and is popular after the show.

Other nighttime action takes place on the Sports Deck, anchored forward by the **Observatory Lounge** with floor-to-ceiling windows—an ideal spot for viewing Caribbean sunsets or the Alaskan wilderness. Open decks are sometimes used for outdoor parties. The informal **Rendezvous Lounge,** next to Four Seasons Dining Room, is a good meeting spot.

SPORTS, FITNESS, AND BEAUTY Sports and fitness programs are offered year-round. The Sports Deck is a mecca for active passengers. Golf instruction and a driving range, plus two outdoor pools, are available. Upstairs on Sky Deck is the basketball and volleyball court. The International Deck offers a small pool.

The **Health Spa and Fitness Center** on the Sports Deck has been enlarged to accommodate a full-service spa with eight treatment rooms for massage therapy, herbal wraps, and facials. A weight room has Cybex training equipment. Aerobics and other exercise classes balance excesses at the Chocoholic Buffet. A wide walking/jogging track wraps around Promenade Deck. The beauty salon is next to the observation lounge.

Tiered teak decks, separated by decorative greenery, are a sunbathers' and people-watchers' delight at the forward pool. It's an innovative design, but it's noisy. On some evenings, the area hosts outdoor events and dancing.

Snorkeling instruction is offered at sea, and hands-on experience is available in ports of call. The Alaskan dive program is a hit.

CHILDREN'S FACILITIES **Kids Korner** playroom is the base for NCL's fleetwide, year-round "Kid's Crew" program. See *Norwegian Star* for details.

Norwegian Crown	QUALITY 7	VALUE B
REGISTRY Bahamas	LENGTH 614 feet	BEAM 92.5 feet
CABINS 552	DRAFT 24 feet	SPEED 20 knots
MAXIMUM PASSENGERS 1,104	PASSENGER DECKS 10	ELEVATORS 4
	CREW 525	SPACE RATIO 32.6

THE SHIP After three years with Orient Lines, NCL's sister company, the *Crown Odyssey* came home to NCL in 2003 and resumed its former name as the *Norwegian Crown,* following a multimillion-dollar refurbishment that added three new restaurants and converted the ship into a Freestyle Cruising vessel with a new look—a white hull—on the outside and many changes on the inside.

Built in 1988, the spacious ship was widely acclaimed for her quality decor by the highly regarded design team of A. and M. Katzourakis. A modern interpretation of classic architectural elements with stunning Art Deco details, the decor in public rooms uses generous amounts of marble, fine woods, original art, antiques, chrome, mirrors, stained glass, smoked glass, reflective ceilings, and brass finishes.

Prior renovations included a redesigned Lido Deck with the addition of an Internet and e-mail center, library, card room, and main lobby. On Marina Deck, a central foyer houses the reception desk, shore excursion office, shop, and a small gallery with fine antique reproductions leading to Seven Continents Restaurant.

At the foot of a circular grand staircase connecting the reception area and Odyssey Deck is a six-foot spherical sculpture in bronze by Italian artist Arnaldo Pomodoro. A mosaic of backlighted stained-glass panels in geometric patterns extends the height of the ship's stairwells.

The *Norwegian Crown*'s sailings from Philadelphia and New York to Bermuda in summer, are part of the line's expanded "Homeland Cruising" program. Afterwards, she sails from Miami to Santiago, Chile, to repeat her former South America series between Santiago and Buenos Aires.

ITINERARIES *See* Itinerary Index.

CABINS *Crown* offers 18 categories on seven decks. About 78% are outside cabins, and more than half of the bathrooms have tubs. Most cabins are large; even the smallest have 154 square feet and the same basic amenities. All have full vanities, two mirrored closets, tie and shoe racks, safe, hardwood furniture and cabinetry, locked drawers, good lighting, and contemporary art. Bathrooms are marble or tiled and have large mirrors, recessed shelves, and hair dryers. Many bathtubs are mid-size. All cabins have direct-dial phones and television with CNN and satellite channels. Four new suites on the Penthouse Deck were added in the most recent renovations, as well as nine new inside passenger cabins.

All penthouse suites have private verandas, a sitting room with a sofabed, refrigerator, walk-in closet, queen or convertible twin beds; marble bathroom with whirlpool tub, and butler service. Four apartments can be combined with adjacent units to provide more than 1,000 square feet. Glass partitions separate sitting and sleeping areas. Beds in the Superior AB Suite category fold into the wall to create a meeting room. The suites on Penthouse Deck have butler and concierge service; those on the other decks have only concierge service.

Specifications 116 inside cabins, 319 outside; 20 penthouse suites with verandas; 20 deluxe suites; 34 junior suites. Standard dimensions, 165 square feet. 284 double cabins; 150 triples; 82 quads; no singles; 32 connecting outside cabins. 4 wheelchair-accessible.

DINING *Norwegian Crown* boasts six restaurants. **Le Bistro,** NCL's popular signature alternative restaurant on the Lido Deck, decorated in coral, green and gold colors, has large, comfortable wood banquettes, classic chairs from France, and etched glass; the **Pasta Café,** high up on the top deck, has modern Italian decor accented by cobalt-blue and cherry wood, and a blue-granite-topped bar where passengers can watch the chefs prepare Italian cuisine; and **Chopsticks,** an Asian-themed restaurant, next to the **Yacht Club** on Odyssey Deck.

The main dining room, the elegantly appointed **Seven Continents Restaurant,** is a two-level room with a sunken central section under Tiffany-style glass domes. It's trimmed with lacquered woods, glass panels, and picture windows. There are two seatings, with open seating for breakfast and lunch and assigned for dinner. Spa cuisine is available. The dining room can be noisy due to the glass ceiling that reverberates the sound. It does benefit from very large windows and has two recessed side sections—the most desirable seats.

The Yacht Club serves as a dining venue for buffet breakfast and lunch with both indoor and outdoor dining. **Café d'Italia** is an al fresco dining venue for lunch aft on Penthouse Deck.

FACILITIES AND ACTIVITIES Daily activities include the Discovery Lecture Series, deck sports, bingo, bridge, dance classes, art, cooking demonstrations, and wine-tasting classes. In addition to Le Bistro, the renovated Lido Deck aft has new **Kids and Teen Centers,** as well as the **Internet Café,** library, and game room. The Lido Bar was expanded to include the original outside area.

Evening entertainment is offered in the multitiered, Art Deco **Stardust Lounge,** where smoky gray mirrors create a sound-wave design in the tiered ceiling. Opaque crystals in Lalique-style glass panels continues the effect on the back wall. A sloping floor gives almost every seat good sight lines. The stage can be lowered to become a dance floor, and the intimate **Rendezvous Bar** next door is popular for cocktails. The **Monte Carlo Court Casino** received a complete renovation, adding glass walls around the perimeter and new upholstery and carpets in rich maroon and gold. The casino offers blackjack, roulette, Caribbean poker, and slot machines.

The ship's crowning glory, you might say, is the **Top of the Crown,** a circular observation lounge and bar with glass domes and floor-to-ceiling windows that offer sweeping views in three directions. A daytime retreat for reading and viewing scenery, it becomes a nighttime disco with an illuminated glass dance floor. The lounge has been enhanced with a new bar topped with blue-pearl granite. The stools, tables and chairs were removed to create an open space and replaced with pull-up cocktail tables attached to a railing that encircles the room. Expansive solarium windows with high-tech stainless-steel support systems make for a modern, more airy space. The teak deck has been restored, complete with large, plush lounge chairs.

SPORTS, FITNESS, AND BEAUTY The ship's **Mandara Spa,** beauty salon, and fitness center on Penthouse Deck were completely rebuilt. Aqua, mint green, and creamy white colors of mosaic tiles and light wood accents on the walls create the spa's serene setting. The spa has nine treatment rooms with a full-time director and offers a wide range of beauty treatments. Passengers can work out in separate aerobic and weight rooms as well as on an array of fitness equipment. The salon features four stations all facing an expanse of floor-to-ceiling windows.

CHILDREN'S FACILITIES The teen center, with bold colors of metallic purples, greens, and oranges, has a dance floor with state-of-the-art sound and light system, juice bar, and large, multicolored banquettes. A video arcade separates the teen center from the children's center. Kid's Crew participants enjoy an arts and crafts center, a computer corner, and a theater with a plasma screen and beanbags for comfortable viewing. See *Norwegian Star* for details of the line's children's year-round program.

Norwegian Majesty	QUALITY 5	VALUE C
REGISTRY Panama	LENGTH 680 feet	BEAM 91 feet
CABINS 731	DRAFT 20 feet	SPEED 20 knots
MAXIMUM PASSENGERS 1,462	PASSENGER DECKS 9	ELEVATORS 6
	CREW 620	SPACE RATIO 28

THE SHIP *Norwegian Majesty,* which was built in 1992, was lengthened in 1999 by 112 feet through insertion of a prefabricated midsection that added 203 new cabins, plus new public areas and facilities. The lengthening also increased the ship's capacity from 1,056 to 1,460 passengers. Interiors throughout were refurbished. The work added a second pool, second dining room, new casino, another outdoor bar, **Le Bistro** restaurant, coffee bar, and substantially more deck space. Crew cabins were expanded to accommodate increased staff. Two new elevators and a third stair tower were incorporated.

The lengthening also gave *Norwegian Majesty* a sleeker, more hydrodynamic profile, enabling the ship to maintain its 20-knot speed with the same power plant, despite increased size. New buoyancy reduced the ship's draft, allowing her to call on all current ports and at some that were previously inaccessible because of shallower waters.

In 2003, the ship started a series of cruises from Charleston, South Carolina, to the western Caribbean. The home porting in Charleston reflected a continuing expansion of NCL's Homeland Cruising program, aimed particularly at the drive markets in nearby states. *Norwegian Majesty* debuted as Majesty Cruises' *Royal Majesty* and was intended to appeal to affluent passengers with understated elegance. Stylish interiors create a refined, harmonious environment of simplicity and clean lines. Contemporary decor employs soft colors, natural wood, leather sofas, glass, mirrors, and fresh foliage. Models of old sailing vessels bow to tradition. The ship is well laid out with many quiet corners. Characteristic of NCL, forward lounges have walls of sloped windows.

Passengers step almost directly into the two-deck atrium that serves as the main lobby and contains the front desk and shore excursion office. Called Crossroads, the circular area has white marble floors and stairs to a white marble island centered with a baby grand piano and furnished with banquettes.

The Atlantic Deck is devoted entirely to public areas. Off the lobby is the **Four Seasons Dining Room;** beyond, the **Seven Seas Dining Room.** Forward are boutiques, library, card room, and meeting room. Small lounges border **Rendezvous,** a large, V-shaped piano bar connecting to **Royal Fireworks,** a lounge with panoramic windows.

ITINERARIES *See* Itinerary Index.

CABINS Ten categories range from royal suites to inside cabins with lower and upper berths. About 71% are outside, and a high percentage are nonsmoking. Standard cabins are modest in size. They have clean, uncluttered lines and are finished in natural wood. Most have twin beds separated by a chest of drawers. A desk unit has drawer space and a dressing mirror, and three closets add to storage. Each cabin has a television carrying CNN, cable sports, shipboard notices, and movies. Bathrooms have showers and a large sink, with ample counter and shelf space and a hair dryer. All cabins have a built-in ironing board.

Upper-category suites and cabins have a minibar, queen beds, and large windows. Forward on Majesty Deck, a group of cabins spans an unusual half-moon contour overlooking the bow. The two Royal Suites on Norway Deck have marble baths and 24-hour butler service.

Specifications 203 new deluxe or standard outside and standard inside. 250 inside, 481 outside; 22 suites. Standard cabins, 108–145 square feet. 487 cabins with 2 lowers (134 convert to doubles); 291 with double beds; 73 with 3 berths; 367 with 4 berths; 22 suites accommodate 3 persons; 4 wheelchair-accessible.

DINING The impressive **Seven Seas Dining Room** has wraparound, full-length windows. A white baby-grand piano plays on a small island at the center. Most tables are set for four or six, contributing to the room's intimate feeling. Seven Seas was the first smoke-free dining room on a major cruise ship.

The **Four Seasons Dining Room** also offers ocean panoramas through floor-to-ceiling windows. Adjacent is the 58-seat **Le Bistro** alternative restaurant ($15), which serves light Italian and continental cuisine in flexible dining hours.

Breakfast and lunch buffets are served inside the casual **Café Royale** on Sun Deck; outside space overlooks two pools. The room is attractively furnished in light wood and wicker chairs. It's tight for buffet lines. Buffets are average, offering a range of hot and cold dishes, daily specialties, and cakes, pastries, muffins, and breads. The cafe is connected to the **Royal Observatory,** a handsome observation lounge/bar below that doubles as a sports bar.

Piazza San Marco Grill, a second Sun Deck serving area, is partially covered. Burgers, hot dogs, pizza, ice cream, snacks, and late-night buffets (different from the nightly midnight buffet) are offered.

SERVICE The crew encompasses 34 nationalities and except, at times, for the dining room, service shipwide has received generally good reviews.

FACILITIES AND ACTIVITIES Daytime offerings include bridge tours, table-tennis tournaments, bridge and Scrabble, fruit- and vegetable-carving demonstrations, poolside fashion show, napkin-folding classes, wine tasting, and dance. The ship has a card room, well-stocked library, and small boardroom. The Internet cafe is also in the card room; fees apply.

The **Palace Theater** show lounge is on one level with a steeply tiered floor. Sight lines to the circular stage are excellent from almost every seat. The ship's midsection has the **Monte Carlo Casino,** offering blackjack, Caribbean stud poker, roulette, and slot machines. Next door, the attractive **Polo Bar** has piano music nightly. One deck below, a small coffee bar and lounge offers coffees, teas, and coffee-flavored drinks, plus bar service. **Royal Fireworks** is a quiet area or meeting space by day and a dance lounge before and after dinner.

In summer, when the ship is in Bermuda, she isn't allowed to stage big productions or open the casino. Instead, the ship offers excursions to local nightclubs. An evening cocktail cruise along Bermuda's pretty shores is another option.

SPORTS, FITNESS, AND BEAUTY Fitness fans pair workouts and ocean views in the gym. Equipment includes Life Circuit machines and a Nordic Track. Exercise and dance classes are held in a mirrored studio. The spa on Promenade Deck has saunas for men and women and offers massage. A small beauty parlor also offers facials and spa treatments. A jogging track circles Promenade Deck.

The top decks were transformed by the addition of a second swimming pool and the **Topsider's Bar,** a second open-air bar. Sky Deck above the Sun Deck provides more sunning area while shading the two pools and whirlpools below. It has lounge chairs, rest rooms, and showers.

CHILDREN'S FACILITIES Supervised program; see "Children's Facilities" in *Norwegian Star* section for details. **Kids Korner** play area has a kiddies' pool, playground rides, ball slide, and a puppet theater. Bathrooms have lowered kiddies' sinks. Older children have a video arcade.

SHORE EXCURSIONS The ship spends four full days in St. George's, in front of King's Square. Nearby are shops, historic St. Peter's church, and motor-scooter rentals (the island's most popular transport; no car rentals are available). The picturesque town is ideal for walking and convenient to beaches, but to reach Hamilton, a town at the island's opposite end, you need to take a taxi or bus or rent a moped. Hamilton is, however, included in some shore excursions. Among other excursions available is a visit to the Bermuda Aquarium Museum and Zoo. The ship's sports program offers sailing, snorkeling, scuba diving, and deep-sea fishing.

NCL AMERICA

In February 2003, NCL Corp. surprised the cruise world when it announced that it would have a U.S.-flagged ship in Hawaii by summer 2004, employing an all-American crew, and subject to all American laws. The announcement came soon after Congress passed a federal spending bill, that included an exemption to the Passenger Services Act. As a result, NCL, in exchange for completing two former Project America vessels (now renamed *Pride of America* and *Pride of Hawaii*) to sail in Hawaii under the U.S. flag, was given an exemption also to re-flag one existing, foreign-flagged NCL ship that would then sail under the U.S. flag within Hawaii (but not Alaska or the Caribbean). The U.S.-flagged ship does not have to make at least one foreign port call on any itinerary, as all foreign-flagged ships are required to do by law. That avoids long ocean journeys and multiple days at sea.

Under the exemption, NCL's *Norwegian Sky*—the first ship to offer Freestyle Cruising when it debuted in 2000—was re-flagged to the U.S. ship registry in June 2004. As the renamed *Pride of Aloha,* it launched NCL America's first Hawaii cruises with all-American crews on July 4, 2004. Now, *Pride of Aloha* passengers enjoy up to 96 hours of port time all within Hawaii on a weeklong cruise.

Pride of America, constructed at the Lloyd Werft shipyard in Germany, is the first new oceangoing passenger ship built in nearly 50 years to sail under the American flag. She was expected to begin service in Hawaii in July offering seven-night, inter-island cruises round-trip from Honolulu. The third Project America ship, *Pride of Hawaii,* is scheduled to enter the Hawaii market in 2006.

On the heels of its Project America purchase, NCL Corp. bought the only two existing U.S.-built oceangoing cruise ships, the *United States* and the *Independence,* and says it plans to completely rebuild the 50-year-old vessels. To rebuild the two U.S.-built ships, the minimum the law requires is to maintain the hull and superstructure as 100% U.S., so all the steel and structural work is done in a U.S. shipyard. Beyond that, NCL can chose a U.S. or European shipyard, or both, for interior work. NCL says renovations are likely to take several years. According to NCL, the purchase was a practical way for NCL to expand its three-ship U.S.-flagged fleet; others say it was a shrewd move to protect its Hawaii position from competition.

Pride of Aloha	QUALITY 6	VALUE B
Pride of America	(PREVIEW)	
Pride of Hawaii	(PREVIEW)	

REGISTRY United States	LENGTH 853/921/971 feet	BEAM 108/106/106 feet
CABINS 983/1,073/1,188	DRAFT 26/27 feet	SPEED 23/22/24 knots
MAXIMUM PASSENGERS	PASSENGER DECKS 15	ELEVATORS 10/12
2,002/2,144/2,400	CREW 920/1,000	SPACE RATIO 37/NA

THE SHIPS   From the ship' exterior with a floral lei painted on her hull to the interior brightened with murals of the South Pacific, blue carpets with tropical fish, birds, flowers and shells, *Pride of Aloha* sings Hawaii. After a multimillion-dollar makeover in San Francisco, the former *Norwegian Sky* was reflagged in June 2004, and on the following July 4th, began her new life of year-round cruises of the Hawaiian Islands.

The focal point of the ship is the eight-deck-high atrium awash with colorful Hawaiian art and motifs. Everywhere in the public areas, bright colors glow everywhere, monkeys peer out from columns, and the **Longboard Bar** honors renowned Hawaii surfer Duke Kahanamoku. At the impressive Kumu Cultural Center, passengers can watch a multi-media presentation on volcanoes or view historic movie posters, menus from vintage cruise ships, and pieces of surfing memorabilia.

Pride of America has as her theme the "Best of America," reflected in the decor and names of public rooms—you can't miss it, starting with the design of the atrium, called the Capitol Atrium, inspired by the Capitol Building and the White House. The eight dining outlets and many lounges have such names as **Liberty Restaurant, Lone Star Steak House, Cadillac Diner,** and **Napa Wine Bar,** among others. In keeping with NCL's new signature, painted on the hull of *Pride of America* is a vibrant, artistic interpretation of the Stars and Stripes and the bald eagle, the U.S. national bird.

In addition to an abundance of public rooms, the ship has state-of-the-art entertainment venues, three pools, extensive children's facilities, and large meeting facilities. It also sports several NCL firsts, including a con-servatory, a new category of family suites, a tennis court, and an art gallery—all named and decorated to reflect America's diversity.

Pride of Hawaii will be a twin of the *Norwegian Jewel* and the seventh new Freestyle Cruising ship to be added to the NCL fleet in only five years. The theme of her decor will be Hawaii's culture and history. The ship will have ten restaurants, including **Cagney's Steak House, Blue Lagoon,** and **Le Bistro,** NCL's signature restaurant, as well as the line's typical Asian complex with a sushi bar, teppanyaki table, and a Pacific fusion restaurant. The ship also has two top-deck garden villas and ten courtyard villas with private courtyard and sundeck. The ship has another new NCL concept—**Bar Central**—including a martini bar, a champagne and wine bar, and a beer and whiskey pub, all connected but each with its own personality.

ITINERARIES *See* Itinerary Index.

CABINS All *Aloha*'s cabins have a refrigerator, small desk, telephone, coffeemaker, in-room safe, and television. Bathrooms have nice storage nooks, but except for suites, all are shower-only. There are several suite categories, including ten penthouse suites at 364 square feet and up, and four owner's suites at 650 square feet.

Pride of America's extensive choice of cabins is highlighted by a grand Grand Suite, as well as NCL's new concept—family suites. The six owner's suites, each with 766 to 875 square feet, are named after Hawaiian flowers; each of six deluxe penthouse suites cover 735 square feet, and 28 penthouse suites range from 504 to 585 square feet. The suites are furnished with a king-size bed and walk-in closet, a bathroom with a separate shower and Jacuzzi bath, dressing area, and flat-screen television; a separate living room has a Bang & Olufsen entertainment center, television with a DVD player and CD/DVD library, and computer access with Internet connection. Each of the eight new family suites covers 360 square feet and has a living room furnished with a double sofabed and entertainment center, separate den with a single sofabed, and a private bedroom with twin beds convertible to a queen. Four additional family suites (330–380 square feet) are interconnecting cabins sleeping up to eight people. The larger of the two cabins is an oversized outside cabin with two single beds that can be combined for a queen-size bed, plus a sitting area with a double sofa bed. The cabin interconnects with another outside cabin that has two single beds and two upper berths. The eight-person family suites have two bathrooms.

The 1,400-square-foot Grand Suite, positioned high atop the ship forward of the main sundeck, offers sweeping views of the ocean and an impressive assortment of amenities. It has a large living room with a Bang & Olufsen entertainment center with television, CD, stereo, DVD player, CD/DVD library, computer access with Internet connection, and a wet bar. The suite also has a dining room with a polished teak table seating six, plus a private butler. The master bedroom has a king-size bed and bathroom with separate shower and Jacuzzi bath, a dressing area with a flat-screen television and a large walk-in closet, and a separate powder room. On the large, wraparound veranda, suite occupants and their guests can enjoy open-air dining, a Jacuzzi for up to six people, and private areas for sunbathing and for entertaining up to 50 visitors.

Pride of Hawaii's cabins will come with NCL standards including cherry wood finishing, refrigerators, tea- and coffeemakers in every room, large bathrooms with separate shower, and wash basin separated by sliding doors. The ship will also have a large number of interconnecting cabins, including suites and junior suites, to create a two-, three-, or more bedroom area suitable for families, as well as expanded kids' and teen centers.

Specifications *Pride of Aloha,* 983 cabins, including 554 outside of which 243 have balconies; 10 penthouse suites; 4 owner's suites.

Pride of America, 1,155 cabins of which 660 have balconies; 250 family accommodations; 1 grand suite; 34 penthouse suites; 5 owner's suites; 8 family suites.

Pride of Hawaii, similar to *Pride of America.*

DINING On *Aloha,* Freestyle Dining gives passengers the option of dining in two open-seating main dining rooms, **Crossings** and the **Palace Restaurant,** as well as the 24-hour buffet-style **Hukilau Cafe,** and other casual venues, for no charge. The three excellent specialty restaurants have a $12.50–$15 charge—**Pacific Heights** for Asian fusion, **Kahili Restaurant** for high-end Italian fare, and the **Royal Palm Bistro** for French cuisine. Outdoor barbecues are nicely presented. Room service is available around the clock.

Pride of America offers eight restaurants and nine different menus every night. These include two main restaurants and alternative gourmet, ethnic, and casual eateries.

On Deck 5, **Skyline,** a main restaurant, has decor inspired by the architecture and skyscrapers of the 1930s; **Liberty,** the second main restaurant one deck up, has colonial design featuring America's founding fathers and large paintings depicting important moments in American history. Both offer traditional dining.

Also on Deck 5, **East Meets West,** an elegant Pacific Rim/Asian fusion restaurant, has a sushi and sashimi bar and a teppanyaki room with two tables accommodating 32 people and offering Japanese-style dining with food prepared in front of guests. **Jefferson's Bistro,** NCL's signature restaurant, has an à la carte menu of nouvelle and classic French cuisine and decor inspired by Thomas Jefferson's home, Monticello. (Jefferson was the U.S. Ambassador to France from 1785 to 1789.)

On Deck 6, the **Lone Star Steak House** is an upscale steakhouse with Texas decor and art depicting the Houston Space Center, Texas Rangers, and Dallas Cowboys. It serves Angus Beef and other grilled meat, seafood, and chicken. The indoor/outdoor **Cadillac Diner,** a 24-hour diner, has decor of 1950s pop stars complete with Cadillac seats and a video juke box. The fare includes hamburgers, fish and chips, pot pie, and wok dishes.

On Deck 11, **Little Italy,** a casual Italian eatery inspired by New York's Little Italy, serves pasta, pizza, and other Italian specialties. **Aloha Café/Kids Café,** the indoor/outdoor buffet with a Hawaiian theme including outrigger canoes and Polynesian carvings and artifacts, has food stations for prepared-to-order omelets, waffles, fruit, soups, and ethnic specialties. It also includes a buffet with small chairs and tables to accommodate 48 kids.

SERVICE When NCL America started its new Hawaii operation, it was bombarded with complaints about service. However, the cruise line has tackled the problems and over the last year has worked hard to correct them with an extensive crew training program and other measures. Approximately 65% of the crew are from Hawaii, which gives us every reason to think that once they have had proper training and time to learn their jobs, the service complaints will be a thing of the past.

FACILITIES AND ACTIVITIES In *Pride of Aloha*'s **Stardust Theater,** passengers can enjoy the the excellent *South Sea Island Spectacular* as well as several Las Vegas–style shows. Enhancing the ship's Hawaii-themed activities are Bishop Museum lectures and classes on how to create tropical jewelry, husk a coconut or do the hula.

The Capitol Atrium, the heart of *Pride of America,* carries her All-American theme with a decorative stone floor, water feature, and a stunning backlit glass dome. Her seven lounges and bars are designed to reflect the diversity of the country, such as the **Mardi Gras Cabaret,** the ship's nightclub; the **Gold Rush Pub;** and two outdoor pool bars, **Key West Bar & Grill** and the **Waikiki Bar**.

The **Soho Art Gallery** offers original works of art, while Newbury Street resembles New England shops in the early 1900s. There is NCL's first conservatory, with a tropical landscaped garden and live exotic birds; the **S.S. America Library,** honoring the famous ship; and the **Hollywood Theater** with large, golden statues adorning the walls. The ship also has WiFi capability and an Internet center. Passengers can obtain an Internet access card for their laptops or rent a laptop with wireless Internet capability.

Pride of America's meeting facilities—among the largest at sea—encompass six meeting rooms ranging from boardrooms for 10 people to an auditorium that can accommodate over 250 persons. Five of the meeting rooms—named for Hawaii and her islands—can be used individually or combined. The **Diamond Head Auditorium** is a multilevel, circular room that boasts a state-of-the-art audiovisual system with multiple screens that lower from the ceiling to be viewed by all participants. The auditorium also splits into two amphitheater-style presentation rooms. The conference area has a business center, a separate large gathering and break area, and the **Lanai Bar and Lounge,** for group cocktail parties and other purposes.

Pride of America's meeting facilities should appeal to the business market on several accounts. As the only large U.S.-flagged ships regularly sailing the Hawaiian islands and visiting only U.S. ports, onboard meetings qualify for corporate and individual tax deductions for meetings expenses.

SPORTS, FITNESS, AND BEAUTY *Pride of Aloha*'s **Body Waves Fitness Center** has a good selection of machines and a spacious aerobics studio. As with NCL's other ships, the spa is operated by Mandara Spa and offers facials, massages, manicures, and hair styling services. The ship also has a basketball/volleyball court, two golf driving nets, two swimming pools, four whirlpools, and a kids' pool.

Pride of America's **Santa Fe Spa and Fitness Center,** a tranquil area decorated with natural elements such as stone, wood, and artifacts from New Mexico, offers an exotic menu of spa and beauty treatments. The Fitness Center has Cybex exercise equipment and Lifefitness cardiovascular machines, each with its own flat-screen television; an aerobics room for yoga, power walking, and other fitness classes; and saunas and steam room.

The Sports Deck has a basketball, volleyball, and soccer court. The large South Beach sunning and swimming area, inspired by Miami's Art Deco district, has some novel distractions and activities capturing the energy and fun of Ocean Drive and Lincoln Road.

Pride of Aloha has the first golf pro shop at sea along with a comprehensive shoreside golf program. The ship features top-of-the-line golf equipment such as Callaway clubs and Adidas shoes for rent, guaranteed tee times, and NCL Golf Hawaii logo items for purchase. The shop offers onboard clinics with local golf pros and three practice nets and play at some of Hawaii's leading courses along the cruise route. Prices start from $95 per person. Transportation is included in all rounds of golf.

CHILDREN'S FACILITIES *Aloha* has a modest **Kids Korner** facility and teens can hang out at The Club. On Pride of America, the **Rascal's Kids Center** and pool offers supervised facilities designed around a theme of native animals of America. Both ships have NCL's age-specific children's program to keep the little ones busy throughout their cruise. See *Norwegian Star* for details.

SHORE EXCURSIONS *Pride of Aloha* offers dozens of shore excursions, as varied as golf and rainforest walks to kayaking and helicopter rides over lava flows. All are listed on the cruise line's Web site, together with their prices. With 96 hours of port time during a week's cruise, there is ample time to explore Hawaii.

Oceania Cruises

8300 NW 33rd Street, Suite 308, Miami, FL 33122
☎ **305-514-2300 or 800-531-5658; fax 305-514-2222**
www.oceaniacruises.com

TYPE OF SHIPS Midsize deluxe ships

TYPE OF CRUISES Upscale cruises with a casual ambience on worldwide, destination-oriented itineraries, usually 10 days or longer.

CRUISE LINE'S STRENGTHS
- nearly-new medium-size ships, newly renovated and refurbished
- diverse foreign home ports and itineraries
- overnights in interesting ports
- gourmet dining; choices of four open-seating restaurants
- casual onboard atmosphere; no formal dress code
- top-of-the-line cabin amenities
- affordable fares, value-added deals

CRUISE LINE'S SHORTCOMINGS
- lack of facilities for children
- few cruise departures from U.S. ports
- no short cruises to sample the product
- limited nightlife

FELLOW PASSENGERS Oceania Cruises attracts a mix of first-time cruisers eager to try a premium cruise line and experienced travelers who simply enjoy the line's longer, destination-focused itineraries. Average passenger age is 55. Many are former Renaissance Cruises fans; others are likely to be experienced travelers who have sailed on other premium and even luxury lines attracted by the value Oceania's prices represent. Oceania passengers prefer smaller ships and savor international travel.

Recommended for Travelers who want to visit far-flung lands; those who appreciate extra time in ports. Intellectually curious couples and mature singles who appreciate a good value and enjoy touches of luxury cruising. Those who prefer medium-size ships.

Not recommended for Families with children; those who seek the party atmosphere of some large cruise ships or seek lots of nightlife and entertainment.

CRUISE AREAS AND SEASONS Europe in spring/summer/fall; Asia, South America, Caribbean in winter/spring; transatlantic in spring/fall.

THE LINE A privately-held company built from scratch, Oceania Cruises was founded in 2003 by two cruise industry veterans—Frank Del Rio,

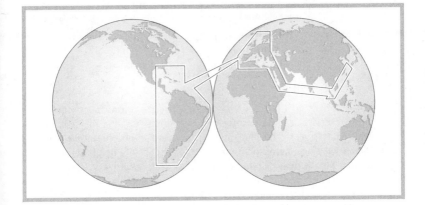

former president and CEO of now-defunct Renaissance Cruises, and Joe Watters, former president of Crystal Cruises. The Oceania team—Del Rio as president and CEO and Watters as chairman—brings complementary talent to the new cruise line. Del Rio runs Oceania's day-to-day operations; he knows the ships well, having previously operated them with Renaissance. Watters has focused on developing the onboard product, designated as premium with luxury touches—an effort to set the line apart from its competitors in the premium cruise category.

Oceania Cruises was launched with the 684-passenger *Regatta,* the former *R2.* Her identical sister, *Insignia,* the former *R1,* was added the following year, and a third copy, *Nautica,* the former *R5,* debuts in November 2005. Oceania selected these three specific ships—of all the available R-class ships on the market after Renaissance's demise—because they had the most high-end suites, an important asset in attracting sophisticated travelers. In addition, Oceania got a great deal for leasing the vessels from the banks that repossessed the ships after Renaissance's collapse, thus enabling the new cruise line to provide its product at very competitive prices.

Oceania's destination focus first centered on Europe, South America, and the Caribbean; new destinations such as North Africa have been added as the line builds its passenger base. Many itineraries have been tailored to include overnight port stays to allow passengers more time to enjoy particular destinations, such as St. Petersburg, Russia, on the Northern Europe cruises, and Venice on Mediterranean ones. When *Nautica* arrives, she is slated to chart a different course, spending winter and spring in the Far East with overnight stays in such cities as Beijing, Hong Kong, Bombay, and Dubai, to name a few.

THE FLEET	BUILT/RENOVATED	TONNAGE	PASSENGERS
Insignia	1998/2004/2005	30,277	684
Nautica	2000/2005	30,277	684
Regatta	1998/2003/2005	30,277	684

STYLE Oceania's goal has been to create a five-star product focused on cuisine, service, and destination-oriented itineraries, and to offer it at reasonable prices. The line's relaxed onboard atmosphere resembles the casual elegance of a country club, neither stuffy nor pretentious. Formal wear is never a requirement for dinner; passengers dress comfortably to enjoy their evenings. Oceania's ships—small compared to today's more typical megaships—provide the intimate atmosphere of a small ship, and at the same time have the facilities of larger ships. For example, each ship has several lounges, a spa, and four restaurants with open seating, enabling passengers to dine when, where, and with whom they choose.

DISTINCTIVE FEATURES Medium-size ships. An upper end premium product with luxury touches. Tranquility Beds. Four restaurants, gourmet open-seating dining, destination-focused itineraries. Affordable pricing; many special deals.

	HIGHEST	LOWEST	AVERAGE
PER DIEM	$1,040	$400	$665

Per diems are calculated from cruise line's nondiscounted *cruise-only* published fares on standard accommodations and vary by season, cabins, and cruise areas.

RATES Gratuities and port charges are additional.

Special fares and discounts Oceania's early booking policy is to open most new itineraries with two-for-one pricing or free economy air, and then to end the promotions as the ships fill. Guests who book early can realize tremendous savings.

- **THIRD PASSENGER:** Fares vary by individual sailing.
- **CHILDREN'S FARES:** None
- **SINGLE SUPPLEMENT:** 200 percent

Packages

- **AIR/SEA:** Yes. First and business-class upgrades for additional charge.
- **PRE/POST:** Yes. Most air/sea packages include one to three nights in a hotel in the departure city.
- **OTHERS:** Yes

PAST PASSENGERS After passengers sail once, they automatically become a member of the Oceania Club, the line's past-passenger club. Then, the more they sail, the higher their level of rewards. All members receive an *Oceania Club Journal* and an invitation to the captain's cocktail party for members. Other awards, depending on level of membership, might include complimentary gratuities, spa or onboard credits, and discounts on future cruises. A dedicated page for the club at **www.oceaniacruises.com** includes information, news, and fun, behind-the-scenes information.

THE LAST WORD Oceania Cruises has developed a substantial following in less than three years. The line is well-run, and passengers have favorably responded favorably to its consistent product. They like the line's midsize ships, their country-club-casual atmosphere, the cuisine, and unusual itineraries. Oceania appears to be doing well financially, but because it is both new and privately-held, it would be prudent to buy third-party travel insurance. Actually, we could say that's a good idea for any cruise.

Oceania Cruises Standard Features

Officers Italian, Croatian, and other Europeans.

Staff Dining and Cabin/European; Cruise/British, North American, and European.

Dining facilities Four restaurants include a main dining room, two alternative restaurants, and a casual buffet-style eatery.

Special diets Request at booking or no later than 30 days prior to sailing.

Room service 24 hours with cabin menu. Top suites may order from any of the four restaurant menus.

Dress code By day, resort casual attire. Evenings are business casual or smart casual. No jackets, ties, or fancy dress. Each cruise has two gala evenings, but formal wear is not required.

Cabin amenities Direct-dial telephone; television with CNN and ESPN; cabin music; hair dryer; safe; deluxe toiletries; and bathrobes. Concierge level and higher cabins and suites: DVD players and minifridge; Owner's and Vista suites: full entertainment system.

Electrical outlets 110/220 AC

Wheelchair access Three inside staterooms.

Recreation and entertainment Several lounges have live music by ship's orchestra or musical trio. Entertainment, typically low key, features cabaret acts, soloists, jugglers, comedians, and dance music. One to two small production shows staged on every cruise.

Sports and other activities Outdoor pool, golf cage, shuffleboard, deck sports, and jogging track.

Beauty and fitness Men's and women's steam rooms, full-service Mandara Spa with treatment rooms, beauty salon, exercise facility, aerobics, and fitness classes. Massages on deck in private cabana.

Oceania Cruises Standard Features (cont'd)

Other facilities Library with 1,000 books, card room, two boutiques, Oceania@ Sea 24-hour Internet cafe, medical center, self-service laundry, dry cleaning and laundry services, four elevators. Nondenominational Sunday services; Jewish Sabbath observance led by crew member or passenger.

Children's facilities None.

Theme cruises None.

Smoking Smoking is permitted only in two designated areas of the ship: the forward starboard corner of the Pool Deck, and in the aft port corner on the Horizon Deck. Smoking is prohibited in all other areas including within cabins and on cabin or suite balconies.

Oceania suggested tipping An $11.50 per person per day and $3.50 per person per day gratuity (for private butlers if in Penthouse, Owner's, and Vista's) added automatically to onboard account. It may be adjusted at the passenger's discretion. Also, 18% added to spa services and bar purchases.

Credit cards For cruise payment and onboard charges: American Express, Diners Club, Discover, MasterCard, and Visa.

Insignia	**QUALITY 9**	**VALUE A**
Nautica	(PREVIEW)	
Regatta	**QUALITY 9**	**VALUE A**
REGISTRY Marshall Islands	**LENGTH** 593.7 feet	**BEAM** 83.5
CABINS 342	**DRAFT** 19.5 feet	**SPEED** 18 knots
MAXIMUM PASSENGERS 684	**PASSENGER DECKS** 9	**ELEVATORS** 4
	CREW 410	**SPACE RATIO** NA

THE SHIPS Because the *Regatta, Insignia,* and *Nautica* are practically identical, the new line has been able to create a consistent product across its fleet. Despite the young age of all three ships—seven years or less—Oceania Cruises gave each of the former Renaissance ships a major renovation prior to entering them in service. These included adding new teak decks on the pool deck, the aft dining terrace, and private balconies. The old patio furniture was replaced with more classy looking lounges, and the pool and whirlpool area resurfaced with an attractive marble and tile look.

Oceania also revamped the decor and use of the interior public spaces, such as the observation lounge, martini bar, atrium and grand staircase area, and the alternative restaurants. Much of the gaudy, heavily patterned furnishings were replaced and toned down with a more elegant, muted look. Decor remains traditional, but some contrast was added with a new $2 million contemporary art collection.

More enhancements were completed recently when all wooden furniture was replaced, doors given a French polish, and brass handles added to cabin doors. Teak decks on balconies were replaced. Public areas, cabins, and the spa were refurbished.

The reception desk, destination services, the concierge, medical center, and an imposing grand staircase are found on Deck 4. One deck above, Deck 5, is totally dedicated to public spaces, including the casino, Martini's Lounge, the Regatta (or Insignia) Lounge, the Grand Bar, photo gallery, two boutiques, and the main dining room.

ITINERARIES *See* Itinerary Index.

CABINS Prior to entering service for Oceania, all cabins were upgraded with luxury appointments; fine linens and bedding, including new Tranquility Bed mattresses; silk-cut duvets and fluffy goosedown pillows; French-milled toiletries; and teak verandas. Passengers also enjoy plush cotton robes and slippers.

The roomy Owner's (aft) and Vista (forward) suites on Decks 6–8 have floor-to-ceiling glass doors with spectacular views from the living room, dining room and master bedroom and lead to a private wrap-around teak veranda. The suites have a separate guest bathroom and butler service. These suites are furnished with queen-size bed, whirlpool, two color TVs, and an entertainment center with DVD and CD players. DVDs are available from the reception desk.

On Deck 8, the Penthouse Suites offer a large living area with sliding glass doors, stylish furniture, and either twin or queen beds, space for in-suite dining, minibar, vanity desk, bath with tub, ample closet space, and butler service that includes arranging priority restaurant reservations and complimentary shoeshine, among other services.

To fill the gap between the more pricey suites and standard cabins, Oceania created a new category called Concierge Level. These 216-square-foot cabins with verandas occupy preferred locations on Deck 7. They have amenities similar to a Penthouse suite, but the space is much smaller. Concierge Level passenger, however, get many perks including priority embarkation with a dedicated check-in desk and priority luggage delivery; welcome bottle of champagne; minibar; 20-inch color television and DVD player; personalized stationery; Hansgrohe hand-held massaging shower heads; and Caswell-Massey toiletries.

Concierge Level cabins as well as deluxe balcony cabins are furnished with cherry wood furniture and dark wood accents and dressed in blue and gold decor. Located on Deck 6, the deluxe balcony cabins have queen or two twin beds, comfortable seating area with sofa, breakfast table, vanity desk, and spacious closets.

Deluxe ocean-view cabins on Decks 4, 6, and 7 have queen or two twin beds and large panorama windows. Standard ocean-view cabins have either a porthole or panorama window with obstructed views. Inside cabins on decks 4, 6, 7, and 8 have a comfortable seating area, vanity desk, ample storage space, and queen or two twin beds.

Specifications 342 cabins and suites of which 314 or 92% are outside and almost 70% have verandas. Six Owner's suites (962 square feet); 4 Vista suites (786 square feet); 52 Penthouse suites (322 square feet); 171 cabins (216 square feet) all with balconies; 83 ocean-view cabins (150–165 square feet) and 26 inside cabins (158 square feet); 3 inside wheelchair-accessible cabins.

DINING The **Grand Dining Room**—open for breakfast, lunch and dinner—is elegantly appointed with a domed ceiling adorned with hand-painted frescoes, soft lighting, and dramatic ocean views. The decor is similar to the room's look during its Renaissance days. While the service is decidedly white glove—and in the evening, waiters wear tuxedos—passengers dine in a relaxing atmosphere in casual attire. The dress code never requires jacket and tie, although many gentlemen do wear jackets with a sport shirt for dinner. On gala nights, passengers might dress more elegantly, if they choose to do so. A classical string quartet or concert pianist usually provides background music during dinner.

The ship's menus have been crafted by master chef Jacques Pepin, the line's executive culinary director and one of America's best-known chefs via his numerous television appearances, food columns, and cookbooks. He has also served as the personal chef to three French heads of state, including Charles de Gaulle. The line offers a selection of more than 150 wines.

The ships have two alternative dining venues, **Polo Grill** and **Toscana;** both require reservations, but there is no extra charge. Resplendent with rich, dark woods and elegant furnishings, they have floor-to-ceiling windows affording views of the seascapes. Polo Grill is a classic steakhouse with an extensive menu of aged prime beef, lamb, pork, and fresh seafood. Desserts might include New Orleans pecan pie or a traditional New York cheesecake, among other choices.

In Toscana, diners enjoy an Italian ambience and may select from such Italian specialties as gnocchi in creamy pesto sauce, risotto with Porcini mushrooms, caramelized shallots and fresh thyme, or sauteed medallions of veal tenderloin with roasted bell peppers in Gorgonzola cheese and Marsala wine sauce—all served on fine china and crystal. Great service enhances the ambience.

According to Oceania's new policy, all suite and Concierge Level passengers may make two reservations at each of the alternative dining venues (total of four nights), while standard-cabin passengers may make one reservation in each venue (total of two nights). After that, the venues are open to more reservations as space permits.

For a more casual dining experience, the buffet-style **Terrace Café**—where casual breakfast and lunch are available—is transformed at dinner into **Tapas on the Terrace.** Passenger serve themselves at a buffet, but the ambience is enhanced by linens and upgraded dinnerware and glassware on the table, and service by waiters who often carry plates to the tables and bring drinks. Menus vary but are decidedly Mediterranean in flair, along with different chef's specials nightly.

Waves, the poolside bar and grill, is a lunchtime option offering grilled meats, seafood, salads, and made-to-order deli sandwiches. All passengers can order room service from a cabin menu 24 hours a day. Those in Penthouse suites and above may also order room service from the four restaurant menus.

SERVICE Passengers praise the service as warm and attentive. The high staff-to-guest ratio of more than one crew member per cabin facilitates a high degree of personalized service.

FACILITIES AND ACTIVITIES The **Regatta** (or **Insignia** or **Nautica**) **Lounge,** dressed in royal blue and gold decor, is furnished with curved couches, upholstered chairs, and cocktail tables. During the day, enrichment lectures might be held here. When the sun goes down, the lounge features entertainment that might include a soloist, comedian, or juggler, and a revue-style production show once or twice during a cruise.

Martini's, reminiscent of a private gentlemen's club, is the place to relax with friends for martinis and live piano music. In the Grand Bar, just outside the main restaurant, you can enjoy a rare vintage or a grappa. **Horizons,** a convivial bar on Deck 10, offers live entertainment and sweeping views to enjoy along with your favorite cocktail. Later in the evening, it becomes the venue for dancing.

Before the ship visits a port, the cruise director provides a talk with historical background and information on the culture, traditions, and language of that destination. The line also offers culinary demonstrations by its executive chef and his staff. Passengers might take a dance lesson, participate in an arts and crafts class, take a golf or bridge lesson, or enjoy bingo or a wine tasting session. The **Library** is stocked with more than 1,000 volumes. **Oceania@Sea** is the line's 24-hour Internet center.

SPORTS, FITNESS, AND BEAUTY Deck 9 has the **Oceania Spa** operated by Mandara, plus a hair salon, fitness center, an outdoor pool, and two whirlpools. The large, airy fitness center has new exercise equipment, a large aerobics area, and offers a variety of fitness classes led by personal trainers. One deck up, on Deck 10, passengers can walk, jog, or run along the fitness track (13 laps equal to one mile). The Deck 11 Sun Deck is the place for a tranquil respite on a cozy lounge chair. Here, golfers can practice their swing in a golf cage.

CHILDREN'S FACILITIES Oceania cruises are not designed for families with children. Given the nature of the cruises, most children would probably be bored to tears. The line's passengers—mostly couples and mature singles—are not likely to appreciate rambunctious kids, either. The ships have no children's facilities, no baby-sitting services, no video arcades, no rock-climbing walls ,or youth activity programs.

SHORE EXCURSIONS Oceania offers two sets of shore excursion packages online: Discovery for those new to the ports of call; or Explorers for experienced cruisers who may have already visited the ports. Prebooking a shore package can bring peace of mind for some, saving their having to stand in line at the shore excursion office onboard ship. Others prefer to wait until they get onboard to book shore excursions individually. Pre-arranged packages provide a 10% discount—a good value. However, these packages are nonrefundable and cannot be changed nor substitutions made. Purchasing excursions onboard costs more, but there's often a wider selection from which to choose. Also, booking onboard offers greater flexibility as passengers often change their mind about excursions after they board the ship.

Also to be considered in making a selection are the ports where the ships overnight. For example, when *Nautica* sails in Asia, her itineraries will feature overnight stays in such cities as Beijing, Hong Kong, Bangkok, Shanghai, Hanoi, Ho Chi Minh City, Kyoto, Bombay, Luxor, and Dubai. Passengers will be able to enjoy two full days and an evening in each of these ports and enjoy the local culture, dining, and sightseeing.

Oceania has also developed pre- and postcruise hotel stays and extended land tours of three to nine days to such locales as Chiangmai, Myanmar, Guilin, Siem Reap, Beijing and the Great Wall, Xian, and the Yangtze River.

POSTSCRIPT For former Renaissance Cruises fans, Oceania was a dream come true. They could once again enjoy sailing on a deluxe midsize ship at an affordable price. Yet, today's Oceania has come a long way from the former Renaissance product. It's better and more complete. Oceania Cruises is attracting a fan base that extends far beyond the former Renaissance cruiser. Most never sailed with Renaissance; rather, they are experienced cruisers who have traveled on other high-quality cruise lines and are attracted by Oceania's itineraries, the ships and their fine onboard product, and the price.

Orient Lines

7665 Corporate Center Drive, Miami, FL 33126
☎ 305-436-4000 or 800-333-7300; fax 305-436-4120
www.orientlines.com

TYPE OF SHIPS Midsize ocean liner.

TYPE OF CRUISES Affordable, destination-intensive, light adventure with first-class amenities, fine cuisine, and refined ambience.

CRUISE LINE'S STRENGTHS
- service by attentive crew
- itineraries
- singles policy
- price
- dock-level gangway door
- expert lecturers on longer voyages
- precruise information

CRUISE LINE'S SHORTCOMINGS
- limited room service
- entertainment

FELLOW PASSENGERS Orient Lines attracts mature, experienced, inquisitive passengers who are friendly and interested in the line's off-the-beaten-track itineraries. On longer cruises, passengers range in age from 50 to 70, have average annual incomes of about $75,000, and are retired or semiretired, business owners, managers, or professionals. Most are North Americans, but some cruises might include Brits and other Europeans, Australians, and South Africans, depending on the itinerary. Many are veteran cruisers, but several are first-timers who have traveled frequently and are drawn to an Orient cruise by its strong destination focus.

Recommended for Orient Lines has two seasons, each with a different appeal. On longer, winter cruises, passengers tend to be seasoned travelers, not necessarily experienced cruisers, who have the curiosity to appreciate exotic destinations, seek a learning experience, but like to travel in comfort. Also, small-ship devotees wanting to sample a cruise on a larger ship but not a megaliner. From April–October, passengers tend to be first-time cruisers, families, and honeymooners; those wanting a land and sea vacation in Europe.

Not recommended for Unsophisticated or inexperienced travelers and those seeking a high-energy, holiday-at-sea, party atmosphere.

CRUISE AREAS AND SEASONS In winter, Antarctica, Africa, and South America, including the Amazon, Caribbean, and Panama Canal. In spring and summer, Mediterranean, Greek Isles, northern Europe, Scandinavia, and Russia.

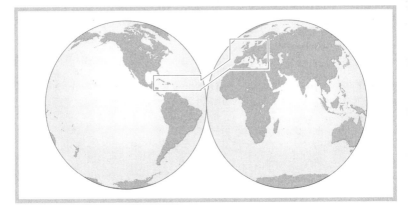

THE LINE Orient Lines originated in 1991 when its former CEO, Gerry Herrod, a British entrepreneur and tour and cruise line veteran, bought the Russian liner *Alexandr Pushkin* for about $25 million. It had been in a Singapore yard for minor repairs and the Soviets couldn't pay their bills. The ship, built in East Germany in 1965 for the Soviets—who hoped to generate hard currency by cashing in on the growing cruise market—was one of four sister ships with ice-strengthened hulls. They served as Soviet troop ships.

At the cost of $75 million, Orient Lines transformed the vessel into a luxury liner and named her *Marco Polo*. At the same time, the cruise line was launched to offer upscale voyages for experienced travelers to exotic destinations at reasonable prices. In its second year, the mission changed somewhat when the line found great success in a summer Mediterranean program.

Orient Lines was purchased by Norwegian Cruise Line in 1998, but continues to operate as a separate entity. Subsequently, NCL, including Orient Lines, was purchased by Asian-based Star Cruises.

THE FLEET	BUILT/RENOVATED	TONNAGE	PASSENGERS
Marco Polo	1965/1993	22,080	826

STYLE "Adventure in elegance" is one way Orient Lines' cruises have been described. From the start, Orient differed from most mainstream cruise lines by focusing on destinations, giving as much weight to developing unusual itineraries as to providing all the comforts and fine cuisine of a deluxe ship.

Meant to be an all-encompassing experience, the line's cruises include detailed port briefings, lectures by distinguished guest speakers (except on Mediterranean cruises) and experts on destination areas, and extended pre- and post-cruise hotel stays with sight-seeing. Some itineraries feature shipboard performances by local groups to showcase the culture of regions visited.

DISTINCTIVE FEATURES Gentlemen social hosts (except on Mediterranean cruises); local cultural performances; helicopter and topside helipad; videotaping of lectures for replay on ship's television; a low single supplement. Antarctic cruises.

	HIGHEST	LOWEST	AVERAGE
PER DIEM	$659	$155	$357

Per diems are calculated from cruise line's nondiscounted *cruise-only* published fares on standard accommodations and vary by season, cabins, and cruise areas.

RATES Port charges are additional.

Special fares and discounts Advance-purchase discounts of up to 50%, 120 days before departure, depending on itinerary and cabin. Savings up to 28% for two or more cruises in sequence.

- **SINGLE SUPPLEMENT:** 125% on all cabin categories except A and suites. For Mediterranean sailings, 50% for categories D–K, 75% for B and C, 100% for A and suites. The line frequently waives the supplement in special promotions.
- **SINGLE GUARANTEE:** Guaranteed share program in some cabin categories.

Packages
- **AIR/SEA:** Yes.
- **PRE/POST:** Cruises are designed as cruise/tours with one- to three-day pre- and postcruise hotel stays in gateway cities. Several Mediterranean itineraries also include two- to six-day escorted motorcoach tours.
- **OTHERS:** Yes.

PAST PASSENGERS After their first cruise, passengers are enrolled in the Polo Club and receive information on new itineraries, the club magazine, cruise discounts, up to $175 onboard credit (depending on cruise length), a bottle of wine in their cabin, a private VIP party with the captain, and certain benefits when sailing on NCL ships.

THE LAST WORD The *Marco Polo* is midsize by today's standards, yet she is among the largest ships cruising to exotic destinations regularly. Her size enables her to provide upscale comfort and a full range of facilities, and her capacity provides a larger passenger base over which to spread costs. Hence, the line can offer cruises at prices considerably lower than its competitors with smaller deluxe ships.

Orient Lines cares about single travelers. In addition to having gentlemen hosts to dine and dance with unaccompanied women passengers, the line offers one of cruising's lowest single supplements as well as occasional singles promotions. Also, it's fastidious in matching participants in its guaranteed-share program. Children are rare aboard the ship but are treated like royalty.

Orient Lines Standard Features

Officers European.

Staff Dining, Cabin/Filipino; Cruise/American and British.

Dining facilities One dining room with open seating for breakfast and lunch and two seatings for dinner with assigned tables; lido restaurant for buffet breakfast, lunch, tea and specialty dinners.

Special diets 60 days advance notice.

Room service Continental breakfast, cabin attendants on call.

Dress code Casual by day; several formal/semiformal nights.

Cabin amenities Direct-dial telephone, safe, television with CNN when available, movies and ship programs, radio, hair dryer, toiletries. Bathrobes and slippers in upper-category cabins; small refrigerators in suites. Deluxe suites with sitting room, marble bathroom with tub and shower, and minibars.

Electrical outlets 110/220 AC.

Wheelchair access Two cabins.

Recreation and entertainment Four lounges, port/country lectures by experts, piano and/or string trio at cocktails and after dinner, folkloric dancers in port; library, card room.

Sports and other activities Small outdoor swimming pool; Ping-Pong.

Beauty and fitness Beauty salon/spa, massage, aerobics studio, exercise equipment, saunas.

Other facilities Medical unit. Zodiacs; helicopter and landing pad; meeting room. Internet access.

Children's facilities No special facilities.

Smoking None in dining room; smoking permitted in designated wing of main lounge bar during shows, but not during lectures and briefings.

Orient suggested tipping Per day per person, $9; 15% of bar and wine bills and spa services are added to passenger's shipboard account. All tips are pooled and divided.

Credit cards For cruise payment and onboard charges: American Express, MasterCard, Visa, Diner's Club, Discover.

Marco Polo	QUALITY 7	VALUE A
REGISTRY Bahamas	LENGTH 578.4 feet	BEAM 77.4 feet
CABINS 425	DRAFT 27 feet	SPEED 20. 5 knots
MAXIMUM PASSENGERS 826	PASSENGER DECKS 8	ELEVATORS 4
	CREW 350	SPACE RATIO 27.6

THE SHIP A lovely vessel with classic lines, *Marco Polo* has been enhanced by handsome Art Deco interiors created by A. and M. Katzourakis of Athens. Reminiscent of grand liners of the 1920s, pastel furnishings are set against etched and beveled glass, brass, chrome, and rich wood accented by Thai and Burmese antiques and prints, plus modern paintings.

Marco Polo is a comfortable ship designed for long cruises. Built for Arctic service, her hull is strengthened for icy waters and ice floes, with many extra frames added. A gangway door enables passengers to enter the ship at the same level as most docks and piers, averting a long walk up a steep gangway. A significant advantage is *Marco Polo*'s superior stability. Twelve-foot waves and rough seas, particularly in such notorious waters as Drake Passage on an Antarctica cruise, are hardly noticeable.

Most cabins are on the main deck, one level below Belvedere Deck, which accommodates most public rooms and includes the lobby, three of four entertainment lounges and bars, the casino, and a library with over 1,000 volumes.

Outside vantage points—especially on the upper deck forward and Promenade Deck aft—are numerous for viewing scenery and wildlife or watching sunsets.

ITINERARIES *See* Itinerary Index.

CABINS Being an older vessel, *Marco Polo* has a variety of cabin sizes and configurations. Almost 70% are outside; those in upper A–D categories have picture windows.

Cabins are light and handsomely appointed with light wood furniture and pastel bedspreads, curtains, and carpeting. Most are comfortably sized for long cruises, with ample storage space, dressing table with pull-out writing desk, and good reading lights. All have a telephone with international direct-dialing; radio; television with CNN in some areas, two channels for movies, and one for ship programs; safe; and a bathroom with shower, built-in hair dryer, and complimentary toiletries. Upper-category cabins provide bathrobes, slippers, and safes. Deluxe suites have a large sitting room, separate bedroom, large marble bathroom with tub and shower, and stocked minibar, replenished without charge. Junior suites and some deluxe cabins have a sitting area and bathroom with tub and shower. Family cabins have curtain-divided sleeping areas.

Views from accommodations on Sky Deck, including junior suites and deluxe cabins and ten cabins on the upper deck, are partially obstructed by lifeboats. These are noted on the deck plan in the line's brochure. Two deluxe suites and some upper-deck and Promenade Deck cabins have windows facing deck areas; however, one-way glass prevents outsiders from seeing in.

Specifications 129 inside cabins, 290 outside; 6 suites. Standard dimensions, 140–180 square feet. 388 cabins with 2 lower beds (42 convertible to double beds); 28 accommodate a third passenger; 10 accommodate 4 passengers. Suites and some upper-category cabins have double or queen-size beds, some have twin beds convertible to doubles. 2 wheelchair-accessible.

DINING Fine cuisine and exemplary service in elegant surroundings with tables set in fine china, crystal, and fresh flowers make dining one of the ship's best features. The **Seven Seas Restaurant** is a large, formal room dressed in mauves and grays. Breakfast and lunch have open seating, but the two dinner seatings have assigned tables with seating for four, six, or eight.

Entry is from the central foyer graced with large abstract paintings and Oriental statues. A central, raised area with Art Deco circular ceiling is separated from lower sides by etched glass partitions. Floor-to-ceiling mirrors on inside walls help create a spacious feeling. Booths and tables for two to ten people are by windows at either side of the room. The room is designated nonsmoking.

Dinner menus offer three appetizers, two soups, four entrees, and two or three desserts, cheeses, and fruits. Lighter, low-fat, low-salt, or vegetarian selections are indicated. Wines from South Africa, Australia, Argentina, Chile, California, and Europe are offered at reasonable prices.

Raffles serves casual breakfast and lunch buffets, plus Asian food on some evenings; at lunch its aft corners have cooked-to-order pasta and specialty stations, and outside, there's a deck grill and an ice cream and dessert bar. Its large windows overlook the pool deck. Chairs and tables with umbrellas are set around the pool. Afternoon tea is served here and in the small **Palm Court.**

Twice weekly in the evenings, Raffles becomes an elegant, very popular bistro for 90 passengers (reservations required) with a changing menu of Chinese, Thai, and other Asian cuisine. A $15 charge per person includes wine and gratuities. On more casual Mediterranean sailings, Raffles' capacity increases to 370, and Italian and regional specialties are served all but one night of the cruise, when the Asian menu is featured.

Surprising for a deluxe ship, room service is unavailable, except for continental breakfast and in case of illness. The line maintains that the ship's fine-dining experience is best enjoyed in the dining room. Some passengers might disagree after a long, tiring day on tour. Despite the official policy, most cabin stewards will bring food to the cabin on request. Another point: On tour days, dress for dinner is casual, and the dining room atmosphere more relaxed.

SERVICE *Marco Polo*'s tone is set by its friendly, service-oriented officers; lively British and American cruise staff; and most of all, its well-trained, hard-working Filipino crew, who win high praise for their attentiveness and cheerful dispositions. The dining staff seems to anticipate your every need, and the restaurant managers must have eyes in the back of their heads, always observing and rushing to correct even the simplest error. Cabin staff know passengers' names minutes after their arrival and address you by name throughout the cruise. This courtesy makes an indelible impression. Overall, the service on the *Marco Polo* is as fine as any we've had on a cruise ship, including the most luxurious ships at triple the price.

FACILITIES AND ACTIVITIES Lectures by experts on the cruise region are well attended. Lectures are not presented on Mediterranean cruises because of itineraries' port-intensive nature. Among other diversions are bridge tours; origami (Japanese paper-folding); art classes, bridge and backgammon lessons and tournaments; workshops on magic; white-elephant sales; passenger talent shows; service club meetings; fashion shows; and joke contests.

The **Ambassador Lounge** showroom features local entertainment brought on board in various ports. These presentations and Filipino crew show are highlights of the cruise and much better than mediocre musical revues and variety shows staged on other nights. Other entertainment might include a classical concert or a piano recital. The lounge, divided into three curved sections, slopes gently toward the stage. Sight lines are good except behind pillars or when the room is completely full. Large windows span both sides of the room, and a marble-topped bar flanked by mirrors is at the rear. Diamond-shaped lighting fixtures, blue carpets and curtains, and pink decor give the room a 1930s look.

The **Polo Lounge** piano bar, with a cream-colored baby grand piano encircled by a bar, is popular for predinner cocktails and late-evening relaxing and sing-alongs. It's also used for afternoon bridge games. The casino offers roulette, blackjack, and slot machines. To one side is an elegant white marble bar, black leather swivel chairs, and photos of famous entertainers. Off the casino are a small card room and a well-stocked library with comfortable leather armchairs and big windows. Guidebooks for the many countries visited by Marco Polo are provided. The **Palm Court,** a small room with marble-topped tables and wicker chairs, is a pleasurable retreat for afternoon tea or quiet conversation. Opposite are two small boutiques. Tucked away in a small area is the Internet center.

The **Charleston Club,** one of several multipurpose lounges, is used for bingo, painting lessons, cocktails, late-evening music and dancing, and midnight pizza. Glass doors open onto a lounge with a white baby grand piano and small bandstand, marble-topped bar, and dance floor. The lounge is a popular late-night gathering spot, though most passengers retire early.

SPORTS, FITNESS, AND BEAUTY On the Pool Deck is a 15-foot-long swimming pool with teak benches on three sides. Ping-Pong and shuffleboard are available. A fitness center on the upper deck has a small, mirrored exercise room with treadmills, stationary bicycles, rowing machine, stair steppers, weight machines, and free weights. Aerobics and exercise classes are offered. Separate saunas for men and women and three outside Jacuzzis are available. The beauty salon, operated by Mandara, offers a full range of services, including facials, massage, and hydrotherapy.

An upper-deck jogging track ringing the ship consists mostly of a narrow, rubberized path behind the lifeboats. For walkers, Promenade Deck has a one-fifth-mile course between the Charleston Club and bridge gangway. It's all on teak decks with sea views.

SHORE EXCURSIONS All cruises feature pre- and postcruise packages and are particularly popular given the distances most passengers travel to the ship. Most cruises also include an unusual highlight ashore Having the helipad is reassuring in case of an emergency in remote areas and for scouting ice conditions in Antarctica.

Note: Shore transport in some remote/primitive locations is not top of the line. Because of this, some shore excursions are inappropriate for passengers with limited mobility. Also, a fee may be charged for upgraded shore accommodations, but it is worth the cost in some out-of-the-way locations.

POSTSCRIPT Writing in 1298, Marco Polo opened his famous *Travels* with the words: "Ye kings, princes, nobles, townsfolk and all who wish to know the marvels of the world, have this book read unto you." If he were writing today, he might say, "All ye who wish to know the marvels of the world, take a cruise on the *Marco Polo*."

Princess Cruises

24305 Town Center Drive, Santa Clarita, CA 91355-4999
☎ 661-753-0000 or 800-PRINCESS; fax 661-753-1535
www.princess.com

TYPE OF SHIPS New superliners and megaliners.

TYPE OF CRUISES Modern, mainstream, worldwide, moderately upscale.

CRUISE LINE'S STRENGTHS
- worldwide itineraries
- Caribbean "private" island
- ScholarShip@Sea enrichment program
- spacious cabins, many with verandas
- 24-hour restaurant on most ships
- Scuba certification

CRUISE LINE'S SHORTCOMINGS
- congestion in 24-hour restaurants
- uneven cuisine in 24-hour restaurants

FELLOW PASSENGERS Princess passengers are difficult to characterize because their ages and incomes vary with the ships, seasons, and destinations. Basically, passengers are age 45 and older with annual incomes of $40,000 and more. They tend to be experienced travelers who cruise frequently and enjoy Princess's mainstream vacations, but they can range from a California schoolteacher or a Midwestern computer systems analyst on a first cruise to affluent retirees on their 20th cruise. On longer cruises and those to "exotic" destinations, the average age is 55 or older; on one-week Caribbean cruises, the average age is younger.

Recommended for Modestly affluent first-timers, frequent cruisers who want easy-paced travel and prefer a balance between sea and land time, and those who understand *The Love Boat* was only a TV show.

Not recommended for Swingers or first-time cruisers in search of the Love Boat; small-ship devotees.

CRUISE AREAS AND SEASONS Caribbean, year-round; Panama Canal, Mexico, Amazon, Orient, Holy Land, Australia/South Pacific, Hawaii/Tahiti, Southeast Asia, Africa, Antarctica, winter; Bermuda, Canada/New England, Alaska, Europe, Scandinavia, Mediterranean, Baltic, summer.

THE LINE Princess celebrated its 40th anniversary throughout 2005. The line marks its beginning in 1965 when a small, one-ship line called Princess Cruises sailed to the Mexican Riviera, using a 6,000-ton ferry vessel named *Princess Patricia*. In the intervening years, the company has grown from a pioneer of the modern-day cruising with a focus on the

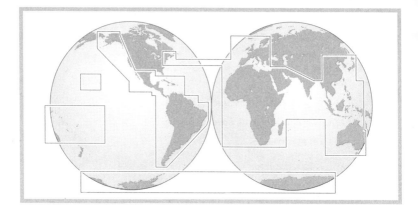

West Coast to a worldwide fleet of 14 modern ships sailing to all seven continents. From its inception, Princess Cruises helped create the relaxed, casual atmosphere that typifies today's cruises.

In 1974, P&O (Peninsular and Orient Steam Navigation Company), a British firm and one of the world's oldest and largest steamship companies, which had entered the cruise business in August 1844, bought the American company, Princess Cruises. It acquired its first *Island Princess* and first *Sun Princess*. The following year, P&O bought *Island Princess*'s sister, *Sea Venture*, and renamed her *Pacific Princess*, better known to TV viewers as *The Love Boat*.

In the early 1980s, Princess became a trendsetter for modern mainstream cruising when it launched the *Royal Princess*. She was hailed as the most stylish ship of the day, setting new standards in comfort and amenities. (Much to the sorrow of her loyal fans, *Royal Princess* was transferred to P&O Cruises in 2005.) In 1988, Princess almost doubled its capacity when it acquired Los Angeles–based Sitmar Cruises, another cruise pioneer, and integrated the Sitmar ships into its fleet. The line continued to benefit from its involvement in *The Love Boat* television series, which had an incalculable impact on modern cruising, popularizing it for a generation of television viewers—those who make up most of cruise passengers today—and helping dispel cruising's elitist image.

In the 1990s, Princess launched $3 billion worth of dazzling megaships. *Sun Princess* ushered in the Grand-class concept and the line's largest vessel when it entered service in 1995. She was followed by triplets over the following four years—all with the same architect, Njal Eide, as the *Royal Princess,* and, like her, with significant new features, including cruising's first 24-hour restaurant, two atrium lobbies, and two show lounges.

The 109,000-ton, $400 million *Grand Princess,* the largest cruise ship ever built when she debuted in 1998, was the first of the Princess fleet too large to transit the Panama Canal. The expansion tripled the line's capacity. Two more like her followed in 2001 and 2002, but that was only the beginning; two more ships, the 92,000-ton *Coral Princess* and *Island Princess,* made their debut in 2003 and ushered in a new class of ship. They were the best yet, combining the best features of the Sun- and Grand-class ships. They came with innovative power generation technology, combining diesel engines and gas turbines (the latter placed in the ship's funnel); and only 10% inside cabins and 80% of outside ones with balconies. In 2004, Princess saw its largest expansion to date with its largest ships: The 116,000-ton *Sapphire Princess* and *Diamond Princess* and the 113,000-ton *Caribbean Princess. Crown Princess,* is a slightly larger version of the *Caribbean Princess,* is scheduled to arrived in 2006, and their sister ship, *Emerald Princess,* in 2007.

Already a major player in Alaska and the Panama Canal, in the last few years, Princess has increased its Caribbean presence by 75%, added itineraries throughout Asia and the Pacific, expanded in Europe, added safaris in Kenya and South Africa, sent the *Royal Princess* on her first around-the-world cruise and her first Antarctic cruise, expanded its Scholarship@Sea program, and opened Internet Cafés fleetwide.

Princess's Alaska role was enhanced in 1997 with the opening of the $20-million Mount McKinley Princess Lodge, featured on the line's cruise tours. The lodge, which has just been expanded, sits on 146 acres inside Denali State Park and has a spectacular view of 20,320-foot Mount McKinley and the Alaska Range. Princess has three other Alaskan properties, including Copper River Princess Lodge, located at the entrance to America's largest national park, Wrangell–St. Elias, that opened in 2002.

On Caribbean cruises, the line offers Princess Cay, its private island in the Bahamas. Princess has one of the industry's best and most extensive selections of shore excursions. Almost all can be booked in advance of your cruise. Princess is also a leader in seasonal savings, deeply discounted advance-purchase fares, and two-for-one promotions. Just about everything you ever wanted to know about Princess Cruises is available on its enormous Web site, which was further enhanced with new features in 2003 and again in 2005.

In 2003, the hard-fought battle between Carnival Corp and Royal Caribbean to buy Princess/P&O Cruises ended in Carnival's favor. As a result, Carnival now owns 12 cruise lines with a total of 77 ships and 13 more on their way by 2009. All, including Princess, continue to operate separately under their own brands.

THE FLEET	BUILT/RENOVATED	TONNAGE	PASSENGERS
Caribbean Princess	2004	113,000	3,100
Coral Princess	2003	92,000	1,970
Crown Princess	2006	116,000	3,100

THE FLEET	BUILT/RENOVATED	TONNAGE	PASSENGERS
Dawn Princess	1997	77,000	1,950
Diamond Princess	2004	116,000	2,670
Emerald Princess	2007	116,000	3,100
Golden Princess	2001	109,000	2,600
Grand Princess	1998	109,000	2,600
Island Princess	2003	92,000	1,970
Pacific Princess	1999/2002	30,277	680
Regal Princess (to 10/2006)	1991/97/99	70,000	1,590
Sapphire Princess	2004	116,000	2,700
Sea Princess	1998	77,000	1,950
Star Princess	2002	109,000	2,600
Sun Princess	1995	77,000	1,950
Tahiti Princess	1999/2002	30,277	670

STYLE California modern in the mainstream, sedate but not staid, a Princess cruise is the essence of mass-market cruising: warm, inviting, and comfortable, suitable for a broad spectrum of people. The fleet has British officers, with their steamship tradition; Italian officers, with their natural charm; and a multicultural dining and hotel staff. Often trendsetters in facilities and amenities, the ships have the look of a well-bred, middle- to upper-middle-class environment (i.e., nothing too flashy or exaggerated) where almost anyone can feel at home. The line has worked hard to improve its entertainment and food, with menus featuring fresh, contemporary selections and now offers some of the best cuisine in its category and superior to most in its alternative Italian restaurant. Shipboard activities are varied and numerous. Ships fleetwide have gyms, saunas, and spa services and offer fitness and sports programs onboard and in port. Princess newest ships have telemedicine technology, giving ships' doctors worldwide access to medical specialists.

The New Waves scuba diving program, associated with PADI (Professional Association of Diving Instructors), offers snorkeling and scuba certification. All Princess ships have Internet access and alternative dining options. "Personal Choice Dining" and "Anytime Dining" are flexible dining room options, available on Sun- and Grand-class ships. With it, an automatic gratuity system for the staffs went into effect on board, adding $10 per person per day to a passenger's shipboard account. "FlightChoice" provides passengers with information on their flight schedule 60 days prior to sailing with the option to choose a customized air schedule. Cruise Personalizers is an online service that enables passengers to book shore excursions, special occasion arrangements, and dietary requirements in advance of their cruise, while Alaska Outfitters links passengers with local guides who can help them customize their wilderness experience.

Princess' latest facility, which the line has dubbed, "Direct to the Wilderness," enables passengers extending their cruise to tour Alaska, boarding their train right at the new Princess terminal in Whittier. From there, they are whisked to one of Princess' two Denali lodges, arriving the same afternoon. The new facility slashes travel time and the number of transfers, and thus gives passengers more time at Denali.

DISTINCTIVE FEATURES Scuba certification; 24-hour restaurants; terry robes and fresh fruit in cabins on request; fresh flowers in suites. Self-service launderettes, private Bahamian island, Alaska lodges. Telemedicine technology; wedding chapels; wedding webcam on Grand class; Personal Choice and Anytime Dining on Sun and Grand class. Wireless Internet capability fleetwide.

	HIGHEST	LOWEST	AVERAGE
PER DIEM	$365	$78	$188

Per diems are calculated from cruise line's nondiscounted *cruise-only* published fares on standard accommodations and vary by season, cabins, and cruise areas.

RATES Port charges included.

Special fares and discounts Frequent two-for-one fares; savings and upgrades on combining consecutive cruises.

- **THIRD/FOURTH PASSENGER:** 50% of fare for suites to 30% of fare for inside cabins.
- **CHILDREN'S FARE:** Same as third/fourth passenger.
- **SINGLE SUPPLEMENT:** 150–200%, Love Boat Savers discounts.

Packages

- **AIR/SEA:** Yes.
- **PRE/POST:** Yes.
- **OTHERS:** Wedding, honeymoon, anniversary, renewal of vows, and grand occasion.

PAST PASSENGERS Captain's Circle past-passenger club members are invited to captain-hosted cocktail party and participate in activities, including a club photo contest with prizes. Each receives a membership number to use when booking a cruise or corresponding with Princess, ensuring that they receive club benefits. Recognition pins are given, from the First Officer's pin for third and fourth cruises to a Commodore pin for ten or more. Quality gifts are presented at onboard parties to passengers who have sailed the most days with Princess. Members receive newsletters reporting new itineraries, new ship plans, staff profiles, chef's recipes, special discounts, and coupons for specific sailings and members-only sailings.

THE LAST WORD For millions of Americans, the popular image of cruising is a Princess cruise. It's perhaps not as luxurious or glamorous as the television image, but it's apparently close enough for the line to attract more than a million passengers a year. Princess's strength is in its consistency, new fleet, itineraries and well-executed shore excursions. Little changes from ship to ship. Your ship will be comfortable, your cruise enjoyable, and you will get a lot for your money, if you have realistic expectations and plan ahead to take advantage of the line's heavily discounted fares.

To its credit, Princess integrated seven enormous ships in four years smoothly—a gigantic job—and has been able to maintain the high standards, particularly of service, that has gained the line its loyal following.

Princess Cruises Standard Features

Officers British and Italian.

Staff Dining/Italian, European, Filipino; Cabin, Filipino; Cruise/American, British.

Dining facilities One main dining room, two seatings for three meals (Sun and Coral groups, two dining rooms; Grand group, three; *Diamond, Sapphire,* five); Personal Choice/Anytime Dining, on Sun, Coral, and Grand groups; alternative Bistro on *Regal,* Sun, Grand group: Italian, Sterling Steakhouse; Coral, Italian and New Orleans. Informal buffet breakfast, lunch in Lido restaurant; pizzeria; patisserie. Grand, Coral, and Sun groups, 24-hour dining. Balcony dinner/breakfast.

Special diets Diabetic, low-calorie/cholesterol/salt, vegetarian.

Room service 24-hour room service with light menu.

Dress code Casual during day; evenings vary, usually there are two smart casual, three informal, and two formal in week's cruise.

Cabin amenities CNN, ESPN, Discovery/Learning Channels and movies on television; fresh fruit daily and terry robes in cabins on request; direct-dial telephone; minifridges; hair dryers.

Electrical outlets 220/110 AC.

Wheelchair access 25–28 cabins on Grand group; 20 on Coral group; 19 on Sun group; 10 on *Regal.*

Recreation and entertainment Las Vegas– and Broadway-style revues, music and dancing, casino, disco, wine and caviar bar, karaoke, theater, dance classes, bingo, bridge. Grand group, virtual reality center, three show lounges. Coral group, two show lounges, one with three revolving stages; demonstration kitchen. Scholarship@ Sea courses.

Sports and other activities Two/three outdoor pools on all ships; Grand group, five; paddle tennis; jogging; scuba program; golf practice. Grand group, swim-against-current lap pool.

Beauty and fitness Spa, saunas, beauty/barber salon, fitness program.

Other facilities Library, hospital, boutiques; self-service laundry; meeting facilities; religious services; Grand group, wedding chapel, wedding webcam. Internet access.

Children's facilities Princess Kids, Princess's youth program on all ships (*Royal*, only if 20 or more children are sailing for ages 3–17); special facilities and full-time youth coordinators: Grand, Sun groups and *Regal*. Group baby-sitting available 10 p.m.–1 a.m. for children ages 3–12 for a $5 per hour charge. No in-cabin baby-sitting. See text.

Smoking No smoking in dining rooms and main showrooms; other public rooms have designated areas.

Princess suggested tipping Gratuities automatically added to passenger's account at $10 per person per day for dining and cabin service. Passengers can add or reduce amount at pursers' desk. 15% is added to bar bills.

Credit cards For cruise payment and on-board charges (settled at the end of the cruise): American Express/Optima, Carte Blanche, Diners Club, Master-Card, Visa, Discover; traveler's and personal checks; U.S., Canadian, and British currency.

Dawn Princess	**QUALITY 8**	**VALUE C**
Sea Princess	**QUALITY 8**	**VALUE C**
Sun Princess	**QUALITY 9**	**VALUE B**
REGISTRY Bermuda	**LENGTH** 856 feet	**BEAM** 106 feet
CABINS 975	**DRAFT** 26 feet	**SPEED** 21 knots
MAXIMUM PASSENGERS 1,950	**PASSENGER DECKS** 14	**ELEVATORS** 9
	CREW 830	**SPACE RATIO** 39.5

THE SHIPS Before its launch, *Sun Princess*—at the time, the largest cruise ship ever built—was described by Princess as offering an intimate feel. Skeptics scoffed.

But guess what? Princess did it. Well, "intimate" is perhaps a stretch, but it certainly managed to diminish the interiors of this big ship to a human scale. The Italian-built ship made her debut in December 1995, the first of Princess's new class of ships. Her mates, *Dawn Princess, Sea Princess,* and *Ocean Princess,* arrived between 1997 and 2000. (*Ocean Princess* left the fleet in September 2002 to join P&O Cruises.) From the outside, the gleaming white liners look colossal, towering 14 decks and stretching nearly three football fields in length. But inside, clever design has created a welcoming, accessible ambience.

The ships are spacious without being overwhelming. Warm colors and refined decor enhance the inviting atmosphere. The group set new standards for megaliners. Their layout is innovative in many ways. Rather than one cavernous atrium, these ships offer two. Instead of one enormous show lounge, there are two main show lounges. Two dining rooms are on different decks, and their layout, decor, and table arrangements help create an intimate ambience. Five dining outlets, including cruising's first 24-hour restaurant, provide options. Small spaces capture the intimacy of a small ship while creating options. Although other ships offer multiple lounges and dining alternatives, few developed the concept to the extent of Princess's Sun- and Grand-class ships. Whatever you choose to do, you can do, and whatever you miss one night, you can catch the next night.

The four-deck Grand Plaza is the ships' main atrium and social hub. It's a showcase of the exquisite Italian craftsmanship evident throughout the vessels and sets the tone for each ship. On the *Sun Princess*, in the elegant space, golden marble suggests the sun, and beige, bronze, and brown accents hint at shade. Sunbursts are set in the marble floors at every level of the atrium, and a backlit stained-glass dome overhead conveys an abstract underwater scene in aqua and turquoise. Glass elevators and a circular, floating staircase connect the decks and provide a stunning setting for the captains' parties.

Among the amenities are five swimming pools; a huge health center and spa; children's and teen rooms; a shopping arcade; computerized golf simulator; library and reading room with "audio chairs," each with its own bay window looking out to sea; and a business and conference center for up to 300 people. Each ship has a $2.5 million collection of paintings, sculptures, ceramic tiles, and Murano glass.

Another significant feature of the ships is their connection with the sea. A wraparound teak promenade lined with canopied steamer chairs provides a peaceful setting to read, daydream, or snooze.

ITINERARIES *See* Itinerary Index.

CABINS About two-thirds of cabins are outside; 70% of those have private balconies. There are 28 cabin categories. Nineteen cabins—among the most on any cruise ship—were designed to Americans with Disabilities Act specifications. Lifeboats obstruct views from 28 outside cabins on Promenade Deck. All standard cabins have a queen-size bed convertible to two singles, refrigerator, safe, ample closet, and bath with shower, terry robes, and hair dryers. All are well appointed and decorated in light, eye-pleasing colors.

Category "A" minisuites with private balcony are lavish in comfort, decor, and size—almost 400 square feet, plus the balcony. A marble-floored foyer with a mirror gives the illusion of a large apartment. Tastefully decorated in beige and butter tones accented by light woods and fine fabrics, each has a separate sitting area with leather chairs and a sofa that converts to a queen-size bed, and an entertainment console with television and music channels. A bar includes a refrigerator.

The bedroom, separated by a curtained archway, has a queen-size bed, vanity/desk, and second television. Drawer space is ample, and the small walk-in closet has a safe. Sliding doors in the sitting area and bedroom lead to a balcony extending the length of the suite. Two lounge chairs and a table make it ideal for breakfast or napping. Etched glass divides the whirlpool tub from a shower stall, and a door separates the toilet and wash basin.

As on all new Princess ships, there are self-service launderettes with washers, dryers, irons, and ironing boards at no charge. You pay for soap, bleach, and dryer sheets from a dispensing machine.

Specifications 372 inside cabins, 603 outside (410 with verandas); 32 minisuites and 6 suites with verandas. Standard dimensions, 135–173 square feet. All with 2 lower beds, convertible to queen; 300 with third berths; no singles. 19 wheelchair-accessible.

DINING Here are the choices: two dining rooms, cruising's first 24-hour restaurant, pizzeria, grill, patisserie, ice cream bar (there's a charge), 24-hour room service, and the newest addition, a steakhouse ($15 surcharge). And now, passengers have the option to dine where and when they want with Personal Choice and Anytime Dining.

The two main dining rooms are on Emerald Deck and Plaza Deck. They have an asymmetrical seating layout and small table groups in various sizes separated by etched-glass dividers. The design gives each group of tables a certain privacy. Separate galleys and service stations in every corner reduce traffic and help ensure that food reaches tables at the proper temperature. The walls are decorated with lovely scenic murals, adding to the gracious surroundings. Lunch and dinner menus offer a selection of appetizers, soups, salads, entrees, and desserts. A pasta special is offered every evening, although it is no longer prepared tableside. Healthy Choice selections, included on the regular menu, provide low-cholesterol, low-fat, and low-sodium alternatives. Wine list choices are reasonably priced, some under $20. Wines are also available by the glass.

Horizon Court on Lido Deck is an innovative 24-hour cafe with 270-degree ocean views through floor-to-ceiling windows, with seating on a trio of terraces. By day, buffets are served at two stations; at night, the center of the room becomes a restaurant with table service and a dance band. Reservations aren't needed, and there's no extra charge.

Breakfast choices range from fresh fruit to hot dishes, with a different special daily. At noon, entrees include ravioli, roast beef, and a salad bar, but selection and preparation do not match the quality or variety in the dining room.

The pizzeria offers a sidewalk cafe setting with marble-top tables and wrought-iron chairs on the balcony overlooking the atrium. Open for lunch and from 6 p.m. to 2 a.m., it serves pizza hot from the ovens, which are in plain sight. Waiters take orders for drinks and pizzas. There's no charge for the pizza, but diners tip the waiters. The outdoor **Grill** serves cooked-to-order hamburgers and hot dogs; the patisserie on the Plaza Deck has espresso, cappuccino, and pastries. **Sundaes,** the poolside ice cream parlor, is a Häagen-Dazs concession, and there's a charge per scoop.

SERVICE Officers are Italian, dining staff European, bar and cabin stewards Filipino, and reception and cruise staff American and British. Most of the crew are friendly and well trained, especially the dining staff, which consistently garners high praise. Service at the reception desk is uneven, and individual cabin stewards, ever smiling and eager to please, have received mixed reviews, often the result of insufficient training.

FACILITIES AND ACTIVITIES The cruise staff presents an enormous variety of entertainment. You might start your day's activities with bridge or dance lessons, or a craft demonstration. In the afternoon you might play golf or Ping-Pong, take a lesson in the casino, join a word or trivia game, or watch a culinary demonstration or horse races. Movies are shown three or four times daily. And then, there's bingo.

The wood-paneled library has a large selection of books, plus "audio chairs" with built-in headsets that are set by large bay windows overlooking the water. The **Card Room** is also used as a meeting room or for private parties. The ships offer a full schedule of daytime diversions, from art auctions and dance lessons to bridge tournaments and bingo. Internet cafes with 20 or more computers are now available on all Princess ships. Internet access costs 35 cents per minute.

Note: Art auctions have become ubiquitous on major cruise ships. Most of the art is terrible and terribly overpriced, despite claims to the contrary. One *Sea Princess* passenger recently wrote:

. . . the tacky, in-your-face display of art for auction [is] everywhere on the ship from embarkation to disembarkation—and it grew day by day . . . on easels, hanging on walls, and even stacked up around the casino lobby, Atrium piano bar, and Wheelhouse and Horizon Court. Tacked on to many were auction announcements with the time and location highlighted in thick orange magic marker. Flyers also appeared in cabin mailboxes almost daily, and, after the "final" auction, another notice appeared announcing the "requested FINAL 'Rocky IV, Death Wish' absolutely final auction." Frankly, Princess has too much class to be using this sort of revenue-generating scheme in the first place, but the carnival hawker's atmosphere and the total lack of knowledge or finesse exhibited by the auctioneer were almost comical. Sea Princess, like her sisters, is an elegant ship with lovely decor, but even the "legitimate" artwork in many passageways and some elevator lobbies was obscured by the easels and announcements of art for sale.

We couldn't agree more.

The Grand Plaza is the ships' hub. The Promenade Deck contains only public rooms and is anchored by the two showrooms. Forward is the **Princess Theatre,** with an enormous stage for Broadway-style productions. Graduated theater seating and an absence of pillars ensure fine sight lines.

Aft is the marble-walled **Vista Lounge** with tiered seating and floor-to-ceiling ocean views. Dancing and cabaret-style entertainment are offered. To one side, a large, free-form bar encourages mingling. Shows in both lounges are repeated—four performances each for early and late seating over consecutive days. The ship's program suggests that passengers attend according to their dining room seating, but some passengers prefer to return to one show for an encore. This hasn't created seating problems because not all passengers attend all performances.

The **Grand Casino** has slot machines, video poker, blackjack, roulette, and craps. The stained-glass ceiling, lighted to simulate a spinning roulette wheel, is visible on the deck below, from where passengers access the casino via a staircase in the second atrium. On the *Sun*, a bronze tubular sculpture by Arizonan Lyle London decorates the lower level.

Flanking the ships' second atrium are the disco and the romantic **Rendezvous Lounge.** The disco's entrance glitters with fiber-optic lights and a video dance floor, rather than video wall. Rendezvous Lounge, an elegant refuge, serves caviar, imported wines, and champagnes by the glass. The **Atrium Lounge,** with a white baby-grand piano and dance floor, is particularly popular for predinner cocktails and late-night sing-alongs. Afternoon tea is also served there as well as in the **Horizon Lounge.**

The **Wheelhouse Bar** near the Princess Theatre is one of the ship's most attractive, inviting rooms. Resembling a British men's club, it's decorated in rosewood and dark burgundy with sumptuous, spruce-green leather chairs. Ship models and P&O memorabilia adorn the walls. Live dance music seems a jarring note in this room that could be ideal for quiet conversation. Yet passengers seem to enjoy the lively atmosphere, packing the dance floor before dinner and late into the night. On the *Sun*, a gallery outside the bar displays costumes worn by opera diva Dame Joan Sutherland.

Before the *Sea Princess* returned to Princess Cruises, after a two-year tour of duty with P&O Cruises, her top deck was outfitted with a special 300-foot Time Square–type outdoor screen for Princess' new, popular "Movies Under the Stars." Passengers can enjoy first-run movies, concerts, and sporting events. Generally, reservations are required.

SPORTS, FITNESS, AND BEAUTY Some of the most innovative architectural designs benefit sports and fitness. One of the ship's pools is open to the sky, though set between two decks. On Riviera Deck are the main pools and the ocean-view spa. Half of this large area is a well-equipped gym;

the other half is a mirrored room where aerobics classes are held. The spa has 11 massage and beauty treatment rooms, saunas, showers, changing facilities, and an ocean-view beauty salon. Next door, a computerized golf center simulates play on a half-dozen top courses ($20 per half-hour for up to four players).

The **Lotus Spa** program features daily exercise and well-being classes as well as traditional and exotic spa and salon services. Start your day with a Lotus Walk on promenade deck followed by a spinning class or aerobics and stretch classes. More leisurely classes include Aqua Aerobics, Pathway to Yoga, and the use of visualization, meditation, and relaxation techniques in the Mind, Body, and Soul classes.

Sunbathing areas are spread across three top decks with a pool and bar (live band during daytime) on one; another pool, whirlpool, and grill on another; and a splash pool, bar, and paddle tennis, volleyball, basketball court on the third. A one-sixth-mile jogging track girdles the top deck; a broad teak promenade encircles the ship. (Three times around equals a mile.)

CHILDREN'S FACILITIES "Princess Kids," Princess's fleetwide youth program provides age-specific activities for three groups: Princess Pelicans (ages 3–7), Princess Pirateers (ages 8–12), and Off Limits (ages 13–17). It also includes in-port programs with lunch, running from 8 a.m. to 5 p.m. at no charge and learning opportunities through a partnership with the California Science Center and the use of National Wildlife Federation educational materials on wildlife and conservation. The program includes studies of the stars, ocean and coral reef, building and racing sailboats, among others, and complements Princess junior ranger program in Alaska and the fleetwide Save our Seas environmental program. Participants take home a "Pete's Pals" booklet reflecting the endangered species including white pelicans, manatees, sea turtles and panda bears in areas Princess sails. Group baby-sitting for ages 3–12 is available from 10 p.m.–1 a.m. for $5 per hour per child. Children can now travel on most itineraries at six months.

Sun Princess's **Fun Zone** is one of the most enchanting children's playrooms at sea. Here, kids romp in a splash pool, play in a castle and big-as-life doll's house, and perform in a little theater. Next door, **Cyberspace** (**Wired** on *Sea*), the teen club, offers video games, a disco, and refreshments.

POSTSCRIPT Of all the megaliners launched since the mid-1990s, *Sun Princess* and her siblings have best reduced behemoth interiors to human scale. They also prove that big can be beautiful, in large part due to their fine Italian craftsmanship. With choices 24 hours a day—in dining, activities, entertainment, and relaxing—anyone seeking less regimented cruising should find happiness on these ships.

Caribbean Princess	QUALITY 8	VALUE B
Crown Princess	2006	
Diamond Princess	QUALITY 8	VALUE B
Grand Princess	QUALITY 8	VALUE B
Golden Princess	QUALITY 8	VALUE B
Sapphire Princess	QUALITY 8	VALUE B
Star Princess	QUALITY 8	VALUE C
REGISTRY Bermuda/Britain	LENGTH 951 feet	BEAM 118/159
CABINS 1,300–1557	DRAFT 26 feet	SPEED 22 knots
MAXIMUM PASSENGERS	PASSENGER DECKS 13	ELEVATORS 16
2,600–3,100	CREW 1,200/1,110	SPACE RATIO 37/42

THE SHIPS Saying the 109,000-ton, $450 million *Grand Princess* was the largest, most expensive cruise ship built when she debuted doesn't say much. But comparisons clarify the image: *Grand Princess is* about four times the length of New York's Grand Central Station. She's 28 feet taller than Niagara Falls, 49 feet taller than the Statue of Liberty, and too wide by 43 feet to transit the Panama Canal.

And what does "most expensive" mean? *Grand Princess*'s price tag was almost twice the cost of the Pathfinder mission to Mars. Happily, there's plenty on this ship to suggest that Princess got its money's worth. Of the ship's 928 outside cabins, 710 have balconies—the most on any other cruise ship at the time. She was the first with three main dining rooms and three main show lounges, each with a different show nightly. Her 13,500-square-foot casino was the largest afloat.

Get the picture? She's big, expensive, and has plenty of wow! But *Grand Princess* also comes with innovations even more exciting than those of the Sun group. For starters, she has cruising's first wedding chapel (Princess is, after all, the company of *The Love Boat*); the first virtual reality arcade with a motion-based ride for up to 18 people, car races, and skiing; a blue-screen video production facility that lets passengers star in their own videos; and the first swim-against-the-current lap pool at sea. She was the first cruise ship with a Southwestern restaurant (one of three alternative restaurants) and the first to have 28 wheelchair-accessible cabins. At the time she debuted, *Grand Princess* was one of few cruise ships with duplicate operational and technical systems to ensure continued operation in emergencies. Her sisters, *Golden Princess* and *Star Princess,* have similar features.

Grand Princess's most unusual and noticeable design feature is the **Skywalkers Nightclub,** an aluminum structure suspended 18 decks above the water at the stern like a skybox at a stadium. Accessed by a glass-enclosed moving walkway, it's an observation lounge by day and a disco by night.

The ship's enormous interior is diminished by being divided into many small spaces offering dozens of activities—so many choices that a week of cruising isn't enough time to try them all. The myriad options should be a comfort to first-time cruisers fearful of feeling confined or having nothing to do.

Among other distinctive features is the bridge, which extends beyond both sides of the ship. It's glass-enclosed to protect the computerized navigational instruments. A bow observation area gives passengers nearly the same view that officers have from the bridge. Balconies, outlined in blue glass, are built out from the ship's body of the ship in stair-stepped tiers. The design opens all balconies to the sun, but the negatives are a loss of privacy (cabins above overlook lower spaces) and noise traveling upward.

In spring 2004, the Grand class more than doubled in cabin count when three more super megaliners were added: the 113,000-ton *Caribbean Princess* in April, the 116,000-ton *Diamond Princess* in May, and. the 116,000-ton *Sapphire Princess* in June. The count will jump again when two more ships similar to the *Caribbean Princess* will be added—the *Crown Princess* in 2006 and the *Emerald Princess* in 2007. From June 14 through October 18, the *Crown Princess* will sail from New York on alternating nine-day Eastern Caribbean voyages to Bermuda, San Juan, St. Thomas, and Grand Turk in the Turks & Caicos, and Western Caribbean to Pt. Canaveral, Grand Cayman, Ocho Rios, and Grand Turk. The itinerary is new for Princess, and the *Crown Princess* will be one of the first cruise ships to call at Grand Turk upon completion of the island's new terminal. The 113,000-ton *Caribbean Princess,* built at Fincantieri shipyard in Italy, is a slightly larger version of the *Grand Princess,* with most of the same features—three dining rooms, three show lounges, several alternative restaurants, a wedding chapel, **Lotus Spa,** nine-hole putting course and golf simulator, library, and Internet cafe. But she has more cabins—261 more to be exact, in all categories. Like her sister ships, 80% of all outside cabins, or 881 cabins, have balconies. The *Sapphire* and the *Diamond* are larger versions of the *Grand* as well, with only minor differences.

A brand-new feature on *Caribbean Princess* is "Movies Under the Stars," a great way for passengers to enjoy the latest movies under the heavens as they relax on deck. The movies are played on a giant, Times Square–style screen built into the superstructure of the vessel at the midship pool. The feature has been so popular, that Princess is extending it to its other ships, starting with *Grand Princess* and *Sea Princess* (which have already been retrofitted for it), and the new *Crown Princess,* where it is being incorporated in the ship's construction. The screen can also show special sports events and be used for the Caribbean night parties held during every cruise. And true to any movie-watching venue, popcorn and other snacks are available. Another new feature is a Caribbean-themed alternative restaurant.

ITINERARIES *See* Itinerary Index.

CABINS These *Princesses* have 35 cabin categories each! Most cabins are on Decks 8–12, with a few on Deck 5 and 14 and the outside cabins, 80% have verandas. The majority range from 215–255 square feet, a spaciousness generally available only in deluxe suites. Decor uses pastels and renders a pleasant ambience. Closet and shelf space is generous; drawers are limited but adequate.

The ships' balconies offer several benefits. First, they entice passengers to spend more time in their cabins, reducing crowds in public areas. Second, with so many available in standard cabin, the amenity is affordable for a wider audience. The ships' wheelchair-accessible cabins are also available in all main categories.

Cabins are more traditional in layout than those on the Sun group. Suites have tiled (not marbled) bathrooms and do not have Jacuzzi tubs. The two 800-square-foot Grand Suites (one on *Golden*) are aptly named. Each has a large balcony with whirlpool, a living room with fireplace, wet bar, three televisions, and walk-in closets.

New amenities have been added for passengers in suites, including expedited embarkation/disembarkation, packing/unpacking service upon request, free Internet access, dry cleaning, laundry, and even shoe polishing. On formal nights, they'll receive a complimentary corsage and boutonniere. They can enjoy tea served in their suites and schedule a private portrait sitting with a shipboard photographer.

Specifications Caribbean Princess, 1,557 cabins, 1,105 outside, 452 inside; 25 suites with balconies; 2 interconnecting family suites; 180 minisuites with balconies; 674 standard with balcony. *Golden, Star/Grand,* 1,301 cabins, 935/928 outside; 366/372 inside (160 square feet); 205/208 suites with balconies (325–800 square feet); 502 outside with balconies (215–255 square feet); 228/218 standard outside (165–210 square feet); 28 wheelchair-accessible including 18 outside/10 inside (240–385 square feet); 609 with upper berths. *Diamond, Sapphire,* 1,337 cabins, 960 outside, 377 inside; 28 suites with balconies; 2 interconnecting family suites; 186 minisuites with balconies; 532 standard with balcony.

DINING Each ship has eight dining venues and offers the line's Personal Choice dining options. This enables passengers to choose between "Traditional Fixed Seating" dining with assigned seats and "Anytime

Dining," thus providing passengers more flexibility in deciding when, where, and with whom they dine, as in a restaurant.

The main dining rooms, named for famous Italian artists—**Botticelli, Da Vinci,** and **Michelangelo** (on the *Star,* the rooms are named for famous Italian places: **Portofino, Amalfi,** and **Capri**)—have low ceilings and clusters of tables in a serpentine layout that breaks the space, so guests don't feel they're dining in a large room with many people. At least one of the three dining rooms is designated for traditional dining; one for Anytime Dining; and the third for either arrangement, depending on demand. Generally, it is wise to make a reservation if you want to dine at a specific time. Otherwise, you can just show up.

Horizon Court, the 24-hour lido cafe, has its own galley and a terrace for outdoor dining. The layout is different from that on *Sun Princess* and causes crowding and confusion. The food, which was sub-par for Princess Cruises on *Grand* in the beginning, seems to have been improved with more variety and selections. Open for brunch (on sea days only) and dinner by reservation are the popular **Sabatini's Trattoria,** an Italian specialty restaurant ($20 surcharge), and the **Sterling Steakhouse** ($15 surcharge)

The *Sapphire Princess* expanded the "Personal Choice" dining concept with a new twist—five main dining rooms, four with a different cuisine and theme. Passengers on the "Anytime Dining" plan can choose the one traditional seating dining room or smaller restaurants, each with its own menu—**Vivaldi** (Italian cuisine), Sterling (steakhouse), **Santa Fe** (Southwestern) and **Pacific Moon** (Asian). They also have the option of ordering from each restaurant's themed dishes in addition to each day's menu. Those in the traditional dining room are not left out; they have changing menu options, including items from the themed restaurants.

Another new feature is Balcony Dinner, $50 per person, and Balcony Breakfast, $25 per person, with cocktails, fresh flowers, champagne, special menus, and in-room service. For now, the breakfast is served on sea days and is available fleetwide, but the dinner is an amenity on Grand-class ships only.

Outdoors are **Prego,** where pizza is served all day; **Trident Grill,** providing hot dogs and burgers; and an ice cream bar (**Sundaes** on *Golden* and **Scoops** on *Star*), a Häagen-Dazs concession where a scoop costs $2. The **Promenade Bar** overlooking the atrium on Deck 7 doubles as a patisserie, serving a light breakfast of croissants and espresso, as does the **Lobby Bar** on Deck 5 on *Golden* and *Star*. Room service is available 24 hours. Because dining is available at all times, passengers do not need to plan shore time around mealtimes. The many dining options also reduce lines and crowds.

FACILITIES AND ACTIVITIES The *Grand Princess*'s **Voyage of Discovery,** the $2.5 million virtual reality center, is an eye-popper. The room has interactive games and a cyberbar, but its main attraction is a wild, motion-based virtual-reality ride that seats 18 people. Passengers buy a Voyager card for $20, which they use to start machines, and the cost of play ($0.75–$3) is deducted. At the blue-screen **Limelight Studio,** passengers can star in their own video, inserted into an existing scene from a popular movie or historical event. Neither the virtual-reality center or blue-screen studio are found on *Golden Princess* or *Star Princess.* Rather, *Golden* has a digital studio which provides a face-replacement computer program. *Star* (and other ships) have a blue-screen portrait type of computer where they can photograph the subject against a variety of backgrounds (similar to the Limelight system). It's a portable system operated off a laptop computer.

Standard diversions are plentiful: bingo, karaoke, cards, board games, and writing room. The small business center has phone, fax, and computer facilities. (There's a charge to use the equipment.) In the 36-seat wedding chapel, couples can be married or renew their vows with the captain presiding. All six ships have webcams in their chapels, enabling folks at home to watch an onboard wedding live.

Shops sell sundries, clothing, jewelry, perfumes, and souvenirs. All are convenient to the Grand Atrium, the heart of the ship. In the **Art Gallery,** reproduction and original prints are for sale; the ubiquitous auctions are held almost daily and, unfortunately, often obscure the ship's $3 million museum-quality collection of contemporary art. The ship's library, **A Quiet Corner,** boasts an extensive book collection and the ever-popular private reading/listening chairs. The newest addition is the **Internet Café,** which is open 24 hours daily; and a florist, who prepares fresh floral arrangements for purchase.

The ships offer a great variety of entertainment. Each of three showrooms has its own shows nightly. **Vista Show Lounge,** the midsize theater, presents cabaret-style entertainment that's quite varied. **Princess Theatre,** a two-deck showroom, stages large-scale production shows and revues and has the best sight lines and most comfortable seats of any shipboard theater we have experienced. The shows, all produced by Princess's production department, are outstanding. The **Explorer's Lounge** nightclub features soloists and bands playing a variety of music. The **Casino,** designed by the architects who created Caesars Palace Forum in Las Vegas, has one of the world's largest examples of holographic art. It also has 260 slot machines, 17 blackjack/poker tables, roulette, and craps.

The ships have many other small entertainment places, some with music and dancing. The **Wheelhouse Bar,** with the ambience of a private club, offers music for dancing; **Snookers** sports bar has a bank of television monitors that broadcast sports programs, also available in cabins (the system can show events on Princess Theatre's big screen, too). **Calypso Bar** and **Oasis Bar,** outdoors and poolside, are frequently the scene of special events, including the Captain's Party. A retractable dome can be closed in bad weather. **Center Court Bar** is near the sports facilities; **Sea Breeze** and the **Mermaid's Tail** are mid-deck bars. **Alfresco's** bar overlooks the aft pool, which can be covered and converted into a stage for live concerts.

On *Sapphire Princess,* the signature Skywalkers Lounge has been moved a bit further forward than on other Grand Class ships, providing 35% more space and a new 125-foot balcony. **Club Fusion,** a multipurpose, high-tech venue, is ideal for dancing or for use as a theater with its 42 high-definition television screens.

SPORTS, FITNESS, AND BEAUTY Each of the Grand-class ships has five swimming pools—including one for children and one for crew—and nine whirlpools. The **Princess Links** computerized golf simulator lets passengers try some of the world's top courses. A landscaped putting green is available, as are paddle tennis, basketball, and volleyball courts. A swim-against-the-current lap pool is the centerpiece of the **Lotus Spa.** The gym has treadmills, Stairmasters, Lifecycles, weight machines, an area for exercise and aerobics classes, and new trainer-led options (all at a charge) like yoga, kickbox press, pulse group cycling, and Pilates, and an outside jogging track. There are changing rooms and saunas (no charge) for men and women. The beauty spa, operated by Steiner, has 11 massage rooms offering a range of pricey treatments, such as aromatherapy massage, mud and seaweed wraps, and reflexology. Also featured are new Asian-influenced treatments, such as chakra stone therapy, a massage with hot, oiled stones. On *Star Princess*, the **Lotus Spa** is even larger than on her sister ships, with more treatment rooms and a thermal suite with steam rooms, heated lounge chairs, cool showers, and an ice bath for use by spa clients only, before or after treatments. A teak promenade encircles the ship; five and a half laps is just shy of a mile.

CHILDREN'S FACILITIES The two-level **Fun Zone Children's Center** offers a whale-shaped splash pool, life-sized doll's house, children's theater, ball jump, games, and more. Programs are age-specific and supervised. The **Off Limits Teen Center,** also bilevel, has a video disco, refreshment bar, video games, and private whirlpool. See "Children's Facilities" in the Sun group for Princess Kids' new expanded program.

SHORE EXCURSIONS Princess shore excursions are well organized, particularly given the size of ship and number of people touring. Excursions on Mediterranean cruises cover the most important attractions; we recommend them, especially for first-timers. Passengers familiar with the ports may want to arrange their own activities. During the *Star*'s calls in Mexico, Princess has introduced a variety of new, adventure-type tours, such as "Dolphin Encounters" and kayaking, certified scuba diving and Sierra Madre excursions in all-terrain vehicles, at a range of prices. Descriptions of shore excursions and prices are available on the Princess Web site; once you have booked your cruise, you can also book shore excursions.

Princess' latest Web site innovation is interactive eBrochures, said to be the cruise industry's first. It offers a clickable table of contents, interactive deck plans, a built-in search function, custom printing of selected pages, the ability to zoom in on maps and deck plans, and direct links to detailed content on **www.princess.com.**

POSTSCRIPT Even with their many innovations and attractions, passengers who have sailed with the line before will recognize these super-megaliners as very much Princess ships. They appeal most to those who see their size as a positive thing, providing options every hour of the day. They are sure to be popular with first-time cruisers. A big dividend of their size is a smooth ride. Those with health problems will be comforted to know the ships have a two-way video system (the first cruise ships to have it) that allows the ships' doctors to confer live with medical specialists and top hospitals ashore and in the United States. *Golden Princess* and *Star Princess*'s telemedicine facilities are even more state-of-the-art and include a digital X-ray machine, defibrillators positioned around the ship as well as in the ship's hospital, and other high-tech equipment.

Regal Princess	QUALITY 7	VALUE C
REGISTRY Bermuda	LENGTH 811 feet	BEAM 105 feet
CABINS 795	DRAFT 26 feet	SPEED 22.5 knots
MAXIMUM PASSENGERS 1,590	PASSENGER DECKS 11	ELEVATORS 9
	CREW 696	SPACE RATIO 44

THE SHIP Anyone familiar with the *Regal Princess* may not recognize her after her recent interior renovation and redesign that added a new 24-hour cafe, a children's center, and a remodeled atrium. The goal of the project, which comprised the largest refurbishment ever done on a Princess ship, was to bring the vessel in line with the newer Grand class, often using design, decor, and color schemes from those ships.

Regal Princess, whose godmother is former British prime minister Margaret Thatcher, was added in 1991. (In 2002, her twin, the former *Crown Princess,* was transferred to Aida Cruises, a Carnival brand serving the German market. The *Regal* is scheduled to leave the fleet in October 2006.) The *Regal,* part of the inventory Princess received from its Sitmar purchase, was very different from any other cruise ship. Designed by Renzo Piano, architect of Paris's Pompidou Center, the Italian-built superliner has sleek lines that Piano says were inspired by the shape of a dolphin. Even now, the unorthodox design garners mixed reviews.

The good news: space and comfort. *Regal* is a superliner, but she carries 25–30% fewer passengers than some of her counterparts. This spaciousness is apparent in wide corridors, lounges with high ceilings, and large cabins. Even standard cabins are the size of some other ships' suites. The ship's appointments range from elegant, with top-quality fabrics, well-made furnishings, and museum-quality works by renowned artists (including Frank Stella, Robert Motherwell, and David Hockney) to the eclectic. Some bars display pop art, and 18th-century romantic landscapes hang in dining rooms. The result is an interesting, stimulating, and entertaining environment.

The main drawback of the interiors is that they look and feel like a hotel. Outside decks are few, and corridors with no ocean view border promenades and lounges. Unless your cabin has a veranda, you must go to the top deck or small, upper aft areas to see the seascape. The forward section, particularly, is closed off from the sea. And the Dome atop of the ship, meant to be a quiet observation lounge, is frenetic: Slot machines buzz in the casino, dance music spills from bars, and the area is thronged. The cavernous space might have been better used for outdoor decks.

The ship's new look is most evident in the three-deck atrium, the Plaza, which serves as the lobby and gathering place. Overall, it has been given a warmer, more inviting appearance. The backdrop of the main staircase is a large vertical water sculpture and a series of small, marble pools intended to create a restful atmosphere with the sound of water. Columns and railings are now covered with cherry wood, and greenery-filled marble planters at their base add warmth. There is a new marble floor at the base of the main staircase, and a large glass chandelier hangs above it. In the **Patisserie** on the first level, windows were added, helping give the space an airy look. Behind the newly paneled reception desk is a dramatic three-dimensional sculpture of swimming dolphins. On the upper decks, rich wood paneling was also added to the facades of the shops and bars around the atrium.

Actually, the most extensive aspect of the recent renovations is not visible. New stern thrusters were installed, increasing the ships' maneuvering capability and allowing them to visit ports without tug facilities.

The *Regal* will introduce a new 21-day round-trip sailing from San Diego, departing November 15, 2005, with an interesting and unusual itinerary calling at San Juan del Sur in Nicaragua and Puerto Quetzal in Guatemala, as well as a unique overnight in the Panama Canal.

ITINERARIES *See* Itinerary Index.

CABINS Spacious cabins are one of the ship's best features. They come in 26 categories and four basic arrangements: inside or outside standard doubles; outside double with a tiny balcony; outside minisuites with small veranda; and full suites with veranda. The six top categories plus the largest of the inside group are on three upper decks; the other 11 categories are spread across four lower decks. All have five-channel television with CNN, ESPN, and Discovery Channel; four-channel radio; direct-dial telephone; refrigerator; safe; walk-in closets, separate dressing area, and generous drawer space; and key card for door locks. Terry robes and fresh fruit are provided in all cabins. Standard outside cabins without a balcony have oversized windows. Lifeboats are midway down the sides of the ship; 26 cabins on Dolphin Deck have obstructed views (they are indicated on the deck plan).

Specifications **171** inside, **440** outside cabins (134 with verandas); 36 minisuites, 14 suites with verandas. Standard dimensions, 190 square feet. All with 2 lower beds, convertible to queen; some have third/fourth berths; no singles. 10 wheelchair-accessible.

DINING The main dining room, which has two seatings for three meals, was extensively redesigned from floor to ceiling with new decorative touches, including new carpets and wall coverings, lighting and dimmer system, artwork, and treatment to the stainless-steel surfaces to soften the room's appearance. Also changing the look is a new table arrangement, adapted from the Grand-class ships, that provides for greater privacy and better service.

Dinner menus are posted at bars and elsewhere aboard the ships. They're similar fleetwide, offering six courses for lunch and seven for dinner, with numerous selections for each course. Pizza lovers will enjoy the poolside pizzeria, complete with checkered tablecloths and Chianti bottles. It's open for lunch and in the evening, serving made-to-order pizzas at no extra cost. The patisserie has excellent espresso and cappuccino and assorted fresh pastries.

Regal's **Café del Sol** has been transformed into a 24-hour restaurant with increased seating capacity by an extension at the aft end of the cafe. It was remodeled with new seating arrangements and serving lines and given new decor; a new galley was added for bistro service in the evening. The extension also provided space for a dance floor and stage. On the open deck, there's a new salad bar and a hamburger bar.

SERVICE Reports indicate that service and food have improved as Princess has worked to correct past flaws.

FACILITIES AND ACTIVITIES Another of the ship's best features is her lounges—greatly varied in size, decor, ambience, and entertainment. The largest is the handsome **International Lounge,** a bilevel show lounge with a horseshoe-shaped stage. **Bacchus** is a small wine-by-the-glass and caviar bar that was given a more intimate setting with lowered ceilings and glass partitions, along with new murals and other decorative accents. The **Bengal Bar** has a stage for a piano, a dance floor, and a mirrored bar. The room sparkles with brass and glass and has ceiling fans suggesting the days of the raj, complete with a brass statue of a Bengal tiger.

Next door, the intimate piano bar displays murals of fashionably dressed revelers from the 1920s. The **Adagio**, as it's called, also has an espresso machine. One flight up, the **Stage Door** cabaret and late-night disco offers a sunken dance floor. **Characters** on the Lido Deck is a colorful poolside bar serving innovative drinks. The huge, top-deck **Dome** with 19-foot ceilings is largely occupied by the casino. It has a dance floor, bar, and 100 trees! A cinema, library, and card room are available.

SPORTS, FITNESS, AND BEAUTY The Sun Deck has two outdoor pools, one with a swim-up bar and the other with waterfalls and whirlpools; a paddle tennis/volleyball court; and a one-sixth-mile jogging track. There's no wraparound deck. **Images,** a beauty and fitness center, has an aerobics area, weight machines, exercise bikes, and a steam room.

CHILDREN'S FACILITIES During the latest renovations, a brand-new, 2,000-square-foot children's center was added to the top sports deck, directly above the cafe extension, replacing the basketball court. The multipurpose center can be divided into separate areas for children and teens or converted into a meeting or conference room. "Princess Kids," Princess's fleetwide youth program, provides supervised activities and facilities. See "Children's Facilities" in the Sun-class section for details. Children younger than age 18 must be accompanied by an adult and have written consent from both parents or legal guardians to cruise.

Coral Princess	QUALITY 9	VALUE B
Island Princess	(PREVIEW)	
REGISTRY Bermuda	LENGTH 964 feet	BEAM 106 feet
CABINS 987	DRAFT 26 feet	SPEED 21.5 knots
MAXIMUM PASSENGERS 2,566	PASSENGER DECKS 16	ELEVATORS 12
	CREW 900	SPACE RATIO 44.6

THE SHIPS In 2003, the 92,000-ton *Coral Princess* made her maiden voyage in and was christened in the Panama Canal by the president of Panama—the first cruise ship ever to have such an honor; and her sister, *Island Princess,* debuted Vancouver, also marking a milestone as the first cruise ship ever christened in the Canadian port city.

These twins are a new class of ships for Princess, built specifically to transit the Panama Canal, and they reverse the line's recent trend of building megaships of over 100,000 tons. Despite their smaller size, they are very spacious and include most amenities and services found on Princess's largest vessels, such as a wedding chapel, alternative dining options, a 24-hour restaurant, **Internet Café,** and a substantial number of balcony cabins. Indeed, the duo appear to combine the best features of the Sun and Grand classes, plus having some great attractions that even the bigger ships can't boast.

Constructed at Chantiers de l'Atlantique, the ships are Princess's first French-built vessels. They are very well laid out, making it easy for passengers to get oriented quickly. Their refined and pleasing decor is sophisticated yet comfortable, interesting in detail, yet easy on the eyes. Among their newest features are the unusual high-tech facilities in the aft show lounge and their innovative power-generation technology—a gas turbine/diesel engine combination, with the gas turbines placed in the ships' funnels. The configuration not only has environmental advantages but also allows for additional space inside the ships used for enhanced passenger facilities. Then, there are the unique features: the first-ever cruise ship kiln—yes, a kiln—and a television-style demonstration kitchen. Emeril would feel right at home.

ITINERARIES *See* Itinerary Index.

CABINS   Nearly 90% of the ships' cabins are outside, and most of these—83%—have private balconies. Although there are 33 different price levels, mostly resulting from location, season, and length of cruise, essentially there are only five types of cabins: suites with balconies (468–591 square feet); minisuites with balconies (323 square feet); outside standard with balconies (214–257 square feet); outside standard (168 square feet); and inside standard (160 square feet). The best value for money are the outside standards with balconies, rightly called "affordable balconies." The wheelchair-accessible cabins range from 217 to 374 square feet and are available in most categories.

Throughout, the cabins are decorated in easy-to-live-with warm colors and mellow wood. All cabins have twin beds that can be converted to a queen; television with CNN, CNBC, ESPN, TNT, Discovery Channel, movies, and several radio channels; minifridge; ample closet and drawer space; two hair dryers; safe; telephone with voice mail; and bathroom with shower. Further amenities are added in the pricier categories: Minisuites have queen-size bed, separate sitting area with sofabed, balcony, two televisions, bathroom with tub and shower, and robes (can be requested in standard cabins). Suites enjoy a larger balcony, walk-in closet, a wet bar, and bath with whirlpool tub. The pebbly nonslip surface of the bathroom floor is a welcome safety feature. There's a self-serve laundromat on every cabin deck—another appreciated amenity.

Specifications   879 outside (527 with balconies), 108 inside; 16 suites and 184 minisuites with balconies; 8 minisuites; 616 upper berths. 20 (16 outside/4 inside) wheelchair-accessible.

DINING   The ships' Personal Choice Dining lineup offers two main dining rooms, **Provence** and **Bordeaux,** which passengers can choose for either Traditional Fixed Seating (Provence Dining Room at either first or second seating each evening) or Anytime Dining (Bordeaux Dining Room 5:30–10 p.m. or by reserving a specific time). Passengers may change from Traditional to Anytime dining during the cruise, if they they prefer. Further options are the 24-hour **Horizon Court** for breakfast, lunch, and bistro dinner for casual evening dining; the **Pizza Bar** where the specialties are varied and excellent; and the patisserie.

Two alternative restaurants carry a surcharge. The new **Bayou Café and Steakhouse,** the first New Orleans–style dinner restaurant at sea ($15 per person, which includes a hurricane cocktail), offers Cajun specialties and live jazz. Reviews on this eatery are mixed. Some thought the food was excellent; we did not, and considering that New Orleans is noted for fabulous cuisine and some of the best restaurants in the country, we were disappointed with the Café's menu. The best aspect of the cafe is the jazz music in the evening, but be sure to avoid the seating at the side tables behind the orchestra; the sound level there is deafening.

Sabatini's ($20 surcharge), the popular Princess signature Italian restaurant, is open for dinner only except on sea days when it serves brunch. Dinner has a set menu of so many courses—all excellent—that it's almost too much food. The outstanding service is as good as the food. And if you are still suffering hunger pangs, there's a poolside hamburger grill, an ice-cream bar (extra charge) near the pool, and 24-hour room service.

SERVICE The service throughout the ship is excellent. The friendly staff greets passengers at all times of day in all parts of the ship, and they are eager to help. The **Sabatini** staff is wonderful, and our Filipino room steward was superb, going out of his way to be helpful. We have never had a more cheerful, attentive, and professional room steward on any ship, including the most luxurious ones. Other passengers have reported enthusiastically the same kudos for the staff of *Island Princess*.

FACILITIES AND ACTIVITIES The ship's design maximizes the public space for passenger activities, with some lounges spanning the ship from port to starboard. Most of the public rooms are on decks 6 and 7. Just as on the larger vessels, the new duo have three show lounges, but with an added dimension—the two-story interactive high-tech aft lounge. Known as the **Universe Lounge,** the decor has been inspired by Jules Verne's classic *20,000 Leagues Under the Sea* and sports three revolving stages with integrated lifts, giant projection screens, and the latest in lighting technology, digital sound, and video systems. The stages are designed for a diverse slate of entertainment, from Vegas-style shows to movie screenings and full television productions to small classroom-style demonstrations.

The Universal Lounge is also home to Princess Cruises' fleetwide enrichment program, ScholarShip@Sea, which Princess calls "edu-tainment." Considering the courses available—cooking, photography, ceramic painting, decorating, visual arts, computers, health, finance, and lectures on a wide variety of topics—the term is accurate. The lounge's demonstration kitchen can be moved into place for cooking classes by the ship's chef or visiting culinary experts. The room has network plug-ins for up to 50 laptop computers and an infrared headset system for the hearing impaired. Each cruise offers a slate of up to 20 courses, with six options offered each sea day. For some there is a small fee, usually about $10. Introduced on the *Coral Princess,* Princess Cruises has now extended the innovative ScholarShip@Sea fleetwide. Other daytime activities are standard cruise-ship fare (which pale by comparison to the edu-tainment) and include the ubiquitous art auctions, bingo, horse racing, ice-carving demonstrations, and pool games.

Evening entertainment is as varied as the venues. Currently, *Coral Princess* has three new musical shows performed by a cast of 17 lively and very professional singers and dancers in the bilevel **Princess Theatre,** the main show lounge, or the multipurpose Universal Lounge. There is also a variety of music from jazz to country, singers, comedians, and novelty acts in other lounges and bars, as well as classical concerts on some days. The **Wheelhouse Bar,** which spans Deck 7, is one of the most handsome rooms on any cruise ship and is very popular with passengers for cocktails and dancing before and after dinner. Further along the deck are some new gathering places, such as the **Churchill Lounge,** a cigar and spirits lounge with its own humidor, and the **Rat Pack Bar,** a 1960s retro martini bar—both firsts for Princess. One deck down is the casino with London-style decor and the **Explorer's Lounge,** which becomes the disco in the late evening. There's also a wedding chapel, an Internet cafe, a library and card room, duty-free shops, and an art gallery.

SPORTS, FITNESS, AND BEAUTY The Lido Deck (14) has a swimming pool, three whirlpools, and a poolside bar. In the **Lotus Spa,** meant to reflect the soothing aura of Bali, there is a swim-against-the-current pool, covered by a retractable glass magrodrome, and two whirlpools. Further aft is the aerobics room and gym. Be prepared for a hard sell of the spa lotions and other products by the staff; your response should be equally firm if you have no interest in purchasing them. The new vessels offer a nine-hole putting course and golf simulator.

CHILDREN'S FACILITIES On Deck 12 aft is action central for Princess's supervised age-specific children's program. The outstanding facilities include **Off Limits,** the teen center with special activities for young adults ages 13–17, including video games and a teen disco. The **Fun Zone** is a special center for Princess Piloteers (ages 8–12), with regular activities designed for this age group. **Pelican's Playhouse** is the children's center for ages 2–7, where **Youth Center** staff host a daily schedule of age-specific activities. The Pelican's Pool is a dedicated children's pool.

Pacific Princess	QUALITY 8	VALUE C
Tahitian Princess	QUALITY 8	VALUE C
REGISTRY Gibraltar	LENGTH 594 feet	BEAM 83.5feet
CABINS 344	DRAFT 19.5 feet	SPEED 20 knots
MAXIMUM PASSENGERS 680	PASSENGER DECKS 9	ELEVATORS 4
	CREW 373	SPACE RATIO 44

THE SHIPS *Tahitian Princess* and *Pacific Princess,* the former *R3* and *R4* of the now-defunct Renaissance Cruises, joined the Princess fleet in late 2002. The twin ships are midgets compared to the other ships in the Princess fleet, but many of the line's passengers who lamented the departure of the former *Pacific Princess* should be pleased with these ships. In addition to their more intimate cruise environment, the ships are quite new, having entered service originally in 1999, and they come with many modern features.

Both ships offer many of the Personal Choice Cruising options that have become Princess trademarks. These include a four restaurant choices: the main dining room, **Sabatini's Trattoria, Sterling Steakhouse,** and the 24-hour **Lido Café,** plus a poolside barbecue grill.

The ships each have a show lounge, eight bars, an observation lounge, casino, a library and card room, two shops, and a medical center. There is a swimming pool, a spa with two whirlpools and beauty salon, a fitness center, and jogging track.

Ninety-two percent of the cabins are outside, and over two-thirds of these come with a private balcony. All have television with CNN, ESPN, and first-run movies, VCR, personal safe, refrigerator, and hair dryer. Passengers have a self-service launderette.

Specifications 344 cabins including 10 suites, 52 minisuites. 317 outside; 27 inside. 232 have balconies. 3 wheelchair-accessible.

POSTSCRIPT *Tahitian Princess* sails year-round in Tahiti and the South Pacific on the region's only 10-day cruises. The three different itineraries sail round-trip from Papeete, Tahiti, call at Bora Bora, Moorea, and Raiatea, and either the Cook Islands, Samoa, or the Marquesas. The *Pacific Princess* operates on a split deployment, sailing half the year throughout French Polynesia and the wider Pacific region for Princess Cruises, and the other half for P&O Cruises.

Radisson Seven Seas Cruises

600 Corporate Drive, Suite 410, Fort Lauderdale, FL 33334
☎ **954-776-6123, 800-477-7500, or 800-285-1835; fax 954-772-3763**
www.rssc.com

TYPE OF SHIPS Small and midsize luxury vessels with big-ship facilities.

TYPE OF CRUISES Quiet, luxury, destination-oriented cruises with personal service and sophisticated amenities.

CRUISE LINE'S STRENGTHS

- service
- itineraries
- cuisine
- single, flex-time/open-seating dining
- all-inclusive prices
- all-outside deluxe accommodations and amenities

CRUISE LINE'S SHORTCOMINGS

- limited, staid shipboard activities

FELLOW PASSENGERS Affluent, well-educated, well-traveled, 45 years and older, $150,000+ annual income. They cherish their individuality and shun group travel. Most are senior executives, professionals, well traveled, and high-end resort vacationers, many own their company. Typical age is 45+; over 75% are Americans. They usually have cruised before on luxury liners, have sophisticated tastes, and care about elegance and service. Some are likely to be special-occasion celebrators and incentive awards winners.

Recommended for Upscale, independent, active, seasoned travelers accustomed to luxury and quality. Small-ship devotees who appreciate the advantages and accept the limitations of such vessels.

Not recommended for Joiners; people who need to be entertained, want a full day of shipboard activity, or thrive in a Vegas atmosphere.

CRUISE AREAS AND SEASONS Asia, Antarctica, Australia, New Zealand, Middle East in winter; Caribbean, transcanal, Mexico, Central and South America, U.S. east coast, Canada in fall/winter/spring; Alaska, Mediterranean, Bermuda, Europe, spring/summer; Northern Europe, summer; South Pacific, year-round.

THE LINE In 1995, Radisson Diamond Cruises and Seven Seas Cruise Line merged to form Radisson Seven Seas Cruises. The deal represented an expansion into cruising by Radisson Hotels International, while the new line brought three market segments—contemporary, traditional, and light adventure—in the luxury cruise market under one umbrella.

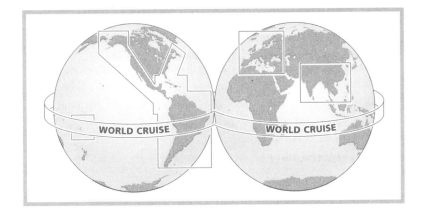

Launched in 1990 by a wealthy Japanese businesswoman who established its high standards, Seven Seas Cruise Line's *Song of Flower* (sold 2003) quickly made her mark by offering deluxe cruises at rates considerably lower than its competitors and winning accolades and awards after only its first year. Radisson Seven Seas introduced the *Paul Gauguin* in 1998, and in a joint venture with Monte Carlo–based V. Ships, it debuted the all-suite luxury *Seven Seas Navigator* in 1999 and the larger, all-suite, all-balcony *Seven Seas Mariner* in 2001, and her sister ship, *Seven Seas Voyager,* in spring of 2003. Each ship can boast some of cruising's highest space-to-passenger and crew-to-passenger ratios. Carlson Hospitality Worldwide is the parent company of Radisson Seven Seas Cruises. In January and February, the cruise line charters deluxe exploration ships, such as the *Explorer II,* for adventure cruises and a series of Antarctica cruises. For 2006, it has two 11-night Antarctic and Falkland Islands cruises departing from Ushuaia on January 16 and 27. Rumors persist that Radisson Seven Seas Cruises will be changing its name soon.

THE FLEET	BUILT/RENOVATED	TONNAGE	PASSENGERS
Paul Gauguin (to 2007)	1998	19,200	320
Seven Seas Mariner	2001	50,000	700
Seven Seas Navigator	1999	30,000	490
Seven Seas Voyager	2003	49,000	700

STYLE The size of the ships, their relatively small number of passengers, and price ensure the cruises a certain exclusivity. They also help define the high level of service and personal attention passengers expect—and receive.

Shipboard life is informal during the day but formal in style (though not necessarily in dress) in the evening. Surroundings are spacious and luxurious, the ambience sophisticated. The ships have loyal fans.

Passengers on these ships are affluent and accustomed to a high level of service and comfort, which the ships deliver in their spaciousness, luxurious surroundings, and attentive staff. There is the usual array of shipboard staples—exercise classes, word and board games, bingo, the ubiquitous art auctions—but nothing too taxing. In fact, if there's a criticism to be made, it would be the need to provide passengers with more imaginative shipboard activities.

Recently, RSSC introduced NewspaperDirect across the fleet. With this new service, passengers may receive daily printed editions of their favorite national or international newspapers, including *USA Today, Financial Times, The Wall Street Journal, Frankfurter Allgemeine Zeitung,* and *Le Monde,* among others.

DISTINCTIVE FEATURES No-tipping policy. Water sports platform and marina on *Paul Gauguin*. Extensive book/video libraries. Cordon Bleu–directed venues on *Mariner* and *Voyager*. Inclusive prices (see Rates below).

	HIGHEST	LOWEST	AVERAGE
PER DIEM	$1,267	$295	$771

Per diems are calculated from cruise line's nondiscounted *cruise-only* published fares on standard accommodations and vary by season, cabins, and cruise areas.

RATES Gratuities and wine with lunch and dinner included. All soft drinks and initial room bar setup included; nonalcoholic drinks restocked daily, depending on ship. Port charges are additional.

Special fares and discounts
- Between 25% and 50% savings on select voyages. Second-passenger savings of 50% savings off standard fares.
- **SINGLE SUPPLEMENT:** Specific amounts per cruise in brochure.

Packages
- **AIR/SEA:** Yes.
- **PRE/POST:** Yes.

PAST PASSENGERS Radisson Seven Seas Society for repeat passengers offers members' sailings with incentives and special prices. Some sailings are hosted by the line's president. Members receive quality gifts based on the number of days they cruise.

THE LAST WORD With the *Diamond* gone, RSSC is left with its newest ships more similar in size and style (*Paul Gauguin* is smaller but similar in style) and should be able to focus on providing its passengers with the ultimate in luxury. However, with the intense competition in the luxury end of the market, not only from the established luxury lines but from new entries and from the new phenomenon of luxury adventure ships, it may have a hard time maintaining the lead it has enjoyed for several years.

Radisson Seven Seas Standard Features

Officers *Mariner,* French, European; *Navigator/Voyager,* European, International, Italian; *Paul Gauguin,* French, International.

Staff Dining and Cabin/European and International; Cruise/American and British.

Dining facilities Two dining rooms on *Navigator;* four on *Mariner, Voyager* with open seating for three meals; informal indoor/outdoor cafe for buffet breakfast and lunch. Reservations-only alternative dining on *Navigator, Mariner, Voyager* four choices.

Special diets Accommodated with advance notice.

Room service 24-hour service with full-meal, in-cabin dining.

Dress code Casual by day; smart casual most evenings; some evenings, jackets required for men. Formal or semi-formal for captain's parties. Visits in some ports of call may require women to cover heads, legs, and arms.

Cabin amenities Direct-dial phone, hair dryer, television, VCR/DVD, radio, stocked minibar; marble bathroom with tub and shower (except *Gauguin*). CNN, *Navigator,* all suites; *Mariner, Voyager* all-suite, all verandas, robes, safe.

Electrical outlets 110 AC.

Wheelchair access *Mariner* 6; *Navigator, Voyager* 4; *Gauguin,* 1.

Recreation and entertainment Nightly shows, nightclub, cabaret, and piano entertainment in two lounges, small casino, dancing, card games, backgammon, book/video library, lecture program.

Sports and other activities One outside pool. See text.

Beauty and fitness Beauty salon. Small gym. Carita spas on all ships; see text.

Other facilities Boutique; hospital; *Mariner, Voyager,* Internet cafe, launderettes; *Navigator* and *Gauguin,* Internet access in library. Meeting space and business facilities.

Children's facilities Club Mariner children's program on select cruises; summer environment program on *Gauguin.*

Theme cruises Yes.

Smoking Smoking sections designated in public areas; no cigar or pipe smoking in dining room.

Radisson Seven Seas suggested tipping Gratuities are included in cruise fare; therefore, no-tipping policy.

Credit cards For cruise payment and onboard charges: American Express, Diners Club, MasterCard, Visa, Discover.

Seven Seas Navigator	QUALITY 8	VALUE B
REGISTRY Bahamas	LENGTH 560 feet	BEAM 81 feet
CABINS 251	DRAFT 21 feet	SPEED 20 knots
MAXIMUM PASSENGERS 490	PASSENGER DECKS 8	ELEVATORS 5
	CREW 324	SPACE RATIO 67.3

THE SHIP In a joint venture with Monte Carlo–based V. Ships, Radisson Seven Seas Cruises launched its all-suite luxury ship, *Seven Seas Navigator*, in 1999. The Italian-built vessel, the fastest in the Radisson fleet at the time, has an ice-strengthened hull giving her the ability to operate virtually anywhere in the world. V. Ships, established in 1984, is a company of the Vlasov Group, one of the world's largest providers of ship management and related services.

A small ship with a big-ship feel, the spacious *Navigator* (with one of the industry's highest space ratios) has half a dozen lounges, superbly appointed outside suites (90% with balconies, walk-in closets, and well-appointed bathrooms), single-seating dining, an alternative restaurant, a wide teak deck surrounding the pool, and a slate of worldwide, port-intensive itineraries.

Designed by Norwegian architects Yran & Storbraaten, *Navigator's* public rooms are strikingly contemporary and minimalist. Yet unusual lamps, exotic chairs, and varied materials and textures provide visual interest. The entire ship is well integrated, with light blue carpeting throughout and bold oil paintings (all for sale) decorating the corridors. A bank of glass elevators offers a bird's-eye view of the gracefully designed ship and a panoramic view of the pool area. Nonetheless, they seem out of place on a small luxury vessel, and the exposed machinery is jarring.

The ship blazed the trail for RSSC's first ventures to South America, Alaska, and a world cruise.

CABINS Particular attention was lavished on the accommodations. They range from roomy standard suites of 301 square feet plus veranda to Master Suites with 1,067 square feet plus a 106-square-foot balcony. All standard suites are identical; price varies by location. Ten suites are interconnected. Four suites are wheelchair-accessible with extra-wide doors and large, shower-only bathrooms.

The suites, like the rest of the elegant ship, are decorated in subdued colors with cherry wood accents. They have sitting areas, twin beds convertible to a queen, marble bathrooms with separate tub and shower, and walk-in closet with safe. Other amenities include a minibar with liquor set-up, bathrobes, hair dryer, television with VCR, and Aveda bath products.

In standard suites, a coffee table rises to dining-table height with the touch of a button, and upper-level suites have proper dining room tables. Passengers can dine en suite, ordering from the dining room menu during meal hours, with dishes served course by course. The ship offers 24-hour room service.

Master and Grand Suites, which come with butler service, have a foyer with a powder room, living/dining area, and a separate bedroom with bathroom that has a bidet. Two other top suite categories (A and B) also offer butler service—a posh touch that includes cocktails served daily.

Specifications 251 outside suites, 90% have balconies. Standard balcony suites, 301 square feet plus balconies; 10 Grand Suites, 538 square feet plus balconies; 4 Master Suites, 1,067 square feet plus balconies. 4 wheelchair-accessible.

DINING The open, single-seating **Compass Rose Restaurant** provides a gracious setting, with a small dance floor for occasional dinner dances. An alabaster compass rose skylight looks down on the pale yellow walls; draperies in soft pastels frame the picture windows; and potted plants are interspersed among the widely spaced tables.

Fine service, gracious ambience, and generous space between tables add to the luxury. Seating is open; neither times nor tables are assigned. Gourmet cuisine is the ship's most outstanding feature. Selections change daily and include fresh seafood and prime meats. Preparation and presentation are varied and sophisticated.

Passengers stroll across a parquet floor to enter the **Portofino Grill,** the alternative restaurant with its own galley. It provides a gorgeous setting of linen-draped tables, blue-cushioned chairs, and filmy white curtains, imparting a true Mediterranean flavor; this venue serves the ship's best dishes. At breakfast and lunch, the indoor/outdoor Portofino provides buffet dining; at night a wing of the spacious room is transformed into an à la carte restaurant featuring northern Italian specialties. Tables must be reserved for dinner, but there is no service charge here or elsewhere on this gratuities-included ship. Complimentary wine is served in both dining venues.

FACILITIES AND ACTIVITIES The two-tiered **Seven Seas** show lounge hosts varied entertainment, ranging from Broadway revues to concert pianists. The Stars Lounge is the disco/after-hours club where sleek, deep-blue leather chairs backed in wood line up along a glass-topped bar.

A few steps away, cigar lovers gather in the **Connoisseur Club's** tobacco-colored leather armchairs near a granite-topped faux fireplace. Next door, the small **Navigator Lounge** serves coffee and cocktails throughout the day. At the large library stocked with books, periodicals, and 800 videos, there is a bank of nine computers where passengers can check their e-mail. Two boutiques sell designer wares.

A dark, rich-looking casino has tables for blackjack, stud poker, roulette, and craps; slots and poker machines are found in an adjacent room. High on Deck 11, passengers walk through a hall of marble and carpet to emerge in the light, attractive **Galileo's,** a piano bar and lounge with indoor/outdoor seating and a dance floor. One deck higher, forward, the **Vista Lounge** provides a hideaway of tambour chairs with thick yellow-and-green striped cushions (private parties welcome).

SPORTS, FITNESS, AND BEAUTY   Adjacent to the **Vista Lounge** are the gym, aerobics rooms, and spa managed by Carita of Paris.

The large midship pool area offers a grill and two whirlpools, plus a venue for moonlight barbecues and dancing. Golfers get two driving cages and a putting green.

CHILDREN'S FACILITIES   "Club Mariner" children's program is available on selected cruises. The age-graded program has two tiers: children ages 6–11 and 12–17. The activities focus on the destination's nature, heritage, and crafts. Special tours are offered and a children's menu is served in the dining rooms.

Seven Seas Mariner	QUALITY 8	VALUE B
Seven Seas Voyager	(PREVIEW)	
REGISTRY Wallis and Futuna/ Bahamas	LENGTH 709/670 feet	BEAM 93/95 feet
CABINS 328/353	DRAFT 21/23 feet	SPEED 20 knots
MAXIMUM PASSENGERS 700	PASSENGER DECKS 8/9	ELEVATORS 8
	CREW 445	SPACE RATIO 71.4/70

THE SHIPS   In another joint venture, Monte Carlo-based V. Ships and Radisson Seven Seas built cruising's first all-balcony, all-suite luxury cruise ship. The *Seven Seas Mariner*, delivered in 2001, and her sister, *Seven Seas Voyager*, delivered in 2003, had the same architects and interior designer, Peter Yran and Bjorn Storbraaten, who have designed many luxury cruise ships. The stylish sisters are the largest ships in the RSSC fleet, with the greatest space ratio of any cruise ships to date.

The two ships, which were built at different shipyards—*Mariner* in France, *Voyager* in Italy—are sisters rather than twins, with some major differences. The latter ship improved over her sister ship by taking some of the best features from *Navigator*, particularly the larger size of its suites and the full bathtub and separate glass-enclosed shower stall, along with some extra marble touches in the bathroom. *Voyager's* hull is wider than *Mariner's*, and she has one additional deck. Two of the alternative restaurants, **Signatures** and **Latitudes,** were relocated to Deck 5 and are serviced by a single galley, and Latitudes was completely redesigned to have a show kitchen visible to passengers from their tables and used for cooking demonstrations and classes. Also, *Voyager* is the first ship to have two independent propulsion and power-generation systems in two separate areas of the ship—a significantly enhanced safety measure.

On both ships, most of the public rooms are located on the first three and top two passenger decks and have as their focal point an eight-deck-high atrium with three glass-enclosed elevators and stairways curving up through the atrium. For some, the lounges on *Mariner* are so spacious they lack atmosphere; for others, the spaciousness of her public areas is the very essence of the ships' luxury. Significantly, the area of the public rooms on *Voyager* was reduced by 23%; two lounges on *Mariner* were combined into one lounge on *Voyager*.

The ships' spaciousness and sparseness are immediately evident in the atrium, whose sculpture decor and visible elevator machinery give it a raw, unfinished look. The starboard side gallery leading off the atrium on Deck Six serves as a wide connecting boulevard running fore and aft past the open-plan library. The promenade deck windows provide natural light, and the generously proportioned space is furnished with wicker chairs, planters and greenery. Art auctions, with some decent paintings for sale, take place here.

The ships' facilities include a spa, a bilevel main show lounge, a small nightclub lounge with a dance floor; a large forward observation lounge; a library; and an Internet cafe. There is a **Club Mariner** for children on select cruises. The ship has the standard RSSC features, such as all gratuities included in the fare, port-intensive itineraries, and single, open-seating dining with complimentary wine at dinner, but it's the choice of four restaurants that makes these ships different.

Also, the duo's innovative pod propulsion system eliminates the traditional shaft-and-rudder system, making the vessel up to 15% more efficient and reducing noise and vibration. The pods have forward-facing propellers that can be turned 360 degrees, which optimizes maneuverability, fuel efficiency, and speed.

ITINERARIES *See* Itinerary Index.

CABINS The cabins are spread over five center decks and come in 12 or 13 categories of outside suites, all with balconies. *Mariner* suites range from 301 square feet to 1,580 square feet including the veranda (*Voyager*, 356 to 1,403 feet). *Voyager* suites are paneled in light wood with fabrics in gold, orange rust, and light green. The deluxe suites are the most numerous and have a slightly partitioned and curtained bedroom with king-size bed (convertible to twins) and lounge, walk-in closet and marble bathroom with a full tub and shower. Curiously, the bath and closet on *Mariner* are smaller than on the *Navigator,* something that was rectified on the *Seven Seas Voyager.*

The Penthouse Suites, somewhat misnamed, are larger than the deluxe category at 449 square feet on *Mariner* (370 square feet on *Voy-*

ager), but not all are located on the top deck as the name might imply. They feature a roomy, partitioned lounge with L-shaped couch, two lounge chairs, and a glass-top table. The 73-square-foot teak deck balcony on *Mariner* (50 square feet on *Voyager*) has rather ordinary white plastic chairs and a low table. Accommodations increase in spaciousness in the higher categories, which also offer butler service. Some suites will take a third person, and the two-bedroom master suites accommodate up to five.

All accommodations have satellite telephone; television with 13 channels, including CNN and ESPN; DVD for American and European systems, and hookups for personal video cameras; safe; bathrobes; hair dryer; in-suite bar setup upon embarkation; and complimentary replenished bottled water, soft drinks, and beer. The suites are attended by European stewardesses.

An expandable table top makes in-cabin dining a pleasure and is very popular, especially at the end of a busy day ashore. A full meal may be ordered from the **Compass Rose Restaurant** or from an in-suite menu 24 hours a day. Valet dry cleaning, laundry service, and tailor service for minor repairs and small alterations are available. The self-service launderettes on cabins decks are complimentary.

Bose Wave music systems have been installed in the *Voyager*, *Mariner*, and *Navigator*. In addition, all suites on *Mariner* and *Navigator* have been upgraded from VCRs to DVD players and an extensive DVD movie library is being developed as well. *Voyager* already had a DVD library and players in all suites. Some 47 of *Mariner's* suites now have new deluxe shower stalls, with rain showers and tile seating.

Specifications Mariner 328/*Voyager* 353 suites. 80 suites (390–1,580 square feet). Limited number of suites accommodate 3 persons. 6 *Mariner*/4 *Voyager* wheelchair-accessible. On *Voyager*, 24 suites are interconnecting.

DINING The choice of four dining venues gives the *Mariner* and *Voyager* their most distinctive quality, and all the venues offer a wide variety of high-quality cuisine. Two restaurants have open seating with no reservations necessary; two take reservations for specific tables; none have an additional charge. Complimentary wines are served with dinner in all four restaurants.

The spacious **Compass Rose Restaurant,** the main restaurant and the largest of the four, accommodates most passengers in open seating dining for three meals. The attractive room has a recessed arched ceiling and faux light-wood columns topped with a band of stainless steel capitals. The menu, changed daily, might offer homemade crab cakes as an appetizer, cream asparagus soup, two salad selections, pasta dish, and main courses, such as sautéed jumbo prawns and Black Angus beef. The choices also include vegetarian dishes and a *menu degustation* (a sampler of dishes appropriate to the cruising region).

La Veranda, an indoor/outdoor venue, serves a buffet with sheltered outdoor seating aft at wooden tables and chairs set under an awning. There is also an outdoor grill here. Inside the room's etched glass doors, the stylish high-back wooden chairs are set around tables under a coffered ceiling; the walls are hung with alluring black-framed Cote d'Azur travel posters. The unusual chairs have double rows of hollow vertical squares cut into the high backs, reminiscent of the work of Scottish designer Charles Rennie Macintosh. In the evening, a portion of La Veranda becomes a Mediterranean bistro for casual dining, offering a tapas, mezze, or antipasti buffet, followed by table service for the soup of the day, salad, pasta, main course, and dessert.

Latitudes, the smallest of the four, is a reservations-only dinner restaurant with a set sampler menu and tableside presentations. Having started with a more Asian menu, the choices now might range from a foie gras mousse, crab and avocado in a light curry sauce, tomato bisque, pan-fried lobster in a lemon grass gravy, and beef tenderloin in salsa. The setting combines a South Seas and oriental decor with black lacquer chairs, walls decorated with wooden masks and headdresses, and large windows with slatted venetian blinds. Recently, the restaurant got a new "Indochine" menu with such exotic selections as Cambodian wafu salad and steamed fresh halibut in a Matsutake mushroom broth with gingered vegetables.

Signatures was the first permanent dining venue aboard a cruise ship directed by chefs from Le Cordon Bleu, the famed French culinary institute. The reserved-table restaurant is repeated on *Voyager,* offering a wide choice of entrees and main courses, and worth several visits on a long cruise. Marinated fillet of red snapper and roast breast of quail with turnips in a morel sauce are two examples from the list of six choices. The appetizing dessert list included warm chocolate tart with cinnamon ice cream. The sophisticated setting features rust-red chairs with gold tassels, an etched-glass divider between the serving and dining area, and black glass against the aft wall. The chefs take their talents a step further by offering Le Cordon Bleu "Classe Culinaire des Croisieres" on certain voyages. Workshops, conducted by Le Cordon Blue–trained chefs, provide a hands-on introduction to the art of French cooking. Classes are limited to 16 guests in three two-hour sessions and cost $295 per person. Upon graduation, participants receive their own chef's apron and short toque, a tea towel, and a Le Cordon Bleu cookbook of classic recipes, as well as a certificate of participation. Inquire from the cruise line for future schedules. Both *Mariner* and *Voyager* have this program on select sailings.

FACILITIES AND ACTIVITIES   Public rooms are varied in location from high up and forward to down low and aft. The **Observation Lounge,** located two decks above the bridge, offers comfy rust- and tan-colored seating to enjoy hot hors d'oeuvres and soothing piano music before dinner, while taking in a grand 180-degree view. From a perch along the horseshoe-shaped bar, the space takes on a magical quality at night.

The semi-circular **Horizon Lounge,** facing aft on one of the lowest passenger decks, is the handsome setting for afternoon tea, with music and light after-dinner entertainment. Additional covered outdoor seating (little used) is a quiet spot for daytime reading. Nearby, the **Connoisseur Club** with tan leather chairs and an electric fireplace makes a sophisticated setting for smoking Cuban and Dominican cigars and sipping liqueurs and wines.

The liveliest venue is the **Mariner Lounge** (**Voyager Lounge** on *Voyager*), drawing a crowd before dining in the adjacent Compass Rose or Latitudes restaurants. *Mariner's* curvy Art Deco design is highlighted by deep blue fabrics covering the chairs and glass tabletops, embedded with a translucent star pattern and framed by raised wooden rims.

Stars nightclub-cum-disco, decorated with black and white photos of Fred Astaire, Ingrid Bergman, Katherine Hepburn, and other movie stars, is an oddly designed space with a spiral staircase in its midst that links to the midsize casino above. The semicircular two-level **Constellation Lounge,** with continuous brushed blue cotton banquette seating, is joined by staircases flanking the stage on each side. Here, full shows and cabarets acts are presented under a starlit ceiling of changing colors.

In the past, production shows have not been a strength of this line, but to their credit, that changed with the two shows that debuted on *Voyager*. The shows are performed by four primary singers plus a production cast of six. On *Mariner,* it is entitled *Lullaby of Broadway,* and highlights Broadway shows from the fifties to today, with a multitude of numbers and costume changes. The second, a very innovative show, at least for a cruise ship, is entitled *On a Classical Note* and features opera, classical music, and light operettas; it is staged on the *Voyager*. The four lead singers have a real opportunity to shine, especially when three different Gilbert and Sullivan operettas were staged in one production. Both ships stage other enjoyable shows, as well. The open-shelf library offers a generous selection of hardbacks, reference books, and videos with tables to spread out an atlas and comfortable seating for reading newspapers and magazines. The adjacent **Club.com** is the plainly decorated Internet center with more than a dozen terminals (three more in the library) and offers very low charges for sending and checking e-mail. Passengers may also browse and enjoy computer games. Computer instruction, free and very popular, is excellent. A long rectangular card room also serves as a conference center.

Amidships on the same deck is a gallery of high-end shops, plus two specialty boutiques placed at two corners of the atrium landings.

SPORTS, FITNESS, AND BEAUTY The ships' spas are operated by Carita of Paris with trained therapists available for a variety of treatments that include thalassotherapy, aromatherapy, seaweed and mud wraps, and a variety of massages. Adjoining the spa is an indoor/outdoor fitness center with treadmills, aerobic benches, Nautilus machine, Lifecycles, Stairmasters, free weights, and other exercise equipment. The center also has a beauty salon.

Deck space centers around the lido pool and three whirlpools, an outdoor bar, and a mezzanine/jogging track above. Outdoor sports include paddle tennis, shuffleboard, and golf nets.

CHILDREN'S FACILITIES "Club Mariner" children's program is available on selected cruises. See *Navigator* for details.

POSTSCRIPT *Mariner's* roominess has pluses and minuses. The latter becomes evident in the public lounges and bars, where except for the cocktail hour before meals, the ship's spaciousness often makes it seem empty of life. After dinner, the show lounge is a draw, but otherwise, most passengers retire to their suites. Occasionally, when younger passengers are on board, they may enliven the bars. On the other hand, it's good to note that the European-modern public rooms are lovely and varied in atmosphere and function. Passengers can now select their shore excursions in advance at the cruise line's Web site.

Paul Gauguin	**QUALITY 9**	**VALUE B**
REGISTRY France	LENGTH 513 feet	BEAM 71 feet
CABINS 160	DRAFT 16.9 feet	SPEED 18 knots
MAXIMUM PASSENGERS 320	PASSENGER DECKS 7	ELEVATORS 4
	CREW 211	SPACE RATIO 59

THE SHIP Named for the French artist whose life and work embodied the romance of French Polynesia, the *Paul Gauguin* is the most deluxe ship of its size to cruise the South Seas year-round. Its space ratio is among cruising's highest, and its shallow draft allows access to small, rarely frequented ports.

The French-built vessel is owned by French investors and managed by Radisson Seven Seas. *Gauguin's* clean lines, understated elegance, and attention to detail are immediately apparent. The yachtlike ship has an airy ambience with stylish touches, such as blond paneling and gray carpets.

ITINERARIES *See* Itinerary Index.

CABINS All accommodations are outside suites with separate sitting area; 50% have verandas. Each is furnished with a queen- or twin-size beds (convertible to queen), closed-circuit television and VCR, safe, direct-dial telephone, and refrigerator stocked with soft drinks, mineral water, and complimentary liquor on arrival. Interiors are enriched by crown moldings and wood accents. Finely crafted furnishings include a love seat and vanity/desk. Storage space includes two closets and built-in drawers. Marble bathrooms have a full-size bathtub and shower, plush towels and cotton robes, hair dryer, and assorted toiletries. Some passengers report being able to hear conversations next door. Cabins above the engine are noisy.

Specifications 160 outside cabins and suites; 80 with balconies. Cabins range from 202 square feet with picture window or portholes and 249 square feet with 56-square-foot veranda to the 457-square-foot owner's suite with 77-square-foot veranda. 1 wheelchair-accessible.

DINING Two restaurants offer single, open seating. Both have ocean views on three sides. An outdoor bistro, **Le Grill,** provides casual dining throughout the day and evening. Dinner for about two dozen people features freshly prepared steaks and seafood. An espresso bar and 24-hour room service are other options. **Restaurant L'Etoile,** the main dining room, features French and continental cuisine. The smaller **La Veranda** is a reservations-only dinner restaurant offering an Italian and other selections. Complimentary wine is served at lunch and dinner; the ship has an excellent wine list. Guests with reservations enjoy predinner cocktails and hors d'oeuvres in the **Connoisseur Club** (open after dinner for drinks and cigars). Evening attire is "country club elegant" (no ties).

SERVICE The crew generally succeeds in its quest to provide outstanding service. A few glitches in the dining room and in cabin maintenance have been reported, but the overall experience is fine.

FACILITIES AND ACTIVITIES   In tribute to Gauguin and French Polynesia, the **Fare** (pronounced "faray") Tahiti Gallery is a small library with books, videos, and other materials on the artist and region. A guest lecturer on every cruise discusses regional history and attractions. The ship has a card room and boutique stocked with Polynesian gifts.

Le Grand Salon is the main lounge for early-evening dancing, entertainment, and daily lectures. Indoor/outdoor **La Palette Lounge** is used for afternoon tea, cocktails, and late-night disco. The small casino has blackjack, roulette, and slot machines, but local regulations bar use of the slots. Nighttime entertainment is minimal. Movies are shown daily on the closed-circuit cabin system; the reception desk lends videos. A singer/pianist performs in La Palette before dinner, and the ship's Filipino band plays for dancing before dinner in Le Grand Salon and afterward in La Palette until 11:30 p.m., when the disco starts up.

SPORTS, FITNESS, AND BEAUTY The fitness center offers free weights and exercise machines that are in use constantly. Aerobics, hydrocalisthenics, and a walkathon are held daily. A separate **Carita of Paris** salon and spa offers a steam room, massage, facials, and beauty treatments, such as aromatherapy. Three- to six-day spa packages are available.

Paul Gauguin has an outdoor pool and splash bar on an upper deck and a retractable marina at sea level where passengers indulge in sports, including diving and snorkeling. Windsurfing and kayaking equipment is available. Snorkeling gear can be signed out at the cruise's start. Diving is a major attraction. The ship provides PADI-certified instructors and dive boats, as well as courses for novices (PADI certification available) and excursions for certified divers.

SHORE EXCURSIONS Many shore excursions are water-oriented. Outings include a Jet-Ski tour of Bora Bora, outrigger/jeep combination tours, shark feeding, and helicopter tours. Weather permitting, a beach party is held on the line's private motu, a small islet.

POSTSCRIPT Passengers concerned about seasickness should know that rough sailing isn't unusual for this ship, owing to her shallow draft and the sometimes rough Pacific waters. The redeeming feature: She travels mostly short distances between ports and is often at anchor in a sheltered bay at night.

Royal Caribbean International

1050 Caribbean Way, Miami, FL 33132
☎ 305-539-6000 or 800-327-6700; fax 800-722-5329
www.royalcaribbean.com

TYPE OF SHIPS Superliners and megaliners.

TYPE OF CRUISES Mainstream, mass market, modestly upscale, wholesome ambience.

CRUISE LINE'S STRENGTHS
- outstanding facilities and activities
- entertainment
- product consistency

CRUISE LINE'S SHORTCOMINGS
- small cabins on older fleet
- limited storage in cabins on older fleet
- impersonal nature of big ships

FELLOW PASSENGERS Moderately upscale couples, singles and families with household income of $40,000+ looking for wide variety in shipboard activities and destinations. Average age is 40s, slightly lower on three- and four-night cruises and slightly higher on ten-night or longer trips. In summer, the age drops because of large number of families traveling with children. About half have cruised at least once, and a quarter are Royal Caribbean repeaters. Genders split evenly, and nine in ten are North Americans. Up to 73% of men and 65% of women are married; 36% are professional, managerial, or proprietors. Educational level, occupations, and age differ on three- and four-night cruises, which are less expensive, shorter cruises appealing to younger people and first-timers.

Recommended for Almost anyone taking a first cruise. Those who like large ships, want an array of options, want to be active, sociable, and don't mind large crowds. Ideal for families, particularly several generations traveling together, because there's something for every age.

Not recommended for Small-ship devotees; those who seek a quiet or intellectual milieu, hate crowds, and have no patience for long lines.

CRUISE AREAS AND SEASONS Caribbean, year-round; Panama Canal, Costa Rica, Mexico, fall to spring; Europe, Mediterranean, Alaska, Bermuda, northeastern U.S., spring to fall

THE LINE Founded in 1969 as a partnership of three prominent Norwegian shipping companies, Royal Caribbean Cruises Ltd. was the first company to launch ships designed for year-round Caribbean cruising. The vessels proved to be so popular that within five years more capacity was

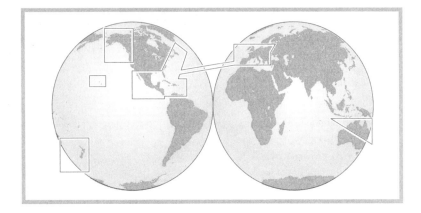

needed. Two vessels were "stretched"—cut in half, then lengthened by inserting prefabricated midsections, and more superliners with unique designs were added. In 1988, *Sovereign of the Seas* was the first of a new generation of megaliners and the largest cruise ship ever built at the time. On *Sovereign's* arrival in Miami, traffic backed up for miles as people on shore tried to glimpse her. That year, too, RCCL merged with Admiral Cruises, a short-cruise specialist.

The line got a jump on the 21st century with Project Vision, a new generation of six megaliners. The first, *Legend of the Seas,* debuted in 1995 with acres of glass and cruising's first 18-hole miniature golf course. In 1999, RCCL launched *Voyager of the Seas,* the first of another new ship class and the industry's first 142,000-ton cruise ship. It came with cruising's first rock-climbing wall and ice-skating rink. The rock-climbing walls proved to be so popular that they have been installed fleetwide.

In 2001, the Radiance group, another new class was introduced with the 2,100-passenger, 90,060-ton *Radiance of the Seas;* she was followed by three more sister ships. And now, not to let any other cruise line get ahead of it in the "largest ship" category, RCCL is building a 158,000-ton ship, dubbed an "ultra voyager," and named, *Freedom of the Seas,* to be delivered in 2006, with two more similar ships scheduled for 2007 and 2008. Roughly 15% larger than *Voyager,* the *Freedom of the Seas* will be 1,112 feet in length, 126 feet in width, and stand 18 stories high. It will carry 3,600 passengers and 1,400 crew.

In a surprise move in 1997, RCCL bought Celebrity Cruises—a deal worth $1.3 billion. Celebrity operates as a separate brand. In 2002, RCCL's attempt to buy Princess Cruises, one of its main competitors, was thwarted by Carnival, which won out in the end after a heavy bidding war. After two decades of focusing solely on the Caribbean, RCCL expanded to other parts of the world such as Canada and Europe, as well as adding more U.S. departure cities and built a new cruise departure point in New Jersey named Cape Liberty Cruise Port. To reflect its growth, the line changed its marketing name to Royal Caribbean International. Recently, the line added the option of advance shore-excursion booking and created Royal Celebrity Tours, a land-tour company in Alaska and the Canadian Rockies.

RCCL has teamed up with Wireless Maritime Services, a joint venture of Cingular Wireless and Maritime Telecommunications Network (MTN), to provide a new service that enables passengers to make and receive calls on their own cell phones—at their personal numbers—while in international waters. RCCL is starting with *Majesty of the Seas, Navigator of the Seas,* and *Celebrity's Summi,* and plans to extend the new capability to all its ships and those of Celebrity by 2006.

For all its firsts and innovative designs, RCCL is still a conservative company that built its success on a solid, consistent product. Royal Caribbean is a public company, traded on the New York Stock Exchange.

THE FLEET	BUILT/RENOVATED	TONNAGE	PASSENGERS
Adventure of the Seas	2001	142,000	3,114
Brilliance of the Seas	2002	90,090	2,100
Empress of the Seas	1990/1998/2004	48,563	1,602
Enchantment of the Seas	1997/1999/2005	80,700	2,252
Explorer of the Seas	2000	142,000	3,114
Freedom of the Seas	2006	158,000	3,600
Grandeur of the Seas	1996/1998	74,140	1,950
Jewel of the Seas	2004	90,060	2,100
Legend of the Seas	1995	69,130	1,800
Majesty of the Seas	1992/1997	73,941	2,350
Mariner of the Seas	2003	142,000	3,114
Monarch of the Seas	1991/1999	73,941	2,350
Navigator of the Seas	2002	142,000	3,114
Radiance of the Seas	2001	90,090	2,100
Rhapsody of the Seas	1997	78,491	2,000
Serenade of the Seas	2003	90,060	2,100
Sovereign of the Seas	1988/1996/2003	73,192	2,250
Splendour of the Seas	1996/1998	69,130	1,800
Vision of the Seas	1998	78,491	2,000
Voyager of the Seas	1999	142,000	3,114

THE FLEET	BUILT/RENOVATED	TONNAGE	PASSENGERS
Freedom 2	2007	158,000	3, 600
Freedom 3	2008	158,000	3, 600

STYLE RCI ships are big ships that hum with activities almost around the clock and are designed for high-volume, year-round, warm-weather cruises. That "C" in RCI could just as well stand for consistency. Whether you take a Royal Caribbean cruise in Europe or the Caribbean, the activities are many and varied and designed primarily for U.S. and Canadian passengers. The ships have acres of sun decks, large pools, and lots of outdoor activity: games, competitions, the ShipShape fitness program, and sports, like golf, that often combine with sports in port. The ships have contemporary decor with such themes as Broadway hits, operas, and the circus. All vessels have extensive programs for children, catering to the 300,000 kids that RCI carries annually.

DISTINCTIVE FEATURES Viking Crown Lounge; rock-climbing wall, golf program; Labadee, RCI's private beach and Coco Cay in the Bahamas; Crown & Anchor lounges in San Juan and St. Thomas. Room service from dining room menus during lunch and dinner; children's program. Internet centers. *Legend's* and *Splendour's* miniature golf courses; Voyager-class ice skating rink; *Explorer's* Oceanography Center.

	HIGHEST	LOWEST	AVERAGE
PER DIEM	$675	$60	$218

Per diems are calculated from cruise line's nondiscounted *cruise-only* published fares on standard accommodations and vary by season, cabins, and cruise areas.

RATES Port charges are included.

Special fares and discounts

- **BREAKTHROUGH FARES:** Capacity-controlled discounts (up to 40%) that change daily; the earlier you buy, the better the discount.
- **THIRD/FOURTH PASSENGER:** Yes.
- **CHILDREN'S FARE:** Third/fourth person rates.
- **SINGLE SUPPLEMENT:** 200%
- **SINGLE GUARANTEE:** Category and cabin assigned by RCI.

Packages

- **AIR/SEA:** Yes.
- **CRUISE/AIR ADD-ONS WITH TRANSFERS:** Yes.
- **PRE/POST:** In departure ports and some vacation spots.
- **OTHERS:** Honeymoon, golf, family, wedding. Crowning Touches and Royal Occasions packages (extra charge) designed for honeymooners or special occasion.

PAST PASSENGERS The Crown and Anchor Society has four membership levels based on how many cruises you take: Gold membership, one to four cruises; Platinum, five to nine; Diamond, ten or more. A new Diamond Plus level recognizes passengers who have completed 24 cruise credits. They receive a cruise credit each time they sail, as well as extra cruise credits when they sail on a cruise/cruisetour of 12 nights or longer and book a suite. The biggest benefit is personalized attention by shipboard personnel. Members get *Crown & Anchor,* a quarterly magazine with information on new programs, itineraries, and ships; special offers and coupons; a color-coded landing card sticker; wine tasting, members-only Web page, sweepstakes, and shoreside events; and on cruises of seven or more nights, a cocktail party. Gold members also receive special offers on future cruises. Platinum members get terry robes for use during the cruise, custom air arrangements, private departure lounge, special 800 number for reservations, and more; and Diamond customers can count on exclusive coupons, boarding privileges, concierge service on select ships, and priority dining room seating, shore excursions, spa services, and disembarkation.

The Diamond Plus level, in addition to the benefits of other levels, gets behind-the-scenes tours, a personalized amenity delivered to their cabin, and a cabin upgrade. After 49 cruises credits, a member gets dinner with a ship's officer and a VIP theater experience, including a backstage tour. When one reaches 100 cruise credits, the member is treated to a free seven-night cruise in a balcony stateroom.

THE LAST WORD RCI is a cruise line of megaliners. It targets 80% of people buying cruises; only budget and luxury customers are excluded. There's no denying that the big ships are big and impersonal, and they have blurred and narrowed the quality that once separated RCI from the pack. If you don't like big ships, this isn't the line for you. But if you want a cruise vacation on ships that have everything, RCI offers good value.

Royal Caribbean International Standard Features

Officers Norwegian, International.

Staff Dining, Cabin/International; Cruise/American and British.

Dining facilities Two seatings for dinner plus midnight buffet; indoor/outdoor cafe with breakfast and lunch buffet; alternative dining for dinner with table service on all ships. Voyager class, three-level dining room, five alternative venues; Radiance class, six venues.

Special diets Low-fat, low-cholesterol, lean cuisine. Full vegetarian menus. Request kosher at time of booking.

RCI Standard Features (continued)

Room service 24 hours with light menu; dining room menus for lunch/dinner.

Dress code Casual but neat by day; informal in evening; one or two nights formal/semiformal. Tuxedo rental available.

Cabin amenities Direct-dial telephone; radio; television; daily world news update; bathtubs in suites; suites with marble baths on *Majesty, Monarch*.

Electrical outlets 110 AC.

Wheelchair access Ramps on all ships; 4 cabins on *Majesty, Monarch, Empress*; 6 cabins on *Sovereign*; 17 on *Legend/Splendour*, 15 on other Vision and Radiance ships; 26 on Voyager class.

Recreation and entertainment Show lounge with entertainment nightly; disco, bingo, horse racing, movies, wine tastings, dance lessons. Viking Crown Lounge, bars/lounges, card room, library, Internet cafe. Voyager, Radiance classes: cyber-cabins

Sports and other activities Two outdoor pools; sports deck with basketball, Ping-Pong, shuffleboard, skeet shooting. Miniature golf course on *Legend, Splendour*, and Voyager class. Rock-climbing walls fleetwide. Ice rink on Voyager class.

Beauty and fitness Beauty/barber shop; massage; sauna; ShipShape fitness program; jogging track; health club/gym. Solarium, elaborate spa on Vision, Voyager, and Radiance class.

Other facilities Boutiques; medical facilities; laundry/dry cleaning services; meeting rooms; Internet and e-mail service; cinema/theater on *Majesty, Monarch, Sovereign*.

Children's facilities Year-round youth programs. Play rooms and teen centers on *Sovereign, Vision, Voyager*, and Radiance class, plus *Empress of the Seas*; teen nightclub on *Majesty, Monarch*, and Vision and Voyager class. Fisher-Price program for infants and their parents.

Theme cruises Jazz, country music, variety of sports.

Smoking Public rooms are nonsmoking except in designated areas.

RCI suggested tipping Per person per day, cabin steward $3.50; dining room waiter, $3.50; $2 assistant waiter; 15% added to bar/wine bill.

Credit cards For cruise payment and on-board charges: American Express, Carte Blanche, Diners Club, Discover, MasterCard, Visa, JCB.

Enchantment/Grandeur	**QUALITY 7**	**VALUE A**
Legend of the Seas	**QUALITY 7**	**VALUE C**
Splendour/Rhapsody	**QUALITY 7**	**VALUE A**

Vision of the Seas	QUALITY 8	VALUE A
REGISTRY Bahamas	LENGTH 867–990 feet	BEAM 105–106 feet
CABINS 902–1000	DRAFT 24–25 feet	SPEED 22–24 knots
MAXIMUM PASSENGERS	PASSENGER DECKS 10	ELEVATORS 11 or 9
1,804–2,435	CREW 735–784	SPACE RATIO 38.32

THE SHIPS *Legend of the Seas,* the first of six megaliners in the Project Vision series, arrived in 1995, and her five sisters followed over the next four years. Constructed in France and Finland, the megaliners were quickly labeled "the ships of glass." Each has two acres of windows, glass windbreaks, skylights, and walls of windows in public spaces. The Centrum, the centerpiece atrium, rises seven decks—two more than on the Sovereign-class vessels—and is topped by the **Viking Crown Lounge**. Bubble elevators whisk passengers to the lounge. The ships embrace the sea and vistas through windows and glass. Natural light sparkles, and open space is abundant.

Each has distinguishing features. At the Centrum's base is the **Champagne Terrace and Bar,** where fine wines and champagne are served by the glass. The elegant setting sets the tone for the ships. *Grandeur's* Champagne Bar covers the Centrum's entire lower level. A white baby grand piano stands next to a stairway to the second level. Decorative screens create conversation corners.

Works of art on *Splendour* were created by more than 50 artists and studios. The ship's atrium sculpture is the fleet's most dramatic. The work consists of three elements symbolizing the solar system. The dominant component, an 18-foot gilded disc representing the sun, hangs on a diagonal, silhouetted by rays from the skylight. Iridescent bulbs around the disc transmit and reflect colored light throughout the atrium. Hundreds of steel cords attached to the upper, outer rim of the disc gather at the top of the atrium and are illuminated, creating a glow.

On the Sun Deck is the Solarium, a landscaped indoor/outdoor area with a second swimming pool, whirlpools, and a cafe. Its Crystal Canopy provides cover in inclement weather. Unlike glass roofs on other ships, this one doesn't fold onto itself; instead, it moves intact. The design uses much more glass, admitting maximum light into the Solarium when the roof is closed. The most celebrated features on *Legend* and *Splendour* are the world's first full-scale floating miniature golf courses. The station where equipment and tee times can be obtained resembles a miniature clubhouse.

Enchantment of the Seas was scheduled to arrive in Boston after completing an extensive renovation. The ship was cut in two in Rotterdam and a 73-foot midship section constructed in Finland was inserted. It brought her overall length to 990 feet, weight to 80,700 tons, and her cabin total to 1,126 with the addition of 151 new accommodations. But lengthening the ship was more than an engineering feat. It was a complete makeover with some unusual features like an on-deck trampoline complete with bungee cords.

One of the most striking additions to *Enchantment* are two suspension bridges on Deck 10, raising the walkway/jogging track and spanning more than 75 feet on either side of the Pool Deck below. Supported by dramatic arches, the bridges cross over two new areas of the Pool Deck, which jut out past lower decks to overhang the water. Each of these deck areas are edged with 14-foot-high sheets of glass, offering great views. They also have peek-a-boo windows in the floor to see the water below. The overhanging space on the port side has a new bar; the starboard side houses a band shell that opens like an orange for poolside musical entertainment.

In total, the main pool area has been expanded by nearly 50%, with two pools, four whirlpools, and a new, circular, kid-focused Splash Deck with 64 water jets. Forty of the jets are connected to an interactive touchpad system, letting kids spray each other or create their own fountain effects. At night, the area closes to become a decorative fountain with a fiber-optic light show.

In addition to the signature rock-climbing wall at the stern, *Enchantment* has four bungee trampolines at the stern on Deck 10. Participants strap into a harness connected to two bungee cords that help them head skyward, while keeping them safely centered when they come in for a landing on the trampolines. The jogging track also offers a new "vitality course" with four fitness stops. In between laps on the quarter-mile track, runners can pause to jump rope; work their arms, back, and stomach at the sit-up/press-up bars; strengthen their legs at a step-up station; and cool down with a series of suggested stretches. Another addition is **Grab and Go**, a fast-food restaurant on deck. The deck also has two ball zones, each with three basketball hoops of different heights to accommodate youth, teen, and adult shooters.

Enchantment's fitness center has been expanded, and the **Day Spa,** one deck below, has five more treatment rooms, including a couples massage room. New entertainment and shopping options were also added. The new **Boleros Latin Club,** a bar with a glass dome ceiling, serves specialty drinks such as mojitos and caipirinhas and features live Latin jazz in the evenings. The new **Latte'tudes** coffee and ice cream shop serve espresso drinks from Seattle's Best Coffee and Ben & Jerry's ice cream. This new area also has computer terminals for Internet access. Next door, **Casino Royale** has been expanded with more slot machines, while the shopping area has new boutiques, including a Fossil watch store, a fine jewelry store, a photo electronics retail shop, an extended art auction gallery, and photo gallery with new digital photo kiosks.

New accessibility features were added throughout the ship, including ramps, pool and Jacuzzi lifts, access to the Splash Deck, and a lift to the bungee trampoline area. The new cabins include two family cabins that sleep six.

ITINERARIES *See* Itinerary Index.

CABINS A major improvement in the Vision class was the size of standard cabins—153 square feet compared to 122 square feet in comparable Sovereign-class cabins. For two decades, Royal Caribbean said cabin size was unimportant because passengers spend so little time in their rooms, but in the Vision class, cabins are larger and more comfortable, with sitting areas and, for the first time, many balconies—one in four. Many more have bathrooms with tubs and showers, too. Pastels and light woods are used in decor. The Royal Suite has a baby grand piano, whirlpool tub, and veranda.

Specifications 327 inside cabins, 575 outside; 83 suites; 4 family suites; 231 with balconies; 388 third/fourth persons; no singles; 17 wheelchair-accessible. *Grandeur/Enchantment*, 399 inside cabins, 576 outside, 18 suites; 4 family suites; 72 deluxe outside; 212 with balconies; 403 third/fourth persons; no singles; 14 wheelchair-accessible. *Enchantment* has 151 more cabins. *Rhapsody/Vision*, 407 inside cabins, 593 outside; 18 suites; 72 deluxe; 4 family suites; 229 with balconies; 287 third/fourth persons; no singles; 14 wheelchair-accessible.

DINING *Legend's* **Romeo and Juliet Dining Room** (the **King and I** on *Splendour* and **Great Gatsby** on *Grandeur*) spans two decks and has 20-foot-tall glass walls on each side, offering spectacular views from every table. The walls are virtually all glass—the load-bearing function is handled by interior columns. A revolving platform with a grand piano is framed by curving stairways to the balcony.

Decor in *Splendour's* King and I is noteworthy. A Thai temple facade has been replicated, and 16 historical paintings plus two epic murals were created by artists of Thailand's royal family. Each painting tells a story.

The nautical-motif **Windjammer Café** on Sun Deck is the indoor/outdoor area for breakfast and lunch buffets and alternative evening dining. Glass walls on three sides and a sloping skylight brighten the room. Each lunch has a theme, and ethnic food joins the regular array of hot dishes, salads, and sandwiches. Dinner, served 6:30–10:30 p.m., offers full table service. The cafe is a popular spot for reading, playing cards, and watching the water.

SERVICE Dining-room service and room stewards have received mixed reviews. Some workers know little English, and they lack training, the latter probably resulting from the line adding so many large ships in a short time.

FACILITIES AND ACTIVITIES Vision-class ships are state-of-the-art at every turn. Computers helped design the bilevel **That's Entertainment Theatre** on *Legend* (**Palladium Theater** on *Grandeur* and **42nd Street Theatre** on *Splendour*) to ensure good sight lines for nightly, full-scale Broadway productions. The venue has a computerized system to move scenery, a device commonly used on Broadway, as well as an orchestra pit that can be raised and lowered.

The **Schooner Bar** is a piano lounge popular for its sing-along sessions. Decor includes authentic rigging and an aroma of tar. **Casino Royale** is next door. On *Grandeur*, passengers enter across a glass floor strewn with "sunken treasure" of jewels and gold coins. The cruise line has a beverage program for adults, which allows up to twelve drinks: nonalcoholic, $29.95, including service charge; fountain packages from $15–$65, depending on cruise length, plus 15% gratuity; and others.

The spacious **Anchor's Away Lounge** on *Legend* (**South Pacific Lounge** on *Grandeur* and **Top Hat Lounge** on *Splendour*) spans the ship's stern. It's a second showroom, used for parlor games, art auctions, daytime dance activities, and late-night shows and dancing. Topside, the glass-sheathed **Viking Crown Lounge** is an observation lounge by day and a nightclub and disco at night. Nightclub action is away from the room's quieter piano bar. On all the ships, the lounge is accessible from the atrium by glass elevators. Aft of the show lounge (to entice you coming and going!) is a mall with varied shops in attractive settings. For example, the **Harbour Shop,** selling liquor and sundries, recalls an old English vintner's shop through aged timber, antique barrels, and stone floors. The casino offers blackjack, Caribbean poker, roulette, craps, and 178 slot machines.

The conference center can be divided into four rooms, each with full audiovisual support. Adjoining is an attractive lounge that also can be divided. A card room can be divided into two sections, and there is a 2,000-volume library that on the *Grandeur* has an amusing lifelike sculpture titled *Snoozin*. **Explorers Court,** off the Centrum on the port side of Deck 8, is the place to relax, read, or converse. Starboard is the **Crown & Anchor Study,** a more formal gathering place.

SPORTS, FITNESS, AND BEAUTY The Sun Deck has an outdoor pool. Contrasting is the quiet Solarium, the second pool area. When the **Windjammer Café** and main dining room are closed, the Solarium's cafe serves snacks, alcoholic beverages, sodas, and juices. The area can be covered by a glass canopy. Beyond the Solarium, the **ShipShape Fitness Center** and spa contain a beauty salon, aerobics area, gym, changing rooms, saunas, steam baths, and seven massage rooms (treatments are pricey). A sports deck is at the stern. Each ship has a padded promenade circling most of the ship.

Legend's much-publicized golf course, **Legend of the Links** (**Splendour of the Greens** on *Splendour*), is above the spa. It was designed by Adventure Golf Services, whose other miniature courses include one at the Mall of America in Bloomington, Minnesota. Each hole of the 6,000-square-foot Links is surrounded by rough to simulate a shoreside layout. On *Legend*, the 17 holes (12 holes on *Splendour*) range in size from 155 to 230 square feet, tees are 5 feet wide, and the longest hole is 32 feet. There is no charge for play. The glass dome over the aft swimming pool can slide to the golf course, where it can be raised to provide almost ten feet of vertical clearance for golfers. A walkway along one edge of the course has benches to encourage spectators. Halogen lights illuminate nighttime play, and baffles redirect wind generated by the motion. A jogging track surrounds the course. Tournaments and children's tee times are available.

CHILDREN'S FACILITIES Outstanding Vision-class facilities for children complement RCI's supervised youth program, Adventure Ocean, available year-round, day and evening, and in port. Activities target ages 3–17, split into five age groups. Daily schedules are delivered to cabins. Among the most original activities is teacher-led Mad Science, which aims to make science entertaining and amusing. Group baby-sitting ($5 an hour per child) is available 10 p.m.–1 a.m. In-room baby-sitting is also available for $8 an hour per room for a maximum of two children (minimum age six months). Family suites have separate bedrooms for children.

Club Ocean is the children's center. On *Grandeur,* it's submarine-themed and includes a tunnel, slide, pool of colored balls, and writing wall. Nearby is **Fanta-SEAS** (**Optix** on *Legend*), the space-themed teen center. The ships also have video arcades.

Note: If you or your children consume a lot of soft drinks, consider buying the "Ocean Potion Card" which allow children up to age 18 to enjoy a dozen nonalcoholic drinks; ranging from $9–$40 depending on cruise length, plus 15% gratuity.

Adventure of the Seas	QUALITY 8	VALUE C
Explorer of the Seas	QUALITY 8	VALUE C
Mariner of the Seas	QUALITY 8	VALUE C
Navigator of the Seas	QUALITY 8	VALUE C
Voyager of the Seas	QUALITY 8	VALUE C
REGISTRY Bahamas	LENGTH 1,020 feet	BEAM 157.5 feet
CABINS 1,900	DRAFT 29 feet	SPEED 23.7 knots
MAXIMUM PASSENGERS 3,114	PASSENGER DECKS 15	ELEVATORS 14
	CREW 1,185	SPACE RATIO NA

THE SHIPS The $500 million *Voyager of the Seas* was the largest cruise ship ever built—142,000 tons—when she made her debut in 1999, and also the first of six similar ships launched over the following five years.

Voyager is awesome. She's twice the size of the largest aircraft carrier ever built, twice as wide as Broadway in New York, and taller than a 20-story building. She has six diesel engines, each the size of a locomotive, and they produce 15,000 horsepower—the equivalent of 150 cars.

Twenty-one million hours worked by a crew of 10,000 people were needed to cut, shape, bend, and weld over 300,000 pieces of steel into the vessel's hull. Her 14 passenger decks cover 646,000 square feet. Furnishings include 538,000 square feet of carpeting, 15,000 chairs, and a $12 million art collection.

Voyager is cruise ship as entertainment. In contrast to other mega-liners, where the goal has been to reduce the behemoth to human scale, RCI has made a virtue of *Voyager's* enormous size, touting her many options and features that only a ship of this size could offer. These include an ice rink, rock-climbing wall, inline skating track, five-story theater, and trilevel dining room.

Voyager also has a television studio, wedding chapel, and the largest youth facilities and largest spa and fitness center afloat. Fifty percent of cabins have balconies. Food and entertainment options and conference facilities rival those at major resorts.

At the heart of the ship, the Royal Promenade stretches the length of one and a half football fields between a 10-story atrium at one end and an 11-story grand atrium at the other. Stores, an ice cream parlor, champagne bar, and pub border the tree-lined boulevard. Around-the-clock entertainment, including jugglers, magicians, and mimes, brings a street-fair atmosphere to the Promenade. Overhead lighting simulates day-to-night conditions outside. Three decks of inside cabins "with a view" overlook the boulevard. The rooms have window seats to watch the scene below, but the idea has not worked as RCI planned because the line failed to put one-way glass on the windows; hence, passengers in these cabins can see and be seen. To avoid being part of the peep show, they must keep their curtains closed.

Studio B is *Voyager's* pièce de résistance. It has a 40-by-60-foot ice-skating rink with arena-style seating for 900 spectators and is available for passenger use during the day (skates may be rented) and for ice shows at night. Fifty television monitors and a broadcast studio are adjacent to the area, which can also serve as a show lounge or conference facility, or be used for game and variety shows and musical concerts.

When we first heard about the ice-skating rink for a ship cruising the Caribbean, we were puzzled, to say the least. But we were pleasantly surprised. The entertainment is wholesome, high-quality, and certainly a welcome alternative, particularly for families, to the stale Las Vegas shows that have become the staple of most cruise ships.

Explorer of the Seas, Adventure of the Seas, Navigator, and *Mariner* are almost identical to *Voyager* and have the same unusual attractions, including the ice-skating rink and rock-climbing wall, as well as the RCI standard features. *Explorer* was the first ship to boast an interactive, state-of-the-art atmospheric and oceanography laboratory. She was also RCI's first ship with Internet access in the cabins. *Navigator of the Seas* is the first of the fleet to get the new service that enables passengers to make and receive calls on their own cell phones—at their personal numbers—while in international waters.

ITINERARIES *See* Itinerary Index.

CABINS Large by RCI standards, cabins are similar in size and decor to those aboard Vision-class ships. Enhancements include larger closets and beds with rounded corners to leave more floor space. All cabins offer telephone, television, electronic minibar, hair dryers, and twin beds convertible to queen.

Specifications Standard inside cabins, including the 138 Category G with atrium views, 150 square feet. 757 cabins with private veranda (50% of the total) have 180-square-foot interiors plus 4.5- by 8.8-foot balcony. 26 wheelchair-accessible.

DINING *Voyager's* main dining room is actually three: the **Carmen, La Boheme,** and **Magic Flute** (**Mozart, Strauss,** and **Vivaldi** on *Adventure;* **Columbus, De Gama,** and **Magellan** on *Explorer*) restaurants connected by a grand staircase. Decor includes a 15-foot crystal chandelier, an antique harp, and gilded marble pillars. Seats—enough for almost 2,000 people—offer views of the staircase and main floor or the ocean.

Other dining venues are **Portofino,** an upscale Italian restaurant for dinner (reservations only; $20 surcharge); **Windjammer Café,** the lido restaurant for breakfast, lunch, and dinner; **Café Promenade,** for Continental breakfast, all-day pizzas, and specialty coffees; **Island Grill,** with a display kitchen, for casual dinner; **SeaSide Diner,** a 1950s all-day/all-night eatery with indoor/outdoor seating and jukebox music; and **Sprinkles,** with around-the-clock ice cream and yogurt. There's a **Johnny Rockets,** a wildly popular seagoing version of the fast food chain. *Mariner* and *Navigator* also have RCI's new steakhouse, **Chops Grill,** specializing in grilled steaks and other meats ($20 surcharge).

FACILITIES AND ACTIVITIES In addition to the ice-skating rink and television studio, *Voyager* has one of the most impressive showrooms afloat. The 1,347-seat **La Scala Theater,** inspired by Milan's famous opera house, rises through five decks and has a stage trimmed with gold leaf, a dome with hand-painted murals, and boxes with satin bunting.

Voyager also offers the $1 million **Aquarium Bar** with 50 tons of water in four huge saltwater aquariums; **Spinners,** a revolving gambling arcade with an interactive roulette wheel that players sit in to play; and **Casino Royale,** cruising's largest casino. Also aboard are a cigar and brandy lounge, champagne bar, English pub, **Schooner Bar,** and a two-deck-tall library. The **Scoreboard** sports bar carries events live on large monitors. Alongside the glass bridge spanning the Royal Promenade is the **Vault,** a two-deck-high late-night disco. **Jesters,** the adults-only nightclub on *Adventure* (the **Chamber** on *Explorer*) is made to look like a gothic castle, with suits of armor, bats, and gargoyles. Sitting atop of *Voyager* is **High Notes,** a jazz club offering nightly performances. Also high on the ship is a chapel where weddings are performed.

Voyager's conference center seats up to 400 people and can be converted into six smaller rooms and a boardroom. Also available are a multimedia screening room, video conferencing, classrooms, and space for exhibition/trade shows. Business services provide typing, copying, and computer access.

SPORTS, FITNESS, AND BEAUTY The 15,000-square-foot health center offers exercise equipment. The Solarium and spa occupy 10,000 square feet. On the ship's funnel is cruising's first rock-climbing wall. Novices and experienced climbers alike are well briefed in advance, and participants work in teams. For most passengers, it's their first rock-climbing experience, and they love it! Other facilities include a nine-hole golf course, driving range, golf simulators ($20/hour), inline skating track, and basketball/volleyball court. Also available are **Sea Quest** dive and snorkel shop and the **19th Hole** golf bar. Little wonder that one passenger, upon touring *Voyager* remarked, "This sure is a guy's ship."

CHILDREN'S FACILITIES **Adventure Ocean,** RCI 's expanded children's facilities, provides age-specific programs: Aquanauts (ages 3–5), Explorers (ages 6–8), Voyagers (ages 9–11), Navigators (ages 12–14), and Optix (teenagers ages 15–17). The latter have a day/nightclub with computers, soda bar, DJ, and dance floor. **Paint and Clay** is a crafts area for young children; **Kids Deck** has deck checkers, shuffleboard, and tic-tac-toe; **Challenger's Arcade** is a virtual reality game center; and **Virtual Submarine** provides underwater virtual reality entertainment for all ages. The **Computer Lab** has 14 stations with games for amusement and education. Adventure Beach, for families, has swimming pools, a water slide, and water games and is convenient to **SeaSide Diner.** Adventure Ocean opens 30 minutes before the morning shore excursions depart to give parents some flexibility in planning for their day.

POSTSCRIPT Passengers have responded to *Voyager* and her sister ships enthusiastically, and almost anyone would enjoy a week on these ships. But you need to understand that it's not cruising in the traditional sense. The ship is the destination; her itinerary is almost immaterial. Like we said, these are cruise ships as entertainment.

Majesty of the Seas	QUALITY 5	VALUE C
Monarch of the Seas	QUALITY 5	VALUE C
Sovereign of the Seas	QUALITY 5	VALUE C

REGISTRY Bahamas	LENGTH 880 feet	BEAM 106 feet
CABINS 1,177/1,140	DRAFT 25 feet	SPEED 19 knots
MAXIMUM PASSENGERS	PASSENGER DECKS 11	ELEVATORS 11
2,744/2,744/2,852	CREW 833	SPACE RATIO 32.3/30.8

THE SHIPS When the *Sovereign of the Seas* was introduced in 1988, she was the largest cruise ship ever built and stirred unprecedented excitement and publicity. More important, she came with innovations that influenced the design of all superliners and megaliners that followed.

Her dramatic atrium, the **Centrum,** was a cruise-ship first. Located amidships and spanning five decks, the atrium opens the space to create a light and inviting environment. Stairs and balconies around the atrium and its glass-enclosed elevators seem suspended in air. A white piano set amid tropical foliage at the atrium's base plays soft music that carries to upper decks and sets the harmonious tone found shipwide. The atrium, similar to a hotel's lobby, provides a friendly focal point. Passengers are dazzled but not intimidated, and the notion of entering a behemoth dissipates. The atrium also separates the forward section of the ship, which contains the cabins, from the aft with all public rooms and dining, sports, entertainment, and recreation facilities.

The arrangement has several advantages. Cabins are quieter; distances among public areas are shorter; and the ship doesn't seem so enormous. The ship looks outward—few areas lack natural light or a view to the outdoors—a feature absent on many new ships. Together with an incredible array of facilities, they explain passengers' immediate acceptance of the megaliner. *Sovereign's* twins, *Monarch of the Seas* and *Majesty of the Seas,* arrived with few changes—a few more cabins, a family suite, and a redesigned **Windjammer Café.** Many public rooms carry the same names. Throughout, contemporary elegance creates a warm, inviting ambience.

The ships are floating resorts, making the most of their size by providing spaces for varying tastes. These include the signature **Viking Crown Lounge** perched high on the stack; wide, outdoor promenades encircling the vessels; and sunny and shaded areas on three decks. They offer so many facilities and activities that even the most frantically active person can't participate in all of the options.

Recently, *Sovereign* was given a stem-to-stern makeover with new decor and new and expanded facilities and amenities that bring her more in line with the newer Voyager-class fleet. Among the new amenities, the new Centrum area on Deck 5 now has **Latte-tudes,** a coffee bar and ice cream shop serving Seattle's Best Coffee and Ben & Jerry's Ice Cream; and nearby **Wi-Fi,** the Internet center. Passengers can use their own or onboard rented Wi-Fi laptops to try out the ship's new wireless "hot spots" to log on to the Internet.

Earlier, *Monarch* was given a complete renovation, adding some of the features of the Voyager class. *Majesty of the Seas* is the first of the group to get the new service that enables passengers to make and receive calls on their own cell phones—at their personal numbers—while in international waters.

ITINERARIES *See* Itinerary Index.

CABINS Each of the trio has 16 categories of cabins. Designed to make the most out of every inch of space, they're fitted with a vanity table, chair, and twin beds convertible to daytime couches. *Monarch* and *Majesty* cabins are similar to *Sovereign's* in size and decor, but came with major enhancements—verandas on 50 deluxe outside cabins, and suites and family suites sleeping up to six. In her recent renovation, balconies were added to 62 suites and junior suites on Deck 10, and bathrooms in these accommodations were completely renewed.

Family suites have two bedrooms, a sitting room, two bathrooms, and veranda. *Majesty* has 146 cabins in the larger outside category, more comfortable than those on *Sovereign,* and the Bridge Deck contains only suites and deluxe cabins with private verandas. Bathrooms, though not large, are well designed with ample space for toiletries, thick towels, hair dryers, and excellent water pressure.

Specifications Sovereign, 427 inside cabins, 722 outside; 12 suites; 62 with balconies. Standard dimensions, inside 119 square feet, outside 122 square feet. 945 with twin beds (convertible to doubles); 196 third/fourth persons; no singles. 6 wheelchair-accessible. *Majesty* and *Monarch,* 444 inside cabins, 721 outside; 12 suites; 62 deluxe cabins and suites with verandas. Standard dimensions, 120 square feet. 917 with twin beds (convertible to queen); 260 third/fourth persons; no singles. 4 wheelchair-accessible.

DINING RCI ships don't serve gourmet fare and don't intend to. Rather, galleys produce tasty food that's plentiful but not excessive, with ample variety. All ships have the same menus (consistency at work), although longer European cruises may feature local dishes. A typical menu offers seven juices and appetizers; three soups; two salads; five entrees with a choice of pasta, fish, chicken, veal, and beef; three desserts; and a selection of cheeses and ice cream.

In keeping with its ShipShape program, all menus have light selections annotated with nutritional information. You can also select vegetarian dishes or request the full vegetarian menu for an entire cruise. Wine lists include California, French, and other vintages. Prices are moderate.

Each ship has two dining rooms serving three meals, all with assigned seating. The *Sovereign's* **Kismet Dining Room** has elaborate columns and lighting fixtures; its twin, **Gigi Dining Room,** has columns styled after palm trees. *Majesty's* **Mikado Dining Room** has a Japanese theme, whereas the springtime theme of its twin, **Maytime,** is expressed in a mural of apple trees in bloom. *Monarch's* **Brigadoon Dining Room** has a Scottish tartan motif; the **Flower Drum Song Dining Room** has sophisticated Oriental decor. Lunch and dinner can be ordered from dining room menus through room service.

A noticeable difference on *Sovereign* is her new **Windjammer Marketplace,** where breakfast, lunch, and a casual alternative dinner are available. In the evening, it offers full table service and a menu that changes daily. Also added is a **Johnny Rockets,** similar to the popular Voyager-class venue, and **Sorrento,** a new parlor. On the *Monarch* and *Majesty,* the **Windjammer Café** spans the ship's width and is wrapped on three sides by windows. The Café also has a mini-atrium with winter garden, waterfalls, and skylight.

SERVICE RCI's crews, from the Norwegian captains to the mini–United Nations of the cabin and dining-room staff, are courteous and eager to please. An affable, largely Caribbean group of stewards tidies rooms twice daily and provides evening turndown service. Dining staff have many Europeans and provide attentive, efficient service. Indeed, the staff is so conscious of the constant evaluation of their work, as reflected in passengers' comment cards, that they sometimes overdo their attention. And it's likely that your waiter, when his supervisors aren't around, will all but beg you to praise him in your comments—his job may depend on it.

FACILITIES AND ACTIVITIES Among activities may be bingo; napkin folding; wine tasting; parlor games; dance classes; bridge; ice carving; parties for singles, children, and teens; a costume party; religious services; and a passenger talent show. The wood-paneled library resembles an English club; it can also be used for meetings. Two levels of sun decks provide peace, privacy, and a place to read.

Almost 24 hours a day, there's music to suit every mood—including big band, steel band, Latin, country, rock, strolling violins, and classical concerts. The **Follies Lounge,** *Sovereign's* richly decorated bilevel showroom, stages two shows nightly. The rooms have video walls with 50 television monitors on movable banks of 25 screens each. Comfortable seats have excellent sight lines, with a few exceptions. Another lounge is *Sovereign's* new **Boleros Nightclub,** the hot new Latin-flavored nightspot with music and drinks to go with it.

Cantilevered from the funnel and encircling it is the extraordinary **Viking Crown Lounge.** The room, 12 stories above the water, provides a fabulous 360-degree view of the sea and sunset.

Among small lounges is the nautical-motif **Schooner Bar,** a favorite casual bar by day and a lively piano bar at night. **Casino Royale** next door offers blackjack, 170 slot machines, and American roulette. **Touch of Class** is a chic champagne bar where 50 people can clink flutes and scoop caviar. Decor lives up to the lounge's name with two lifelike bronze statues of 1920s flappers. Other options include **Flashes,** the teen nightclub, karaoke, a shopping boulevard, and a movie theater.

SPORTS, FITNESS, AND BEAUTY Fitness enthusiasts have a one-third-mile outside deck encircling the vessel and a second jogging track. The well-equipped health club offers saunas and locker rooms, a large exercise room with ballet bars, an array of exercise equipment, and a high-energy staff. The sports deck has twin swimming pools, two whirlpools, and a basketball court. ShipShape Fitness activities start with a sunrise stretch class or water exercises, low-impact aerobics, and walkathons, basketball, and Ping-Pong tournaments. Participants earn "dollars" for each activity, redeemable for T-shirts and visors. Vitality Unlimited is designed for senior citizens. All menus offer low-fat, low-calorie entrees, prepared to American Heart Association guidelines. The beauty salon/barber shop offers massage and beauty treatments at additional cost.

On *Sovereign,* the spa and fitness center were moved to Deck 9 and re-designed and enlarged with 11 treatment rooms, including a "couples" massage room. There are also new state-of-the-art cardiovascular and resistance machines, free weights, and an aerobics center with free classes; yoga, Pilates, and spinning classes are available for $10 per session.

CHILDREN'S FACILITIES RCI was among the first lines to create a children's program with youth centers, play rooms, and counselors. Sovereign-class ships offer the program year-round. They also have video arcades and teen centers. *Majesty* and *Monarch* have teen nightclubs. Kids get their own daily agenda, slipped under the cabin door each night. Among the activities are ice cream and pizza parties, dance classes, golf putting, face painting, midnight basketball, autograph hunts, talent shows, and shore tours. Baby-sitters (extra cost), cribs, and high chairs are available. Captain Sealy's Kids' Galley, a menu for children ages 4–12, offers such favorites as peanut butter sandwiches, hamburgers, and pizzas, along with salads, fruit, and alphabet soup.

The *Sovereign* has a new **Adventure Ocean and Teen Club** with learning and play areas with computers, toys, and books. **Fuel** is the teen's own disco and the **Living Room** is their place to chill out, watch large-screen televisions, or surf the Web. Teens also have a new, no-adults-allowed area, the **Back Deck**—it's a sun deck with an outdoor dance floor.

SHORE EXCURSIONS Except for its golf programs and cruises that include Labadee in their itinerary, RCI's shore excursions are similar to those of other lines cruising the Caribbean. They include island tours, beach trips, and snorkeling and diving. RCI's private resort, **Labadee,** created in 1987 on the north coast of Haiti, offers one of the best days at the beach of any line. Its setting is beautiful—lush mountains rise behind a lovely cove with a series of crescent-shaped beaches. There are pavilions for dining, entertainment, water sports equipment, and a marketplace with Haitian crafts, which are the Caribbean's best. Music, dancing, and performances by a local folklore group are provided.

Recently at Labadee, RCI opened a new pirate-themed water playground, sponsored by the Coca-Cola Company, and featuring a "sunken" pirate ship and a new mascot, Labadee Luc, who appears on signage throughout the peninsula. The **Splash Bash,** a special play area for kids ages 3–5, has a central pipe that sends water into three play areas with dams, water wheels and other fun activities. Admission to the water playground is $5 per person for a two-hour period. Volleyball courts were also added.

Some itineraries call for a day at **Coco Cay,** a small Bahamian island. Diversions for a range of ages include beach games, pedal boats, shopping, steel-band music, visits to a shipwreck led by snorkeling instructors, a barbecue, palm-shaded trails, six sandy beaches for swimming, and hammocks and beach chairs for lounging. Children's programs are available.

Empress of the Seas	QUALITY 5	VALUE C
REGISTRY Bahamas	LENGTH 692 feet	BEAM 100 feet
CABINS 801	DRAFT 25 feet	SPEED 19.5 knots
MAXIMUM PASSENGERS 2,020	PASSENGER DECKS 9	ELEVATORS 7
	CREW 685	SPACE RATIO 30.4

THE SHIP With a new look and a new name, *Empress of the Seas* (formerly *Nordic Empress*) took up her home at the brand new Cape Liberty Cruise Port in Bayonne, New Jersey, in May 2004. Changing the ship's name was meant to reflect the scope of the redesign that brought her facilities more in line with RCI's newer ships. Among the changes are new dining, entertainment and fitness areas, and a general facelift to the lobbies, elevators, landings, corridors, and restrooms, and enhancements to the shopping areas and Pool Deck.

Even before the changes, the *Empress* dazzled, from light that streams in by day to nighttime glitter. Passengers board at the nine-deck-tall atrium called the Centrum. Two of four elevators are glass and overlook a waterfall and greenery. Most public rooms flow from here. Two center decks contain the dining room, showroom, casino, and lounges. The Sun Deck topside is an all-day center of activities—from sunning and swimming to entertainment and dancing under the stars. It also contains the fitness and kids' centers.

ITINERARIES *See* Itinerary Index.

CABINS The dozen categories include many inside and lower-priced outside cabins. All are designed to be light and tropical in feeling. All have
two lower beds, color television, three-channel radio, telephone, and
private bath. Sixty percent are outside cabins with large windows. All
suites and deluxe cabins have balconies. All cabins were renovated with
new and upgraded bathrooms. Cabins, including the Royal Suite; superior outside cabins were given new decor, while the Owner's Suites
were completely redesigned with new furniture and finishes.

Specifications 338 inside cabins, 463 outside; 6 suites; 69 deluxe cabins with verandas. Standard dimensions, 194 square feet. 495 with twin
beds (all convertible to double); 358 with upper/lower berths accommodating third/fourth berths; no singles; 4 wheelchair-accessible.

DINING *Empress of the Seas* has an elegant new specialty restaurant,
Portofino ($20 surcharge); an upgraded **Windjammer Café;** and a
refurbished, bilevel **Carmen Dining Room,** the main dining room with
walls of floor-to-ceiling windows spanning two decks. There are two
seatings for the three meals. Menus are the same as offered on other
RCI ships and include theme dinners. At the new **Latte'tudes,** a combined coffee bar and ice cream shop, passengers can enjoy specialty
espresso drinks from Seattle's Best Coffee or 16 different flavors from
Ben & Jerry's ice cream.

Meals and snacks are served around the clock, starting with early-
riser's breakfast at 6:30 a.m. and ending with the midnight buffet. A
typical seven-course menu lists a wide choice of juices and appetizers;
soups; salads; pasta; entrees with fish, chicken, veal, and beef; desserts;
cheese; and ice cream. All menus have health-conscious selections.

Breakfast and lunch buffets are served in the upgraded, glass-domed
Windjammer Café. It's also an alternative dinner restaurant, offering
full table service 6:30–10:30 p.m., and a midnight buffet. A Sun Wor-
shipper's lunch and afternoon tea are served poolside. The full dining
room menu is available for room service at lunch and dinner.

SERVICE *Empress'* crew are eager to please. Stewards, most of them
Caribbean, make up rooms twice a day and provide evening turndown
service. The friendly dining staff quickly learn your preferences. As on
all other RCI ships, they will encourage good reviews on your passenger
comment cards.

FACILITIES AND ACTIVITIES Passengers on short cruises usually pack in as
many activities as possible. *Empress* provides abundant choices. Topside
by day are outdoor games and entertainment; elsewhere are dance
classes, cards, crafts, bingo, and karaoke.

Nighttime entertainment is some of RCI's best, with good shows,
music, and dancing for many tastes. Big, Broadway-style productions

are staged in the impressive, tiered **Strike Up the Band** lounge. Sight lines are good from almost any seat. The lounge also has a dance floor. The ship's most dazzling feature is the **Casino Royale,** offering slot machines, nine blackjack tables, roulette, craps, and wheel of fortune. Between the casino and Centrum is the newly created **Card Room.** The former High Society lounge was transformed into **Bolero's,** a Latin-themed bar offering specialty tequilas and cocktail favorites like mojitos and live entertainment. *Empress of the Seas* also now has the line's popular **Schooner Bar,** a nautical-themed lounge with sing-along piano entertainment. The **Viking Crown Lounge** is at the stern on Sun Deck, rather than cantilevered from the stack as on other RCI ships. Nonetheless, with three walls of windows, it's a fine observation area. Late night, it's a disco.

Note: When the ship is in Bermuda during summer, much of this entertainment won't be available. Bermudan regulations don't allow ships to open their casinos or stage shows while they're in port. However, the ship offers Bermuda-by-Night shore excursions, or you can explore local nightlife independently.

SPORTS, FITNESS, AND BEAUTY The large, bilevel **ShipShape Fitness Center** has a glass-enclosed exercise area and an array of equipment, plus saunas, showers, and massage rooms. On deck are three whirlpools and two fountains that cascade into two pools (one for children). The beauty salon offers hair, facial, and beauty treatments (additional charge). Video golf in the **Golf Ahoy! Center** enables participants to try their skill at world-famous courses projected on the screen ($20 per hour). A computer analyzes the stroke and scores the game. ShipShape activities range from aquadynamics to basketball free throws. "Dollars" earned for participation can be redeemed for T-shirts and visors.

CHILDREN'S FACILITIES **Kids' Konnection** is a multipurpose, 95-square-foot play room for children ages 5–12. Designed with a space-station theme, the room has an 11-foot ceiling, making room for the **Tubular Time** labyrinth of suspended tubes that are lighted and carpeted inside. Children can crawl through the tubes to a slide and clubhouse platform.

The youth program provides participants with a daily agenda, slipped under the cabin door at night. It's packed with activities, including ice cream and pizza parties, face painting, midnight basketball, talent shows, and shore tours. Menus designed for children ages 4–12 offer such favorites as peanut butter sandwiches, hot dogs, and pizzas, plus salads and fruit. Baby-sitters (extra cost), cribs, and high chairs are available.

SHORE EXCURSIONS Descriptive booklets accompany documents mailed to passengers. Excursions target varied interests but essentially are off-the-shelf programs, among them island tours, beach trips, snorkeling, and diving.

Brilliance of the Seas	QUALITY 8	VALUE C
Jewel of the Seas	(PREVIEW)	
Radiance of the Seas	QUALITY 8	VALUE C
Serenade of the seas	QUALITY 8	VALUE C
REGISTRY Bahamas	LENGTH 962 feet	BEAM 106 feet
CABINS 1,050	DRAFT 26.7 feet	SPEED 25 knots
MAXIMUM PASSENGERS 2,501	PASSENGER DECKS 12	ELEVATORS 9
	CREW 859	SPACE RATIO NA

THE SHIPS With sunshine shimmering through walls of glass, Royal Caribbean's *Radiance of the Seas* lives up to her name. The ship is so bright and airy you'll want to keep your sunglasses on when you come in from an outside deck.

Launched in 2001, *Radiance* has floor-to-ceiling windows on all levels of its nine-deck atrium and in 16 public areas, plus exterior glass elevators spanning 12 decks. Passengers never have to miss a minute of the beauty of Alaska and the Caribbean or the connection with the sea.

First of the new class of ship for Royal Caribbean, *Radiance of the Seas* is a classy lady—smaller than the giant Voyager class and larger than the Vision group. She incorporates the best of her predecessors: the many entertainment and activity options of *Voyager* (including the famous rock-climbing wall), the sleek profile of *Sovereign*, and glass galore. Her twin, *Brilliance of the Seas,* debuted in Europe in 2002. *Serenade of the Seas* followed in 2003 and *Jewel of the Seas* in 2004. The ships are Panamax class, meaning they are narrow enough—just barely—to pass through the Panama Canal.

And these ships have highlights of their own: the most balconies of any RCI ships; Internet ports in every cabin; a bookstore/coffeehouse; and gas and steam turbines said to reduce emissions, noise, and vibration. The ships reflect RCI's "resort-like" style, with the purser's desk called Guest Relations, its staff wearing resort-wear (rather than nautical uniforms), and a general manager and vacation experience director intended to foster guest satisfaction.

Radiance also boasts a first-at-sea: self-leveling pool tables. These high-tech tables are the big attraction in the **Bombay Billiard Club,** one of four lounges clustered in the **Colony Club.** The others are the **Calcutta Card Club; Jakarta Lounge,** an intimate bar with gaming tables; and **Singapore Sling,** a piano bar with floor-to-ceiling windows offering spectacular views aft. The Centrum, a dramatic, airy atrium and an RCI signature, is decorated in light woods and soft tones of sand, coral and aqua, set off with greenery, a waterfall, and colossal abstract sculpture—all part of the ship's $6-million-plus art collection.

Another memorable area is the African-themed Solarium, with three life-sized stone elephants, a bronze of a lion cub dipping his paw in the water, a waterfall, stone relief art panels depicting gazelles and antelopes, greenery, and piped-in sounds of chirping birds. It also has a raised pool (with a counter-current), two whirlpools, a bar and pizzeria, all under a retractable glass roof.

On the new *Jewel of the Seas,* passengers enjoy unobstructed views of the sea and landscapes afforded by the ship's nearly three acres of exterior glass in the dining rooms, lounges, ocean-facing glass elevators, and floor-to-ceiling windows in most public areas. The ship also has the highest percentage of cabins with balconies in Royal Caribbean's fleet and an eclectic, $5.3 million dollar art collection with themes of landscape and light in paintings, sculptures, textiles, ceramics, and mosaics throughout the ship. The nine-story Centrum has a modern art interpretation of the Northern Lights: a stainless steel, wire, and glass sculpture with an integrated lighting system.

Other highlights include the **Coral Theater,** introducing three new productions: a tango show, *Tango Buenos Aires,* starring Argentinean dancers and musicians; and two musical reviews, *City of Dreams,* featuring the music of top artists including Billy Joel, Elton John, and Celine Dion; and *From West End to Broadway,* a variety of music from Cole Porter to Les Miserables.

ITINERARIES *See* Itinerary Index.

CABINS Accommodations are spacious and attractively decorated; 70% have verandas. The most lavish, the Royal Suite, is a palatial 1,035 square feet, with 173 square feet of balcony and such amenities as a baby grand piano, wet bar, and entertainment center with 42-inch flat screen TV, stereo, and VCR, and bath with whirlpool, bidet, and steam shower. Veranda cabins measuring 179 square feet with a 41-square-foot-balcony are situated on Decks 7, 8, 9, and 10, with the ones on Deck 10 closest to the pools and other outdoor amenities. The lowest-priced cabins are inside cabins measuring 166 square feet.

All cabins are equipped with an interactive television, telephone, computer jack, vanity table with an extendable working surface for a laptop computer, refrigerator/minibar, hair dryer, 110/220 electrical outlets, two single beds convertible to double; and reading lights by the beds. There are wheelchair-accessible cabins are available in most categories.

The needs of physically challenged passengers are addressed not only in the cabins and oversized hallways, but also with special devices to aid the hearing impaired. Listening devices are available, as well as telephone amplifiers and strobe-light door knockers and telephone ringers. For the visually impaired, cabin doors, service directories, and even elevator buttons and dining menus are written in Braille. The personalized service sometimes extends to extra assistance at the pier, early-boarding orientation, sign language interpreter, special diet accommodation, or onboard medical services.

Specifications 1,055 cabins; 238 inside; 817 outside (577 with balconies); 62 suites; 62 deluxe; 6 family suites; 65 third/fourth persons; no singles; 15 wheelchair-accessible.

DINING **Cascades,** the elegant, two-level main dining room, has a grand staircase, etched-glass mural, and a cascading waterfall. The upper level has floor-to-ceiling windows; the lower level, large windows. Two smaller dining rooms, **Breakers** and **Tides,** are ideal for private parties. Breakfast and lunch are open seating; dinner is served in two seatings. ShipShape (or low fat) selections are offered for lunch and dinner. The casual **Windjammer Café** serves buffet-style breakfast and lunch with a choice of indoor and outdoor seating. The **Seaview Café** cooks up burgers, hot dogs, and nachos. The food ranges from mediocre to delicious.

Alternative eateries include **Chops Grill,** serving steaks and other grills from an open kitchen; and **Portofino,** an upscale Euro-Italian restaurant with Tuscany-inspired decor. Fee is $20 per person at each which covers gratuities; reservations required.

FACILITIES AND ACTIVITIES The three-level **Aurora Theatre,** the setting for Broadway-style revues, has Arctic-themed decor with sculptured balconies, side walls, and parterre divisions resembling glacial landscapes. The futuristic **Starquest** (with a revolving bar) and **Hollywood Odyssey** are two nightspots housed in RCI's hallmark **Viking Crown Lounge** perched high over the sea. The latter features jazz ensembles, comedians, pianists, and vocalists. The ship has a large casino, several bars, and a library reminiscent of a traditional English study, as well as **Royal Caribbean Online,** the Internet center with 12 stations.

SPORTS, FITNESS, AND BEAUTY The ocean-view **ShipShape Spa,** the beauty and health center, has 12 treatment rooms, including rasul and a thermal suite ($15–$42 for a half-hour); gym with 18 treadmills and an array of equipment; and fitness activities and exercise classes. Out on deck, passengers have more challenges at the rock-climbing wall with five separate climbing tracks, golf simulator ($20 per hour), nine-hole miniature golf course, basketball court, and jogging track.

CHILDREN'S FACILITIES The line's **Adventure Ocean** youth program offers supervised activities by age group (ages 3–5, 6–8, 9–12, and 13–17) in age-appropriate activity centers. Kids earn gift coupons for participating. Facilities include a computer lab, play stations with video games, and Adventure Beach with splash pools and a water slide. Teens have their own coffeehouse/disco with flat-screen televisions and soda bar. Children's menus and group baby-sitting are available.

POSTSCRIPT Royal Caribbean's reputation for delivering consistency holds up on all its ships. But remember, these are megaliners; you need patience for crowds and long lines, no matter how smoothly the ships operate. At the same time, their size and array of facilities and activities are treats in themselves, and they and serve to fuel the action-packed, high-energy atmosphere aboard.

Freedom of the Seas	(PREVIEW)	
REGISTRY NA	LENGTH 1,112 feet	BEAM 184 feet
CABINS 1,800	DRAFT 28 feet	SPEED 21.6 knots
MAXIMUM PASSENGERS 4,370	PASSENGER DECKS 15	ELEVATORS NA
	CREW 1,360	SPACE RATIO NA

THE SHIP At 158,000 tons with a maximum capacity of 4,370 passengers, *Freedom of the Seas,* under construction in Finland, will be the largest cruise ship in the world when she debuts in May 2006. The first of three in Royal Caribbean's new Freedom class, the giant vessel is being billed as the most innovative ship the company has built to date.

The innovations revealed thus far (RCI is releasing only pieces of the design at a time to build the suspense), has an unusual top-deck aquatic playground with three massive pool areas. They include an interactive water park, two dramatically situated whirlpools, and a dedicated sports pool—each with a different audience appeal.

The most interesting space is the **H₂0 Zone,** a colorful wonderland of large, bright sculptures doubling as interactive fountains that spray, sprinkle, and spurt water in every direction. The oversized sculptures are in all shapes and sizes and will give passengers numerous playful opportunities—by turning wheels, setting off sensors, and dodging dumping buckets—to get soaked or to soak others.

In one corner of the water playground, a circular pool will shoot a current of water in a river around a central island. Passengers can float with the flow as they are misted by one of the fountain sculptures. A shallow pool area, fed by a flamingo-shaped fountain, is a secluded space for the youngest kids. At the back of the park, a rectangular swimming pool is flanked by wading areas and fed by a waterfall cascading from an overhanging bridge. At night, the water park will turn into a dramatically lit sculpture garden.

The **Solarium,** an adults-only oasis, offers a cruise-ship "first." Two hot tubs, large enough for 16 people, are cantilevered out 12 feet from the sides of the ship and suspended 112 feet above the ocean. Its panoramic views from here will definitely not be for those with acrophobia. The Solarium's jungle decor has tropical foliage, rainforest-inspired mosaics and murals, tall metal palm trees and hammocks, and seven-foot-tall parrot sculptures. Passengers swimming in the Solarium's pool will be treated to music piped in underwater, a simulation of a coral reef, and a glass wall that allows them to get an underwater view of the atrium adjacent to the pool.

Another first for RCI is in the main pool area at the center of the ship where there are two parallel pools. One of the pools will be designated as a sports pool for activities ranging from pool volleyball to contestants trying their hand at synchronized swimming competitions. The sports pool has lane markers for lap swimming. At night, the main pool area will be transformed into an open-air nightclub, with a large dance floor situated between the two pools. The ship's combined pool areas—the family pool area, adults-only Solarium, and the main pool area—are 43% larger than on the Voyager-class ships.

CABINS Another innovation on *Freedom of the Seas* will be its six categories of family cabins designed especially for large families and groups of friends. These accommodations come in several new configurations, sizes, and price ranges.

The largest is the 14-person Presidential Suite, with a 1,215 square-foot interior and an 810 square-foot balcony equipped with a whirlpool, wet bar, eight lounge chairs, and a 14-person table for dining alfresco. The oversized suite has dual entryways, two master bedrooms with 30-inch, flat-panel televisions, and bathrooms with bathtubs. Two other bedrooms will accommodate four people each, with convertible twin/queen and Pullman beds. Both rooms will have a 23-inch, flat-panel television. In fact, all cabins on *Freedom* will have flat-panel television. The suite's common area will include two additional bathrooms with showers, a spacious living room with a sectional sofa that sleeps two, a card/dining table, and an entertainment center with a 42-inch plasma television.

The five other types of family accommodations are in addition to the ship's standard triples and quads. Each category includes twin beds, convertible to a queen bed and bunks.

Four eight-person Royal Family Suites (600 square feet with a 270-square-foot balcony), each with two bedrooms, including a master bedroom with a bathroom with bathtub, a second bathroom with shower, and a living area with a sectional sofa and an entertainment center with a 30-inch, flat-panel television and an alfresco dining table for eight. Each suite can be expanded to accommodate up to 10 people via a connecting cabin.

Three categories with a total of 15 cabins, each for six persons, have a curtained-off sleeping alcove with bunk beds, sleeper sofa, a bathroom and shower or tub; some with walk-in closets: One Accessible Family (400 square feet with a 120-square-foot balcony); 8 Family Oceanview (up to 495 square feet with windows); 4 Promenade Family (335 square feet, two windows with window seats overlooking Royal Promenade); and 2 Inside Family (330 square feet).

Freedom of the Seas will have RCI standard features, such as production shows in the main theater; ice-skating shows and free-skate parties on the ice rink; the Royal Promenade, a 445-foot-long shopping, dining, and entertainment boulevard with nightly activities and festive parades; and the Adventure Ocean Program for kids ages 3–17. Teens particularly will be catered to with three areas just for them: **Fuel** nightclub, the **Living Room** hangout, and the **Back Deck** sundeck. For tiny tots ages 6–36 months and their parents, *Freedom of the Seas* will offer the line's Aqua Babies and Aqua Tots playtime programs developed by partner Fisher-Price.

Freedom's rock-climbing wall, 43 feet tall and 44 feet wide, is 30% larger than the original on Voyager-class ships. The free-standing wall has a central spire, adding a new dimension to the experience. Passengers have 11 different routes to choose, from easy to expert.

Freedom of the Seas will sail on seven-night Western Caribbean itineraries from Miami to Cozumel, Grand Cayman, Montego Bay, and Labadee.

Seabourn Cruise Line

6100 Blue Lagoon Drive, Suite 400, Miami, FL 33126
☎ **305-463-3000 or 800-929-9391; fax 305-463-3010**
www.seabourn.com

TYPE OF SHIPS Small, modern, ultraluxurious ocean liners.

TYPE OF CRUISES Top-shelf luxury cruises on worldwide itineraries.

CRUISE LINE'S STRENGTHS
- impeccable service
- luxurious accommodations
- exclusivity
- ship size/maneuverability
- open-seating dining
- cuisine
- worldwide itineraries

CRUISE LINE'S SHORTCOMINGS
- limited activities
- limitations on use of water-sports facilities

FELLOW PASSENGERS Sophisticated, discriminating, well-heeled, experienced travelers; 80% from North America; others are from Europe and elsewhere. Age varies, depending on season and destinations. Most are age 50 and older; active business owners and professionals—doctors, lawyers, entrepreneurs—and honeymooners and some semiretired. They come mainly from the Northeast, Florida, California, and Chicago area. Fifty percent or more are repeaters. The mix could include a childless couple in their 30s or multigenerational families ages 4–70. Passengers are likely to have sailed on other luxury vessels and stayed in five-star hotels. They know and understand quality; their expectations are high, and their judgment tough.

Recommended for Sophisticated, seasoned travelers accustomed to the best; affluent passengers whose first priority is service; those who seek exclusivity; yacht owners who want to leave the driving to others; those who shun big-ship, glitzy cruises; first-timers who seek and can afford small-ship ambience; honeymooners with rich parents; lottery winners.

Not recommended for Those unaccustomed to luxury or a sophisticated environment; anyone uncomfortable in a fancy restaurant or five-star European hotel; flashy dressers, late-night revelers, inexperienced travelers, children.

CRUISE AREAS AND SEASONS Caribbean, Panama Canal, South America, Australia/New Zealand, Southeast Asia in winter. Europe, Mediterranean, Black Sea, Norwegian fjords, Baltic, British Isles in spring/

summer. New England, Canada, Caribbean, Red Sea and Africa in autumn; Transatlantic, spring, fall.

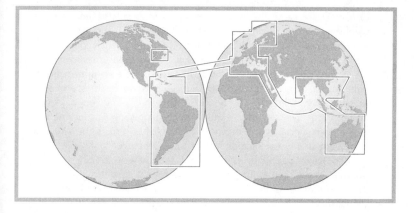

THE LINE Founded in 1987 by Norwegian industrialist Atle Brynestad, Seabourn Cruise Line's goal has always been to offer the world's most luxurious cruises on the most elegant ships afloat for the most discriminating travelers. Seabourn quickly won enough fans with its first ship, *Seabourn Pride,* to complete a second one. Seabourn's posh ships with sleek, yachtlike profiles are small enough to be exclusive yet large enough to be spacious and offer most facilities of a large ship. The ambience is carefree elegance. Cruises follow the sun on worldwide itineraries that circle the globe in a year's time.

In 1996, with the demise of Royal Viking and Royal Cruise lines, Seabourn acquired the *Royal Viking Queen,* which was originally intended to be the third Seabourn ship. In 1999, Carnival, which had owned 50% of Seabourn Cruises, acquired 100% ownership. Seabourn remains a separate brand. With the purchase, Carnival became a major player in the luxury market.

THE FLEET	BUILT/RENOVATED	TONNAGE	PASSENGERS
Seabourn Legend	1991/96/2000/03	10,000	208
Seabourn Pride	1988/97/2000/03	10,000	208
Seabourn Spirit	1989/99/2000/03	10,000	208

STYLE Elegant but not stuffy, glamorous but not glitzy, Seabourn ships are like tony private clubs. Quality is key, starting with a nearly effortless embarkation and a white-gloved attendant to escort you to your suite (as luxurious as the brochure promises), where fruit and champagne await you. Decor exudes understated elegance. Service—always attentive, never intrusive—is as polished as the silver with which you dine. You will be addressed by name by the staff after your first appearance.

Seabourn attracts both old-money travelers who disdain mainstream cruise ships and newly rich who appreciate the line's status symbolism. It also caters to stressed-out professionals and others seeking privacy. Whatever their background, they're affluent enough to be accustomed to a high level of service and style without excessive fuss.

Days at sea are for relaxing. Dress and atmosphere are informal, and time is unstructured. The usual announcements, pool games, and contests are absent. In fact, a Seabourn cruise is so low-key, you may need to read your daily agenda to know what's happening. Each cruise has one or two special events meant to be highlights. It might be a special concert in an unusual location for Seabourn passengers only; a visit to a private island, marina, or estate; or a sporting event. Evenings aboard ship are more formal; fine dining is the day's highlight. On evenings when you prefer to relax, a full-course dinner will be served en suite.

All three ships are now wired for Wi-Fi access, enabling passengers with suitable laptop computers to receive and send email and Web-surf from all suites and most public areas on board. A new satellite service has lowered costs: Internet access is $0.50 per minute, with lower bulk rates available. Phone service is $4.95 per minute. The ships offer an expanded menu of television channels, with additional sports, news, and entertainment programming.

Seabourn offers the ultimate in vacation flexibility by enabling passengers freedom to choose from varied options. These include tailoring their cruise with separate and independently priced cruise fares, air-travel options, pre- and postcruise tours, hotel, and transfers. For air, the choices are Seabourn's air program with preselected carriers, economy, business, or first class; the cruise line's independent air program, booked through Seabourn; or a chartered Gulfstream to and from the ship anywhere in the world. The ships are to be renovated again in late 2005 and early 2006.

DISTINCTIVE FEATURES Unusual care for solo passengers. Foldout watersports marina. Personalized stationery, walk-in closets, complimentary self-service laundry/dryer. Computer learning centers. Luggage shipping. Visiting chefs. Wi-Fi access. Personal Shopper services in many ports.

	HIGHEST	LOWEST	AVERAGE
PER DIEM	$1,422	$417	$839

Per diems are calculated from cruise line's nondiscounted *cruise-only* published fares on standard accommodations and vary by season, cabins, and cruise areas.

RATES Tips are included; port charges are additional. Prestocked minibar in cabins; wine with meals.

Special fares and discounts **Advance-purchase, capacity-controlled discounts, known as EBS (Early Booking Savings) reward early birds with up to 50% savings. Combo savings of 10% are added for booking consecutive cruises totaling up to 17 days. Longer combinations of 18 days or more get 50% or more "Grand Voyage" savings. Future cruises booked aboard a cruise earns an extra 5% savings. For the line's other special fares, consult its brochures. Those who have sailed on Seabourn or any of the other Carnival member lines qualify for Club Signature Savings of 50% on an array of cruises throughout the world. Club Signature Value Sailings are clearly marked in Seabourn's cruise catalog and on the Web site.**

- **THIRD PASSENGER:** 50% of per-person published tariff.
- **CHILDREN'S FARE:** Same as third-person rate. No infants under one year; children ages 1–2 sail free.
- **SINGLE SUPPLEMENT:** 110–200% of per-person double-occupancy basic suite, depending on cruise.

Packages
- **AIR/SEA:** Yes. First- and business-class upgrades at extra charge.
- **PRE/POST:** Yes. Many basic air/sea packages include one hotel night in the departure city; extensions available in all major gateways.
- **OTHERS:** Yes.

PAST PASSENGERS Members receive fare reductions for accumulated days of sailing up to the plateau of a free 14-day cruise after 140 days. For a second Seabourn cruise, members get free trip cancellation/interruption insurance, plus other insurance and medical coverage. There are also savings for early payment.

THE LAST WORD To compete in the growing ultra-deluxe market, Seabourn widened its price range and began offering much more flexibility. The per diems on some sampler and promotional cruises are no more than those of mainstream cruises. In any year, Seabourn visits more than 300 ports in over 100 countries. Very few cruise lines can match those numbers. If you can afford the price, you're unlikely to find any finer cruising—even on your own yacht.

Seabourn Cruise Line Standard Features

Officers Norwegian, International

Staff Dining/European; Cabin/Scandinavian; Cruise/British, European, and American.

Dining facilities Two open-seating restaurants; one more formal, the other a casual indoor/outdoor cafe. En suite dining. Complementary wine.

Special diets On request, four weeks prior to sailing.

Room service 24 hours, cabin menu and full service.

SCL Standard Features *(continued)*

Dress code By day, casual but conservative, comfortable. Dinner is a dressy affair, informal (jacket but no tie for men) or formal (two black-tie evenings in the dining room on one-week cruise; four formal dinners on two-week cruise); there are casual alternative for dinner.

Cabin amenities Television with CNN; financial fax service; VCR, direct-dial telephone; marble bathroom with twin sinks (one on *Legend*), tub and shower, deluxe toiletries, hair dryer, bathrobes, walk-in closet, minifridge; safe. Stocked bar. Bose Wave radio and CD player.

Electrical outlets 110/220 AC.

Wheelchair access Four suites.

Recreation and entertainment Three lounges with entertainment/dance music nightly; cabaret, classical music concerts, folkloric performances in ports of call; weekly dinner-dance; casino; cruise-related lectures, bridge instructor/lessons; enrichment programs.

Sports and other activities Water-sports marina, outdoor pool, deck sports; golf program.

Beauty and fitness Several saunas, outdoor whirlpools, gym, exercise classes, beauty salon, spa with massage, beauty treatments.

Other facilities Self-service laundry, laundry/dry cleaning; library; boutique; hospital; nondenominational religious services. Wi-Fi access, medical facilities and computer center.

Children's facilities None; children under age 18 must be accompanied by parent or adult with written permission.

Theme cruises Classical music, food and wine, others.

Smoking Public rooms are designated as nonsmoking. One lounge is smoking after dinner.

Seabourn suggested tipping No-tipping-expected policy.

Credit cards For cruise payment and on-board charges: American Express, Diners Club, Discover, MasterCard, Visa.

Seabourn Legend	**QUALITY 9**	**VALUE C**
Seabourn Pride	**QUALITY 9**	**VALUE C**
Seabourn Spirit	**QUALITY 9**	**VALUE C**
REGISTRY Bahamas	**LENGTH** 439 feet	**BEAM** 63 feet
CABINS 104	**DRAFT** 16 feet	**SPEED** 18 knots
MAXIMUM PASSENGERS 208	**PASSENGER DECKS** 6	**ELEVATORS** 3
	CREW 150	**SPACE RATIO** 49

THE SHIPS In this age of glitzy ships, the Seabourn triplets (they are nearly identical) are the epitome of understatement. Clean lines, fine fabrics, and subtle styling are meant to soothe. Passengers board through a lobby that instantly reveals the ships' character. Quietly elegant, the small atrium spans five decks with a double circular stairway accented by brass railings and etched glass. A glass dome above illuminates the stairs and adjacent hallways with diffused natural light. Pastel carpeting complements blush marble and wood used throughout the vessel. The sense of space and serenity is immediate and is among the ships' most appealing features.

Public rooms occupy all of the two top levels and are aft on the two center decks. The dining room is on the lowest passenger level. In 2000, all three ships were given a stem-to-stern multimillion-dollar renovation, along with the addition of French balconies to 36 suites, a computer learning center, a cigar humidor, and an expanded gym, among other improvements. Again, in 2003, the ships were refurbished and new amenities added. More enhancements are to be added when the ships are renovated in late 2005 and early 2006.

The main showroom, **Magellan Lounge** (**King Olav** on *Legend*; **Amundsen Lounge** on *Spirit*), has a stage and dance floor. It is used for daytime lectures and evening entertainment. In the lobby area are the tour desk, cruise director's office, writing room, and computer center.

One flight up is a second entertainment lounge, which is cleverly glass-partitioned in three sections: a small casino; an informal bar; and a piano lounge used for activities, socializing, daytime parties, and predinner cocktails. After dinner, it's a nightclub. There's also a small book-and-video library.

The first of the two top levels contains the sports and spa deck and indoor/outdoor **Veranda Café.** Another flight up is the **Observation Lounge,** a beautiful room with sloping floor-to-ceiling windows. Early-bird continental breakfast and afternoon tea are served here–both stellar times for ocean panoramas. Reference material on shore excursions, board games, and puzzles are available. A bar outside serves morning bouillon and is a popular gathering spot in fair weather. A promenade used by walkers and joggers connects the bar to a sunning deck.

ITINERARIES *See* Itinerary Index.

CABINS Accommodations—all spacious, outside suites—are among the ships' finest features. Even standard Seabourn Suites are large. Their practical design maximizes space, and appointments—wall coverings, carpets, draperies, bed covers of fine, lightly textured fabrics—enhance harmony and elegance.

They have well-defined sitting and sleeping sections. The roomy conversation area has a sofa, two chairs, and a coffee table that can be transformed into a dining table. Two cushioned stools provide extra seating for guests. The sitting area is next to a five-foot-wide picture window placed low enough that you can lie in bed and watch the passing scenery. The window has a mechanical shade operated by a switch near the desk and a device to clean the outside automatically.

Now, 36 of each ship's 104 suites have French balconies in place of the five-foot picture window. The balconies consist of two full-length sliding glass doors opening onto a narrow, Riviera-style balcony with a waist-high glass balustrade. The sliding doors can be opened to enjoy sea breezes without cutting into the interior space of the room. In the ships' tariff, these suites are designated by categories B2 and B3, and their locations are shown on deck plans. Unfortunately, the French balconies have shown not to ride well in high seas when water has seeped in to such an extent that the wall-to-wall carpets and furniture had to be changed completely. Upon the first experience of this problem, all seals on balcony doors were replaced and closures changed—making for significant improvement.

A curtain separating the sitting and sleeping areas can be drawn to put sleepers in darkness. Beds can be configured as twins or a queen. The bedroom section has a long dresser/desk and a large, lighted mirror. A wall-mounted minifridge and bar is stocked with two bottles of spirits or wine that you select when you book. Replenishments cost extra. Mineral water and soft drinks are free. The bar contains Norwegian crystal glassware. On the opposite wall is a pull-out writing desk, containing your personalized stationery and a small sewing kit. The cabinet conceals a flat-screen television and DVD player. CNN and other channels are available, depending on the location of the ship The suites also have a Bose Wave stereo radio and CD player. The walk-in closet contains extra shelf space and a safe.

The marble bathroom has twin sinks (*Legend*, one sink), mirrored storage shelves, a large tub, and a shower. Thick terry robes, a hair dryer, and toiletries are supplied. Fine bed and bath linens are used throughout.

Cabin doors have a thoughtful touch: a brass clamp to hold the daily agenda, messages, and menus. A hall-side door can be used to convert adjacent standard suites into doubles.

Sixteen larger suites are in four configurations. Classic suites have queen beds only, a larger sitting area, and a small veranda. Regal suites have a separate bedroom and living room, two bathrooms (one with shower and one with tub), a table with four chairs, two walk-in closets, and two sofas. Two owner's suites are the largest and have small private verandas.

Specifications All suites: 88 are standard Seabourn suites; 2 larger Classic suites and 4 Owner suites—all with verandas, 36 with French balconies. Standard dimensions, 277 square feet. 102 with twins (convertible to queen); no singles; 4 wheelchair-accessible.

DINING Fine dining is central to a Seabourn cruise, and the choices are diverse. For any meal, you dine when and with whom you like in the

Restaurant dining room or the casual **Veranda Café,** an indoor/outdoor venue for buffet breakfast, lunch, and dinner. Both offer open seating, but reservations are recommended for the Veranda Café. Or dine en suite, choosing from the 24-hour cabin menu or the dining room menu, served course by course. Morning bouillon is served in the **Sky Bar,** and afternoon tea with cucumber sandwiches can be enjoyed in the **Observation Lounge.**

With Seabourn, the emphasis is on fresh ingredients, such as seafood, fruits, and vegetables, obtained in ports. Breads, pastries, and ice cream are prepared onboard. Menus, changed daily and repeated on a 21-day cycle, are created by celebrity chef Charlie Palmer, and offer three appetizers, two soups, two salads, five entrees, three desserts, cheese, and ice cream. Generally, dishes are innovative and sophisticated. You will find a familiar fettuccine alfredo, but you may be tempted by seared reindeer or grilled marlin with strawberry and cilantro sauce. Vegetarian and lean specialties are available daily, as are classic steak, chicken, and fish.

Menu entrees are cooked to order, and presentation is outstanding. Suggested wines are usually moderately priced; the wine list is more elaborate. Wine is available by the glass. Caviar available by request.

The Restaurant is a pretty room dressed in pastels where tables are set with Wedgwood china, fine crystal, silverware, and fresh flowers. Most tables seat four or six, but two, eight, and tens are available.

Breakfast and lunch appeal most to those who prefer a quiet environment and full service. Dinner is a lavish, somewhat formal affair. Two evenings each week call for formal attire, and for all but casual nights, dress suitable for fine dining in New York or Paris is expected. Recently, Seabourn expanded its passengers' choices by offering a more casual dining alternative in the Veranda Café on evenings when the suggested attire for the Restaurant is black tie.

Service is unfailingly superb. In fact, service in the Restaurant is the best and most professional we have encountered on any cruise ship. Unlike on other cruise ships, singles are invited to join an officer's table or one hosted by management or a social-staff member. An invitation will be clipped to your door almost daily, and the maitre d' will seat singles with other guests, unless you indicate that you prefer to dine alone. At least once each cruise, a dinner dance is held in the Restaurant.

The informal, convivial atmosphere of the Veranda Café makes it the most popular choice for breakfast and lunch or for dinner after a long shore excursion. In the ships' most recent refurbishing, the Café got fresh new decor and new contemporary menus. The lively cafe bustles with people and conversation indoors. Outside, tables are set under protective awnings. In fair weather, the deck is one of the most delightful dining places anywhere. During the upcoming renovations, new seamless awnings will be installed which will allow for greater use of the deck, even in inclement weather.

The breakfast buffet offers fruit, fresh breads and pastries, smoked fish, cheeses, and eggs, pancakes, and waffles made to order. The lunch buffet includes salads, made-to-order pasta, hot and cold seafood, chicken and meats, or grilled fish or meat on request. Hard to resist are the daily surprises: guacamole, an Asian buffet, or a cheese and dessert bar. The homemade ice cream is a passenger favorite. But these aren't your ordinary self-service buffets. An army of attentive stewards take drink orders, assist you with your plate, and bring seconds.

Every evening, the Veranda Café becomes a trattoria or bistro with a special menu and lively music. The meal and the evening are wonderful and very popular. Reserve early.

Seabourn is continuing its highly appreciated "Chef's Circle," a guest chefs program that brings America's most creative and celebrated chefs onboard, features their signature dishes in the Restaurant, and has them give cooking demonstrations during the cruise.

SERVICE Most passengers rate service as the single best feature—and with good reason: It's impeccable. Shipwide, the thoroughly professional staff is gracious and attentive, but never intrusive. The Norwegian captain and officers, European hotel staff and stewardesses, and British and American cruise and social staff work harmoniously and are visibly proud of their ship. The ships' small size lends them to personalized service impossible on larger ships. The luxury setting offers more opportunities to provide good service, and the high crew-to-passenger ratio enables staff to deliver it.

The ship's no-tipping policy appeared to work very well, but we've recently been told that it's being modified to allow staff to accept tips for unusual service. We thought it was the result of the line's lowering its cruise prices (20% or more), but we were wrong. Gratuities are still included in the cruise price. We hope the change won't impact service. Also, to note, some guest give donations to a crew fund through the purser's office; it pays for crew parties and other activities during their free time.

FACILITIES AND ACTIVITIES The daily agenda isn't taxing but might include a cooking demonstration; afternoon lecture by a well-known person from the arts, academia, politics, or show business; port talks; bridge lessons or play; art class; galley tour, wine-and-cheese party; ice cream social; or folkloric show. A movie on one of Seabourn's other cruises—and a not-too-subtle sales pitch—may be presented. Not on the schedule are bingo, horse racing, pool games, or costume parties.

The library has music and books, including some on CD. Also, cabin stewardess will deliver DVDs to suites, upon request. The boutique beckons to shoppers. The **Computer Learning Center** with four computers offers classes for a fee. In the **Observation Lounge,** a humidor cabinet was installed at the rear of the room, and cigar tastings are held nightly.

Or you can do nothing at all. If the weather is fair, you'll probably be out on deck, relaxing, snoozing, soaking in the Jacuzzi, or enjoying a "massage moment" (complimentary from the spa staff). Some places offer protection in hot or cool weather.

Evening entertainment is tony, designed for sophisticated people. The ship's small orchestra plays easy listening and dance music in the **Club,** or a pianist/vocalist performs at the cocktail hour. Evening cabaret and variety shows staged in the **Magellan Lounge** are usually very good. They feature the cruise director and three or four social-staff members. Lounge seats are slightly tiered, providing excellent sight lines. A classical concert or program by a young artist may be offered, or the **Restaurant** becomes a supper club with dancing. The casino offers roulette, blackjack, slot machines, and gaming lessons.

SPORTS, FITNESS, AND BEAUTY Decks have ample space for sunning and a teak promenade for walking or jogging. Whirlpools and a small, deep swimming pool are in a peculiar spot near the Veranda Café—the pool is often shaded by the ship's superstructure, inhibiting swimmers.

The ships have a water-sports platform with a 30-by-30-foot steel-meshed cage that drops into the sea, creating a protected saltwater pool. A teak border provides a launch area for paddleboats, wind-surfers, and sailboats in warm weather ports. Two high-speed boats pull water-skiers or banana boats and also transport snorkelers and divers to choice locations. Although the ships try to use these marinas at least once a week, rough water may preclude it.

In the 2003 renovations, fitness facilities were upgraded substantially, with the gym doubled in size and more state-of-the-art equipment added, along with new cabinets and lockers. Daily stretch and exercise classes at varied workout levels, individual training, sauna, and steam rooms are available. The **Spa at Seabourn** has enhanced selections of beauty treatments and services, along with fitness classes in yoga, Pilates, and cardio Ki Bo Circuit training.

Seabourn no longer has a golf program; however, the line can make arrangements for tee times on request. Seabourn's ships visit 90 ports around the world where passengers have access to more than 100 golf courses, including most of the major and famous ones.

CHILDREN'S FACILITIES Although Seabourn doesn't offer the ideal family vacation, it's a testimony to staff that three children younger than nine years old reported having the time of their lives on a recent cruise.

SHORE EXCURSIONS Excursions are well-organized and orchestrated by an experienced, knowledgeable staff. On a Norwegian fjord cruise, the briefing was the most thorough heard on any but expedition-type cruises accompanied by specialists. There's no push to sell excursions, and even off-the-shelf motorcoach tours tend to be pricey. Information on excursions is available on Seabourn's newly expanded and enhanced Web site.

Each cruise offers one event designated as an "Exclusively Seabourn" excursion for all passengers. These often are a cruise highlight and may be visits to private homes or local sites off the tourist track. Refreshments and entertainment are provided, and guests may be introduced to local dignitaries. For example, a Norwegian voyage offered a concert of Edvard Grieg's music at his lakeside home near Bergen, presented by Norway's foremost pianist.

In addition, the line recently added over 75 new and unusual shore excursions created exclusively for Seabourn passengers that include special entry to sites of interest, meetings with famous personalities, and a variety of special-interest pursuits such as racecar driving, yacht racing, photography, and river rafting. There's a visit to Hong Kong's Cantonese Opera to watch artists apply their makeup; a tour of the Ngorongoro Crater and the Olduvai Gorge with a member of the Leakey family; and shopping in Florence markets for an Italian Cordon Bleu Cooking School class, to name a few.

POSTSCRIPT One of Seabourn's most useful innovations has been "Personal Valet Luggage Shipping," particularly these days considering the frequent hassle travelers encounter at airports and customs. By teaming up with DHL Worldwide Express, it enables passengers to ship their luggage directly from their home to their ship. The service prepares all the shipping and customs paperwork, picks up the luggage, maintains 24-hour online tracking, insurance, and delivers the shipment. The cost is based on weight. As an example, 30 pounds from the United States to Seabourn's Scandinavia/Russia cruise cost about $200.

Silversea Cruises

110 East Broward Boulevard, Ft. Lauderdale, FL 33301
☎ 954-522-4477 or 800-722-9955; fax 954-522-4499
www.silversea.com

TYPE OF SHIPS Ultraluxury, all-suite, small ships.

TYPE OF CRUISES Luxury cruises on worldwide itineraries.

CRUISE LINE'S STRENGTHS
- luxurious all-suite accommodations, most with verandas
- open-seating dining
- cuisine
- impeccable service
- worldwide itineraries
- congenial atmosphere
- comprehensive, all-inclusive prices

CRUISE LINE'S SHORTCOMINGS
- somewhat staid evening activities and entertainment
- shallow draft in rough seas

FELLOW PASSENGERS Diverse demographically, experienced cruisers. Many have made the rounds of the luxury ships. Well-traveled and out-going, passengers range from young professionals in their 30s to lively 80-year-olds. The majority are older than 50; couples are the rule. Passengers come from throughout the United States, and Silversea has a sizable European following. A high number of passengers are repeaters.

Recommended for Sophisticated, knowledgeable travelers who prefer a finely crafted ship and low-key atmosphere to the glitz and games of big ships; those who appreciate exacting service in casual elegance.

Not recommended for Those for whom subtle luxury and attention to detail are unimportant, and anyone uncomfortable among non-Americans. Late-night revelers or children.

CRUISE AREAS AND SEASONS Africa, India, Seychelles, Madagascar, Mediterranean, Baltic, Canada, New England, Far East, China, Northern Europe, South Pacific, Amazon, South America, Alaska, Australia, New Zealand, Caribbean, seasonally.

THE LINE Silversea Cruises was created in the early 1990s by the Lefebvre family of Rome with the Vlasov Group of Monaco, commercial and passenger shipping families that previously owned Sitmar Cruises. The name was chosen to suggest quality, luxury, and the romance of the sea.

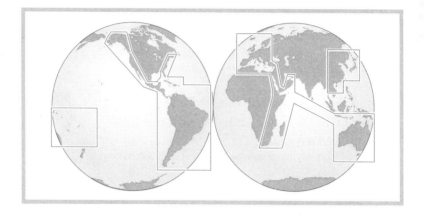

When the Italian-built fleet of identical twins was launched in 1994 and 1995, Silversea took the luxury market by storm with reasonable pricing, uncompromising service, outstanding accommodations, and a space ratio of 55.74, among the highest of any cruise ship. The ultra-deluxe, six-deck ships were substantially larger than most of their direct competitors, offering big-ship facilities and all-suite accommodations in a comfortable small-ship atmosphere. Their biggest advantage was their high number of cabins with verandas. Prices cover beverage service throughout the ship (wine, liquors, and nonalcoholic drinks), stocked in-suite beverage cabinet, in-suite hors d'oeuvres and full meals, a special shoreside event on some sailings, baggage handling, and gratuities. The ratio of crew to passengers is 1 to 1.34.

Encouraged by its initial success, the line added another set of larger twins: *Silver Shadow* in 2000 and *Silver Whisper* in 2001. They are about a third bigger and carry about a third more passengers than the line's first twins. The design is similar, but with enhancements based on passengers' comments: larger bathrooms and closets, more top-grade suites, 80% of cabins with verandas, a poolside dining venue, computer center, cigar lounge, and larger spa and fitness center. The ships were built at the T. Marrotti Shipyard in Italy, where the first two ships were built. Also in 2001, the line debuted its first cruise around the world.

THE FLEET	BUILT/RENOVATED	TONNAGE	PASSENGERS
Silver Cloud	1994/2001	16,800	296
Silver Shadow	2000	28,258	382
Silver Whisper	2001	28,258	382
Silver Wind	1995/2003	16,800	296

STYLE Sparkling clean, impeccably maintained, and luxurious in an under-stated way consistent with fine yachts, the ships offer elegance undisturbed by pretense or formality. From boarding to disembarking, passengers are attended by a crew that makes a genuine effort to know each individual and anticipate their every need. This attention is direct and friendly, but never obsequious.

Suites are exceptionally comfortable and exceed their representa-tion in the line's brochure. Public areas are inviting and elegant. Structured activities are available, but they tend toward the relaxing and cerebral. Announcements, games, and contests are the exception rather than the rule.

At sea and in port, days are casual. Evenings are low-key but dressier. Most cruises include a "Silversea Experience" signature event—usually an excursion with dining and drinks in a beautiful setting, perhaps a pri-vate island, private club, or deserted coast.

Silversea attracts gregarious and adventuresome passengers. Although the atmosphere is social and conducive to meeting new friends, dozens of delightful nooks offer solitary time.

Through several exclusive arrangements, Silversea is introducing a series of new features and amenities. With the Italian Factory, special-ists in the new Italian art scene and representing such new art masters as Petrus, Velasco, Pignatelli, Frangi, Neri, and Rapetti, Silversea ships will display some of these sought-after Italian artworks, providing a new level of decor for the ships and an enhanced ambiance for passen-gers. Select pieces will be available for purchase.

With Viking Range, manufacturer of ultra-premium kitchen appli-ances, Silversea will introduce the first Viking Cooking School at sea. Silversea passengers can participate in cooking classes led by Relais & Châteaux–Relais Gourmands chefs hosting Silversea's popular culinary cruises. The new Viking culinary theaters feature a custom-designed cooking station, fully equipped with Viking professional-caliber cook-ware, cutlery, and countertop appliances.

Another addition is the new Loro Piana boutiques fleetwide. Loro Piana, a six-generation Italian luxury brand, creates elegant, top-quality pieces for men and women, including accessories, gifts, and made-to-measure products—all crafted in Italy.

Through Silversea's exclusive partnership with the National Trust for Italy (Fondo per l'Ambiente Italiano) passengers will enjoy an enhanced program of shore excursions, cultural events, and access to some of Italy's most historical sites. FAI protects and maintains some of Italy's most beautiful architectural and cultural treasures, including ancient castles, villas, a monastery, gardens, and stretches of pristine countryside and coastline.

DISTINCTIVE FEATURES All-suite accommodations; comprehensive air/sea travel with personalized service at intermediate travel stops; all-inclusive prices. Silversea Experience on most sailings. Moderate single supplements. Golf program. Internet access. Personalized Voyage program.

	HIGHEST	LOWEST	AVERAGE
PER DIEM	$1,439	$488	$865

Per diems are calculated from cruise line's nondiscounted *cruise-only* published fares on standard accommodations and vary by season, cabins, and cruise areas.

RATES Tips, onboard beverages, including select wine and spirits in cruise-only rate; an optional air/hotel program includes round-trip airfare (with upgrades to business class available), one-night precruise deluxe hotel, transfers, and baggage handling.

Special fares and discounts Early booking incentive savings range from 5–20%; they are capacity controlled and subject to availability. An additional advanced payment savings of 5% may be combined with the early booking savings when payment is made in full by a specified date. Silversea continues its "Silver Savings" program into 2006, enabling passengers to save up to 50% off cruise-only fares on certain cruises. Generally, discounts are valid for some Caribbean, South America, South Pacific, Australia/New Zealand, Mediterranean, and Africa cruises and have set, pre-assigned savings on particular voyages. The Silver Savings offers are subject to availability; they are valid only for new cruise bookings and do not apply to land, hotel, and air programs.

- **THIRD PASSENGER:** Approximately 50% of the Vista or Veranda Suite per-person published rate.
- **SINGLE SUPPLEMENT:** 110%, 125%, 150%, 175% of per-person double-occupancy basic suite, depending on cruise.

Packages
- **AIR/SEA:** All cruises packaged with economy-class air; upgrades available for an additional charge, but still at special rates.
- **PRE/POST:** Extensive pre- and postcruise tours. Many air/sea packages include one or more hotel nights in the departure or termination city; extensions are available.

PAST PASSENGERS Past passengers automatically become members of the Venetian Society, named to reflect the line's Italian ownership. On their second voyage, members receive a silver pin bearing the society's winged-lion emblem, a symbol of Venice. After they have sailed for 100-, 200-, and 500-plus days, they receive sapphire, emerald, and diamond pins, respectively. Members also receive a newsletter three times yearly containing information on special discounts. Other benefits include shipboard events hosted by the captain. Members get fare reductions of 5%, 10%, and 15%, combinable with early-booking incentives, advance-payment bonus, and consecutive-cruise savings.

Members may bring friends in an additional suite at some savings. They also receive $250 or $500 shipboard credits and a credit to their Society account for the days their friends cruise. Members may accrue days toward a free cruise.

THE LAST WORD Silversea got off to a great start with its first two ships, setting exceptionally high standards for itself and the industry. The second two larger ships did not draw the same level of praise initially, and the line fell into a slump. Now, after a determined effort to improve the product across the board, Silversea has made a comeback. The new food, entertainment, and enrichment programs are innovative, and the itineraries are creative, calling on some ports seldom visited by cruise ships. Officers and crew are actively involved in providing highly personalized service. If there are shortcomings, they are in the lack of innovative daily programs or evening entertainment that makes it worth staying up past 10:30 p.m.

Highlighting the 2006 schedule, Silversea will visit 23 ports for the first time, including Eden and Kangaroo Island, Australia; Khasab, Oman; Kura Kura, Indonesia; Comodoro Rivadavia, Argentina; Ilheus, Brazil; Bocas del Toro, Panama; Grand Turk Island, Turks and Caicos; St. Eustatius; San Juan del Sur, Nicaragua; Libya; Brest, France; and Isafjordur, Iceland, among others.

Silversea has expanded its guest lecturer program with a new series called "The Spirit of Exploration." On select voyages, an internationally acclaimed adventurer will serve as the ship's Resident Explorer, hosting a series of presentations and accompany passengers on selected shore excursions.

Silversea Cruises remains a good value for those who can afford it, and increased competition keeps a constant pressure on price. The cruise line's Personalized Voyages program provides prospective passengers with the utmost flexibility and convenience to customize a cruise to suit their needs. For a minimum of five consecutive nights, a passenger can cruise for as little or as long as they want.

Here's how it works: Passengers choose the length of their voyage (five nights minimum) and the embarkation and disembarkation ports from Silversea's list of over 200 approved ports of call or on its Web site (**www.silversea.com**). To determine your cost, you select a suite category, then add up the daily rate for the days you plan to be onboard. You must arrange your own air transportation, but Silversea will assist you with hotel and/or transfers in select ports, as needed, for a fee.

Silversea Cruises Standard Features

Officers Italian.

Staff Dining/European; Cabin/European; Cruise/British and American.

SC Standard Features (continued)

Dining facilities All meals served at one seating in restaurant; indoor/outdoor cafe for casual breakfast and lunch. Alternative dining specialty dinners on most evenings. In-suite dining.

Special diets Available on request.

Room service 24 hours, cabin menu and full-service dining room menu.

Dress code By day, casual but conservative and comfortable. Dinner is more dressy. Informal (jacket, tie optional for men) or formal (two black-tie or dark suit nights on one-week cruise; four on two-week cruise).

Cabin amenities Stocked bar, mini-fridge; interactive television with CNN, VCR, direct-dial telephone; marble bathroom with sink, tub, and shower, hair dryer, bathrobes, walk-in closet, safe.

Electrical outlets 110/220 AC.

Wheelchair access Limited.

Recreation and entertainment Three lounges with entertainment/dance music nightly; cabaret, classical music concerts, folkloric performances in ports of call; nightly dancing; casino; cruise-related lectures. Internet access.

Sports and other activities Outdoor pool, deck sports; bridge instructor and lessons; enrichment programs.

Beauty and fitness Two saunas, two outdoor whirlpools, small gym, exercise classes, beauty salon, spa with massage, beauty treatments.

Other facilities Self-service laundry, laundry/dry cleaning; library with books and video; hospital; cigar lounge, computer center, nondenominational religious services.

Children's facilities None; children under age 18 must be accompanied by parent or adult with written permission.

Theme cruises Cuisine, wine, golf, music, and others.

Smoking Dining and public rooms nonsmoking except designated areas in lounges and bars.

Silversea suggested tipping No-tipping policy.

Credit cards For cruise payment and on-board charges: American Express, Diners Club, MasterCard, Visa.

Silver Cloud/Silver Wind	**QUALITY 8**	**VALUE C**
REGISTRY Bahamas	**LENGTH 514 feet**	**BEAM 70 feet**
CABINS 148	**DRAFT 18 feet**	**SPEED 20.5 knots**
MAXIMUM PASSENGERS 296	**PASSENGER DECKS 6**	**ELEVATORS 4**
	CREW 210	**SPACE RATIO 56.8**

THE SHIPS Styled to soothe, the first Silversea twins are the antithesis of the huge floating hotels that dominate cruising. Elegance is anchored in simplicity, clean lines, earth-tone fabrics, and polished wood and brass.

The entry lobby surprises with its modest proportions. No six-story atrium here. The feeling is of boarding a yacht. The ships' layout is simple. On topmost Deck 9 are a fitness center and jogging/walking track that circles the ship. It overlooks the pool and pool bar on Deck 8, which also contains the bridge, twin whirlpools, **Panorama Lounge** with indoor and outdoor seating, and the **Champagne Room,** an elegant wine and cigar lounge.

On Decks 4–7, all cabins are forward, all public areas aft. Elevators and a circular stairwell are aft of amidships. Deck 7 offers the library (on *Silver Cloud*), spa, beauty salon, and **Terrace Café** for informal dining and breakfast and lunch buffets. Deck 6 has the main lobby, travel desk, reception desk, card and conference room, and showroom, which is large enough for small production shows but small enough to be intimate. Deck 5 has a sundries shop, casino, and the **Bar,** where the showroom audience gathers. The **Library** (on *Silver Wind*) and **Restaurant** are on Deck 4. Public areas are extensive for ships of this size. Dozens of quiet places throughout the ship invite reading or watching the water. *Silver Cloud* was completely refurbished in 2001 and additional renovations were made before returning her to service in April 2004. *Silver Wind* had a similar treatment in 2003.

ITINERARIES *See* Itinerary Index.

CABINS The spacious, all-outside suites are among the ships' signature features. Suites provide twin beds convertible to queen, walk-in closet, sitting area with loveseat, coffee table and side chairs, writing desk, dressing table with hair dryer, marble bathroom with full-size tub and shower, stocked refrigerator and cocktail bar, entertainment center with satellite interactive television and VCR, and direct-dial telephone. A curtain separates the sleeping and living areas.

Seventy-five percent of the suites have private teak verandas; the remainder provide picture windows. All suites are decorated in light earth tones or pastel blues with nautical trim of polished wood and brass. Other ultra-deluxe extras are fine, pure cotton bed linens and robes, down pillows, personalized stationery, fresh fruit, large umbrellas in the closets, complimentary shoeshine, and 24-hour room service.

Added in 2005 are luxury bath amenities by Acqua di Parma, the century-old Italian fragrance house, which has produced in-suite toiletries characterized by natural ingredients, delicate production processes, and meticulous attention to detail; most products are still packaged and bottled by hand.

Specifications 102 veranda suites (295 square feet); 34 vista suites (240 square feet, no veranda), 3 silver suites (541 square feet), 2 royal suites (1,031 square feet in the 2-bedroom configuration), 2 grand suites (1,314 square feet with 2 bedrooms), and 1 owner's suite (827 square feet). No singles. 2 wheelchair-accessible.

DINING The main dining room, called the **Restaurant,** is reminiscent of an exclusive club. Tables are set with Eschenbach china, Christofle silver, linen, and Schott crystal. Draped picture windows flank the elegant room, and a domed center section adds to its spaciousness. A small marble dance floor allows for occasional dinner dances. Though formal, the Restaurant is also comfortable, relaxed, and unpretentious.

Passengers aren't assigned seating times or tables; they may eat any time during published hours. Lunch and breakfast buffets in the **Terrace Café** provide an informal option. No late-night buffet is offered. Room service is available 24 hours and is delivered with the same attention to detail characteristic of the dining room. Service is outstanding.

Carrying fewer passengers enables Silversea ships to cook dishes to order, as in a restaurant. (However, we have received complaints from some passengers that the kitchen isn't as accommodating as the line claims, or as it should be for this price, or as some competitors are.)

Silversea also provides for picky eaters, health-conscious diners, and the meat-and-potatoes set. Only the finest ingredients are used, regardless of how simple or complex the dish. Meat eaters in search of a cruise ship that can prepare a good steak, chop, or prime rib will find nirvana here. Menus offer three appetizers, a pasta, two soups, two salads, sherbet, three main courses, and usually a grilled selection. In addition are a "Light and Healthy" and a vegetarian entree. The dessert menu is separate. Wines are included in the cruise price.

The food is excellent in quality and presentation, but for those unaccustomed to rich sauces and creams, it could be overwhelming—although you can order meals without creams or sauces. Freshness of ingredients is not a problem. One day, returning to ship aboard the tender, we were assaulted by an unexpected smell. Peering around the bulkhead, we discovered a grinning chef with a huge string of fish just purchased from local fishermen—a luxury that could never be provided on a large ship.

The casual Terrace Café high on the stern offers a commanding view of the sea. A wall of windows faces the sheltered outside dining area. Tables are always set with china, crystal, and silver. Buffet waiters take orders for drinks and hot entrees. Theme dinners take diners through eight delectable regions of Italy plus cuisine of the cruise's area. Several times each cruise, the Terrace Café offers a special multicourse meal on a reservation basis. These meals provide a change of scenery and let the chefs re-create traditional European fine dining.

The recently refurbished *Silver Cloud* and *Silver Wind* boast a new **Champagne Room,** bringing them more in line with Silversea's newest ships, *Silver Shadow* and *Silver Whisper*. The Champagne Room, located on Deck Eight and adjacent to the Panorama Lounge, is a new wine and cigar room offering guests a cozy venue where they can relax and settle back into sumptuous leather chairs to enjoy a select vintage or fine cigar.

Recently, too, the dining options were expanded by a new alternative gourmet dining venue, called **Saletta,** which means "a small room" in Italian, offering signature creations of chef Joachim Koerper. A native of Germany, Koerper is considered one of Europe's finest chefs. His Michelin two-star restaurant, Girasol, in Moraira, Spain, is a member of Relais & Châteaux–Relais Gourmands.

SERVICE Passengers rate service in a dead heat with accommodations as these twins' best feature. Without exception, the staff is professional and attentive, but never intrusive; friendly without being familiar; and thoroughly gracious in the European manner.

Working harmoniously, officers and crew form a highly effective and responsive team. A concierge is available for special services. These ships' size lends itself to more personalized service than larger ships can offer. There's no tipping. Period.

FACILITIES AND ACTIVITIES The next-day's programs, delivered nightly to your suite, are more mainstream than you might expect on an ultraluxury cruise, but they prove that even the pampered and sophisticated play bingo! A typical day might include an early power walk with the fitness instructor, a visit to the bridge, a lesson about computers or multimedia, aerobics, wine tasting by the sommelier, a bridge lecture; bingo, backgammon, shuffleboard competition; water volleyball; golf-putting competition; afternoon tea; team trivia; and line-dancing lessons.

In conjunction with Relais & Châteaux–Relais Gourmands, Silversea has a series of culinary cruises highlighted by cooking demonstrations, gala dinners, signature dishes, and regional specialties created by master chefs from around the world.

Experts lecture on the cruise area and a folkloric show might be staged by a local group. A morning port talk will include a sales pitch for tours. Doing nothing is an option. In fair weather, you'll probably be on deck, relaxing in a lounge chair or soaking in the Jacuzzi. There are ample places in shade or sheltered from wind. In foul weather, the library stocks books, magazines, periodicals, and videos; it's open around the clock, and sports computer terminals with Internet access. Also available are daily printed news and market-wrap reports.

In the evening, there's music for dancing before and after dinner and evening entertainment—a variety show, comedy, and magic. The ship's small orchestra plays easy listening and dance music in the **Bar,** and a pianist or vocalist duo perform in the **Panorama Lounge.** The casino offers roulette, blackjack, slot machines, and gaming lessons. Entertainment in the **Main Lounge** spotlights individual entertainers and production shows by a six-member group. All passengers can be accommodated in the steeply tiered, two-level room. Murals of sinuous women add an Art Deco touch. Most sight lines are good. Late-night diversions consist of audience-participation games, dancing, and piano music in the Panorama Lounge.

SPORTS, FITNESS, AND BEAUTY The pool deck has a large swimming pool, plentiful sunbathing space, two whirlpools, and a pool bar. Blue-and-white striped chair cushions create a nautical atmosphere. The uppermost deck has an Astroturf-carpeted promenade for walking or jogging. The fitness center, recently expanded and moved to the top deck, now offers a panoramic ocean view in addition to ample exercise equipment and free weights. One or more daily stretch and exercise classes for various workout levels is offered; individual training is available. The spa offers sauna, steam rooms, and beauty treatments and a comprehensive program of fitness, beauty, and spa treatments crafted for Silversea by Mandara Spa, an international spa specialist. It uses naturally blended treatments and Balinese techniques, incorporating its signature blend of exotic, traditional, and cutting-edge health and beauty programs, offering such unusual indulgences as a hot lava rock massage and a Japanese honey steam wrap. Spa treatments can now be booked on Silversea's Web site.

CHILDREN'S FACILITIES Children are rare on Silversea cruises, and no children's facilities or programs are offered. The occasional child receives lots of attention and generally enjoys the cruise. The nice pool and all-included drinks and snacks help.

SHORE EXCURSIONS Shore excursions are administered efficiently onboard, and the line has a good batting average with them. Silversea passengers' expectations that excursion operators will provide the same level of service they receive aboard ship may be unrealistic in some regions of the world, no matter how hard the cruise lines tries. This problem is, of course, not unique to Silversea; only that the contrast from the ship to the land operation is sometimes sharper.

Excursion sales are low-key, and some cruise directors do an excellent job of matching passengers with the tours most suited to their tastes. Even off-the-shelf motorcoach tours tend to be pricey. Shore excursions can now be booked online. Many cruises include one "Silversea Experience," a special shore excursion showcasing an area's culture. This may be a private tour or dinner in an extraordinary location. For example, the line has hosted wine tastings at a private chateaux and dinner at a palace in St. Petersburg.

Silver Shadow	QUALITY 8	VALUE C
Silver Whisper	QUALITY 8	VALUE C
REGISTRY Bahamas	LENGTH 610 feet	BEAM 82 feet
CABINS 194	DRAFT 19.6 feet	SPEED 21 knots

| MAXIMUM PASSENGERS 382 | PASSENGER DECKS 7 | ELEVATORS 5 |
| CREW 295 | | SPACE RATIO 73.9 |

THE SHIPS *Silver Shadow,* launched in 2000, was followed by her twin, *Silver Whisper,* in 2001. The noted Norwegian architectural team of Petter Yran and Bjorn Storbraaten, designers of *Silver Cloud* and *Silver Wind,* created the ships, which are slightly larger and accommodate 100 more passengers than the line's first ships. Otherwise, they are similar, more or less, to their sister ships in layout and contemporary decor. Throughout the ships, mellow wood furnishings and fine fabrics combine with marble floors and crystal chandeliers to create an elegant, stylish setting. Their passenger space ratio of 73.9 may be the highest of any cruise ship.

Silversea's hallmarks—veranda suites, single-seating dining, in suite dining, Christofle silverware, fine linens, down pillows—are found aboard these ships. Among the new features were a casual poolside dining venue, a computer center, conference center, and cigar lounge, and a champagne bar. The ships also have an observation lounge, show lounge, boutique, a larger spa, swimming pool, and whirlpools.

ITINERARIES *See* Itinerary Index.

CABINS More than 80% of the suites have teak verandas. A standard Veranda Suite measures a spacious 345 square feet, including veranda. The smallest cabins measures 287 square feet. All cabins have a walk-in closet and large Italian marble bathroom with telephone, double-basin vanity, full bath and shower, and separate toilet, and are equipped with small refrigerators and cocktail bar; entertainment center with interactive television and VCR, and fresh fruit and flowers.

The largest suites range from 701 to 1,435 square feet and include the Owner's, Grand, and Royal suites in six variations. They have enlarged balconies, separate bedrooms and living rooms, large-screen televisions, and private bars. Owner's suites also have a guest powder room and CD stereo system. Larger suites are located amidships. Two Medallion suites, 501 square feet each, are extremely comfortable, with enough storage space for a family of five.

Room service, available 24 hours a day, offers a full room service menu. Passengers can order from the Restaurant's menu and have their meal served course-by-course in their staterooms. Self-service laundry facilities are available.

Specifications 194 outside suites. 2 Owner's, 4 Grand, 13 Silver, 2 Medallion, 134 Veranda, 35 Vista (no veranda); 2 wheelchair-accessible with verandas.

DINING The **Restaurant,** the main dining room, has an elegant ambience with tables set with fine linens and Christofle silverware. It offers open seating and a variety of table configurations for two to six people. The popular bistro-style **Terrace Café,** with floor-to-ceiling windows opening onto panoramic views off the ship's aft deck, serves buffet breakfast and lunch, and makes a charming setting in the evening, when it is transformed into a casual alternative restaurant serving Asian, French, and Italian fare. The **Grill** is a casual poolside dining venue.

Recently, another dining alternative was added. The new gourmet restaurant, **Le Champagne,** offers signature creations by chef Joachim Koerper, one of Europe's leading chefs. A native of Germany, his Girasol in Moraira, Spain is two-star Michelin restaurant and a member of Relais & Châteaux—Relais Gourmands.

FACILITIES AND ACTIVITIES The **Humidor,** an elegant wine and cigar bar, adjoins Le Champagne. Designed in the style of a traditional English smoking club with rich wood floors and deep galley chairs, it has a walk-in humidor stocked with Davidoff products, a Swiss-based purveyor of fine cigars and luxury merchandise, as well as a selection of Dominican, Honduran, and Cuban cigars. The lounge seats 25 and offers complimentary cognacs and cordials, along with cigars.

Of the ship's four bars, the **Casino Bar,** a small nook adjoining the casino, seems to be the most popular place. Simply furnished with a semicircular cherry wood bar with ebony leather stools, it has two small leather sofas and modern-style halogen lamps and fixtures.

The ships have a shopping arcade, a library with books in varied languages, videos, and seven computer terminals with Internet access. Silversea has an unusual way of charging for their use: The $0.75 per minute is only charged for as long as it takes a Web page to download and come into view. The charges then stop until another Web page is requested. Silversea is preparing to install keyboards into suites to provide in-room Internet access as well.

SERVICE These ships do not have as high a crew-to-passenger ratio as the smaller twins, and thus, conceivably cannot deliver the same level of service. However, a new program designed to enhance service and improve consistency of Silversea's onboard product has aimed at precisely this problem.

SPORTS, FITNESS, AND BEAUTY The ships have large health clubs and spas which occupy most of Deck 10 and are operated by Mandara Spa, specializing in Asian-type treatments. Decorated in a soothing combination of aqua and blue tiles and blonde carpets, the facility has a beauty salon and an aerobic and fitness center with weights, treadmills, stationary bikes and other equipment. There are separate steam rooms, saunas, and changing facilities for men and women. The ships also have a heated outdoor pool and two whirlpools.

POSTSCRIPT *Silver Shadow* and *Silver Whisper* are almost 70% larger than their predecessors, but not everyone agrees that bigger is necessarily better. Some passengers like the spaciousness and new facilities that the larger size provides; others prefer the more intimate experience that the smaller ships offer. Still, all Silversea ships carry an impressive number of repeat passengers, and during the last two to three days of a cruise, many passengers are seen in front of the concierge desk waiting to book their next voyage.

Star Clippers, Inc.

4101 Salzedo Avenue, Coral Gables, FL 33146
☎ 800-442-0551 or 305-442-0550; fax 305-442-1611
www.starclippers.com

TYPE OF SHIPS Replicas of 19th-century clipper sailing ships.

TYPE OF CRUISES Casual, active, sports-oriented, sailing under canvas to out-of-the-way places.

CRUISE LINE'S STRENGTHS
- traditional sailing with some cruise-ship comforts
- camaraderie
- ship size/maneuverability
- itineraries

CRUISE LINE'S SHORTCOMINGS
- meager port information
- potential language/cultural collisions among passengers
- small cabins

FELLOW PASSENGERS International mix. About half are American, Canadian, and Latin American; the other half are European, particularly Germans, including non-English speakers. The average age is 45, but some cruises have 20- and 30-year-olds. The majority are couples, usually including about a dozen newlyweds.

As many as 50% may be repeaters, attracted by sailing on a square rigger. Many appreciate the beauty and authenticity of the clipper ships and have no interest in the nightclubs, casinos, and glitter aboard mainstream cruise ships, which they probably have shunned.

Recommended for Independent, active travelers who seek light adventure and off-the-beaten-track itineraries, small-ship devotees, stressed-out urbanites, honeymooners and romantics captivated by the notion of sailing on a tall ship. Also, avid sailors, water sports enthusiasts, experienced cruisers weary of crowded large ships, and conservationists who appreciate environmentally friendly travel aboard ships that use their engines only when necessary. It's a great experience for children ages seven and older who mix well with adults.

Not recommended for Those seeking gourmet cuisine, pampering, around-the-clock activity, and resort facilities of a superliner. Physically impaired travelers.

CRUISE AREAS AND SEASONS Caribbean, South Asia, winter; Mediterranean, summer; transatlantic, trans–Indian Ocean, April and October.

THE LINE Launched in 1991, Star Clippers is the dream come true of Swedish shipping entrepreneur Mikael Krafft, whose passion for sailing

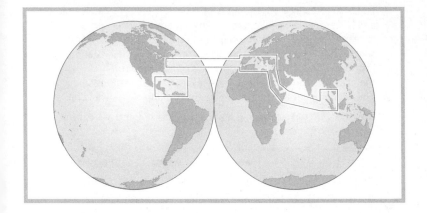

and building yachts and love of the clipper ship (one of America's greatest inventions, he says) led him to create an unusual cruise line with replicas of the sleek, mid–19th-century trading ships. Called greyhounds of the sea, they were the fastest ships afloat until the arrival of the steam age in the late 1860s.

About 100 feet longer than the original clippers and equipped with the latest marine technology, these clippers combine the romance of yesteryear's sailing with some modern amenities. They offer the excitement of manning an authentic square rigger and cruising out-of-the-way waters of the Caribbean, Mediterranean, or South Asia.

The success of Star Clipper's twins lead the line to build a third ship, which is reported to be the world's largest sailing vessel. She entered service in July 2000.

THE FLEET	BUILT/RENOVATED	TONNAGE	PASSENGERS
Royal Clipper	2000	5,000	227
Star Clipper	1991	2,298	170
Star Flyer	1992	2,298	170

STYLE Cruises have the freewheeling spirit of a private yacht and are intended to fit between budget-priced Windjammer Barefoot Cruises and pricey Windstar Cruises. They're designed for active, healthy folks who want their travel to be interesting, educational, and fun. Daytime dress is very casual (shorts and deck shoes); evenings are only a bit dressier. Cabins are of average size and public rooms few, but the teak decks are roomy.

Cruises offer island-hopping in a laid-back atmosphere with varied options at each port of call. The clippers can anchor in bays where large cruise ships cannot go. Launches take passengers to isolated beaches and places for scuba diving, snorkeling, and other water sports.

After a week's cruise, you will know on a first-name basis many passengers and most of the crew, who are both deck hands and sports instructors. You can help hoist the sails or laze about on deck watching the canvas and the sea. Itineraries ensure daylight cruising under sail. The environment is great for families with children ages 7 and up.

DISTINCTIVE FEATURES The ship and helping sail it. Captain's daily briefings. PADI certification.

	HIGHEST	LOWEST	AVERAGE
PER DIEM	$575	$97	$272

Per diems are calculated from cruise line's nondiscounted *cruise-only* published fares on standard accommodations and vary by season, cabins, and cruise areas.

RATES Port charges are additional.

Special fares and discounts 10% discount on published rates for booking 120 days in advance on selected cruises.

- **SINGLE FARE:** Guaranteed rate, depending on season, with cabin assigned two weeks before departure.
- **SINGLE SUPPLEMENT:** 150% for categories 2–6 (selected seasons) of published fare. 200% for highest-category cabins, deluxe suites, and owners' suites.

Packages

- **AIR/SEA:** Yes.
- **PRE/POST:** Yes.
- **OTHERS:** Honeymoon.

PAST PASSENGERS Membership cards for the Past Passengers Club are sent after your first voyage. Members receive special discounts and a bottle of champagne in their cabins on boarding and are placed on the ship's VIP list.

THE LAST WORD Star Clippers provides an unusual experience on unique ships that are modern and comfortable, yet steeped in tradition. More affordable than *Sea Cloud* and more upscale than Windjammers, Star Clippers' ships are more authentic than those of Windstar. Yet, they definitely aren't for everyone.

The ships cannot readily accommodate disabled passengers and aren't for people who want mainstream cruising's comforts and options. English is the ships' language, but announcements are likely in other languages, depending on passenger makeup. Language can become a problem when English speakers are outnumbered by non-Anglophones, and some may feel left out of activities. Onboard charges are in Euros.

Star Clippers Standard Features

Officers European.

Staff Dining, Cabin/International; Cruise/Swedish, Australian, and Hungarian.

Dining facilities One dining room for three meals with open, unassigned seating. Light breakfast, occasional buffet lunch, hors d'oeuvres on deck at 5 p.m.

Special diets Inquire in advance. Vegetarian, low-calorie standard on menus.

Room service None.

Dress code Relaxed and casual. Walking shorts, bathing attire with cover-up, skirts, slacks for daytime; slacks with polo or casual shirts, no jackets required for men in evening.

Cabin amenities Radio, hair dryer, safe, cellular-satellite phone; movies, ports of call videos, and music; bathrooms with showers; upper category with whirlpool bath and minifridge.

Electrical outlets *Star Clipper/Flyer,* 110 AC; *Royal Clipper,* 220 AC, American adapter needed.

Wheelchair access None.

Recreation and entertainment Piano bar with entertainer, outdoor deck bar for dancing and local entertainment, library/writing room, backgammon, and bridge.

Sports and other activities Two outdoor pools; water sports and equipment; sailing dinghies, windsurfers, water-skiing, underwater viewing craft, water-jet launches, and inflatables carried onboard. Learn-to-sail and dive programs.

Beauty and fitness No beauty/barber service on *Star Clipper/Flyer;* spa, hair salon, gym on *Royal Clipper.* Exercise sessions.

Other facilities Dining room doubles as conference room with audiovisual equipment. Nurse on seven-day cruises; doctor and nurse on transatlantic. Ship's officers trained in emergency medicine.

Children's facilities None; younger than age 18 must be accompanied by adult.

Theme cruises None.

Smoking No smoking in cabins. At first briefing, captain emphasizes that smoking is allowed on deck or in rear of dining room.

Star Clippers suggested tipping $8 per person per day; 15% added to bar bills.

Credit cards For cruise payment and onboard charges: American Express, MasterCard, and Visa.

Star Clipper/Star Flyer	QUALITY 7	VALUE A
REGISTRY Luxembourg	LENGTH 360 feet	BEAM 50 feet
CABINS 85	DRAFT 18.5 feet	SPEED 17 knots
MAXIMUM PASSENGERS 170	PASSENGER DECKS 4	ELEVATORS None
	CREW 72	SPACE RATIO 15

THE SHIPS *Star Clipper* and *Star Flyer* are identical, with four masts and square-rigged sails on the forward mast—a barquentine configuration—with a total of 16 sails (36,000 square feet of Dacron). They are manned, not computerized, and are capable of attaining speeds up to 19 knots. A diesel engine is in reserve for calms and maneuvering in harbors.

At 226 feet, they are among the tallest ships and the first true sailing vessels to be classified by Lloyd's Register of Shipping since 1911. Built in Belgium, they comply with the latest safety regulations for passenger vessels on worldwide service.

The ships have four passenger decks; all but eight cabins are on the lower two. Public spaces, which were recently refurbished, are on the top two. There, amid sails and rigging, every Walter Mitty begins to salivate with anticipation. They can help hoist the sails or watch in wonder. The ships are generally under sail from late evening to the following midmorning. Under normal conditions, they use the engine only to maneuver in port. For true salts and romantics, balmy tropical air filling the white sails against a star-filled sky is the essence of bliss. Many stay up half the night savoring it.

ITINERARIES *See* Itinerary Index.

CABINS Small but comfortable, cabins are carpeted, air conditioned, and tastefully furnished with a counter/desk and built-in seat, large mirror, wood paneling, brass lamps, and prints of sailing scenes. Two portholes admit light. Under-bed storage holds luggage or scuba gear, and closet and drawer space is adequate for informal cruising.

Most cabins are outside and have twin beds convertible to a double. They have multichannel radio, phone, hair dryer, safe, ceiling-mounted television/video monitor (videotapes are available from the library in English and German), and 24-hour news prepared in British English, American English, Canadian English, and German. Each version includes news of interest to that group.

Bathrooms are very small. They have marble-trimmed fixtures and showers. Eight top-category cabins have a whirlpool bathtub, hair dryer, and minifridge stocked at cruise's start (occupants pay for restocks). These cabins open onto the deck; some people may feel that decreases their privacy. Cabin service is limited to cleaning. Aft cabins on lower decks are the least desirable due to engine noise.

Specifications 6 inside cabins, 78 outside; 1 suite. Standard dimensions, 120 square feet. 66 cabins with 2 lower beds (convertible to queen); 18 cabins with fixed double beds; 12 cabins accommodate third passenger; 6 inside cabins have uppers and lowers; no singles.

DINING The **Clipper Dining Room,** resplendent with shining brass and etched glass, is rather formal for such an informal ship. Seating is at tables for six among or around a forest of columns, and banquettes line the walls by portholes. All passengers and officers are accommodated at one open seating. When the ship is full, the room is crowded.

The buffet breakfast has made-to-order omelets; lunch has a different pasta daily and a self-service salad bar. A light, early-morning breakfast and occasional lunch buffet are also served on deck.

Dinner selections include beef, chicken, and fish; vegetables; cheeses; and desserts. The food is plentiful but appeals mostly to those with minimal interest in epicurean delights. During a week, food can range from adequate to good, but not gourmet. The menu emphasizes fresh ingredients, fruit, salads, vegetables, and seafood. Wines are available at reasonable prices.

SERVICE Officers and deck crew are friendly, energetic, and easygoing. They mix freely and easily with passengers, helping create the ship's relaxed atmosphere. The dining and hotel staff is low-key and congenial. An easy camaraderie between officers, staff, and passengers is part of the ships' appeal.

FACILITIES AND ACTIVITIES Passengers might be found playing backgammon or bridge. The teak-paneled library/writing room resembles an English club, with large brass-framed windows, paintings of nautical scenes, and a nonworking fireplace (snuffed by the U.S. Coast Guard). Furnished with card tables and comfortable chairs, it's a reception desk at boarding and a small meeting room. A good selection of popular fiction, travel, and coffee-table books is stocked. A tiny shop sells film and souvenirs. The dining room converts to a meeting room with screen projectors and video monitors for port lectures. The captain and cruise director hold "story time," an informal briefing, on deck in late afternoon or the morning before arriving in port. Passengers congregate around the open bridge, where they can hear the captain and his mates at work and watch the sails being raised and lowered. Many lend a hand with the rigging, but few hang in for the full cruise.

A small, U-shaped piano lounge wraps the landing of the stairway between the main deck and dining room. It has brass-framed panoramic windows and small tables with cushioned banquettes that seat about two dozen people. The skylight overhead is actually the transparent bottom of a pool on the sun deck. A pianist or vocalist entertains before and after dinner. Swinging doors connect to the outdoor **Tropical Bar.** Depending on the hour, it's a social center, meeting area, stage (where the captain speaks daily), spot for light breakfast or buffet lunch, or dance floor (taped music or electronic keyboard). There's no casino.

SPORTS, FITNESS, AND BEAUTY There are two tiny outdoor pools, one filled with fresh water and one with sea water. Beginning scuba lessons are offered at the forward pool.

Exercisers can walk from the stern to the bow around the open parts of the main and sun decks. At 8 a.m. daily, one of the water sports teams leads a half-hour aerobics session.

In the Caribbean and South Asia, water sports are a more important element of the cruise than in the Mediterranean. The ships carry sailing dinghies, windsurfers, underwater viewing craft, boats for water-skiing and skis, snorkel gear (issued for cruise duration), scuba equipment for certified divers, volleyballs, and oversized, solid-surface kadima paddles for beach sports. The ships might anchor in a remote cove or off a deserted beach and shuttle passengers to and from shore for snorkeling, sailing, windsurfing, and swimming.

The sports and recreational staff includes multilingual instructors. Snorkeling is organized almost daily in the Caribbean. Certified divers with C cards can join trips to reefs and underwater wrecks. A charge of $52 for a daytime dive or $60 for a nighttime dive covers air tank refill, personal supervision, and transport by Zodiac.

Two dive programs are available: A PADI refresher course costs 75 euros, for those whose certification has lapsed within the past year; and a full PADI certification course costing 410 euros. For the latter, the line requires that divers spread the course over a two-week cruise.

SHORE EXCURSIONS Guided tours (usually $25–$85) focus on a destination's architectural, historical, and environmental points of interest and are likely to be more interesting than those offered by mainstream ships. Fewer passengers and unusual itineraries help ensure more stimulating, personalized tours for participants.

The ships tie up in port as seldom as possible. Patented stabilizing tanks keep the ship steady at anchor. Tender service is offered every half-hour until sailing time, usually around 6 p.m.

Royal Clipper	QUALITY 9	VALUE A
REGISTRY Luxembourg	LENGTH 439 feet	BEAM 54 feet
CABINS 114	DRAFT 18.5 feet	SPEED 20 knots
MAXIMUM PASSENGERS 227	PASSENGER DECKS 5	ELEVATORS None
	CREW 106	SPACE RATIO NA

THE SHIP *Royal Clipper* made her debut in 2000 as the world's longest, largest sailing vessel ever built. Her gross tonnage of about 5,000 tons is more than twice that of *Star Clipper* or *Star Flyer*. Her appearance contrasts sharply with her running mates, which resemble large, white-hull racing yachts. *Royal Clipper* is a full-rigged ship, with square sails on all five masts; the earlier four masters are barquentine-rigged. *Royal Clipper* carries 56,000 square feet of Dacron sail, compared to 36,000 square feet on each of the small twins.

The vessel's interior, created by noted megayacht interior designer Donald Starkey of London, is more upscale than her sisters and has many new features. One of her three outdoor swimming pools—an oval, center pool—has a glass bottom, which allows light into the three-deck atrium below. A circular staircase links the atrium with lounges, cabins, and public rooms. **Captain Nemo's Lounge,** on the lowest passenger deck, has 16-inch portholes looking out on marine life day and night.

On the Main Deck below the bridge is an observation lounge with wraparound windows; it is used for meetings, informal talks, and Internet connections. The main deck also has the purser's office, a large piano lounge, an indoor/outdoor bar, and library.

The main lounge, located amidships, is as comfortable as they come with banquette, soft couch, and chair seating. It has a sit-up bar and a central well that looks down into the dining room two decks below. Leaving via the aft doors, the covered **Tropical Bar** recalls the earlier *Star Clipper* pair; so too, does the paneled Edwardian library, though aboard *Royal Clipper* both rooms are on a much larger scale.

When there is no wind, the twin Caterpillar 2,500-horsepower diesel engines can drive the ship at up to 14 knots. When maneuvering in and out of port, the captain may put up most of the sails, then use a very quiet generator to turn the ship and drive it forward to leave the harbor.

ITINERARIES *See* Itinerary Index.

CABINS Standard cabins, each with 148 square feet, are 35% larger than those on sister ships; 32 have a third fold-down bed. There are two deck cabins of 125 square feet and six inside cabins of 100 square feet. The cabins are furnished in much the same style and vary mostly by location. They have marble bathrooms with shower, television, satellite telephone, radio channels, private safe, and hair dryers.

The outstanding deluxe suites are located along a narrow central mahogany-paneled companionway with a thick sloping mast penetrating the corridor at the forward end. These luxurious cabins, measuring 215 square feet, are mahogany-paneled with rosewood framing and molding against an off-white ceiling and upper portion walls. Pale gold-framed mirrors enlarge the space, and brass-framed windows bring in light to bathe the far corner sitting alcove. Brass wall lamps and sailing ship prints round out the feel of an upward sloping ship's cabin, not a hotel-style room on a hull. One door opens to a huge marble bathroom with Jacuzzi bath—a nod to upscale cruise ship amenities. Another heavy wooden door leads to a private teak veranda with shrouds passing upward from the ship's side.

The two owner's suites at the stern are even larger at 355 square feet and have a private entrance and butler service. There are also two 226-square-foot deluxe cabins that open onto the after deck.

Specifications 114 cabins: 6 inside with double bed; 90 outside—all but 4 have 2 lowers, convertible to doubles; 32 convertible to triples; 2 owner's suites; 14 deck suites with verandas; 2 deck suites.

DINING The handsome bilevel dining room accommodates all passengers at a single seating for all meals. The paneled room with brass wall lamps has rectangular, round, and banquette-style tables and is set low enough that in any kind of sea, the water splashes in washing-machine fashion over the portholes.

An omelet chef cooks to order at breakfast, and a carvery features roast beef, ham, and pork at lunch. The lunch buffets are the biggest hits on the menu for the first day at sea, providing such fare as jumbo shrimp, foie gras, artichoke hearts, herring, potato salad, lots of salad fixings, hot and cold salmon, meatballs, and sliced roast beef.

SERVICE The international crew provides friendly service, though the pace can be slow at dinner when passengers order from the menu.

SPORTS, FITNESS, AND BEAUTY At least once during the cruise, passengers with a Walter Mitty fantasy may climb (wearing safety belts) the steel mast to a crows nest, 60 feet above the deck. They may also climb out on the netting that cascades from the bowsprit. Although passengers do not handle the sails as on Windjammers, they can enjoy being part of the navigation by helping the helmsmen on a raised platform above the bridge and chart room. They can also take lessons in sailing and rope tying.

The lower deck has an exercise room, spa, tiled Turkish bath, and beauty salon. A hydraulic platform stages the water sport activities, which include banana boats, water-skiing, diving, snorkeling, and swimming from the 16-foot inflatable raft. An interior stairway gives access to the marina. Two 60-passenger tenders, resembling military landing craft, take passengers for beach landings. Two 150-passenger fiberglass tenders ferry passengers between the anchored ship and pier.

POSTSCRIPT The ship has no special facilities for children, but when they are aboard, they are looked after well by the crew and staff, and there is much for them to observe, learn, and enjoy.

Although the overall experience and attraction of *Royal Clipper* is similar to the smaller clippers, comparisons are difficult. *Royal Clipper* is truly different. Her size, her 42 sails, the sheer amount of deck equipment, and her lavish Edwardian interiors are a sharp contrast to the smaller-scale, relatively simple, sleek sisters. As one passenger saw it, "For an ocean crossing, I would want the full-rigged *Royal Clipper;* for sailing the Caribbean or Mediterranean, I would be happy with either."

Windstar Cruises

300 Elliott Avenue West, Seattle, WA 98119
☎ 206-281-3535 or 800-258-7245; fax 206-281-7110
www.windstarcruises.com

TYPE OF SHIPS Deluxe sailing yacht/cruise ships.

TYPE OF CRUISES Low-key, laid-back, yet luxurious, for active, affluent travelers with cosmopolitan tastes for offbeat corners in sunny climes.

CRUISE LINE'S STRENGTHS
- appealing lifestyle
- private yacht exclusivity on small ships
- cabins
- romantic escape
- water sports

CRUISE LINE'S SHORTCOMINGS
- evening activity
- port-intensive itineraries with minimal time under canvas

FELLOW PASSENGERS The mix is broader than generally perceived. Not all drive BMWs and Porsches: 40% have Jeeps and Fords, and 77% of those are the family version rather than sports model. Passengers range from 20 to 80 years in age, but the majority are 35–65 years old, and the median age is 50. Incomes differ, and they might be first-time or experienced cruisers. Despite many differences, they share one aspect in common—a lifestyle preference, even if they cannot enjoy it 365 days of the year. Passengers are likely to be well-traveled; from the United States, Europe, and Latin America; and about 75% are professionals—lawyers, doctors, business executives—and probably work in high-pressure jobs. The remainder are apt to be retirees from similar pressure cookers, plus a few honeymooners. They are active and enjoy individual and low-energy sports, such as golfing, walking, and swimming.

Recommended for Active, affluent, Type-A individualists, 25–75 years old, who really mean it when they say they want to chill out; those who abhor mainstream cruising; divers and others who enjoy water sports; experienced cruisers looking for something different; those attracted by the romance of sailing ships who want upscale luxury.

Not recommended for Anyone who prefers large ships, thrives on nightlife, or enjoys wearing fancy clothes; those who need to be entertained, don't relate to a sophisticated ambience; those who prefer a burger to brûlée.

CRUISE AREAS AND SEASONS Caribbean, Bahamas, Costa Rica, Panama, winter; Mediterranean, Greek Isles, spring/summer/fall; transatlantic, March/April and November.

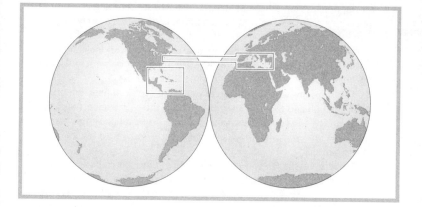

THE LINE Four masts in a row, each with enormous triangular sails and as tall as a 20-story building, tower above a deck one and a half times the length of a football field and half its width. The great sails are manned by computers designed to monitor the direction and velocity of the wind to keep the ship from heeling more than 40 degrees. The sails can be furled in less than two minutes.

These ships are windcruisers, which on their introduction in 1985 were called the most revolutionary vessels since the introduction of the steamship. The vessels use wind power alone up to 50% of the time at sea, depending on itinerary; electrical power and back-up propulsion are provided by diesel-electric engines. The ships marry the romance and tradition of sailing with the comfort and amenities of a cruise ship. Their all-outside cabins are larger, better designed, and better appointed than most standard cabins on mainstream cruise ships. The French-built vessels' shallow draft enables them to call at less-visited ports, private marinas, and secluded beaches.

Windstar Cruises was acquired by Holland America Line in 1987, and the next year both companies were purchased by Carnival Corporation. Windstar continues to operate as a separate entity. In 1997, Windstar bought the five-masted *Club Med 1*, a larger version of the Windstar ships, and after remodeling, renamed her *Wind Surf*.

THE FLEET	BUILT/RENOVATED	TONNAGE	PASSENGERS
Wind Spirit	1988/2003	5,350	148
Wind Star	1986/2003	5,350	148
Wind Surf	1990/98/2000/01/03	14,745	308

STYLE Laid-back, romantic, and informal, the cruises combine the atmosphere of a private yacht with the amenities and services of a cruise ship. From the outset, the ships have offered exclusivity because of their size, ambience, and the people they attract: upscale professionals who can afford a luxury cruise but want a less-structured environment and more unusual vacation than is available on traditional cruises.

The ships are wonderfully quiet under sail; you can hear the ocean wash the hull and the sails snap as wind fills them. Passengers visit the open bridge to see how everything works. The captains—their hands never far from the wheel—usually give eager passengers a few minutes at the helm.

There's a casual elegance and easygoing informality about the ship and its occupants. Regardless of age, passengers seem to blend easily; by week's end, they're good friends. Pressure to keep a schedule is nonexistent. You decide how to spend your day. Even ardent Type-A personalities can unwind.

DISTINCTIVE FEATURES The ship. Water sports platform; use of most sports gear is free. A passenger lucky enough to hook a fish on a deep-sea outing can have it cooked by the chef.

	HIGHEST	LOWEST	AVERAGE
PER DIEM	$659	$89	$303

Per diems are calculated from cruise line's nondiscounted *cruise-only* published fares on standard accommodations and vary by season, cabins, and cruise areas.

RATES Port charges and tips are included.

Special fares and discounts Booking six months in advance saves up to 50%. Windstar frequently offers two-for-one promotions. Other discounts are on a quarterly basis.

- **SINGLE SUPPLEMENT:** 175% of the published per-person rate.

Packages
- **AIR/SEA:** Yes. Packages are available for some European cruises from select air gateways across the United States and Canada.
- **PRE/POST:** Yes.
- **OTHERS:** Yes.

PAST PASSENGERS The Foremast Club is open to all who take a Windstar cruise. They receive a quarterly newsletter, e-mails, and other literature highlighting new itineraries and special discounts, including alumni savings on select cruises.

THE LAST WORD On our first Windstar cruise, having expected passengers on the level of royalty, the ones who seemed to be enjoying themselves most were a blue-collar couple from Massachusetts on their second honeymoon—and first cruise. A Windstar cruise is a relaxing, romantic escape, but the perception more than the reality seems to put it out of reach in price and ambience for most people. Although it's definitely a way to impress your friends, deciding whether this cruise is for you shouldn't be based on price (although you get a lot for your money), but on the type of cruise it offers. Those who relate to it think it's heaven; those who don't would probably be bored.

Our only complaint is that the itineraries are so port-intensive they leave little time for passengers to enjoy the ships, particularly under sail. Windstar recently added a day at sea to some Mediterranean cruises. We think two would have been better.

Windstar has a "no-tipping-required" policy. It supposedly means staff cannot solicit tips but can accept them. We think that's confusing, especially to first-time cruisers who already worry excessively about tipping. Further, tipping should never be "required." Period. It should be a passenger's prerogative. So, why does Windstar pretend? If they want passengers to tip, they should say so.

Windstar Cruises Standard Features

Officers British

Staff Dining, Cabin/Indonesian and Filipino; Cruise/American, British, some European.

Dining facilities One open-seating restaurant; indoor/outdoor cafe for breakfast and lunch buffet featuring traditional and tropical specialties; occasional barbecues on the beach. *Wind Surf,* lunch, dinner in Bistro.

Special diets Sail Light menus with low-calorie, heart-smart, and vegetarian selections. Advance notice requested for others.

Room service 24 hours.

Dress code Casual and elegantly casual.

Cabin amenities Color television, flat screen LCD television and DVD player, CD player, three-channel radio; international direct-dial telephone; safe; minibar and refrigerator; hair dryer and terry robe.

Electrical outlets 110 AC (220 *Wind Surf*).

Wheelchair access None. Seeing-eye dogs have been permitted.

Recreation and entertainment Piano bar, casino, lounge with local musicians or ship's band, library, videocassette/CD library.

Sports and other activities Water-sports platform for sailboats, windsurfers, motorized inflatables, water-skiing, scuba diving; snorkeling equipment carried onboard; saltwater pool. Charge for diving.

Beauty and fitness Beauty salon; hot tub/Jacuzzi, sauna, masseuse, fitness room with weight-training equipment. Spa on *Wind Surf*.

Other facilities Laundry; doctor, infirmary, e-mail/Internet access.

Windstar Cruises Standard Features *(cont'd)*

Children's facilities None. Children's videos.

Theme cruises Wine, culinary, life-enrichment on some repositioning cruises, which are packaged with airfare and pre-/postcruise hotel packages.

Smoking Allowed in designated areas, but not in dining room.

Windstar suggested tipping Tipping-not-required policy.

Credit cards For cruise payment and onboard charges: American Express, Discover, MasterCard, Visa, travelers checks.

Wind Spirit	QUALITY 9	VALUE C
Wind Star	QUALITY 9	VALUE C
REGISTRY Bahamas	LENGTH 440 feet	BEAM 64 feet
CABINS 74	DRAFT 13.5 feet	SPEED 8–12 knots
MAXIMUM PASSENGERS 148	PASSENGER DECKS 4	ELEVATORS None
	CREW 81/91	SPACE RATIO 36

THE SHIPS   The ships are identical inside and out. If not for their itineraries, they would be difficult to tell apart. Throughout, the tasteful appointments are well-designed and inviting. They have the feel of a sailing ship—wood and leather, portholes, and nautical blue and white—yet they're modern, with expanses of windows creating spaciousness and space-station-white walls adorned with contemporary art.

Because the number of passengers is small, boarding is speedy. You're greeted with a glass of champagne or chilled fruit drink and escorted to the main lounge to complete paperwork. Then, you're escorted to your cabin, where your luggage should be waiting.

The cabins, gym, and sauna are on the bottom two of four passenger decks. The third deck contains a main lounge and dining salon—both handsome. Through a lounge skylight, passengers have dramatic views of the majestic sails overhead. You'll also find a tiny casino, boutique, and beauty salon. The top deck offers a pool, bar, and veranda lounge.

ITINERARIES   *See* Itinerary Index.

CABINS   With the exception of the owner's suite, cabins are identical: large and outside. Larger than those on mainstream cruise ships, these well-designed, nicely appointed cabins make optimum use of space and are fitted with twin beds or a queen-size bed.

The marriage of tradition and technology is apparent in cabins. Each has twin portholes with brass fittings and wood cabinetwork, including a foldout vanity with makeup mirror. Modern amenities include flat-screen LCD television and DVD player, international direct-dial telephone, CD player, safe, and minibar stocked daily with beer, wine, spirits, and soft drinks. Note that drinks are expensive. A beer, for example, costs $5. However, Windstar offers several beverage packages: per person, per day, nonalcoholic, $18; all-inclusive, $45; and others.

Bathrooms have showers, teak decking, well-lighted mirrors, hair dryers, terry robes, and adequate storage.

Specifications 74 outside cabins; 1 suite with queen-size bed. Standard dimensions, 185 square feet. 73 with twin beds (convertible to queen); 11 (20 on *Wind Star*) with third berths; there are no singles and none wheelchair-accessible.

DINING The teak-lined dining room—nautical in design with rope-wrapped pillars—has low ceilings and subdued lighting, giving it an intimate atmosphere. Seating is open, restaurant-style. Cuisine continues to be uneven, ranging from super to ordinary. Generally, the smaller ships get better reviews.

Menus by celebrity chef Joachim Splichal of Patina and Pinot Bistro in Los Angeles, whose French cooking incorporates light California style, match Windstar's casual style of cruising. For 2005 and beyond, Splichal is creating one hundred new dishes. The line serves California wines to complement the cuisine; tastings are offered. "Sail Light" menus by Jeanne Jones, who developed the spa menus for Canyon Ranch and the Pritiken Center, are also available.

Coffee, tea, juices, and breakfast rolls are served poolside for early risers. Breakfast in the glass-enclosed veranda offers tropical fruits and freshly baked breads. Afternoon tea on the pool deck with pastries and finger sandwiches is popular. Room service is available 24 hours a day. In the Caribbean, a highlight is the pool deck barbecue, serving grilled lobster tails, shrimp, and other seafood accompanied by local music.

SERVICE The captain and European officers are affable, accessible, and visible, inviting passengers to watch the ship in operation, visiting with them, and participating in activities when possible. They welcome questions. Cabin staff and most restaurant personnel are Indonesian; deck stewards, bar personnel, and section captains are Filipino. All get very high marks.

FACILITIES AND ACTIVITIES Windstar ships don't have scheduled daily activities. You set your own schedule and make your own activities, independently or with new friends. That's what this cruise is all about. Days are passed sunbathing, reading, deep-sea fishing, swimming, and watching the ship's operation. (Readers should bring their books; selection aboard is limited.) Ship's television features two current movies daily, plus satellite news around the clock.

Nightlife is low-key and minimal. The tiny casino has blackjack tables, a Caribbean stud poker table, and slot machines. An easy listening trio plays nightly for dancing in the lounge. Topside, rock videos play in the disco. You also can watch a movie in your cabin; a selection of videos is available at the reception desk. A Caribbean night showcases a reggae band, and passengers young and old dance on the pool deck.

SPORTS, FITNESS, AND BEAUTY Water sports from the ships' fold-out platform more than compensate for the absence of onboard sports. Furthermore, the ships' shallow draft enables them to stop at less visited ports and secluded beaches and coves. On Caribbean more than Mediterranean cruises, water sports are a main attraction. Carried aboard are sailboats, windsurf boards, snorkeling and diving equipment (including tanks), and Zodiacs (inflatable boats) to take passengers snorkeling, scuba diving, water-skiing, and deep-sea fishing. Except for scuba, gear is available free of charge. Scuba costs $70 for one tank dive; $120, two tanks; divers must show certification. Beginning dive lessons are available; a Discover Scuba resort course is $140. Kayaking is also available. Dive masters and water-sports directors are well-qualified, personable, and eager to help. Snorkeling and scuba trips and lessons are organized daily. When the ships anchor off deserted islands, passengers often must wade from Zodiacs to the beach. Each ship has a fitness room with some exercise equipment, sauna, and masseuse; Jacuzzis are on the pool deck. The salon offers aromatherapy.

SHORE EXCURSIONS Most excursions are half-day tours with an emphasis on tropical gardens, national parks, and other natural attractions. Prices are on the high side, costing $25–$150. Excursions at St. Kitts in the Caribbean, for example, include a rain forest hike and horseback riding. In the Mediterranean, sight-seeing is emphasized.

Wind Surf	QUALITY 7	VALUE C
REGISTRY Bahamas	LENGTH 617 feet	BEAM 66 feet
CABINS 152	DRAFT 16 feet	SPEED 12 knots
MAXIMUM PASSENGERS 308	PASSENGER DECKS 6	ELEVATORS 2
	CREW 191	SPACE RATIO 48

THE SHIP *Wind Surf,* acquired by Windstar Cruises in 1997, is the former *Club Med 1,* a larger version of Windstar. After extensive remodeling, the ship was rechristened *Wind Surf* and entered Windstar service in 1998.

During renovations, 31 deluxe suites were created, reducing the ship's capacity some, although it remains double that of her Windstar sisters. Reducing the number of passengers was intended to offset the ship's larger size, which dilutes the intimate Windstar experience. The suites are double the size of already spacious standard cabins. A spa was also added.

In 2000, *Wind Surf* got another refit that corrected its most serious problem—the steep gangway was replaced by a new shorter one, lowering it from Deck 4 to Deck 2. To do so, two cabins (one from the port and one from the starboard side) were eliminated, thus lowering its passenger capacity from 312 to 308 and changing the ship's space ratio to 48. The new gangway has also improved the embarkation/debarkation process.

The ship has a **Computer Center,** and the **Cinema/Meeting Room** was remodeled into a fully equipped conference center with meeting facilities for up to 50 people. The **Wind Surf Lounge & Casino** was completely redesigned with a new nautical design and color scheme and furniture, a beautiful teak bar, and relocation of the stage and dance area resulting in clear sight lines to the stage from every seat. The casino has additional gaming tables and slots. The floorplan has enhanced passenger flow and allowed for smaller, more intimate groupings.

Other public rooms include a library well-stocked with CDs, books, and videos; a signature shop; and fitness center. The captain maintains an open bridge. Also available are 24-hour room service, laundry service, and a doctor's office.

ITINERARIES *See* Itinerary Index.

CABINS The deluxe outside cabins encompass 188 square feet each and offer queen-size beds (convertible to twins) and a work/desk/vanity area. They are similar in layout and decor to standard cabins on Windstar's other ships. All have flat-screen LCD television and DVD player, CD player, safe, minibar and refrigerator, and direct-dial telephone. The bathroom has a shower, hair dryer, toiletries, and terry robe.

The 31 new ocean-view suites in selected areas of top decks measure 376 square feet. Their decor, in maroon and cream, is accented by teak wood, linen wall coverings, and original art. Each suite has a queen bed convertible to twins and a sofa bed. A curtain can be pulled across the bedroom to separate it from the living room for dining or entertaining. In addition to standard amenities, suites boast his-and-her bathrooms with shower, teak flooring, plush towels and robes, and vanity lighting.

Specifications 31 deluxe outside suites; 123 outside cabins with queen beds (convertible to twins) and sitting area. Standard cabin dimensions, 188 square feet. Some cabins have third berth; some side-by-side have adjoining private door.

DINING The ship's two dining rooms—the **Restaurant** and the smaller **Bistro**—accommodate all passengers at one open seating. Menus for both were developed by Joachim Splichal, chef and founder of the Patina group of top restaurants in Los Angeles. Passengers have the opportunity to dine in both during a cruise. Light and vegetarian menus are available. The **Verandah Café** serves breakfast and lunch.

The Bistro, Windstar's alternative restaurant, is modeled after Splichal's Pinot Bistro. Splichal and his partner, Octavio Becerra, developed 132 recipes for the Bistro.

All three venues have been improved with increased capacity. The Bistro has a new look with French- and Italian-inspired colors, fabrics, and furniture. The glassed-in Verandah had its aft wall pushed back to enclose a portion of the deck to allow for additional indoor seating, which is preferred by guests on hot or windy days.

SPORTS, FITNESS, AND BEAUTY The 10,000-square-foot **WindSpa,** operated by Steiner, has a staff of ten and offers three kinds of treatments. Health and exercise includes aerobics, yoga, and other exercise classes; a water aerobics pool; and a fitness room with trainers. Pampering includes Swedish, deep tissue, sports, and other massage; aromatherapy; hair care; manicures, pedicures, and facials; and hand, foot, and spa bath treatments. Purification treatments include herbal wraps, algae and fango body masks, and mineral baths. Treatments can be purchased in advance or onboard. The Windstar brochure outlines options.

Wind Surf offers a complimentary water-sports program. The ship has a water-sports platform and equipment similar to that on the other Windstar vessels, two saltwater pools, and two hot tubs.

POSTSCRIPT Affluent clients attracted to Windstar for casual elegance, small ships, fewer passengers, and the chance to sail with passengers of similar means and interests will find that *Wind Surf* is different. One passenger observed, "*Wind Surf* is too large to get the true feeling of a yacht. It's more of a cruise-ship experience than a sailing experience." Like so many ships sailing the Mediterranean in summer, Windstar's cruises are so port-intensive that there is little time—not enough time, in our opinion—to enjoy the ship, which as we said in the beginning, is the best thing about the cruise line. Recently, the line added some overnights in port, enabling passengers to take in some of a destination's nighttime pleasures and, perhaps, satisfying those who prefer more time in port than under sail.

EUROPEAN, ASIAN, *and* SMALLER CRUISE LINES

IN ADDITION TO THE CRUISE LINES and ships in the American mainstream of cruising already profiled in this section, another group of lines, with ships based mostly in Europe, may be of interest to readers. Space doesn't allow the same in-depth treatment, but generally they are small to midsize ships operated in the European tradition. Their interesting itineraries often visit places many Americans would need an atlas to find. Ships have English-speaking staff, although the majority of passengers may be Europeans speaking other languages. A few ships operate from U.S. or Asian ports.

The degree of luxury varies widely. Some are luxury vessels launched only in the last year or so; others are renovated vintage ships forming a flotilla of new cruise lines.

Cruises appeal particularly to those who have traveled the main routes often and are looking for new destinations or a new environment in which to return to places seen previously. They also appeal to those who might never consider a typical cruise ship, preferring to explore less traveled waters.

Also described are a few lines and ships that cater mainly to the U.S. market but weren't profiled in depth for other reasons, such as the fact that they're sold mainly through tour companies in combination with larger tour programs, they're under charter much of the year, or we had difficulty obtaining information.

Note: In parentheses after each ship name is information about the number of cabins and passengers; officers and crew; and the ship's length and tonnage (cabins/passengers; officers/crew; ship length/tonnage).

Abercrombie & Kent, Inc.

1520 Kensington Road, Suite 212, Oak Brook, IL 60523-2141; ☎ 630-954-2944 or 800-323-7308; fax 630-954-3324; www.abercrombiekent.com

Abercrombie & Kent is a prestigious international tour operator specializing in exotic journeys worldwide for affluent, sophisticated travelers with an avid interest in nature and wildlife. The cruise programs focus on Antarctica; barge and river cruises in Europe and on the Amazon, Nile, Yangtze, and Ayeyarwaddy Rivers; and a wide selection of other areas, such as the Galapagos, Tahiti, Alaska, Mediterranean, and the Caribbean. All emphasize culture and ecologically sound tourism. Most passengers are professional, retired or semi-retired, well-educated, well-traveled, usually age 50 and older, in good health, and fit enough to enjoy hikes in Antarctic snows or Zodiac rides on the Amazon. Singles make friends easily on these trips.

Marco Polo is a club for A&K veterans and offers a quarterly newsletter, members-only trips, a 5 percent discount on land arrangements on most tours, luggage tags, priority on new destinations, tailored itineraries, a free lending library of A&K videotapes, and eligibility to compete in the annual Marco Polo Photo Contest. Annual membership is $95; five-year, $325; lifetime, $950; and children's memberships are available.

Explorer II (111 CABINS, 12 BALCONY SUITES/300; BRITISH, INTERNATIONAL/146; 436 FT./12,500 TONS)

In early 2003, Abercrombie and Kent replaced its venerable *Explorer I,* the world's first expedition cruise ship, with the new, spacious *Explorer II,* and with one stroke changed the nature of its adventure cruises, bringing a new level of comfortable and informal refinement to Antarctic travel.

Gone are the small, spartan cabins and antiquated bathrooms of the old ship. Now passengers can enjoy modern, well-appointed, and comfortable accommodations and public rooms on a ship with more facilities and greater flexibility than might have ever been imagined in the past.

Explorer II, the former *Minerva I* of Swan Hellenic launched in 1996, is a stylish yet unpretentious ship that has been likened to a country-house inn, with gleaming brass, polished wood, fresh flowers, and original art decorating the walls. But beneath these amenities, there's strong steel, including an ice-strengthened hull, stabilizers, and bow thrusters that give the ship the power, stability, and agility to handle open-water cruising and the icy channels of Antarctic seas.

The Lounge on Main Deck forward is a favorite place for passengers to congregate before the day's Zodiac excursion, listen to talks by onboard naturalists and other experts, or join friends for after-dinner coffee. Two bars—the **Shackleton** and the **South Cape**—provide additional corners in which to relax. The ship's library is exceptional, with a wide range of books, as well as newspapers, games, and puzzles. The Main Deck also has the dining room aft and a beauty salon (which also offers massage) at midship. On Bridge Deck is the swimming pool, a bar and informal restaurant, lounge, card room, cinema, library, exercise room, and sauna. The ship also has a gift shop, medical center, and two elevators.

Explorer II can carry in excess of 300 passengers, but on her Antarctica voyages, A&K limits her complement to 199 passengers. The smaller number enhances the comfort level for all passengers, including the use of outside cabins and suites only, so that all passengers have their own window onto the Antarctic landscape. The price of the cruise begins at $4,995 per person, double occupancy. Children ages 18 and under receive a 50 percent discount off the adult price when sharing a cabin (except suites) with adults.

The atmosphere onboard *Explorer II* is informal, unregimented, and sports an easy camaraderie among the passengers and the experts (naturalists, geologists, zoologists, historians, and ornithologists) who accompany every cruise. Each day, passengers gather for informal preexcursion briefings or posttrip wrap-ups in the ship's lounge or auditorium. Throughout the trip, they interact with the experts to exchange ideas and ask questions—at dinner, at the rail, or on a Zodiac. Staff and crew add to the experience with their informal talks and entertainment.

No formal entertainment or shows are offered; days are packed with intellectual and physical activities and the day's recap before dinner. Socializing resumes after dinner, sometimes continuing into the wee hours. A passenger may tickle the ivories or sing, but guests generally just converse. Slides, a film, or a Hollywood movie may be shown. The library is popular at any hour. Lectures are well attended. Most talks are accompanied by audiovisuals.

Explorer II offers among the most spacious and comfortable accommodations in Antarctica, many with private balconies. All cabins have vanity table/writing desk and chair, television and radio, refrigerator, direct-dial telephone, hair dryer, and binoculars. There are 2 owner's suites and 10 outside suites on Bridge Deck forward, with floor-to-ceiling patio doors leading to a balcony and furnished with queen or twin beds, bathroom with tub, large double wardrobe, ample drawer space, and separate sitting area with sofa, chair, and table. The 12 outside deluxe cabins on Promenade Deck forward have twin beds or queen bed, and some have a pull-out sofa for triple occupancy; bathroom with tub; separate sitting area with sofa, chair and table; a large picture window mirrored for privacy. Promenade Deck, midship and aft, also has 20 outside superiors with twins or queen bed, bathroom with tub, walk-in closet, armchair, and large picture window.

The standard categories (A, B, SA) are spread on two decks: 54 on A Deck, and 26 on B Deck. All are outside and have twin beds or queen; bathroom with shower; single and double wardrobes; love seat; and a picture window or porthole. Four cabins are handicapped accessible, and four are single cabins. Laundry service is available on Deck A. For its 199 passengers, *Explorer II* carries a staff and crew of 146, who provide a high level of warm, personal service.

Explorer II has two dining rooms with open seatings and indoor and outdoor service. The menus offer international cuisine as well as selections of light fare and vegetarian dishes. Special diets can be accommodated with sufficient advance notice. "Smart casual" wear is the attire of the evening. Smoking is not permitted in most areas of the ship, but there is a dedicated smoking room on the Bridge Deck and designated areas on the outer decks.

In addition to accommodations and meals, A&K's all-inclusive cruise prices include all bar drinks and house wines, onboard gratuities, and sightseeing. You receive a backpack, parka for Antarctica cruises, and very good precruise information.

Explorer II sails on diverse itineraries in Antarctica and neighboring islands. She claims to operate under guidelines to do all that is possible to protect the fragile Antarctic environment. Antarctic cruises are intended for serious travelers who cherish unusual opportunities and draw interesting, intellectually curious people, among whom many lasting friendships are forged. If you don't have a similar thirst for knowledge or the flexibility to deal with frequent changes caused by weather and sea, you could find yourself on the wrong ship a long way from home. Gadabouts and tourists wanting to add exotic destinations to their tally should look elsewhere.

A&K also markets some deluxe yachts, such as the famous *Sea Cloud* and the luxurious *River Cloud*. For A&K's river cruises, see Part Three.

American Canadian Caribbean Line

(See Part Two, Cruise Lines and Their Ships.)

American Cruise Lines

741 Boston Port Road, Suite 200, Guilford, CT 06437; ☎ 800-814-6880 or 203-453-6800; fax 860-453-0417; www.americancruiselines.com

American Eagle **(31/49; AMERICAN/AMERICAN; 165 FT.)**

American Glory **(31/49; AMERICAN/AMERICAN; 168 FT.)**

American Spirit **(51/93; AMERICAN/AMERICAN; 235 FT.)**

The small coastal ship *American Eagle*, completed in 2000 at the owner's Chesapeake shipyard in Salisbury, Maryland, takes only 49 passengers on close-to-shore trips from Maine and New England through the Chesapeake Bay to the Deep South and Florida via the Intracoastal Waterway from March to December. (For the eagle-eyed, some of the company ads and brochure photos might be familiar. American Cruise Lines first surfaced in 1974 with a previous *American Eagle*, and after operating six ships for 15 years, the company quietly went bust.)

In 2002, the *Eagle* was joined by *American Glory*, which is three feet longer and three feet wider at the beam and has 14 veranda suites. The larger *American Spirit*, scheduled to depart on her first cruise in June 2005, has 23 veranda cabins.

The ships' public spaces are roomy, considering they have only four decks. The forward-facing **Nantucket Lounge** (**Chesapeake Lounge** on *Spirit*) seats all passengers; and amidships, a shipwide foyer offers additional comfy couch seating. A library has television, VCR, and books. The decor is a bit plain, with utilitarian-looking walls and ceilings, but the carpets and fabrics help to dress it up. The ships have an elevator with access to each floor, and equipment for the handicapped is available.

The dining room, glass-enclosed on three sides, has open seating at large, round tables. The ships do not have a liquor license; instead, there is a complimentary bar and sumptuous predinner hors d'oeuvres for the very popular cocktail hour, and there are carafes of wine on the dinner table.

Each ship has chefs from the Culinary Institute of America and Johnson and Wales. Their expertise shows in the delicious, creative meals. The food is uniformly excellent throughout the cruise. Lunch is light fare, such as crab cakes and chicken Caesar salad. The set dinner menus, with a choice of two entrees, might be grilled artichoke hearts, hearts of palm in balsamic vinegar, Cornish game hen with wild rice, grilled catfish, broiled live lobster, and desserts such as pecan peanut butter pie.

The fourth or Sports Deck, open to the sky, has deck chairs for all passengers plus tables and chairs and a putting green. Additional covered deck space faces aft, and the open deck forward of the lounge is excellent for viewing ahead.

There are five cabin categories, all with private bath and outside with windows that slide open to allow in fresh air. AA, the second grade up, measures 192 square feet and compares favorably to the line's competition. The six AAV cabins are 249 square feet, including veranda; *Glory* has 14 cabins with verandas.

The average size of *Glory*'s cabins is slightly larger at 220 square feet. All ships have five single cabins priced at about a 50 percent premium over the AA category. Cabins are furnished with comfortable couches. The American Cruise Lines' ships offer a low-key cruising experience with itineraries from Maine and New England to Florida that celebrate Americana, sometimes with the help of an enrichment lecturer. The passengers are mostly an amiable retired lot who like sailing in a small club setting. There may also be mothers, grandmothers, daughters, and sons. The all-American crew includes college-age men and women, some just out of high school, serving as deck hands, cleaning cabins, and waiting tables. The level of service is friendly, if sometimes haphazard. The line offers early-bird discounts to those who book six months in advance. Fares begin at $2,475 per person for a six-night cruise.

American Safari Cruises

19921 36th Avenue West, Suite 208, Lynnwood, WA 98036; ☎ 425-776-4700 or 888-862-8881; fax 425-776-8889; www.amsafari.com

Safari Escape (6/12; AMERICAN/6; 112 FT.)
Safari Quest (11/22; AMERICAN/9–10; 120 FT.)
Safari Spirit (6/12; AMERICAN/6; 105 FT.)

Formed in 1996, American Safari Cruises offers nature-oriented adventure cruises for affluent travelers on three small luxury yachts. The Alaska itineraries are off the beaten track, close-up experiences of wildlife, or scenery viewing at a leisurely pace with the pampering of a luxury cruise. The line's three-, four- and seven-night fall and spring cruises sail in the Pacific Northwest and from San Francisco to the heart of the California wine country, where passengers tour private villas, dine in winery caves, and enjoy onboard wine tastings and lectures conducted by experts. There also is a winter series of weekly cruises of Baja California and the Sea of Cortés, departing from La Paz.

All cabins on the vessels are outside and deluxe. Each is furnished with a king or queen bed or two twin beds (except for one cabin with one twin on *Safari Quest*), television with DVD/VCR, and private bathroom with shower or tub. Amenities include evening turndown service, terry robes, and fresh flowers.

The main gathering spot is a salon furnished with comfortable couches and chairs. A self-service bar separates the dining area and salon. The salon opens onto the sports platform, where passengers can board a launch or a two-passenger kayak. A spiral staircase links all public decks, the library and lounge, and the bridge. A promenade circles the entire yacht. The yachts have a top-deck hot tub for an under-the-stars spa experience. Upon request, fishing charters can be arranged for an additional charge.

On Alaskan itineraries, binoculars, rain jackets, and rubber boots are provided. A skilled and personable expedition leader accompanies each cruise and serves in lieu of a cruise director. A trained naturalist and usually university educated, the expedition leader, organizes hikes and biking excursions, leads kayak explorations, and identifies wildlife en route. In the evenings and when appropriate during the day, the expedition leader lectures on the flora, fauna, geology, and the history of the areas visited. Praised by passengers as caring, enthusiastic, and knowledgeable, the expedition leaders elevate the experience from a luxury cruise to a horizon-expanding voyage of discovery.

Food aboard American Safari Cruises is as good as it gets on a cruise ship. Each day, the chef joins the passengers to discuss the menu and to describe special dishes to be prepared. An early-bird breakfast of fresh fruit, pastries, cereal, juices, and hot beverages starts at 6 a.m., with a full-service, cooked-to-order breakfast available at 8 a.m. A full-course lunch is served at 1 p.m. Hors d'oeuvres are offered nightly during the cocktail hour preceding dinner at 7 p.m. Two entrees are offered each evening—usually fresh local seafood as well as chicken, lamb, or beef. Wine with meals and all other alcoholic beverages are included in the price of the cruise. The wine selection is stellar, as are the upscale labels in the well-stocked bar. Beer drinkers will love the draft beers from a prize-winning Alaskan microbrewery.

The yachts travel in daytime for wildlife viewing and scenic exploration. In late afternoon, they anchor in a scenic, secluded cove or bay for the night, offering further discovery on foot or by Zodiacs. Sighting wildlife—whales, porpoises, harbor seals, black bears, brown bears, sea lions, bald eagles, cormorants, herons, sandhill cranes, oystercatchers, and gulls—is all but guaranteed. The yachts are small enough that the captain can change course immediately to approach something for closer inspection. Long summer days allow kayaking, whale-watching by Zodiacs, and hiking until late evening.

All meals, excursions, and events on these cruises are strictly informal. Jeans, khakis, and shorts, along with outdoor gear appropriate to the cruise venue and time of year, are all you need. Though the expedition leader has lots of activities on tap each day, the decision to participate is yours. Soaking in the hot tub, reading, napping, and watching movies on your cabin

VCR are some of the alternatives available. Each ship also has at least one aerobic exercise machine.

The Alaska itineraries explore remote areas and small villages. They range from 7 nights starting at $3,895 to 14-nights for $4,995 per person, double. Prices cover shore excursions, including unlimited use of kayaks, guided nature walks, all private transfers, open bar, and port charges. Tips are extra. The Sea of Cortés 8-night series operating from December to April has a starting price of $3,895, while the 7-night cruises of the Pacific Northwest in September and October start at $2,795; and a longer 11-night one on the Columbia and Snake rivers is priced from $4,995—all per person double. Safari Quest offers three- and four-night California Wine Country cruises in October and November, starting at $1,695. Golf and spa packages are available in conjunction with the California Wine Country and the Sea of Cortés cruises; Kids in Nature programs are featured on some Alaska and Sea of Cortés cruises. All three vessels are available for private charter.

Although a luxury product, American Safari cruises represent a good value, offering a highly personalized and intimate private yacht experience for less than most upscale cruises of comparable length. Indeed, with early booking discounts and the inclusion of wine, liquor, and all shore excursions in the price of the cruise, American Safari cruises are among the most affordable luxury cruises afloat.

American Safari passengers are typically over 40 years old, well educated, and adventurous individuals who revel in learning and discovery and who enjoy making new friends. Life aboard is, after all, an intimate experience, one that practically ensures you will become well acquainted with your fellow passengers.

ITINERARIES *See* Itinerary Index.

Bora Bora Cruises
P. O. Box 40186, Fare Tony–Vaiete, 98713 Papeete, Tahiti, French Polynesia; ☎ 689-544 505; fax 689-451 065; www.boraboracrusies.com

---

Tu Moana/Ti'a Moana (37/74; FRENCH; 230 FT.)

Bora Bora Cruises, launched in 2003, sails on weekly cruises of French Polonesia with its two custom-built, luxury super yachts. The boutique cruise-yachts are aimed at a market niche of exclusive, stylish cruises with great attention to detail, a high level of service, gourmet cuisine, and designer furnishings and amenities.

The twin vessels take their names from the native Tahitian language: *Moana* is the universal Polynesian word meaning "the sea," *Tu* and *Ti'a* carry similar meanings "to stand erect, to be upright" and "to fit, agree, answer the purpose." Thus, each ship's name literally means "comfortably upright in the sea."

Built in Australia by Austal Ships, with interiors by well known Tillberg-Design, and technical oversight by V-Ships of Monaco, *Tu Moana* and *Ti'a Moana* have the sleek lines of a private luxury yacht. The vessels are identical in all areas except interior decor. Their fine finishes combine exotic hardwood interiors, original artwork, and glass staircases with the latest technologies.

All cabins are outside ones with large windows and lovely furnishings, located on three decks. They have three different layouts with an average size of about 170 square feet. Each cabin has a queen bed with an exclusive Kenzo throw, high quality European bed and bath linens; flat screen television and DVD/CD player, phone, safe, mini-bar and refrigerator, writing desk and stationery; hand-blown glass bowl with fresh fruit; bedside reading lamps; bathrobes and BBC logo beach bag. In the glass-enclosed bathroom, there are Phillipe Starck–designed bath fixtures, hairdryer, adjustable shower-head, BBC bathrobe, and exclusive hypo-allergenic bathroom toiletries.

The crew speaks three languages, and the French chef's creations have garnered rave reviews. Special touches include breakfast served on linen and china at tables in the warm waters of the lagoon, movies shown on a deserted island under the stars, and a canoe expedition for two up a tropical river. Passengers can snorkel, get a massage on the beach, or enjoy other options, including 4x4 island safaris, horseback riding, mountain climbing, shark and manta ray feeding, aft-deck night fishing, and lagoon photo excursions.

The ships have an unusual "flat-water" design, which draws only 7.5 feet and allows for safe navigation in the lagoons inaccessible to larger vessels, providing passengers with a unique experience. The shallow draft enables the yachts to travel close to the shoreline and to the most beautiful coral reefs in these islands; at the same time, the ships' advanced stabilization technology provides smooth sailing in open water.

Both vessels depart Bora Bora on Monday mornings, returning to Bora Bora Sunday evenings, gliding across the calm lagoons of Huahine, Raiatea, Taha'a, and Bora Bora on 6-night, 7-day cruises. Bora Bora Cruises has a sales and marketing partnership with Orient-Express Hotels, Trains & Cruises. Travelers can book a 7-day cruise to the islands or a 10- or 14-day Motu Miti (island and sea) package combining a cruise with a stay at Orient-Express's newly renovated Bora Bora Lagoon Resort & Spa. Most passengers are from Spain, France, and the United States.

Bora Bora Cruises is the dream of its founder, owner, and chairman, Mehiti Degage, a young Polynesian woman whose a love for the sea and lagoons inspired her to provide visitors with an experience that captures the essence of these islands in a stylish, intimate manner.

ITINERARIES *See* Itinerary Index.

Discovery World Cruises
1800 SE Tenth Avenue, Suite 205, Fort Lauderdale, FL 33316;
☎ **866-623-2689; fax 954-761-7768; www.discoveryworldcruises.com**

Discovery (351/650; SCANDINAVIAN, BRITISH, DUTCH/AMERICAN, EUROPEAN, FILIPINO; 553 FT./20,186 TONS)

Founded in 2002 by well-known travel industry entrepreneur Gerry Herrod, this new cruise line has been designed to offer deluxe cruises to less traveled destinations at affordable prices, much like Orient Lines and other niche-market companies that Herrod headed in the past. The cruises focus on giving passengers in-depth exposure to their destinations, while providing the traditional comforts of a deluxe ocean liner.

Before entering service in 2003, the *Discovery*, built as *the Island Venture* in 1972 in Germany by century-old shipbuilder Rheinstahl Nordseewerke (and best-known as Princess Cruises' *Island Princess*) underwent extensive, multimillion-dollar renovations that, in effect, created a new ship. She has retained her handsome, classic profile and grand ocean liner ambience, but now boasts modern safety features and amenities. At 20,000 tons—small compared to today's megaliners—*Discovery* is large enough for cruising to faraway places, yet small enough to enter remote harbors that larger vessels must bypass.

Facilities on the eight-deck ship include three restaurants; five lounges; lecture theater/cinema; a well-stocked library; modest casino; modern health club and beauty center; two swimming pools, one with a retractable dome; two Jacuzzis; card room; Internet center, boutiques; and four elevators. There is nightly entertainment, classical music concerts, and folkloric performances by local groups.

The ship has 351 cabins and suites, all equipped with private facilities, air-conditioning, television, hair dryer, and safe. Cabins on Bridge and Promenade Deck have bath and a shower; those on other decks have showers. Cabins have two lower beds or a double bed. Some cabins have one or two upper berths or a sofa bed, allowing for third or fourth person sharing (when only one or two passengers are occupying a cabin the upper berths are folded away). Most beds in twin cabins are arranged parallel to each other, although some are arranged in an L shape. A small number of cabins have an inter-connecting door, and can be booked as adjoining cabins. Outside cabins on Bridge and Promenade Decks have picture windows (the view of the Owner's Suite is obscured by lifeboats). Outside cabins on the Pacific Deck have two windows; those on Bali and Coral Decks have two portholes. Outside and inside standard cabins measure 135 square feet; outside superior cabins have 194 square feet.

Most itineraries are being marketed as cruise-tour vacation packages, which include extended stays and sightseeing in embarkation and/or disembarkation cities, detailed briefings on each port of call, and local cultural performances on board. A hallmark of Discovery World Cruises is its enrichment program of lectures and workshops at sea, with noted expedition leaders and area experts on each voyage. Early-bird savings up to 50 percent are available.

During the winter season, *Discovery* sails on cruises in South America, Antarctica, New Zealand, and the South Pacific. After visits to Peru and Central America, *Discovery* sails through the Panama Canal, stopping in the San Blas Island, Costa Rica, and Belize before making a transatlantic voyage to England from Fort Lauderdale. During the remainder of the year, the ship operates under the banner of Voyages of Discovery, cruising the British

Isles, the Baltic, Greenland, Iceland, and the Faroe Islands, Scandinavia, the Mediterranean, the Black Sea, Red Sea, Suez Canal, and North African.

Discovery has run an unusual lecture series sponsored by the Mayo Clinic that includes a comprehensive team of distinguished medical professionals aboard eight select cruises. The lecture series debuted during the ship's first year, it was repeated in 2005, and is likely to be offered again in 2006. Contact the cruise line for a schedule.

The ship's senior officers are Scandinavian, British, and Dutch; the cruise staff is American and European; and the service staff, Filipino. In September 2004, All Leisure Group of the United Kingdom announced its intention to buy the *Discovery*. Upon the expected completion of the transaction in May 2005, All Leisure Group will manage *Discovery*'s cruise-tours year-round. In the United States, the cruise-tours will be marketed as Discovery World Cruises; in Europe, they will be sold as Voyages of Discovery.

ITINERARIES *See* Itinerary Index.

easyCruise
easyGroup (UK) Ltd., The Rotunda, 42–43 Gloucester Crescent, London NW1 7DL; ☎ 0207-241-9000; fax 0207-482-2857; www.easycruise.com

Upstart easyCruise, launched in May 2005, is both a new cruise line and a new concept. Billed as "no frills cruising," the new line has "unbundled" the cruise package, selling cabins on board the ship on a night-by-night basis, for a two-night minimum. Prices start at about $60 per person per night for a simply furnished, basic cabin; passengers are charged for meals, housekeeping, and other onboard services.

Passengers make their own air connections to and from the ship, presumably using the abundance of low-cost European airlines, such as easyJet, which serve the Mediterranean. Dubbed "city-hopping by sea," the product enables passengers to hop on and off the ship, cruising for as many or as few nights as they wish, and provides a travel experience probably more akin to European ferry service than a cruise.

The new venture is the brainchild of 38-year-old Stelios Haji-Ioannou, known to one and all simply as Stelios, the founder of easyGroup which includes easyJet.com, the successful British no-frills airline; easyHotel.com, easyCar.com, easyCinema.com, and other enterprises in the same mode. Now he is applying the no-frills concept to cruises.

The ship, the 4,077-ton *easyCruise One* (previously called *Neptune*), is the former 114-passenger luxury *Renaissance II*, built in Italy in 1990. It has been completely refitted with new interiors in Singapore to carry 170 passengers in a no-frills style. Cabins, pictured on easyCruise's Web site, are in the same style as easyHotel, striped down to the basics. The line wants you to think of them as being in the currently fashionable minimalist style. Each, measuring about 100 to 150 square feet, has a shower unit, a lavatory and a wash basin, and one double bed or two twins. The six-deck ship has four suites with balcony (220 square feet), seven quads, 74 standard cabins, and one disabled double. Housekeeping will be an optional extra.

The Mediterranean-based ship will sail for no more than about six hours a day, departing in early morning, arriving at her next port by noon or early afternoon, and staying through the night to give passengers the opportunity to dine and enjoy the evening in port. Entertainment onboard the vessel will be limited, since presumably an evening in Cannes, Monaco, or St. Tropez would top anything the ship could offer. Food and beverages are available for purchase from the ship's restaurant and shop.

V. Ships Leisure, the passenger ship arm of V. Ships, one of the world's leading ship management and marine services group, has been hired to manage the new easyCruise venture. The veteran company, with offices in 26 countries providing services to some 650 vessels, is involved in marine planning, technical management, and provisioning the deck and engine crew for easyCruise's first three years of operation.

The no-frills, unbundled cruising product is being marketed mostly to Europeans in their 20s, 30s and 40s and sold via the Internet. Following a cruise industry practice, the best prices are available to customers who book early at **www.easyCruise.com.** In fact, the earlier they book, the less they pay. Peak periods cost more than off-peak periods. The new easyCruise is calculating that its flexibility and low prices will attract a wider customer base of new travelers who have never cruised. During her maiden summer, the ship is scheduled to sail the western Mediterranean from Nice (Friday), Cannes (Saturday), St. Tropez (Sunday), Monaco (Monday), Genoa (Tuesday), Portofino (Wednesday), and Imperia (for San Remo, Thursday). In winter, easyCruise will offer Caribbean cruises. Ports of call are Barbados (Saturday and Sunday), St. Vincent (Monday), Martinique (Tuesday), Bequia (Wednesday), Grenada (Thursday), and St Lucia (Friday). *easyCruise One* will remain in Barbados for two days and nights to provide greater flexibility for passengers in making flight arrangements. Her ports of call are tied to those with frequent, low-cost air service.

An impression of the vessel, painted in the unmistakable orange that is splashed on the sides of easyJet planes, the company's offices, easyInternet cafes, and the ship's cabin interiors, can be seen on the company's Web site.

ITINERARIES *See* Itinerary Index.

Fred Olsen Cruise Lines (The Cruise Broker)

**Fred Olsen House, White House Road, Ipswich IP1 5LL, United Kingdom;
☎ 01473-292-200; fax 01473-292-201; www.fredolsencruises.co.uk; or
c/o Borton Overseas, 5412 Lyndale Avenue South, Minneapolis, MN
55419; ☎ 612-822-4640; fax 612-822-4755; www.bortonoverseas.com**

Black Prince **(234/472; EUROPEAN/FILIPINO; 480 FT./11,209 TONS)**

Built in 1966 and renovated in 1999, the ship caters to Britons. It sails on 9- to 49-night cruises from Southampton, England, year-round, to South

America and the Amazon, Canary Islands, Baltic Sea, Norwegian coast, Caribbean, Mediterranean, and Middle East. The ship—a good choice for gregarious travelers age 50 and older—has a gym, pool, sauna, beauty salon, disco, and casino, and provides international entertainment and sports. On this and other Fred Olsen Lines cruises, early-bird discounts of 30 percent are available for booking six months in advance; last-minute values might be reduced 50 percent. The *Black Prince,* as well as the other two ships, offer theme cruises, such as music, dance, painting, bridge, wine, antiques, and more, throughout the year. Details are available on the cruise line's Web site.

ITINERARIES *See* Itinerary Index.

Black Watch (400/761; NORWEGIAN/INTERNATIONAL; 674 FT./ 28,492 TONS)

Formerly the *Royal Viking Star,* the much-loved *Black Watch* was judged too small and too old to compete in the U.S. market and was sold to Fred Olsen Lines and given an $8 million refurbishment.

Black Watch cabins come in a bewildering number of configurations. Thirty-nine are singles. Though most are small, all are nicely appointed. Ninety percent are outside with portholes, picture window, or private veranda. Baths are well designed but very plain. All cabins have televisions and phones, and many have refrigerators.

The ship's public areas are exceptional. The library is among cruising's largest and most splendidly appointed. (Unfortunately, it's only open a couple of hours each day.) Contiguous is an equally impressive card and game room. Both rooms display artifacts from earlier ships named *Black Watch.* Observation lounges overlook the bow and stern. Both provide live music well into the night. A third lounge adjoins the main showroom; decor honors the Scottish Black Watch Regiment.

The clubby **Braemar Room,** a large lounge adjacent to the dining room, is packed with brightly colored stuffed chairs. It's given over entirely to the British passion for tea, which is available around the clock.

Well-designed public areas continue outside with a promenade that encircles the ship. Also available are pools, Jacuzzis, bars, cafes, an Internet center, and outdoor areas (some covered) for sunning or relaxing.

Entertainment is professional, varied, and appealing to a range of ages and backgrounds. It puts to shame the offerings aboard many superliner competitors. During a recent voyage, we enjoyed Las Vegas–style production shows, an incredibly talented opera company, an illusionist, a comic, a celebrity vocalist, and classical music concerts. Lounges, the casino, and the **Star Night Club** dance venue bustle into the wee hours. Theme cruises are varied.

For an American, the greatest pleasure aboard *Black Watch* is meeting Britons—delightful, interested, and interesting. Many hours are spent with new English, Scottish, and Irish friends exploring the subtleties that make our cultures so similar yet so different. Some misunderstandings of idiom and accent are uproarious: Announcement of a "folkloric presentation" was heard by the Americans as a "full colonic presentation.". . . We couldn't wait! Because the British are gracious and friendly, being the minority was a special pleasure.

Black Watch makes a three-and-a-half month world cruise annually. *Black Watch* is expected to be joined soon by a former sister. In early 2005, Fred Olsen Line bought the 28,000-ton *Grand Latin* from Spain's Iberojet Cruises, which had had her for about a year. The 800-berth ship was built in 1973 as the *Royal Viking Sky;* she became the *Sunward* for Norwegian Cruise Lines in 1991, and later joined Princess Cruises as the *Golden Princess.* Three years later she was acquired by Star Cruises as *Superstar Capricorn.*

Following her 2005 world cruise, *Black Watch* was scheduled for major surgery during a 63-day refit that will include the installation of four new engines and renovations to her passenger cabins, including the addition of 36 balconies to her Bridge Deck cabins.

ITINERARIES *See* Itinerary Index.

Braemar (377/820; EUROPEAN/INTERNATIONAL; 537 FT./20,000 TONS)

The former *Crown Dynasty* of Crown Cruise Line and *Norwegian Dynasty* of Norwegian Cruise Lines, she is one of the nicest ships in her size and price category in cruising. She is small enough to be cozy but large enough to offer modern cruise-ship amenities and facilities.

Elegant but not stuffy, *Braemar*'s decor communicates a sophistication that is apparent the moment you step onboard. Expansive glass windows throughout the ship, large open decks and terraces, and a five-story atrium with walls of glass create a feeling of space and openness. Polished woods, gentle lighting, and soft hues contribute to the stylish comfort.

Built in Spain in 1993 and originally designed by Scandinavian architect Petter Yran, known for his work on many luxury ships, the pretty *Braemar* was given a facelift by the eminent British ship-interior designer John McNeese prior to beginning her new life in August 2001.

The layout of the eight-deck ship is unusual, if not unique. The five-deck, greenery-filled atrium lobby is aft, rather than amidships. Also, it's on the starboard side rather than at the center, with windows spanning Decks 4 to 8, admitting natural light and sea views, and helping connect passengers with the sea. Four of the main public rooms are stacked vertically at the stern, allowing for large windows in virtually every area. The decks are connected by outdoor stairways and open decks.

Deck 5 is devoted to public rooms. It's anchored at both ends by lounges oriented to the port side horizontally and facing large windows (rather than the usual arrangement of lounges facing the bow or stern). The multilevel show lounge, for example, is semicircular, with the stage and dance floor on the port side. Between the lounges are shops, a casino, and a bar.

Cabins are on five decks; about two-thirds are outside. They are nicely appointed in pastels with light wood furniture and brass fixtures. All have television, phone, safe, and card-key door lock. Closet space is good, but drawer space is minimal. Many cabins are fitted with twin beds that can be converted to a queen. Bathrooms are small but have large medicine cabinets, mirrored doors, and vanities. Deluxe cabins and suites have refrigerators and sitting areas with large windows. Ten suites have private balconies. Four wheelchair-accessible cabins have large bathrooms with grab bars and wide doorways. There are four elevators.

The dining room has a skylight and panoramic windows on three sides, providing natural light and sea views for all diners. Although tables are close, noise is low. The room, decorated in muted colors with lively, contemporary art, has a variety of table configurations separated from service areas by frosted glass.

Above the dining room on Deck 6 is a casual indoor/outdoor cafe—more elegantly decorated than usual for a lido cafe. It's also a lounge with a full-service bar and is used as the disco at night. Adjacent to the casino is a tastefully decorated bar separated from the main thoroughfare by frosted glass and wood paneling. The ship also has a cozy library with good sea views, a card room, an Internet center, and medical center.

The top deck has a swimming pool, Jacuzzis, bar, and a spa with large windows facing the bow. The spa is equipped with state-of-the-art exercise equipment, an aerobics area, and a juice bar. It also has a beauty salon with hair and body treatments, two saunas, and steam and massage rooms. A jogging track rims the pool on an overhang and windscreens line the deck's perimeter. A wide outside promenade circling Deck 5 provides an uninterrupted track for walking or jogging. The ship also has a golf program which is available on most Caribbean itineraries and on selected Mediterranean ones. It combines individual instruction onboard ship and play at clubs on shore.

Despite the increasing numbers of seasoned cruisers who prefer smaller ships, their choices in the midprice range are limited. As one of the few midsize ships built in the 1990s, *Braemar* helps fill the void.

ITINERARIES *See* Itinerary Index.

Hapag-Lloyd Cruises
c/o Euro Lloyd Tours, 1640 Hempstead Turnpike, East Meadow, NY 11554; ☎ 516-228-4970 or 800-334-0284; fax ☎ 516-228-8258; www.hl-cruises.com; www.eurolloyd.com

Hapag Lloyd Cruises traces its origins back to the mid-nineteenth century and two venerable German shipping companies, Hamburg America Line of Hamburg and North German Lloyd of Bremen. Until World War II, the two companies operated some of the world's largest and fastest liners and were pioneers in the operation of pleasure cruises. With today's combined company, the cruising arm is a very small part of a giant container-shipping operation based in Hamburg. The current fleet names recall some of the two lines' most famous ships, and while greatly reduced in size, today's vessels offer the very high standards of the past.

In recent years, Americans have come aboard Hapag Lloyd ships when chartered by special interest and university groups, and for individual bookings when the *Hanseatic* was chartered by Radisson Seven Seas Cruises for Antarctica and the *C Columbus* began sailing on the Great Lakes. Now the firm has mounted a campaign to increase the numbers of North Americans by establishing fully bilingual cruises with menus, programs, entertainment, and announcements in English. Most of the crew, mainly German and Filipino, speak English.

The vessels can boast high space-to-passenger and crew-to-passenger ratios. They are decidedly European, yet each has her own distinct character and distinctive features. Most of the time daytime has everyone in an adventure mode and dress; nighttime brings out conservative fineries.

Hapag-Lloyd does not have a U.S. office; rather it uses several agencies that are listed on its Web site.

Europa (204/408; GERMAN/INTERNATIONAL/275; 651.5 FT./28,600 TONS)

The flagship of Hapag-Lloyd Cruises, *Europa* is primarily a German ship, but to attract English-speaking travelers, Hapag-Lloyd has begun to extend its bilingual sailings to attract more U.S. and Canadian passengers.

The all-suite ship, known for its attention to detail, is designed for cruisers who have refined tastes and are interested in the music, food, and art of the places the ship visits. Onboard, there are wine masters, three-star Michelin guest chefs, and an PGA professional to help golfers improve their game. The line provides renowned lecturers; arranges excursions for passengers to view art, architecture, and nature; and looks for cruises that provide once-in-a-lifetime experiences. *Europa*'s size allows her to dock at smaller ports or anchor off remote beaches. She carries Zodiacs to reach remote areas.

Europa's spacious suites, ranging from 290 to 914 square feet, have large living and bedroom areas, a luxurious bathroom, and a mini-bar. An infotainment system includes television, VCR, music center, as well as an information medium with which guests can send and receive personal e-mails free of charge.

Europa's penthouse deck has ten deluxe suites, and two grand suites, each with its own sauna, whirlpool, guest bathroom, and a dining table for six. Passengers on penthouse decks are served by personal butlers 24/7. Most of the other 192 outer suites have balconies. Two suites are specially designed for disabled persons.

The *Europa* restaurant, which can accommodate all passengers at one-seating for all meals, serves haute cuisine. Two specialty restaurants, **Oriental** and **Venezia,** offer Asian and Italian cuisine. Europa Deck has a cigar bar, piano bar, the **Clipper Lounge** for cocktails and snacks, and a boutique. On the Lido Deck, an informal indoor/outdoor cafe serves a buffet and snacks three times a day. The Lido Deck also has a club and bar, a well-stocked library, and an auditorium where lectures and films are presented frequently. The ship's entertainment ranges from classical musicians to well-known popular acts.

During *Europa*'s 2004 refurbishing, an expanded fitness area, a new bar, and new children's area were added. The **Spa Futuresse Center** on Sports Deck is fitted with a sauna, steam bath, massage parlor, Japanese bath, and solarium. The fitness center covers three levels—all with ocean views. Top-of-the-line equipment for cardiovascular training and other exercises are available, as is a personal trainer for individual programs and fitness counseling. The golf training unit has a golf simulator, video analysis, two tee-offs, and a putting green. The swimming pool, one of the longest on any cruise ship, has a magrodome for use as an indoor as well as an outdoor pool.

The new **Sansibar** at the stem of the *Europa,* designed in cooperation with its namesake's creators on the island of Sylt, enjoys great ocean views. The sophisticated **Club Belvedere** is almost entirely glassed-in, providing another venue for sea views.

Families with children are welcome on the *Europa,* with a special children's program and staff during vacation periods. During the ship's refurbishment two children's areas—for younger and older children—were added.

Europa also has a fully equipped hospital and two self-service laundrettes.

ITINERARIES *See* Itinerary Index.

Bremen (82/164; GERMAN/INTERNATIONAL; 366 FT./6,752 TONS)

Described as a world-class private club aboard a first-class exploration cruise ship, the *Bremen* (former *Frontier Spirit*) was constructed at the Kobe Shipyard in Japan by Mitsubishi Heavy Industries in 1990. Slightly smaller than the *Hanseatic,* the *Bremen* is a fine expedition vessel with an ice-hardened hull, which means she can sail in places such as Antarctica. Her 16-foot draft enables her to sail to remote areas of the Amazon and Orinoco rivers, and her Zodiac landing craft enables her to take passengers even farther into areas where large ships cannot go.

Public rooms include a light-filled observation lounge that is used for lectures, a roomy main lounge and bar with a small dance floor and band, and a well-stocked library. The restaurant operates on an open-seating plan for breakfast and lunch and assigned seating for dinner. Meals are prepared with high-quality ingredients. Additional amenities include a sauna, small fitness room, and a heated outdoor swimming pool, usable for polar bear types in cold-weather conditions, with a pool bar and awnings covering 60 percent of the deck.

All cabins, arranged in four categories, are outside and measure a standard 149 square feet. They have a sitting and bedroom area, large panoramic windows or portholes, and private bath. Eighteen cabins have private verandas. All cabins are fitted with closed-circuit television, satellite telephone, writing desk, a moderate amount of closet space for a casual cruise, and a stocked minibar; bathrooms have a hair dryer and bathrobes. In addition to the cabin amenities, suites have a large, comfortable entertaining area and separate sleeping area with twin beds convertible to queen. All cabins have a special niche for keeping personal expedition gear and a warming drawer for drying wet clothing.

The *Bremen,* besides cruising for the German market, is often chartered for worldwide cruising by American special-interest and alumni groups, among whom her reputation is high.

ITINERARIES *See* Itinerary Index.

C Columbus (205/420; GERMAN INTERNATIONAL; 473 FT./14,903 TONS)

The *C Columbus* is marketed to North Americans only for two or three Great Lakes cruises in the late summer and early fall. When built in 1997, her design included bridge wings that swivel inward to allow the ship to enter the extremely deep lock chambers in the Welland Canal linking Lakes Erie and Ontario. These bilingual cruises, but with German-speaking passengers in the majority, offer English-language printed materials, entertainment, enrichment programs, and shore excursions. Currently, the *Columbus* is the only oceangoing cruise ship plying these waters.

Cabins are of moderate size, with some inside and only two with balconies. Colorfully decorated public rooms include a forward observation lounge, adjacent to the buffet and used for breakfast, lunch, and afternoon tea seating; a sprawling, low-ceiling main lounge for lectures and cabaret shows; a cozy corner wine bar; a library with mostly German-language books; and several small gallery lounges ideal for daytime reading.

The restaurant operates with one fixed seating, and while the menu does not feature the same level of gourmet dishes as on the *Europa,* the quality of the ingredients is of the same fine standard. The menu is international with a German specialty—venison, wild boar, and wild duck are offered every night. German selections also appear at breakfast—herring, meats, and cheese—in the buffet. An Octoberfest with free beer takes place at picnic tables around the lido pool once every cruise.

ITINERARIES *See* Itinerary Index.

Hanseatic (92/184; GERMAN/INTERNATIONAL; 403 FT./8,378 TONS)

A small ship offering adventure-in-luxury cruises, *Hanseatic* was launched in 1993 as one of the most luxurious, technologically advanced adventure-cruise vessels afloat, and at the time set a new level of luxury for adventure cruises. The small ship offers a high crew-to-passenger ratio and amenities typical of small luxury ships. Her rich wood, brass interiors, and fine appointments create the atmosphere of a private yacht.

Hanseatic is said to be one of the most environmentally friendly cruise ships ever built, with a nonpolluting water disposal system, a pollution-filtered incinerator, and full biological treatment plant. The sleek vessel, designated "1A Super Ice" class—the highest rating for a passenger vessel—can carry passengers into the far reaches of the Arctic and Antarctica, while her shallow draft, small size, and maneuverability enable her to penetrate deep into the Amazon and other areas inaccessible to most cruise ships.

The *Hanseatic* has six passenger decks with public rooms on all of them. The reception area and all-purpose **Explorer's Lounge** is on Explorer Deck, the dining room is one flight below on Marco Polo Deck, and the **Columbus Lounge** for casual dining is one flight up on Bridge Deck. **Darwin Hall,** the lecture hall, is located on the lowest deck.

Topside, the Observation Deck is a combination sports and sun deck with a small outdoor swimming pool and a glass-enclosed indoor hot tub. The ship has a small health club with exercise equipment, sauna, massage therapy, and a beauty salon. Forward, the **Observation Lounge** with a 180-degree span of windows is the ship's most popular room, where passengers socialize and relax while viewing the passing scene. The lounge has a library, ocean charts, maps, and a radar monitor to follow the progress of the ship. Sometimes, alas, this lounge may be filled with smoke. It is the one place on the ship where smoke is noticeable. Passengers are allowed to smoke in all lounges and restaurants that usually have clearly marked smoking areas.

Hanseatic's all-outside cabins come in six categories and are located on four of the ship's seven decks. All are large (standard average dimension, 236 square feet) with separate sitting areas and large windows. They are furnished with twin or queen beds, writing desk, spacious closets, a flat-screen television and VCR, radio, and a refrigerator restocked daily with soft drinks and water. The marble bathroom has a full-size bathtub, shower, and hair dryer. Some cabins accommodate third/fourth persons. Four deluxe suites have a separate sleeping area, walk-in closets, and a large entertaining area. The suites and eight deluxe cabins on Bridge Deck have butler service. The ship also has a small boutique for gifts and clothing.

The **Marco Polo Dining Room,** an attractive setting with large windows on three sides at the stern, accommodates all passengers at a single, open seating for breakfast and lunch and assigned seating for dinner. Some passengers give the food high marks; most call it uneventful. Casual breakfast and lunch buffet are served in the airy Columbus Lounge with an indoor/outdoor seating—weather permitting. At night on select evenings, the Columbus Lounge is transformed into the intimate, reservations-only (no extra charge) "Ethno Restaurant" and serve a fixed menu with a regional theme related to the area of cruising. Daily in the Explorer's Lounge, an English tea is served with piano background music. Room service offers in-cabin dining.

Life aboard is casual, unregimented, and leisurely paced, with none of the organized activity that typifies mainstream cruise ships. Every cruise has lecturers, who might include naturalists, marine biologists, geologists, zoologists, research scientists, or anthropologists. They make daily presentations with films and slides and accompany shore excursions, acting as guides; and in the late afternoon, they recap the day's visit. Four tenders and 14 Zodiac landing craft take passengers ashore, from the Far North or the Galapagos to Antarctica. Parkas and rubberized boots are issued gratis to all passengers on Arctic and Antarctic voyages; snorkel equipment is provided in the tropics.

Hanseatic cruises are designed for passengers seeking off-the-beaten-path voyages in comfort. Her passengers are small-ship devotees, affluent, 50+ in age, adventurous, interested in natural history, and committed to preserving the environment. They are independent, active, seasoned travelers accustomed to luxury and quality. The ship globe-trots throughout the year. Although most of her cruises are light adventures, many entail considerable walking, wet landings, and climbing in and out of Zodiacs in remote areas. Anyone with physical limitations or health problems should not underestimate the difficulties they could encounter. The Antarctica itineraries involve traversing the Drake Channel, a notoriously rough stretch of water. Often, this ship is on charter to an American cruise line or group.

ITINERARIES *See* Itinerary Index.

Hebridean Island Cruises
Griffin House, Broughton Hall, Skipton, North Yorkshire, United Kingdom BD23 3AN; ☎ 011-44-1756-704-704 or 800-659-2648; fax 011-44-1756-704-794; www.hebridean.co.uk

Hebridean Princess (30/49; BRITISH/SCOTTISH/38; 235 FT./1,420 TONS)

Built in 1964 to carry 600 passengers, the ship was redesigned in 1994 to carry only 47 passengers in the style of a deluxe country inn. Accommodations vary from singles with shared facilities to suites. The ship has a lounge, restaurant, library of books and videos, and shop. She visits lochs, estuaries, and Scotland's Inner and Outer Hebrides islands on 3- to 14-night cruises from March to November, usually departing from the West Highlands port of Oban. Prices start at £690 for a three-night Highland cruise.

ITINERARIES *See* Itinerary Index.

Hebridean Spirit (49/80; BRITISH/SCOTTISH/72; 300 FT./4,200 TONS)

In 2000, Hebridean Island cruises bought the *MegaStar Capricorn* from Star Cruises, Asia's largest cruise line, and renamed her *Hebridean Spirit.* She was given a $4.7 million renovation and redesigned to accommodate 79 guests (down from 114 passengers) in a style similar to the *Hebridean Princess.* The crew of 72 (for a maximum of 80 passengers) includes seven chefs! Even her superstructure has been "aged" to give the ship the style and outline of ships from the "golden era of cruising."

The 49 cabins, decorated in a classical English yet contemporary style, include 18 singles (no supplementary charge). Each cabin has a sitting area and is decorated individually and named after familiar places. They have marble bathrooms with full tub and shower, a large or walk-in closet, and a tea and coffee maker. Eight cabins have balconies, and there are two suites.

The ocean-going vessel has enabled Hebridean Island to cruise in new waters and to offer itineraries for north European and Mediterranean destinations in summer, and from the Greek Islands through the Red Sea and the Indian Ocean to Sri Lanka in winter, on weekly cruises and normally with no repetition of ports of call. Passengers' departure points are reached by private charter to and from London. Prices for an eight-night Mediterranean cruise start at £3,915 per person for a single cabin and £3,500 per person double, and include air travel, transfers, entrance fees to attractions, house wine, shore excursions, meals, gratuities, and port or passenger taxes. Brits account for 84 percent of the line's passengers, with 50 percent repeaters.

ITINERARIES *See* Itinerary Index.

Kristina Cruises
Kirkkokatu 16, 48100 Kotka, Finland; ☎ 358-5-211-4230; fax 358-5-211-4500; www.kristinacruises.com

Kristina Cruises, the Finland-based shipping company, has more than 50 years' experience in the cruise business. Today, the second generation of the Partanen family heads the company and operates two cruise ships.

Kristina Regina **(119/245; FINNISH/55; 327 FT./4,295 TONS)**

The ship, which has a receptive audience among well-traveled Americans, sails on multi-length on itineraries that visit West Africa, the Mediterranean, the Baltic region, and Iceland. In spring of 2001, she underwent a million-dollar renovation. She has an English-speaking staff, several bars and lounges, library, health center, sauna laundry, and sun decks. Dining is at one seating; menus vary. Her small size enables her to dock within walking distance of town centers.

Kristina Brahe **(57/137; FINNISH/24; 186 FT./1,105 TONS)**

Regina's sister ship, in summer of 2003, inaugurated cruises on the route of the Russian Czars between the Finnish archipelago and Lake Saimaa, taking passengers to the destinations westbound from Helsinki through the Finnish Archipelago National Park and different outer islands. The eastbound cruise leads through the Saimaa canal to Lappeenranta and on the Saimaa to Savonlinna, a town noted for its opera festival. These cruises won the Scandinavian Travel Award in 2004.

ITINERARIES *See* Itinerary Index.

Lindblad Expeditions
(See Part Three, Cruising Alternatives, Adventure and Cultural Cruises)

MSC Cruises
6750 N. Andrews Avenue, Fort Lauderdale, FL 33309; ☎ 800-666-9333 or 954-772-6262; fax 954-776-5881; www.msccruises.com

Part of a Swiss group operating a global fleet of 210 container ships and 36 fast ferries, Mediterranean Shipping Company acquired three cruise ships in less than four years and in the past year added another four ships, including the purchase of two ships of bankrupt First European (Festival) Cruises. That increased its fleet from three to seven ships almost overnight and launched the line's bid to be a major player in Europe and North America. To underscore the latter, the line expanded its presence in North America with new offices in Fort Lauderdale and hired one of the cruise industry's best-known executives, Rick Sasso, to head up the operation.

One of the largest cruise lines in the Mediterranean, the firm also sails to South Africa and South America. With Italian staff and ambience, the ships offer classic cruises with good food and service. MSC is aiming for a mix of 85 percent American and 15 percent international passengers when its two Florida-based ships sail the Caribbean, and the reverse of those percentages in Europe. Onboard, MSC is making changes to appeal to American tastes. For example, prices are in dollars rather than euros; cabin television carries CNN and American movies; breakfast and lunch buffets offer choices that American passengers prefer, and a new alternative dinner service is soon to be available.

Armonia (783/1566; ITALIAN/INTERNATIONAL; 824 FT./58,625 TONS)

Lirica (795/1,590; ITALIAN/INTERNATIONAL; 763 FT./59,058 TONS)

Opera (878/1,756; ITALIAN/INTERNATIONAL; 763 FT./59,058 TONS)

Sinfonia (783/1,566; ITALIAN/INTERNATIONAL; 824 FT./58,600 TONS)

The first of MSC's newships, the *Lirica* (or "Lyric" in English), built by the French shipyard Chantiers de L'Atiantique, made her debut in 2003, with actress Sophia Loren doing the christening honors. *Lirica* was followed by her similar sister ship, *Opera,* in the spring of 2004, the first phase of the line's expansion plans. The ships are powered by a technically advanced propulsion system to reduce engine noise and increase comfort levels.

Among their amenities, the new ships each have two swimming pools, a fully equipped gym and jogging track, two hot tubs, and a sauna. They are equipped with a **Virtual Reality Center** and an Internet cafe with 16 terminals. Each ship has a disco and theater with shows nightly, a supervised **Mini Club** for children, and a shopping gallery.

The nine-passenger-deck ships each have six elevators. Out of 795 cabins, 132 cabins have verandas. There are 387 outside standard cabins, 272 inside standard cabins, and four cabins for disabled passengers. All cabins have satellite television, mini-bar, safe, radio, and 24-hour room service.

Each of the sister ships has two restaurants as well as a grill and pizzeria; they serve authentic Italian cuisine. The staff and crew of the *Lirica* number 760 and of the *Opera* 800.

For the winter season, the ships sail on 7-, 10- and 11-day cruises in the Caribbean and Panama Canal, departing from Fort Lauderdale.

The *Armonia* has many of the same facilities as her sister ships, but her interior architecture is different. She is dedicated to the European and South American market, sailing from Brazil in the winter and the Mediterranean from April to October.

Sinfonia, MSC Cruises'seventh ship, was purchased at auction in Barcelona in 2004 for 220 million euro. The *Sinfonia,* the former *European Stars,* and her sister ship, *Armonia,* were both constructed at Chantiers de l'Atlantique in France. Each ship has a show room, two pools, children's club, dining room, indoor/outdoor restaurant, spa, golf simulator, and conference and Internet center. The *Sinfonia* was launched in 2002 by the now-bankrupt First European (Festival) Cruises; she began sailing for MSC Cruises in March 2005, on seven-night Mediterranean cruises.

ITINERARIES *See* Itinerary Index.

Musica (1,275/3,000; ITALIAN/INTERNATIONAL; 90,000 TONS)

MSC Cruises' newest flagship, *Musica,* under construction at Chantiers de l'Atlantique in France, is scheduled to debut in spring 2006. The Panamax vessel is part of the line's $3 billion expansion program launched in 2003 with the introduction of the *Lirica.* She will be the largest member of the MSC Cruises' fleet, carrying up to 2,550 passengers. In response to guests preference for outside cabins, 85 percent of the cabins are outside accommodations and 65 percent of the total 1,300 passenger cabins have balconies.

Genoa-based De Jorio Design International, designers of the *Lirica* and *Opera,* are creating interiors that blend Art Nouveau and Art Deco geometric 1930s designs with high-tech and contemporary styles, along with Italian design for which MSC Cruises is known. Taking the name of the ship as a key, one of the ship's highlights is a three-deck waterfall in the central foyer, where guests will be entertained by a piano suspended, by means of a clear crystal floor, above a pool of luminous water.

Other features will be a three-deck show lounge for 1,200 passengers; another lounge that can be used as a theater, concert room, and conference room; a music hall equipped for orchestras and cabaret performances, and dancing; a panoramic disco complete with plasma screens; a well-equipped stage in the pool area; and locations throughout the ship for musical performances such as small jam sessions and karaoke.

Dining venues include an elegant panoramic **Garden Restaurant,** with columns and frescoed ceilings; a sushi bar with a Zen garden; a self-service pizzeria; and a large grill cafeteria. Bars and lounges are numerous and varied: **Cyber Cigar Room, Wine Tasting Bar, Piano Bar,** and **Cozy Bar** for an after-dinner aperitif or cappuccino; a 46-foot-long bar in the casino; and a **Well-Being and Fitness Center Bar** in the spa.

Musica has two large swimming pools, a wading pool, four hot tubs, shopping mall, card room, library, art gallery, home cinema/conference room, virtual games room, children's playroom, hair salon, tennis and volleyball court, minigolf and golf training, and a jogging track.

Musica is expected to sail in the Caribbean and Mediterranean waters. Her sister ship is scheduled to be delivered in 2007, and the line has an option for a third new ship.

ITINERARIES *See* Itinerary Index.

Melody (549/1,076; ITALIAN/INTERNATIONAL/535; 671 FT./35,143 TONS)

Formerly the *Star/Ship Atlantic* of Premier Cruise Lines, *Melody* was acquired in 1997 by MSC. She has several lounges, a showroom, piano bar, disco, casino, fitness center, two outdoor pools, and beauty salon. Cabins are moderate in size and have radio, direct-dial telephone, and private bathrooms. The ship is scheduled to have a major renovation, including adding cabins with balconies.

ITINERARIES *See* Itinerary Index.

Monterey (290/576; ITALIAN/INTERNATIONAL/200; 563 FT./20,046 TONS)

Built in 1952 and refurbished in 1991 and 1997, *Monterey* underwent her most extensive upgrade yet in 2004. She once belonged to Matson Line and sailed for Aloha Pacific Cruises. The steam-operated vessel has been well maintained and is a pleasant older ship with a fine style and a friendly crew. She complies with new safety requirements. The classic Art Deco vessel gleams with brass and polished mirrors and has two swimming pools, fitness center with two whirlpools, sauna, hospital, library, beauty salon, boutiques, casino, disco, and two elevators. The attractive dining room offers two seatings. Cabins on the top three decks are large and have private bathrooms. Disabled-accessible cabins are available. Most passengers are middle-income Italian and British, age 55 and older. She sails on 11-night cruises in the Mediterranean from spring to fall.

ITINERARIES *See* Itinerary Index.

Rhapsody (384/850; ITALIAN/250; 541 FT./16,852 TONS)

Built in 1977 as *Cunard Princess, Rhapsody* was first refurbished in 1995 after purchase by MSC, and once again in 1997. Facilities include a swimming pool, whirlpool, fitness center, conference room, library, cafe, bars, casino, video arcade, cinema, beauty and barber shops, and medical center. Two elevators and dry cleaning services are available. A comfortable ship enhanced by a friendly atmosphere, she offers international cuisine with an Italian emphasis. Passengers dine in the window-lined **Meridian Dining Room** at two seatings. In her most recent renovation, the original buffet area was replaced by an extensive indoor/outdoor casual dining area. Cabins are small with limited storage space and thin walls; all have private bathrooms. Passengers are middle-income Europeans older than age 50. They tend to be smokers. *Rhapsody* spends summer in northern Europe and the fall in the Mediterranean.

ITINERARIES *See* Itinerary Index.

P&O Cruises

Mountbatten House, Grosvenor Square, Southampton S0152BF, United Kingdom; ☎ 023-8065-6652; fax 023-8065-6502; www.pocruises.com

P&O Cruises stems from the original steamship company founded in 1837, whose principal routes served the British empire from India to New Zealand. In 1974, P&O Cruises purchased Princess Cruises, and through it had a big impact on modern cruising, particularly on the U.S. West Coast market.

The introduction of the *Oriana* in 1995, P&O Cruises' first brand-new ship in more than two decades, signaled the start of a modern era for the cruise line, replacing her old ships and building new ships designed for British passengers. *Oriana*'s sister, *Aurora,* was delivered in 2000 with even more new features. In 2003, the *Oceana,* formerly the *Ocean Princess* of Princess Cruises, joined the fleet. The line's recent addition is *Arcadia,* to be followed by the new *Artemis.* In 2003, P&O Cruises, along with Princess Cruises and the company's other cruise lines, were bought by Carnival Corporation after an intensive bidding war with Royal Caribbean Cruises.

P&O's cruises are moderately priced, classic cruises and offer worldwide itineraries. Their British style cannot be overemphasized; it's what P&O passengers want. The atmosphere is very social, helped by friendly British officers who mingle with passengers and host tables at dinner, a popular feature. The ships are well organized, aboard and ashore, with excellent programs that include outstanding lecturers on port history and culture, classical pianists, afternoon teas, Sunday religious services (Anglican) with a passenger-staff choir, and nighttime entertainment. The dress code tends to be dressier than on similar ships catering to Americans. Men wear jacket and tie on most nights at sea and on formal evenings they wear tuxedos or dinner jackets, and women don cocktail and long dresses.

P&O focuses generally on three programs: cruises departing from Southampton, those based in the Caribbean in winter, and annual around-the-world voyages. Most passengers are British, of all ages and incomes. Americans, Australians, and New Zealanders are a sizable minority on around-the-world voyages.

Arcadia **(984/1,952; BRITISH/INTERNATIONAL; 952 FT./83,000 TONS)**

Aurora **(939/1,874; BRITISH/INDIAN AND EUROPEAN; 886 FT./76,000 TONS)**

Oriana **(914/2,016; BRITISH/INDIAN AND EUROPEAN; 853 FT./69,153 TONS)**

The *Oriana* is big and beautiful. New and modern, she nonetheless has the design and decor of a classic liner with traditional oil paintings, historic documents, and ship models on the walls. Interiors are as fine and refined as tea in a British parlor. No flashy neon or glitz here. The ship has an inviting calm and numerous nooks where it's easy to relax, read, write postcards, and let the world go by. It's cruising as it should be.

Aurora, which debuted in 2000, came with new features and a bit more glitz as well as some "firsts" for a ship dedicated primarily to the British market. These include two-deck penthouse suites, four decks of cabins with balconies, and interconnecting family cabins. She also had P&O's first 24-hour bistro-style restaurant, coffee and chocolate bar, champagne bar, tea- and coffee-making facilities in all cabins, a retractable dome over one swimming pool, and a virtual-reality center. Her four-deck atrium has a waterfall and Lalique glass–style sculpture, and is surrounded by shops and a tour desk.

The size and spaciousness of these ships allow for a variety of public rooms and entertainment facilities, as well as some larger public rooms enabling passengers of all types to find comfortable and familiar surroundings. Vast amounts of open deck call to British sun worshippers and those who take a daily "constitutional" walks.

Oriana's cabins are spacious and more luxurious than on previous P&O ships and come in a wide range of configurations with ample storage space. The ship has 114 singles—an unusual feature for today's superliner. Almost all cabins, including suites, are on the three middle decks. *Aurora*'s cabin choices are even wider, and range from two-deck penthouse suites to interconnecting cabins suitable for families. Over 40 percent of the cabins, including some standard ones, have balconies. Cabins on both ships have tea- and coffee-makers, safe, refrigerator, television, direct-dial telephone, air-conditioning, and music system; some have bathtubs, hair dryers, and minibars.

Two main restaurants offer two sittings for three meals. The cuisine is very British: lots of meat and potatoes and sauces, excellent soups but few salads. The **Conservatory** on Lido Deck, with indoor/outdoor seating, serves a buffet breakfast and lunch. The area can become very crowded at peak lunch hours.

The ships' elaborate activities programs ranges from bingo and crafts to bridge and dance classes. Port lecturers are very knowledgeable and generally have a dry, British sense of humor. They wouldn't dream of giving the shopping sales pitch heard on many Caribbean cruise ships. The comfortable library is well supplied.

Public rooms spread over two main decks offer a variety of atmospheres catering to class-conscious Brits. Many reflect in name and style the company's 165-year history, such as classical music in the elegant **Curzon Room,** cabaret in the **Pacific Lounge,** and large production show in **Theatre Royal.** There's **Lord's Tavern,** a cricket-themed pub; and the spacious **Crow's Nest** observation bar and lounge, with wraparound windows and a trio playing dance music before and after dinner. **Monte Carlo Casino** is small, compared with casinos on big ships sailing the Caribbean.

On *Aurora*, a West End–style theater has the latest production technology, and the new-concept main show lounge comes with a spacious bar, large dance floor, and retractable stage. Amidships is an intimate, futuristic nightclub with small dance floor and stage. One deck above, a large concert hall/cinema shows first-run films and stages concerts; there's also a business center with computers.

Activities on *Oriana*'s vast open decks include deck tennis, quoits, shuffleboard, golf nets, and trapshooting. Cricket matches between passengers and officers are popular. One of two adult pools is a generous 42 feet long.

Passengers take daily walks on a wide promenade sprinkled with deck chairs shaded by lifeboats. A large spa offers aerobics, a gym, whirlpools, sauna, massage, beauty and therapy rooms, and a hair salon.

On *Aurora,* a pool between decks 11 and 12 has a waterfall and is surrounded by tiered decks. Another pool can be covered by a dome in inclement weather; still another is reserved for families at certain times of year. A netted deck area is adaptable for cricket, soccer, and tennis, and golfers can practice on the golf simulator. A well-equipped gym and aerobics studio overlook the forward pool. The spacious area is linked by stairs to health and beauty facilities.

P&O's children's program is highly praised. In peak times, four age-specific areas have separate, supervised well-designed programs; two age groups are used at other times. Children have their own pool and lido area, and they eat at an early sitting, with or without their parents. A staffed night nursery is available for children under age 5 and cabins have baby "listening" facilities.

Arcadia, which was scheduled to join the fleet in 2005, will be the largest ship in the fleet. She will be "children-free" and dedicated exclusively to British passengers. Among her spacious public rooms, the 11-passenger-deck ship has array of dining options, a three-tier theatre, 12 bars, nightclub, coffee and chocolate bar, spa with a thermal suite and hydrotherapy pool, an outdoor pool, five Jacuzzis, and an indoor/outdoor swimming pool with retractable dome, shops, casino, library, an observation lounge with panoramic views, Cyb@study, hair salon, art gallery, touch-screen photo gallery, and 14 passenger elevators, including two panoramic glass ones on the sides of the ship.

More than two-thirds of the cabins on the British registered ship have balconies. **The Belvedere,** a food court so named because it commands fine views, offers informal dining around the clock with a wide choice of menus, from Oriental and Italian to bistro-style dishes and a delicatessen counter. Light and airy, the decor has a soft, calm Japanese theme and is furnished with outside seating for dining alfresco. There is a two-tier main restaurant, and the ship's specialty restaurant, **Arcadian Rhodes,** is the creation of Gary Rhodes, one of Britain's best-known chefs noted for his innovative take on contemporary British cuisine. Rhodes has created the menu and several signature dishes for the restaurant.

ITINERARIES *See* Itinerary Index.

Oceana (1,008/2,016; BRITISH; 856 FT./77,000 TONS)

Oceana (formerly *Ocean Princess*) joined the P&O fleet in fall 2003. She was part of Princess Cruises' Sun Princess group. (For a description of these ships, see Princess Cruises earlier in Part Two.)

ITINERARIES *See* Itinerary Index.

Artemis (520/1,196; BRITISH/INTERNATIONAL; 757 FT./45,000 TONS)

The *Artemis* (the former *Royal Princess*), which joined P&O Cruises in spring 2005, was launched in 1984 and christened by Diana, Princess of Wales.

Both made an indelible mark on the 1980s. At the time, *Artemis* was the most expensive passenger ship ever built. Her sleek lines and tapered bow looked traditional, but she had so many innovations inside that she was called revolutionary and set new standards in passenger comfort for the cruise ships that followed.

Artemis was the first cruise ship to have all outside cabins, and television with remote control, minifridge, and full bathroom with tub and shower in all cabins. She was first to have verandas in all suites, deluxe cabins, and even in some lesser categories; and large windows instead of portholes in every category. The ship, with nine passenger decks, has two acres of open teak decks, three swimming pools, and a fully equipped spa. Her decor is refined. Interiors are defined less by walls than by art, sculpture, glass with brass railings, and live plants. The varnished wood hand rails are a rarity today. Muted colors and abundant windows create openness throughout the ship.

Artemis's layout is unusual. Most public rooms are on the two lower levels, and virtually all cabins are on upper decks. A large foyer on the lower Plaza Deck spans two decks—the first shipboard atrium, perhaps. This greenery-filled area is dominated by a large David Norris sculpture consisting of a bronze spiral with seagulls rising over rocks. A dramatic staircase with glass balustrade curves in two wings upward to a balcony with piano lounge overlooking the foyer; it is a gathering spot where passengers enjoy prelunch or predinner drinks, entertained by a pianist-vocalist. This deck also holds the main showroom, cabaret-style lounge, casino, boutique, card room, and a theater. The ship has six elevators.

Artemis's cabins are all outside and spacious, and each with picture windows, a tiled bathroom with tub and shower, retractable clothesline, mirrored medicine-cabinet door, minifridge, safe, multifunction phone, television and four-channel music radio, and door key cards. High quality interiors and attention to detail are reflected in a large dressing table with makeup lights and mirrors, an easy-to-reach hair dryer, ample drawers, and large closets. In many cabins, a twin bed folds into a wall, providing extra sitting space by day. Some cabins have obstructed views, indicated on the deck plan.

Suites and cabins with verandas are very roomy; the outside deck accommodates a small table and chair; some have a chaise lounge. The two largest suites have separate sitting and dining rooms, Jacuzzi bathtub, separate bedroom with queen bed, and large veranda. Minisuites are similar, but they don't have walls between bedrooms and sitting areas. Self-service launderettes offer washers, dryers, irons, and ironing boards at no charge. There are 600 outside cabins (150 with verandas, including 52 minisuites, 12 suites, 2 deluxe suites); standard dimensions, 168 square feet. Some cabins accommodate a third person and there are ten wheelchair-accessible cabins.

The warm, pleasant **Continental Dining Room** has a raised perimeter level delineated with brass railings. Small islands of round tables break up the space, provide privacy, and help lower the noise level and allow easy conversation. Senior dining staff is Italian and very attentive. The **Lido Café** is an indoor/outdoor café with tile-topped tables, which serves an informal buffet breakfast, lunch, and snacks.

The show lounge has seats tiered in a semi-circular fashion; sight lines are generally good, except from the back. There are several other lounges offering entertainment and playing dance music every evening, as well as a casino.

A cluster of five small pools is the centerpiece of the Lido Deck, the main outdoor recreation area. On Sun Deck, passengers sunbathe on a raised platform, play table tennis and shuffleboard, swim in one of cruising's largest lap pools, and exercise in the spa. The fitness complex has a gym with state-of-the-art equipment, sauna and massage rooms, and a large whirlpool. Joggers and walkers circle the wraparound teak promenade (four laps equal one mile). The spa and beauty salon offers hair and body treatments.

From the time of her launch, this classy ship was admired by competitors as much as her owners. Like fine wine, she has mellowed nicely.

ITINERARIES *See* Itinerary Index.

Peter Deilmann Cruises
1800 Diagonal Road, Suite 170, Alexandria, VA 22314; ☎ 703-549-1741 or 800-348-8287; fax 703-549-7924; www.deilmann-cruises.com

Peter Deilmann Cruises' *Deutschland,* launched in 1998, was built in the Art Nouveau and Art Deco style of grand ocean liners of the past as a traditional luxury liner in the grand European style. She has three restaurants and a promenade deck and accommodates 513 passengers in a variety of mostly outside staterooms. The ship, because of its name, is renowned in Germany, and the majority of the passengers are from German-speaking countries. But it also attracts different nationalities, including up to 20 percent from England, Canada, and the United States, especially on Mediterranean cruises. In addition to German food, the menu includes selections reflecting the cuisine of each port of call. Underscoring Deilmann's effort to appeal to Americans, hamburgers and brats are available on the Lido Deck each day for lunch. There's also a wealth of vegetarian dishes. There are two seatings for dinner in the **Berlin Restaurant,** the ship's main dining salon. The wait staff are especially friendly and the service is excellent in this plush dining venue. An alternative gourmet restaurant, the **Four Seasons,** requires advance reservations. Both intimate and quiet, the Four Seasons serves as many as six courses at a leisurely pace (dinner is routinely a two- to three-hour affair). A buffet on the Lido Deck offers breakfast, lunch, and dinner, and frequently offer dishes from the menu of the main dining salon. In the **Lili Marleen** lounge, nightly music varies. The mainstay is American pop and oldies, occasionally punctuated by special classical recitals. The **Old Fritz Pub,** a cozy wood-paneled bar, opens to additional seating outdoors. Entertainment here features a singing pianist playing German, French, and American standards and pop. The two-story **Emperor's Ballroom** serves as the ship's theater and primary dance venue. Though English is as common as German in the lounges, German is king in the ballroom. Shows range from Las Vegas–style production shows to classical concerts to stand-up comics (totally incomprehensible to non-German speakers).

Cabins on the *Deutschland* feature polished burl walnut paneling and pastel yellow softgoods. Well designed bathrooms in Italian marble are unusually spacious, but for the most part offer showers only. Amenities include a radio and color television, a minifridge, two armed chairs and a table, a desk, robes, a hair dryer, and for outside cabins, a medium to large picture window.

The *Deutschland* provides a small but adequate fitness center and a full-service spa. Although a notable array of outdoor activities are available, there is no place on board to run or jog. On another sour note, the swimming pool is saltwater.

Announcements are conducted in German. When there are enough English speaking passengers to warrant it, announcements are repeated in English. There are many English-speaking staff members aboard; cabin crews are often from eastern Europe and speak English rather than German. Passengers get news and daily activity reports in English or German. English-language shore excursions are offered in a package at up to 50 percent discount when prepurchased. (For Peter Deilmann River Cruises, designed for English-speaking passengers as well as European ones, see Part Three, Cruising Alternatives.)

ITINERARIES *See* Itinerary Index.

SeaDream Yacht Club
2601 South Bayshore Drive; Penthouse 1B, Coconut Grove, FL 33133-5417; ☎ 800-707-4911; www.seadreamyachtclub.com

---

SeaDream I/SeaDream II (55/110 SCANDINAVIAN/ INTERNATIONAL/89; 344 FT./4,260 TONS)

SeaDream Yacht Club, a venture of Seabourn Cruise Line veterans, Norwegian entrepreneur Atle Brynestad, who was Seabourn's founder, and Larry Pimentel, its former president, began operating in late 2001 and early 2002, offering seven-day summer Mediterranean and winter Caribbean cruises on the luxury twin ships *SeaDream I* and *II* (formerly *Sea Goddess I* and *II*). The twin megayachts, as the line calls them, were redesigned and refitted at Lloyd Werft's shipyard in Bremerhaven, Germany, prior to their entering service.

The handsome twins are meant to provide a totally different experience from today's typical cruise, one that more closely resembles yachting. Like yachts, the ships offer an open and unstructured ambience and provide passengers the ability to move at their own pace and to make personal choices. "No clocks, no crowds, no lines, no stress" could be the company's motto.

These are the SeaDream differences the owners cite:

- **Flexible Schedules and Itineraries** *SeaDream's* yachts depart their first port and arrive at their last port as scheduled, but the port calls in between are not run by a strict timetable. Captains have the authority to adjust for local opportunities. If they want to visit a small island fish market so the chef can pick up the catch of the day, that's fine. If the weather and the snorkeling are perfect in a small secluded bay and passengers want to remain longer, that's okay, too.

- **Overnight in Key Ports** Most cruise ships arrive at ports of call at about 8 a.m. and sail at 5 or 6 p.m. of the same day. *SeaDream* yachts overnight at such ports as Monte Carlo and St. Tropez, where the action doesn't even get started until late in the evening.

- **Officers and Staff as Guides** Passengers might visit a small town pastry shop with the chef, go snorkeling with the captain, or go hiking, biking, or golfing with the officers. What better guides to have, *SeaDream* says, than those who know their sailing regions like the backs of their hands?

- **No Tuxedos or Gala Gowns** *SeaDream* has no dress code; rather it stresses the casual nature of yachting.

The outdoor features of *SeaDream I* and *II* include alcoves for sunning on double sun beds, a private massage tent on deck, a large-screen golf simulator that can also be used to watch sports events or movies, and a water sports marina at the stern where there is equipment for kayaking, water skiing, windsurfing, wave running, snorkeling, and Sunfish sailing. Tai chi, yoga, and aerobics classes are also offered.

Indoors, passengers have an Asian-style spa with fitness center with elliptical treadmills mounted with flat-screen televisions, as well as free weights, and recumbent bikes. A personal trainer is available. The ships also have a **Main Lounge** with a 61-inch, flat-screen television, a piano bar, casino, and a library with books, CDs, DVDs, and computer outlets. Laptop computers are available. Passengers are given their own onboard e-mail address.

Each ship accommodates from 47 to 55 couples, depending on the configuration. Of the 55 cabins, all but one are Yacht Club–category with 195 square feet. Sixteen of these are convertible to Commodore Club–cabins of 390 square feet with his and her bathroom facilities and a dining area accommodating four. The 450-square-foot Owner's Suite has a bedroom, a bathroom with a tub and separate shower with a view of the sea, a living room and dining area, and a guest bathroom.

All cabins are Internet-ready and have an entertainment center with a flat-screen television, CD and DVD systems with an extensive selection of movies and other offerings, and a personal jukebox with more than 100 digital music programs. All bathrooms have multiple-jet massage showers and lighted magnifying mirrors.

Staff and crew number 89; most have been sailing on their respective ships for several years. The yachts, suitable for small meetings and incentive groups, are available for charter.

ITINERARIES *See* Itinerary Index.

Star Cruises
Ocean Center, 5 Canton Road, Suite 1501, Tsimshatsui, Kowloon, Hong Kong; ☎ 852-2378-2000; fax 852-2314-3809; ☎ 60-3-3101-1313 (Malaysia); www.starcruises.com

Malaysian-based Star Cruises, owned by Genting Group, a publicly traded investment group, is a phenomenon in Far Eastern cruising. Launched in 1993 with two ships, it grew rapidly to a fleet of ten ships despite the Asian financial crisis in 1998. In 2000, it purchased Norwegian Cruise Lines and Orient Lines and their eight ships. Today, Star Cruises commands the bulk of the Asian cruise market. The Star Group, taken as a whole, has 20 ships in service. The Star fleet is now somewhat smaller than in its initial years, having transferred several ships to NCL, and divides into several brands: Star, SuperStar, and Mega-Star, with more under construction or planned.

Star Pisces (780/1020; SCANDINAVIAN/INTERNATIONAL; 581 FT./ 40,053 TONS)

The ship is a former Baltic ferry designed for the regional Asian market. The ship sails on short, one-night cruises from Hong Kong to the South China Sea, catering largely to families and first-time cruisers. The ship is exceedingly well maintained and has no fewer than ten food and beverages options. Child-care facilities are extensive. Activities and entertainment are geared to the whole family, with karaoke, Ping-Pong and other sports, a library, spa, boutiques, and big-name performances. The line earns high marks for its food and incredibly friendly crew.

ITINERARIES *See* Itinerary Index.

SuperStar Gemini (400/800; INTERNATIONAL/470; 538 FT./19,093 TONS)

Built in 1992 in Spain for more than $100 million, *SuperStar Gemini* (the former *Crown Jewel*) was the first of the SuperStar group launched in 1995 and offers deluxe, one- to three-night cruises from Port Klang (Malaysia) and Singapore to Southeast Asian ports. She has an inside/outside buffet, several bars and entertainment venues, swimming pool, gym and sauna, shops, Internet room, and children's center.

ITINERARIES *See* Itinerary Index.

SuperStar Virgo (980/1960; INTERNATIONAL/1,100; 879 FT./76,800 TONS)

SuperStar Virgo arrived in 1999. One of the largest and first world-class megaships in the Asia–Pacific market, she set new standards with extensive facilities for those who prefer activity-filled cruises. *SuperStar Virgo* has a high crew-to-passenger ratio of one to two. Dining options include a standard dining room and eight specialty dining venues serving Chinese, Japanese, Indian, Italian, Mediterranean, or international cuisine. Unusual features include a public observation area of the bridge, with videos detailing bridge and engine operations. The ship offers a casino, spa and fitness center, shops, library and Internet facility, a computer center, and children's facilities. The ship's cruising speed is a zippy 25.5 knots, enabling her to include more ports of call on her itineraries. She sails on multinight cruises around Malaysian waters, departing from Singapore.

ITINERARIES *See* Itinerary Index.

MegaStar Aries/MegaStar Taurus (36/72; INTERNATIONAL/ INTERNATIONAL; 270 FT./3,264 TONS)

The *MegaStars* are the most deluxe of Star's brands. Formerly *Aurora I* and *II*, the ships were among the most luxurious small ships built in the 1990s. The ships each carry only 72 passengers and 80 crew members and operate short cruises year-round from Malaysia, Singapore, and Kuala Lumpur. They are most often chartered to corporations, groups, or wedding parties.

ITINERARIES *See* Itinerary Index.

Swan Hellenic Cruises
631 Commack Road, Suite 1A, Commack, NY 11725; ☎ 631-858-1263 or 877-800-7926; fax 631-858-1279; www.swanhellenic.com

Swan Hellenic, which was owned by P&O Line and now, by Carnival Corporation as a result of the latter's purchase of P&O/Princess Cruises, has a large following in the United States as well as the United Kingdom, Australia, and Canada. The line caters to travelers (most age 50 or older) who are intellectually curious and interested in the art and culture of destinations they visit.

Minerva II (342/600; BRITISH/EUROPEAN; 594 FT./30,277 TONS)

Swan Hellenic's new ship, *Minerva II,* was launched in April 2003. The ship originally debuted in 2001 as the *R8* of the now-defunct Renaissance Cruises. She is Swan Hellenic's most luxurious ship to date, with the most modern facilities and amenities, although she has been given many country house-style touches to fit Swan Hellenic's image.

Minerva II's outstanding features include 93 percent outside cabins, of which 73 percent have private balconies. There also is a range of single cabins at affordable prices. Open seating dining in four restaurants with a wide choice of cuisine is also available. The ship has three bars, a library, spa facilities and fitness center, and an outdoor swimming pool with a hot tub. She offers a choice of venues for classical music recitals and other activities, such as art classes, tai chi, and music and dance performances by local groups.

The ship is able to visit a wider range of destinations than its predecessor ship, thanks to its increased speed. Itineraries continue to focus on well-known as well as off-the-beaten-track places, with a team of guest speakers (the latest tour book devotes six full pages to descriptions of guest speakers) on each cruise and a wide choice of excursions at ports of call. Prices include excursions and all tips. In 2004, the ship made Swan Hellenic's first trip to Central America, departing from New Orleans, as well as to South America and the Amazon, the Bahamas, and the eastern seaboard of the United States and Canada. These voyages were slated to be repeated in 2005 and 2006, along with new cruises of Belize, Costa Rica, the Panama Canal, and the U.S. West Coast, as well as India and the Mediterranean. The cruise line offers substantial early-bird savings, particularly for those booking two consecutive cruises.

ITINERARIES *See* Itinerary Index.

Travel Dynamics International
**132 East 70th Street, Suite 1501, New York, NY 10021;
☎ 212-517-7555 or 800-257-5767; fax 212-774-1545; www.traveldynamicsinternational.com**

The former Classical Cruises has been folded into its owner's operation, Travel Dynamics International, a long-established incentive-travel company. As in the past, the company continues to specialize in educational and cultural cruises, using a variety of well-known deluxe and luxury ships. Programs are designed for well-traveled, destination-oriented individuals who want a learning experience but don't want to forgo comfort. Itineraries span the globe and include exotic as well as familiar destinations. Lecturers and academics knowledgeable about the destination accompany the cruises. The company usually uses such ships as described below.

Callisto (17/34; GREEK/EUROPEAN/18; 164 FT./435 TONS)

This small luxury yacht, built in Germany, underwent comprehensive renovation and refurbishment prior to her debut in 2000. The ship has 17 outside cabins, 11 with large panoramic windows and 6 with three large portholes each; a spacious lounge, a dining room accommodating all passengers at one open seating, and alfresco dining on two decks. There is piano bar, two broad decks for sunbathing, a swimming platform at the vessel's stern, and a gym. All cabins are air-conditioned and have full- or queen-sized beds, marble bath, radio, telephone, refrigerator, and television with VCR. The four-deck ship has a draft of eight feet and a speed of 14 knots. It is equipped with Zodiac landing crafts. The bridge is outfitted with state-of-the-art navigational and communications equipment.

Callisto sails to the Greek Islands, Turkey, the Adriatic, Mediterranean, and West Africa. A 12-day cruise of Croatia's Dalmatian coast starts at $6,595 per person double.

ITINERARIES *See* Itinerary Index.

Orion (53/106; GERMAN/EUROPEAN; 337 FT./4,050 TONS)

Billed as a vessel for a new age of exploration cruising, the *Orion,* which made her maiden voyage in 2003, combines the latest advances in ship design and communication technology with the style and comfort of a luxury cruise ship. From her ice-strengthened hull (rated E3, the highest rating available) to the remote viewing cameras atop its mast, no expense was spared in *Orion's* construction.

Built at the Cassens Shipyard in Emden, Germany, *Orion* is a model of German craftsmanship and engineering, with such features as technologically advanced stabilizers, bow and stern thrusters for easy maneuverability, a surround-sound audio system in the lecture hall, and direct Internet access in every cabin.

But it's *Orion's* luxurious accommodations that distinguish her from older, more traditional expedition ships. Each of the 24 standard cabins measures between 175 and 180 square feet, while each of the 29 suites measures from 215 to 345 square feet; eight have French balconies. All cabins are outside; many outside suites and the Grand Suites have a balcony. All cabins include a sitting area or living room, television/DVD and CD player, minifridge, private marble bathroom, ample closet space, and twin beds that can be converted to a queen. Large oval, rectangular, or sliding glass floor-to-ceiling windows offer panoramic views.

Orion's facilities include a spa, sauna, whirlpool, massage services, hairdresser, boutique, several lounges, and a computer center equipped with Internet access. At the center of the ship is a glass atrium that wraps around the elevator and serves *Orion's* seven decks. The **Constellation Restaurant** accommodates all guests at a single unassigned seating; an open deck off the main lounge is available for dining alfresco.

The spacious observation lounge on the top deck opens onto a wraparound deck for optimal viewing. The bridge also leads out to an open observation area. A mud room on the lower deck stores parkas, boots, and other equipment used during and after a day of exploration. Ten heavyduty Zodiac inflatable motorized boats are used for landing in shallow areas and to navigate small waterways. Several two-seater kayaks are available for individual exploration.

Classified with Germanischer Lloyd, *Orion* meets the latest international safety rules and regulations. The ship is served by 70 European officers and crew. She sails to such exotic locales as Easter Island and Polynesia, as well as Antarctica.

Corinthian II (114/57; EUROPEAN/70; 297 FT./4,200 TONS)

The *Corinthian II* is the newest member of Travel Dynamics International's fleet, offering a classic yacht-like atmosphere and fine accommodations. Originally built in 1992 and refurbished in 2004 and 2005, *Corinthian II* accommodates all guests in 57 outside suites, each affording sea views. Suites have a sitting area, television, minifridge, safe, and other amenities, as well as a marble-appointed bathroom. Several suites include private balconies accessed via sliding glass doors.

The *Corinthian II*'s spacious and finely decorated public areas include a library stocked with books related to the itinerary and other volumes. Four computer terminals are accessible for e-mail access. The ship has an elegant lounge as well as **The Club,** a space for relaxation, with picture windows for panoramic views. The restaurant serves fine cuisine prepared by European chefs and can accommodate all guests at a single unassigned seating. Other facilities onboard include a gym, beauty salon, a sun deck with whirlpool, and an outdoor bar and café for alfresco dining. *Corinthian II* has an ice-strengthened hull for voyages into Antarctic waters and is equipped with a fleet of Zodiac inflatable craft for excursions ashore.

ITINERARIES *See* Itinerary Index.

The World/ResidenSea Ltd.

Regent Centre West, Building No. 2, Suite D; P.O. Box F-40967, Freeport, Grand Bahama Island, Bahamas; ☎ 800-970-6601 (North America rentals); ☎ 305-259-5151; fax 305-269-1058; www.residensea.com

---

The World **(88 SUITES, 106 APARTMENTS; 19 STUDIO APARTMENTS; 40 VERANDA STUDIOS; NORWEGIAN/320; 644 FT./43,000 TONS)**

The World, the first residential cruise ship ever built, was launched from Oslo in March 2002 to begin her cruising odyssey and confounded the skeptics (us included), who said it would never happen. Five weeks later, she sailed to America on her maiden voyage.

Billed as the world's first residential resort community at sea continuously circumnavigating the globe, *The World* has 165 residences, most available for rent. A staff of about 250 attends them.

Here's what she offers on her 12 decks: two- and three-bedroom private apartments ranging from 1,100 to 3,242 square feet, with decor by four top designers and fully furnished down to the Christofle flatware and Wedgewood china; four theme restaurants featuring French, Mediterranean, and Asian cuisine, plus a delicatessen; enrichment activities such as lectures and seminars; full-size tennis court; a retractable marina for water activities; two pools; a top-deck, open-air, full-shot driving range, 40-course golf simulators, real grass putting greens, two artificial greens, a sand bunker, and a PGA-certified golf director; a fitness center; the Swiss spa, **Clinique La Prairie;** an art gallery, casino, Internet café, library, two conference rooms, nightclub, meditation chapel, and several boutiques. Oh, yes, and three emergency wards, full-time doctor, and nurse, as well as a telemedicine hookup with Mt. Sinai–Cedars Hospital in Miami Beach. Activities on board are deliberately kept to a minimum, but there are some typical cruise pastimes such as bridge and other games, trivia, lectures, movies, afternoon tea, and enrichment programs.

Passengers enjoy all this while traveling the world: 140 ports in more than 40 countries with planned itineraries of 6 to 17 days, and attending such special events as the Cannes Film Festival, the Grand Prix of Monaco, and the British Open in Scotland. And the price (ah yes, if you have to ask): Apartments ranged from $1.3 million to $7.5 million, with an average price of $2.8 million. And then there's the annual maintenance fee, which includes housekeeping, of $160,000. More than 85 of the 110 apartments were sold before the ship sailed.

Who, you ask, would pay such a price? According to its marketing company, they are homeowners who have two or three residences, are age 55, and are first-generation entrepreneurs who have built their worth as computer-chip makers, real-estate developers, and the like. They are very active, have an affinity with the sea, maybe own a yacht or have cruised a lot, and they guard their privacy.

North Americans constitute the largest number of buyers, followed by Norwegians, Brits, Germans, Australians, and Swiss. Some owners stay aboard for three months a year, just as they would, say, at their condo in Aspen or their villa in the south of France.

The World's promoters say that the ship is for people who hate having to pack a suitcase to travel, who really miss sleeping in their own beds when they're away, and who long to see the world without ever having to leave the comforts of home. It seems such a simple idea that it's surprising no one ever floated it before.

The World operates on an all-inclusive basis: roundtrip economy air transportation, transfers, porterage, port charges, and meals with beverages, including an extensive selection of fine wines and spirits. (No tips, please.)

Recently, the apartment owners bought out the original owners/developers and now they own the ship. ResidenSea Ltd. remains the managing company of *The World*. Rentals can be booked through travel agents or ResidenSea.

ITINERARIES *See* Itinerary Index.

PART THREE

CRUISING ALTERNATIVES

■ RIVER *and* BARGE CRUISES

A RIVER CRUISE IS NOT ONLY a different way to see a country; it's a different country you will see. Whether you sail down the Danube or the Yangtze, up the Hudson or the Nile, or float on European channels or the Erie Canal, the cruise will be a new travel experience, even if you have visited the same area by land.

The river cruise most familiar to U.S. travelers is probably steamboating on the Mississippi, but there are many kinds of river cruises, their character shaped by the location and nature of the waterway. An adventure cruise on the Amazon, for example, is quite different from barging in Burgundy. Nonetheless, river cruises share certain characteristics, and all are light years from an ocean cruise.

To begin with, boats (a vessel is a ship on the ocean, but a boat on a river) offering river cruises are small. Most boats carry 100 to 200 passengers, although some of the new riverboats accommodate 250 or more, and Delta Queen Steamboat Company's *American Queen* takes 436 passengers. Barges that glide along small canals and waterways are much smaller, taking as few as 6 and never more than 24 passengers.

The small size of vessels and the nature of the waterways provide an intimate look at the cruise locale, heightening the sense of place and history in a way oceanliners never can. The destination, not the boat, is the main attraction on a river cruise.

Cabins are small but comfortable. The ambience is informal, the dress casual. Except on some large riverboats, nightly entertainment is absent. Passengers are left to their own devices, and many rediscover the pleasure of conversation and friendship.

RIVER AND BARGE CRUISES IN EUROPE

RIVER CRUISES ARE AVAILABLE on major rivers worldwide, but the largest selection is in Europe on the Rhine, Rhone, Seine, Danube, and Volga, where rivers have been thoroughfares of commerce and culture for centuries.

European cruises—most between April and November—take you to the continent's great cities through beautiful scenery laced with ancient forts, mighty cathedrals, and storybook castles. They dock in the heart of a different town each day. Some river cruise lines include sightseeing tours in their cruise fare. If not, passengers may book optional tours for a fee or they can easily sight-see on their own.

River cruises reveal Europe the way it was meant to be seen. Almost all historic buildings were built facing the river, so when the boat docks in front of Pillnitz Palace on the Elbe, for example, passengers enter the way guests of Augustus the Strong did centuries ago.

Some itineraries overnight in port, allowing passengers to attend local shows or dine ashore. Others sail at night so passengers wake refreshed for the next day of sightseeing.

More than a dozen companies offer such cruises; the largest, Viking River Cruises, is typical in its itineraries. Its fleet of 25 ships sails the length of the Rhine, as well as the Elbe, Moselle, Seine, Saone, and Rhone. The Danube and Rhine-Main-Danube Canal were added in 1994, when the North and Black Seas were linked for the first time.

Riverboats and barges have completely different styles. Canals and smaller rivers deep in the countryside are traversed by barges, which glide gently through some of the most beautiful and historic areas of England and Europe. The pace is so leisurely (three or four miles per hour) that passengers can get off to walk in the woods or bike in the village and not be left behind. The tortoise-like pace, the utter peace and relaxation, are for some the best vacation they ever had. For others, it's like watching grass grow.

By day, passengers lounge on deck, play cards, read, and watch the boat navigate the locks. They can walk or bike, discovering interesting places and friendly people, and reboard at the next lock. The price usually includes a choice of guided tours by minibus or bicycle to nearby castles, wineries, and medieval towns.

Hotel barges, as they are known, are like floating country inns. They vary in size, carrying from 6 to 51 passengers on cruises of 3, 6, or 13 days. Cabins are small and bathrooms are tiny, but the barges, such as those of French Country Waterways, are luxurious. Many serve outstanding gourmet cuisine prepared by Le Cordon Bleu chefs. Regional wines, normally included in the cruise price, flow generously. The atmosphere is very informal—and very romantic.

Dozens of boats and barges cruise Europe. The season runs April through October. Here's a sampling with U.S. offices or representatives. Note that several companies offer the same boats; agreements may not be exclusive.

Note: In parentheses after each boat name is information (where available) about the number of cabins and passengers; officers and crew; and the boat's length (cabins/passengers; officers/crew; boat length).

Abercrombie & Kent Inc.
1520 Kensington Road, Suite 212, Oak Brook, IL 60523-2156;
☎ **630-954-2944 or 800-323-7308; fax 630-954-3324;**
www.abercrombiekent.com

(Also see Abercrombie & Kent under Yangtze River Cruises, Nile River Cruises, and Amazon River Cruises, all later in this chapter.)

Actief **(6/11; BRITISH; 100 FT.)**
Six nights on the upper Thames.

Alouette **(3/6; FRENCH/BRITISH; 98 FT.)**
Six nights in southern Burgundy, Canal du Midi, Provence, and Beaujolais.

Amaryllis **(4/8; FRENCH; 129 FT.)**
Six nights on various routes in France, including Burgundy, Franche-Comte, and Beaujolais.

Anjodi **(4/8; FRENCH; 100 FT.)**
Six nights Canal du Midi, and Provence.

Fleur de Lys **(3/6; FRENCH/BRITISH; 129 FT.)**
Six nights in Burgundy, Franche-Comte, and Beaujolais; for charter only.

Hirondelle **(4/8; FRENCH/BRITISH; 129 FT.)**
Six nights in Burgundy and Franche-Comte.

L'Art de Vivre **(4/8; FRENCH/BRITISH; 100 FT.)**
Six nights in Burgundy and Nivernais.

La Belle Epoque **(6/12; FRENCH/BRITISH; 128 FT.)**
Outdoor spa/pool as well as sauna and fitness area. Six-night cruises in Burgundy and Chablis.

La Bonne Amie **(4/8; FRENCH; 126 FT.)**
Six nights in Alsace-Lorraine.

Le Bon Vivant **(4/8; FRENCH; 126 FT.)**
Six nights in upper Loire.

L'Impressionniste **(6/12; FRENCH; 128 FT.)**
Six nights in Provence, Camargue, and Languedoc.

Libellule **(10/20; BRITISH/FRENCH; 128 FT.)**
Six nights in southern Burgundy and Beaujolais.

Litote **(10/20; BRITISH/FRENCH; 128 FT.)**
Six nights in central Burgundy.

Lorraine (11/22; FRENCH/BRITISH; 128 FT.)
Six nights in Alsace-Lorraine.

Magna Carta (4/8; BRITISH; 117 FT.)
Six nights on the lower Thames.

Marjorie (4/8, FLEMISH; 128 FT.)
Six nights in Holland and northern Burgundy.

Marjorie II (6/12; FLEMISH; 128 FT.)
Six nights Holland, Burgundy, and Chablis.

Napoleon (6/12; FRENCH; 129 FT.)
Six nights on the Saone in Burgundy and Rhone in Provence.

Prosperite (4/8; FRENCH; 128 FT.)
Six nights on the Bourgogne Canal; charter only.

Roi Soleil (3/6; DUTCH; 98 FT.)
Six nights in Provence, Camargue, Languedoc, and Canal du Midi; charter only.

Scottish Highlander (4/8; SCOTTISH; 117 FT.)
Six nights on the Caledonian Canal in the Scottish Highlands.

Shannon Princess II (5/10; IRISH; 105 FT.)
Six nights on the Shannon River in Ireland and Lough Derg.

Avalon Waterways
5301 South Federal Circle, Littleton, CO 80123; ☎ 877-380-1544 or 877-797-8791; www.avalonwaterways.com

Artistry (87, 2 SUITES/178 PASSENGERS)

Poetry (84, 4 SUITES/176 PASSENGERS; CREW OF 43; 426 FT.)

Symphony (73/146 PASSENGERS)

Avalon Waterways, a new division of Globus Tours, offers a new generation of river cruise boats built specifically for the North American market, with non-smoking interiors and English speaking crews. The new boats feature some of the largest cabins and suites available on river cruises, with comfortable beds and large windows to view the passing scenery. European cuisine tailored to North American tastes is served at an open, single seating in a spacious restaurant; wine is included with all onboard dinners; coffee and tea are available throughout the day. The company says that its enrichment program is "geared for the way North Americans like to travel, with lively itineraries, time for individual discovery, and onboard entertainment."

The well-appointed boats have a two-story lobby, lit by a central glass skylight, and both the dining room and lounge have floor-to-ceiling windows with panoramic views. The boats are equipped with state-of-the-art technology and have a **Sky Bar, Club Lounge,** exercise room with fitness equipment, walking track, whirlpool, hair salon, massage service, and gift shop. The Sky Deck is fitted with newly developed shade systems, which are lowered when passing under a bridge then promptly raised again.

All cabins are outside ones; some have picture windows, while 70% have a floor-to-ceiling sliding glass doors to enjoy the passing scenery. The *Poetry* has four junior suites (two on the *Artistry*), each 258 square feet, and standard cabins of 172 square feet. On the *Artistry,* for example, all cabins have a granite bathroom, ample closet, radio, telephone, satellite television, minibar, safe, and hair dryer. Beds may be configured as twins or one queen; connecting cabins are available.

The cruise-tour itineraries range from 9 days in Holland and Belgium from Amsterdam to 12 days on the Lower Danube/Black Sea from Budapest to Bucharest with two nights in Budapest; or three nights in Prague and a cruise from Nuremberg to Budapest. Other cruises and land combinations from 14 to 20 days are available with time in Paris or Berlin. Discounts for AARP members are available.

The Barge Lady
101 West Grand Avenue, Suite 200, Chicago, IL 60610; ☎ 312-245-0900 or 800-880-0071; fax 312-245-0952; www.bargelady.com

A variety of barges on the canals of France, Holland, Belgium, Scotland, Ireland, Germany, and Great Britain; multigenerational, small group, and wine-tasting cruises featured. More recently, the company has added European rivers (*River Cloud* on the Danube, Rhine and others), Alaska (American Safari Cruises), and Asia (*Road to Mandalay* in Myanmar, Burma).

Crown Blue Line
980 Awald Road, Suite 302, Annapolis, MD 21403; ☎ 888-355-9491; fax 410-280-2406

Specializes in self-drive boats with a large fleet of small boats operating in England, Ireland, Scotland, and others in France, Italy, Germany, and Holland. Recently, the company became affiliated with Le Boat, Inc. (see listing further in this section).

Peter Deilmann Cruises
1800 Diagonal Road, Suite 170, Alexandria, VA 22314; ☎ 703-549-1741 or 800-348-8287; fax 703-549-7924; www.deilmann-cruises.com

This European line markets nine riverboats and the luxury oceanliner, *Deutschland.* The line added its newest riverboat, the *Heidelberg,* in 2004. In addition to traditional cruises, the line has special interest ones for music, golf, gardens, and cycling.

Casanova (48/96; GERMAN/EUROPEAN; 338 FT.)
Built in 2001, this deluxe boat offers spacious outside cabins with French doors on the upper deck and picture windows on the lower. All cabins have a private bathroom, telephone, radio, desk, and chair. Facilities include a

single-seating dining room, lounge, bar, library, dance floor, fitness area, conference room, boutique, and beauty salon. The boat sails seven-day cruises from on the Rhine, Moselle, Rhine-Main Canal, and Danube.

Cezanne (50/100; EUROPEAN; 356 FT.)
Built in 1993, the line purchased this boat and completely renovated her in 2000, with elegant furnishings and a panoramic dining room and lounge. In 2005, the boat introduced weekly cruises on the Seine River, sailing from Paris and Rouen on two different itineraries.

Danube Princess (94/198; EUROPEAN/GERMAN; 364 FT.)
Facilities include an outdoor swimming pool, single-seating dining room, two bars, conference room, library, gift shop, and beauty salon. Cabins have a private bathroom, telephone, radio, and television. Between March and early November, the ship sails on seven-day Danube cruises from Munich to Austria, Hungary, Serbia, and Romania to the Black Sea.

Dresden (53/106; EUROPEAN/GERMAN; 320 FT.)
Facilities include a single-seating dining room, bar, gift shop, beauty salon, fitness equipment, sauna, library, infirmary, and laundry room. All cabins have a private shower and toilet, telephone, radio, and television. *Dresden* sails seven-day Elbe cruises from Hamburg and Dresden, visiting Meissen, Magdeburg, and Wittenberg.

Frederic Chopin (41/79; EUROPEAN/GERMAN; 272 FT.)
The *Frederic Chopin,* a luxury vessel that debuted in 2002, sails on seven-night cruises on the Oder River in Germany and Poland between Potsdam and Stralsund Prague and on the Elbe between Prague and Berlin.

Heidelberg (56/110; EUROPEAN; 360 FT.)
On the new ship, all cabins on two upper decks have French windows, and four cabins on the lower cabin deck have large portholes. Cabins are a spacious 190 square feet and the ship's facilities include a fitness center and spa with sauna, steam room, and massage facilities. She sails on the Rhine and Moselle rivers in Holland, Germany, France, and Switzerland from April through October.

Katharina (41/79; EUROPEAN/GERMAN; 272 FT.)
Double- and twin-bedded cabins have French doors on upper decks, picture windows on the lower deck. The vessel operates various itineraries on the Elbe River between Potsdam and Prague.

Mozart (100/200; EUROPEAN/GERMAN; 396 FT.)
This deluxe boat, renovated in 2003, has large, all-outside cabins with spacious private bathrooms, television, minibar, hair dryer, and telephone. Facilities include an indoor/outdoor swimming pool, whirlpool, sauna, and fitness center. From March to October the boat sails seven-day Danube cruises departing from Passau and calling at Bratislava, Budapest, Kalocza, Esztergom, Duernstein, and Melk. Classical music summer cruises are also scheduled.

Princesse de Provence (70/140; GERMAN/EUROPEAN; 363 FT.)
All cabins have a private bathroom, hair dryer, telephone, and radio. Facilities

include fitness equipment, single-seating dining room, two bars, conference room, library, infirmary, gift shop. Between March and November, the boat sails seven-day cruises round-trip from Lyon or between Arles and Lyon calling at Chateauneuf-du-Pape, Viviers, Trevoux, and Avignon.

Elegant Cruises & Tours
24 Vanderventer Avenue, Port Washington, NY 11050; ☎ 516-767-9302 or 800-683-6767; fax 516-767-9303; www.elegantcruises.com

River Cloud (45/90; EUROPEAN; 360 FT.)
Launched in 1996, the splendidly appointed *River Cloud* is one of the finest boats on European waterways. Interiors convey 1930s luxury reminiscent of the Orient Express. She offers the impeccable service and fine cuisine for which her famous sister ship, *Sea Cloud,* is known.

The elegant dining room serves meals in a single, open seating in a relaxed, friendly atmosphere. Breakfast and lunch are buffet-style; dinner is served at tables. Menus feature continental specialties and complimentary fine wines, beer, and soft drinks. The centerpiece of the handsome lounge—encircled by windows at the bow—is a seven-foot Steinway grand piano. It's much in use during afternoon tea and music cruises, when renowned pianists and opera stars are aboard. Amenities include a library, boutique, hair salon, exercise room, sauna, putting green, and large-scale chessboard. All cabins have telephone, radio, television, air-conditioning, safe, and marble bathroom with shower and hair dryer. The Dutch-built *River Cloud* sails on the Rhine, Main, Moselle, and Danube, April through October.

River Cloud II (44/88; EUROPEAN; 338 FT.)
Launched in late spring 2001, this boat sails on Italy's historic Po River between Cremona and Venice, on seven-night itineraries with the debarkation port alternating each week. Her public rooms include a lounge and library, restaurant, boutique, and hair salon. The air-conditioned ship has 13 junior suites with windows, 20 double-bed cabins with portholes, and 10 twin-bedded cabins. All have direct-dial telephone, television with video player, radio and music channels, minibar, emergency button, and bath with shower, hair dryer, bathrobes, and toiletries. A fruit basket, half-bottle of champagne, bottled water, and soft drinks are replenished daily.

A typical cruise would include two nights in Venice, cruising the lagoon to the islands of Murano, Burano, Torcello, and Chioggia, before entering the Po. Other ports and sites to be visited include Taglio di Po, the Abbey of Pomposa, Ferrara, Mantua, Verona, and Parma. Shore excursions include the Violin Museum in Boretto, where passengers hear a private Stradivarius recital.

The cruises are also sold through Dailey-Thorp Travel of New York, ☎ 212-307-1555; Abercrombie & Kent, ☎ 800-323-7308; European Waterways, ☎ 800-217-4447; and other U.S. companies.

In addition to the European river boats described above, Elegant Cruises also markets the *Andrea* in Antarctica and on expedition cruises in the Mediterranean, Adriatic, and Baltic regions; *Sea Cloud* in the Caribbean and Mediterranean; and the *Monet* in Europe and the Dalmatian Coast.

Les Etoiles
c/o Karen Bull Associates, 3355 Lenox Road, Suite 750, Atlanta, GA
30326; ☎ 800-280-1492 or 404-237-1841; www.lesetoilesbarges.com

La Nouvelle (4 SUITES/8; DUTCH; 128 FT.)
Seven- and thirteen-day trips to Holland, Belgium, France, Germany, and
Mosel Valley, April through September.

European Waterways
c/o 35 Wharf Road, Wraysbury, Staines, Middlesex, TW19 5JQ, England;
☎ 44-0-1784-482-439 or 800-394-8630; fax 44-0-1784 483 072;
www.gobarging.com

Actief/Anjodi/La Belle Epoque/La Dolce Vita/
L'arte de Vivre/L'Impressioniste/Magna Carta/
Meanderer/Nymphea/Rosa/Scottish Highland/
Serenite/Shannon Princess
(3–6/6–12; FRENCH/FRENCH AND ENGLISH; 80–128 FT.)
The company offers six-night cruises on the rivers and canals of England,
Scotland, Ireland, France, Germany, Italy, and the Czech Republic. European
Waterways also owns a medley of barges and riverboats for 6 to 12 passen-
gers on the Shannon River in Ireland, the Thames of Scotland, as well as
waterways in France, Italy, Germany, and the Czech Republic. All cruises can
be geared to special interests, such as golf, sport fishing, horseback riding,
fine dining, cycling, wildlife, poetry, and more.

French Country Waterways
P.O. Box 2195, Duxbury, MA 02331; ☎ 781-934-2454 or 800-222-1236;
fax 781-934-9048; www.fcwl.com

As its name implies, French Country Waterways' six boats, or hotel-barges,
as they are known, concentrate on the small rivers and canals that crisscross
France, through a navigational system that began in the early 17th century.
The line's handsome brochure details each of the barges and its itineraries
with descriptions and photographs that convey an accurate and inviting
look at its cruises.

Adrienne (6 SUITES/12; FRENCH/ENGLISH; 128 FT.)
Upper Loire Valley.

Esprit (9/18; FRENCH/ENGLISH/7; 128 FT.)
Cote d'Or wine region (Burgundy Canal, Saone River, Canal du Centre from
Dijon to St. Leger-sur-Dheune).

Horizon II (6/12; FRENCH/ENGLISH/6; 128 FT.)
Upper Burgundy (Burgundy Canal from Tonnerre to Venarey-les-Laumes).

Liberté (4/8; FRENCH/ENGLISH/4; 100 FT.)
Western Burgundy region (Canal du Nivernais from Auxerre to Clamecy).

Nenuphar **(6/12; FRENCH/ENGLISH/6; 128 FT.)**
Champagne region.

Princess **(4/8; FRENCH/ENGLISH/6; 128 FT.)**
Alsace-Lorraine region.

Global Quest Journeys
185 Willis Avenue, Second Floor, Mineola, NY 11501; ☎ 516-739-3690 or 800-221-3254; fax 516-739-8022; www.globalquesttravel.com

The company represents a variety of cruise lines and vessels which cruise in different areas: Europe and Russia; Mediterranean, Galapagos, Central and South America; Antarctica; and East Africa/Indian Ocean. Information on the Galapagos and Indian Ocean is found in the next section, "Adventure and Cultural Cruises."

Novikov Priboy **(242 PASSENGERS; RUSSIAN OR UKRAINIAN)**
This boat features all outside cabins, an informal atmosphere, local enter-tainment, and guest lecturers on history and culture. On 12-night voyages, passengers arrive in a different port each morning and have most of the day for sightseeing (guided tours optional). Boats sail from June to September on the rivers, lakes, and canals connecting Moscow and St. Petersburg. On three nights each in Moscow and St. Petersburg, passengers sleep aboard and can take guided shore excursions.

The company also has a 14-night Russian Cruise aboard the *Peter the Great.*

Amadeus/Amadeus Classic/Amadeus Rhapsody/Amadeus Royal
(73–236 PASSENGERS; EUROPEAN; 347–370 FT.)
Danube cruises of seven nights, linking central and southeastern Europe and the Balkans. Passengers may extend their trips with cruise/tour options from Amsterdam to Prague. Itineraries include entertainment, guest lectur-ers, and shore excursions. Ships have all outside cabins, an informal atmosphere, and regional cuisine. Ports may include Passau, Budapest, Vienna, Bratislava, Tulcea, and Weissen-kirchen. *Amadeus Rhapsody* has a library, sun deck, and heated pool. A *Holland-at-Tulip-Time* cruise on the *Amadeus Royal;* a Classical Music Festival on *Amadeus;* and the Po River on the *River Cloud II* are among the offerings. The company also has a cruise of Italy, Croatia, and Greece on the *Royal Clipper;* and the Adriatic from Venice on the *Monet* that can include diving in Dubrovnik.

Le Boat, Inc.
980 Awald Road, Suite 302, Annapolis, MD 21403; ☎ 800-992-0291; fax 410-280-2406; www.leboat.com; www.connoisseurafloat.com

Le Boat, now affiliated with the self-drive specialist Crown Blue Line, offers a wide range of cruises in Europe and specializes in barge charters, often representing owner-operated barges, and self-drive canal boats on canals in Britain, Scotland, France, Germany Holland, Ireland, Italy, and Belgium. At most of the European destinations, one-way cruises that start and finish in different places are available. Discounts for early bookings, family, and groups are also offered.

Overseas Adventure Travel
One Broadway, Suite 600, Cambridge, MA 02142; ☎ 800-527-3850; www.oattravel.com.

In 2004, OAT, which is owned by Grand Circle Travel, acquired Continental Waterways, one of the leading operators of European barge cruising. The company has designed seven itineraries in Alsace, Bordeaux, Provence, Burgundy, Holland, and Belgium which can be combined with several days visit at the beginning and end of the cruise in Paris, Amsterdam, and other cities. OAT puts the emphasis on the local experience, providing opportunities to visit local markets, bakeries, cheese shops, and vineyards; to hike or bike; and to share time with local people at their homes.

Abercrombie **(11/22; 128 FT.)**
Burgundy.

Caprice **(11/21; 128 FT.)**
Provence and the Camargue.

Chanterelle **(14/24; 128 FT.)**
Burgundy, Alsace, Rhone Valley.

Lafayette **(12/22)**
Alsace-Lorraine.

Marguerite **(10/20; 128 FT.)**
Holland and Belgium.

Mirabelle **(12/24; 128 FT.)**
Bordeaux and Loire Valley.

Princesse Royale **(2 SUITES, 10 CABINS; 128 FT.)**
Holland and Belgium.

Peter the Great Cruises
2610 East 16th Street, Brooklyn, NY 11235; ☎ 718-934-4100 or 800-828-7970; fax 718-934-9419; www.cruise-russ.com

Peter the Great **(157/280; RUSSIAN; 425 FT.)**
Thirteen- to sixteen-day tour of waterways connecting Moscow and St. Petersburg. Multiple ports of call, including four days in Moscow and five in St. Petersburg on longer tours, May through September. The line also offers cruises in the Ukraine from Kiev to the Black Sea on the Dnieper River.

Viking River Cruises
21820 Burbank Boulevard, Woodland Hills, CA 91367; ☎ 818-227-1234 or 877-668-4546; fax 818-227-1231; www.vikingrivercruises.com

Viking River Cruises, a Switzerland-based company with 25 river boats, offers European, Russian, Ukrainian, and Chinese cruises. In Europe, the line has a variety of itineraries ranging from 7 to 14 days on the Rhine, Main, Danube, Seine, Saone, Rhone, Elbe, Volga, and Dnjepr rivers. Those sold in North America cover inclusive programs created specifically for English-speaking passengers. (See the China cruises section later in this chapter for the line's Yangtze River program.) The following is a sampling of the fleet in Europe that caters to North Americans.

Viking Burgundy/Viking Seine (76/154; FRENCH/INTERNATIONAL; 365 FT.)
Two seven-night cruises along the Rhone and Saone rivers through Burgundy, Provence, and the scenery of the Ardeche region as well as Paris and the heart of Normandy.

Viking Europe (75/150; 40/365 FT.)
Fourteen-night Eastern European Odyssey from Budapest to the Black Sea and back. Sailing through Eastern Europe.

Viking Kirov/Viking Pakhomov/Viking Surkov (103/212; 430 FT.)
From May to October, these boats sail on ten- and eleven-day "Waterways of the Czars" cruises between St. Petersburg and Moscow.

Viking Lavrinenkov (103/212; 114; 430 FT.)
Dnieper River cruises in Ukraine, roundtrip from Kiev to the Black Sea.

Viking Neptune/Viking Pride/Viking Spirit (75/150; 365 FT.)

Viking Schumann (60/124; 311 FT.)
Six-night cruise on the Elbe (Berlin to Prague).

Viking Sky (75/150; 360 FT.)
Seven- to nine-night roundtrip cruises from Amsterdam sail Holland and Belgium's waterways. Seven to fourteen nights along Rhine, Main, and Danube also offered.

Viking Sun (99/198; 44; 433 FT.)
Twelve-night Rhine cruises from Antwerp to Basel through Holland, Germany, France, and Switzerland.

YANGTZE RIVER CRUISES IN CHINA

THE CHINESE APTLY CALL the Yangtze "Changjiang" (long river). Rising from the Tibetan plateau, it plunges through mountain passes into Sichuan to form a border between Hubei and Hunan before reaching the fertile plains of Jiangsu and Shanghai, a journey of almost 4,000 miles.

The Yangtze (a local name) is more than a scenic wonder. It was the site of epic battles in the second century B.C., and archaeological excavations suggest that the area was a cradle of Chinese civilization.

The river remains the great highway of central China, carrying passenger ferries, patrol boats, and barges piled with coal, limestone, timber, and cement. Small freighters deliver supplies to towns built into the cliffs and collect the fruit grown in terraced orchards.

The river is always busy, especially as it narrows into gorges. There, traffic control is essential, and cruise ship captains are in telephone contact with shore pilot stations as they steer the shallow-draft vessels between gravel shoals.

The Three Gorges: Qutang, Wu, Xiling

Qutang Gorge, also known as Wind Box Gorge, is five miles long, but never wider than 490 feet. Limestone cliffs erupt on either side in sheer walls up to 4,000 feet tall. The cliff face is pitted with caves, and there remains visible an old towpath—the only way through the gorge before the biggest boulders were cleared from the river.

Less than an hour after leaving the Qutang, cruise-ship passengers enter 25-mile-long **Wu Gorge.** Its cliffs are so high and steep that the sun rarely touches the water. Twelve peaks dominate the skyline. According to myth, they're a goddess and her handmaidens who chose to be turned to stone to stand sentinel over the river.

Midway through the gorge is the border between Sichuan and Hubei Provinces. The exit from the gorge is only 164 feet across, the narrowest part of the river.

It takes another day for cruise ships to reach **Xiling Gorge,** the longest canyon, which winds 47 miles through small gorges amid fierce rapids. On either side are examples of the mountains beyond mountains of classic Chinese scenery.

Three Gorges Dam

Three Gorges Dam is under construction at Sandouping, at the eastern mouth of the gorges. It's massive. The dam wall will be almost two miles long and 607 feet tall. Behind it, a lake will stretch 373 miles and cover 418 square miles, inundating most of the Xiling and half of the Wu Gorge. A million or more people are being evacuated in anticipation of the dam's completion in 2009.

Supporters say the multibillion-dollar dam will control flooding and generate 84.7 billion kilowatt hours of electricy a year for Shanghai and the Lower Yangtze Basin. Opponents say it will destroy the environment and build a reservoir of toxic silt in an earthquake-prone region. Either way, it adds poignancy to a Yangtze cruise.

With Stage Two finished in June 2003, the eastern section at Sandouping is virtually complete, and the reservoir continues to fill. The lake behind the dam will raise water levels in the Xiling and Wu Gorge. Cruise boats journey through a new, five-stage lock to go around the dam wall.

The first westerners to sail up the Yangtze River were British colonial administrators who established the inland port of Hankow (now part of Wuhan) in the 1840s. The most adventurous continued into the sparsely populated wilderness upstream and found the Three Gorges.

Transport was by sailing ships, which were hauled by teams of trackers through raging rapids and over great boulders, until English trader Archibald Little pioneered steamship service from Wuhan, finally reaching Chongqing (formerly Chungking) in 1898. The voyage remained extremely hazardous until the 1950s, when the Chinese blasted away the largest boulders.

Regular cruises through the gorges were introduced in the early 1980s and became an established part of many all-China itineraries. The gorges are on the 120-mile (192-kilometer) stretch of river between Baidicheng and Yichang. Some itineraries between Chongqing and Yichang reduce the trip by a day and night. However, it has often proven difficult to arrange air or land passage to or from Yichang. Most cruises thus cover the full 850-mile (1,370-kilometer) section between Chongqing and Wuhan.

Shore Excursions (Upstream or Downstream)

SHENNONG STREAM/DANING RIVER GORGES All cruises offer a side trip up one of the Yangtze's tributaries for a closer look at its natural grandeur. Excursions feature fast-flowing, crystal-clear streams with shifting, pebbled shoals and sheer cliffs pocked with caves, clad in waterfalls, and encrusted with ferns. With the rising waters of the river, some of the lesser gorges are also now fully accessible by larger boats, and previously unexplored tributaries are available to visitors.

Shennong Stream is a better option than Daning River, partly because the journey is taken in wooden longboats, which are steered, pushed, and sometimes hauled by husky young men of the Tujia minority. Shennong Stream is also a good option because it is one of the shallower tributaries. The half-day excursion includes a visit to a Tujia-style house, where local dance is performed and worthwhile souvenirs are sold.

ZIGUI This historic town, poised on the cliffs at the entrance to Xiling Gorge, exudes an air of ancient certainty, but it will be swallowed by the dam's reservoir. Only one building will be preserved: The temple dedicated to Chu Yuan, the scholar and statesman who drowned himself in 278 B.C. in protest of his government's policy, will be moved downstream with the population. Travelers will lose a town whose main street is packed with sidewalk kitchens, vegetable stalls, alfresco hairdressers, one-room tailors, and an alley of pool tables.

SHASHI/JINGZHOU Upstream from Wuhan, this bustling port contains the remains of a royal capitol from the seventh century B.C. Some original walls are maintained, and the museum contains a 2,000-year-old mummy.

YUEYANG TOWER This gold-tiled pavilion on the Hunan banks of the river, upstream from Wuhan, was built in A.D. 716 as a military lookout. It was later expanded to provide a belvedere over scenic Dongting Lake.

FENGDU Near the western entrance of Qutang Gorge, this ancient cliff town is reputed to be where people's spirits go after death. To placate unhappy and potentially dangerous phantoms, a temple sells "passports to hell" and other souvenirs.

SHIBAOZHAI This cliffside town, between Chongqing and the first gorge, has a 12-story red pagoda and hilltop temple. Built right into the cliff and called the "Pearl of the Yangtze," the temple is an architectural treasure from the Ming Dynasty, dating to the mid-16th century. Some excursions visit it.

Cruise Lines and Ships

Dozens of ships offer cruises through the Yangtze gorges. Many are Chinese-owned and marketed internationally by Changjiang Cruise Overseas Travel Company (**www.ccotc.com**), with offices throughout Asia.

A new generation of vessels caters to travelers whose interest has been fueled by reports that the gorges' days are numbered. These ships operate on regular itineraries designed to allow passage through the gorges during daylight. The timing concerns produce shore excursions that are conveniently located, interesting, varied, and appropriate to the area's history. The season lasts from late February to early December. Summer is extremely hot; in winter, the water level is low and temperatures are colder, often below freezing. There are almost weekly departures of the four-day, three-night downstream cruise from Chongqing and the five-day, four-night upstream trip from Wuhan.

However, those reports that the gorges' days are numbered are a bit exaggerated. Overall, the river will rise some 575 feet in total, but the gorges themselves are so deep that they will be less affected than some have claimed. While the landscape will change, the reality is that the water will not submerge the gorges. In fact, since Stage Two of the dam is already complete, the river will rise only about another 131 feet at the dam's completion. In addition, the deeper water will open even newer vistas to cruisers, since the lesser gorges, which previously held little water, will be fully navigable, and visitors will have the opportunity to explore previously inaccessible areas of the river.

Note: In parentheses after each boat name is information (where available) about the number of cabins and passengers; officers and crew; and the boat's length (cabins/passengers; officers/crew; boat length).

Abercrombie & Kent Inc
1520 Kensington Road, Suite 212, Oak Brook, IL 60523; ☎ 630-954-2944 or 800-323-7308; fax 630-954-3324; www.abercrombiekent.com

---

East King/East Queen (80–88/160–176; CHINESE; 300 FT.)
The twin boats *East King* and *East Queen* (operating March through November) are fast and modern. All cabins are spacious—about 183 square feet—and have picture windows, minibars, satellite television, international

direct-dial telephones, safes, terry robes, hair dryers, and well-designed bathrooms. There are two suites, which can be combined with a tea lounge for seminars, groups, or small meetings. The main dining room serves western and Chinese meals. Public facilities include a nightclub, five karaoke rooms, an enclosed observation deck with cafe, a business center, and a 100-seat function room. Recreational facilities include a swimming pool, card rooms, gym, and sauna.

Victoria Cruises
57-08 39th Street, Woodside, NY 11377; ☎ 212-818-1680 or 800-348-8084; fax 212-818-9889; www.victoriacruises.com

---

Victoria Anna **(2006; 132 CABINS, 22 SUITES/308; CHINESE; 348 FT.)**

Victoria Empress **(91 CABINS, 8 SUITES/198; CHINESE; 3,868 TONS)**

Victoria Katarina **(119 CABINS, 14 SUITES/266; CHINESE; 324 FT./ 5,780 TONS)**

Victoria Prince/Victoria Queen/Victoria Star **(93 CABINS, 10 SUITES/ 206; CHINESE; 4,587 TONS)**

Victoria Rose **(63 CABINS, 2 SUITES; 130; CHINESE; 2,428 TONS)**
Victoria Cruises, a New York–based Sino-American joint venture, with American management, operates vessels with the wedding-cake look and character of Mississippi riverboats. Each has four decks and an observation area and offers single-seating dining with Chinese and western cuisine.

Ships come in two categories: premier and classic. Premier ships include all of the vessels listed above, with the exception of the *Victoria Rose,* a classic ship and smaller than the others; it was rebuilt in 2001, and maintains the same quality standards onboard. The premier ships are new or newly rebuilt vessels, and have a higher level of comfort and decor as well as private balconies for every cabin. Introduced in 2004, *Victoria Katarina* is the newest of these vessels, with floor-to-ceiling windows and a mix of modern and traditional architecture.

All cruises have professional, multi-lingual, western cruise directors and trained local staff. Meals on all boats are served in a single-seating **Dynasty** dining room. Western and Chinese buffets are offered at breakfast and lunch; dinners are served family style. Passengers can enjoy cultural immersion both ashore and onboard; tai chi is offered mornings on the boats, as are lectures in Chinese culture and history and live traditional performing arts. An onboard boutique sells Chinese gifts and souvenirs. The boats have cocktail lounges, game rooms, business centers, health, and other facilities.

Victoria Anna, another premier vessel, is scheduled to debut in April 2006. She will be the largest ship in the company's fleet, with 132 standard cabins, 16 junior suites, 4 deluxe suites, and 2 Shangri-La suites. The cabins have bathrooms with a shower and bathtub, television with HBO and BBC broadcasts, and private balconies. There is a single-seating main restaurant and an à la carte restaurant on the top deck. The boat has a three-story atrium lobby, two lounges, three bars, a fitness room, lecture room, library, beauty salon, massage room, foot-massage center, gift shop, observation deck, Internet access, and two elevators.

Four- to nine-day itineraries are operated roundtrip from Chonqqing; between Chonqqing and Yichang; between Chonqqing and Shanghai; and between Chonqqing and Wuhan. Victoria Cruises provides cruises on the Yangtze exclusively for such tour operator partners as Pacific Delight Tours, Uniworld, and a host of others.

Viking River Cruises, Inc.

21820 Burbank Boulevard, Woodland Hills, CA 91367; ☎ 877-66-VIKING (668-4546) or 818-227-1234; fax 818-227-1237; www.vikingrivercruises.com

Viking Century Sky (153/306; EUROPEAN/CHINESE; 415 FT.)

Viking Century Star (93/186; EUROPEAN/CHINESE; 285 FT.)

Viking Century Sun (2006)

Europe's largest river-cruising company launched its first boat in China on the Yangtze River in March 2004, offering five different seven-night cruise-tour itineraries on the newly-built, deluxe *Viking Century Star.* With offices in Beijing and Chongqing, Swiss-based Viking River Cruises oversees all its program components, from ship operations and shore excursions to land programs, tours, hotel selections, meals, and cultural performances. Each program has English-speaking escorts and guides.

The purpose-built *Century Star* is one of the most deluxe of the Yangtze cruise vessels, with all-outside cabins (86 standard, 5 deluxe, 2 suites) with balconies, baths with shower, telephones, televisions, and air-conditioning. The boat has a restaurant, observation lounge and bar, gym, sauna, massage room, sun deck, business center, beauty salon, doctor, and laundry service.

Viking's Swiss hotel-management staff oversees all food and beverage service and a crew of 135. A variety of food, from the traditional family-style Chinese cuisine to western selections and even an on-deck barbecue, is available. English is the primary language onboard as well as during shore excursions and tours.

Passengers have an adventure on a traditional Chinese sampan to the Lesser Three Gorges—formerly inaccessible to travelers. One itinerary includes a visit to Lhasa, Tibet. Pre- and post-cruise land extensions are available for Hong Kong and Guilin. In addition to the river cruise, the 9- to 18-night programs include all shore excursions and tours, meals, five-star and deluxe hotels, intra-Asia flights, and English-speaking escorts. With its policy of contributing to the regions in which it sails, Viking River Cruises has built an elementary school in Jingzhou in the Hubei province that passengers have the opportunity to visit.

In April 2005, Viking introduced another ship, almost twice as large as the *Viking Century Star.* The five-deck *Viking Century Sky* is air-conditioned and all her cabins have a balcony, private bathroom and shower, telephone, television, safe, and hair dryer.

Also in 2006, Viking River Cruises will launch the *Viking Century Sun,* on the Yantgze. The new, five-deck vessel will have an observation lounge, restaurant, sauna, sun deck, bar, massage room, beauty salon, Internet bar, and two elevators. All cabins will be air-conditioned and have private bathroom with shower and a balcony.

Other Yangtze River Cruises

Several other U.S.-based companies offer Yangtze cruises. All include the cruises as part of longer China itineraries ranging from 12 to 24 days.

CHINA VACATION	☎ 888-285-8933	www.china-vacation.com
GENERAL TOURS	☎ 800-221-2216	www.generaltours.com
MAUPINTOUR	☎ 800-255-4266	www.maupintour.com
ORIENT FLEXI-PAX TOURS	☎ 800-223-7460	www.orientflexipax.com
PACIFIC BESTOURS	☎ 800-688-3288	www.bestour.com
PACIFIC DELIGHT TOURS	☎ 800-221-7179	www.pacificdelighttours.com
SITA WORLD TRAVEL	☎ 800-421-5643	www.sitatours.com
TRAVCOA	☎ 800-992-2003	www.travcoa.com
UNIWORLD	☎ 800-360-9550	www.uniworld.com
VACATIONS TO GO	☎ 800-338-4962	www.vacationstogo.com
VISITS PLUS	☎ 800-321-3235	www.visitsplus.com

OTHER ASIAN RIVER CRUISES

Orient Express Hotels, Trains, and Cruises
1114 Avenue of the Americas, 38th Floor, New York, NY 10036;
☎ **800-524-2420; fax 401-351-7220; www.orient-express.com**

Road to Mandalay **(66/118; EUROPEAN/BURMESE; 305 FT.)**
Unusual cruises in Myanmar (formerly Burma) are offered by Orient Express Hotels, Trains, and Cruises, the company that operates the famous Orient Express. The boat sails from fall to spring on three- to seven-night itineraries on the Irrawaddy (Ayeyarwady) River between Mandalay and Pagan and round trip from Mandalay. The cruises are part of a package departing from Bangkok, Thailand, with round-trip flights to Yangon.

The German-built *Road to Mandalay,* a deluxe cruiser, previously sailed the Rhine and Elbe. Before starting these cruises in 1996, the boat was renovated. Facilities include a pool, large sun deck, observation lounge, and several bars. The dining room accommodates all passengers in a single seating and serves international and Asian cuisine. The three cabin types include some singles. All have a private bath and air-conditioning. Doubles have twin beds; larger cabins have a sitting area. Two even more exotic journeys: One eight-night cruise heads up the Chindrin River, while an 11-night adventure visits a little-known region north of Mandalay to beyond Bhamo, stopping just short of the China border. Unlike the tranquil flood plains surrounding the lower Irrawaddy, the northern landscape changes as the ship enters the Three Narrows region, marked with lush forests and towering cliffs.

NILE RIVER CRUISES

NO TRIP TO EGYPT is complete without a cruise on the Nile. It is the perfect way to enjoy the Egyptian countryside as well as to see ancient temples and monuments, because the most famous sites are clustered along the great river. Your first view of the Nile snaking through the desert will illustrate dramatically why the river has been so important throughout Egypt's history. Quite literally, Egyptian civilization would not exist without the Nile. Beyond the green ribbon—the land irrigated by the Nile—the desert stretches endlessly into the horizon. The Nile flows so gently that ships glide as though unmoving. Riverbanks, always near, give passengers an intimate view of rural life in Upper Egypt. Along the riverbanks and in the fields of the green valley, Egyptians live today much as they have for thousands of years. Life and land have a continuity bridging the centuries, as visitors will see in the ancient drawings on temple and tomb walls and the present scenes of the countryside. The sense of tranquility is an overwhelming sensation throughout a Nile cruise and is a total contrast from the roar and clamor of Cairo—the juxtaposition makes the pastoral setting of the Nile Valley all the more remote.

Nile Itineraries

Those beginning their cruise in Upper Egypt may travel from Cairo to Luxor or Aswan by plane, train, or road. They can begin their trip in Aswan and cruise to Luxor or do the reverse. We recommend the former, as the trip then saves the best for last: climaxing with sightseeing at **Karnak** and the **Valley of the Kings** at Luxor.

Aswan was the capital of Nubia in ancient times and an important trading place. Today, it's primarily a winter resort and the administrative center for the **High Dam** and surrounding region. Aswan is dotted with antiquities. The most important is the **Temple of Philae**—one of many temples saved from the High Dam's reservoir—on an island in the river. The botanical gardens, also on an island, and the Aga Khan's mausoleum are standard stops on the popular excursion made by local felucca, the graceful sailboats of the Nile.

From Aswan, Nile steamers sail downstream (north) to Luxor, stopping at **Kom Ombo, Edfu,** and **Esna**—sites of temples dating from the Ptolemaic, or Greek, period. One temple has a wall carving bearing the only known likeness of Queen Cleopatra. Luxor is the modern town next to the ancient city of Thebes, capital of Egypt for most of its illustrious early history. Boats dock on the east bank near the **Sofitel Winter Palace Luxor** hotel, which is walking distance from **Luxor Temple** and a short carriage ride from the colossal **Karnak Temple.** A full-day excursion visits the west bank to the **Valley of the Kings,** where tombs of Tutankhamen and other pharaohs were found; the **Valley of the Queens;** and the **Tombs of the Nobles,** which contain important art.

Many cruises also sail north to the **Temples of Dendera** and **Abydos,** considered the most important temple in Egypt for its artwork. A limited number of cruises sail beyond Abydos on longer itineraries, stopping at **Tel al Amarna,** capital of revolutionary pharaoh Akhenaten and his wife, Nefertiti; Minya, central Egypt's largest town; and **Beni Hassan,** site of tombs containing drawings showing ancient Egyptians at play.

Lake Nasser and Abu Simbel

Construction of the Aswan High Dam created Lake Nasser, which stretches more than 300 miles south from Aswan to the Sudanese border. As waters rose, the famous temple of **Abu Simbel** would have been inundated had it not been moved to higher ground in a colossal 1950s international project. For decades while the waters rose, visitors flew or drove to the site of Abu Simbel. Now, they can go by Nile steamer, departing from the south side of the dam. (See Misr Travel below.)

Nile River Journeys

Nile river boats range from cozy, friendly, and clubby to very luxurious. Some accommodate as few as 20 passengers; the largest carry 150 or more passengers. Cabins, smaller than those on standard cruise ships, are well-appointed and comfortable; on many new ships, suites are available. Most have twin lower beds (some have pull-down bunks for a third person), a dressing table or night-stand, closet, and private bathroom with shower. Boats holding 80 or more passengers have lounges for reading and relaxing, a bar, sun deck, dining room with table service, and evening entertainment. Laundry service is available. Some offer table tennis or a tiny swimming pool.

The boat's small size limits its recreational and entertainment facilities, but these aren't important on a Nile cruise, where antiquities and scenery are the attractions. "Roaming" room is surprisingly ample. Deck chairs invite lounging and watching history float by.

Newer four- and five-star vessels offer three- to five-night cruises between Luxor and Aswan. Some add **Abydos** and **Dendera** and feature cruises of six or seven nights plus optional land excursions.

Nile cruises are divided into three seasons (prices include all meals, service, taxes, and guided sightseeing).

HIGH SEASON (OCTOBER TO APRIL) Five-star boats range from $200–$450 per person per night; four-star, approximately $150–$210.

SHOULDER SEASON (MAY AND SEPTEMBER) 10% to 15% off high-season rates.

LOW SEASON (JUNE TO AUGUST) 15% to 50% off high-season rates. Generally, U.S. tour companies do not visit Upper Egypt during this period.

Although prices are lower in summer and many of the boats are air-conditioned, the heat in sight-seeing areas can be intense. Large groups walking generate dust in which it's difficult to breath; a dust mask or handkerchief over the mouth is helpful. Boat food usually is quite good. Be very careful to eat only fruits and vegetables that can be peeled.

More than 200 boats sail on Nile cruises. Unless you have the opportunity to inspect a vessel yourself, book only with established companies. Five-star boats operated by Mena House Oberoi, Movenpick, Sheraton, and Sonesta are among those used by major U.S. tour companies.

If you arrive in Egypt without reservations and decide to cruise, make inquiries and reservations through the managing company's office in Cairo, where cabin space is controlled. If you wait until you arrive in Luxor or Aswan to find space, you might have to walk among ships and ask the boat manager if a cabin is available.

If you have ample time, however, the latter method lets you see the ship, its cabins, and cleanliness (important, especially on boats of less than five stars) before booking. And, if you're good at bargaining, you may negotiate a price better than you would have received in Cairo.

A selected list of companies and Nile river boats marketed in the United States follows. *Note:* In parentheses after each boat name is information (where available) about the number of cabins and passengers; officers and crew; and the boat's length (cabins/passengers; officers/crew; boat length).

Abercrombie & Kent Inc
1520 Kensington Road, Suite 212, Oak Brook, IL 60523;
☎ 800-323-7308; fax 630-954-3324; www.abercrombiekent.com

Sun Boat III (18 CABINS)

Sun Boat IV (40 CABINS)
Cruises of five to eight days between Luxor and Aswan are included in various small group and independent itineraries in Egypt.

Esplanade Tours
160 Commonwealth Avenue, Suite L3, Boston, MA 02116; ☎ 617-266-7465 or 800-426-5492; fax 617-262-9829; www.esplanadetours.com

Regency/Regina/Royale (30–70/50–102; EGYPTIAN; 238 FT.)
This luxury group's boats, owned and operated by Travcotels of Egypt, are

fully air-conditioned. Each has lounges, bars, panoramic windows, single-seating dining, two sun decks, a swimming pool, gift shop, beauty salon, and laundry facilities. Cabins measure 230 square feet; suites have 380 square feet. All have a television, video, minifridge, and bathroom with shower, toilet, bidet, and hair dryer. The boats offer three-, four-, and seven-night cruises between Luxor and Aswan or a Lake Nasser cruise between Aswan and Abu Simbel.

Mena House Oberoi Hotels
Pyramids Road, Giza, Cairo, Egypt 12556; ☎ 20-2-383-3222; fax 20-2-383-7777; www.oberoihotels.com

Nephtis (59 CABINS AND SUITES)

Oberoi Philae (50 DOUBLE CABINS, 4 SINGLES, 4 SUITES)

Shehrayar/Shehrazah (59 CABINS AND SUITES)

These boats are operated by Oberoi Hotels, an international chain with hotels in Cairo. The *Oberoi Philae* resembles a paddlewheeler. Each cabin has floor-to-ceiling sliding glass doors leading to a private balcony. Jacket and tie are preferred for men at dinner. The ships sail on three- to seven-night cruises between Luxor and Aswan.

Misr Travel
630 Fifth Avenue, Suite 1460, New York, NY 10111; ☎ 212-332-2600 or 800-223-4978; fax 212-332-2609; www.misrtravel.org

Misr Travel has been taking tourists to Egypt for more than 70 years, and its network of 29 local offices at all major Egyptian tourist sites and in many of Egypt's leading hotels can be comforting to travelers. Misr offers a myriad of packages in Egypt and neighboring countries, with different cruise options. Packages can be customized with add-ons as well.

Currently, Misr offers several cruise-tours that included a Nile cruise. For example, a nine-day "Classic Egyptian Tour" with year-round departures, includes four nights at a Hilton or Sheraton Hotel in Cairo with full breakfast buffet and a four-night cruise on a Sonesta-, Movenpick- or Oberoi-managed Nile cruise boat. Also included are air transportation between Cairo and the ship, transfers, and sightseeing. During the cruise portion of the journey, passengers visit the Valley of the Kings and Queens, the Colossi of Memnon, the Temples of Karnak, Luxor, Edfu, Kom Ombo, and Philae and Aswan.

For those short on time and low on funds, Misr also offers a lower cost option on their "Extraordinary Egypt" package. Passengers spend several nights in Cairo and three nights onboard a Movenpick- or Oberoi-managed Nile cruiser, and also get local flights, transfers, a full-day guided tour of Cairo, and roundtrip air from New York. An optional excursion to Abu Simbel by air from Aswan is available for an additional cost.

Misr Travel also has boats—*Eugenie* (50 cabins/100 passengers)/*Nubian Sea* (60/120)/*Kasr Ibrim* (60/120)/*Prince Abbas* (60/120)—that make three- and four-night cruises on Lake Nasser between Aswan and Abu Simbel. The boats have outside cabins with private baths. The four-night program sails south from Aswan on Monday and ends at Abu Simbel on Friday; three-night cruises sail north on Friday from Abu Simbel to Aswan. The highlight is a daylight visit to Abu Simbel, and a special feature is a candlelight dinner on deck in front of the floodlit temple of Ramses II and a performance of the son et lumiere. The price is about $200 per person, per night, double occupancy in winter; it is lower in off-season. All meals and shore excursions are included.

Nabila Nile Cruises
605 Market Street, Suite 507, San Francisco, CA 94105; ☎ 415-979-0160 or 800-443-6453; www.nabilatours.com

---

King of Thebes (65 CABINS)

Queen Nabila of Abu Simbel (60 CABINS, 2 SUITES)

Queen of the Nile (70 CABINS)

Queen of Sheeba (78 CABINS)

Ramses King of the Nile (71 CABINS)
Four, five- and eight-day cruises between Luxor and Aswan. Three- and four-night cruises on Lake Nasser between Aswan and Abu Simbel.

Sonesta Hotels, Resorts & Nile Cruises
116 Huntington Avenue, Ninth Floor, Boston, MA 02116; ☎ 800-SONESTA (766-3782); www.sonesta.com; Sonesta Nile Cruises, 4 El Tayaran Street, Nasser City, Cairo, Egypt; ☎ 20-2-2628111; fax 20-2-2628765; www.sonesta.com

---

Sonesta Moon Goddess (48 CABINS/2 SUITES; EGYPTIAN)

Sonesta Nile Goddess (63 CABINS/2 SUITES/136; EGYPTIAN)

Sonesta Sun Goddess (58 CABINS/4 SUITES; EGYPTIAN)
Four- to six-night cruises between Luxor and Aswan are offered.

UNITED STATES AND CANADIAN RIVER CRUISES
THE MISSISSIPPI HAS NORTH AMERICA'S best-known river cruises, but there are others. Spectacular scenery is the main attraction. In the Northeast, the favorite season is autumn, with its brilliant foliage.

Note: In parentheses after each boat name is information about the number of cabins and passengers; officers and crew; and the boat's length (cabins/passengers; officers/crew; boat length).

American Canadian Caribbean Line
(See Part Two.)

American Cruise Lines
(See Part Two, under "European and Smaller Cruise Lines.")

American West Steamboat Company
**2101 Fourth Avenue, Suite 1150, Seattle, WA 98121; ☎ 206-292-9606 or
800-434-1232; fax 206-340-0975; www.americanweststeamboat.com**

Empress of the North (112/235; AMERICAN/84; 360 FT.)

Queen of the West (72/161; AMERICAN/47; 230 FT.)

The deluxe paddlewheeler *Queen of the West* was launched in 1995 to offer cruises on the Columbia, Snake, and Willamette rivers. In 2003, the line launched a second paddlewheeler, *Empress of the North,* which came with an important new feature—105 cabins have balconies.

The comfortable, all-outside cabins and suites are large and richly decorated and have picture windows or verandas and private baths. All cabins also have a telephone, minibar, television, and DVD player, among other amenities. Each vessel has a show lounge and several bars. Onboard entertainment includes lectures, cabaret singers, and showboat-style revues. Several new revues—including one highlighting the music of the 1950s, 1960s, and 1970s and another dedicated to female singers—were introduced in 2005.

The elegant main dining room offers open seating for all meals, with one set dinner seating time on *Queen of the West* and two dinner times on *Empress of the North.* Recently, the AWSC engaged a senior executive chef to add flair and consistency to the cuisine. A casual, top-deck bar and grill serves sandwiches, hot dogs, cookies, popcorn, and other snacks.

An AWSC cruise has a strong focus on history, culture, wildlife, and sternwheeler cruising, with both a fun and educational approach. A historian or naturalist accompanies every cruise. Passengers enjoy the small-ship cruise experience with an American staff who will be addressing them by name soon after they have come aboard. The onboard atmosphere is casual but with a touch of elegance.

Passengers will find a 24-page art and artifacts brochure in their cabins, enabling them to take a self-guided tour of each ship's impressive art collection, ranging from cowboy art to Gold Rush–era photos. Many paintings in the ships' corridors also reflect the Native American heritage and Pacific Northwest or Alaska scenery. On the *Empress of the North,* guests will relish a rare collection of Russian nesting dolls, Fabergé eggs, and native Alaskan masks and carvings.

Queen of the West recently received an interior refurbishment and *Empress of the North* was slated to introduce several GPS navigational screens in public areas so passengers can see exactly where they are on a waterway or river.

Queen of the West sails from Portland, Oregon on seven-night cruises on the Columbia, Snake, and Willamette rivers from February to December. *Empress of the North* has Juneau and Portland as home ports, and sails on a series of seven-night Alaska cruises roundtrip from Juneau, as well as two 11-night Alaska cruises; a four-day Puget Sound cruise (which will become a seven-night one in 2006); and spring and fall seven-night Pacific Northwest cruises. All shore excursions are included in the price of all AWSC cruises.

Great American River Journeys
2101 Fourth Avenue, Suite 2200, Seattle, WA 98121;
☎ **800-901-9152 or 206-388-0444; fax 206-388-0445;**
www.greatamericanriverjourneys.com

Columbia Queen (81/161; AMERICAN; 218 FT.)
In April 2005, Great American River Journeys, a new cruise company, launched the *Columbia Queen,* after a three-year absence, on eight-night cruises of the Columbia, Snake, and Willamette rivers. The company, headed by a cruise industry veteran, is a division of a hospitality and travel group comprised of American Rivers Journeys, Glacier Bay Cruiseline, and Coastal Hotel Group, which operates seven small lodges and resorts.

The *Columbia Queen* was built in 2000 for a reported $43 million in early 20th-century riverboat style by the Mississippi River–based Delta Queen Steamboat Company to start a new operation in the Pacific Northwest. In August 2004, Great American River Journeys purchased the finely appointed vessel from the U.S. Maritime Administration after Delta Queen's former parent company, American Classic Voyages, fell on hard times. Although the *Columbia Queen* was found to be in good condition, the new owners refurbished her and added some upgraded amenities and special passenger features prior to her return to service.

The U.S.-owned and -operated boat features a blend of Victorian and Pacific Northwest decor, using warm mahogany wood paneling, plush leather furniture, Tiffany-stained glass chandeliers and lamps, brass accents and Northwest artwork. The *Columbia Queen*'s cabins offer modern amenities similar to those found on ocean-going cruise ships. All cabins are equipped with satellite television and a DVD player, boat-to-shore telephone, bath with a glass-enclosed shower, and robes. Most cabins have private verandas, French doors with balconies, or doors that open directly onto the deck.

The **Astoria Room,** a handsome two-tiered space on the main deck, serves a dual purpose. Dressed in richly upholstered banquettes and chairs, tables are set for dinner with Tavern-on-the-Green china and ecru damask linens. The room is large enough to seat all passengers at one time. Later in the evening, the room is transformed into the main show lounge and theater for passengers to dance under authentic Tiffany stained glass chandeliers or enjoy a variety of entertainment.

Other facilities include the **Explorer Bar,** a piano bar with large windows revealing panoramic views, and the **Lewis & Clark Lounge,** an intimate space for cocktails and hors d'oeuvres, reached by a large stairwell with a mahogany banister and ornate iron grillwork reminiscent of the stately homes of Portland. The Lounge is furnished with overstuffed library chairs and a mahogany bar with an eight-foot mirrored bar back. The **Back Porch,** at the rear of the observation deck, provides a venue for passengers to enjoy breakfast, a light lunch, or cocktails, or to relax in the ladder-back rocking chairs and read or watch the world go by. The ship also has a gift shop, two elevators, and an e-mail center.

Cruise West
(See Part Two.)

Delta Queen Steamboat Company
(See Part Two.)

RiverBarge Excursion Lines, Inc.
201 Opelousas Avenue, New Orleans, LA 70114; ☎ 504-365-0022 or 888-462-2743; fax 504-365-0000; www.riverbarge.com

---

River Explorer (98/198; AMERICAN; 295 FT.)
Similar in concept to European barges, *River Explorer* was the first boat of its kind when it was inaugurated in 1998. She's a modern, American-built, American-flagged, and American-crewed hotel-barge; the vessel consists of two connected custom-built barges propelled by a 3,000-horsepower tow-boat. The forward barge contains public rooms, including a dining room accommodating all passengers at a single, open seating for all meals; a two-deck showroom; exercise and games area; library; gift shop; and **Pilot House Lounge,** a re-creation of a river pilothouse complete with equipment and windows overlooking the bow. Art depicting river exploration decorates public areas. Among the amenities are a never-empty cookie jar, a "raid the fridge" policy for sandwiches and snacks, and 24-hour coffee service.

The aft barge contains all 98 cabins, each measuring 200 square feet. All are outside and have picture windows. Upper-deck cabins have balconies. All have twin or super-queen-size beds, satellite television, VCR, telephone with computer port, minifridge, coffeemaker, iron, and bathroom with tub.

River Explorer sails from New Orleans on four- to ten-day excursions encompassing six geographic regions. Itineraries feature the Mississippi, Ohio, Cumberland, and Tennessee rivers; Atchafalaya basin; and Gulf of Mexico Intracoastal Waterway.

Prices begin at $865 per person, double, for a four-day excursion. Taxes, port charges, most shore activities, and tipping are included. Alcoholic beverages cost extra.

St. Lawrence Cruise Lines/ Canadian River Cruise Vacations
253 Ontario Street, Kingston, Ontario, Canada K7L 2Z4; ☎ 613-549-8091 or 800-267-7868; fax 613-549-8410; www.stlawrencecruiselines.com

---

Canadian Empress (32/66; CANADIAN; 108 FT.)
Three, five, and six nights on the St. Lawrence and Ottawa rivers. Boarding

ports include Kingston, Ottawa, and Quebec City. Cruise fares include most sightseeing tours and attractions.

AMAZON RIVER CRUISES

MANY MAINSTREAM SHIPS with South American itineraries include an Amazon River cruise. They enter on the Atlantic delta and sail up-river to Manaus. The river is very wide; any intimate view must be obtained aboard small crafts on tributaries. More exotic regions of the upper Amazon are reached mainly from Iquitos, Peru, or via Ecuador.

Note: In parentheses after each boat name is information (where available) about the number of cabins and passengers; officers and crew; and the boat's length (cabins/passengers; officers/crew; boat length). Many companies offering tours from the United States use the same boats on the Amazon; these include the following:

Amazon Clipper **(8/16; PERUVIAN; 65 FT.)**
Three-night cruises explore the tributaries to bird-watch, fish for piranha, and visit Amazon Ecopark, a nature reserve and wildlife rehabilitation sanctuary. Clipper's cabins have private bathrooms, bunk berths, as well as nighttime air-conditioning. Facilities include a covered salon, bar, dining area, library, and fully equipped kitchen with freezer. Local cuisine is served—mainly fresh fish. Mineral water is provided.

Amazon Explorer **(8/16; PERUVIAN; 85 FT.)**
Three- or six-night round-trip cruises upriver from Iquitos. The steel-constructed boat has a small air-conditioned lounge, dining room/bar, and sun deck. The cabins are outside doubles with bunk beds; all are air-conditioned and have private bath/shower.

Arca **(13/31; PERUVIAN; 98 FT.)**
Three- to six-night trips on the Upper Amazon. The air-conditioned, steel-hull riverboat operates between Iquitos and the twin cities of Tabatinga, Brazil, and Leticia, Colombia. She offers ten twin-bedded cabins with upper/lower berths and three triples with lower beds. All cabins have private bathroom and shower. The boat has a lounge/bar and covered and uncovered deck areas.

Rio Amazonas **(21/44; PERUVIAN; 146 FT.)**
Three- to six-night explorations of the Upper Amazon, sailing downriver on Sunday from Iquitos to the twin cities of Tabatinga, Brazil, and Leticia, Colombia; upriver on Wednesday from Leticia. Itineraries can be combined. The ship has an air-conditioned dining room and library, covered and uncovered deck areas, and hot tub. Upper-deck cabins have picture windows and private bathrooms with shower. Sun-deck cabins are larger, offering three twin beds, a closet, and a chair.

Most of the following companies also offer Galapagos cruises as well as Amazon ones. See listings in the next section, Adventure and Cultural Cruises.

Abercrombie & Kent Inc.
(See Part Two.)

Ecotour Expeditions
P.O. Box 128, Jamestown, RI 02835-0128; ☎ 800-688-1822 or
401-423-3377; fax 401-423-9630; www.naturetours.com

Tucano (9/18; PERUVIAN/7; 80 FT.)
The boat, which recently underwent seven weeks of renovation and refurbishing, is air-conditioned and has wood-paneled walls, a large observation deck, a living room, a wide balcony around the front of the vessel and a collection of science and nature reference books. Seventy-six windows showcase the forest. All cabins have private bathrooms with shower, toilet, and sink.

Nine-day cruises depart year-round. Air transportation can be arranged from Miami. The trips on the Amazon and tributaries are accompanied by naturalists. The company also offers Galapagos cruises.

Iberostar Grand Amazon Cruises
2566 Le Jeune Road, Coral Gables, FL 33134; ☎ 888-923-2722 or
305-774-9225; fax 305-774-4810; www.iberostar.com

Iberostar Grand Amazon (74/148; BRAZILIAN; 270 FT.)
In May 2005, the Spanish hotel company, Iberostar, launched its first cruise ship on the Amazon River in Brazil. The *Iberostar Grand Amazon,* which is one of the most luxurious ships on the Amazon, has 72 cabins and two superior suites on three decks, all with air-conditioning, private balcony, private bathroom, hair dryer, twin beds, writing desk, television, and phone.

The boat has two restaurants serving local and international cuisine, two bars, a conference room for 148 passengers, fitness center, elevator, laundry, paramedic, Internet access, and a Jacuzzi on the top open deck. Departing from Manaus, she will sail on three- and four-day itineraries which can be combined into a seven-day one. The boat will stop at several points along the Amazon jungle, offering excursions on small boats to explore certain areas close up.

International Expeditions
1 Environs Park, Helena, AL 35080; ☎ 205-428-1700 or 800-633-4734;
fax 205-428-1714; www.ietravel.com

La Amatista (15/30; 125 FT.)

La Turmalina (14/28; 115 FT.)

La Turquesa (23/46)
This 25-year-old company uses exploratory vessels sailing from Iquitos, past the start of the Amazon, exploring its tributaries. These include the Ucayali, Maranon, and Tapiche rivers and the Pacaya-Samiria National Reserve viewed from excursion craft and on foot along jungle trails. Naturalists/guides accompany

the outings. All cabins have private facilities and air-conditioning. Nine-day cruises make weekly departures throughout the year. The company also offers Galapagos cruises and others in Central and South America.

Ladatco Tours
2200 South Dixie Highway, Suite 704, Coconut Grove, FL 33133; ☎ 305-854-8422 or 800-327-6162; fax 305-285-0504; www.ladatco.com

Ladatco is a tour company that promotes and sells cruises on the following boats:

Amazon Clipper Premium (8/16; PERUVIAN; 66 FT.)

La Amastista/La Esmeralda/La Turmalina (11–15/22–30; PERUVIAN; 91–115 FT.)

Amazon Clipper Premium, a two-deck riverboat refurbished for overnight touring, has cabins with bunk beds, private baths, and air-conditioning. Three- to four-day cruises depart Monday and Wednesday from Manaus on the Amazon and Negro rivers; a six-day cruise combines the two. Multilingual local guide accompanies all cruises.

La Amastista, La Esmeralda, and *La Turmalina* offer six-day cruises, round trip, departing Sunday from Iquitos. Three-night cruises are also available. Itinerary includes bird-watching, jungle walk, and fishing in the Ataquari River.

Marco Polo Expeditions/PTS, Inc./Galapagos Cruises
1467 Industrial Avenue, Escondido, CA 92029; ☎ 866-672-4533 or 858-672-4533, fax 858-672-4505; www.marcopolovacations.com; www.ptsincorporated.com

Three-night *Desafio* cruises depart year-round from Manaus to the Amazon and tributaries accompanied by a multilingual naturalist. Continental and Brazilian cuisine is served buffet-style. The three-day *Tucano* program includes jungle walk to explore flora. The *Uncano* also sails on a nine-day Amazon adventure. The company also uses the *Amazon Clipper, Arca, Delfin, Orellana, Rio Amazonas,* as well as offering three- to seven-night cruises in the Galapagos on a variety of vessels, including the *Galapagos Legend, Coral I,* and *Coral II* on year-round departures.

Tara Tours
6595 Northwest 36th Street, Suite 306, Miami, FL 33166; ☎ 305-871-1246 or 800-327-0080; fax 305-871-0417; www.taratours.com

The tour company utilizes a variety of vessels and offers Amazon cruises from both Iquitos and Manaus. Among its vessels are *Rio Amazonas* (21/44; Peruvian; 146 ft.)/*La Amastista, La Esmeralda, La Turmalina* (11–15/22–30; Peruvian; 90–125 ft.)/*La Aquamarina* (16/29).

Eight-night Amazon packages offered year-round from Miami to Iquitos include boat trips and one night at a hotel in Lima, plus jungle walks, visits to native villages, and English-speaking naturalists. The company also offers cruises of the Galapagos.

ADVENTURE *and* CULTURAL CRUISES

THE DIFFERENCE BETWEEN an adventure or expedition cruise and an educational or cultural cruise is often a matter of semantics or marketing. And although there are differences, there are also similarities, particularly in the type of person to whom they appeal—namely, experienced travelers who prefer an intellectually stimulating or educational environment when they travel and do not need (or want) the activities and entertainment typical of mainstream cruises. They prefer the hands-on learning that adventure and educational cruises provide as well as the companionship of like-minded travelers.

Ships offering adventures or expeditions generally are informal and small, accommodating fewer than 150 passengers. Their small size enables them to visit places large ships cannot go. Vessels providing educational or cultural cruises might be larger and more formal. In all cases, the itineraries (which tend to be two weeks or longer) and the opportunity to learn from experts are the main attractions.

In the last two or three years, more deluxe ships have been added in the adventure and cultural cruises category, bringing with them a new level of comfort and expanded facilities. But the majority are still comfortable workhorses that safely ply icy waters or jungle rivers. They have cozy, functional cabins; friendly service; and good food, served at one open seating, often family-style. Dress is casual. Most ships maintain an open bridge.

Cruises are almost always seasonal to take advantage of optimum weather and wildlife conditions. On board, passengers attend lectures by specialists and have time to enjoy fellow shipmates. Ports are likely to be remote and passengers travel by Zodiac boats to the most inaccessible areas, often making wet landings where no docks are available.

On shore, participants view wildlife and scenery, hike into coastal forests, or encounter remote cultures. Not all cruises require heavy exertion—many are light adventure, nothing more than a short walk. In the evening, staff naturalists and guest lecturers recap the day's excursion in well-attended sessions. On educational or cultural cruises, lecturers are likely to be historians, anthropologists, museum authorities, and area specialists. Many such trips are sponsored by universities and museum groups, often as an alumni fund-raiser.

Destinations might be world-renowned sites visited by general tours, but participants on cultural cruises get in-depth information and excursions led by experts rather than the commercial guides that regular cruise lines use. Participants also are likely to attend cultural and folklore events. It isn't unusual for adventure and cultural cruises to overlap in their activities, particularly those offering light adventure (or soft adventure, the unappealing term the travel trade uses).

Not only do these cruises appeal to the same type of people—they may appeal to the same exact people.

If you've never tried an adventure/expedition cruise, there are a few things you need to consider. Adventure cruises are not exactly laid-back affairs. You might be rousted out of bed at 5:30 a.m. to see a whale, a penguin, or nearly anything else within the purview of the cruise's educational program. Even if you're not rolled out at 5:30 a.m., you'll probably have to rise by 6:30 or 7 a.m. to dress and have breakfast before the day's activities commence. If you try sleep in, you can often count on some announcements over the public address speaker that can be heard in your cabin. Such cruises tend to pack a lot into a day. On some ships, you scarcely have time for a shower and a change of clothes before dinner is served, except on days at sea.

Before you book an adventure/expedition cruise, carefully scrutinize the itinerary and make some inquiries about the likelihood of rough seas. An Antarctic cruise, for example, must traverse the Drake Passage for two days southbound and two days northbound from South America. The Drake Passage can be one of the roughest seas on the planet—perhaps not the place to be if you've never cruised before or if your experience is limited to the calm waters of the Caribbean. But if you're lucky, as Kay was on her Antarctic expedition, the passage can be as smooth as a lake.

Because many adventure/expedition cruises are at the ends of the earth or halfway around the world, you need to pay attention to all aspects of your travel plans. We recommend an intermediate layover both coming and going, as well as an extra day in the port of embarkation. If you're going to the Far East or Australia, try to arrange a night in Hawaii or California before continuing to your final destination. If you're headed to Antarctica, you might want to spend a night in Santiago or Buenos Aires on the return. Once when coming home from Antarctica, Bob ignored his own advice. After two days bouncing across the Drake Passage, he disembarked the ship at 8:30 a.m., then had to wait until 1 p.m. for a four-hour flight to Santiago. He had another four-hour layover in Santiago before boarding a nine-hour flight to Houston and connecting on to his final destination. By the time he got home, he'd been traveling for 32 hours (not counting the Drake Passage).

If your cruise package includes a stopover (and many do), it pays to check out the city where you'll be stopping. A Galapagos Islands adventure cruise included an overnight in Quito, Ecuador. Those folks who didn't check out Quito before leaving home were astonished to learn upon arrival that it sits in the Andes at an elevation of 9,350 feet. Not only did most not have warm clothing—they were heading for the equator and sea level, after all—but they discovered it was quite impossible to acclimate to that altitude in one day. An equally compelling reason for an overnight stopover and an extra night in the port city is the opportunity to deal with lost luggage. Believe us, the worst time to have your luggage disappear is when you're about to embark on an adventure/expedition cruise. Chances are you've spent weeks rounding up the specialized clothing and gear required for the cruise, but if you have a day or more prior to boarding for your luggage to catch up with you, you'll be fine 90 percent of the time. In a worst-case scenario, when your lost luggage stays lost, you'll still have time to re-equip in local stores before sailing.

Another precaution we take is to avoid luggage transfers between airlines. On an itinerary from Fort Lauderdale to Iceland for an expedition cruise out of Reykjavik, for example, we took an early Delta flight to New York's JFK International Airport where we claimed our bags and then personally rechecked them with Icelandair. We were perfectly happy to suffer an extra hour or two at JFK for the peace of mind of knowing that our bags were safely checked with Icelandair to Reykjavik.

Adventure/expedition cruises don't require physical training, but participants should be in good condition and able to endure some exertion. More importantly, they need to be flexible in temperament as well as body. They should be good sports, keep a sense of humor, and be ready to forgo comforts occasionally. Adventure or expedition cruises take participants off the beaten path worldwide. They tend to be more expensive than mainstream cruises because fewer people share the cost and because it costs more to operate a ship in remote areas. Also, shore excursions are usually included, and lecturers must be accommodated in cabins that otherwise draw revenue.

Participants tend to be strong environmentalists who expect fellow travelers to share their views. They like to be outdoors, are active, well-traveled, well-educated, intellectually curious, affluent, and perhaps semi-retired professionals age 50 or older. They often belong to a museum or natural history group. They probably read *Audubon, National Geographic,* or *Smithsonian* magazines, watch public television, and support the local zoo.

Following is a representative list of companies offering adventure/expedition or educational/cultural cruises. They provide brochures, usually with deck plans of vessels they use, and descriptions of itineraries. Being specialists, they usually can answer questions with more firsthand authority than a travel agent—unless it's an adventure travel specialist—or a mainstream cruise line can.

Regarding Galapagos cruises, in an effort to prevent overcrowding at certain visitor sites, the Galapagos National Park Service has revised the itineraries of many tour boats. Check with the tour company for the latest information.

Note: In parentheses after each boat name is information (where available) about the number of cabins and passengers; officers and crew; and the boat's length (cabins/passengers; officers/crew; boat length).

Abercrombie & Kent Inc

(See Part Two.)

Small boats are chartered for Galapagos cruises, including *Eclipse* (27/48; Ecuadorian; 210 ft.), among others. In Antarctica, the company uses *Explorer II*.

American Safari Cruises

(See Part Two under "European and Smaller Cruise Lines.")

Canodros, S.A.

Canodros 2735, P.O. Box 59-9000, Miami, FL 33159-9000;
☎ **800-613-6026; www.canodros.com**

Galapagos Explorer II (50/100; ECUADORIAN; 295 FT.)

The luxury, all-suite ship, built in 1990 as the *Renaissance III,* sails on three-, four-, and seven-night cruises weekly in the Galapagos Islands. Cruises can be combined with three or more nights at Kapawi Ecological Reserve, an unusual native Indian-owned and -operated base camp in the Amazon.

Ecuadorian-owned and -operated, the ship has classic lines and interiors throughout. Cabins, all with sitting rooms, are air-conditioned and have queen or two twin beds, telephone, television for VCR use, refrigerator-bar, full-length wardrobe, marble bath, and 110-volt electric outlets. Also onboard are an outdoor pool and whirlpool, boutique, library, observation deck, karaoke bar, and massage suite. The vessel has satellite communications and carries a doctor onboard.

The elegant, nonsmoking restaurant offers one informal, open seating. International and Ecuadorian cuisine is served; special diets can be accommodated. A lunch buffet is served on deck. Staff will prepare additional dishes on request. All bar drinks—including bottled water—are complimentary; only name wines, champagne, and minibar contents cost extra. Cruise price also includes twice-daily tours escorted by naturalists.

The ship always anchors offshore, and passengers are tendered on dinghies for dry or wet landings. In keeping with the company's environmental commitment, all soaps, detergents, and shampoo used on board are biodegradable. The ship produces its own fresh water and is equipped with a sewage treatment system to minimize environmental impact. Chlorine isn't used on board. Paper and nontoxic solids are incinerated, metal cans are compacted for recycling, and nonbiodegradable trash is returned to port.

Clipper Cruises

(See Part Two.)

Compagnie Polynesienne de Transport Maritime

☎ **650-574-2575 or 800-972-7268; www.aranui.com**

Arnaui III (85/200; MARQUESAN)

The world has shrunk to the point that most places on earth can be reached by air, but there are a few exceptions such as the French Polynesian Marquesas and Tuamotu (or Tuomotu) Islands in the South Pacific. These islands have been accessible by passenger freighters named *Aranui* (meaning "great highway" in the Maori language) since 1959. In 2003, a brand-new one arrived, the 200-passenger *Aranui III*, to take over the 16-day round trips from Papeete, Tahiti. She carries all manner of cargo and 20-foot containers to the remote archipelago and is crewed mostly by Marquesans.

The passengers' quarters are of a high standard and include a main lounge, library, video room, gym, small shop, laundry, and outdoor swimming pool with a bar. The dining room can accommodate all passengers at one seating, and the food is both international and Polynesian, with ingredients such as pork, poultry, fish, fruits and vegetables, and imported beef. French wines are included with lunch and dinner, which are served family-style while breakfast is a buffet. Many passengers are French (French Polynesia is still part of France), and others are European, Australian, and American.

The ship has a total of 85 cabins and suites. They include 63 standard, moderate-size twins with portholes, shower, and toilet that are plainly appointed with light wood furnishings; 12 larger deluxe cabins with windows, more colorful decor, darker wood furnishings, a refrigerator, and bathtub; and 10 suites, 8 with private balconies. Some cabins will accommodate a third person.

The ship sails year-round from Papeete, about every three to four weeks, on a 16-day voyage, calling at two Tuamotu and 15 Marquesas islands, all with spectacular scenery and some with beautiful volcanic peaks. Most days are spent at anchor off an island, while the ship loads and unloads cargo; three days are spent at sea. Time in port varies from a few hours to a full day. The *Aranui*'s arrival is a major event for each of these islands.

Activities include watching locals harvest black pearls, swimming from fine sandy beaches, snorkeling over coral reefs, exploring archeological ruins by jeep and on foot, buying handicrafts, and enjoying barbecues. Shore excursions are included in the fare. Scuba diving, horseback riding, and helicopter tours are extra. A 16-day voyage on *Aranui III* starts at about $3,000 per person, double occupancy.

Although assistance is provided, passengers need to be able to negotiate ladders into whale boats and disembark through the surf. March to August is the dry season, but with an occasional shower. September to February is the rainy season. Daytime temperatures hover in the 80s and fall into the 60s and 70s after dark.

Cruise North Expeditions Inc.
1920 Avenue Road, Toronto, Ontario, M5M 4A1 Canada;
☎ **866-263-3220 or 416-789-3752; fax 416-789-1974;**
www.cruisenorthexpeditions.com

Ushuaia **(28 CABINS, 5 SUITES/66; ARGENTINE, CANADIAN, INUIT/ 38; 278 FT.)**
Cruise North Expeditions, the brand new, Inuit-owned cruise line launched in July 2005, plans to revolutionize travel to the remote Canadian Arctic, a

virtually undiscovered part of the world, by making it affordable, accessible, and authentic. The Inuit are the indigenous people of the Canadian Arctic, popularly known as the Eskimo.

The U.S.-built, ice-class ship, *Ushuaia,* will be the only passenger ship docked in the Canadian Arctic with cruises starting in Kuujjuaq at the northern limit of the great Boreal Forest. That's a clear advantage over other cruise ships that must sail into the region from distant locations, such as Greenland, requiring extra travel days at sea.

The Cruise North package includes a short two-hour flight from Montreal to Kuujjuaq on its sister company, First Air, a Canada airline that has served of the northern region for more than 50 years. Thus, Cruise North's Arctic wildlife experience begins immediately upon the flight's arrival in Kuujjuaq. Through the savings in travel time, Cruise North is able to offer its expeditions at about half the price of other cruise lines calling in the North. Its prices start at $2,490 per person, double occupancy for a seven-night package that includes air, land, and sea.

Rather than exclude the Inuit, as cruise tourism has done in the past, Cruise North has the local inhabitants actively involved in the cruise operation. At the same time, the new venture helps the Inuit preserve their culture by sharing their traditions and customs with passengers. By being in direct contact with Cruise North passengers and welcoming them to their homeland, Inuit hosts expect to help passengers understand the indigenous people's deep reverence for the natural world, its scenic wonders, and abundant wildlife of the North.

For its maiden year, Cruise North was scheduled to operate a series of eight, seven-night Arctic cruises from July 10 to September 4, 2005. Normally during that time, the average temperature is about 50 degrees and can even reach 70 degrees. The Arctic wildlife and scenery are certain to delight passengers when they see polar bears standing upwards of 11 feet tall, walrus, Beluga whales, bearded seals, and musk-ox against a stunning backdrop of icebergs, soaring cliffs, mountains, and fjords. The cruises feature an experienced expedition team and a lecture series by leading naturalists, historians, and ornithologists. Cruise North's three itineraries—Arctic Explorer, Baffin Adventure, and In Hudson's Wake—include visits to ancient Inuit archaeological sites, a traditional Inuit community feast, drum dancing, and throat singing. Pre- and post-cruise options in the Arctic for small groups are offered and include kayaking, hiking, and a stay at a wilderness lodge.

The ship has four decks plus the Bridge Deck. The five suites and four twin cabins on Upper Deck have two lower beds, a television with DVD player, minifridge, and private facilities. The 20 twin cabins on the lower two decks and four on the Upper Deck have upper and lower beds, a private wash basin inside the cabin, and semi-private facilities (shared by two cabins). All cabins have a desk and storage space. The ice-strengthened ship's facilities include a library stocked with Arctic-related literature, dining room, observation lounge and bar, conference room, gift shop, and several observation decks.

Cruise North Expeditions is owned by the Makivik Corporation of Quebec, a successful investment corporation born of the first modern-day Aboriginal land claim settlement agreement in Canada (the JBNQA of 1975). Makivik also owns First Air and Air Inuit. The new cruise line is headed by Adamie Alaku, the Inuk chairman, and Dugald Wells, a professional engineer and expedition cruise veteran who began his career in the Arctic 20 years ago as a research scientist onboard Canadian icebreakers. The deck staff and engine crew are Argentine. The expedition leader, guides, lecturers, chef, and bartender are mostly Canadian, including some Inuit. The cruise line plans to train the Inuit in assistant positions for the first year and groom the best for more senior positions in future.

Reservations can be made through travel agents or The Travel Network in Toronto, Canada at ☎ 866-263-3220 or 416-789-3752.

Ecotour Expeditions
P.O. Box 128, Jamestown, RI 02835-0128; ☎ 800-688-1822 or 401-423-3377; fax 401-423-9630; www.naturetours.com

This operator uses three small sister ships, *Eric, Flamingo,* and *Letty* (10/20; 83 ft.) as well as the *Beluga* (8/16; 110 ft.) All cabins and dining rooms are air-conditioned and all cabins have private bathrooms with showers. The vessels are comfortable, but not luxurious. On the upper Dolphin Deck, cabins have two twin lower beds and picture windows, except one cabin which has one double bed. Booby Deck cabins have one double bed and picture windows; while the lower Iguana Deck cabins have two twin lower beds and portholes. Two Iguana cabins have an upper berth and can be used as triples. The *Beluga* has a large dining room, salon, and a full sun deck. Of its eight cabins, two have queen size beds, three bunk beds, and three have two twin beds. The cruises depart on Mondays and Fridays; on each island passengers visit two to three different sites.

Ecoventura S.A.
(See entry for Galapagos Network.)

Esplanade Tours
(See "Nile River Cruises" earlier in Part Three.)

Galapagos Cruises
c/o Adventure Associates, 13150 Coit Road, Suite 110, Dallas, TX 75240; ☎ 972-907-0414 or 800-527-2500; fax 972-783-1286; www.metropolitantouring.com or www.adventure-associates.com

Adventure Associates is the U.S. representative of Quito-based Metropolitan Touring, Ecuador's leading tour company, and the oldest company offering Galapagos cruises. Ships are well-run and have excellent guides.

Isabela II **(211/40; ECUADORIAN; 166 FT.)**
Completely renovated in February 2000, this ship's new look includes an

enlarged reception area, a redesigned library, and a new multimedia system for briefings and lectures. The mahogany-paneled dining room and library were totally refurbished along with the lounge and cabins. The redesigned sun deck now has a bar, observation area for whale- and dolphin-watching, and a solarium. The air-conditioned ship offers satellite telephone, e-mail, and fax service. She sails from Baltra on Fridays on seven-night cruises of the Galapagos Islands; shorter cruises are offered on Tuesday departures. Children under age 12 who share a cabin with adults get a 25% discount off the regular price. Prices do not include Ecuador/Baltra flights or national park entrance fee.

Santa Cruz (46/90; ECUADORIAN; 237 FT.)

Offering three-, four-, and seven-night Galapagos cruises, this ship, renovated in 1998, is one of the largest and most comfortable sailing in Galapagos waters. Food and service are good, and the ship is well-run. All cabins were refitted, and passengers can choose singles, doubles, or suites. The air-conditioned ship is mostly carpeted and has a large dining room, cocktail lounge, bar, library, Jacuzzi, and spacious decks. Three-night cruises visit the southern islands; four-night tours visit the central and northern groups. The two can be combined. Naturalist/guides, trained and licensed by Galapagos National Park, give nightly briefings on the next day's visit and accompany passengers on excursions. Passengers are divided into groups of 20 people or less. In 2005, the company introduced enhancements to its established routes with visits to Sante Fe Island, home to endemic land iguanas, a large sea lion colony and the Galapagos' oldest rocks; Dragon Hill on Santa Cruz, where marine iguanas bask on black lava and a lagoon attracts flamingos; La Galapaguera, the giant-tortoise breeding station; and Stephen's Bay on San Cristobal, with indigenous Chatham mockingbirds, lava lizards, and a white coral beach.

Galapagos Network

5805 Blue Lagoon Drive, Suite 160, Miami, FL 33126; ☎ 305-262-6264 or 800-633-7972; fax 305-262-9609; www.ecoventura.com

This tour company offers year-round, five- to ten-night cruises in the Galapagos Islands on its fleet of small vessels. Cruises are designed for the well-educated, well-traveled, and those eager to learn about nature, ecology, and environmental issues. The boats' size allows them to visit remote islands. Naturalist/guides lecture and lead walks. Passengers are ferried to the islands by launches.

Life aboard a Galapagos Network cruise, especially on the *Letty, Eric,* and *Flamingo I,* is, well, familial. The small number of passengers and Ecuadorian crew connect almost immediately in a friendship that only ripens over the duration of the cruise. The whole crew—from the captain to the cook—is invested in sharing the rugged beauty and abundant wildlife of the Galapagos, and their enthusiasm is impossible to resist.

Dining features Ecuadorian specialties, which in spice, aroma, and taste are always a surprise. Some dishes exhibit characteristics of provincial

Mexican cuisine; others, remarkably, would be at home in an Indian (as in Bombay) restaurant. But it's all good, even if it keeps you guessing.

One of the Galapagos Network's greatest strengths is its land support. From the time you step off your international flight, there is someone to watch over you. Most itineraries include an overnight in either Quito or Guayaquil in quirky but totally wonderful (and totally Ecuadorian) local hotels. Following an overnight, passengers continue on by plane the next day to the Galapagos.

Sky Dancer (8/16; ECUADORIAN; 100 FT.)
Built in the United States, this vessel has a spacious dining area which serves both Ecuadorian and international cuisine, fully stocked bar, main salon with entertainment center, allocated personal dive storage, and sun deck. Cabins are air-conditioned and have private bathrooms. *Sky Dancer* attracts hard-core divers who can take as many as four dives per day on a preplanned, seven- or ten-night itinerary. Dive in the Northern Islands of Wolf and Darwin, famous for hammerhead sharks, giant manta rays, and whale sharks.

Eric/Flamingo I/Letty (10/20; ECUADORIAN; 83 FT.)
Built in 1993, *Letty* is the newest of three luxury yachts. All are air-conditioned. Cabins have private bathrooms, VCRs, and stereo equipment. *Letty* departs on Monday; the others depart on Sunday. Approximately four hours per day are spent on each island. The boats are well-suited for families or groups. Five- to seven-night itineraries include the western islands of Fernandina and Isabela, as well as Espanola, Tower, Santa Cruz, Bartolome, South Plaza, Santiago, and San Cristobal. In addition, passengers may lunch at a ranch on Santa Cruz.

Galapagos Yacht Cruises
c/o Galapagos Inc., 7800 Red Road, Suite 112, South Miami, FL 33143; ☎ 305-665-0841 or 800-327-9854; fax 305-661-1457; www.galapagoscruises.net

---

Cruz del Sur/Dorado/Estrella del Mar (8/16; ECUADORIAN; 75 FT.)
Cruz del Sur and *Estrella del Mar* sail from San Cristobal; *Dorado* sails from Baltra with stops at the main Galapagos islands and others where larger ships don't go.

Yolita (6/12; ECUADORIAN; 53 FT.)
Three-, four-, and seven-night cruises from San Cristobal to Islas Lobos, Espanola, Punta Suarez, Gardener, Darwin Station, North Seymour, Baltra, Bachas, Rabida, Puerto Egas, Bartolome, Sullivan, Islas Plazas, Santa Fe, and Santa Cruz.

Glacier Bay Cruises
(See Part Two.)

Global Quest Journeys
185 Willis Avenue, Second Floor, Mineola, NY 11501; ☎ 516-739-3690 or 800-221-3254; fax 516-739-8022; www.globalquesttravel.com

GlobalQuest has diverse offerings, including cruises to the Galapagos, Kenya, Antarcia, and Chile, among other destinations. GlobalQuest partners with Quark Expeditions for its Antarctic cruises on the *Professor Multanovskiy* and *Professor Molchanov* (see Quark Expeditions further in this section for a description). Global has also expanded its U.S. coastal cruises on the *Nantucket Clipper, as* well as the Adriatic on the *Monet* and Russian Waterways on the *Novikov Priboy.*

Galapagos Legend I (50/90; ECUADORIAN/68; 300 FT.)
Built in Germany in 2002, this ship has 50 outside cabins, of which four are large suites and 24 are junior suites, and 3 inside cabins. All cabins have a private bathroom, hair dryer, and television. The ship is air-conditioned and has a lounge, library, pool, 24-hour coffee bar, observatory, jogging track, auditorium, boutique, clinic, and dining room where continental cuisine and Ecuadorian specialties are served. The ship sails on three-, four-, and seven-night cruises year-round from Baltra to the Galapagos Islands, accompanied by naturalist guides. Longer itineraries can include stayovers in Quito, Ecuador.

Pacific Explorer (50/100; COSTA RICA; 185 FT.)
Built in 1995, and completely remodeled, this ship has an English-speaking Costa Rican crew and American exploration leader. All cabins are air-conditioned with private baths and showers and have picture windows that open, teak beds (either twin or one double), a television monitor and VCR, a storage closet, and private facilities. Maneuverable and versatile, the ship is equipped with Zodiacs for beach landings on remote shores and it carries kayaks for those who want to explore on their own. International cuisine with Central American specialties is prepared daily using fresh products. The ship sails on nine-night cruise/land programs in Costa Rica and Panama.

Royal Star (111/200; GERMAN/130; 472 FT.)
On this boat, most cabins are outside and have air-conditioning, bathroom with shower, and phone. Some triples and quads are available. The one dining room has two seatings; cuisine is international with local specialties. The ship sails on 14- to 21-day cruises from Mombasa to Zanzibar and Mahe in the Seychelles. The ship sails on 14 to 21 day cruises from Mombasa to Zanzibar and the Seychelles. Safari packages are available in Kenya before or after the cruise.

Skorpios III (49 CABINS, 125 PASSENGERS)
For its southern Chile program, the company uses *Skorpios III* constructed in 1994 and 1995 to international standards for SOLAS and A-1 Ice, among others. She is equipped with fire, navigational, security, and lifesaving equipment and satellite phone service. The ship sails every Sunday from Puerto Natales, about 153 miles north of Punta Arenas, on a five-day cruise through the channels and fjords that border the Southern Ice Field in the Chilean Patagonia, considered the third largest reserve of fresh water on the planet and home to the most spectacular glaciers in the southern hemisphere.

International Expeditions
**One Environs Park, Helena, AL 35080; ☎ 205-428-1700 or
800-633-4734; fax 205-428-1714; www.ietravel.com**

Evolution (18/32)
This new four-deck expedition ship is fully air-conditioned and has 14 cabins and 4 suites that measure about 200 square feet each, with generous-size bath with shower and hair dryer. There is an observation deck, a sun deck with a small pool, a canopied bar on the roof deck, a library/video room, and an infirmary with a doctor aboard every voyage. Meals are served in the dining room in one seating or outdoors, weather permitting. Satellite phone and e-mail access is available from the bridge when necessary. The ship carries regular kayaks and special acrylic sea kayaks for underwater viewing; SNUBA and snorkeling equipment; and wet suits. All cruises are accompanied by naturalist guides. Ten-day Galapagos itineraries are offered monthly year-round.

Kleintours
**Avenue Eloy. Alfaro N 34–151 and Catalina Aldaz, Quito, Ecuador;
☎ 888-50-KLEIN or 593-2-2267-000; fax 593-2-2442-389;
www.kleintours.com**

Coral I/Coral II (20/26 PASSENGERS)
These two vessels offer three-, four-, and seven-night cruises. Three-night cruises depart on Sunday; four-night cruises, Wednesday.

Galapagos Legend (110 PASSENGERS)
This boat offers three-, four-, and seven-day cruises. Three-day cruises depart on Monday; four-day cruises depart on Thursday. Seven-night cruises depart on Monday, Wednesday, or Thursday.

Lindblad Expeditions
**96 Morton Street, Ninth Floor, New York, NY 10014; ☎ 212-765-7740 or
800-397-3348; fax 212-265-3770; www.expeditions.com**

Lindblad Expeditions describes its mission as "providing travelers with a more thoughtful way to see the world, avoiding crowded destinations, and seeking out natural ones." The company offers a wide selection of light adventure cruises using six different small ships in various parts of the world. The globe-roaming company was founded in 1979 by Sven-Olof Lindblad, son of the late Lars-Eric Lindblad, who pioneered modern expedition cruising. Each cruise is designed to take travelers to remote areas in comfort and safety.

Lindblad Expeditions occasionally charters other ships and operates cruises for universities or groups.

In 2004, Lindblad took two major steps: the company added a second ship, the *Islander,* to its Galapagos series and joined forces with the National

Geographic Society to combine their travel and expedition strengths in three broad areas:

1. Create an education program to enhance passengers' expedition experience and bring the findings to an audience far beyond expedition participants;

2. To add technological innovations across the Lindblad fleet, with particular focus on the *Endeavor*, newly renamed *National Geographic Endeavour*, where new, state-of-the-art equipment will allow for more extensive underwater exploration; and

3. Establish an expert advisory panel of researchers, scientists, and explorers, including oceanographer and National Geographic explorer-in-residence Sylvia Earle and National Geographic contributing photographer-in-residence Emory Kristof, to help shape the alliance's conservation, research, and education initiatives. The best part for Lindblad passengers is the opportunities to interact with the National Geographic team as well as Lindblad's expedition leaders and naturalists.

National Geographic Endeavour (61/110; SCANDINAVIAN/INTERNATIONAL; 295 FT.)

The *Endeavor*, after being renamed, sailed on its inaugural voyage in April 2005. Throughout the year, the ship operates from Antarctica to Scandinavia. Recently, she was outfitted to allow for more extensive exploration, including Zodiac landing craft, sea kayaks, snorkel gear, and high-tech underwater equipment like a remotely operated video camera (ROV) that transmits live underwater pictures back to the ship.

The five-deck ship has a lounge with a bar and facilities for films and lectures, a library, small swimming pool, fitness center, sauna, hair salon, gift shop, and observation deck. Meals are served in one seating with unassigned tables in an informal setting. All cabins are outside above the waterline and have windows or portholes and private baths; there are a few singles. The ship provides a passenger e-mail station, and laundry services. A doctor and massage therapist are on board.

Islander (24/48; ECUADORIAN; 164 FT.)

This new, fully air-conditioned ship has a lounge with bar and facilities for films and lectures, a library, small gift shop, doctor's office, and deck space for lounging in the sun or shade. All meals are served in one seating and offer a international menu with Ecuadorian specialties. All cabins on the three deck ship are outside and have windows and private baths. The ship carries Zodiac landing craft, snorkeling gear, and wet suites. The ship sails in the Galapagos year-round.

Lord of the Glens (29/54; SCOTTISH; 150 FT.)

A classic luxury yacht with rich mahogany finishes and teak decks, the vessel has two lounges, a small library and bar, and two open-air viewing areas. The cabins are outside with large windows (some have portholes), bathrooms with shower, bathrobes, hair dryer, phone, television, and safe. Meals that stress local fare and fresh products are served in a single seating in the room-with-a-view dining room. From May to September, the vessel offers ten-night or longer cruises in the heart of the Scottish highlands, seeing historic places and extraordinary scenery. For a 14-day trip, the Heart of the Highlands cruise is combined with a Royal Scotsman Train ride through countryside between Edinburgh and Inverness.

Polaris **(41/80; SWEDISH/FILIPINO AND SWEDISH; 238 FT.)**
Polaris offers Galapagos cruises year-round. Ten-day land and sea itineraries are accompanied by outstanding naturalists, such as Dr. Lynn Fowler, who has conducted wildlife research in the area for over 20 years. The fully air-conditioned ship has a lounge with bar and facilities for films and lectures, a library, gift shop, doctor's office, and covered deck with tables and chairs. All meals are served in one seating and offer an international menu with Ecuadorian specialties. All cabins on the four-deck ship are outside and most have windows (except a few on the lower deck that have portholes) and private bath. The ship carries Zodiac landing craft, a glass-bottom boat, snorkeling gear, and wet suits.

Sea Bird/Sea Lion **(37/70; AMERICAN; 152 FT.)**
The twin ships have a lounge with bar and facilities for films and lectures, a library, and outside deck with chairs. All meals, prepared by American chefs, are served in one seating. All cabins on the four-deck ship are outside and have windows (except four on the lower deck that have portlights) and private bath. The ship carries Zodiac landing craft, kayaks, snorkeling gear, and wet suits and has an e-mail station. From May to September, the ships sail on 7- and 11-night Alaska cruises; in autumn and spring they move to the Columbia and Snake rivers to Hells Canyon and Lewis and Clark sites, as well as Idaho and Montana. In winter, they offer a series of cruises to Baja California and the Sea of Cortés timed for optimum whale-watching.

Sea Voyager **(32/62; COSTA RICAN; 175 FT.)**
Acquired in summer 2001 from Temptress Cruises, this ship has all-outside cabins with private bathrooms and air-conditioning. She was completely refurbished in 2001 and sails most of the year on Baja California, Costa Rica, and Panama cruises.

MTS (Melanesian Tourist Services)
P.O. Box 707, Coastwatchers Avenue, Madang, Papua New Guinea; or USA Sales Office, MTS, P.O. Box 65515, Tucson, AZ 85728; ☎ 310-785-0370 or cell 310-809-6700; fax 310-785-0314; www.meltours.com

MTS Discoverer **(21/42; NEW GUINEAN; 117 FT.)**
The *MTS Discoverer* was built exclusively for expeditionary cruising up the mighty Sepik River and around the Bismarck and Trobriand islands. She can cruise for 30 days without the need to take on fuel and water. She is fast, comfortable, and equipped with five tenders and a helicopter (subject to conditions). The vessel is air-conditioned; her facilities include a restaurant,

library, in-house television system, bar, lounge, covered deck space, dive shop, laundry, and gift shop. All cabins have private bathroom, satellite phones, and public address system.

The ship meets international safety requirements and is the only vessel of its kind in Papua New Guinea. She sails on four- and five-night cruises on the Sepik River, and seven-night cruises of the Trobriands and the remote islands of Bismarck and North Solomon seas. The cruises remain flexible to take advantage of the opportunity to witness an authentic local ceremony that may occur along the way or insure maximum shore time in the villages.

MTS, a Papua New Guinea owned and operated company, was founded in 1975 to develop the country's tourism in a sustainable manner. MTS operates full inbound services and is based in Madang with offices in Port Moresby, Japan, and North America.

Metropolitan Touring
(See entry for Galapagos Cruises.)

National Geographic Expeditions
P.O. Box 65265, Washington, D.C. 20035-5265; ☎ 888-966-8687; www.nationalgeographic.com/ngexpeditions

National Geographic Expeditions offers a wide selection of worldwide programs including more than 20 cruises or journeys that include a cruise as part of the itinerary. The programs use a total of 13 ships as different as the 320-passenger luxury *Paul Gauguin* in Tahiti and the 48-passenger sailing vessel *Panorama* in the Mediterranean; five of the ships are operated by Lindblad Expeditions. In 2004, the National Geographic Society and Lindblad Expeditions joined hands to offer excursions that combine the expertise of both. (See Lindblad Expeditions above for details.) As a start, Lindblad's 110-passenger *Endeavor* was renamed *National Geographic Endeavor* and has been outfitted with new equipment such as sea kayaks and high-tech underwater equipment to enhance the expeditions.

Orient Lines
(See Part Two.)

Quark Expeditions
1019 Post Road, Darien, CT 06820; ☎ 203-656-0499 or 800-356-5699; fax 203-655-6623; www.quarkexpeditions.com

This tour company, a pioneer in Arctic and Antarctic expedition cruises, handles a group of Russian and Yugoslavian-built ships, all with Russian officers and crew. They are accompanied by an expedition leader, assistant expedition leader, lecturers, and Zodiac pilots who may be from the United States, Europe, Australia, or South America, depending on destinations and their expertise. Antarctica departures include a combination of the Antarctic Peninsula, Weddell Sea, South Georgia, Falkland Islands, Chilean fjords, Ross Sea, New Zealand, and Australian subantarctic islands. Most cruises depart from Ushuaia, Argentina, but some depart from Auckland, New Zealand, or Hobart, Tasmania. Some ships sail around the Arctic Circle and to the North Pole.

Akademik Shokalskiy (28/49; RUSSIAN; 234 FT.)

Professor Molchanov (28/49; RUSSIAN; 226 FT.)

Professor Multanovskiy (28/49; RUSSIAN; 226 FT.)

The *Professor Multanovskiy,* built in Finland in 1982 for polar and oceano-graphic research, has been refurbished since her conversion to a passenger ship. She has two dining rooms, a lounge, bar, library, lecture room, sauna, and infirmary. There are twin and triple cabins; some with private baths and others with shared baths. From November to March, the ship sails to the Antarctic Peninsula, South Shetlands, South Georgia, and the Falklands round-trip to Ushuaia. *Professor Molchanov* and *Akademik Shokalskiy* are sister ships of *Professor Multanovskiy.*

Orlova (62/110; RUSSIAN/53; 328 FT.)

Built in 1976, refurbished in 1999, and upgraded in 2002, this ship is fully equipped with a lecture hall, library, bar and lounge, and a dining room. Accommodations include twin and triple cabins and suites, all with a lower berth, private bathroom, porthole or window, writing desk, sitting space, and ample storage. Meals, prepared by European chefs, are served at a sin-gle seating in a window-lined dining room. *Orlova* operates cruises to the Antarctic Peninsula and South Georgia.

Kapitan Khlebnikov (54/112; RUSSIAN; 433 FT.)

This Antarctic icebreaker, built in 1980 and refurbished in 1992, became the first ship to circumnavigate Antarctica with passengers in 1997. All cabins and suites are outside ones and have two lower berths, private bath, desk, and large closet. There are two dining rooms, a lounge and bar, conference room, indoor swimming pool, gym and sauna, library of polar books and videos, shop, small infirmary with doctor, and an elevator. The ship's satellite commu-nication system provides phone, fax, and e-mail facilities when necessary.

From December to March, the ship sails on three Antarctica cruises, ranging from three weeks to one month. Early booking discounts are avail-able. In July and August, she sails to Russia's Far East and Wrangel Island, the Northwest Passage, and Tanquary Fjord, Ellesmere Island, and Greenland. The ship has Zodiacs and an onboard helicopter offering spec-tacular views.

Yamal/Sovetskiy Soyuz (50/100; RUSSIAN; 492 FT.)

One of the world's most powerful icebreakers, the *Yamal* has a lounge, bar, li-brary, gift shop, infirmary, dining room, lecture room, gym, sauna, pool, and two helicopters. She departs on 15-day expeditions round-trip from Murmansk to the geographic North Pole. *Sovetskiy Soyuz* is a sister ship to the *Yamal.*

St. Helena Line

Andrew Weir Shipping, Ltd., Dexter House, 2 Royal Mint Court, London EC3N 4XX, England; ☎ 44-020-7575-6480; fax 44-020-7575-6200; www.aws.co.uk

---

St. Helena (49/128; BRITISH/ST. HELENIAN)

The island of St. Helena, a British South Atlantic territory located 1,200 miles off the coast of Africa, may be the world's most significant place with no airport. For the mountainous island's 4,000 inhabitants, the 6,767-ton Royal Mail Ship (RMS) *St. Helena* provides the sole link to the outside world (at least until the island's new airport opens in 2010). For visitors, the voyage is one of the last true ocean liner experiences, plus it gives passengers the bonus of a full week on the island. The trips begin either at Cape Town, South Africa and sail via Namibian ports to St. Helena and Ascension islands and return south (about three weeks) or, less frequently, sail from England and call at Las Palmas, Ascension, St. Helena, and onto Cape Town (about four weeks).

The passenger, mail, and cargo service began in 1978 and operates under a contract with the British Government. The present ship was purpose-built in a Scottish shipyard in1989 to serve the islands, offering the comfortable facilities of a small liner for 128 passengers and a British and St. Helenian crew of 65. One-way fares between Cape Town and St. Helena range from 288 to 1,107 British pounds.

The homey public rooms include a two-section forward observation lounge with a bar, and a video lounge for screening films and reading. The **Sun Lounge** looks onto the outdoor pool. Here, a light breakfast and lunch are served daily. The dining room, on a lower deck, operates with two reserved sittings at dinner. The food is good British fare, such as tasty soups, curries, roasts, and well-prepared fish.

All plainly furnished cabins are outside, with windows or portholes, twin beds, and upper and lower berths. Most have a private shower and toilet. Budget accommodations, reserved for the Saints, as the St. Helenians are called, are sometimes available for non-island passengers.

The local passengers are Saints—a people of mixed British, South Asian, East Indian, and Madagascar origin—and visitors from Britain, Germany, France, South Africa, and the United States. Cargo includes mail and parcels, refrigerated and frozen food, medical equipment and drugs, construction materials, textbooks, and vehicles. In short, everything the islanders require.

During the daily cycle, passengers establish a routine of reading, socializing on deck, visiting the bridge or engine room, and taking a swim or playing deck tennis with the officers. In the evening, the purser hosts games, quizzes, and pantomime, all old-fashioned shipboard fun. There's also a captain's cocktail party.

St. Helena, the principal destination, spreads across the horizon beneath a low cloud clinging to the mountain peaks. The ship anchors off

Jamestown, a pastel-colored 19th-century Georgian town sandwiched into a deep valley. Through and round-trip passengers get the bonus of a week on the island while the cargo is discharged and the ship makes a passenger run to Ascension and back. Most visitors stay at two small hotels in Jamestown, while others choose self-catering cottages up in the hills. Jamestown offers a small museum, a pretty Anglican church, a few shops, and a couple of restaurants, but the principal attraction is main street, the island's social center where everyone gathers to talk.

Napoleon spent six years here from 1815 until his death in 1821; Longwood, his permanent residence and gardens, is open to visitors. Nearby, Deadwood Plain is home to the island's indigenous wirebird. The governor's house, a handsome 1791 Georgian mansion, is home to a giant Seychellois tortoise named Jonathan, reputed to about 175 years old. There are miles of walking trails around the coast and down to secluded bays. After a week, the ship returns on the island and embarks passengers for a continuation of the voyage. Once a year, the St. Helena also makes a three-week round-trip voyage to the even more remote island of Tristan da Cunha, located about halfway between South Africa and South America. This one sells out well in advance.

Wilderness Travel
1102 Ninth Street, Berkeley, CA 94710; ☎ 510-558-2488 or 800-368-2794; fax 510-558-2489; www.wildernesstravel.com

---

This adventure tour company offers Galapagos programs almost year-round, some with up to three departures monthly. The company combines cruises on small yachts with hiking in areas not usually covered by conventional excursions. As an example, the *Sagitta* (10/16; 120 ft.), a sailing yacht, boasts three full masts, two decks, and cabins with private bathrooms, hot-water showers, and air-conditioning; a library, dining room, salon, and conference room with video. The crew is made up of the captain, first mate, engineer, two sailors, a cook and assistant, cabin attendant, and naturalist guide. The *Diamante* (6/12; 112 ft.), a brigantine schooner motor sailer, is a modern, scaled-down version of the great naval training ships. She has an airy deck house which includes the main salon/dining room. The beamed salon is decorated with beautiful mahogany and teak wood and offers 360-degree visibility onto the passing scenery. It is also possible to dine outside, around a teak table aft of the pilot house. The six cabins have upper/lower berths, private facilities with fresh, hot and cold water showers.

The company also has a combination cruise of the Galapagos and the haciendas of Ecuador, with an optional extension to the Kapawi rainforest.

NORWEGIAN COASTAL CRUISES *and* CRUISE FERRIES

THE CRAGGY COAST OF NORWAY, deeply indented like the fingers on your hand, was carved eons ago by massive glaciers. Crevices, which we call fjords, can be ten miles long. From their dark, mirror-like waters rise almost vertical cliffs, and awesome mountains climb to several thousand feet on each side.

Often at the head of fjords are snow-capped peaks. In some places, glaciers inch toward the North Sea. Along the shores are tiny fishing villages and isolated farmhouses. Farther up the mountains are lodges where hikers bed down in summer and Olympic hopefuls fine-tune their skiing in winter.

The setting is beautiful; late May through early autumn are ideal for cruising. Most major lines with ships in Europe offer Norwegian fjord cruises. Itineraries differ slightly, but the program is essentially the same: departing from Copenhagen, Oslo, Bergen, Harwich, or Dover and going as far north as Trondheim, Norway's original capital and third-largest city, or Tromso, the largest town north of the Arctic Circle. Others continue to the North Cape, the northernmost point in Europe, and to Spitsbergen, a group of islands studded with massive glaciers. Another way to cruise the coast—the way Norwegians do—is on the Norwegian Coastal Express.

NORWEGIAN COASTAL VOYAGE

ELEVEN WORKING PASSENGER-CARGO SHIPS, known as the Hurtigruten ("fast route" in Norwegian), operate a daily passenger and cargo service from Bergen to 35 ports on Norway's coast, well beyond the North Cape to Kirkenes, near the Russian border.

A Norwegian institution since 1893, the ships operate year-round through all weather and are a lifeline for the people in small, often isolated communities along the way. The vessels, while increasingly cruise-oriented, provide transportation for locals and haul cargo ranging from automobiles and farm equipment to frozen fish.

The ships also carry tourists who may board and disembark at any port. Many visitors, however, take the 2,500-mile round-trip voyage as a 12-day cruise. Others sail one-way and return by road or air. (Some open-water passages can be rough; passengers should come prepared.)

Time in port varies from as little as 15 minutes to several hours. There are shore excursions (about $20 to $40) at a few ports, and more costly trips leave the ship at one port, travel inland, and rejoin it at another.

The best time to make the trip is mid-May to July, the period with 24 hours of daylight. Some travelers prefer the quieter months of early spring and fall. Summer sailings fill quickly, although space is often available at short notice. During the off-season, cabins are plentiful.

In the height of summer, some stretches are crowded with deck passengers, especially between the mainland and islands. Generally, about half of the passengers are local commuters or those attending an onboard conference; the balance is an international mix. There are usually quite a few English-speaking people, and always many Germans. Announcements are made in the languages required by passenger makeup. Meals are served at two seatings when traffic warrants. Breakfast and lunch are buffet-style. Dinner is from a set menu; tables are reserved. Dietary requests should be made when booking. Continental and Norwegian dishes are served. Lunch offers the widest selection of hot and cold foods. Because of hefty taxes, alcoholic beverages are expensive—$6 or more for a beer is common. Entertainment is limited to the gorgeous scenery, enlivened by commentary, good conversation, cargo handling, and the festive occasion of crossing the Arctic Circle. The line provides an excellent guidebook. In summer, the newest ships might have a band for dancing.

Norwegian Coastal Voyage, Inc. markets the service in North America. The service has 11 ships in four classifications: Millennium, Contemporary, Mid-generation, and Traditional.

Millennium Ships

The *Finnmarken* and *Trollfjord*, completed in spring 2002, and the *Midnatsol* in 2003 are 15,000 tons and take 643, 674, and 674 passengers, respectively. Of the three new ships, the *Finnmarken* appears to be the more innovative with features such a Jugend-style (Art Nouveau) interiors, an indoor/outdoor cafe, wine bar, two panoramic lounges, an indoor pool, a racquet court and gym, four conference rooms, and 14 suites with private balconies. The *Trollfjord* has 21 suites (8 with balconies), glass elevators, a sauna and fitness room, and eight conference rooms. The cargo is handled via ramps through the side doors. The standard amenities are the same as the new ships. The *Midnatsol*, meaning the midnight sun, has its interiors dedicated to the Norwegian summer, and natural light pours in through the big glass windows. Like the *Trollfjord*, the ship has some suites with balconies as well as amenities like a sauna, gym, and library. All three Millennium vessels have an Internet cafe.

Contemporary Ships

The *Kong Harald, Nordkapp, Nordlys, Nordnorge, Polarlys,* and *Richard With,* all completed since 1993, add to the Hurtigruten the concept of the cruise ferry, with its greater comfort (well-established and popular in Baltic waters). Large and boxy (390 feet long and 63 feet wide), the ships take as many as 490 passengers in relatively roomy accommodations. Cargo is handled via ramps.

The modern cabins are mostly outside. They have foldaway beds and two lower berths, audio channels, automated wake-up calls, tiled baths with showers, and hair dryers.

Public rooms have the fashionable look of modern cruise ships, with rich fabrics, thick carpets, and ample use of brass, glass, and veneers. Norwegian sculptures and painted seascapes are attractive features. A top-deck, wraparound observation lounge is for viewing. A middle deck offers a cocktail lounge, library/card room, conference rooms, a souvenir shop, playroom, video arcade, 24-hour cafeteria, 240-seat restaurant, and private dining room. Also aboard are a sauna, small gym, and passenger laundry.

Mid-generation Ships

The *Narvik* and the *Vesteraalen,* were built in 1982 and 1983, then rebuilt and enlarged later in the same decade, and refurbished in 1995, carry up to 320 passengers. Cabins are smaller and decidedly plainer, but most are outside and all have private bathrooms with showers. The ships' have forward-facing observation lounges and glass-enclosed top-deck lounges. Freight and vehicles are handled via roll-on ramps.

Traditional Ships

The 1956-built *Nordstjernen* is one of two remaining Traditional ships. She has 179 very small outside and inside cabins, some without private facilities. The best cabins sell out fast. The ship possesses rich character, teak decks, and a battered hull from thousands of dockings. There are two lounges (the forward facing one is nonsmoking), a restaurant, and a cafeteria, the latter used by short-run passengers. Cargo and vehicles are loaded by crane. This ship is no longer in year-round service.

The *Nordstjernen* summer cruises around Spitzbergen are marketed in the United States as "The Adventure Expedition," and feature naturalist guides and Zodiac landings. The packages combine roundtrip flights from New York to Oslo and Spitsbergen, hotel and breakfast in each capital, selected cabin category, all meals on the cruise, shore excursions, transfers, port charges, air taxes, and gratuities. The eight-day voyage ranges in cost from $3,615 to $4,420 per person double occupancy. Norwegian Coastal Voyage also sells the 94-passenger *Polar Star,* an expedition ship rebuilt from a Swedish icebreaker, on 11- to 15-day Spitzbergen circumnavigation packages from Longyearbyn.

The *Lofoten,* the second of the classic ships, was completed in 1964 and given a major refit in 2003. Like the *Nordstjernen,* she substitutes for the *Nordnorge* and *Nordkapp* when these ships leave the rotation in October for cruises to Antarctica and the Chilean fjords, returning in April. The *Lofoten*'s maritime character and paneled interiors are a well-maintained delight. With berths for 171 passengers, her cabins are small, with the majority having upper and lower berths; about half have private facilities. There are two forward observation lounges from which to watch the cargo handling, a dining room spanning the width of the ship, a cafeteria, and a bar aft. In the summer, the *Lofoten* is used on a fjords cruise program including the 11-day "Lofoten Islands" and "Western Fjords" and 10-day "Fjords to the North" cruises.

On the Coastal Express

Billed as the world's most beautiful voyage, especially when the weather cooperates, the Coastal Express offers relaxed and informal adventure. Aboard the *Kong Harald,* the feeling is that of a small, modern, floating hotel. On the first morning at sea, a sheer mountain wall plunges into the narrow channel, and, to port, Norwegian Sea breakers pile up against low-lying islands. At a briefing, the courier reminds everyone that this is a working ship and that local passengers will be boarding and leaving at each port. The diesel engine throbs rhythmically in the background. At Bodo, a city at the northern end of Norway's main rail line, about 100 passengers typically board for the six-hour crossing to the Lofoten Islands. Automobiles come aboard, and fork-lifts maneuver whole fish, bundles of evergreen saplings, and building materials.

During brief port calls, you can walk briskly to the main shopping street to buy souvenirs and newspapers. On one excursion, during the stop at Harstad, passengers attend a short worship service in a fortress church. There are visits to the North Cape promontory; an excursion from Kirkenes, the voyage's turnaround port, to the Russian border; and a cruise into the **Trollfjord,** a one-mile passage between vertical rock cliffs bubbling with falling water. The moon reflects in the turning basin as the captain revolves his ship in a tight half circle. During the warmer months, the ship sails well inland to take in the spectacular **Geirangerfjord.** By voyage's end, round-trip passengers have shared a 2,500-mile feast of dramatic scenery, shore visits, fresh—if somewhat repetitious—food, and constantly changing weather.

EUROPEAN CRUISE FERRIES

"CRUISE FERRY" IS AN INADEQUATE TERM for a sophisticated breed of ship that takes passengers on overnight sea voyages but provides most of the comforts and amenities of a deluxe liner. Still, that's the name. And cars, recreational vehicles, and large trucks are indeed below deck.

Operating throughout northern Europe, the ferries crisscross the Baltic and North Seas, linking cities such as Copenhagen and Oslo, Stockholm and Helsinki, Newcastle and Bergen. Creative train-ferry itineraries often include the Eurailpass network. Most passengers are Scandinavians (Danish, Finnish, Norwegian, Swedish), traveling to visit Scandinavian friends and relatives or simply cruising. Germans are second-most numerous among passengers. North Sea sailings also attract Britons.

Larger, newer ships offer varied restaurants. Options include quality à la carte dining, a 60-item smorgasbord, and simpler, cheaper cafeteria meals. The *Silja Europa* even has a McDonald's. After-dinner entertainment includes cabarets, dancing, gambling, and films. There are children's playrooms, video arcades, saunas, and on some ships, duty-free shopping (purchases can be rolled to check-out in supermarket carts). English is widely spoken.

Cabins vary from well-appointed rooms with windows and cruise-ship amenities to large family cabins with private showers. Most accommodations are away from the activity and noise of public rooms. Young Scandinavians come aboard to party on weekend sailings, so be prepared for some public drunkenness.

The following lines are represented in North America. They offer the most extensive routes and some of the newest and most sophisticated ships. However, they're only a sampling of a wider network spanning all European seas, including the Mediterranean. Most major inter-city services operate year-round. Ships occasionally may change routes or be sold.

Color Line

THE FLEET	BUILT/RENOVATED	TONNAGE	PASSENGERS
Bohus	1971	8,772	1,422
Christian IV	1982	21,699	1,860
Color Fantasy	2004	76,600	2,770
Color Festival	1985/1986	34,314	2,000
Color Viking	1985	19,763	1,720
Kronprins Harald	1987	31,914	1,432
Peter Wessel	1981/1988	29,704	2,100
Prinsesse Ragnhild	1981/1992	35,438	1,875
Silvia Ana (fast day ferry)	1996	7,895	1,043

Norwegian-based Color Line operates five international cruise ferry lines between eight ports in Norway, Germany, Demark, and Sweden. For example, it sails between Oslo, Norway, and Kiel, Germany; between Bergen, Stavanger, and Hirtshals in northern Denmark; and between Oslo or Kristians, Norway, and Hirtshals, Denmark. The largest and most impressive of its ships is the *Color Fantasy* which is more than twice the size of the *Kronprins Harald;* both of those vessels operate the Oslo-Kiel route, and leave daily from either port for the 20-hour overnight run. The ships enter and leave Oslo via the scenic Oslofjord, a two-hour stretch. Most passengers are German or Norwegian.

The departures from Newcastle that connect two to three times weekly in Bergen with Norwegian Coastal Express evening northbound departures are operated by the Fjord Line's 20,581-ton *Jupiter,* formerly the *Color Viking.* The Fjord Line also operates the *Fjord Norway* between Norway and Denmark.

DFDS Seaways

THE FLEET	BUILT/RENOVATED	TONNAGE	PASSENGERS
Crown of Scandinavia	1994	35,498	2,026
Dana Sirena	2002	22,400	600
Duchess of Scandinavia	1993	16,794	698
Duke of Scandinavia	1978/1991	19,589	1,131
Pearl of Scandinavia	1989/2001	40,039	2,166
Princess of Scandinavia	1976/1991	22,528	1,534
Queen of Scandinavia	1981/1998	34,093	1,756

Danish-owned DFDS Seaways operates cruise ferries between England and Denmark; England and Sweden; England and Germany; England and the Netherlands; Denmark and Sweden; Denmark and Norway; and Copenhagen and Gdynia.

The largest ships operate between Copenhagen and Oslo, with scenic departures from both cities at 5 p.m. and arrival about 9 a.m. the next morning. The northbound route from Copenhagen passes Hamlet's Castle at Helsingor, calls at Helsingborg (Sweden), and enters the Oslofjord at dawn. Two-night round-trip cruises are popular from Oslo and Copenhagen. They give passengers time ashore between the morning arrival and late-afternoon departure. The Copenhagen pier is adjacent to the central business district, and the Oslo pier is a short bus ride from the city's center.

DFDS departs year-round from Harwich, England, which can be reached by boat or train from London. It has year-round, overnight services three to four times a week to Esbjerg on the Danish west coast, and Cuxhaven near Hamburg, from where trains connect to all of Germany. Additional sailings operate from Newcastle to Gothenburg, Kristiansand, and Amsterdam.

Silja Line

THE FLEET	BUILT/RENOVATED	TONNAGE	PASSENGERS
Finnjet	1977	32,940	1,781
Silja Europa	1993	59,914	3,013
Silja Festival	1986/1992	34,414	1,916
Silja Opera	1980/1992/1995	25,611	1,400
Silja Serenade	1990	58,376	2,852
Silja Symphony	1991	58,377	2,852
SuperSeaCat Three	1999	NA	640
SuperSeaCat Four	1999	NA	722

Operating some of the largest cruise ferries, Silja Line is the best-known Scandinavian ferry company. The ships are cities at sea; some carry as many as 3,000 passengers.

Though busy, they're designed to avert crowding and long queues. Cruise ship–style atriums are the centerpiece; nearby are eateries, lounges, and bars for all incomes. The prestige route is Stockholm to Helsinki. A ship leaves each port at 5 p.m. every night year-round (the sun shines until 10 p.m. or later in summer, this being the Land of the Midnight Sun) and arrives the next day at 9:30 a.m. The extended passage time includes a middle-of-the-night call in the Aland Islands that permits the continuation of duty-free shopping, a major attraction for high-taxed Scandinavians. The two-hour passage through the Stockholm archipelago is a highlight; to enjoy the entire transit, be up before 7 a.m. The ship docks conveniently next to central Helsinki; passengers on the two-night round-trip have the day ashore. Extended stopovers are easily arranged. Arrival in Stockholm is slightly less convenient with a subway connection to the city center.

The overnight Stockholm to Turku, Finland route is offered daily. A companion daylight service takes about 11 hours.

One of the fastest single-hull ships in northern Europe is the gas turbine *Finnjet,* whose summer schedule between St. Petersburg, Russia, Tallinn, Estonia, and Rostock, Germany, calls for speeds of up to 30 knots. In the off-season, the ship operates a more relaxed schedule.

In 2000, the line introduced the even faster *SuperSeaCat IV* on Baltic daylight service between Helsinki and Tallinn. The $30 million ship cruises at 37.8 knots and takes one hour and 40 minutes to make the crossing. The 328-foot monohull carries 707 passengers, 140 cars, and four motor-coaches. Facilities include a bar and cafeteria, 50-seat business-class lounge, shop, and observation area.

Viking Line

THE FLEET	BUILT/RENOVATED	TONNAGE	PASSENGERS
Alandsfarjan	1972	NA	963
Amorella	1988	34,384	2,450
Cinderella	1989	46,398	2,500
Gabriella	1992	35,492	2,420
Isabella	1989	35,154	2,450
Mariella	1985	37,860	2,500
Rosella	1980	16,850	1,700

The red-hulled ships of Viking Line, Silja Line's main competitor, cruise similar routes. The Stockholm-to-Turku daylight voyage calls at Mariehamn in the beautiful Aland Islands, about halfway between Sweden and Finland. The Stockholm–Helsinki route may be taken as a two-night round-trip cruise that includes two dinners and two breakfasts. The berth in Stockholm is closer to the city center than Silja's, while the Helsinki location is similar.

INFORMATION AND RESERVATIONS

Borton Overseas (for Viking Line)

5412 Lyndale Avenue South, Minneapolis, MN 55419

☎ 612-822-4640 or 800-843-0602; fax 612-822-4755

www.bortonoverseas.com; www.vikingline.fi

DFDS Seaways (USA) Inc. and Silja Line

6801 Lake Worth Road, Suite 107, Lake Worth, FL 33567

☎ 800-533-3755 ext. 114; fax 561-432-2550

www.seaeurope.com; www.europeonsale.com; www.silja.com

Norwegian Coastal Voyage

405 Park Avenue, New York, NY 10022

☎ 212-319-1300 or 800-323-7436; fax 212-319-1390

www.norwegiancoastalvoyage.us

Nordic Saga Tours (for Color Line)

303 Fifth Avenue South, Suite 109, Edmonds, WA 98020

☎ 800-848-6449 or 425-673-4800; fax 425-673-2600

www.nordicsaga.com; www.colorline.com

The tour operator also represents Scandinavian Seaways, Fjord Line, and other European cruise ferries.

Traghettionline S.r.l.

Via Brigata Liguria 4

16121 Genoa, Italy

www.traghettionline.net

Traghettionline, an Italian company with years of experience in sea transportation, provides information on some 90 ferry companies in Europe, North America, Australia, and Asia on its Web site. The Internet service enables users to book a ferry, receive the ticket directly at home, and pay with a credit card or bank transfer.

SAILING SHIPS

PEOPLE CHOOSE TO CRUISE for reasons as diverse as the amazingly wide range of ships, itineraries, and services available. For many, however, there is a longing that transcends midnight buffets, luxurious cabins, and myriad ports of call. These are individuals who are transfixed and enchanted by the lure of the sea itself. The feeling of being underway, the buffeting wind, the salt sea spray over the bow, and the twinkling phosphorescent wake are to them the stuff of dreams. There is no bingo, afternoon tea, or stylish air-conditioned lounge for these folks. Rather, you'll find them on deck leaning on the starboard rail, taking in every white-capped wave.

Almost all are landlubbers—individuals whose imagination draws them to the sea—and many of them first experience the sea aboard a large, modern cruise ship. It doesn't take long for them to realize, however, that no matter how grand a particular floating resort might be, they desire a much more intimate relationship with the sea. Opting for a smaller cruise ship does the trick for some, but for others it's not enough. Sooner or later, these folks discover the wonderful world of cruising under sail.

Cruising under sail is cruising in concert with the sea. By definition, sailing uses currents, tides, and winds to the advantage of the sailor, always working with natural forces and never against them. Pursuing this harmony precipitates any number of outcomes (the elements are not always cooperative, you know), but it's always an adventure. Bringing home the reality of weather and sea conditions, sailing is for many a life-changing experience—an epiphany.

If you want to try sailing on for size, you have a wide selection of alternatives. Choices range from medium-sized cruise ships with computer-controlled sails and powerful, supplemental engines, to tiny schooners with no motor at all, where every passenger must help work the boat. Accommodations range from conventional cruise-ship staterooms to tiny cabins accessible only by descending a ladder through a hatch. Some voyages are veritable courses in sailing and seamanship; others demand nothing beyond normal cruise ship passenger passivity.

If you've not sailed before, enjoy the amenities of a larger cruise ship, or are uncertain how much of an adventure you want, consider sailing with either **Star Clippers** or **Windstar Cruises** (both described in detail in Part Two, Cruise Lines and Their Ships). Star Clippers operates four- and five-masted, square-rigged ships with small (by cruise ship standards), air-conditioned cabins with private baths. You'll find a small pool, a library, and even a piano lounge. Star Clippers vessels carry a maximum of 170 or 227 passengers, depending on the vessel.

Windstar, which operates three, four-masted ships with triangular sails, costs about $350 to $550 per day before any applicable discounts, compared to an average non-discounted per diem of about $268 on Star Clippers. Two Windstar ships carry about 150 passengers, and one ship, *Wind Surf*, accommodates 308. Cabins on these ships approximate the size of those on mainstream cruise ships, and there's even a casino and a disco. Whereas a crew sets the sails in the traditional way aboard Star Clippers ships (you can pitch in if you want), sails on Windstar are computer-controlled. Ships of both lines have powerful diesel-electric engines. Windstar uses its engines for propulsion up to 50% of the time, whereas Star Clippers employs its engines primarily to get into and out of port.

Similar to Windstar's *Wind Surf* is **Club Med's** five-masted, computer-controlled sailing ship *Club Med 2*. The length of two football fields, *Club Med 2* carries almost 400 passengers with a per diem ranging from $130 to more than $350, depending on season and itinerary. Smaller, luxury ships with large cabins and many main line cruise ship amenities are **Sea Cloud's Cruises'** *Sea Cloud* (64 passengers) and *Sea Cloud II* (94 passengers). The sailing cruise lines mentioned in this section offer itineraries that can take you all over the world.

Less expensive, but offering a more authentic, hands-on experience are the **Maine Windjammer Association** cruises and **Windjammer Barefoot Cruises.** The Maine Windjammer Association is the marketing arm for 14 individually owned and operated traditional tall ships, all schooners, ranging in size from 46 to 132 feet. The fleet operates exclusively along the mid-coast region of Maine, with the majority of itineraries in the verdant, island-studded waters of Penobscot Bay. Most of the schooners were built between 1871 and 1945 as working boats for hauling cargo or fishing and were converted to passenger-carrying ships within the last 20 years or so. Nine of the fourteen schooners are designated National Historic Landmarks.

Cruises depart Camden, Rockland, or Rockport from May through October for three- to six-day itineraries which include short ports of call at small islands and at historic Maine coastal villages. Days, for the most part, are spent sailing. The schooners anchor in protected coves or tie up at small, picturesque maritime communities at night. Meals are served family style, sometimes in the galley and sometime on deck, and feature local produce and seafood among other selections. A lobster bake on a forested island is a highlight of many cruises. While most of the schooners accommodate 12 to 29 guests, the 46-foot *Mistress* carries only 6, and the *Victory Chimes,* the largest sailing vessel flying American colors, carries 40.

About a thousand miles south, the Caribbean is home water to Windjammer Barefoot Cruises. Though the names are similar ("windjammer" is nautical slang for a seaman on a sailing ship), Windjammer Barefoot Cruises is related to the Maine Windjammers in concept only. Windjammer Barefoot Cruises operates four sailing vessels and one motorized vessel year-round, on a variety of 6- to 13-day Caribbean and the Bahamas itineraries, particularly the Eastern Caribbean, including the Grenandines, and further south to Aruba, Bonaire, Curaçao, and occasionally, Panama and Costa Rica.

All of its sailing craft are larger than those of the Maine fleet, with the largest carrying 122 passengers and the smallest 64. Facilities are not as extensive as those of the *Sea Clouds, Club Med 2,* or Clipper and Windstar ships described earlier, but are more luxurious than those of the relatively spartan Maine fleet. Most Windjammer Barefoot cabins are air-conditioned and offer a private bath. Air-conditioning isn't generally needed in Maine, and schooner passengers usually share toilet and bathing facilities. Dining is of comparable quality in both fleets, with meals distinguished by fresh, locally available meat, seafood, vegetables, and fruit. On both Maine Windjammer and Windjammer Barefoot vessels, you can help the crew sail the ship. On the Barefoot cruises, however, such activity is take-it-or-leave-it, while Maine schooner captains frequently count on passengers to help out. On ships of either fleet, you can avail yourself of a fairly extensive sailing education during your time aboard.

For all the similarities, however, there are likewise some striking differences. The Maine experience is all about sailing, while the Barefoot ships spend most of the day in port or anchored in a secluded cove, where diving, water sports, or sunning are the main attractions. In fact, on a Barefoot cruise, most of the sailing is done between the hours of dinner and breakfast—the exact opposite of a Maine schooner.

If you think this type of cruising will appeal to you, take a moment to check out the respective Windjammer Web sites (**www.sailmainecoast.com** and **www.windjammer.com**), potentially critical differences will become immediately apparent. The Caribbean cruise line's site screams fun, sun, and warm weather delights. The Maine Windjammers' site, in contrast, emphasizes the peace and serenity of sailing, rugged Maine coastline scenery, and maritime skills and history. On Barefoot cruises, morning Bloody Marys, afternoon Rum Swizzles, and wine with dinner are provided in the price of the cruise. On a Maine schooner, no alcohol at all is served or sold, except at lobster bake events, though passengers are invited to bring aboard their own private stock. Days start early in Maine, while in the Caribbean, sleeping in is definitely an option.

Climate additionally differentiates the two sail cruise options. The Caribbean is a perfect destination during the cold-weather months of the year, while Maine offers a great escape from the heat during the summer and early fall.

Finally, regardless which cruise line you choose, you should know that seasickness is rare on sailing ships. This is because the wind stabilizes the ship in the water and prevents almost all of the side-to-side rolling motion that is the primary cause of seasickness.

Note: In parentheses after each boat name is information about the number of cabins and passengers; officers and crew; and the boat's length (cabins/passengers; officers/crew; boat length).

Classic Cruises of Newport
Christie's Landing, Newport, RI 02840; ☎ 800-395-1343 or 401-849-3033; dock office ☎ 401-847-0298; fax 401-849-3023; www.cruisenewport.com; www.cruisearabella.com

---

Arabella (20/42; AMERICAN; 160 FT.)

Favored by sailing enthusiasts, romance seekers, and travelers who enjoy soft adventure, *Arabella,* a new luxury schooner, offers cruises throughout the British and U.S. Virgin Islands from late December through early May, and the New England coast in summer and fall.

The Caribbean excursions, combining sailing, swimming, and snorkeling with day trips and island dining, depart from St. Thomas on six-night sails. One sample itinerary might include St. John, U.S.V.I. and Norman Island, Jost Van Dyke, Tortola, Virgin Gorda, and Peter Island B.V.I., and Culebra and Vieques, Puerto Rico.

Arabella has 20 air-conditioned cabins, each with satellite television, viewing portholes, and communications capabilities that allow guests to conduct business while at sea. She also houses an on-deck hot water spa, a lounge and bar, and water sports equipment for passenger use.

Rates for Caribbean cruises range from $1,295 to $2,195 per person, based on double occupancy and include all daytime meals, four dinners ashore, and optional excursions. The cruise departs Sunday afternoon and returns to St. Thomas on Saturday at or before noon. At the end of her Caribbean season, *Arabella* sails north with spring (and south with fall on the return) for cruises of Chesapeake Bay and spends June through September along the New England coast. Summer and fall cruises of four and five nights from Newport stop in Nantucket, Martha's Vineyard, Cuttyhunk, and Provincetown. Those cruises start at $999 per person, double occupancy. In September, the ship sails on a wine tasting cruise that visits vineyards from Rhode Island to Martha's Vineyard.

Arabella is part of the Newport-based Atlantic Stars Hospitality Group which has hotels in New York City, Newport, and Martha's Vineyard; a restaurant in South Beach, Miami; and cruise vessels on day trips around Newport Harbor and Narragansett Bay.

Club Med
75 Valencia Avenue, Coral Gables, FL 33134; ☎ 800-CLUB MED or 800-258-2633; fax 305-443-0562; www.clubmed2.com/FR/clubdescroisires

---

Club Med 2 (190/392; FRENCH; 614 FT.)

One of the world's largest cruise ships with sails offers casual, sports-oriented, all-inclusive vacations with an easy lifestyle for active, upscale vacationers. The ship sails on seven-day Caribbean cruises in winter, Mediterranean cruises in summer, and transatlantic voyages in spring and fall.

After two decades of spreading the gospel of all-inclusive resort vacations, Club Med applied its resort formula to a cruise ship, *Club Med 2.* Built in 1992, the 14,000-ton vessel marries today's technology to yesteryear's seafaring. She is as long as two football fields and rigged with five 164-foot masts and seven computer-monitored sails; there's no listing or heeling and no officers on deck—they are on the bridge monitoring computers.

Club Med 2 has an open, nautical feeling and is glitz-free, but loses much of the intimacy that makes the Windstar line's smaller version so appealing. She is spacious and has multiple Burmese teak decks. Interiors by the well-known European designer Albert Pinto evoke understated luxury through meticulous craftsmanship and the use of fine mahogany, quality fabrics, and leather reminiscent of classic sailing ships. Walls of windows afford sea and shore views.

The cabins are large, comfortable, and handsomely decorated with hand-rubbed mahogany cabinetwork. All cabins are outside and have twin portholes. They're fitted with twin or queen-size beds, a mahogany desk, large mirrors, ample closets, a television, radio, safe, refrigerator, minibar, and satellite telephone, which is also used to order room service. The teak-floored baths have showers, hair dryers, and fluffy bathrobes. Electrical outlets are 110/220 AC. In all, there are 190 outside cabins; 6 suites. Standard dimensions are 188 square feet. There are no single cabins but you can book a cabin as a single by paying a supplement of 40 percent on the Deck C price.

The cruises are basically a French product with the same informal, care-free ambience of Club Med villages, but in deluxe surroundings with cruise ship amenities. Integral to both operations are GOs—gentils organisateurs—the social hosts and hostesses who keep the action and smiles going day and night. Most GOs are French, other Europeans, or Americans who speak very good French. Their first task when you board is to familiarize you with the ship and answer questions. They organize shipboard activities and can usually give valuable tips on the best bars and restaurants in ports of call.

The ship has two ocean-view dining rooms, each with a different menu featuring French cuisine. Le Grand Bleu, an open-air veranda cafe on the top deck, serves a casual breakfast, luncheon buffets, and theme dinners featuring cuisine from around the world. Le Deauville is a more intimate, formal dining room. The à la carte menu offers several choices for each course.

Dinner is a serious affair lasting up to two hours or longer. Complimentary wine from Club Med's private label, beer, and bottled water accompany lunch and dinner. Smokers are in the majority on board and have the run of the ship. Restaurants have nonsmoking sections, but smoking is allowed in all public areas. Unlike at Club Med villages, breakfast can be enjoyed in your cabin. There is 24-hour room service, and laundry service is available for an extra charge.

Both restaurants have waiters and unreserved, unassigned seating at tables for two or more, with continuous service during dining hours. Officers and staff dine with passengers. Most seven-night Caribbean itineraries offer a lobster beach picnic.

The ship has several lounges, a nightclub, piano bar, and disco. The St. Tropez Piano Bar, one of several bars, is the most popular for afternoon tea with French pastries and music and for after-dinner drinks (at prices higher than average). A lounge that doubles as a theater has a bar, stage, bandstand, and dance floor. A different show or program is presented here each evening by GOs—some more entertaining than others and all amateur. Some passengers find this fun, while others say that the luxury prices they pay merit more professional entertainers.

There's a small library, card tables and chairs in a lounge, and a boutique. Party-seekers make their way to the disco with its lighted dance floor. One night in the Caribbean is Carnival.

Sports facilities include a teak sports platform at the stern that unfolds into the sea to become a marina when the ship is at anchor. The vessel carries sailboards, sailboats, snorkels, fins, and masks and provides free lessons in water-skiing, windsurfing, sailing, and snorkeling. Two ski boats with scuba equipment take certified divers on diving trips. The scuba program is a good value.

The less ambitious can retire to a chaise lounge around the two outdoor, saltwater swimming pools. Even when the ship is full, space to lounge is ample. The supervised fitness center has exercise equipment that passengers use while enjoying a panoramic view from the top deck. Aerobics and water exercise in the pool are offered daily. Several decks below are a sauna and massage room. *Club Med 2* also has a beauty salon and spa with massage therapists and treatments—all at additional cost.

The Club Med imprint is obvious. Officers are French; the crew, Filipino. The staff, dressed in impeccable white shirts, shorts, and socks, handle dining and hotel duties and earn praise for their friendly, professional service. The energetic, attractive GOs are managed by the Chef du Village, the cruise director. These cheery camp counselors do it all: the reception desk, run activities, teach sports, and entertain. In the Caribbean, the ship visits a port each day and sails at night. Unfortunately for those who love sailing, passengers get very little opportunity to experience the pleasure of sailing under canvas.

The ship attracts a range of passengers that changes with the cruise, season, and location. Typically, passengers are 30 to 60 years old. The majority are couples. Children younger than age 8 are not accepted. Most passengers like the informality and sociability of the GO concept. On the other hand, the constant interaction between the young, bouncy GOs and passengers creates a summer camp atmosphere that is not for everyone.

The GO team is bilingual in English and French, but French is the ship's primary language. That could be a problem for English speakers who aren't up to the language challenge, or who might feel there's unequal treatment.

Club Med's attitude is: This is a French-European product. The cruise is, after all, an experience where Americans might lunch with people from Normandy, snorkel with Italians, and have cocktails with Austrians. That's part of the attraction.

Per diems start at about $350 per person but may vary by season, cabin, and cruise areas. Tips, wine and beer at lunch and dinner, and most water sports are included in the fare; port charges are additional. Club Med offers specially priced cruises occasionally, but it does not discount prices.

Coastal Cruises
P.O. Box 798, Camden, ME 04843; ☎ 207-785-5670 or 800-992-2218; www.schoonermaryday.com

---

Mary Day (15/30; AMERICAN; 90 FT.)
This two-masted schooner sails on three- to six-day cruises along the Maine coast. Some cruises are themed ones, such as "Lighthouses" or "Audubon Naturalist," while others focus on special events like the Great Schooner Race or a folk festival.

Maine Windjammer Association
P.O. Box 1144P, Blue Hill, ME 04614; ☎ 800-807-WIND; www.sailmainecoast.com

---

Formed in 1977, the Maine Windjammer Association is made up of 14 privately owned and operated traditional tall ships that once belonged to commercial fleets. They delivered everything from fish and granite to coal and Christmas trees along U.S. coasts. The two- and three-masted schooners range from 46 to 132 feet long. Nine are National Historic Landmarks, some older than 100 years.

The windjammers offer three- to six-day cruises from mid-May to October, departing Rockland, Rockport, and Camden on the scenic Penobscot Bay, Maine. With more than 3,000 islands, the Maine coast is one of the best and most beautiful sailing areas anywhere. Ships sail by day, about 10 a.m. to 4 p.m., and anchor each night at a deserted inlet or quiet port or village where passengers can go ashore. Passengers may participate in all aspects of sailing, from hoisting sails and taking the wheel to helping in the galley.

Meals are served family-style and include fresh seafood, roasts, garden salads, chowder, and homemade breads and desserts. A lobster bake on an island is featured on every six-day trip and most three-day cruises. Accommodations are simple: single, double, or triple cabins with comfortable mattresses, fresh linens, and plenty of blankets. Shipboard life is relaxed and informal.

Each windjammer carries 6 to 40 passengers and a crew of 2 to 10. Cruises are ideal family vacations, appropriate for most ages. (Check with individual captains regarding children. Teens ages 12 years and up are accepted on most boats. However, because of an increasing demand for family cruises, three of the vessels are now offering cruises with a minimum age of 5, 6, and 8, respectively. Some windjammers have theme cruises. The tall ships gather annually for an all-day race in which passengers can participate.

Three- to six-day cruises range from $395 to $915 per person. Charter rates are available. All vessels undergo rigorous U.S. Coast Guard inspections and carry ship-to-shore radios and electronic navigational devices.

Air transportation is available to departure ports via Portland International Jetport, with limousine service to the Rockland/Camden area. Commuter air service is available from Boston, and buses run from Boston and Portland. All vessels offer free parking.

Member vessels are *American Eagle, Angelique, Grace Bailey, Heritage, Isaac H. Evans, J&E Riggin, Lewis R. French, Mary Day, Mercantile, Mistress, Nathaniel Bowditch, Stephen Taber, Timberwind,* and *Victory Chimes.* The association provides descriptive brochures.

Although all are schooners, each boat is different and special in its own way. The *Angelique,* for example, has a deck house salon—a passenger lounge above deck. This gives passengers a warm, cozy alternative to the galley on rainy days. The *Grace Bailey* offers a combination lounge/galley below deck large enough to accommodate an upright piano. Most toilet and bath facilities are shared. Some schooners, like the *American Eagle,* with hallways running fore and aft below decks, offer toilets and hot showers situated adjacent to passenger cabins. On other ships, the communal heads are accessed from the main deck. A few vessels, including *Victory Chimes,* may have some cabins with private toilets in the cabin.

Cabins for the most part are very small—a place to sleep or change clothes, but not a place to hang out. Most cabins include a reading light and private sink, sometimes with hot and cold fresh running water, sometimes just with cold water. Storage space in the cabins is minimal, sometimes problematic when two or more share a cabin. A few ships offer 110-volt electrical outlets for hair dryers and such, but this is more the exception than the rule.

During fair weather, almost everyone hangs out on deck, where lunch and sometimes other meals are served. Some ships have built-in benches on deck, while others provide collapsible chairs. On rainy days, a galley with a hot wood stove affords refuge from the elements during and between meals. While anchored, both in dry and wet weather, a canvas tarp is deployed over much of the deck.

Passengers should be reasonably agile. Access to lower decks is almost always by ladder, with the exception of the *Victory Chimes* and the *Heritage,* which substitute rather steep stairs. One ship, the *Stephen Tabor,* offers two main deck–level pilot cabins.

Music, in the form of informal jam sessions or sing-alongs, is a favorite evening's entertainment on many schooners, including the *Stephen Tabor, J&E Riggin, Grace Bailey, Victory Chimes, Angelique,* and *Mary Day.* Two ships, the *Grace Bailey* and *Angelique,* carry upright pianos, and the *Mary Day* carries an organ. Passengers are strongly encouraged to bring along any sort of acoustic (i.e. nonelectrical) instrument. On ships without captain or crew of a musical bent, storytelling is a preferred pastime. Regardless of the activity, it's a rare night when festivities go beyond 11 p.m.

In a rather marked departure from the rest of the cruise industry, no alcoholic beverages are sold or served on Maine Windjammer schooners (with the exception of educational wine tasting events or on some vessels, a lobster bake). Although guests are invited to bring aboard their own stash, most precruise instructional material makes it clear that excessive imbibing will not be tolerated.

Itineraries are quite flexible, with no particular urgency to be at a certain place at a particular time. Many captains ad-lib their itineraries en route, responding to the weather and the stated preferences of the passengers. And speaking of captains, they are as diverse as the ships. There are several husband-and-wife teams, some partnering gentlemen captains, and on the *Isaac H. Evans,* the fleet's only solo female captain. Some of the couple-captains bring their children along (amazingly socially acclimated and well-behaved).

Summer weather in Maine is all over the map, although you can usually count on good wind. May and June are very unpredictable both in terms of temperature and rainfall. July is almost always warm, but with more rain than the predictably dry and warm August and September. Regardless of the time of year, good rain gear is essential.

Sea Cloud Cruises
32–40 North Dean Street, Englewood, NJ 07631; ☎ 201-227-9404 or 888-732-2568; fax 201-227-9424; www.seacloud.com

Sea Cloud (32/64; INTERNATIONAL; 360 FT.)
One of the world's most luxurious sailing ships, the *Sea Cloud* was built in 1931 as a wedding present from financier E. F. Hutton for his bride, Marjorie Merriweather Post. The ship has 32 air-conditioned cabins with phone, safe, hair dryer, and bathrobes. The elegant dining room accommodates all passengers at one seating; complimentary wines are served at lunch and dinner. A library and boutique are available.

The four-masted barque sails on different itineraries year-round. She plies the Eastern Caribbean in winter and the Mediterranean during the remainder of the year, and she is marketed by several U.S. companies. Sea Cloud Cruises also owns the luxurious River Cloud sisters, which sail European rivers (see "River and Barge Cruises in Europe" earlier in Part Three).

Sea Cloud II (47/94; INTERNATIONAL; 384 FT.)
The legendary *Sea Cloud* got a sibling in 2001. The 384-foot, $40 million vessel is square rigged with three masts (rather than *Sea Cloud*'s four), and her 29,687 square feet of sail are manually operated, with the crew climbing the masts and clambering along the spars to set the square-rigged sails. Modern with the highest safety standards, the vessel is traditional in

appearance and offers opulent 1930s decor. Forty-seven luxurious cabins range from 129 to 236 square feet, those on the promenade deck with ornate marble bathtubs and marble mantels; two owner's suites each contain 290 square feet, with separate shower stalls and four-poster beds. Large deck areas and a swimming platform provide plentiful outside space for jogging, walking, lounging, sunning, and dining. The ship has an alfresco bar, and attractive restaurant, an elegant lounge with large arched windows, an inviting sauna and gymnasium, and a sunny, well-stocked library with windows overlooking the foredeck. The European/Asian crew is attentive and efficient—you could almost be on a private yacht—and the cuisine, predominantly French and German, is outstanding. Many of the cruises are chartered to museum and alumni groups (but there are normally cabins available for non-members). Nightlife tends to consist of lectures, wine tastings, and recitals by soloists or chamber groups.

Sea Cloud II's all-weather cruising ability sets her apart from *Sea Cloud*, which is generally restricted to sunny climes. The new ship cruises through the North Sea and Baltic in summer, the Mediterranean in autumn, and the Caribbean in winter.

Star Clippers, Inc.
(See Part Two.)

Windjammer Barefoot Cruises
P.O. Box 190120, Miami Beach, FL 33119-0120; 1759 Bay Road, Miami Beach, FL 33139; ☎ 305-672-6453 or 800-327-2601; fax 305-674-1219; www.windjammer.com

---

For sailors young or just young at heart with good sea legs and a Captain Mitty spirit, Windjammer Barefoot Cruises offers a chance to stand watch at the wheel or climb the mast and live out your fantasies. The line has a fleet of famous tall ships, including those once owned by Aristotle Onassis, the duke of Westminster, and financier E. F. Hutton. Most cabins have bunk beds, private facilities, and steward service. Itineraries are super, including the Grenadines (often called the world's most beautiful sailing waters) and less-visited destinations in the Eastern and Southern Caribbean. Most cruises are six days; some have different southbound and northbound legs that can be combined. A sample six-night St. Vincent and the Grenadines cruise starts at $900 per person double.

Amazing Grace **(92 PASSENGERS; BRITISH/WEST INDIAN; 257 FT.)**
This is the fleet's only freighter. In winter, *Amazing Grace* offers 13-day cruises alternating between Freeport, Grand Bahamas, and Port of Spain, Trinidad. In summer, she alternates weekly homeports between Panama and Costa Rica, exploring the San Blas Islands. On summer sailing between May and August, Windjammer's Junior Jammer Kids Club, a program of chaperoned activities for children age six and older, allows the kids to sail for free when accompanied by two full-fare adults or for half fare when

accompanied by one adult. The kids learn to sail and have full days of activities. In the fall and winter, the ship sails on seven-day cruises between Tortola, British Virgin Islands, or Antigua and Port of Spain, Trinidad. When the vessel is in Trinidad for provisioning, she stays in port for two days.

Legacy (61/122; AMERICAN/WEST INDIAN; 294 FT.)

Built in 1959, this ship was a meteorological research and exploration vessel for the French government. She was acquired by Windjammer in 1989, stripped to her hull, and converted into a four-masted tall ship, debuting in 1998.

The well-designed vessel has her original portholes, wide stairways, hand-carved South American wood, and custom interiors. All cabins are air-conditioned and have private bathrooms with showers. They are simply decorated and have wooden wardrobes, full-length mirrors, and either bunk, double, or twin beds (some have sofa beds). The most luxurious cabin, Burke's Berth, has a platform double bed, entertainment center, bar, and picture windows.

The top deck, with its large bar, entertainment by local bands, and hermit crab races, is action central. The captain gives a morning briefing there on the day's activities. Meals are served family style in the dining room, which is air-conditioned. A small lounge contains the only television and VCR, along with books and games. *Legacy* offers Junior Jammers Kids Club, a summer program of chaperoned activities for children age 6 to 11.

Legacy is based in St. Thomas in winter and sails on six-day itineraries to the U.S. and British Virgin Islands. In summer, she sails on three-, four-, or seven-day cruises between Miami and Nassau and through the Bahamas, visiting lesser-known islands with great beaches and diving. Daily, she offers scuba diving courses for beginners and one- and two-tank and night dives for certified divers.

Mandalay (72 PASSENGERS; BRITISH/WEST INDIAN; 236 FT.)

Mandalay is queen of the fleet. Formerly the yacht of financier E. F. Hutton and an oceanographic research vessel of Columbia University, she has three masts and 22,000 square feet of sail. Under Hutton's ownership, she was considered the world's most luxurious private yacht. When she retired in 1981 from Columbia, nearly half the existing knowledge of the ocean floor had been gathered by the ship.

In winter, *Mandalay* alternates on 13-day cruises between Grenada and Antigua, exploring the British, French and Dutch West Indies and the Grenadines. In summer, she is based in Tortola and does six-day cruises through the British Virgin Islands. In fall, she alternates between six-day sailings of the British Virgin Islands and 13-day cruises alternating between Grenada and Antigua.

Polynesia (54/112; BRITISH/WEST INDIAN; 248 FT.)

This legendary fishing schooner has been featured in articles in *National Geographic* magazine and various television productions. She was added to the Windjammer fleet in 1975 after extensive remodeling added 12 deck cabins, 40 regular cabins, and two admiral suites, all double occupancy. All have private bathrooms and showers, wood paneling, and tile floors. Three bachelor quarters were built, each accommodating six. New plumbing, air-conditioning, and a teak deck were installed. The curved stern contains a specially designed dining salon with large tables, each depicting an island on *Polynesia*'s itinerary.

Probably the most popular Windjammer ship, *Polynesia* sails in winter on six-day Caribbean itineraries from St. Maarten to St. Barts, St. Kitts, Saba, Nevis, Anguilla, and Montserrat, depending on wind. In summer through early fall, she is based in Aruba and offers the Junior Jammers Kids Club summer program. Occasionally, she offers singles' cruises as well as theme cruises.

Yankee Clipper (64 PASSENGERS; BRITISH/WEST INDIAN; 197 FT.)
In 1927, German industrialist Alfred Krupp built this ship as the *Cressida*, probably the world's only armor-plated private yacht. Adolf Hitler was aboard during World War II to award the Iron Cross to a U-boat captain. She was confiscated as a war prize and commandeered by the U.S. Coast Guard. After the war, she was acquired by the wealthy Vanderbilt family, renamed *Pioneer*, and sailed off the West Coast. Joining Windjammer's fleet in 1965, she was rechristened *Yankee Clipper*. Extensive remodeling gave her a third mast, continuous upper deck, and cabins with private bathrooms and showers. She's one of the fastest tall ships.

Yankee Clipper offers six-day Caribbean cruises year-round, leaving Grenada for St. Vincent, Bequia, Mayreau, Union Island, Carriacou, and a host of other isles.

Windstar Cruises
(See Part Two.)

Zeus Tours and Yacht Cruises
c/o Tourlite International, 120 Sylvan Avenue, Englewood Cliffs, NJ 07632; ☎ 201-242-1770; 800-272-7600; fax 201-242-8085; www.zeustours.com

The Zeus Group, which has been in operation for more than half a century, offers Greek Isles, eastern Mediterranean, and South American cruises in its own and chartered vessels. The cruises are sold in the United States through Tourlite International.

Among their current offerings are several set itineraries with frequent sailing dates on the following vessels:

Diogenis V (24/49; GREEK; 165 FEET)
From April to October, this vessel operates seven-night "Aegean Mosaic" cruises roundtrip from Heraklion, Crete, visiting such destinations as Aghios Nicolaos, Karpathos, Rhodes, Simi, Astypalea, and Santorini. The vessel offers air-conditioned cabins with private facilities, a dining room, lounge bar with stereo music/TV, and a sun deck equipped with sun chairs.

Panorama (25/50; GREEK; 175 FT.)

Also from April through October, this ship sails on seven-night "Cycladic Pearls" cruise roundtrip from Marina Zea, with stops at Sounion/Lavrion, Sifnos, Milos, Folegandros, Santorini, Mykonos, Delos, and Kea. Built in 1993 and rebuilt in 2003, the air-conditioned vessel has two lounges and two wet bars. Amenities include a television and audio-visual equipment in one lounge; sun decks with sofas, sun bathing mattresses and lounge chairs; and kayaks and snorkeling equipment carried onboard for passenger use. Cabins have private facilities and such amenities as a mini-refrigerator, VCR, and central music.

Viking Star (24/42; GREEK; 106 FT.)

The vessel operates seven-night "Ionian Odyssey" cruises roundtrip from Corfu, with port calls at Albania and such Greek Isles as Scorpios and Parga. The vessel was constructed in the mid-1990s, and has 24 outside cabins, 19 on the main deck, and 5 on the lower deck; one dining room; and adjacent bar/lounge; and a sun deck with sun beds and chairs.

FREIGHTERS

FREIGHTER TRAVEL MAY BE the least-understood segment of the cruise industry. You don't read or hear much about it, and cargo lines that offer passenger service rarely advertise in the mainstream media. Most travel agents, too, lack experience and expertise in booking freighter cruises.

Freighters roam the globe, visiting ports famous and exotic but usually industrial and removed from city centers and tourism attractions. They offer a carefree, informal environment conducive to total relaxation, and they may cost less than conventional cruise ships on a per diem basis.

Before the post–World War II boom in air travel and cruises, freighters were a significant mode of international travel. Expanding air routes, lower fares, and the growth of the cruise industry gradually relegated freighter travel to a minor niche in the cruise market.

Cargo lines have since recognized a revival of interest and the economics inherent in carrying passengers. Ten passengers at roughly $100 a day each adds up to good found money over the course of a year, and at the small cost of perhaps providing one extra steward and additional food. A few companies operate combined container and passenger vessels that can accommodate large numbers of passengers. But more typical are the 100 or more traditional freighters currently in service—mostly container ships—that accommodate from 2 to 12 passengers. Many enjoy brisk bookings and operate at capacity during peak seasons. However, extra regulations since 9/11 have caused several freight lines to reconsider the practicality of passenger service. Always call to confirm all information before making travel plans or reservations, and then, deal with a freighter travel specialist who can keep you apprised of departure, embarkation time, and arrangements.

FREIGHTERS: DEFINING THE BREED

WHAT EXACTLY IS A FREIGHTER? First, let's say what it is not. A modern freighter isn't a rusty tramp steamer sailing on a mission of intrigue or romance as popularized in movies and novels. The vast majority of cargo vessels today are less than 30 years old. Imposing and boxy, they're loaded with sophisticated navigation and communication equipment. Most are containerized, that is, their freight is carried in large metal containers resembling railway box cars systematically stacked below and above decks. Some carry bulk items in holds such as iron ore or grain.

The International Conventions and Conferences on Marine Safety define the passenger-carrying freighter as a vessel principally engaged in transporting goods that is licensed to carry a maximum of 12 passengers. Those licensed to carry more than 12 are defined as combination passenger-cargo ships. The latter must meet stricter safety standards and carry more staff, including a doctor. They also have the advantage of gaining preferred docking privileges over ordinary freighters.

Nowadays, most cargo ships run on fixed schedules along established routes, except for those in so-called tramp service. Tramps don't sail regular routes or schedules and can be hired to haul almost anything, anywhere, anytime. A few take passengers. However, many of today's freighters are often chartered for specific periods of time, so their "fixed schedules" and routes may change.

Why People Choose Freighters

Traveling by freighter offers a rare opportunity to truly get away from it all. There are no crowds, no planned activities, no lines, no dress code, and no hoopla. The atmosphere aboard a freighter is relaxed and unstructured. Passengers can be as active or as lazy as they choose.

Freighters are for travelers who want to see the world on their own terms and are flexible about schedule changes and port substitutions. Most are veteran travelers who have become bored or disillusioned with conventional tours, cruises, and popular vacation destinations. Their sense of adventure and yearning for discovery demand something different.

A glance at freighter itineraries often reveals ports that would be impractical or prohibitively expensive to visit any other way. While some ships will dock in ports close to places you will want to visit, others may be berthed at a sprawling container terminal miles from the city. Often the ship and/or its port agents will help with hiring taxis or provide some basic touring information. But veteran freighter travelers know to come prepared with some knowledge of what they want to see, then perhaps ask local residents to suggest how to get there and back by their vessel's posted "All Aboard" notice. Time ashore is often limited, as modern ships can load or off-load hundreds of containers in only a few hours; a long stay rarely exceeds 24 hours.

Freighter travelers recognize good value, and, on a per diem basis, there are few better travel values than freighters. With careful research and planning, you can roam the world for months aboard a freighter for roughly $90 to $250 per day. And unlike cruise ships with their large assortment pay-as- you-go activities and amenities, there are few opportunities to spend more money on board a freighter beyond the fare.

Some people are attracted by the camaraderie they enjoy with fellow passengers. Sailing with usually no more than a dozen like-minded, well-informed veteran travelers in a low-key, relaxing atmosphere is their ideal travel environment and often leads to lasting friendships. On the other hand, if you have a list of books that you have been eager to read, here's your chance. Be aware, some pas-

sengers are avid bridge players, and others can't wait to bend an
elbow when the sun is over the yard arm.

Is Freighter Travel for You?

Judging from the high rate of repeat bookings, once a freighter traveler, always a freighter traveler. If you haven't tried it but you've read
this far, you may be a good candidate.

You must usually have plenty of time, as most trips are long, although voyages of one to two weeks also exist. Most folks just can't get
away for a 30-, 60-, or 90-day trip. For that reason alone, the majority of
freighter travelers are retirees, teachers and professors, self-employed
professionals, and the occasional artist or writer. Common characteristics include an extensive travel background, love of the sea, preference
for independent travel, and a general dislike of formality.

Wherever on this planet your imagination might roam, chances are
you can go there on a freighter. Some of the more exotic and popular
routes (round-trip from the United States) include South Africa from
New York (46 days), the East or West Coast to New Zealand and Australia (38 to 66 days), around the world from New York (90 days or
longer), Marquesas Islands from Tahiti (16 days), Mediterranean from
the East or West Coast (42 to 60 days), and South America from the
East or Gulf Coast (42 to 70 days). Shorter one-way transatlantic trips,
such as Montreal, Canada, to England, France, or Belgium, are an average of 8 to 11 days and trips from the U.S. East Coast to the Mediterranean, some ranging from 10 to 20, days are available.

Accommodations and Facilities

The majority of cargo-liners have spacious, comfortable accommodations equal to, and often better than, those found on cruise ships.
Normally they are located in a multi-story superstructure at the
stern. The cabins and public spaces may be on two to four different
decks, so vertical movement is often the norm. Cabins have showers
and sometimes bathtubs. In most cases they're air-conditioned and
have a tastefully furnished lounge area. Often, they have taped music,
service phones, VCRs or DVD players, minifridges, and picture windows rather than portholes.

Comfy, smartly decorated public lounges invite card games, conversation, and evening cocktails. Most vessels have large-screen
televisions and an extensive library of videos and DVDs. The lounge
may be shared with the officers, or there may be a separate one for
passengers. Smoking policies will vary, too. Many cargo-liners have
small pools, exercise rooms, and saunas for officer and passenger
use, and plenty of deck space for walks.

Some lines offer single cabins; others charge a single supplement,
usually less than 50 percent. You should ask if your assigned cabin
window is likely to be blocked by container during any part of the
voyage. Because freighters are working vessels, most lines won't

accept pre-teen children for passage. Those that do usually charge the adult fare for children. Pets aren't permitted.

An open bridge policy prevailed among freighters in the past; some freighters may still have one, others may not. Policies on bridge access are more strict since 9/11. Some lines and governments in port destinations may prohibit non-crew passengers from gaining bridge access. When the vessel does have an open bridge, you're welcome to watch officers and crew in action, except during critical maneuvers such as docking. On some freighters, passengers are free to go almost anywhere, while on others there are sensible security and safety rules. Obviously during rough weather, the container decks are off-limits. Pampering is not part of the program, although the crew may be very attentive. Basic services are handled by stewards who usually double as cabin attendants and waiters. A washer and dryer are generally available for passenger use. Phone and fax services are always available in emergencies, but policies on casual use vary.

Ships carrying more than 12 passengers have a doctor on board and generally have a small hospital or treatment center. But medical services aboard freighters carrying 12 or fewer passengers are limited. All, however, carry basic medical supplies and someone aboard will be trained in first aid. In case of serious illness, the captain will contact the nearest ship or shore station with a doctor available for advice. In a grave emergency, the victim will be transferred to a ship with appropriate medical facilities or be put ashore at the nearest port. Costs incurred in medical evacuation and treatment are the passenger's responsibility. All freighters taking less than 12 passengers have age limits; many will not take passengers over age 79, and some have a cutoff as low as 70 years of age.

In view of this, you're advised to take out travel health insurance with medical evacuation coverage and to carry more than enough of any medications you require. (See Part One of this book for insurance information.)

Dining and Food

Every freighter has a comfortable dining room shared by officers and passengers. On some ships, the officers share their tables with passengers; on others, they eat at separate tables. Dining is the day's special event and an opportunity to socialize. Most officers are congenial, eager to please, and happy to share their knowledge of the ship, the sea, and the world. Most freighter food is of good restaurant quality, well-prepared, and plentiful. Menus often feature the national cuisine of the ship's and/or officers' origin, which are as wide-ranging as British, German, Ukrainian, or Indian. The deck crew's nationality may be entirely different.

Breakfast and lunch are usually presented buffet-style, while dinners are served at tables, often in four or five courses. Coffee and tea are available anytime, and between-meal snacks are provided. While beer, wine, and liquor is available on most ships, it may be necessary for you to BYOB.

PLANNING YOUR FREIGHTER VOYAGE

THE MAJORITY OF FREIGHTERS book up early, especially for peak summer months and on voyages to tropical climes during northern winters. Start early yourself—six months or more—to get your choice of ship and routing, and a year ahead is not unusual on popular voyages. Planning, booking, and confirming your voyage can take much longer than you imagined. Depending on itinerary, you may have to obtain travel documents, such as visas, make arrangements concerning your home or business, get a physical check-up and inoculations, and decide on trip and travel health insurance options. Fewer than 40 nations require U.S. citizens to carry visas, but those that do will require some advance planning to avoid a potentially nasty situation. These are all reasons to engage a freighter travel specialists, especially when it is your first trip on a freighter.

Ford's Freighter Travel Guide
19448 Londelius Street
Northridge, CA 91324
☎ 818-701-7414

You might start by consulting a current issue of **Ford's Freighter Travel Guide,** a comprehensive twice-a-year guide listing almost all passenger-carrying freighter itineraries. Your local university library may have a copy. A subscription costs $24 (plus $1.98 sales tax for California residents). Single copies are $15.95.

A smart move would be to join **TravLtips Cruise and Freighter Association;** membership costs $20 per year per couple or $35 for two years). You'll connect with this loose-knit group of thousands of freighter and off-beat cruising buffs and receive bi-monthly issues of *TravLtips,* the association magazine; periodic issues of *Roam the World by Freighter,* which includes members' reports of voyages; access to the association's travel planning and reservation services; and member-only invitations on special and unusual cruises.

TravLtips Cruise and Freighter Association
P.O. Box 580188
Flushing, NY 11358-0188
☎ 718-224-0435 or
800-872-8584
fax 718-224-3247
www.travltips.com

Another very useful resource is California-based **Freighter World Cruises**. Printed twice monthly, *The Freighter Space Advisory* reports cabin availability, descriptions, departure dates from the U.S. and foreign ports, en route ports of call, and fares. You can subscribe online at **www.freighter world.com;** a one-year subscription costs $29. Both of these resources can help you select a vessel or voyage and book it, plus handle air and other travel arrangements.

Freighter World Cruises
180 South Lake Avenue
Suite 335
Pasadena, CA 91101-2655
☎ 626-449-3106 or
800-531-7774
fax 626-449-9573
www.freighterworld.com

Canada-based **The Cruise People** have been in business since 1972, and employs a full-time freighter travel specialist. By accessing their Web site, **www.thecruisepeople.ca,** you can get on their e-mail list for promotions on freighter voyages and cruises.

The Cruise People
1252 Lawrence Avenue East
Suite 210
Don Mills, Ontario
Canada M3A 1C3
☎ 416-444-2410 or
800-268-6523
fax 416-447-2628
www.thecruisepeople.ca

All three companies' Web sites list the ever-changing freighter voyage opportunities, and access is free.

Many cargo lines are represented by the above or similar specialized agents. These services can be a real blessing, particularly to first-timers, because booking passage on a freighter is neither quick nor easy.

You need lead time. Because freighter schedules are prone to change, some lines require wait-listing (no charge) until firm schedules are released. Only then will waiting passengers be given an option on a cabin. A deposit—usually 10 to 20 percent—is required only after a cabin option is accepted. Final payment is usually due 45 to 60 days before sailing.

During the months before sailing, the departure date may shift a few days and the routing may change. (For example, you may be going to Wellington rather than Auckland.) This proves the value of having an experienced agent to keep you informed of changes and to help deal with them, as well as your need for flexibility in schedule and attitude.

Every freighter company has its own policies affecting passengers. Most have literature outlining these policies and describing their ships and itineraries. Obtain such materials through your travel agent or freighter travel specialist or directly from the line, and read everything thoroughly—including the fine print. Pay particular attention to the company's cancellation policy, and take it into account when you consider trip cancellation insurance. Also, it may be wise to take out deviation insurance in case a voyage suddenly becomes longer by a week or more, because some lines will charge you for the extra days.

Your Health and Safety

Cargo lines require passengers ages 65 or older to present a certificate of good health from their doctor before booking can be completed. Review your itinerary with your physician regarding potential risk of disease or infection and any immunizations or protective medicines needed. Up-to-the-minute immunization recommendations are available from the **U.S. Centers for Disease Control's** 24-hour hotline in Atlanta: ☎ 877-394-8747. You'll need a touch-tone phone and fax machine to receive faxed messages. You may also check for information on the CDC Web site at **www.cdc.gov.** You may also want to stay informed about potential unrest in the countries you are visiting. The State Department publishes travel advisories at **travel.state.gov/travel/**

warnings.html. If something happens en route, the shipping line may change the itinerary. Or, if it is safe to call for handling cargo, you may be advised or even required to stay aboard.

Clothing and Essentials

Packing for a 90-day freighter voyage should be no different from selecting your gear and garments for a 10-day trip. Nor should it weigh more; cargo lines, unlike cruise lines, aren't obligated to provide baggage service. Don't bring more than you can handle, although crewmembers are likely to help you carry your luggage up a steep gangway.

Casual attire is the rule. It's possible there might be a special occasion calling for slightly dressier clothes, or that restaurants ashore may require them. For everyday wear, bring low-heeled, nonskid, rubber-soled shoes. They are essential for safe maneuvering aboard ship in rough seas and during normal rolling conditions. Be prepared for just about any kind of climate. Light wraps (even in the tropics) and rain gear are essential.

Foul weather is almost a certainty during any long voyage, and many freighter veterans pack a lightweight, two-piece rain suit (parka and pants) and rubber boots. They also are handy for wading through the dust and residue that cakes bulk-loading docks. Bring binoculars, some reading material (don't overdo; most ships have extensive libraries), washcloths, and facial tissue.

Electrical current on most foreign-flagged freighters is 220/250 AC. You'll need a voltage converter and plug adapter to use your appliances. Funds for shipboard expenses should be in U.S. currency. Traveler's checks are generally accepted, but very few lines take credit cards or personal checks.

Some lines say they have no policy on tipping. A few say that their stewards who serve passengers get extra pay and suggest that tipping be reserved for exceptional or special service. The norm seems to be $1.50 per person per day to the room steward and an equal amount to the dining steward.

Smoking is allowed on nearly all freighters because many officers and crew members smoke. A few lines bar smoking in dining rooms. The majority of officers and crew who smoke are courteous around nonsmoking guests, and most passengers say smoking is not a big problem.

FREIGHTER TRAVEL COMPANIES

BELOW IS A SMALL SAMPLE of freighter companies offering cruises; all can be booked through The Cruise People, Freighter World Cruises, and TravLtips. These agents are able to supply detailed information on these and other freighter companies and ships with the facilities to carry passengers.

BANK LINE/ANDREW WEIR SHIPPING LTD. General cargo ships take 12 passengers sailing from Dunkirk and Le Havre, France on a round-the-world service via the Panama and Suez Canals. The route includes South Pacific islands, Papua New Guinea, Singapore, Malaysia, then Algeciras, Spain, ending at Hamburg, Germany. 100 to 105 days.

CANADA MARITIME Container ships accommodating from three to eight passengers operate regular transatlantic services on three routes from Montreal to two or three European ports—Liverpool and Thamesport, England; Le Havre, France; Antwerp, Belgium; and Hamburg, Germany. 18 to 20 days round trip; one-way passage is also available. **www.canmar.com.**

CMA CGM, THE FRENCH LINE Four container ships take six passengers sailing from New York, Norfolk, and Savannah, then via the Panama Canal to the South Pacific, Australia, Singapore, Saudi Arabia, and Egypt; through the Suez Canal to Mediterranean and Northern European ports; and then west to New York. All in about 84 days.

GRIMALDI FREIGHTER CRUISES Roll-on/roll-off ships take nine to ten passengers from Southampton, England to ports in Italy, Greece, Turkey, Cyprus, Israel, and Egypt, and return via several Northern European ports back to Southampton. Complete voyage takes about 35 days. **www.Grimaldi-Freightercruises.com.**

LYKES LINES LTD. Four container ships accommodating five passengers sail from Houston to New Orleans, San Juan, then transatlantic to Italian and Spanish ports, returning via Mexican ports to Houston. Complete voyage takes about 42 days. **www.lykesline.com.**

PZM POLISH STEAMSHIP COMPANY Bulk carriers taking six passengers sail from Amsterdam (Ijmuiden) to the Great Lakes ports of Cleveland, Ohio; Burns Harbor, Indiana; Duluth, Minnesota; and Thunder Bay, Ontario. The one-way westbound trip lasts about 12 to 21 days. The return is a tramp service with eastbound ports not known in advance. They could be in Northern Europe, the Mediterranean, and North Africa. Complete voyage takes about 60 days.

REEDEREI F. LAEISZ Four container ships taking four passengers leave from Long Beach, California for Pusan, South Korea, and Shanghai, China, and return to Long Beach in about 28 days. The company also operates nine ships that accommodate eight passengers and sail from Long Beach to East Asian ports, Sri Lanka, then via the Suez Canal to Northern European ports, returning via Suez to East Asian ports and back to Long Beach in about 84 days. **www.laeiszline.de.**

ITINERARY INDEX

Abercrombie & Kent International, Inc.

Explorer II **HOME PORT** Ushuaia
November–February, 14–19 nights, Antarctica. Tour programs include flights between Miami and Santiago (Chile), 1 night hotel in Santiago, and flights between Santiago and Ushuaia—all round-trip from Ushuaia.

November, December, February, 18–19 nights, Antarctica, Falkland Islands, and South Georgia Island.

January, 15 nights, Antarctica and the Falkland Islands.

December, February, 14 nights, "Classic Antarctica" to the Antarctic Peninsula only.

Abercrombie & Kent also offers luxury and educational cruise packages aboard yachts, barges, river boats, cruise ships, and sailing ships in South America, the Galapagos, Caribbean, Alaska, Tahiti, Baltic, and on rivers in Europe, Russia, China, and Myanmar.

American Canadian Caribbean Line

Grande Caribe **HOME PORTS** Warren (RI), others vary with itinerary
November–May, 14 nights, Intracoastal waterways between Florida and Rhode Island.

December–January, 11 nights, Virgin Islands.

January–February, 11 nights, St. Maarten/Antigua.

March–April, 11 nights, Bahamas/Caicos or Bahamas/Eleuthera/Exumas.

May, 7 nights, Chesapeake Bay.

June–July and September, 12 nights, Erie Canal/Saguenay.

July–August, 5 nights, New England Islands.

October, 12 nights, Erie Canal Fall Foliage between Warren (RI) and Quebec City.

Grande Mariner **HOME PORTS** Warren (RI), Chicago, others vary with itinerary
November and May, 14 nights, Intracoastal waterways between Florida and Rhode Island. December–January, Panama/Colon/Balboa.

February–March, 11 nights, Belize/Barrier Reef/Guatemala; or 7 nights, Belize/Barrier Reef.

April, 7 nights, Colonial Intercoastal.

June and August, 6 nights, Lake Michigan.

August–September, 15 nights, Chicago/Great Lakes/Erie Canal/Warren.

September, 5 nights, New England Islands.

September–October, 12 nights, Erie Canal/Fall Foliage.

Niagara Prince **HOME PORTS** Warren (RI), others vary with itinerary
May, 7 nights, Jacksonville/St. Petersburg, positioning cruise; 11 nights, St. Petersburg/New Orleans, positioning cruise; 14 nights, New Orleans/Chicago

June, 6 nights, Lake Michigan; June–July, Chicago/Great Lakes/Erie Canal/Warren.

July–August, 7 nights, Coast of Maine, round-trip from Portland.

September–October, 10 nights, Hudson River/Lake Champlain round-trip Warren.

November, 14 nights, Intercoastal waterways.

American Safari Cruises

Safari Escape **HOME PORTS** Juneau, Friday Harbor
September–October, 7 nights, San Juan Islands and fjords of Canada, round-trip from Friday Harbor (WA) to Sidney, Victoria, Princess Louisa Inlet, and Vancouver; Roche Harbor, Jones Island (WA).

May–September, 8 nights, Alaska, between Juneau and Prince Rupert (BC); mid-May to late August, calling at Tracy Arm and the twin Sawyer Glaciers, Stephens Passage, and Frederick Sound, Petersburg, Canoe Pass, Meyers Chuck, Misty Fjords, Ketchikan. Includes kayaking, hiking, whale-watching.

May and September, 14 nights, Inside Passage positioning cruises between Seattle and Juneau.

Safari Quest **HOME PORTS** Juneau, La Paz, Astoria, Lewiston, San Francisco
September–October, 11 nights, Columbia and Snake Rivers from Lewiston (ID) to Astoria (OR) or reverse.

October–November, 3 and 4 nights, round-trip from San Francisco to Petaluma and Carneros regions and Napa Valley.

December–April, 8 nights, Sea of Cortés cruise-tour, round-trip from San Jose del Cabo, with overnight hotel before sailing from La Paz to explore islands,watch for whales and birds, and calling at Isla Partida, Isla San Jose, Isla Coyote, Loreto, Isla Espiritu Santo, Bahia Aqua Verde.

May–September, 7 nights, Alaska, between Juneau and Sitka; late May to late August, calling at Tracy Arm, Sawyer Glaciers, Frederick Sound, Petersburg, Admiralty Island, and secluded bays and channels along the route. Includes kayaking, hiking, whale-watching. Positioning cruises from Seattle to Juneau, 14 nights, mid-May and September, Inside Passage.

Safari Spirit **HOME PORTS** Juneau, Friday Harbor
September–October, 7 nights, San Juan Islands and fjords of Canada, round-trip from Friday Harbor (WA) to Sidney, Victoria, Princess Louisa Inlet, and Vancouver; Roche Harbor, Jones Island (WA).

May–September, 7 nights, Alaska, round-trip from Juneau, Icy Strait, Elfin Cove, Tenakee Springs, Baranof, and Chichagof Islands, the Brother's Islands (part of Admiralty Island National Monument), Endicott Arm, Dawes Glacier. The adventure cruise includes whale-, wildlife-, and bird-watching and kayaking.

Bora Bora Cruises

Tu Moana/Ti'a Moana **HOME PORT** Bora Bora
Year-round, Monday, 6 nights, Society Islands lagoon cruising, round-trip from Bora to Taha'a, Raiatea (2 days), Huanine, overnight in Bora Bora.

Carnival Cruise Lines

Carnival Conquest **HOME PORT** New Orleans
Year-round, Sunday, 7 nights, Western Caribbean round-trip from New Orleans to Montego Bay, Grand Cayman, Cozumel.

Carnival Destiny **HOME PORT** San Juan
Year-round, Sunday, 7 nights, Southern Caribbean round-trip from San Juan to St. Thomas/St. John, Dominica and 15-hour calls at Barbados and Aruba.

Carnival Freedom (debuts February 2007) **HOME PORT** t.b.a.

Carnival Glory **HOME PORT** Port Canaveral
Year-round, Saturday, 7 nights, alternating Eastern and Western Caribbean round-trip from Port Canaveral to Nassau, St. Thomas/St. John, and St. Maarten; or Key West; Belize City, Cozumel, and Progreso/Merida (Mexico).

Carnival Legend **HOME PORTS** Ft. Lauderdale, New York
November–April and from October 23, 2006, 8 nights, Southern Caribbean or Panama Canal round-trip from Ft. Lauderdale to St. Maarten,

Barbados, Martinique; or Belize City; Puerto Limon (Costa Rica); Colon (Panama) (optional Panama Canal/Gatun Lake excursions available).

April 20, 2006 and April 19, 2007, Bermuda, 6 nights, depart from New York and overnight visit to King's Wharf, Bermuda as well as a full day at Newport (RI)

April–October, 8 nights, Eastern Caribbean round-trip from New York, calling at San Juan, St. Thomas/St. John, and Tortola with excursions to Virgin Gorda available.

Carnival Liberty **HOME PORTS** Ft. Lauderdale, Rome
November–April, 6 and 8 nights, Caribbean round-trip from Ft. Lauderdale. 8 nights, Saturday, to either Puerto Limon (Costa Rica), Colon (Panama), and Cozumel (passengers can visit the Panama Canal on excursions from Colon); or San Juan, St. Thomas/St. John, Antigua, Tortola/Virgin Gorda, and Nassau. 6 nights, alternate Sundays to Freeport, Grand Cayman, and Cozumel.

April and November, 14–16 nights, transatlantic, Ft. Lauderdale to Rome or reverse.

May–October, 12 nights, Mediterranean, round-trip from Rome (Civitavecchia) to Naples (Italy), Dubrovnik (Croatia), Venice (Italy) (2-day call), Messina (Sicily), Barcelona (Spain), Cannes (France), and Livorno (Italy) for Pisa (Florence, Italy).

Carnival Miracle **HOME PORT** Tampa
Year-round, Sunday, 7 nights, Western Caribbean round-trip from Tampa to Grand Cayman, Costa Maya, Cozumel, Belize City.

Carnival Pride **HOME PORT** Los Angeles (Long Beach)
Year-round, 7 nights, Mexican Riviera round-trip from Long Beach to Cabo San Lucas, Puerto Vallarta, Mazatlán.

Carnival Spirit **HOME PORTS** Vancouver, San Diego
October–April, 8 nights, Mexican Riviera round-trip from San Diego to Acapulco, Zihuatanejo/Ixtapa, and Manzanillo.

April, September, October, 12 nights, Hawaii, between Honolulu (overnight) and either Ensenada or Vancouver, calling at Kona and Hilo (Hawaii); Lahaina and/or Kahului (Maui); and Nawiliwili, Kauai (except on Vancouver-to-Honolulu itinerary).

May–September, Wednesday, 7 nights, Alaska between Vancouver and Whittier, calling at Prince William Sound, College Fjord, Lynn Canal, Sitka, Juneau, Skagway, Ketchikan, and the Inside Passage; or Alaska Inside Passage round-trip from Vancouver to Juneau, Glacier Bay, Skagway, Ketchikan.

Carnival Triumph **HOME PORT** Miami
Year-round, Saturday, 7 nights, alternating Eastern and Western Caribbean, round-trip from Miami to San Juan, St. Thomas, St. Maarten; or Cozumel, Grand Cayman, Ocho Rios.

Carnival Valor **HOME PORT** Miami
Year-round, Sunday, 7 nights, alternating Eastern and Western Caribbean
round-trip from Miami to Nassau, St. Thomas, and St. Maarten; or Belize
City (Belize); Isla Roatan (Honduras); Grand Cayman and Cozumel.

Carnival Victory **HOME PORTS** Miami, New York, Norfolk, Charleston
September–May, Sunday, 7 nights, alternating Eastern and Western
Caribbean round-trip from Miami to San Juan, St. Maarten and St. Thomas,
or Cozumel, Grand Cayman, Ocho Rios.

June and October, 2 and 6 nights, Bahamas and weekend getaways from
Norfolk to Nassau (overnight onboard) and Freeport (6 nights); or weekend getaway to nowhere (2 nights).

June–September, 4–5 nights, Canada, round-trip from New York to Halifax
(4 nights); or Saint John and Halifax (5 nights).

October, 5 nights, Bahamas, from Charleston (SC) to Nassau (overnight)
and Freeport.

November, 7 nights, resumes alternating Eastern and Western Caribbean
cruises from Miami.

Celebration **HOME PORT** Jacksonville
Year-round, 4–5 nights, Bahamas round-trip from Jacksonville (FL).
4 nights, alternate Thursdays to Freeport and Nassau; or 5 nights, alternate
Mondays and Saturdays to Key West and Nassau.

Ecstasy **HOME PORT** Galveston
Year-round, 4–5 nights, Western Caribbean from Galveston. 4 nights, alter-
nate Thursdays to Cozumel; 5 nights, alternate Mondays to Cozumel and
Calica/Playa del Carmen.

Elation **HOME PORT** Galveston
Year-round, Sunday, 7 nights, Western Caribbean cruises round-trip from
Galveston to Progreso, Cozumel, Belize.

Fantasy **HOME PORT** Port Canaveral
Year-round, 3–4 nights, Bahamas cruises round-trip from Port Canaveral.
3 nights, Thursday to Nassau; 4 nights, Sunday to Freeport and Nassau.
Both have 1 day at sea.

Fascination **HOME PORT** Miami
Year-round, 3–4 nights, Bahamas and Western Caribbean round-trip from
Miami. 3 nights, Fridays to Nassau; 4 nights, Monday to Key West, Cozumel.

Holiday **HOME PORT** Mobile
Year-round, 4–5 nights, Western Caribbean round-trip from Mobile (AL).
4 nights, alternate Thursdays to Cozumel; 5 nights, alternate Mondays to
Cozumel, Calica/Playa del Carmen; 5 nights, alternate Saturdays to
Cozumel and Costa Maya.

Imagination **HOME PORT** Miami
Year-round, 4–5 nights, Western Caribbean round-trip from Miami.

4 nights, alternate Thursdays to Key West and Cozumel; 5 nights, alternate Mondays to Key West and Belize; 5 nights, alternate Saturdays to Grand Cayman and Ocho Rios.

Inspiration **HOME PORT** Tampa
Year-round, 4–5 nights, Western Caribbean round-trip from Tampa.
4 nights, alternate Thursdays to Cozumel; 5 nights, alternate Mondays and Saturdays to Grand Cayman and Cozumel.

Paradise **HOME PORT** Los Angeles (Long Beach)
Year-round, 3–4 nights, Mexico round-trip from Long Beach. 3 nights, Friday to Ensenada; 4 nights, Monday to Ensenada and Catalina Island.

Sensation **HOME PORT** New Orleans
Year-round, 4–5 nights, Western Caribbean round-trip from New Orleans.
4 nights, alternate Thursdays to Cozumel; 5 nights, alternate Mondays to Cozumel.

Celebrity Cruises

Celebrity Xpedition **HOME PORT** Baltra (Galapagos Islands)
Year-round, 7 nights, Galapagos Islands round-trip from Baltra to North Seymour, Española, Santa Cruz (Darwin Station and Cerro Dragon), Bartolome, Isabela, Fernandina, Rabida, Santiago, and Santa Maria. 10-night cruise-tours from North America include round-trip air, 2 nights hotel in Quito (Ecuador), and a city tour.

Century **HOME PORTS** Ft. Lauderdale, Amsterdam
October, 15 nights, transatlantic Barcelona to Ft. Lauderdale.

October to April, 9–10 nights, Southern Caribbean/Panama Canal round-trip from Ft. Lauderdale. 9 nights to St. Maarten, St. Lucia, Barbados, Antigua; or Grand Cayman, Ocho Rios, Aruba, Curaçao. 10 nights to Ocho Rios (Jamaica), Puerto Limon (Costa Rica), Colon (Panama), and Aruba.

May–August, 12 nights, Northern Europe, round-trip from Amsterdam.

September–October, 10–11 nights, Mediterranean, round-trip from Barcelona.

November 2006–April 2007, 4–5 nights, Caribbean, round-trip from Miami.

Constellation **HOME PORTS** San Juan, Cape Liberty (Bayonne, NJ), Dover
September–October, 12–13 nights, Canada/New England round-trip from Cape Liberty at Bayonne (NJ) to Boston, Bar Harbor, Halifax, Quebec City (2 days), Saguenay River, Portland Maine, and Martha's Vineyard on the 13-night sailing.

November–March, 7 nights, Southern Caribbean round-trip from San Juan to Casa de Camp, Barbados, Grenada, St. Kitts, St. Thomas; or St. Maarten, Dominica, St. Lucia, Margarita Island, Aruba. March 18, 2006 8 nights, San Juan to Cape Liberty.

March, September–October, 12 nights, Caribbean or Canada/New England, round-trip from Cape Liberty to either Charleston, Grand Bahama, Nassau, St. Maarten, St. Thomas, San Juan; or Boston, Bar Harbor, Halifax, Quebec City (2 days), Saguenay River, Portland Maine.

May–August, 14 nights, Northern Europe, round-trip from Dover.

November 2006–April 2007, 10–11 nights, Caribbean round-trip from Ft. Lauderdale. 5 nights alternate Saturdays to Cozumel and either Costa Maya or Calica.

Galaxy **HOME PORTS** Galveston, Rome, San Juan
October, 14 nights, transatlantic Rome to Galveston.
November–April, 11 and 12 nights, Panama Canal, round-trip from Galveston to Cozumel, Belize City, Cristobal, Panama Canal partial transit, Puerto Limon, Grand Cayman plus Montego Bay on the 12-night cruises.

May–October, 10–11 nights, Mediterranean, round-trip from Rome to either Naples (Italy), Mykonos and Santorini (Greece), Messina (Sicily, Italy), Villefranche (Nice, France), and Genoa (Italy) (10 nights); or Mykonos, Rhodes, and Santorini (Greece), Istanbul and Kusadasi (Ephesus, Turkey), Piraeus (Athens, Greece), and Naples (Italy). October 16, 2006, Med/Black Sea, 14 nights, calls at Mykonos, Rhodes, and Santorini (Greece); Istanbul (Turkey); Constanta (Romania); Odessa (Ukraine); Kusadasi (Ephesus, Turkey); Piraeus (Athens, Greece); and Naples (Italy).

November 2006–April 2007, 10–11 nights, Southern Caribbean, round-trip from San Juan.

Infinity **HOME PORTS** San Diego, Vancouver, Buenos Aires, others vary with itinerary
October–December, 14 nights, Hawaii round-trip from San Diego.

October, December, April, 3, 6, 11 nights, Mexican Riviera round-trip from San Diego or San Francisco.

December and April, 14 nights, Panama Canal between San Diego and Ft. Lauderdale.

December–March, 12–14 nights, South America, Ft. Lauderdale to Valparaiso; between Valparaiso and Buenos Aires; or round-trip from Buenos Aires.

May–September, Sunday, 7 nights, Alaska, round-trip from Vancouver to Ketchikan, Juneau, Sitka, and cruising the Inside Passage and Hubbard Glacier.

October 2006–April 2007, returns to South America.

Mercury **HOME PORTS** San Diego, Seattle
September–October, 3–8 nights, Pacific Northwest/British Columbia round-trip from Seattle.

October and April, positions from Seattle to San Diego and reverse.

October–April, 10 and 11 nights, Mexican Riviera round-trip from San Diego to Cabo San Lucas, Mazatlán, Puerto Vallarta, Acapulco, Ixtapa/ Zihuatanejo plus Manzanillo on the 11-night sailings.

May–September, 7 nights, round-trip from Seattle to Juneau, Skagway, Hubbard, Ketchikan, Prince Rupert (BC).

November 2006–April 2007, 10–14 nights, Mexican Riviera, Hawaii, or Panama Canal, round-trip from San Diego.

Millennium **HOME PORTS** Ft. Lauderdale, Barcelona, Venice
November and April, 14 nights, transatlantic, Barcelona to Ft. Lauderdale or reverse.

November–April, Sunday, 7 nights, Caribbean round-trip from Ft. Lauderdale to San Juan, Catalina Island (Casa de Campo), Dominican Republic, St. Thomas; or Nassau or San Juan, Antigua, St. Maarten.

May–November, 12 nights, Mediterranean, between Barcelona and Venice via Villefranche (Nice, France), Florence (Italy), Civitavecchia (Rome, Italy), Naples (Italy), Mykonos (Greece), Santorini (Greece), Piraeus (Athens, Greece), and Dubrovnik (Croatia).

December 2006–April 2007, 7 nights, Eastern Caribbean round-trip from Ft. Lauderdale

Summit **HOME PORTS** Los Angeles, Ft. Lauderdale, Vancouver
October, 6–7 nights, Mexican Riviera round-trip from Los Angeles.

October–April, 14–15 nights, Panama Canal between Los Angeles and Ft. Lauderdale (14 nights); or Hawaii round-trip from Los Angeles, calling at Nawiliwili, Honolulu, Hilo, Kona, Lahaina, Ensenada (15 nights).

May–September, 7 nights, Alaska, between Vancouver and Seward, via Hubbard Glacier, Juneau, Skagway, Ketchikan, and either Icy Strait or Valdez and College Fjord.

October 2006–April 2007, repeats Panama Canal and Hawaii sailings round-trip from Los Angeles.

Zenith **HOME PORTS** Miami, Cape Liberty
October–April, 4–5 nights, Caribbean round-trip from Miami. 4 nights to Key West, Cozumel. 5 nights to Port Antonia (Jamaica) and Grand Cayman.

April–October, 7 nights, Bermuda, round-trip from Cape Liberty (Bayonne, NJ) to Hamilton and St. George Island (Bermuda).

November 2006–April 2007, 10–11 nights, Eastern and Western Caribbean, round-trip from Tampa.

Clipper Cruise Line

Clipper Adventurer **HOME PORT** Varies with itinerary
October, 12–15 nights, South America: Panama to Callao (Peru); Callao

(Peru) to Puerto Montt (Chile); or Santiago to Ushuaia.

November–February, 15 and 21 nights, Antarctica:

November 9, 2005 round-trip from Ushuaia: Antarctic Peninsula, 15 nights; December 17, 2005 Antarctica, the Falklands, and South Georgia, 21 nights; November 20, 2005, January 21, 2006, and February 1 and 12, 2006, Antarctica and the Falklands, 15 nights. Cruise-tour packages include air from the United States, pre-cruise Santiago and post-cruise Buenos Aires, or reverse.

March–May, 9–12 nights, Mediterranean and Adriatic, Rome–Athens; Athens–Malta; Dubrovnik–Malta; Malta–Rome.

June–September, 11–19 nights, Western Europe, British Isles, Iceland, Greenland, Arctic Circle, Norwegian Fjords, cruise-tours Lisbon–London; Leith, Edinburgh (Scotland)–Reykjavik (Iceland); Reykjavik to Ottawa (Canada); Ottawa–Oslo (Norway); Oslo–Bergen (Norway); Bergen–Dublin (Ireland); Dublin–Greenock, Glasgow.

November, 17 nights, Argentina/Falkland Islands from Buenos Aires to Ushuaia via Montevideo, San Clemente, Mar del Plata, Viedma, Valdez Peninsula, Punta Tombo, Camarones, Puerto Deseado, Falkland Islands.

December, resumes sailings to Antarctica from Ushuaia.

Clipper Odyssey **HOME PORT** Varies with itinerary
September, 12 nights, Vietnam between Hanoi to Ho Chi Minh City.

November–February, 13 nights, New Zealand, between Queenstown and Auckland via Milford Sound (Embark), Doubtful Sound, Dusky Sound, Dunedin, Akaroa, Lyttelton, Queen Charlotte Sound, Motuara Island, Picton, Wellington, Napier, Tauranga.

January–February, 13 nights, Australia/New Zealand between Queenstown and Auckland via Milford Sound (Embark), Doubtful Sound, Dusky Sound, Dunedin, Akaroa, Lyttelton, Queen Charlotte Sound, Motuara Island, Picton, Wellington, Napier, Tauranga; Auckland to Cairns (Australia); Sydney to Brisbane (Australia).

February–June, 14–18 nights, New Zealand/Great Barrier Reef/Australia/South Pacific/Japan: Queenstown (New Zealand)–Sydney; Sydney–Guam; or Himeji (Japan) to Tokyo via Uno Ko, Miyajima Island, Hiroshima, Uwajima, Nagasaki, Pusan, Hagi, Sakai–Ko, Kanazawa, Sado Island, Aomori, Hakodate.

June, 13–15 nights, Russian Far East/Alaska, from Tokyo to Anchorage and round-trip from Anchorage.

August–September, 12–18 nights, China/Vietnam, Yokohama to Ho Chi Minh City or between Ho Chi Minh City and Hanoi.

November, 16 nights, South Pacific, Noumea to Auckland (New Zealand).

Nantucket Clipper **HOME PORT** Varies with itinerary
September–December, 7–14 nights, Canada/New England, Hudson Valley,

and Antebellum South; Halifax to New York City; round-trip from New York; New York to Alexandria; Washington, D.C. to Charleston; Charleston to Jacksonville. Special golf cruise-tour, Orlando to Miami, 7 nights, December 5, 2005.

December–January, 7–10 nights, Caribbean round-trip from St. Thomas to Jost Van Dyke, Tortola, Virgin Gorda, Salt Island, Norman Island, St. John, Christmas Cove. 10-night sailing January 7, Culebra, Ponce, Vieques replace Jost Van Dyke.

February, 7 nights, "The Rain Forests, Reefs, and Mayan Temples of Belize and Honduras" cruise-tour between Puerto Cortez, Honduras, and Belize via Co-coa Plum Cay, Livingston, Puerto Barrios (for Tikal), Punta Sal Peninsula, and Roatan Island.

March–June and September–November, 7 and 14 nights, U.S. East Coast on various itineraries, including Antebellum South along the Intracoastal water-ways from Jacksonville (FL) to Charleston (SC); Colonial America and Civil War Battlefields from Jacksonville to Washington, D.C./Alexandria; Spring-time on the Chesapeake Bay and Hudson River, Alexandria to New York City; Coastal Waterways and Fall Foliage of Maine, Boston to Bangor; Fall Foliage on the Hudson, round-trip from New York. Fall sailings operate in reverse.

June–September, 7–14 nights, Canada/New England and Great Lakes be-tween Quebec City and Buffalo or Chicago; or round-trip from Chicago.

December, resumes sailings round-trip from St. Thomas.

Yorktown Clipper **HOME PORT** Varies with itinerary
September–October, 5 nights, Pacific Northwest between Seattle and Van-couver to either Roche Harbor, Sucia Island, Matia/Puffin Island and Victoria; or Victoria, Friday Harbor, Roche Harbor, Sucia Island, Matia/Puffin Island. Optional Rockies rail tour add-on, Calgary/Vancouver available.

October, 5 nights, California wine country, round-trip from Redwood City to Sausalito, Sacramento, Vallejo, and San Francisco.

November–December, February, 8 nights, Panama Canal/Costa Rica cruise-tours between Balboa (Panama) and San Jose (Costa Rica) via Panama Canal, Bahia Garachine (for Darien Jungle), Marenco, Manuel Antonio National Park, Quepos, Punta Leona (for Carara Biological Reserve), Curu, Puerto Caldera.

January and December, 7 nights, Caribbean, round-trip from St. Thomas to Jost van Dyke, Tortola, Virgin Gorda, Salt Island, Norman Island, St. John, Christmas Cove.

February–March, 8 nights, Sea of Cortés, round-trip from La Paz to Isla Par-tida, Los Islotes, Isla Espiritu Santo, Cabo San Lucas, Bahia Magdalena, Boca De Soledad, La Entrada (for Magdalena Bay), San Carlos.

April–May, October–November, 7 nights, California wine country round-trip from Redwood City to Sacramento, Napa Sea Ranch (for Sonoma and Napa Valley), Sausalito, San Francisco.

May–September, 7 nights, Alaska, round-trip from Juneau to Skagway, Haines, Elfin Cove, Idaho Inlet, Glacier Bay National Park, Sitka, Tracy Arm.

May and September, 11 nights, positioning cruises between Seattle and Juneau or reverse.

September–October 2006, 7 nights, between Seattle and Vancouver, Friday Harbor, Sucia Island, Matia/Puffin Island, Victoria, Powell River, Jervis Inlet, Squamish (for Whistler).

November 2006 resumes Panama, Costa Rica, and Caribbean sailings.

Costa Cruises

Costa Allegra **HOME PORTS** Savona, Amsterdam
September–November, 10–12 nights, Mediterranean, round-trip from Savona (Genoa) to Egypt/Turkey/Greece (10 nights) or Libya/Greece/Egypt (12 nights).

May–August, 11 nights, Norwegian Fjords and North Cape or Fjords and Scotland; 12 nights to Fjords and Iceland; 12 nights, Baltic; 14 nights to North Cape and Spitsbergen or North Cape and Iceland, round-trip from Amsterdam.

May and August, 9 nights, positioning cruises from Savona to Amsterdam or reverse.

Costa Atlantica **HOME PORTS** Copenhagen, Genoa
September–November, 10 nights, Eastern Mediterranean, round-trip from Genoa to Egypt, Turkey, and Greece.

May–September, 7 nights, Baltic or Norwegian Fjords, round-trip from Copenhagen to either Stockholm, Helsinki, St. Petersburg, Tallinn; or Hellesylt, Geiranger, Flam, Bergen, Kristiansand, and Oslo (Norway).

Costa Classica **HOME PORT** Venice
September–October, 7 nights, Eastern Mediterranean, round-trip from Venice to Ancona (Italy), Athens and Corfu (Greece), Heraklion (Crete), Dubrovnik (Croatia).

Costa Concordia (debuts Spring 2006) **HOME PORT** t.b.a.
Year-round Mediterranean sailings.

Costa Europa **HOME PORTS** Amsterdam, Savona
May–November, 11 nights, Mediterranean/Canary Islands, round-trip from Savona to Barcelona, Casablanca, Agadir, Arrecife, St. Cruz de Tenerife (Canary Islands), Madeira, Malaga.

May and September, 9 nights, positioning cruises between Savona to Amsterdam.

May–August, 10–14 nights, Baltic or Norwegian Fjords, round-trip from Amsterdam to either either Ronne, St. Petersburg, Tallinn, Stockholm, Copenhagen, Visby; or Bergen, Hellesylt, Geiranger, Trondheim, Honningsvag, Tromso, Gravdal, and Olden.

Costa Fortuna **HOME PORT** Savona
October, Sunday, 7 nights, Mediterranean, round-trip from Savona to Naples (Italy), Palermo (Sicily), Tunis (Tunisia), Palma de Mallorca, Barcelona, Marseille.

November, 11 nights, Canary Islands/Mediterranean, round-trip from Savona to Barcelona; Casablanca, Morocco; Arrecife, St. Cruz de Tenerife, Canary Islands; Funchal, Madeira and Malaga, Spain.

January–April, 11 nights, Mediterranean, round-trip from Savona to Italy, Egypt, Cyprus, and Greece.

May–September, Sunday, 7 nights, Mediterranean, round-trip from Savona, as above.

Costa Magica **HOME PORTS** Ft. Lauderdale, Rome
November, Sunday, 7 nights, Mediterranean, round-trip from Rome to Savona (Italy), Barcelona, Palma de Mallorca, Tunis (Tunisia), La Valetta (Malta), Palermo (Sicily).

November–April, 7 nights, Caribbean, round-trip from Ft. Lauderdale to either San Juan, St. Thomas/St. John, Catalina Island, Casa de Campo/ Santo Domingo, Nassau; or St. Maarten, Tortola, Nassau with 3 days at sea; or Western calls at Key West, Cozumel, Ocho Rios, Grand Cayman. April 21 and 28, 2006 sailings spend 2 days in both Hamilton (Bermuda) and Nassau (Bahamas).

May to November, Sunday, 7-night cruises from Rome as above.

Costa Mediterranea **HOME PORTS** Ft. Lauderdale, Venice
May–October, 7 nights, Adriatic/Greek Isles/Turkey, round-trip from Venice to Bari (Italy), Katakolon (Greece), Izmir and Istanbul (Turkey), Dubrovnik (Croatia).

November–April, 7 nights, Caribbean, round-trip from Ft. Lauderdale to either San Juan, St. Thomas/St. John, Catalina Island, Casa de Campo/Santo Domingo, Nassau; or St. Maarten, Tortola, Nassau with 3 days at sea; or Western calls at Key West, Cozumel, Ocho Rios, Grand Cayman.

November and April, 16 nights, transatlantic from Savona to Ft. Lauderdale and reverse.

Costa Romantica **HOME PORT** Savona
May–November, 10 and 11 nights, round-trip from Savona, on four different itineraries to either the Canary Islands/Morocco/Spain; Egypt/ Cyprus/Greece/Turkey; Spain/Portugal/Morocco; or the Black Sea (Naples, Istanbul, Yalta, Odessa, Santorini, Katakolon).

Costa Victoria **HOME PORT** Venice
September–November, Monday, 7 nights, Mediterranean, round-trip from Venice to either Bari (Italy), Katakolon, Santorini, Mykonos, and Rhodes (Greece), Dubrovnik (Croatia); or Naples, Athens, Marmaris (Turkey), Rhodes, Katakolon.

January–March, 3–7 nights, round-trip from Santos, Brazil (Sao Paolo) to ports in Brazil including Rio de Janeiro, Salvador, Maceio, Buzios, Ilheus, and Porto Belo.

Cruise West

Pacific Explorer **HOME PORT** Colón, Los Sueños, Panama City
December–April, 9 nights, Costa Rica and Panama, cruise-tours including San Blas Islands, Portobelo, Panama Canal, Darién Jungle, Isla de Coiba, Golfo Dulce, Corcovado National Park, Manuel Antonio National Park.

November–December, June–July, 7 nights between Panama and Costa Rica including the Panama Canal, Darién Jungle, Isla de Coiba, Golfo Dulce, Corcovado National Park, Drake Bay, Manuel Antonio National Park. Summer departures are eco adventures geared to families.

Spirit of Alaska **HOME PORTS** Juneau, Portland
May–August 3–4 nights, Alaska Glacier Bay, round-trip from Juneau to Skagway, Haines, Sitka, Glacier Bay. Positions between Juneau and Seattle, 10 nights, May and September.

September–October, 7 nights, Columbia River, round-trip from Portland to Columbia River Gorge, Snake River, Hells Canyon, Walla Walls, The Dalles, Maryhill Museum, Astoria, Fort Clatsop, 8 sets of locks.

Spirit of Columbia **HOME PORTS** Whittier, Seattle
May–August, 3–4 nights, Prince William Sound round-trip from Anchorage/Whittier to Blackstone Bay, College Fjord, Knight Island, Chenega Glacier, Cordova, Turnagain Arm. Positioning cruises between Juneau and Seattle, 10 nights, May and September.

September, 7 nights, Gulf Islands/British Columbia, round-trip from Seattle to Vancouver, Granville Island, Princess Louisa Inlet, Nanaimo, Gulf Islands, Sidney, , Victoria, Friday Harbor, San Juan Islands, Port Townsend.

Spirit of Discovery **HOME PORTS** Portland, Juneau, Ketchikan
September–October, April, 7 nights, Columbia and Snake rivers round-trip from Portland to Columbia River Gorge, Snake River, Hells Canyon, Walla Walls, The Dalles, Maryhill Museum, Astoria, Fort Clatsop, eight sets of locks.

June–August, 8 nights, Alaska Inside Passage, round-trip from Juneau to Endicott Arm, Tracy Arm, Frederick Sound, Sitka, Icy Strait, Elfin Cove, Glacier Bay National Park. Positioning cruises between Juneau and Seattle, 10 nights, May–June and September.

Spirit of Endeavour **HOME PORTS** Cabo San Lucas, Juneau, Ketchikan, San Francisco

December–March, 7 nights, Sea of Cortés, round-trip from Cabo San Lucas to Isla Espiritú Santo, Loreto, Los Islotes, Isla Partida, La Paz. Includes whale-watching and island exploration. Optional Copper Canyon rail excursion, 4 nights, available.

May–September, 8 nights, Inside Passage between Juneau and Ketchikan. via Misty Fjords, Metlakatla, Petersburg, Frederick Sound, Tracy Arm, Sitka, Glacier Bay, Skagway and Haines. Positioning cruises between Juneau and Seattle, 10 nights, May and September .

October–November, 3–4 nights, California wine country, round-trip from San Francisco to Sacramento River Delta, Napa Valley wineries, Sausalito, Sonoma Valley wineries. Includes exclusive events and tastings.

Spirit of '98 **HOME PORTS** Portland, Ketchikan, Juneau
September–October, April, 7 nights, Columbia and Snake rivers round-trip from Portland to Columbia River Gorge, Snake River, Hells Canyon, Walla Walls, The Dalles, Maryhill Museum, Astoria, Fort Clatsop, eight sets of locks.

May–August, 8 nights, Inside Passage between Ketchikan and Juneau via Misty Fjords, Metlakatla, Petersburg, Frederick Sound, Tracy Arm, Sitka, Glacier Bay, Skagway, Haines. Positions between Juneau and Seattle, 10 nights, May and September.

Spirit of Oceanus **HOME PORTS** Vancouver, Anchorage, Papeete, others vary with itinerary
March and October, 2006, 13 nights, Japan between Kobe and Niigata via Okayama, Kurashiki, Takamatsu, Inland Sea cruising, Miyajima, Hiroshima, Beppu, Nagasaki, Pusan, Kyongju, Hagi, Izumo Taisha, Matsue, Kanazawa.

May–September, 11 nights, Alaska between Vancouver and Anchorage via Petersburg, Juneau, Sitka, Metlakatla, Misty Fjords, Tracy Arm, Glacier Bay, Prince William Sound. Can be combined with Bering Sea cruise below for a 24-night sailing.

June–August, 13 nights, Alaska/Bering Sea cruise-tour, round-trip from Anchorage to Kodiak, Dutch Harbor, Russian Far East, Arctic Circle, Shumagin Islands, Katmai National Park, Pribilof Islands, Bering Sea. Can be combined with Inside Passage cruise above for a 24-night sailing.

December 2006–February 2007, 11–18 nights, South Pacific including Hawaii/Tahiti from Honolulu to Papeete; Tahiti/Society Islands/Marquesas, round-trip from Papeete; 13 nights, Society Islands/Samoa/Fiji from Papeete to Lautoka, Fiji; World War II Islands of the Pacific from Lautoka, Fiji to Guam.

Sheltered Seas **HOME PORTS** Juneau, Ketchikan
May–August, 4–5 nights, between Juneau and Ketchikan to Petersburg, Wrangell, Frederick Sound, Tracy Arm, Sawyer Glaciers, Misty Fjords. Cruising by day with overnight in hotels ashore. Optional Glacier Bay tour connects with *Spirit of Alaska,* 3 nights.

Crystal Cruises

Crystal Harmony **HOME PORT** Los Angeles
September–November, 2005, 7 and 10 nights, Mexican Riviera, round-trip from Los Angeles. *Crystal Harmony* will leave the fleet following the November 18 sailing.

Crystal Serenity **HOME PORT** Varies with itinerary
September–November, 2005, 11–12 nights, Mediterranean and Canary Islands, from Rome, Venice, Athens, Barcelona. November 16, 10 nights, transatlantic, Lisbon to Ft. Lauderdale.

November–December, 10–15 nights, Caribbean, Panama Canal, Mexican Riviera, round-trip from Ft. Lauderdale; Ft. Lauderdale to Los Angeles; round-trip from Los Angeles.

January–May, 106 nights, World Cruise, Los Angeles to Southampton, via Mexico, Ecuador, Peru, the islands of the South Pacific, New Zealand, Australia, Mauritius, Cape Town, Tanzania, Kenya, Seychelles, Dubai, Egypt, Libya, Rome. Seven segments available, 14–19 nights, Los Angeles to Lima (Peru); Lima to Papeete (Tahiti); Papeete to Melbourne (Australia); Melbourne to Cape Town; Cape Town to Dubai; Dubai to Rome; Rome to Southampton.

May–September, 10–14 nights, Western Europe, British Isles, Norwegian Fjords, round-trip from Southampton or Dover; Stockholm to Dover; Copenhagen to Dover; Dover to Monte Carlo.

June–August, 7–11 nights, Baltic, including 2 overnights onboard in St. Petersburg (Russia) from Dover to Stockhom, Stockholm to Copenhagen, or reverse.

September–November, Mediterranean and Canary Islands, from Monte Carlo to Venice; Venice to Rome; Rome to Athens; Athens to Monte Carlo; Monte Carlo to Lisbon. November, 10 nights, transatlantic, Lisbon to Miami.

November–December, 7–14 nights, Caribbean, round-trip from Miami.

Crystal Symphony **HOME PORT** Varies with itinerary
September–October, 2005, 7–11 nights, Canada/New England, between New York and Montreal or round-trip from New York.

November 2005–February, 2006, 8–15 nights, Caribbean/Panama Canal, between Ft. Lauderale and Caldera (Costa Rica); round-trip from Ft. Lauderdale; between Caldera and Miami.

February–April, 11–16 nights, South America, from Miami to Manaus; Manaus to Buenos Aires; Buenos Aires to Valparaiso (for Santiago) or reverse; Buenos Aires to Maimi.

April–May, 9 and 10 nights, transatlantic/Mediterranean, from Miami to Athens in 2 segments: Miami to Lisbon, 9 nights, and Lisbon to Athens, 10 nights.

May–August, 7–12 nights, Mediterranean and Black Sea, from Venice, Rome or Athens; 12 nights, Western Europe, from Rome to Dover; 14 nights, transatlantic, from Dover to New York via Scotland, Iceland, Greenland.

September–October, 7 and 11 nights, Canada/New England, between New York and Montreal, or round-trip from New York.

November–December, 11–16 nights, Panama Canal/Mexican Riviera, from

Miami to Caldera (Costa Rica); Caldera to Tampa; Tampa to Los Angeles; or round-trip from Los Angeles.

Cunard Line, Ltd.

QE2 **HOME PORT** Southampton, others vary with itinerary
September–October, 15–16 nights, Eastern Mediterranean round-trip from Southampton to Greece, Egypt, Turkey.

November, 31 nights, South America/transatlantic round-trip from Southampton to Canary Islands, Salvador de Bahia (Brazil), Montevideo (Uruguay) (2 days), Stanley (Falkland Islands), Rio de Janeiro (2 days), Dakar (Senegal), Gran Canaria, Lisbon.

December, 16 nights, Canary Islands/Mediterranean round-trip from Southampton to Lisbon, Gibraltar, Barcelona, Gran Canaria, Dakar (Senegal), Tenerife and Madeira for the famous New Year's Eve fireworks display.

January–April, 109 nights, World Cruise round-trip from New York via the Panama Canal to Los Angeles, across the South Pacific to New Zealand and Australia, through the Far East to India, Arabia, and Europe, transatlantic to New York. Five "Liner Voyages" from 37–72 days available.

May–September, 4–20 nights, Europe, round-trip from Southampton to Baltic, Norwegian Fjords, Channel Islands, England/Ireland/France, Iberia; Canary Islands; Western and Eastern Mediterranean; or Egypt/Turkey.

Queen Mary 2 **HOME PORTS** Southampton, New York, Ft. Lauderdale
September, 12 nights, Canada/New England, round-trip from New York.

December–January, 12–14 nights, Caribbean, round-trip from New York.

January–April, 12, 14, 38 nights, South America, New York to Los Angeles via Cape Horn or reverse (38 nights). Available in segments from New York to Rio de Janeiro or reverse (12 nights), Rio de Janeiro to Valparaiso (Chile) or reverse (12 nights), Valparaiso to Los Angeles or reverse (14 nights).

April–November, 6 nights, transatlantic, between Southampton and New York, interspersed with occasional cruises in Europe, New England/Canada and to nowhere.

Queen Victoria (debuts December 2007) **HOME PORT** t.b.a.

Itineraries t.b.a.

Delta Queen Steamboat Company

American Queen **HOME PORTS** New Orleans, Memphis
September–June, 3–4 nights, round-trip from New Orleans. 3 nights to Vacherie, Baton Rouge; 4 nights to Natchez, Baton Rouge. 7-night vacation pakcages include pre- or post-cruise New Orleans hotel stay.

June–August, 7 nights, Mississippi, round-trip from New Orleans or between New Orleans and Memphis.

Delta Queen **HOME PORTS** New Orleans, others vary with itinerary
September–November, 4–12 nights, Upper Mississippi, Ohio, Cumberland
and Tennessee Rivers, from St. Louis, St. Paul, Nashville, Mobile,
Chattanooga, Cincinnati, or Pittsburgh.

November–April, 5–7 nights, Mississippi, round-trip from New Orleans; or
between New Orleans and either Galveston or Pensacola.

April, resumes Upper Mississippi and Wilderness River routes.

Mississippi Queen **HOME PORTS** New Orleans, others vary with itinerary
September–November, 3–7 nights, Upper Mississippi and Ohio Rivers,
round-trip from Cincinnati; between Cincinnati and Pittsburgh; Cincinnati
and St. Louis; or between St. Louis and St. Paul.

November–June, 5–7 nights, Mississippi, round-trip from New Orleans; or
between New Orleans and Memphis; or Memphis and Nashville.

June–September, 11 nights, Great Steamboat Race from New Orleans to St.
Louis followed by Upper Mississippi cruises.

Discovery World Cruises

Discovery **HOME PORT** Harwich, others vary with itinerary
September–November, 7–24 nights, Iberia, Mediterranean, Black Sea, Red
Sea, North Africa from Harwich (England); Barcelona (Spain); Istanbul
(Turkey); Larnaca (Cyprus); Alexandria or Sharm El Sheikh (Egypt).

November and May, 15–16 nights, transatlantic, from Lisbon to Barbados
or Nassau to Harwich (England).

December–January, 7–20 nights, Caribbean/South America, round-trip
from Barbados; Amazon, from Barbados to Manaus and Manaus to Buenos
Aires; Antarctica and the Falkland Islands, round-trip from Buenos Aires;
Cape Horn, from Buenos Aires to Valparaiso (Chile).

February–April, 16–26 nights, South Pacific, from Valparaiso to Papeete or
reverse; Papeete to Auckland or reverse; round-trip from Auckland; Papeete
to Quito (Ecuador); Panama Canal from Quito to Nassau. Combine voyages
for extended sailings of 34, 43, and 53 nights.

Disney Cruise Line

Disney Magic **HOME PORT** Port Canaveral
Year-round, 7 nights, Saturday, round-trip from Port Canaveral alternating
Eastern and Western Caribbean to either St. Maarten, St. Thomas (with
excursions to St. John), and Castaway Cay, Disney's private Bahamian island;
or Key West, Grand Cayman, Cozumel, and Castaway Cay. Additional
itineraries: Calls at Grand Cayman, Cozumel, and makes 2 different day calls
at Castaway Cay, November 19, 2005 and November 18, 2006; Calls at
Costa Maya, Cozumel, and spends 2 days at Castaway Cay on the May 27,
June 24, July 22, August 19, September 16, October 14, November 11,

December 9, 2006 departures. 10 nights, December 16, 2006 to Key West, St. Maarten, St. Lucia, Antigua, St. Thomas/St. John, Castaway Cay.

Disney Wonder **HOME PORT** Port Canaveral
Year-round, 3–4 nights, round-trip from Port Canaveral on Thursday to Nassau and Castaway Cay (3 nights); or on Sundays to Nassau, Castaway Cay, plus a full day at sea (4 nights). Cruise can be combined with Disney World packages for a 7-night vacation.

easyCruise

easyCruiseOne **HOME PORT** varies with itinerary
June–September, 2–7 nights, French and Italian Rivieras, flexible 1 week itineraries allow passenger to embark and disembark at any port on the route for a minimum of 2 nights. Ports of call are St. Tropez, Cannes, Nice, Monaco, Imperia (for San Remo), Genoa, Portofino.

November–April, Caribbean ports, including Barbados, St. Vincent, Martinique, Bequia, Grenada, and St. Lucia.

Fred Olsen Lines

Black Prince **HOME PORTS** Southampton, Liverpool, Dublin, Belfast, Leith, Greenock
October–January and February–April, 3–25 nights, Mediterranean, Iberia, Canary Islands/Iberia, or mini-cruises to England/France/Ireland/Channel Islands, round-trip from Southampton, Liverpool, Dublin, Greenock, and Belfast.

January–February, 35 nights, Caribbean, round-trip from Southampton to Bermuda, Bahamas, Caribbean, Azores.

May–July, 7–13 nights, Norwegian Fjords, Baltic, or Greenland and Iceland, round-trip from Greenock and Leith (Scotland).

Black Watch **HOME PORTS** Southampton, Dover
October–December and March–May, 3–21 nights, Mediterranean, Black Sea, Canaries/Iberia, or mini-cruises to England/France/Ireland/Channel Islands/Holland, round-trip from Southampton or Dover.

January–February, 69 nights, South America circumnavigation, round-trip from Southampton, available in segments of 23–25 nights from Southampton to Buenos Aires; Buenos Aires to Lima; Lima to Southampton.

May–September, 8–15 nights, Baltic or Norwegian Fjords, round-trip from Dover with one Mediterranean or Canaries/Iberia cruise in each of July, August, and September; an Iceland and Greenland cruise in July; around the U.K. in August.

September 2006, 23 nights, Canada, round-trip from Southampton.

January–March, 2007, 78 nights, World Cruise (Circle Africa), round-trip from Southampton on a route to Spain, West Africa, Cape Town (3 days),

Reunion, Mauritius, Madagascar, Mombasa (3 days), Seychelles, Maldives, Muscat, Qatar, Dubai (3 days), Egypt, Jordan, Crete, Malta, Spain.

Boudicca **HOME PORT** Dover
February–December, 2006, 3–28 nights, Mediterranean, Adriatic, Canary Islands, Iberia, Scandinavia, Norway, Baltic, Iceland, Caribbean, round-trip from Dover.

Braemar **HOME PORTS** Barbados, Montego Bay, Dover, Newcastle
October–April, 15–32 nights, Caribbean, Panama Canal, or Amazon, fly-cruises from the U.K., sailing from Dover to Montego Bay; Montego Bay to Acapulco; round-trip from Montego Bay; Acapulco to Barbados; round-trip from Barbados to the Caribbean or Amazon; Barbados to Southampton.

May–July, 7–13 nights, Norwegian Fjords, North Cape, or Baltic, round-trip from Dover.

July–September, 3–14 nights, alternating Norway, Baltic, Mediterranean, Canaries, and Iberia, or mini-cruises round-trip from Dover or Newcastle.

October, 2006, resumes Caribbean sailings, positioning from Southampton to Montego Bay.

Glacier Bay Cruiseline

Executive Explorer **HOME PORTS** Juneau, Ketchikan
April–May, August, 9 nights, positioning cruises between Seattle and Juneau and reverse

May–September, 7 nights, between Juneau and Ketchikan, via Haines, Skagway, Glacier Bay, Sitka, Frederick Sound, Tracy Arm and the twin Sawyer Glaciers, Petersburg, Wrangell, Metlakatla, Misty Fjords.

Wilderness Adventurer **HOME PORT** Whittier
June–August, 8 nights, Alaska cruise-tours, round-trip from Anchorage, includes a night at the Alyeska Resort on Turnagan Arm and a cruise on Prince William Sound, round-trip from Whittier calling at Valdez, Beartrap Bay and visiting the Chenega Glacier, Columbia Glacier and College Fjord.

Wilderness Discoverer **HOME PORTS** Juneau, Sitka; Vancouver and Richland (WA), Portland (OR)

September–October and May, 7 nights, Columbia River, between Vancouver and Richland (WA) or between Richland and Portland (OR) via the Columbia Gorge, Bonneville Dam, Hood River, Hanford Reach National Monument, Pelouse River, Miller Island, Astoria, with opportunities for kayaking, hiking, bird-watching, and jet-boating.

April–May, August, 9 nights, positioning cruises between Seattle and Juneau.

May–September, 7 nights, Alaska active-adventure cruises between Juneau and Sitka via Tracy Arm and the twin Sawyer Glaciers, Endicott Arm, Frederick Sound, Chichagof, Baranof, and Admiralty Islands, Icy Strait, Glacier Bay. Includes whale- and wildlife-viewing and kayaking.

Wilderness Explorer **HOME PORT** Juneau
May–September, 7 nights, Alaska, active–adventure cruises round-trip from
Juneau to Glacier Bay and Icy Strait with a call at Glacier Bay Lodge, featur-
ing opportunities for sea kayaking and hiking.

Global Quest

Royal Star **HOME PORT** Mombasa
Year-round, 13–21 nights, in East Africa/Indian Ocean, from Mombasa.
Cruise/safari packages in conjunction with African Safari Club. Destinations
include Kenya, the Seychelles, Mauritius, Reunion, Zanzibar, Shangu Mbili,
Mayotte, Madagascar, South Africa.

Global Quest also offers packages aboard small ship expedition cruises to
Antarctica and Patagonia as well as cruise-tours to the Galapagos, Costa
Rica, and Panama, North America's Great Lakes, Canada/New England, the
Adriatic, the Mediterranean, and the rivers of Europe and Russia.

Hapag Lloyd Cruises

Bremen **HOME PORT** varies with itinerary
September–November, 10–13 nights, Western Europe, Mediterranean,
Canary Islands, from Hamburg to Lisbon; Lisbon to Nice; Nice to Venice;
Venice to Piraeus; Piraeus to Malta; Malta to Palma de Mallorca; Palma to
Gran Canaria.

November–January, 12–18 nights, South America, from Gran Canaria to
Recife (Brazil); Recife to Buenos Aires; Buenos Airea to Ushuaia; round-trip
from Ushuaia.

April–September, Mediterranean and Northern Europe, from Malaga,
Bordeaux, Hamburg, Kiel, Flensburg, Reykjavik, Cuxhaven.

Columbus **HOME PORT** varies with itinerary
September–October, 9–13 nights, Great Lakes and New England, between
Toronto and Chicago or between Chicago and Sarnia; Toronto to
Philadelphia.

October–November, 12 nights, Caribbean/South America, Philadelphia to
Progreso; Progreso to La Guaira.

November–December, 14 and 18 nights, South America, La Guaira to Rio
de Janeiro; Rio to Valparaiso.

December–February, 12–17 nights, South Pacific, Valparaiso to Papeete;
Papeete to Sydney; Sydney to Bali; Bali to Singapore.

February–March, 13–18 nights, Asia, Middle East, Singapore to Chennai;
Chennai to Dubai; Dubai to Venice.

Europa **HOME PORT** Varies with itinerary

September–October, 4–12 nights, Western Europe and Mediterranean,
from Kiel, Hamburg, Santander, Monte Carlo, Piraeus, Istanbul.

October–January, 13–17 nights, Middle East, Indian Ocean, Africa, from Istanbul, Dubai, Mumbai, Seychelles, Mauritius, Durban, Cape Town.

January–May, South America, South Pacific, Southeast Asia, Middle East, on a route from Cape Town to Puerto Montt (Chile), Papeete (Tahiti), Auckland, Sydney, Padang Bay, Yangon, Dubai, Limassol (Cyprus).

May and September–October, 10–14 nights, Mediterranean, from Limassol (Cyprus) to Lisbon; round-trip from Lisbon; Lisbon to Rome; Rome to Istanbul.

May–September, Western Europe, Baltic on various itineraires from Lisbon to Hamburg, Kiel to Hamburg, or reverse; round-trip from Kiel; round-trip from Hamburg; Kiel to Warnemünde; Warnemünde to Hamburg; Hamburg to Lisbon.

Hanseatic **HOME PORT** Varies with itinerary
September, 3–4 nights, Baltic round-trip from Hamburg, Hamburg to Portsmouth.

September–October, 5–8 nights, from Portsmouth, Liexoes, Barcelona.

October–November, 10–16 nights, Middle East, Indian Ocean, South Africa, on a route from Athens to Muscat, Seychelles, Mauritius, Cape Town.

April–May, 12–13 nights, Mediterranean from Istanbul and Naples.

June–September, 12–16 nights, Baltic, Norway, Iceland, Greenland, from Lisbon to Hamburg; Hamburg to Reykjavik; Reykjavik to Kangerlussuaq; Kangerlussuaq to Hamburg; Hamburg to Tromsoe; Tromsoe to Kiel; Kiel to Hamburg.

Hebridean Island Cruises

Hebridean Princess **HOME PORT** Oban
March–November, 3–7 nights, Scotland's "Highlands and Islands" round-trip from Oban including the Inner and Outer Hebrides, Iona, Rum, Muck, Eigg, Harris, Lewis, Skye, Staffa and River Clyde. Several cruises from Invergordon and between Oban and Manchester .

Hebridean Spirit **HOME PORT** Varies with itinerary
September–November, 7 nights, Mediterranean, Adriatic, Greek Isles, Turkey, from Seville, Nice, Palermo, Trieste, Dubrovnik, Kalamata, Thessaloniki, Kusadasi, Catania, Valetta.

December–April, 10–21 nights, South Africa and Namibia from Cape Town or Durban. December and April, positions from Tenerife to Cape Town and reverse

April–May, 3–9 nights, Mediterranean, French Riviera, Monaco Grand Prix, Spain from Valetta, Kalamata, Pula, Nice.

Summer 2006 not available.

Holland America Line

Amsterdam **HOME PORTS** San Diego, Copenhagen, Ft. Lauderdale, others vary with itinerary
October–December, 30–62 nights, Orient/South Pacific, Seattle to San Diego via the Aleutian Islands, Petropavlovsk (Russia); Kuril Islands, Korskov, Sakhalin (Russia); Yokohama (overnight), Osaka/Kyoto, and Nagasaki (Japan); Cheju City (South Korea); Dalian, Xingang (overnight for Beijing), Hong Kong (overnight); Singapore; Bali (Indonesia); Perth, Adelaide, Sydney, and Brisbane (Australia); New Caledonia; Fiji; Apia (Samoa); Christmas Island, Honolulu. Available in two segments, Seattle to Singapore (30 nights) and Singapore to San Diego (32 nights).

December, February–April, 15 nights, Hawaii, round-trip from San Diego to Hilo (Hawaii), Honolulu (Oahu), Nawiliwili (Kauai), Lahaina (Maui), Kona (Hawaii), and Ensenada (Mexico).

January, 30 nights, South Pacific, round-trip from San Diego to Hilo, Honolulu (2 days), Nawiliwili, Lahaina, and Kona (Hawaii); Christmas Island, Kiribati; Raiatea, Bora Bora (2 days), Moorea in the Society Islands; Nuku Hiva, Marquesas Islands.

April and from October 2006, 13–18 nights Panama Canal from San Diego or round-trip from Ft. Lauderdale.

May and August, 14 and 17 nights, transatlantic.

May–August, 10 nights, Baltic, round-trip from Copenhagen to Tallinn (Estonia), St. Petersburg (2 days), Helsinki, Stockholm, Visby, Warnemünde/Berlin.

September–October, 2006, 10 nights, Canada/New England.

Maasdam **HOME PORTS** Norfolk, Boston, Montreal
April–June and August–October, 2006, 7 nights, Canada/New England, between Montreal and Boston via the Saguenay River fjord, Quebec City; Charlottetown PEI; Sydney and Halifax, Nova Scotia and Bar Harbor (ME). Positioning cruises: 10 and 11 nights Montreal to Norfolk (VA), October 2006; 15 nights, Ft. Lauderdale to Montreal, April 28, 2006.

October–December, 2005, 10–11 nights, Eastern/Southern Caribbean, round-trip from Norfolk to Half Moon Cay, San Juan, St. Thomas and either Nassau or St. Maarten (10 nights) or Half Moon Cay, St. Thomas, Dominica, Barbados, St. Kitts, San Juan (11 nights).

December 2005–March 2006, October–December, 2006, 11 nights, Southern Caribbean, round-trip from Norfolk to Half Moon Cay, St. Thomas, Dominica, Barbados, St. Kitts, San Juan.

July, 2006, 35 nights, transatlantic/Europe, round-trip from Boston to Iceland, Shetland Islands, Norway, Holland, France, England, Ireland, Faroe Islands, Iceland, Greenland, Newfoundland. Available in 2 segments: Boston to Rotterdam, 17 nights; Rotterdam to Boston 18 nights.

Noordam **HOME PORTS** New York, Rome
February–April and October–December, 2006, 10–11 nights,
Eastern/Southern Caribbean, round-trip from New York to either Turks
and Caicos, Tortola, St. Maarten, St. Thomas, San Juan; or Tortola, St.
Thomas, Dominica, Barbados, St. Maarten, San Juan.

April and September, 15 nights, transatlantic, New York to Rome or reverse.

May–September, 10 nights, Eastern/Western Mediterranean, round-trip
from Rome to either Monte Carlo, Livorno, Barcelona, Palma de Mallorca,
La Goulette (Tunisia), Palermo, Naples (Western), or to Dubrovnik, Corfu,
Katakalon, Santorini, Kusadasi, Malta, Messina (Eastern).

Oosterdam **HOME PORTS** San Diego, Seattle
October 2005–April, 2006, October–December, 2006, 5–8 nights, Mexican
Riviera, round-trip from San Diego to Cabo San Lucas, Puerto Vallarta, and
Mazatlan.

April–May, October, 3–4 nights, Pacific Coast/Pacific Northwest, from San
Diego to Vancouver or reverse, or Vancouver to Seattle.

May–September, 7 nights, Alaska round-trip from Seattle to Juneau,
Hubbard Glacier or Glacier Bay, Sitka, Ketchikan and an evening call at
Victoria (BC).

Prinsendam **HOME PORT** Varies with itinerary
October–November, 12 nights, Mediterranean, Rome to Athens; Athens to
Venice via Black Sea ports; Venice to Lisbon. November, 15 nights, transat-
lantic, Lisbon to Ft. Lauderdale.

November and April–May, 26 and 28 nights, South America/Amazon
River, round-trip from Ft. Lauderdale, November, calls at La Romana,
Dominican Republic; Ponce, Puerto Rico; St. Kitts; Grenada; Santarem, Boca
da Valeria, Manaus (overnight onboard) and Parintins (Brazil); Devil's
Island; Barbados; Guadeloupe; St. Maarten; Tortola and Half Moon Cay, the
line's private island in the Bahamas. Round-trip from New York or Ft.
Lauderdale, April–May, same ports except Port Antonio (Jamaica); Aruba
and Bonaire replace Dominican Republic, Puerto Rico, and St. Kitts.

December, 15 nights, Southern Caribbean Holiday, round-trip from Ft.
Lauderdale.

January–April, 108 nights, World Cruise, round-trip from Ft. Lauderdale on
a route to South America and the Amazon, Antarctica, South and East
Africa, India, Egypt and the Suez Canal, North Africa and the
Mediterranean.

May–June, 34 nights, transatlantic/North Cape, from Ft. Lauderdale.

June–July, 14–21 nights, Baltic/Norwegian Fjords-North Cape/Western
Europe.

August–October, 16 nights, Mediterranean.

October–November, 46 nights, West Africa/South America, from Lisbon to Ft. Lauderdale via Cape Town and the Amazon in two segments, Lisbon to Cape Town (22 nights) and Cape Town to Ft. Lauderdale (24 nights).

Rotterdam **HOME PORTS** Venice, Rio de Janeiro, Valparaiso, others vary with itinerary
September–October, 10 nights, Mediterranean, round-trip from Venice to either Missina, Rome, Livorno (Florence), Monte Carlo, Corsica, Sardinia, Dubrovnik; or Santorini, Rhodes, Kusadasi, Athens, Katakolon, Malta. October 28, 10 nights, Venice to Lisbon.

November and April, 15–17 nights, transatlantic, Lisbon to Rio de Janeiro, 17 nights, November 3, 2005. Rio de Janeiro to Lisbon, 15 nights, April 15, 2006. Lisbon to Rio de Janierio, 15 nights, November 5, 2006.

November–March, 12 and 20 nights, South America between Valparaiso and Buenos Aires via Montevideo; Buenos Aires (2 days); Stanley, Falkland Islands; Cape Horn; Ushuaia, Tierra del Fuego; Beagle Channel, Strait of Magellan, Punta Arenas, Chile; Chilean Fjords and Amaila Glacier; Puerto Montt, Chile.

December–January, 20 nights, Antarctica/South America, between Valparaiso and Rio de Janeiro, with overnight onboard in Rio and calling at Montevideo (Uruguay), Buenos Aires (Argentina), Stanley (Falkland Islands) (on January 11, 2006 sailing); the Antarctic Peninsula cruising past Elephant Island, Paulet Island, Deception Island, Errera Channel and Paradise Bay, Neumayer Channel, LeMaire Channel, and Petermann Island. Heading back to South America, cruises past Cape Horn to Ushuaia, Beagle Channel, Punta Arenas, Strait of Magellan, Chilean Fjords, and Glacier visit and Puerto Montt. Ports can vary depending on conditions in Antarctica.

April–May and September–October 2006, 10–15 nights, Mediterranean, Lisbon to Athens; Athens to Venice and reverse; Athens to Lisbon.

May and September 2006, 14–15 nights, Western Europe, Athens to Harwich and Rotterdam to Athens.

June–September 2006, 12 nights, Baltic and Scandinavia.

Ryndam **HOME PORTS** San Diego, Tampa, Vancouver
October–December, 10 nights, Mexico/Sea of Cortés, round-trip from San Diego to either Puerto Vallarta, Mazatlan, Topolobampo, Loreto, La Paz, Cabo San Lucas plus scenic cruising of Sierra de la Giganta; or to Manzanillo, Acapulco, Zihuatanejo/Ixtapa, Puerto Vallarta, Mazatlan, Cabo San Lucas.

January, April, September, 14–19 nights, Panama Canal, San Diego to Tampa or reverse; or Tampa to Vancouver or reverse; or San Francisco to Tampa.

January–April and October–December, 14 nights, Southern Caribbean, round-trip from Tampa to San Juan, St. Thomas, Dominica (Cabrits and

Roseau), Barbados, Grenada, Islae Margarita, Bonaire, Aruba, Grand Cayman.

May–September, 7 nights, Alaska, between Vancouver and Seward. Northbound calling at Ketchikan, Juneau, Sitka and either Hubbard Glacier and Skagway or Glacier Bay and College Fjords. Southbound calling at College Fjord, Glacier Bay, Sitka, Juneau, Ketchikan. May 7, 14, 2006, 7 nights, Inside Passage, round-trip from Vancouver to Juneau, Skagway, Glacier Bay, Ketchikan.

Statendam **HOME PORTS** Sydney, Auckland, Vancouver others vary with itinerary
October–November, 15 nights Hawaii, round-trip from San Diego to Hilo, (Hawaii), Honolulu (Oahu), Nawiliwili (Kauai), Lahaina (Maui), Kona (Hawaii), and Ensenada (Mexico).

November–December, 35 nights, South America/South Pacific, San Diego to Auckland, Cabo San Lucas, Zihuatanejo, and Acapulco (Mexico); Manta (Ecuador); Salavery and Calloa/Lima (Peru) (2 days); Easter Island; Papeete (Tahiti) and Bora Bora (2 nights); Tonga and Bay of Islands (New Zealand).

January–February, 14 nights, Australia/New Zealand between Auckland and Sydney via Tauranga, Napier, Wellington, Picton, Christchurch, Dunedin, Fjordland, and Milford Sound (New Zealand), Burnie Tasmania and Melbourne (Australia).

March–May, 14–18 nights, Asia and transpacific, from Sydney to Hong Kong; Hong Kong to Osaka or reverse; Osaka to Vancouver.

May–September, 7 nights, Alaska, between Vancouver and Seward. Northbound calling at Ketchikan, Juneau, Sitka and either Hubbard Glacier and Skagway or Glacier Bay and College Fjords. Southbound calling at College Fjord, Glacier Bay, Sitka, Juneau, Ketchikan. September 22, 2006, 7 nights, Inside Passage cruise round-trip from Vancouver to Juneau, Skagway, Glacier Bay, Ketchikan.

September–October, 23–28 nights, South Pacific, Vancouver to Auckland, San Francisco to Auckland, or Los Angeles to Auckland. Full cruise from Vancouver, calls at San Francisco, Los Angeles, Hilo, Honolulu, Lahaina, Christmas Island, American Samoa, Apia Samoa, Tonga, Fiji, Bay of Islands, Tauranga.

October 27, 2006, resumes Australia/New Zealand sailings.

Veendam **HOME PORTS** Vancouver, Tampa, others vary with itinerary
October–December, 7–14 nights, Eastern/Western/Southern Caribbean round-trip from Tampa.

January–April, 7 nights, Western Caribbean, round-trip from Tampa to either Grand Cayman, Montego Bay and Cozumel; or Key West, Belize City, Santo Tomas de Castilla, Guatemala, Cozumel.

April, 17–22 nights, Panama Canal, Tampa to San Diego, Seattle or Vancouver.

May–September, 7 nights, Alaska, between Vancouver and Seward. Northbound calling at Ketchikan, Juneau, Sitka and either Hubbard Glacier and Skagway or Glacier Bay and College Fjords. Southbound calling at College Fjord, Glacier Bay, Sitka, Juneau, Ketchikan. September 22, 2006, Inside Passage cruise round-trip from Vancouver to Juneau, Skagway, Glacier Bay, Ketchikan.

September–October, 30–34 nights, Panama Canal/Amazon, Vancouver to Tampa via Seattle, Los Angeles, Cabo San Lucas (Mexico), Puerto Caldera (Costa Rica), Golfo Dulce, scenic cruising, transit Panama Canal, Grenada, Santarem, Boca da Valeria, Manaus (overnight) and Parintins (Brazil), Barbados, and either Half Moon Cay or Dominican Republic. Available in segments: 33 nights from Seattle to Tampa; 30 nights from Los Angeles to Tampa.

November, resumes 7-night Caribbean sailings from Tampa.

Volendam **HOME PORTS** Ft. Lauderdale, Vancouver
October–December, 5–10 nights, Southern/Western/Eastern Caribbean and Bahamas, round-trip from Ft. Lauderdale.

January–March, 10 night round-trip from Ft. Lauderdale to Aruba, Curaçao, Dominica, St. Thomas, Half Moon Cay.

April and September, 16–20 nights, Panama Canal, Ft. Lauderdale to either Los Angeles, Astoria or Seattle and Vancouver or San Diego to Ft. Lauderdale.

May–September, 7 nights, Alaska, round-trip from Vancouver to Juneau, Skagway, Glacier Bay, Tracy Arm and Ketchikan.

October resumes 10-night Caribbean sailings from Ft. Lauderdale.

Westerdam **HOME PORTS** Ft. Lauderdale, Seattle, others vary with itinerary
October, 10–15 nights, Mediterranean between Rome and Barcelona and transatlanic from Rome to Ft. Lauderdale.

November–April, Eastern/Western Caribbean, round-trip from Ft. Lauderdale to either Cozumel, Grand Cayman, Ocho Rios or Montego Bay, Half Moon Cay; or Nassau, St. Maarten, Tortola, Half Moon Cay.

April and September, 17–21 nights, Panama Canal, from Ft. Lauderdale to Los Angeles or Seattle, and, Vancouver, Seattle or Los Angeles to Ft. Lauderdale.

May–September, 7 nights, Alaska, round-trip from Seattle.

October 2006, resumes Eastern/Western Caribbean, round-trip from Ft. Lauderdale. Turks and Caicos replaces Nassau and the call at Jamaica.

Zaandam **HOME PORTS** Ft, Lauderdale, Seattle, San Diego
October–April, 10 nights, Panama Canal/Caribbean, round-trip from Ft. Lauderdale to Half Moon Cay, Curaçao, Aruba, Gatun Lake, Colon (Panama), and Puerto Limon (Costa Rica).

April 17–21 nights, Panama Canal, from Ft. Lauderdale to San Diego, Astoria, or Seattle.

May–September, 7 nights, Alaska, round-trip from Seattle to Juneau, Skagway, Glacier Bay, Ketchikan.

September, 1 and 3 nights, Pacific Northwest and Pacific Coast, positions from Seattle to Vancouver and Vancouver to San Diego.

October–December, 10 and 15 nights, Hawaii and Mexico round-trip from San Diego.

Zuiderdam **HOME PORTS** Ft. Lauderdale, Vancouver
To April, 2006, Saturday, 7 nights, Eastern Caribbean round-trip from Ft. Lauderdale to Half Moon Cay, St. Thomas, Tortola, Nassau.

April and September, 21 nights, Panama Canal, from Ft. Lauderdale to Vancouver or reverse, available in segments.

May–September, 7 nights, Alaska, round-trip from Vancouver to Tracy Arm and the twin Sawyer Glaciers, Juneau, Skagway, Glacier Bay, and Ketchikan.

October–December, Saturday, 7 nights, Eastern Caribbean round-trip from Ft. Lauderdale to Half Moon Cay, St. Thomas, Tortola, Turks and Caicos.

Kristina Cruises

Kristina Brahe **HOME PORT** Kotka, Helsinki, others vary with itinerary
September–December, 1–4 nights, Finland and the Finnish Archipelago, on evening, Sunday lunch and mini-cruises, round-trip from Helsinki; round-trip from Kotka; between Helsinki and Kotka; round-trip from Hamina.

April–August, 1–7 nights, Finland, Finnish Archipelago, Lake Saimaa on lunch cruises and mini-cruises round-trip from Kotka, round-trip from Helsinki; round-trip from Lappeenranta; between Kotka and Helsinki, Lappeenranta and Puumala; Lappeenranta and Savonlinna. Special bird migration sailings in May and midsummer sailings in June.

Kristina Regina **HOME PORTS** Helsinki, Dakar, Las Palmas, others vary with itinerary
September–November, 7 nights, Mediterranean, , fly-cruise including air from Helsinki, sailing from Bordeaux, Gibraltar, Valetta, Athens, Haraklion, Dubrovnik, Monaco, Nice.

November–December and February–March, 7 nights, Canary Islands, fly-cruise including air from Helsinki, round-trip from Las Palmas to Arrecife, Puerto del Rosario, Santa Cruz de Tenerife, San Sebastian de la Gomera, Santa Cruz de la Palma, Puerta la Estaca, El Hierro.

December–January, 7 nights, West Africa/Cape Verde Islands, fly-cruise including air from Helsinki, round-trip from Banjul (Gambia) to Dakar (Senegal) and the Cape Verde Islands.

March–June, 7 nights, Mediterranean, Adriatic and Western Europe as ship positions from Las Palmas to Helsinki for summer cruises.

July–August, 3–7 nights, round-trip from Helsinki, visa free cruises to St. Petersburg, round-trip from Helsinki (3 nights); Norwegian Fjords; Baltic Sea; Iceland, Faroe Islands and Shetland Islands.

MSC Cruises

Armonia **HOME PORTS** Rio de Janeiro, Venice
October and April, 5 nights, positioning from Venice and Genoa and reverse.

November and March, 17 nights, transatlantic, Genoa to Rio de Janeiro and reverse.

December–March, 3–7 nights, Brazil, round-trip from Rio de Janeiro.

April–October, 7 nights, Greek Isles/Turkey/Croatia, round-trip from Venice to Bari, Corfu, Santorini, Athens, Katakolon, Dubrovnik.

Lirica **HOME PORTS** Ft. Lauderdale, Rome
November and May, 17 nights, transatlantic, Genoa to Ft. Lauderdale and reverse.

December–January, 6–10 nights, Eastern and Southern Caribbean round-trip from Ft. Lauderdale.

December–April, 11 nights, Panama Canal, round-trip from Ft. Lauderdale to Ocho Rios or Montego Bay, Cartegena (Colombia), San Blas Islands, Cristobal (Panama), Puerto Limon (Costa Rica), Roatan Island (Honduras).

May–October, 7 nights, Mediterranean, round-trip from Rome to Messina, Tunis, Palma de Mallorca, Barcelona, Marseille, Genoa.

Melody **HOME PORTS** Rio de Janeiro, Genoa
November and March, 16–17 nights, transatlantic, from Genoa to Rio de Janeiro and reverse.

December–February, 8–9 nights, Brazil, round-trip from Rio de Janeiro to Santos, Punta del Este, Buenos Aires (2 days), Ilhabela plus Buzios on the 9-night sailing January 19, 2006.

March–April, 11 nights, round-trip from Genoa to the Black Sea or Canary Islands.

May–October, 7 nights, Mediterranean, round-trip from Genoa to Naples, Malta, Tunia, Ibiza, St. Tropez.

November, 9 nights, round-trip from Genoa to Rome, Katakolon, Athens, Tripoli (Libya), Malta, Naples.

Musica (debuts June 2006) **HOME PORT** Ft. Lauderdale
Europe, summer, 2006; Caribbean, winter, 2006–2007. Itineraries t.b.a.

Opera **HOME PORTS** Ft. Lauderdale, Venice
December and April, 17–18 nights, transatlantic, Genoa to Ft. Lauderdale and reverse.

January–April, 7 nights, Eastern Caribbean round-trip from Ft. Lauderdale to San Juan, St. Marteen, La Romana, Cayo Levandado.

December–April, 11 nights, Panama Canal, round-trip from Ft. Lauderdale to La Romana and Cayo Levantado, Dominican Republic; San Juan, St. Maarten.

April–October, 7 nights, Saturday, Greek Isles/Turkey/Croatia, round-trip from Venice to Bari, Katakolon, Kusadasi, Istanbul, Dubrovnik.

October–November, 11 nights, Mediterranean, round-trip from Venice to Croatia, Greece, Italy, Egypt, Cyprus; and Venice to Genoa via Italy, Croatia, Greece, Egypt, Libya, Malta.

Rhapsody **HOME PORT** Copenhagen
November and May, 20–21 nights, positioning to and from South Africa, from Genoa to Durban via Suez, the Seychelles, Mauritius, Reunion; and, Cape Town to Dover, via Namibia, Senegal, Canary Islands, Madeira, Lisbon, Vigo, Le Havre.

December–May, sails from South Africa under charter.

May–September, Baltic and Norwegian Fjords, round-trip from Copenhagen to either Visby, Stockholm, Tallin, St. Petersburg, Helsinki (Baltic); or Flaam, Hellesylt, Geiranger, Bergen, Kristiansand, Oslo (Norwegian Fjords).

Sinfonia **HOME PORT** Genoa
October–November, 11 nights, Canary Islands, round-trip from Genoa to Barcelona, Casblanca, Arrecife, Tenerife, Madeira, Malaga.

December–March, 11 nights, Eastern Mediterranean or Canary Islands, round-trip from Genoa to either Naples, Port Said (Egypt), Cyrpus, Rodi (Greece), Tripoli (Libya), Rome; or Barcelona, Casablanca, Tenerife, Canary Islands, Madiera, and Malaga and Alicante (Spain).

March–April, 11–12 nights, Black Sea or Egypt/Libya for the Solar Eclipse, round-trip from Genoa to either Naples, Athens, Yalta, Odessa, Istanbul, Catania, and Capri; or Naples, Siracuse, Alexandria, Tobruk (overnight), Tripoli, Malta, and Salerno.

Norwegian Cruise Line

Norwegian Crown **HOME PORTS** Buenos Aires, Valparaiso, Philadelphia, New York, Miami
October, 6–7 nights, Bermuda, round-trip from New York and Philadelphia to St. George's, Hamilton, and King's Wharf.

November, March, April, 13–15 nights, Caribbean and Panama Canal, round-trip from Miami; round-trip from Philadelphia; or positioning between Miami and Philadelphia; or between Miami and Valparaiso (Chile).

November–February, 14 nights, Cape Horn between Valparaiso and Buenos Aires calling at Montevideo (Uruguay); Puerto Madryn (Argentina); Port Stanley (Falkland Islands); cruise Cape Horn; Ushuaia (Argentina); cruise

Beagle Channel, strait of Magellan and Patagonic channels; Puerto Chacabuco and Puerto Montt (Chile).

2006: April–September resumes Bermuda sailings from Philadelphia and New York.

Norwegian Dawn **HOME PORT** New York
October–April, 10 and 11 nights, Eastern and Western Caribbean, round-trip from New York to St. Thomas, Tortola, St. Maarten, San Juan, Great Stirrup Cay, NCL's private island in the Bahamas (10 nights); or Ocho Rios (Jamaica), George Town (Grand Cayman), Roatan (Honduras), Belize City (Belize), Cozumel (Mexico), and Great Stirrup Cay (Bahamas) (11 nights).

2006: April–October, Sunday, 7 nights, round-trip from New York to Port Canaveral (15 hours), Miami, Nassau, and Great Stirrup Cay.

Norwegian Dream **HOME PORTS** Houston, Dover
October–April, 7 nights, Western Caribbean round-trip from Houston to Cozumel (Mexico), Roatan (Honduras), Belize City (Belize), and Cancún (Mexico).

April, September, 15 nights, transatlantic, Dover to Miami or reverse.

April–May, 12 nights, Western Europe, Rome to Dover or reverse, via Livorno, Pisa (Florence), Genoa (Italy); Cannes, Marseille (France); Barcelona, Cadiz (Spain); Lisbon; and Le Havre (Paris).

May–September, 12 nights, Scandinavian Capitals, round-trip from Dover to Kiel Canal, Tallinn (Estonia); St. Petersburg (2 days); Helsinki; Stockholm; Copenhagen; Oslo (Norway).

Norwegian Jewel **HOME PORTS** Miami, Barcelona
November–April, 7 nights, round-trip from Miami, alternating Eastern and Western Caribbean, to either San Juan, St. Thomas, Antigua, Great Stirrup Cay (Eastern); or Great Stirrup Cay, Ocho Rios, Grand Cayman, Roatan Bay Islands.

May–September, 7 nights, Western Mediterranean, round-trip from Barcelona to Messina, Naples, Rome, and Livorno (Florence) and Villefranche (Nice, France).

September–October, 12 nights, Barcelona to Istanbul (overnight onboard) or reverse via Rome, Naples, Venice (overnight onboard), Dubrovnik, Athens; Istanbul to Athens or reverse via Izmir (Turkey), Mykonos and Santorini (Greece), Iraklion (Crete), Alexandria and Cairo (Egypt) (2 days), and Corfu and Katakolon (Greece).

Norwegian Jewel 2 (debuts February 2007)
Itineraries t.b.a.

Norwegian Majesty **HOME PORTS** Charleston, Boston
November–April, 7 nights, Western Caribbean, round-trip from Charleston (SC) to Grand Cayman, Cozumel, and Key West.

April and October, 15 nights, Caribbean/Colonial America positioning between Charleston (SC) and Boston.

May–October 2006, t.b.a.

Norwegian Spirit **HOME PORT** New York
November–April, 7–11 nights, Caribbean/Bahamas/Florida, round-trip from New York to St. Thomas, Antigua, Barbados, St. Maarten, Tortola (10 nights); same ports plus Dominica and Grenada replaces St. Maarten (11 nights); or Port Canaveral, Miami, Nassau, and Great Stirrup Cay (7 nights).

May–September 2006, t.b.a.

Norwegian Star **HOME PORTS** Seattle, Los Angeles
October–April, nights, Mexican Riviera, round-trip from Los Angeles to Acapulco, Zihuatanejo/Ixtapa, Puerto Vallarta, Cabo San Lucas.

May and September, 3 and 4 nights, Pacific Coast positioning between Vancouver and Los Angeles.

May–September, 7 nights, round-trip from Seattle to Juneau, Skagway, Glacier Bay, Ketchikan, Victoria.

Norwegian Sun **HOME PORTS** New Orleans, Seattle
October–April, 7 nights, Western Caribbean, round-trip from New Orleans to Cozumel and Playa del Carmen (Mexico), Belize City (Belize), and Roatan (Honduras).

December, 10 and 11 nights for Christmas and New Year's.

October and April, 16–17 nights, Panama Canal, Los Angeles to New Orleans or New Orleans to San Francisco, and 4–5 nights, Pacific Coast, Vancouver to Los Angeles and San Francisco to Vancouver.

May–September, Saturday, 7 nights, Alaska round-trip from Seattle to Ketchikan, Juneau, Skagway, Prince Rupert.

Norwegian Wind **HOME PORTS** Honolulu, Vancouver
To April, 2006, 10–11 nights, Hawaii, round-trip from Honolulu to Fanning Island in the Republic of Kiribati, Hilo, Kona, Nawiliwili, and Lahaina with 2 days in Lahaina on the 11-night cruise. Honolulu to Vancouver, 11 nights, April 1, 2006 calling at Hilo, Kahului, Lahaina, Nawiliwili and 6 days at sea.

April, 2006, 3 and 5 nights, Pacific Coast, Vancouver to San Francisco and reverse.

May–September, Sunday, 7 nights, Alaska round-trip from Vancouver to Ketchikan, Juneau, Skagway, Tracy Arm.

NCL America

Pride of Aloha **HOME PORT** Honolulu
Year-round, 7 nights, round-trip from Honolulu (Sunday) or Kahului (Maui) (Saturdays) to Nawiliwili (Kauai) (overnight), Hilo (Hawaii); cruise by Mt. Kilauea; Kona (Hawaii), Kahului (Maui) (overnight); Honolulu.

Pride of America **HOME PORT** Honolulu
Year-round, 7 nights, Saturday, round-trip from Honolulu to Hilo (Hawaii), Kahului (Maui) (2 days), Kona (Hawaii), Nawiliwili (Kauai) (2 days), Kona (Hawaii), and Nawiliwili (Kaui) (2 days). The ship is in port every day and offers scenic cruising on Sunday evening (Mt. Kilauea) and Thursday morning.

Pride of Hawaii (debuts Summer 2006)
Itineraries t.b.a.

Oceania Cruises

Insignia **HOME PORT** Varies with itinerary
November and March, 11–12 nights, transatlantic, Barcelona–Rio de Janeiro or Barbados–Genoa.

December–March, 10–15 nights, South America, between Rio de Janeiro and Buenos; or between Buenos Aires and Valparaiso via Montevideo (Uruguay), Stanley (Falkland Islands), Ushuaia (Argentina), Puerto Arenas (Chile) (overnight onboard), Chilean Fjords, Puerto Montt; or Rio de Janeiro to Manaus on the Amazon (overnight in both ports and Recife, Brazil); or Manaus to Barbados.

April–May and September–November, 10–14 nights, Mediterranean/Greek Isles, from Rome, Athens, Barcelona, or Venice.

June and August, Western Europe and British Isles, from Lisbon to London; London to Barcelona; or round-trip from London.

July–August, 10–14 nights, Baltic, from London to Stockholm or reverse; or from Stockholm to Copenhagen or reverse. Includes 2 or 3 days in St. Petersburg (Russia).

Nautica **HOME PORT** Varies with itinerary
November–April, 15–35 nights, Asia, from Athens to Singapore; Singapore to Hong Kong or reverse; Hong Kong to Bangkok; Bangkok to Beijing; Beijing to Hong Kong; Hong Kong to Athens.

May–November, 10–14 nights, Mediterranean/Geek Isles/Black Sea from Athens, Istanbul, Rome, Venice, or Barcelona.

Regatta **HOME PORT** Miami, others vary with itinerary
November–December, 25 nights, round-trip from Miami to the Caribbean and Amazon with overnight onboard in Manaus (Brazil).

December–March, 10–16 nights, Eastern Caribbean and Panama Canal, either round-trip from Miami or between Miami and Los Angeles.

March, 12 nights, transatlantic, from Miami to Barcelona.

April–May and September–November, 10–14 nights, Mediterranean/Greek Isles, from Rome, Barcelona, Venice, Athens, or Istanbul.

May and September, 10 and 16 nights, Western Europe/Baltic, from Barcelona to Stockholm and London to Rome.

June–August, 14 nights, Baltic, between Stockholm and London via St. Petersburg (3 days), Stockholm (overnight onboard), Tallinn (Estonia), Gdansk (Poland), Warnemünde/Berlin (Germany), Helsinki, Copenhagen, Kiel Canal, Amsterdam, Bruges.

Orient Lines

Marco Polo **HOME PORT** Varies with itinerary
October–November, 9–35 nights, , Western Europe, Mediterranean, various itineraries from London, Barcelona, Venice, Athens or Rome.

November and April, 17, 20, 27 nights, transatlantic, Barcelona to Barbados; Montego Bay to Barcelona, Montego Bay to Athens.

December, February, March, 17–30 nights, South America, Barbados to Santiago (10 nights); Barbados to Ushuaia (32 nights); Rio to Santiago (20 nights); Santiago to Montego Bay (30 nights)

December–January, 10, 17, 19 nights, Antarctica, Cape Horn, Falkland Islands, South Georgia, Chilean Fjords (Only 450 passengers allowed by authorities; ship's normal complement is up to 800). Includes lectures by scientists, wildlife-viewing from Zodiacs, and visits to scientific stations. Antarctic ports may vary depending on ice conditions. Cruise tours include flights from Miami, pre- and/or post-cruise hotel and tours. Sail round-trip from Ushuaia (10 nights); Santiago to Ushuaia (17 nights) or Ushuaia to Rio de Janeiro (19 nights).

April–June and September–November, 10–38 nights, Mediterranean, Greek Isles, Iberia, Western Europe, from Athens, Venice, Rome, Barcelona, Dover.

June–August, 10–31 nights, Baltic and Norwegian Fjords, from Dover, Stockholm, Copenhagen, and Warnemünde.

P&O Cruises

Arcadia **HOME PORTS** Southampton, Barbados
September–October, 7–16 nights, Mediterranean/Canary Islands/Iberia, round-trip from Southampton.

October and March, 2005 and 2006, 14 nights, transatlantic, Southampton to Barbados or reverse.

October–March, 14 nights, Caribbean fly-cruises from the U.K, sailing round-trip from Barbados or between Barbados and New Orleans.

December and February, 15–16 nights, Panama Canal/Latin America, between Barbados and Acapulco.

April–October, 2–17 nights, Mediterranean, Western Europe, Iberia, Norwegian Fjords, Canary Islands, Baltic, sailing round-trip from Southampton.

October, 2006 resumes Caribbean/Panama Canal sailings from Barbados.

Artemis **HOME PORT** Southampton

October 2005–February 2006, 110 nights, Grand Odyssey, round-trip from Southampton on a route via the Canary Islands and Cape Verde Islands to Brazil, Argentina, Falkland Islands, Cape Horn, Chile, Pitcairn Island, Tahiti, Fiji, Brisbane, Sydney, Tasmania, New Zealand, Samoa, Hawaii, Los Angeles, Panama Canal, Caribbean, and the Azores. Available in segments of 21–71 nights.

February 2006, 38 nights, transatlantic, Amazon and Caribbean, round-trip from Southampton.

June–October, 4–17 nights, round-trip from Southampton to either the Mediterranean, Canary Islands, Baltic, Norwegian Fjords, North Cape, or Iceland.

Aurora **HOME PORTS** Southampton, others vary with itinerary
August–December, 2–21 nights, Iberia, Black Sea, Adriatic, Mediterranean, Caribbean, Western Europe, round-trip from Southampton.

January–April, 80 nights, World Cruise, westbound from Southampton via Caribbean, Panama Canal, Acapulco, San Francisco, South Pacific, New Zealand, Australia, Hong Kong, Singapore, India, Suez Canal. Available in segments of 16–51 nights.

May–July, 4–18 nights, Mediterranean, Norway, Baltic, or Greenland, round-trip from Southampton.

Oceana **HOME PORTS** Southampton, Barbados
September–October, 3–14 nights, Canary Islands, Mediterranean, Western Europe, round-trip from Southampton.

October and March, 14–15 nights, transatlantic, Southampton to Barbados and reverse. October-March, 14 nights, Caribbean, fly-cruises from the U.K., sailing round-trip from Ft. Barbados on various Circle Caribbean itineraries.

May–September, Canary Islands, Iberia, Mediterranean, Norwegian Fjords, round-trip from Southampton.

Oriana **HOME PORTS** Southampton, others vary with itinerary
September–December, 2–21 nights, Canary Islands, Canada/New England, Caribbean, Iberia, Mediterranean, round-trip from Southampton.

January–April, 100 nights, World Cruise, round-trip from Southampton on a route via the Mediterranean, Suez Canal, India, Hong Kong, Brisbane, Sydney, Melbourne, Perth, Singapore, Cape Town. Available in segments of 18–61 nights.

May–Septemer, 2–17 nights, Norway, Canary Islands, Mediterranean, round-trip from Southampton.

Peter Deilmann Cruises

Deutschland **HOME PORTS** Cuxhaven, Kiel, others vary with itinerary

September–October, 13–15 nights, Mediterranean, from Lisbon to Venice; Venice to Istanbul, Istanbul to Limassol (Cyprus).

November–March, 10–18 nights, Middle East, Indian Ocean, Africa, on a route from Limassol, Cyprus to Dubai, Colombo, Mauritius, Cape Town, Mombasa, Dubai, Aqaba, Istanbul, with segments starting in each of these ports.

March–April, 8–12 nights, Mediterranean from Lisbon, Venice, Monte Carlo.

May–September, 3–17 nights, Western Europe, Baltic, Norwegian Fjords, British Isles, round-trip from Lisbon (Portugal), Kiel, Cuxhaven, or Travemünde (Germany); Lisbon to Cuxhaven; Cuxhaven to Kiel or reverse; Travemünde to Hamburg; Hamburg to Lisbon.

Princess Cruises

Caribbean Princess **HOME PORT** Ft. Lauderdale
Year-round, Saturdays, 7 nights, round-trip from Ft. Lauderdale to St. Thomas, St. Maarten, Princess Cays.

April–October, alternates with a Western itinerary calling at Grand Cayman, Ocho Rios (or Montego Bay), Cozumel, Princess Cays.

Coral Princess **HOME PORTS** Vancouver, Ft. Lauderdale
October–April, 10 nights, Panama Canal round-trip from Ft. Lauderdale to Belize City (Belize), Cozumel, Grand Cayman, Puerto Limon (Costa Rica), partial transit of the Canal.

April and September, 15–17 nights, Panama Canal, positions between Ft. Lauderdale and Vancouver, available in segments.

May–September, 7 nights, Alaska, between Vancouver and Whittier via Ketchikan, Juneau, Skagway, Glacier Bay, College Fjord.

Crown Princess **HOME PORT** New York
June–October 2006, 9 nights, round-trip from New York, Bermuda/ Eastern/Western Caribbean to either West End (Bermuda); San Juan, St. Thomas, Turks and Caicos; or Port Canaveral, Grand Cayman, Ocho Rios, Grand Turk.

Dawn Princess **HOME PORTS** San Francisco, Seattle, Sydney,
September–May, 10 nights, Mexican Riviera, round-trip from San Francisco to Catalina, Puerto Vallarta, Mazatlan, Cabo San Lucas, and San Diego.

May–September, 7 nights, Alaska, round-trip from Seattle to Juneau, Skagway, Ketchikan, Tracy Arm, Sawyer Glaciers, and Victoria.

October 2006–March 2007, 8-28 nights, South Pacific, Australia, New Zealand, round-trip from Sydney and between Sydney and Auckland.

Diamond Princess **HOME PORTS** Sydney, Auckland, Vancouver, others vary with itinerary

September–November 2005, 11–17 nights, Asia, from Seattle to Osaka; Osaka to Beijing; between Beijing and Bangkok; Beijing to Singapore.

December–April, 12 nights, Australia/New Zealand, between Sydney and Auckland via Tauranga, Christchurch, Dunedin, Fjordland National Park (New Zealand); Hobart (Tasmania) and Melbourne (Australia)

December and April, 19 and 29 nights, positions from Singapore to Sydney and Sydney to San Francisco.

May–September, 7 nights, between Vancouver and Whittier via Skagway, Juneau and Ketchikan, plus cruising College Fjord, the Inside Passage and Glacier Bay National Park.

Golden Princess **HOME PORTS** New York, San Juan, Southampton
September–October 2005, 7 nights, Canada/New England, round-trip from New York to Halifax, Saint John, Bar Harbor, Boston, Newport.

October–April, 7 nights, Southern Caribbean, round-trip from San Juan to either Barbados, St. Lucia, Antigua, St. Maarten, St. Thomas; or St. Thomas, St. Kitts, Grenada, Caracas, Aruba.

May, 16 nights, transatlantic, New York to Venice.

June, September, October, 12 nights, Greek Isles, between Rome and Venice.

June and September, 14 nights, Western Europe, between Rome and Southampton,

July–August, 10 nights, British Isles and Western Europe, round-trip from Southampton.

November, 20 nights, transatlantic, Rome to Rio de Janeiro.

Grand Princess **HOME PORTS** Galveston, Rome, Venice, Barcelona
September–October, 12 nights, Greek Isles/Mediterranean, between Rome and Venice; or Grand Mediterranean between Barcelona and Venice.

November, 16 nights, transatlantic, Rome to Galveston.

November–April, 7 nights, Western Caribbean, round-trip from Galveston to Belize, Majahual, Grand Cayman, Cozumel.

April and October, 15–19 nights, transatlantic, Galveston or Ft. Lauderdale to Rome, and, Barcelona to Ft. Lauderdale.

May–October, 12 nights, Greek Isles/Mediterranean, between Rome and Venice; or Grand Mediterranean between Barcelona and Venice.

Island Princess **HOME PORT** Los Angeles, Vancouver
September–April, 15 nights, Hawaii, round-trip from Los Angeles to Hilo, Kona, Lahaina, Honolulu, Nawiliwili, Ensenada.

May, 7 nights, Pacific Coast, Los Angeles to Vancouver.

May–September, 7 nights, Alaska, between Vancouver and Whittier via Ketchikan, Juneau, Skagway, Glacier Bay, College Fjord.

Pacific Princess **HOME PORT** Sydney, others vary with itinerary
September, 28 nights, South Africa/Indian Ocean/Australia, Cape Town to Sydney.

October–April, Australia/ South Pacific/New Zealand cruises from Sydney for P&O Cruises, Australia.

April–September, 12–28 nights, South Pacific/Asia/Indian Ocean, on a route from Sydney to Papeete; Papeete to Honolulu; Honolulu to Osaka; Beijing to Bangkok or reverse; Bangkok to Cape Town; Cape Town to Sydney.

Regal Princess **HOME PORTS** San Diego, Santiago, Buenos Aires, others vary with itinerary
September–November, 10 nights, Mexican Riviera, round-trip from San Diego to Cabo San Lucas, Acapulco, Ixtapa/Zihuatanejo, Puerto Vallarta and Mazatlan.

December–April, 13–18 nights, South America/Antarctica, December, 18 nights, Ft. Lauderdale to Rio de Janeiro; January 21, nights, Rio to Santiago, Chile via Buenos Aires, Montevideo, Puerto Madryn, Falkland Islands, 5 days cruising the Antarctic Peninsula, Cape Horn Ushuaia, Punta Arenas, Puerto Chacabuco, Puerto Montt; January–March, 13 nights, between Santiago, Chile and Buenos Aires, via Puerto Montt, Pio XI Glacier, Punta Arenas, Beagle Channel, Ushuaia, Cape Horn, Falkland Islands, Puerto Madryn and Montevideo; March, 16 nights, Santiago to Ft. Lauderdale; April, 12 nights, Ft. Lauderdale to Manaus (Brazil) (overnight onboard) or reverse, calling at Tortola, Dominica, Trinidad, Devil's Island, Santarem, Boca de Valeria.

March and May, 15–16 nights, Panama Canal, from Santiago (Chile) to Ft. Lauderdale; or Ft. Lauderdale to San Francisco.

May–August, 10 nights, Alaska, round-trip from San Francisco to Victoria, Ketchikan or Sitka, Skagway or Haines, Juneau, and the Sawyer Glaciers in Tracy Arm.

Sapphire Princess **HOME PORTS** Los Angeles, Vancouver, Sydney, Auckland, others vary with itinerary
September and April, 5–6 nights, Pacific Coast, positioning between Los Angeles and Vancouver.

October–April, 7 nights, Mexican Riviera, round-trip from Los Angeles (Long Beach) to Puerto Vallarta, Mazatland, and Cabo San Lucas.

May–September, 7 nights, between Vancouver and Whittier via Skagway, Juneau and Ketchikan, plus cruising College Fjord, the Inside Passage and Glacier Bay National Park.

December 2006–April 2007, 12 nights, Australia/New Zealand, between Sydney and Auckland via Tauranga, Christchurch, Dunedin, Fjordland National Park (New Zealand); Hobart (Tasmania) and Melbourne (Australia).

Sea Princess **HOME PORTS** New York, Ft. Lauderdale, Barbados, Southampton
September–October, 10–12 nights, Canada/New England, between New York and Quebec City via Newport, Boston, Bar Harbor, Saint John, Halifax, Sydney, Saguenay River. October, 12 nights, Quebec City to Ft. Lauderdale.

November–April, 14 nights, Southern Caribbean, round-trip from Ft. Lauderdale or Barbados to either Princes, Cays, Tortola, St. Maarten, St. Kitts, St. Lucia, Barbados, St. Vincent, Trinidad, Bonaire, Curaçao; or Princess Cays, Tortola, Antigua, Dominica, Martinique, Barbados, Grenada, Isla Margarita, Aruba, Grand Cayman.

April and September, 14 and 16 nights, transatlantic, Ft. Lauderdale to Southampton and Southampton to Quebec City.

April–September, 7–14 nights, Europe, round-trip from Southampton to the Mediterranean, Western Europe, British Isles, Norwegian Fjords/North Cape, Iceland.

Star Princess **HOME PORTS** Ft. Lauderdale, Copenhagen
October–April, 7 nights, Western Caribbean, round-trip from Ft. Lauderdale to Princess Cay, Montego Bay, Grand Cayman, Cozumel.

April and September, 15 nights, transatlantic, Ft. Lauderdale to Copenhagen or Copenhagen to New York.

May–September, 10 nights, Baltic, round-trip from Copenhagen, calling at Stockholm, Helsinki, St. Petersburg (overnight), Tallinn (Estonia) and Gdansk (Poland), plus either Oslo and Oslo Fjord or the port of Warnemünde for an excursion to Berlin.

Sun Princess **HOME PORTS** Ft. Lauderdale, Seattle
September–April, 10 nights, Eastern/Southern Caribbean, round-trip from Ft. Lauderdale to either St. Vincent, Grenada, St. Lucia, Martinique, St. Thomas and Princess Cays, or Curaçao, Isla Margarita, Barbados, Dominica, St. Thomas, Princess Cays.

September and April, 15 nights, Panama Canal positioning cruise San Francisco to Ft. Lauderdale; Ft. Lauderdale to Los Angeles.

May–September, 7 nights, Alaska, round-trip from Seattle to Juneau, Skagway, Ketchikan, Tracy Arm, Sawyer Glaciers and Victoria.

Tahitian Princess **HOME PORT** Papeete
Year-round, 10 nights, Polynesia, round-trip from Papeete: Polynesia/Cook Islands to Bora Bora (overnight onboard), Moorea, Huahine, Raiatea, Rarotonga plus scenic cruising of Tahaa and overnight onboard in Papeete;

or Polynesia/Marquesas to Moorea, Nuku Hiva, Hiva Oa, Rangiroa, Raiatea, Bora Bora, plus scenic cruising of Tahaa and the Tuamotu Atolls and overnight onboard in Papeete.

Radisson Seven Seas Cruises

Paul Gauguin **HOME PORT** Papeete
Year-round, Saturday, 7 nights, French Polynesia from Papeete, Tahiti to Raiatea, Tahaa (Motu Mahana), Bora Bora and Moorea with an overnight onboard ship in Bora Bora, Moorea and Papeete.

January 29, 2006, 17 nights, Brisbane to Papeete, following drydock.

February, June, and December, 10–11-night sailings add Huahine and Rangiroa in the Tuamotu Islands. November and April, 14 nights, Society Islands/Marquesas sailings.

Seven Seas Mariner **HOME PORTS** Vancouver, Whittier, others vary with itinerary
October–December, 2005 and 2006, 7–18 nights, Asia/ South Pacific on a circle Pacific route from Vancouver to Whittier, Tokyo, Hong Kong, Singapore, Sydney, Auckland, Los Angeles available in segments from these ports.

December, 2005 and 2006, 8–14 nights, Mexican Riviera/Panama Canal, round-trip from Los Angeles and Los Angeles to Ft. Lauderdale.

January–February, 12–20 nights, Circle South America in segments: Ft. Lauderdale to Manaus; Manaus to Buenos Aires; Buenos Aires to Callao (Lima); Callao to Ft. Lauderdale.

March, 7–15 nights, Caribbean/Panama Canal, round-trip from Ft. Lauderdale or Ft. Lauderdale to San Francisco.

April, 26 nights, Hawaii/Tahiti, round-trip from San Francisco.

May–September, Wednesday, 7 nights, Alaska, between Vancouver and Whittier. Positions San Francisco to Vancouver, 10 nights, May 14, 2006 via Alaska.

Seven Seas Navigator **HOME PORTS** New York, Ft. Lauderdale, San Juan, Copenhagen, Stockholm, others vary with itinerary
October, 7–9 nights, Canada/New England, between New York and Montreal.

October and December, 14 and 17 nights, Panama Canal, New York to Los Angeles and Los Angeles to Ft. Lauderdale.

November, 26 nights, Hawaii/Tahiti, round-trip from Los Anglges, available in two segments: 10 nights, Los Angeles to Papeete; 16 nights, Papeete to Los Angeles.

December–April, Caribbean, 4–11 nights, Ft. Lauderdale to San Juan or reverse, round-trip from Ft. Lauderdale, or round-trip from San Juan.

April and October, 8 nights, transatlantic, Ft. Lauderdale to Madeira or reverse.

April–June, August–October, 7–14 nights, Mediterranean/Western Europe, from Madeira, Monte Carlo, Venice, Dover, Athens, Istanbul, Rome, Nice.

July, 7 nights, Baltic, between Copenhagen and Stockholm via Tallinn (Estonia); St. Petersburg (3 days); Visby, and either Helsinki or overnight onboard in Stockholm. July, Stockholm to Dover, 11 nights.

Seven Seas Voyager **HOME PORTS** Ft. Lauderdale, Copenhagen, Stockholm others vary with itinerary
October, 7–8 nights, Mediterranean, from Monte Carlo, Rome, Athens.

November 2005 and 2006, and April 2006, 8 nights, transatlantic, Madeira to Ft. Lauderdale and reverse.

November–Decemer 2005 and 2006, 7–15 nights, Caribbean/Panama Canal, round-trip from Ft. Lauderdale and Ft. Lauderdale to Los Angeles.

January–May, World Cruise, 109 nights and segments of 14–23 nights, Los Angeles to Ft. Lauderdale on a route to French Polynesia, New Zealand, Australia, Indonesia, China, Vietnam, Thailand, Singapore, Malaysia, Myanmar, India, United Arab Emirates, Oman, Egypt, Jordan, Libya, Italy, Monaco, Spain, Portugal, Bermuda, and the Bahamas.

May and August–September, 7–10 nights, Mediterranean/Western Europe, from Madeira, Rome, Monte Carlo, Rome, Athens. Western Europe positioning cruises, 10 nights, from Monte Carlo to Dover (May) and Greenwich to Monte Carlo (August).

June–August, 7 nights, Baltic, between Copenhagen and Stockholm via Tallinn (Estonia), St. Petersburg (3 days), Visby, and either Helsinki or overnight onboard in Stockholm. Positioning cruises from Dover to Copenhagen, 12 nights (June); Copenhagen to Greenwich, 11 nights (August).

Royal Caribbean International

Adventure of the Seas **HOME PORT** San Juan
Year-round, Sunday, 7 nights, Southern Caribbean round-trip from San Juan to Aruba, Curaçao, St. Maarten, St. Thomas. April to October, alternate Sundays, cruises to St. Maarten, Antigua, St. Lucia, Barbados.

Brilliance of the Seas **HOME PORTS** Miami, Barcelona
October–November 2005 and April–November, 2006, 12 nights, Mediterranean, round-trip from Barcelona to either Villefranche (Nice/Monte Carlo, France), Livorno (Florence/Pisa), Naples, Rome, and Venice (Italy), Dubrovnik (Croatia), and Corfu (Greece); or Villefranche (Nice/Monte Carlo, France), Livorno (Florence/Pisa), Naples, and Rome (Italy), Athens, Santorini, and Mykonos (Greece), and Kusadasi (Ephesus, Turkey).

November and April, 11–13 nights, transatlantic, Barcelona to Miami or reverse.

November–April, 2005–2006 and 2006–2007, 10 and 11 nights, Southern Caribbean/Panama Canal, round-trip from Miami to Grand Cayman, Aruba, Cristobal (Panama), and Puerto Limon (Costa Rica) (10 nights); or Labadee, Aruba, Curaçao, Panama Canal, Cristobal, Puerto Limon (11 nights).

Empress of the Seas **HOME PORTS** San Juan, Philadelphia
November–April, 2005–2006 and 2006–2007, 3 and 11 nights, Southern Caribbean, round-trip from San Juan, alternating itineraries to St. Maarten, St. Barts, St. Kitts, St. Lucia, Barbados, Grenada, Isla Margarita, Curaçao, Aruba (11 nights); or St. Thomas, St. Maarten (3 nights); or St. Kitts, St. Maarten (3 nights).

May–October, Sunday, 7 nights, Bermuda, round-trip from Philadelphia.

Enchantment of the Seas **HOME PORT** Ft. Lauderdale
Year-round, 4 and 5 nights, Western Caribbean, round-trip from Ft. Lauderdale, 4 nights, alternating Thursdays to Key West, Cozumel; 5 nights, alternating Mondays to Belize City, Cozumel, Key West; 5 nights, alternate Saturdays to Ocho Rios, Grand Cayman.

Explorer of the Seas **HOME PORTS** Miami, Bayonne
To April, 2006, Saturday and November 2006 to April, 2007, Sunday, 7 nights, alternating Eastern and Western Caribbean from Miami to San Juan, St. Maarten, St. Thomas, Nassau (Eastern); or Belize City, Costa Maya, Cozumel, Grand Cayman (Western).

May–October, 5 and 9 nights, alternating Bermuda and Caribbean, round-trip from Cape Liberty (Bayonne, NJ)

Freedom of the Seas **HOME PORT** Miami
Year-round beginning June 4, 2006, Saturday, 7 nights, Western Caribbean round-trip from Miami to Cozumel; Grand Cayman; Montego Bay, and Labadee, the line's private resort in Haiti.

Grandeur of the Seas **HOME PORTS** New Orleans, Baltimore
October–November, 5 and 9 nights, alternating Western Caribbean and Bermuda, round-trip from Baltimore to either Grand Bahama, Coco Cay, Key West, Cozumel, Port Canaveral (9 nights); or docking for 2 days at King's Wharf (Bermuda) (5 nights).

December–April, 2005–2006 and November–April 2006–2007, 7 nights, Western Caribbean, round-trip from New Orleans to Cozumel, Grand Cayman and Costa Maya.

May–November, 5 and 9 nights, alternating Western Caribbean and Bermuda, round-trip from Baltimore to either Grand Bahama, Coco Cay, Key West, Cozumel, Port Canaveral (9 nights); or docking for 2 days at King's Wharf (Bermuda) (5 nights).

Jewel of the Seas **HOME PORTS** Harwich, Boston, Ft. Lauderdale
October–November 2005 and 2006, 10 nights, round-trip from Boston to
either Kings Wharf (Bermuda), St. Maarten, Tortola, and Labadee; or
Labadee, Tortola, St. Maarten, Kings Wharf (Bermuda).

November–April, 5 and 8 nights, alternating Eastern and Western
Caribbean, round-trip from Ft. Lauderdale to either San Juan, St. Maarten,
Antigua, St. Thomas, Nassau; or Key West, Cozumel, Costa Maya, Grand
Cayman.

May and August, 12 and 14 nights, transatlantic, Ft. Lauderdale to Harwich
and Harwich to Boston.

May–August, 12 nights, Baltic or Norwegian Fjords, round-trip from
Harwich to either Oslo, Copenhagen, Stockholm, Helsinki, St. Petersburg (2
days), Tallinn; or Paris, Plymouth, Cork, Belfast, Glasgow, Bergen, Alesund,
Flam, Amsterdam.

December 2006–April 2007, 6 and 8 nights, alternating Eastern and
Western Caribbean, round-trip from Ft. Lauderdale.

Legend of the Seas **HOME PORTS** Southampton, Tampa
October, 14 nights, Mediterranean, round-trip from Southampton to Praira
Da Rocha (Portugal), Gibraltar, Rome, Nice, Corsica, Barcelona, Lisbon,
Vigo.

October and April, 14 nights, transatlantic, Southampton to Tampa or
reverse.

November–April, 2005–2006 and 2006–2007, round-trip from Tampa,
Western Caribbean to Grand Cayman, Costa Maya, Belize City, Cozumel.

May–October 2006, 4–14 nights, Europe, round-trip from Southampton.

Majesty of the Seas **HOME PORT** Miami
Year-round, Bahamas from Miami, 3 nights on Fridays to Nassau, and Coco
Cay (RCI private island); 4 nights on Mondays adds Key West.

Mariner of the Seas **HOME PORT** Port Canaveral
Year-round, Sunday, 7 nights, Eastern/Western Caribbean, round-trip from
Port Canaveral to either Nassau, St. Thomas, St. Maarten; or Labadee,
Ocho Rios, Grand Cayman, Cozumel.

Monarch of the Seas **HOME PORT** Los Angeles
Year-round, 3 and 4 nights, Mexican Riviera, round-trip from Los Angeles; 3
nights, Fridays, to Ensenada; 4 nights, Mondays, to Ensenada, San Diego,
Catalina Island.

Navigator of the Seas **HOME PORT** Miami
Year-round, Saturday, 7 nights, alternating Eastern/Western Caribbean,
round-trip from Miami to either Nassau, San Juan, St. Thomas, St. Maarten,
Nassau (Eastern); or Labadee, Ocho Rios, Grand Cayman, Cozumel
(Western).

Radiance of the Seas **HOME PORTS** Vancouver, Miami
October, Saturday, 7 nights, Alaska Inside Passage, round-trip from
Vancouver to Juneau, Skagway, Hubbard Glacier, Ketchikan; 10 and 11
nights, Hawaii, Vancouver to Honolulu and Honolulu to Ensenada via Hilo,
Kailua, Kona, Nawiliwili, and 2 days in Lahaina; 14 nights, Panama Canal,
San Diego to Miami.

November–April, Sunday, 7 nights, round-trip from Miami to either Coco
Cay, St. Thomas, St. Maarten; or Labadee, Ocho Rios, Grand Cayman,
Cozumel.

April and October, 14 and 15 nights, Panama Canal, Ft. Lauderdale to San
Diego or San Diego to Miami.

May–September, Saturday, 7 nights, Alaska, between Vancouver and
Seward via Ketchikan, Skagway, Juneau, Icy Strait, Hubbard Glacier plus
Misty Fjords on the southbound.

Rhapsody of the Seas **HOME PORT** Galveston
Year-round, Sunday, 7 nights, round-trip from Galveston to either Key
West, Grand Cayman, Cozumel; or Grand Cayman, Montego Bay, and
Cozumel.

Serenade of the Seas **HOME PORTS** San Juan, Vancouver
October, Sunday, 7 nights, Alaska Inside Passage, round-trip from
Vancouver to Juneau, Skagway, Hubbard Glacier, Ketchikan; 11 nights,
Hawaii, Vancouver to Honolulu and Honolulu to Ensenada via Hilo, Kailua,
Kona, Lahaina, Nawiliwili; 12 nights, Panama Canal, San Diego to San Juan.

October–April, Saturday, 7 nights, round-trip from San Juan to St. Thomas,
St. Maarten, Antigua, St. Lucia, Barbados.

May–September, Sunday, 7 nights, Alaska Inside Passage, round-trip from
Vancouver to Juneau, Skagway, Hubbard Glacier, Ketchikan, Misty Fjords.

Sovereign of the Seas **HOME PORT** Port Canaveral
Year-round, Thursday and Sunday, 3 and 4 nights, Bahamas from Port
Canaveral to Nassau and Coco Cay.

Splendour of the Seas **HOME PORTS** Barcelona, Galveston, Venice
October–November, Saturday, 7 nights, round-trip from Barcelona to
Villefranche (France), Florence/Pisa (Livorno, Italy), Rome (Civitavecchia,
Italy), Naples (Italy), Valletta (Malta). November, 14 nights, transatlantic,
Barcelona to Galveston

November–April, 4 and 5 nights, round-trip from Galveston, 4 nights on
Thursdays to Cozumel, and 5 nights on Mondays or Saturdays to Cozumel
and Costa Maya.

May and October, 14 nights, transatlantic, Galveston to Venice or reverse.

May–November, Sunday, 7 nights, Mediterranean, round-trip from Venice.

Vision of the Seas **HOME PORTS** Los Angeles, Seattle
October–April, Sunday, 7 nights, Mexican Riviera, round-trip from Los
Angeles to Cabo San Lucas, Mazatlan, and Puerto Vallarta.

May–September, Friday, 7 nights, Alaska Inside Passage, round-trip from
Seattle.

Voyager of the Seas **HOME PORTS** Bayonne, Miami, Barcelona
October–November, 5 and 9 nights, alternating Bermuda/Western
Caribbean, round-trip from Cape Liberty/Bayonne (NJ) to Bermuda for 2
days at King's Wharf (5 nights) or to Labadee, Ocho Rios, Grand Cayman,
Freeport (9 nights).

November–April, Saturday, 7 nights, alternating Eastern/Western
Caribbean, round-trip from Miami to either Nassau, St. Thomas, San Juan,
Labadee; or Labadee, Ocho Rios, Grand Cayman, and Cozumel.

May–November, Saturday, 7 nights, Mediterranean, round-trip from
Barcelona.

Seabourn Cruise Line

Seabourn Legend **HOME PORTS** St. Thomas, Monte Carlo, Rome,
Barcelona, others vary with itinerary
September–October, 7–31 nights, Western Mediterranean, from Barcelona,
Monte Carlo, or Rome.

November and April, 2005 and 2006, 11, 12, 16 nights, transatlantic,
Tenerife to Ft. Lauderdale; Ft. Lauderdale to Lisbon or Malaga to Ft.
Lauderdale. Can be combined with Caribbean or Mediterranean sailings for
Grand Voyages or 19–28 nights.

November–February, 14 nights, Panama Canal/Costa Rica/Belize, between
Ft. Lauderdale and Puerto Caldera (Costa Rica). Special Christmas and New
Year Caribbean sailings, 16 and 18 nights, round-trip from Ft. Lauderdale or
between Ft. Lauderdale and Barbados.

March–April, 7 and 14 nights, Caribbean, round-trip from St. Thomas to
either Martinique, St. Kitts, Nevis, St. Croix, St. John; or Guadeloupe,
Antigua, St. Barts, St. Martin, Virgin Gorda. Combine for 14-night sailing.

May–October, 7–35 nights, Western Mediterranean/French and Italian Rivieras plus Greek Isles in July, from Lisbon, Rome, Barcelona, or Monte Carlo.

November 2006–February, 2007, resumes Panama Canal cruises between
Ft. Lauderdale and Caldera (Costa Rica) and Caribbean Christmas and New
Year sailings plus additional Mexican Riviera cruises between Caldera and
Los Angeles.

February–March, 2007, resumes Caribbean sailings round-trip from St.
Thomas.

Seabourn Pride **HOME PORT** varies with itinerary
October, 3–21 nights, Canada/New England/Colonial United States, New York to Quebec City; Quebec City to New York; round-trip from New York; or Quebec City to Nassau.

November–December, 7–23 nights, Caribbean, Ft. Lauderdale to Barbados; Barbados to Ft. Lauderdale; or round-trip from Ft. Lauderdale.

January–February 2006 and 2007, 6–72 nights, South America circumnavigation, round-trip from Ft. Lauderdale available in segments, on a route via Panama Canal, Ecuador, Peru, Chile, Argentina (Buenos Aires 2 days), Brazil (Rio de Janeiro 2 days), the Amazon (Manaus 2 days), Devil's Island, Barbados (overnight), St. Barts, St. Thomas.

March and September, 12 and 23 nights, transatlantic, Ft. Lauderdale to Lisbon; or London to Gloucester (MA). Can be combined with Mediterranean sailings for 24–65 night Grand Voyages.

March–May, 9–55 nights, Iberia/Canary Islands/Mediterranean/North Africa, from Lisbon, Monte Carlo, or Istanbul.

April–May, 13 and 58 nights, Western Europe, Monte Carlo to London; Istanbul to London; Istanbul to Copenhagen; Lisbon to London; Lisbon to Copenhagen.

May–August, 9–27 nights, Baltic/Scandinavia, alternating itineraries round-trip from Copenhagen to either Gudvangen, Flaam, Aalesund, Bergen, Ulvik, Eidfjord, and Oslo (Norway) and Skagen (Denmark) (Norwegian Fjords 9 nights); or Tallinn (Estonia), St. Petersburg (3 days), Helsinki, Stockholm (overnight), Warnemünde (Berlin), Roenne (Scandinavia/Russia 12 nights). Combine for a 21-night cruise. Copenhagen to London adds the Orkney Islands, Invergordon, Dublin, Waterford, Falmouth (27 nights).

September–October 2006, 7–28 nights, Canada/New England/Bermuda, round-trip from Gloucester (MA); between Gloucester and Quebec City; Gloucester to Nassau, Quebec City to Nassau, Boston to Nassau.

November–December 2006, 7–21 nights, Caribbean, round-trip from Barbados; Ft. Lauderdale to Barbados or reverse; Ft. Lauderdale to St. Maarten or reverse.

Seabourn Spirit **HOME PORT** Varies with itinerary
October, 7–21 nights, Greek Isles/Adriatic, from Ahtens, Istanbul, or Venice.

October–November, 2005 and 2006, 7–32 nights, Middles East, Africa, Indian Ocean, on a route from Istanbul to Singapore via Alexandria, Mombasa, the Seychelles.

November–January, 13–17 nights, Southeast Asia, round-trip from Singapore, Singapore to Hong Kong, or Hong Kong to Cairns.

January–March, 14–29 nights, Australia/New Zealand/Fiji from Cairns (Australia), Christchurch and Auckland (New Zealand), Lautoka (Fiji).

March–April, 15–62 nights, Barrier Reef/Southeast Asia/Middle East from Cairns to Athens on a route via Singapore, Dubai, Alexandria, and Rome, available in segments from these ports.

May–October, 7–35 nights, Greek Isles/Adriatic/Turkey from Rome, Athens, Istanbul, or Venice. July sailings include Black Sea ports.

October 2006 to May 2007, 7–32 nights, positions from Istanbul to Singapore via Athens, Alexandria, Mombasa, Seychelles followed by Asia sailings round-trip from Singapore or Hong Kong; Hong Kong to Singapore or reverse; Hong Kong to Bangkok; Bangkok to Singapore. Returns to Europe, May 2007 from Singapore to Alexandria via Dubai and the Suez Canal.

SeaDream Yacht Club

SeaDream I **HOME PORTS** San Juan, St. Thomas, others vary with itinerary
October, 7 nights, Mediterranean, round-trip from, Istanbul; Istanbul to Piraues (Athens) or reverse; Athens to Barcelona; Barcelona to Seville.

October, 2005, May and November, 2006, 11–13, nights, transatlantic, Seville to San Juan; San Juan to Malaga; Seville to St. Thomas.

October–April, 4–7 nights, Eastern Caribbean, round-trip from St. Thomas; round-trip from San Juan; St. Thomas to San Juan, or reverse; St. Thomas to St. Martin; St. Martin to San Juan.

May–November, 3, 4, 7 nights, Mediterranean, Adriatic, Greek Isles to Malaga, Nice, Venice, Istanbul, Piraeus, Dubrovnik, Alexandria, Naples, or Palma de Mallorca.

November–December, 2006, 7 nights, Eastern Caribbean, round-trip from St. Thomas to either San Juan, St. Martin, Nevis, Saba, St. Barts, Jost van Dyke; or Guadeloupe, Antigua, Anguilla, Virgin Gorda, Jost van Dyke.

SeaDream II **HOME PORT** Varies with itinerary
October 2005, 7 nights, Mediterranean from Nice, Rome, Barcelona, or Seville.

October 2005, April and November 2006, 7–12 nights, transatlantic from Tenerife to West Palm Beach; Barbados to Madeira; Tenerife to San Juan.

November–April, 4–9 nights, Southern/Eastern Caribbean, round-trip from Barbados, St. Thomas, Antigua or St. Maarten; St. Thomas to Barbados or St. Maarten; Antigua to Barbados.

May–November, 7–12 nights, Mediterranean, Canary Islands and French and Italian rivieras, from Madeira, Nice, Venice, Monte Carlo, Rome, Barcelona, Piraeus, Seville.

November–December 2006, 6, 7, 8 nights, Caribbean round-trip from St. Thomas, San Juan or Barbados; San Juan to Barbados; Barbados to St. Thomas.

Silversea Cruises

Silver Cloud **HOME PORT** Varies with itinerary
October 2005, 7–14 nights, Western Europe/Mediterranean from Southampton, Malaga, Nice, Barcelona, or Rome.

October and April, 14 nights, transatlantic, Lisbon to Barbados and Barbados to Lisbon.

October to April, 6–16 nights, South America from Barbados to Manaus; Manaus to Rio de Janeiro; Rio to Buenos Aires; round-trip from Buenos Aires; Buenos Aires to Valparaiso or Ushuaia; Valparaiso to Buenos Aires or Ushuaia; Ushuaia to Buenos Aires; Buenos Aires to Rio de Janeiro; Rio to Barbados.

May–June and September–October, 7–12 nights, Mediterranean/Western Europe, from Lisbon, Genoa, Barcelona (spring) and London, Lisbon, Monte Carlo, Rome, Alexandria (fall).

June–August, 7–15 nights, Baltic, London (Tower Bridge) to Stockholm or reverse; Stockholm to Copenhagen or reverse; round-trip from Copenhagen; Copenhagen to London or reverse.

November–December, 8–16 nights, Middle East/Asia/Australia from Port Said, Dubai, Mumbai, Singapore en route to Sydney.

Silver Shadow **HOME PORT** Varies with itinerary
October, 7–15 nights, Mediterranean, from Athens, Istanbul, Venice, Rome, or Monte Carlo.

November–February, 8–16 nights, Middle East/Asia/Australia/New Zealand from Port Said, Dubai, Singapore, Sydney, Auckland, or Fremantle.

February–May, 8–14 nights, Southeast Asia/China/Japan from Singapore, Hong Kong, Bangkok, or Tokyo.

June–September, 9–12 nights, Alaska from Anchorage to Vancouver; Vancouver to Seattle or reverse; round-trip from Seattle; Vancouver to San Francisco or reverse; round-trip from San Francisco; Vancouver to Los Angeles.

September–October, 9 and 17 nights, Mexican Riviera and Panama Canal, round-trip from Los Angeles to San Diego, Mazatlan, Puerto Vallarta, Cabo San Lucas, Ensenada; or Los angeles to Miami via Puerto Vallarta, Acapulco, Guatemala, Nicaragua, Costa Rica, Colombia.

October–December, 7–14 nights, Caribbean/Panama, Miami to Barbados, round-trip from Barbados, Ft. Lauderdale or San Juan , Barbados to San Juan, San Juan to Ft. Lauderdale, Ft. Lauderdale to Barbados or reverse.

Silver Whisper **HOME PORT** Varies with itinerary
October, 9–12 nights, Canada/New England/Colonial Coast, from Boston to Montreal; Montreal to New York or reverse; round-trip from New York; Montreal to Ft. Lauderdale.

November–February and March–April, 4–14 nights, Caribbean/Panama, from Ft. Lauderdale to Barbados, or reverse; round-trip from Ft. Lauderdale, or Barbados, or Antigua, or San Juan; Ft. Lauderdale to Antigua, or reverse.

February–March, 10–15 nights, Panama Canal, Ft. Lauderdale to San Diego; San Diego to Puerto Caldera (Costa Rica); Puerto Caldera to San Juan.

April, 14 nights, transatlantic, San Juan to Las Palmas (Canary Islands).

May–July and September–October, 7–12 nights, Mediterranean from Las Palmas, Barcelona, Nice, Rome, Monte Carlo, Villefranche, Athens, or Venice.

July and September, Western Europe, 12–14 nights, Monte Carlo to Dover and Amsterdam to Barcelona; July–September, 7–11 nights, Baltic, from Dover to Copenhagen; Copenhagen to Stockholm or reverse; Copenhagen to Amsterdam.

October–December, 12–15 nights, Middle East/Asia from Port Said; Dubai; Singapore; Hong Kong; Bangkok; or round-trip from Singapore.

Silver Wind **HOME PORT** Varies with itinerary
October 2005, 8–10 nights, Mediterranean from Venice, Athens, Rome, Monte Carlo.

November to February, 8–17 nights, Indian Ocean/Africa/Middle East from Port Said to Mahe, Seychelles; round-trip from Mahe; Mahe to Mauritius; Mauritius to Cape Town; round-trip from Cape Town; Cape Town to Mauritius; Mauritius to Mombai; Mombai to Dubai; round-trip from Dubai; Dubai to Port Said; Port Said to Athens.

March–November, 7–15 nights, Mediterranean/Adriatic/Black Sea/Canary Islands, from Athens, Lisbon, Las Palmas, Barcelona, Rome, Venice, Monte Carlo, Villefranche, Istanbul, Genoa.

November, 14 nights, transatlantic, Las Palmas to Rio de Janeiro.

November 2006–January 2007, 7–16 nights, South America, Rio de Janeiro to Buenos Aires, round-trip from Buenos Aires, Buenos Aires to Valparaiso, Buenos Aires Ushuaia, Ushuaia to Valparaiso.

Star Clippers, Inc.

Note: All ports may not be included on every Star Clipper cruise, as itineraries are subject to weather conditions and alterations by the captain, in search of calm sailing and best anchorage.

Royal Clipper **HOME PORTS** Barbados, Rome, Venice
November–April, Saturday, 7 nights, Southern Caribbean round-trip from

Barbados alternating to either St. Lucia, Iles des Saintes, Antigua, St. Kitts, Dominica, Martinique; or Grenadines, Grenada, Tobago Cays, St. Vincent; St. Lucia, Martinique.

April and October, 21–22 nights, transatlantic, between Barbados and Rome available in segments.

May–June, 7 nights, Western Mediterranean, alternating cruises round-trip from Rome to either Sicily, Malta, Panarea and Venotere (Italy); or Ponza, Sorrento, Amalfi, and Lipari (Italy) and Taormina (Sicily).

July–September, 10 and 11 nights, Mediterranean, alternating cruises between Rome and Venice calling at Capri, Lipari, Taormina, Corfu and Dubrovnik, Korcula, Hvar, and Pula (Croatia) (11 nights) or Pula, Losinj, Hvar, and Dubrovnik (Croatia), Corfu, Taormina, and Lipari (10 nights).

Star Clipper **HOME PORTS** St. Maarten, Cannes
November, 28 nights, transatlantic, Cannes to St. Maarten.

November–April, Sunday, 7 nights, Caribbean, round-trip from St. Maarten to either St. Barts, Nevis, Guadeloupe, Dominica, Iles des Saintes, Antigua; or Anguilla, Virgin Gorda, Norman Island, Jost van Dyke, St. Kitts, St. Barts.

May–September, 7 nights, Western Mediterranean, round-trip from Cannes to Rome via Monaco, the islands of Corsica and Elba as well as Italy; 10–11 nights, between Cannes and Dubrovnik (Croatia) via France, Italy, and Greece.

October, 26 nights, transatlantic, Cannes to St. Maarten available in segments.

Star Flyer **HOME PORTS** Phuket, Athens, Istanbul
November–March, Saturday, 7 nights, Far East, alternating southern and northern routes, round-trip from Phuket or between Phuket and Singapore: Round-trip from Phuket to either Ko Adang, Ko Lipe, Ko Khai Nok, Phang Nga/Ko Dam Hok, Similian Islands, Thailand and Penang, Malaysia; or Surin Islands, Similian Islands, Ko Rok Nok, Phi Phi Islands, Phang Nga/Ko Knai Nok, Thailand and Langkawi, Malaysia. Between Singapore and Phuket calling at either Similian Islands, Phang Nga/Ko Dan Hok, Ko Adang, Thailand; Penang and Malacca, Malaysia; or Malacca and Langkawi, Malaysia; Ko Lipe and Ko Khai Nok, Thailand.

March and October, 37 nights, positioning cruises between Athens and Phuket.

May–October, Saturday, 7 nights, Eastern Mediterranean, alternating cruises, round-trip from Athens to either Kamilimani Beach and Kusadasi (Turkey), Pythagoria, Patmos, Delos, and Sifnos (Greece); or Rhodes, Santorini, and Hydra (Greece) and Bodrum and Dalyan (Turkey); or 7 nights between Athens and Istanbul via Delos, Patmos, Bodrum, Kusadasi, Dikkili.

Star Cruises

MegaStar Aries (chartered)

MegaStar Taurus (chartered)

Star Pisces **HOME PORT** Hong Kong
Year-round, 1 night to nowhere from Hong Kong catering to gamblers and first-time cruisers. Subject to change.

SuperStar Gemini **HOME PORT** Singapore
November–April, 7 nights, Malaysia and Thailand, round-trip from Singapore (aimed at Australian market) to Port Klang (Kuala Lumpur), Langkawi Island and Penang (Malaysia); Krabi and Phuket in Thailand. Three sailings in April 2006 call at Ko Samui (Thailand) and Ho Chi Minh City (Vietnam).

SuperStar Libra **HOME PORT** Mumbai
September–April, 1–4 nights, India, round-trip from Mumbai to Kadmat (Lakshadweep) and Goa, or Kochi and Goa (4 nights); to Goa (2 nights) or weekend getaway cruises (1 night).

SuperStar Virgo **HOME PORT** Singapore
Year-round, 2, 3, or 5 nights, Malaysia/Thailand, round-trip from Singapore to Langkawi Island and Penang or Phuket (3 nights); or to Malacca and Port Klang (2 nights); combine for 5-night cruise. Round-trip from Singapore to Port Klang, Phuket, Langkawi and second call at Port Klang (5 nights); or to Bangkok, Ko Samui (5 nights).

Swan Hellenic Cruises

Minerva II **HOME PORT** Varies with itinerary
October, 13–15 nights, Mediterranean, Black Sea, Canary Islands, from Malta, Dubrovnik, Venice, Cadiz, Athens, Istanbul, Cyprus.

November–January, 11–22 nights, South America, from Manuas, Buenos Aires, Ushuaia, Callao.

January–February, 15 nights. Central America, Panama Canal, from Caldera to San Francisco and reverse; Caldera to New Orleans.

February–March, 15–17 nights, Caribbean, South America from New Orleans to Barbados and round-trip from Barbados.

April, 15 nights, transatlantic, Barbados to Cadiz.

May and August–October, 13–15 nights, Mediterranean, Black Sea, Canary Islands, from Malta, Dubrovnik, Venice, Cadiz, Athens, Istanbul, Cyprus.

June–August, 9–15 nights, Western Europe, Baltic, Norway, British Isles from Genoa to Dover, round-trip from Dover, Dover to Cadiz.

Travel Dynamics International

Callisto **HOME PORT** Athens, Dubrovnik, Dakar
October–December, 9–13 nights, Greece, Greek Isles, Turkey, Crete, in-

depth educational fly-cruise tours from the United States, sailing round-trip from Athens plus pre-cruise tours of Greece (Athens or Thessaloniki).

December–March, 16 nights, Rivers of West Africa, fly-cruise tours from the United States, sailing from Dakar, Senegal to the Casamance River, the Gambia, and Saloun River plus pre-cruise tour of Mali and Timbuktu.

April–August, 11–12 nights, Adriatic, Greece, Greek Isles, in-depth educational fly-cruise tours from the United States, sailing round-trip from Athens, between Dubrovnik and Athens, or between Dubrovnik and Rab, plus pre- and post-cruise tours.

Corinthain II **HOME PORT** Athens, Ushuaia, others vary with itinerary
September–November, 11–13 nights, Mediterranean, Greece, Greek Isles, Turkey, Libya, Tunisia, in-depth educational fly-cruise tours from the United States, sailing from Barcelona to Venice; Venice to Istanbul; round-trip from Athens to Black Sea; Athens to Naples, or reverse; Athens to Tunis; each with a special theme plus pre- and post-cruise tours.

December–February, 13 nights, Antarctica, fly-cruise tours from the United States, sailing round-trip from Ushuaia to the Antarctic Peninsula plus a pre-cruise stay in Buenos Aires.

April–June, 10–14 nights, Mediterranean, in-depth educational fly-cruise tours from the United States, sailing from Malaga to Nice; Seville to Venice; round-trip from Palermo (Sicily); Palermo to Athens, round-trip from Athens; Athens to Anzio (Italy).

Windjammer Barefoot Cruises

Amazing Grace **HOME PORTS** Balboa, Antigua, Tortola, Trinidad
October–November, 6 nights, Panama, Costa Rica, and Las Perlas Islands, sailing between Balboa (Panama) and Playa Herradura (Costa Rica).

November–February, 7 nights, Caribbean on 4 itineraries, either from Trinidad to Antigua via Grenada, Tobago Cays, Bequia, St. Vincent, St. Lucia, Nevis; or Antigua to Trinidad via Isles Des Saints, Dominica, St. Lucia, Bequia, Tobago; or Tortola to Antigua via Virgin Gorda, Anguilla, St. Barts, St. Kitts, Montserrat; or Antigua to Tortola via Antigua, St. Martin, St. Barts, Saba, Virgin Gorda, Jost Van Dyke.

June–October, 6 nights, Costa Rica sailings above.

Legacy **HOME PORTS** St. Lucia, St. Thomas, Miami, Nassau
October–November, 5 nights, round-trip from St. Lucia to St. Lucia, Grenada, Tobago Cays, Union Island, St. Vincent.

December to May, 5 nights, round-trip from St. Thomas to Water Island (USVI), Jost Van Dyke (BVI), St. John, Norman Island, Tortola, Virgin Gorda.

May–August, 3, 4, 7 nights, Bahamas, round-trip from Miami to Bimini, Gun Cay, Berry Islands, Great Abaco, Freeport, Nassau (7 nights) available in 3- and 4-night segments, one-way between Miami and Nassau.

Mandalay **HOME PORTS** Tortola, Antigua, Grenada
September, 5 nights, British Virgin Islands round-trip from Tortola to
Cooper Island, Jost Van Dyke, Norman Island, Peter Island, Salt Island,
Tortola, Virgin Gorda.

November–April, 12 nights, between Antigua and Grenada, calling at
Antigua, Bequia, Tobago Cays, Carriacou, Dominica, Grenada and to Iles
des Saints, Martinique, Mayreau, Nevis, St. Lucia, St. Vincent.

April–September, resumes 5 nights, British Virgin Islands.

Polynesia **HOME PORTS** Aruba, St. Maarten
September–October, 5 nights, ABC Islands round-trip from Aruba to
Aruba, Bonaire, Curaçao, Klein Curaçao.

December through 2006, 5 nights, round-trip from St. Maarten to a selection of the following islands: St. Maarten, St. Barts, Anguilla, Tintamarre,
Saba, St. Eustatius (Statia), Nevis, St. Kitts.

Yankee Clipper **HOME PORT** Grenada
Year-round, Monday, 5 nights, round-trip from Grenada to Bequia,
Carriacou, Grenada, Mayreau, St. Vincent, Tobago Cays, Union Island.

Windstar Cruises

Wind Spirit **HOME PORTS** St. Thomas, Athens, Istanbul, others vary with
itinerary
December–April, 7 nights, round-trip from St. Thomas to St. Martin, St.
Barts, Tortola, Jost Van Dyke, and overnight onboard in St. John and Virgin
Gorda.

April and November, 14 nights, transatlantic, St. Thomas to Lisbon and
reverse.

April and October, 7 nights, Western Mediterranean, from Lisbon to
Barcelona; Barcelona to Rome; Rome to Athens or reverse.

May–October, Saturday, 7 nights, Eastern Mediterranean/Greek Isles, from
Athens to Istanbul or reverse; to either Mykonos, Santorini, Rhodes,
Bodrum, and Kusadasi; or Canakkale and Izmir (Turkey); Patmos, Agios, Kis,
and Naxos (Greece); and Nikolaos (Crete).

December 2006–March 2007, resumes Caribbean cruises from St. Thomas.

Wind Star **HOME PORTS** Puerto Caldera, Athens, Istanbul, others vary
with itinerary
November and April, 14 nights, transatlantic, Barbados to Lisbon, or
reverse.

November 2005 and 2006, 14 nights, Panama Canal from Barbados to
Puerto Caldera (Costa Rica).

December–March, Saturday, 7 nights, Costa Rica, round-trip from Puerto Caldera to San Juan del Sur (Nicaragua); Playas del Coco, Quepos, Bahia Paraiso, Curu, and Tortuga Island (Costa Rica).

April and October, 7 nights, Western Mediterranean, from Lisbon to Barcelona; Rome to Athens, or reverse; Rome to Barcelona.

May–July and September–October, Saturday, 7 nights, Eastern Mediterranean from Athens to Istanbul, or reverse, to Mykonos, Santorini, Rhodes, Bodrum, and Kusadasi.

July–August, 7 nights, Saturday, Athens to Venice or reverse, via Monemvasia, Katakolon, and Corfu (Greece) and Dubrovnik (Croatia) (northbound); or Rimini (Italy), Hvar and Dubrovnik (Croatia), and Cephalonia and Kythira (Greece) (southbound).

December 2006–March 2007, resumes Costa Rica sailings from Puerto Caldera.

Wind Surf **HOME PORTS** Barbados, others vary with itinerary
November and April, 13–14 nights, transatlantic, Lisbon to St. Thomas; Barbados to Lisbon or reverse.

December–April, 7 nights, Caribbean, round-trip from Barbados to either Tobago, Bequia, Dominica (Roseau and Cabrits), St. Lucia, Mayreau; or St. Kitts and Nevis, St. Martin, St. Barts, Isles des Saintes, St. Lucia.

April–October, 7 nights, Western Mediterranean from either Marseille, Rome, Nice, or Barcelona. May 21, 2006, Monte Carlo Grand Prix sailing, 14 nights round-trip from Nice.

December 2006–April, 2007, resumes 7-night cruises from Barbados. Guadeloupe replaces St. Kitts on northbound itinerary.

The World/ResidenSea

The World **HOME PORT** Varies with itinerary as it continually sails around the world.
October 2005 to December 2006, sails a route from Iceland to Greenland, Labrador, Montreal, Boston, New York, Bermuda, Bahamas, Caribbean, New Orleans for Mardi Gras, Mexico, Panama Canal, Mexican Riviera, San Diego, Hawaii, Japan, Korea, China, Hong Kong, Vietnam, Thailand, Singapore, Indonesia, Australia, Tasmania, New Zealand, South Pacific to Chile for New Year in the Chilean Fjords.

CRUISE SHIP INDEX

KEY A = Adventure | E = European Cruise Ferry | F = Freighter

G = Galápagos | GR = Greek Islands | M = Mainstream | NC = Norwegian Coastal

O = Others | R = River | SS = Sailing Ship

KEY   A = Adventure | E = European Cruise Ferry | F = Freighter

G = Galápagos | GR = Greek Islands | M = Mainstream | NC = Norwegian Coastal

O = Others | R = River | SS = Sailing Ship

KEY A = Adventure | E = European Cruise Ferry | F = Freighter
G = Galápagos | GR = Greek Islands | M = Mainstream | NC = Norwegian Coastal
O = Others | R = River | SS = Sailing Ship

SHIP	CRUISE LINE	TYPE	PAGE
Mirabella	Overseas Adventure Travel	R	538
Mississippi Queen	Delta Queen Steamboat Company	R	277–278, 284–285
Mistress	Maine Windjammer Association	S	567, 583, 589
Monarch of the Seas	Royal Caribbean International	M	425, 436–441
Monterey	MSC Cruises	M	515
Moon Goddess	Sonesta Cruises	R	550
Mozart	Peter Deilmann Cruises	R	534
MTS Discoverer	MTS	A	569–570
Musica	MSC Cruises	M	514
Nantucket Clipper	Clipper Cruise Line	M	204, 207–209
Napoleon	Abercrombie & Kent	R	532
Narvik	Norwegian Coastal Voyage/Bergen Line	NC	576
Nathaniel Bowditch	Maine Windjammer Association	SS	589
National Geographic Endeavour	Lindblad Expeditions	A	568, 570
Nautica	Oceana Cruises	M	366–374
Navigator of the Seas	Royal Caribbean International	M	525, 433–436
Nenuphar	French Country Waterways	R	537
Nephtis	Mena House Oberoi Hotels	R	549
Niagara Prince	American Canadian Caribbean Line	M	144, 147–149
Nile Goddess	Sonesta Cruises	R	550
Noordam	Holland America Line	M	311, 331–334
Nordkapp	Norwegian Coastal Voyage	NC	575–576
Nordnorge	Norwegian Coastal Voyage	NC	575–576
Nordstjernen	Norwegian Coastal Voyage	NC	576
Norwegian Crown	Norwegian Cruise Line	M	338, 354–356
Norwegian Dawn	Norwegian Cruise Line	M	338, 342–346
Norwegian Dream	Norwegian Cruise Line	M	338, 350–354
Norwegian Jewel	Norwegian Cruise Line	M	342–346
Norwegian Majesty	Norwegian Cruise Line	M	338, 357–359
Norwegian Spirit	Norwegian Cruise Line	M	346–350
Norwegian Star	Norwegian Cruise Line	M	338, 342–346
Norwegian Sun	Norwegian Cruise Line	M	338, 342–346
Norwegian Wind	Norwegian Cruise Line	M	338, 350–354
Novihov Priboy	Global Quest Journeys	R	537
Nubian Sea	Misr Travel	R	549–550
Nymphea	European Waterways	R	536
Oberoi Philae	Mena House Oberoi Hotels	R	549
Oceana	P&O Cruises	M	518
Oosterdam	Holland America Line	M	311, 331–334
Opera	MSC Cruises	M	513–514
Orellana	Marco Polo Expeditions	R	556
Oriana	P&O Cruises	M	516–518
Orion	Travel Dynamics International	R	526
Orlova	Quark Expeditions	R	571

KEY   A = Adventure | E = European Cruise Ferry | F = Freighter
G = Galápagos | GR = Greek Islands | M = Mainstream | NC = Norwegian Coastal
O = Others | R = River | SS = Sailing Ship

SHIP	CRUISE LINE	TYPE	PAGE
Sonesta Moon Goddess	Sonesta Cruises	R	550
Sonesta Nile Goddess	Sonesta Cruises	R	550
Sonesta Sun Goddess	Sonesta Cruises	R	550
Sovereign of the Seas	Royal Caribbean International	M	424–425, 436–441
Sovietskiy Soyuz	Quark Expeditions	A	571
Spirit of Alaska	Cruise West	M	236, 244–246
Spirit of Columbia	Cruise West	M	236, 244–246
Spirit of Columbia	International Expeditions	R	236
Spirit of Discovery	Cruise West	M	243–344
Spirit of Endeavour	Cruise West	M	235, 240–242
Spirit of '98	Cruise West	M	236, 242–243
Spirit of Oceanus	Cruise West	M	235–236, 239–240
Splendour of the Seas	Royal Caribbean International	M	425, 428–433
Star Clipper	Star Clippers, Inc.	M	475, 478–480
Star Flyer	Star Clippers, Inc.	M	475, 478–480
Star Pisces	Star Cruises	M	523
Star Princess	Princess Cruises	M	386, 395–401
Statendam	Holland America Line	M	311, 315–322
Stephen Taber	Maine Windjammer Association	SS	589
Summit	Celebrity Cruises	M	182, 193–200
Sun Boat III	Abercrombie & Kent	R	548
Sun Boat IV	Abercrombie & Kent	R	548
Sun Goddess	Sonesta Cruises	R	550
Sun Princess	Princess Cruises	M	384, 386, 389–394
SuperSeaCat III and IV	Silja Line	EC	579–580
SuperStar Gemini	Star Cruises	M	523
SuperStar Virgo	Star Cruises	M	523–524
Symphony	Avalon Waterways	R	532–533
Tahiti Princess	Princess Cruises	M	386, 408
Tia Moana	Bora Bora Cruises	M	499–500
Timberwind	Maine Windjammer Association	SS	589
Trollfjord	Norway Coastal Voyage	NC	575
Tu Moana	Bora Bora Cruises	M	499–500
Tucano	Marco Polo Expeditions	R	555
Uncano	Marco Polo Expeditions	R	556
Ushuaia	Cruise North Expeditions Inc.	A	561–562
Veendam	Holland America Line	M	311, 315–322
Vesteraalen	Norwegian Coastal Voyage	NC	576
Victoria Anna	Victoria Cruises	R	543
Victoria Empress	Victoria Cruises	M	543
Victoria Katarina	Victoria Cruises	R	543
Victoria Prince	Victoria Cruises	R	543
Victoria Queen	Victoria Cruises	R	543
Victoria Rose	Victoria Cruises	M	543–544
Victoria Star	Victoria Cruises	R	543

KEY   A = Adventure | E = European Cruise Ferry | F = Freighter
G = Galápagos | GR = Greek Islands | M = Mainstream | NC = Norwegian Coastal
O = Others | R = River | SS = Sailing Ship

KEY A = Adventure | E = European Cruise Ferry | F = Freighter
G = Galápagos | GR = Greek Islands | M = Mainstream | NC = Norwegian Coastal
O = Others | R = River | SS = Sailing Ship

DESTINATION INDEX

Note: This index is organized according to continents, oceans and seas.

SUBJECT INDEX

Note: Ship names are found in a separate ship name index; destinations are found in a separate destination index.

If you would like to express an opinion about your cruise or this guide-book, complete the following survey and return to:

Unofficial Guide Reader Survey
P.O. Box 43673
Birmingham, AL 35243

Name of ship: Today's date:
Date, duration, and destination of cruise:
Please circle one of the following:

—*Was this your*   1st   2nd   3rd   4th   5th   6th
or more cruise?
—*Would you take another cruise on this ship?*   Yes   No
—*Recommend it to a friend?*   Yes   No
—*Do you plan to cruise*   within a year   within next 3 years   longer?
—*Your age:*   teens   20s   30s   40s   50s   60s   70s   over 80
—*You are:*   employed   self-employed   retired
—*Line of work:*

Please score items below from 1 to 10 with 10 being the highest or best.
Feel free to add your comments.

Value for money:

Total cruise experience:

Your overall impression of the ship (*appearance, appeal, furnishings and decor, cleanliness, sports and recreation facilities, consistency, comfort, boarding/disembarking procedures*):

Cruise director (*available, helpful, friendly*):

Cruise staff:

Dining room food (*choices, quality, taste, presentation*):

Breakfast and lunch buffet:

Dining room service:

Bar service:

Cabin (*size, layout, soundproofing, cleanliness, appearance, condition*):

Bathroom:

Cabin attendant (*service, attitude*):

Enrichment programs, lectures, games (*variety and quality*):

Entertainment in the main lounge:

Entertainment in other lounges:

Children's programs:

Youth counselors:

Shore excursions (*guides, variety, advanced information, value*):

Some more questions:

—Was the food quality better, worse, or about what you expected?

—Were wine and bar prices low, moderate, or high?

—Was the music level tolerable or too loud, especially by the pool?

—Were you bothered by announcements over the public address system?

—Was the promotion of shipboard shops low key, moderate, or hard sell?

—Was the lifeboat drill well executed?

—Did you choose your cruise for its itinerary?

—Which ports of call did you like best?

—Were port talks poor or helpful?

—Did the speakers plug specific shops?

—Was passenger information available prior to the cruise? in your cabin? during the cruise?

Your hometown:

How did you learn about your cruise?

How did you learn about this book?

Where did you buy your cruise?

When and where did you buy this book?

(*Optional*) If you are available for a telephone interview, please give us your name, address, telephone number, and a convenient time to call.

THANK YOU!